AUSTRALIA

NEW ZEALAND

AND THE

SOUTH PACIFIC

Fodor's Australia, New Zealand and the South Pacific:

Editor: Debra Bernardi
Area Editors: Emery Barcs, Lois Brett, John P. Campbell, Robert Gilmore, Kathleen Hancock, Don Hook, Jan Prince, Jennifer Pringle-Jones, David Swindell, James Tully, John Young
Drawings: Sandra Lang
Photographs: Australian Tourist Commission, Lois Brett, New Zealand Tourist Office, Victoria Arts Centre, Western Samoa Visitors Bureau
Maps and plans: Pictograph

AUSTRALIA
NEW ZEALAND
AND THE
SOUTH PACIFIC
1986

FODOR'S TRAVEL GUIDES
New York & London

The following Fodor's Guides are current; most are also available in a British
edition published by Hodder & Stoughton.

Country and Area Guides

Australia, New Zealand
 & The South Pacific
Austria
Bahamas
Belgium & Luxembourg
Bermuda
Brazil
Canada
Canada's Maritime
 Provinces
Caribbean
Central America
Eastern Europe
Egypt
Europe
France
Germany
Great Britain
Greece
Holland
India, Nepal &
 Sri Lanka
Ireland
Israel
Italy
Japan
Jordan & The Holy Land
Kenya
Korea
Mexico
North Africa
People's Republic of
 China
Portugal
Scandanavia
Scotland
South America
Southeast Asia
Soviet Union
Spain
Switzerland
Turkey
Yugoslavia

City Guides

Amsterdam
Beijing, Guangzhou,
 Shanghai
Boston
Chicago
Dallas–Fort Worth
Greater Miami & The
 Gold Coast
Hong Kong
Houston
Lisbon
London
Los Angeles
Madrid
Mexico City &
 Acapulco
Munich
New Orleans
New York City
Paris
Philadelphia
Rome
San Diego
San Francisco
Stockholm, Copenhagen,
 Oslo, Helsinki &
 Reykjavik
Sydney
Tokyo
Toronto
Vienna
Washington, D.C.

U.S.A. Guides

Alaska
Arizona
California
Cape Cod
Colorado
Far West
Florida
Hawaii
New England
New Mexico
Pacific North Coast
South
Texas
U.S.A.

Budget Travel

American Cities (30)
Britain
Canada
Caribbean
Europe
France
Germany
Hawaii
Italy
Japan
London
Mexico
Spain

Fun Guides

Acapulco
Bahamas
London
Montreal
Puerto Rico
San Francisco
St. Martin/Sint Maarten
Waikiki

MANUFACTURED IN THE UNITED STATES OF AMERICA
10 9 8 7 6 5 4 3 2 1

CONTENTS

CONTENTS

CONTENTS

THE NEW ZEALAND SCENE

THE FACE OF NEW ZEALAND

THE SOUTH PACIFIC

PLANNING YOUR TRIP

PLANNING YOUR TRIP

by
LOIS BRETT

The writer is a journalist and a Pacific specialist, having lived and traveled in that area for the past fifteen years. She has written extensively on 33 destinations within the Pacific basin.

WHAT WILL IT COST? Traveling in the South Pacific can be confusing to the ordinary tourist because of the multiplicity of standards of accommodations available. Many small hotels lack restaurants but have kitchens. Large hotels usually have dining and bar facilities. Tourists can find a number of international standard hotels in the major cities and resort areas.

In general it will cost two people about $155 a day—excluding liquor, gasoline for rented cars, which can be quite expensive, and the car rental itself—to travel in the area. But this is a deceptive figure that may vary widely from island group to island group, from cities to small towns within a single group, and from main islands to outer islands. The figure is also high because it includes sizable amounts for tours and excursions, most of which involve fairly expensive boat and plane trips. And, of course, currency exchange rates vary.

Typical Daily Budget for Two Persons	
Room at a moderate hotel	$60.00
Light breakfast for two	14.00
Lunch for two at a moderate restaurant	16.00
Dinner for two at a moderate restaurant	30.00
Touring and excursions	35.00
	$155.00

According to this book's system of categories, a moderate hotel room for double occupancy ranges from $50–70. An inexpensive restaurant is one where dinner will cost less than $10 per person. (All $ prices are U.S.$ unless otherwise noted.)

In addition to a realistic amount for touring and excursions, you will need to include adequate funds for souvenirs, postage, and extra film.

You can cut costs somewhat by taking advantage of free coffee or tea heaters in most Australian or New Zealand hotels (also available on many Aust. or N.Z.-oriented islands) and by picnicking for lunch as much as is possible when you have a car to carry coolers, thermos bottles, and other picnic paraphernalia.

With these general rules stated, we can take an overview of the regions included in this book to see how much they depart from the norm. Prices listed below were in effect in 1985 and are subject to change.

Australia offers a variety of accommodations—luxury hotels, smaller hotels, TraveLodge hotels & (far superior to their US equivalents) motels, more moderate motels, camping grounds, etc. Single rooms run from about $25 per night outside the larger cities and from about $45 in Melbourne and Sydney, with doubles beginning at about $50. Breakfast is often included.

Australia is the one place in the South Pacific where camping is widespread. There are also camping tours from less than a week to over a month.

There is a wide variety of restaurants in the larger cities, offering a range of international cuisines.

New Zealand also has hotels in every category and in every kind of setting—urban, rural, and resort. Rooms can cost anywhere from $25–80 for singles and $30–90 for doubles, depending upon location and facilities.

Few of the scenic and historic spots are served by rail, and travel is mostly by coach or air. The longest day journey by coach would cost $16–40.

Like Australia, New Zealand has a wide range of restaurants in its major cities. You can dine on simple fare or enjoy gourmet meals, as your budget dictates.

In the **Cook Islands** you can get a room for as little as $6 (for one); the international Rarotongan Resort Hotel is even considered a bargain: $25–39. Small hotels with kitchens are becoming a bargain. Some offer discounts for lengthy stays.

You can rent cars, motorcycles, and bicycles in Rarotonga; charter flights are available but they are expensive.

Fiji has bargains. There are places you can stay, usually on the smaller islands, for as little as $7 a night per person—with breakfast—and for $7 more you get full meals! But these guest houses are on the outer islands. Fancier accommodations cost about $24 for a single, $30 for a double. Rates for deluxe hotels such as the Regent in Nadi, run around $88–116 for a double.

Getting around the islands can cost as much as $20 per person by plane and $40 per person per day by boat with meals.

American Samoa has the Rainmaker Hotel, which is the only international standard hotel in Pago Pago. Singles run $45; $60 double; suites $65–75. Samoan fares: single $37; double $38, additional person $6. Children under 12 are free. The Apiolefaga Inn, P.O. Box 336, Pago Pago, has 8 rooms at $30.

Western Samoa. On Savai'i Island you can stay in the Safua Hotel at Lalomalava for around $30.

In Apia, at establishments such as Aggie Grey's Hotel, rates start at $51 single; $76 double, including meals. Smaller hotels are available for $12–24. The international Tusitala Hotel runs around $35.

French Polynesia is a paradise—but with perhaps the most expensive accommodations of all the Pacific Islands, with virtually no hotel room available for less than $20 for a single. Beach-side bungalows can cost up to $100 per day and meals are commensurately high.

Prices in **Papua New Guinea** are expensive. In the highlands, you can pay $115 and up (meals and sightseeing included); in Port Moresby rates range $25–102. There is virtually no overland travel to the interior, so the only way to get around is by air and sea, which generally is more expensive.

Kiribati (formerly Gilbert Islands) has few accommodations. The Captain Cook Hotel on Christmas Island has 24 units. Rates are about $50 with a/c. Meals are inexpensive. The Otintai Hotel P.O. Box 270, Bikenibeu, Tarawa, has 20 a/c rooms at $31–38 with bath. Meals moderately priced. Robert Louis Stevenson Hotel, Abemama, is about $15 and up, depending on facilities, and meals included.

New Caledonia is getting less expensive due to the strong exchange rate of the U.S. dollar. Rates range $18–45, depending on the island, for average-priced accommodations. The luxury resort or international standard hotels start at around $35 single and $40 double. Boat cruises run about $25 per person for an all-day trip to an outer island. The French enjoy their food and price does not seem to matter—consider it expensive. Hotel reservations before arrival are a must.

Vanuatu (formerly New Hebrides) hotel space is also at a premium and tourists should make sure they have guaranteed reservations before arriving. Rooms can be obtained for as little as $25 single. Resorts have rates that range from $39 single to $77 double. French restaurants are expensive compared to the Chinese restaurants. But there are hamburger and snack facilities where you can budget food dollars.

Solomon Islands can be a bargain. Even in Honiara you can get a single room—without shower and air conditioning—for around $18 and most doubles go for $20 or under. You can also travel from island to island by boat at relatively moderate prices.

Tonga is not considered expensive. Moderate accommodations can be had for around $10–15, and the International Dateline Hotel, where diplomats and royalty from around the world have stayed, starts at around $29.

 HOW TO GO? Between the all-expenses-paid-in-advance type of travel and the pay-as-you-go there are enormous variations and unless you are a widely experienced traveler you will be wise to consult a travel agent on the various possibilities. We list below the four principal ways of traveling:

The group tour, in which you travel with others, following a prearranged itinerary hitting all the high spots, and paying a single all-inclusive price that covers everything—transportation, meals, lodging, sightseeing tours, guides. These can range from two weeks to several months and can be taken on luxury or budget levels. Usually accompanied by experienced multilingual guides.

Furthermore, there are possibilities for special interest tours in which you are ensured of companions with similar interests or hobbies to your own. Whether you want to visit World War II sites or enjoy the South Pacific horticulture, your travel agent will be able to find you a specialized tour.

The freelance tour is now defined as following a set itinerary planned for you by the travel agent or by tour operators, with all costs in advance. You are strictly on your own, not with any group. This type of tour allows for a great deal of flexibility. Hotel reservations and transportation facilities are all taken care of by the travel agent, but no sightseeing is included—you do this on your own. If your arrangements are through one of the larger operators, their representative may meet you on arrival and help you with your luggage. This same rep can book you on sightseeing tours, if you want them, but you will pay extra for this.

The FIT (foreign independent travel) tour is the custom-made type of program, all arranged for you by your travel agent prior to your departure. The agent tailors the tour to your preferences. There's a charge for this type of service, so it's an expensive way to travel. Your air or sea travel is paid in advance; you can pay for tours as you go.

The majority of the islands in the Pacific and Australia and New Zealand require you have a visa and a paid-for onward ticket to your next destination. You must also be able to prove you have enough money, traveller's checks, or a bank draft to be able to stay within their country for the period of your visit.

TRAVEL AGENTS. Travel agents are experts in the increasingly complicated business of tourism. A good travel agent (and they are located everywhere) can save you time and money through knowledge of details which you could not be expected to know about. Your agent can help you take advantage of special reductions in air fares and the like, save you time by making it unnecessary for you to waste precious days abroad trying to get tickets and reservations. In the all-important phase of planning your trip, even if you wish to travel independently, it is wise to take advantage of the services of these specialists. Whether you select a large or small organization is only a matter of your preference. But be sure the agent is reliable.

If you wish your agent merely to arrange a steamship or airline ticket or to book you on a package tour, the services should cost you nothing as the agent almost certainly has a commission from the tour operator.

If, on the other hand, you wish your agent to plan an individual itinerary for you, there will be a service charge on the total cost of the work done. This may amount to 10 or 15 percent, but it will save you money on balance. If your travel budget is limited, you should frankly explain this to your agent and have an interesting itinerary worked out accordingly.

If you cannot locate a travel agent near your home, we recommend the following:

The Pacific Area Travel Association (PATA) is a non-profit corporation to promote and facilitate travel and tourism to and among Pacific destinations. Contact PATA, 228 Grant Avenue, San Francisco, California 94108.

Membership totals over 2,200 and represents 34 destination countries. Included in this membership are carriers (airlines, cruise ship operators, railways, road transport companies), hotels and publications having a primary interest in the Pacific and travel as a whole.

Another place to write in the United States is to the American Society of Travel Agents, 3 East 54th Street, New York, New York 10022. In Britain, write to the Association of British Travel Agents, 55 Newman Street, London W1P 4AH. Any agency affiliated with these organizations is almost sure to be thoroughly reliable.

 MONEY MATTERS. Many of the rates in this book are in the local currency. Rates below show only approximations and should be used only as a rough guide. Check with your bank or travel agent for rates before departure.

U.S. ($) DOLLAR COST					
American Samoa:					
(US$)	(US$1)	$1.00	(US$5)	$5.00	(US$25)	$25.00
Australia: (A$)	(A$1)	$0.68	(A$5)	$3.40	(A$25)	$17.00
Cook Islands:					
(New Zealand $)	(NZ$1)	$0.45	(NZ$5)	$2.25	(NZ$25)	$11.25
Fiji: (Fiji $)	(F$1)	$0.84	(F$5)	$4.23	(F$25)	$21.18
Kiribati:					
(Australia $)	(A$1)	$0.68	(A$5)	$3.40	(A$25)	$17.00
New Caledonia:	(100CFP)	$0.62	(500CFP)	$3.10	(1,000CFP)	$6.20
(French Pacific Franc, CFP)					
New Zealand: (NZ$)	(NZ$1)	$0.45	(NZ$5)	$2.25	(NZ$25)	$11.25
Papua New Guinea:					
(Kina)	(K1)	$0.80	(K5)	$4.00	(K25)	$20.00
Solomon Islands:					
(SBD)	(SBD1)	$0.73	(SBD5)	$3.65	(SBD25)	$18.25
Tahiti:					
(French Pacific Franc, CFP)	(Fr 100)	$0.62	(Fr 500)	$3.10	(Fr 1000)	$6.20
Tonga: (T$)	(T$1)	$0.67	(T$5)	$3.35	(T$25)	$16.75
Vanuatu (New Hebrides):					
(Vatu franc)	(V100)	$1.00	(V500)	$5.00	(V2500)	$25.00
Western Samoa:					
(Tala WS$)	(WS$1)	$0.60	(WS$5)	$3.00	(WS$25)	$15.00

These figures represent exchange rates valid at publication time. However, check with your bank or travel agent for the latest rates.

Credit Travel and Credit Cards. A number of organizations in the United States, Canada, and Britain make credit cards available which enable you to sign for hotel and restaurant bills, car rentals, purchases, and so forth, and pay the resulting total at one time on a monthly bill, either pay-as-you-go or in installments after you return home. In these days of currency exchange rate fluctuations, cards save you the trouble of converting, as you'll be billed in dollars back home at current exchange rate on date of purchase. If you want to be certain of the rate at which you will pay, insist on the establishment entering the current rate onto your credit card charge at the time you sign it—this will prevent the management from holding your charge until a more favorable rate (to them) comes along, something which could cost you more dollars than you counted on. (On the other hand, should the dollar be revalued upward before your charge is entered, you could gain a little.) Some credit card organizations are *American Express, BankAmericard (VISA), Carte Blanche, Diner's Club, Eurocard, Japan Credit Bureau, MasterCard, Motel Federation of Australia, New Zealand Bank Card, Overseas Trust Bank, Union Card,* and *Barclaycard.*

Also on credit, airline tickets can be bought on the installment plan with a ten percent down payment securing the reservations; the balance, plus interest, being paid in monthly installments.

Finally, you can borrow money specifically for travel, from your bank or from special firms handling travel loans.

Travelers' checks are the best way to safeguard travel funds. They are sold by various banks and companies in terms of American and Canadian dollars, pounds sterling, and other foreign currencies. We recommend buying them in the local currencies you will be using, whenever possible. These are called destination-currency checks, and have the double advantage of being cashed free of service charge, and protecting you against loss on exchange rates. Those issued by *American Express, First National City Bank (Citibank)* and *Bank of America* are best known and their offices are most widespread. The *Bank of America* has 28,000 correspondent banks around the world; *Thomas Cook & Son* has 20,000; *Barclay's Bank,* about 8,000.

It usually helps to buy foreign currency up to the maximum permissible, or in amounts to meet your anticipated expenses. This also helps to get you through airports, porters, taxis, bellhops at your next stop . . . Sometimes you can do this at larger banks. There are a number of private firms that buy and sell foreign money; look under Foreign Money Brokers and Dealers in the Yellow Pages of large-city phone books.

Don't ever have any truck with characters who sidle up to you on the street with offers to change money.

Changing travelers' checks or cash is easiest at your hotel, but will cost you more (and it will be worse in shops and restaurants!). Some small South Pacific shops do not cash or change travelers' checks. So change at banks, if you can afford the extra time, and try to avoid doing so at weekends, when rates are less advantageous. Rates at main downtown banks are often better than those at airport branches. So try to have on hand enough local currency for arrival at next port of call, to get you through the unnerving procedures at airports with porters, taxi drivers, bellhops at the hotel, etc.

 SPECIAL INTEREST TRAVEL. More and more people are looking for unusual methods of travel and off-beat, but purposeful, pastimes. The standard tours are still popular with those on limited time and those who expect to be in the Pacific only once in their lifetime. However, special interest tours are rocketing into popularity. There are literally hundreds of different tours in special interest categories ranging from artifacts to scuba diving. The problem is to select the right one from such an abundance. No matter what your interest, there is a package holiday to suit you. If you don't like packages, you can still go it alone, putting purpose into travel by fixing up special visits before you leave. If you don't want to plan ahead, you can wait until you arrive before choosing a special interest tour.

If you want a change from your usual holiday and in complete contrast to your normal routine, try variety. It brings an extra dimension to travel which should be just the thing to give your vacation added zip. For specific information, write to the National Government Tourist Office. Your special interest may be one which has clubs or other activities in which you may wish to become involved.

Of particular interest to visitors to the Southern Hemisphere in 1986 will be the return of Halley's Comet. Astronomers feel the best views will be had below the Equator between February and April. A number of cruise ship lines are offering voyages centered around the comet (contact individual cruise lines; see below). The U.S. Naval Observatory has a recorded message about the comet's whereabouts and visibility: 202-653-0258.

Here are examples of the diverse interests to be enjoyed or explored.

American Samoa: anthropology, dressmaking, LBJ Tropical Medical Center, photography, Sadie Thompson's hotel (of Maugham fame and now Max Halleck's store No. 3), tapa cloth, tuna canneries.

Australia: arts, astronomy, casino (gambling), cattle, crafts, farming, fauna, flora, gemstones, historical sights, horse breeding, horticulture, national parks, ornithology, railroading, sheep shearing, wine making.

Cook Islands: fruit processing, horse racing (but not the serious type—Cook Islanders never guarantee their horses will cross the finish line. It all depends on how the horses feel that day), museum, numismatics, philately.

Fiji: fauna, Fijian dancing, firewalking, gold mines, photography, pottery making, rail tour through sugar cane fields, tapa cloth making and weaving.

Kiribati: bird sanctuary (largest in Pacific, on Christmas Island); WWII historical sites (Tarawa, Abemama); Robert Louis Stevenson site and hotel (Abemama).

New Caledonia: aquarium, botanical garden and zoo, nickel mining, shopping for French items such as lingerie, shoes, fabrics and clothing as well as ties and shoes for men.

New Zealand: anthropology, archeology, cultural artifacts, dairying, farming, fiords, glaciers, meat industry (65% of world exports of lamb and mutton come from New Zealand), greenstone (a type of jade), railway museum, research museum of New Zealand Geological Survey, sheep-wool industry.

Papua New Guinea: anthropology, archeology, historical walks (covering trails from WWII), ornithology, plantation visits (coffee, tea, rubber), philately, shells, singsings (village festivals).

Solomons: bird watching, garden touring, philately, WWII artifacts.

Tahiti: aerial sightseeing, anthropology, archeology, botany, exploring different islands of French Polynesia, Gauguin Museum.

Tonga: birdwatching; Captain Cook's discovery tour, Christianity affinity tours, coconut processing, dancing/feasting, farming, handicrafts (Tonga weaving, basketware and tapa cloth), philately, whaling.

Vanuatu (formerly New Hebrides): artifacts, art centers, bird watching, Pentecost land divers, shell collecting, stone age people (the Big Nambas).

Western Samoa: aerial tours, feasts and dancing, island exploring, plantation visiting (copra), shell collecting, tapa cloth making and weaving.

Note: All of the destinations in this book have many more special interest categories. (Also check the sport section). Write to the Official Tourist Information Bureaus if your particular hobby or interest is missing.

TOURIST INFORMATION. All the major tourist countries maintain official information bureaus in important cities: New York, San Francisco, London, Toronto and many others. They have a wealth of free printed matter to help you in planning your trip and they are at your service to give you any additional special information you may require. There is no charge for any of this. They do not, however, issue tickets or make hotel reservations.

There are many special holidays and events in the Pacific that are well worth seeing. Take advantage of these cultural experiences by planning ahead. Write to the tourist bureaus listed below for specifics.

Remember that in the case of Australia and New Zealand the amount of information available is so great that you should try to specify which areas within these two countries you wish to visit, or indicate your special interests.

Addresses of the official tourist information bureaus in the South Pacific Islands, Australia, New Zealand, the United States, Canada, and the United Kingdom are:

American Samoa: Director of Tourism, Government of American Samoa, PO Box 1147, Samoa, Pago Pago, American Samoa 96799.

Australian Tourist Commission, Head office: 324 St. Kilda Rd., Melbourne, Victoria 3004, Australia; 5 Elizabeth St., Sydney NSW 2000, Australia. North America: 3550 Wilshire Blvd., Los Angeles, California 90010; 489 5th Ave., New York, New York 10017. United Kingdom: 20 Savile Row, 4th flr., London W1X 1AE. Europe: Australische Fremdenverkehrszentrale, D6000, Frankfurt am Main, Neue Mainzerstrasse 22, Federal Republic of Germany or any Air New Zealand office.

Cook Islands Tourist Authority, PO Box 14, Otera, Rarotonga, Cook Islands.

Fiji Visitors Bureau, Head office: PO Box 92, Thomson St., Suva. Also in Fiji: PO Box 9217, Nadi. North America: Fiji Consulate General Office, 3701 Wilshire Blvd., Los Angeles, California 90010. New Zealand: PO Box 1179, Auckland. Australia: 38 Martin Place, Sydney, NSW 2000.

Kiribati (formerly the Gilbert Islands), Government of the Republic of Kiribati, Ministry of Natural Resources, PO Box 261, Bairiki, Tarawa.

New Caledonia Office Du Tourisme, Head office: PO Box 688, Nouméa. Australia: 39 York St., 13th flr., Sydney, NSW 2000; New Zealand: UTA French Airlines, 11 Commerce St., Auckland.

New Zealand Govt. Tourist Office, Head office: New Zealand Govt. Tourist & Publicity Dept., Private Bag, Wellington, New Zealand. Australia: 115 Pitt St., (GPO Box 614), Sydney NSW 2000; 330 Collins St. (PO Box 2136T), Melbourne 3000 Victoria; 288 Edward St., Box 62, Brisbane, Queensland 4000; 16 St. George's Terrace, Perth, Western Australia 6000. Europe: 6000 Frankfurt am Main, Kaiserhofstrasse 7, Federal Republic of Germany. North America: Alcoa Bldg., Suite 970, One Maritime Plaza, San Francisco, California 94111; 10960 Wilshire Blvd., Suite 1530, Los Angeles, California 90024; 630 5th Ave., Suite 530, New York, New York 10111; IBM Tower, 701 West Georgia St., Vancouver, British Columbia Y7Y 1B6, Canada. United Kingdom: New Zealand House, Haymarket, London S.W.1Y. 4T.Q.

Papua New Guinea National Tourist Authority, PO Box 7144, Boroko, Port Moresby, Papua New Guinea.

Solomon Islands Tourist Authority, PO Box 321, Honiara, Solomon Islands.

Tahiti Tourist Board, Head office: BP Box 65, Papeete, Tahiti. North America: 2330 Wilshire Blvd., Suite 200, Los Angeles, California 90064. Australia: BNP Bldg., 12 Castlereagh St., Sydney, NSW 2000.

Tonga Visitors Bureau, Head office: PO Box 37, Nuku'alofa, Tonga Islands. Australia: 61 Cross St., Double Bay, NSW 2028. United Kingdom: Tongan High Commission, New Zealand House, Haymarket, London. SW1Y4TQ.

Vanuatu (formerly New Hebrides):*Tourist Information Bureau,* Head office: PO Box 209, Port Vila.

Western Samoa Department of Tourism, Government of Western Samoa, PO Box 862, Apia. North America: c/o Polynesian Airlines, 9841 Airport Blvd., Room 418, Los Angeles, California 90045.

PASSPORTS. A valid passport is required for all destinations. The following are the requirements for individual areas covered in this book:

American Samoa. A valid passport is required of all except United States citizens; however, United States citizens must have proof of citizenship. American Samoa is not a port of entry for the United States—foreign citizens intending to proceed or return to the United States must have the appropriate visa.

Australia. A passport valid for at least 3 months longer than intended stay and a return or onward ticket is required of all passengers. (Passport not required for New Zealanders.)

Cook Islands. A valid passport is required, except for nationals of Australia and New Zealand whose stay does not exceed 31 days. Note: Australian nationals will need a passport to re-enter New Zealand. On direct flights from the Cook Islands, New Zealand nationals must have proof of national status.

Fiji. A passport valid for 6 months beyond date of departure from Fiji is required, plus reserved onward transportation.

Kiribati (formerly Gilbert Islands). Valid passport required by all.

New Caledonia. A valid passport is required of all except nationals of France.

New Zealand. A passport valid for 3 months beyond intended stay is required, except for nationals of Australia and the Commonwealth countries who have permission to reside indefinitely in Australia and New Zealand, but passports are necessary for reentry into Australia.

Papua New Guinea. A valid passport is required.

Solomon Islands. A valid passport is required.

Special Note: Bougainville and Buka (part of the Solomon Islands) also require a valid passport.

Tahiti. A valid passport is required, except for nationals of France and African countries of the former French community.

Tonga. A valid passport is required, except for nationals of Cook, Niue, and Tokelau Islands.

Tuvalu (Ellice Islands). Valid passport required by all.

Vanuatu (formerly New Hebrides). A valid passport is required.

Western Samoa. A valid passport is required.

Wallis Islands require a valid passport.

VISAS. American Samoa. Not required of U.S. citizens. Foreign visitors do not need visa for stay of one month. Onward confirmed reservations to a point outside American Samoa required of all visitors.

Note: Pago Pago is not a port of entry to U.S. Non-U.S. citizens who plan on proceeding to U.S. from American Samoa must comply with appropriate regulations, and multiple-entry visa is required if non-U.S. citizen travels from U.S. to Pago Pago and plans to return to U.S.

Australia. Required of all visitors except New Zealanders and passengers in transit for up to 72 hours who arrive and depart on same mode of transportation.

Tourist visas valid for up to four years for American citizens, with a maximum stay of six months. Multiple entry is usually granted U.S. citizens.

Visas available from Australian government representatives for no charge, with application form and one passport-size photo in North America. Allow 21 days if applying by mail.

Cook Islands. Entry permit is not required for bona fide visitors for stay of 31 days or less. For others, entry permits may be applied for through Principal Immigration Officer, Ministry of Labour and Commerce, P.O. Box 61, Rarotonga, Cook Islands, or New Zealand embassy or consulate offices. All visitors must hold valid documents and tickets with confirmed bookings for onward or return journey.

Ellice Islands. (See Tuvalu)

Fiji. None required for citizens of U.S. and Commonwealth countries (except Pakistan). Many other countries are also exempt. Citizens of these countries are issued visitor permits on arrival, good for 30 days and extendable up to six months. Sufficient funds for length of stay and onward ticket also required.

For information on citizens of other countries or other visa details write: Fiji Mission to the United Nations, 1 UN Plaza, 26th Floor, New York, N.Y. 10017. Allow 14 days.

Kiribati (formerly Gilbert Islands). Required of all except British subjects and British Commonwealth citizens. Visitors may, upon arrival, apply for a visitor permit entitling them to a stay of a maximum of four months in any period of 12 months, provided they hold tickets for return or onward tickets and sufficient funds for their maintenance. Visa applications can be obtained at British consulates or from the Principal Immigration Officer, Office of the Chief Minister, P.O. Box 261, Bairiki, Tarawa, Kiribaki.

New Caledonia. Not required for stay of up to 30 days provided visitor has return or onward ticket. Visa may be obtained for stay of up to three months, good for multiple entries and extendable upon arrival. No group visas. Visas can be obtained from French consulate or embassy. Two photos needed.

New Zealand. None required for tourists from U.S. (except American Samoa), Japan, New Caledonia and Tahiti for stay of up to 30 days; citizens of West Germany, Iceland and Malta for stay of not more than three months; citizens of Belgium, Denmark, Finland, France, Liechtenstein, Luxembourg, Monaco, Netherlands, Norway, Sweden and Switzerland for stay of not more than six months. Commonwealth citizens require only temporary entry authority which may be granted on arrival; those not wholly of European origin must obtain it before departure. Sufficient funds for length of stay and onward ticket required.

Visa applications at nearest New Zealand embassy or consulate or at British consulates. Allow two weeks by mail.

Papua New Guinea. A visa will be issued on arrival for tourist visit up to 30 days. Visas available prior to arrival for stays up to 60 days. Onward ticket required.

Note: A visa for Australia does not qualify the holder for entry into Papua New Guinea—a separate entry permit is essential.

Solomon Islands. None required for most Western European, British Commonwealth or U.S. citizens. All visitors must have onward travel ticket and sufficient funds for stay.

Tahiti. Not required for citizens of 44 countries, including U.S., for up to 30 days.

Also required: onward ticket or deposit equivalent to onward airfare or guarantee of repatriation.

Tonga. Visitors are given entry permits on arrival at the airport, good for a maximum stay of 30 days. Onward or return tickets required.

Tuvalu (Ellice Islands). No visa required of British or British Commonwealth citizens. Visitor permits, however, are issued upon arrival for tourist stay up to a maximum of four months. Tickets for return or onward travel plus adequate funds for self-maintenance during stay required.

Vanuatu (formerly New Hebrides). Not required for stays of 30 days or less. Onward tickets required.

Western Samoa. None required for tourists up to 30 days, providing they hold tickets with reserved seats and documents for onward or return travel.

Wallis Islands. No visa required for a maximum of 30 days. A tourist visa may be obtained at normal cost for stays up to 90 days. The French in New Caledonia will want to know why you are going to Wallis, so it is wise to secure in advance written entry permission from the Chief Administrator for Overseas Administration of the French Republic in the Pacific, Noumea, New Caledonia. Or, the Commissariat a la Promotion de Departements et Territoires d'Outre-Mer, 83 Boulevard du Montparnasse, 75006, Paris, France.

 HEALTH CERTIFICATES. In 1985, the International Association for Medical Assistance to Travelers (IAMAT) issued a release warning tourists of the *malaria* increase throughout the world. Many destinations in the South Pacific fit into this category. Chloroquine has been the usual treatment, however, in Papua New Guinea and the Solomon Islands, there is a tolerance problem and visitors should take both the drugs Fansidar and Chloroquine, as designated by your personal physician. Malaria medication must be continued for 6 weeks after leaving infected area. For IAMAT's free folder *How to Protect against Malaria,* which gives complete details about the disease, its control, and high risk areas, write: IAMAT, 736 Center St., Lewiston, New York 14092.

The U.S. Department of Health and Human Services, Public Health Service Centers for Disease Control, Atlanta, Georgia 30333, also makes a few suggestions for visitors to South Pacific destinations:

Gamma globulin, typhoid/tetanus: 2 shots 30 days apart, if you've had no immunization before, or typhoid/tetanus booster, polio booster, if it has been 10 years since your last. *These are not requirements to enter these countries but they are strongly recommended.* Please consult your physician.

Listed below are Health Certificate requirements necessary to enter each country. Single asterisk (*) indicates a requirement; double asterisk (**) indicates immunization strongly suggested by the health organizations mentioned above; you should check with your personal physician.

American Samoa: Gamma globulin, typhoid/tetanus, and polio.**

Cook Islands: Gamma globulin, typhoid/tetanus, and polio.** Special Note: All luggage except hand luggage loaded in Honolulu, Nadi, or Papeete is fumigated on arrival in the Cook Islands. Cabin may be fumigated before passengers disembark.

Fiji: No shots required unless coming from endemic zones. Gamma globulin, typhoid/tetanus, and polio.**

Kiribati and **Tuvalu:** *Yellow fever* and *cholera** (even required of those not leaving the airport). Gamma globulin, typhoid/tetanus, and polio.**

New Caledonia: Gamma globulin, typhoid/tetanus, and polio.**

New Zealand: Gamma globulin, typhoid/tetanus, and polio** if you will be stopping over in any destination listed, other than Australia.

Papua New Guinea: *Cholera* and *yellow fever.** *Malaria* exists throughout the country. Fansidar and Chloroquine recommended strongly; gamma globulin, typhoid/tetanus, and polio.**

Solomon Islands: Same as Papua New Guinea.
Tahiti: No shots required unless coming from endemic zone.**
Tonga: Gamma globulin, typhoid/tetanus, polio.**
Vanuatu: No shots required unless coming from endemic zone. Malaria risk; Chloroquine suggested if recommended by your physician; also gamma globulin, typhoid/tetanus, polio.**
Wallis and Futuna. None required unless coming from afflicted areas. Typhoid and paratyphoid.**
Western Samoa: *Yellow fever.** Gamma globulin, typhoid/tetanus, polio.**

PETS. There is so much red tape in traveling with pets that it is best not to even consider taking them along. Long quarantine periods are the main reason; problems often arise from not being able to transit from one island area to another.

Exception: Seeing eye dogs may accompany any passenger traveling to New Zealand. For regulations on seeing eye dogs to other destinations, it is best to check with embassy or consulate when applying for passport or visa.

INSURANCE. Always a wise investment wherever you travel. In the South Pacific it would be more for loss of luggage than for sleight-of-hand. The great majority of the population in the South Pacific is basically honest. However, this does not mean you should not lock up your valuables or other items considered irreplaceable.

Contact your insurance broker or travel agent for types and costs of personal liability insurance coverage.

WHAT TO WEAR. The smart, sophisticated traveler usually packs light. And don't forget to save space in your suitcase for your purchases. A plus for travelers to the Pacific, according to Air New Zealand, is that your baggage allowance has been changed from the old 44/66 pound weight. Now you are allowed two pieces of luggage, plus one carry-on. The total for economy is two pieces with an overall length/width/height no more than 104 inches. No single piece may be over 62 inches. For first-class passengers, the rules are the same, except they have a 124-inch limit. Total weight for both classes is 70 pounds per piece of luggage. Carry-on luggage may not exceed 44 inches.

Drip dry summer clothes or cottons that can be easily and quickly laundered are a boon. Just remember that nylon can be hot in the tropics. The dacron/cotton dries just as fast and just as smooth and is pleasantly cool to wear. Cotton knits stay comparatively wrinkle-free. Better take along one sweater. It can get cool in the hill areas of the tropics after the sun goes down, especially in the winter months. If you are going to a posh resort, you may want tropical dinner clothes, but few places insist upon them these days. The emphasis everywhere is on comfortable, casual and colorful clothing. In general, it's safe to plan your wardrobe as you would for summer at home, but with more bathing suits. A small folding umbrella with or without case is a must for sudden showers.

For men: A lightweight sportcoat, a couple of dress shirts, several sportshirts, walking shorts and a bathing suit should cover the basic outfit. A tie or two for fancy restaurants, a pair of dress shoes, sandals and tennis shoes for beach exploring among the coral are the other more important items. Use your own discretion on how much underwear, socks, etc. you want to tote along.

For women: Pantsuits with matching skirt are ideal. Remember, you will be traveling in territory where shorts and bathing suits are worn only at resorts, beaches or on boats. Shorts are not worn in town nor is any outlandish or questionable attire. Do bring shorts, bathing suits and a couple of tropical type evening dresses. Bring sandals, comfortable walking shoes and tennis shoes for beach exploring, and, of course, dress shoes for special occasions. Some modish sandals can serve for both day and evening wear. You might save some of your travel wardrobe money for a shopping spree in Tahiti or New Caledonia where some very smart items from France, Italy, and London can be purchased in the local boutiques, and can be worn with comfort and flair throughout the South Pacific Islands.

Note: Australian and New Zealand ladies dress more formally than those in the other destinations in this book. Dresses are worn in town, to dinner at the deluxe type restaurants and hotels, or when dining with friends.

It appears that everything shuts down on Sundays throughout the Pacific, Australia, and New Zealand. Mornings are devoted to church services and evenings, too, on most of the island communities. Everyone dresses in his best and the entire day on the islands is devoted to religion and family outings. So, plan on bringing along something to wear to at least one Sunday service. The choirs on any of the islands make it worthwhile. (Refer to section on "Special Events.")

 WHAT TO TAKE. Travel light. Double check what you have packed in clothing—then eliminate half. Decide what else you want to take along. If possible, switch from heavy duty suitcases to the lightweight canvas type; this saves weight for more important things. Not only that, it's amazing how much you can squeeze into the corners of those flexible bags.

Miscellaneous items: *Camera* (movie and still); loads of film as it's extremely expensive abroad. Ask your travel agent if there are restrictions on how much film you can take into the country you'll be visiting.

A *portable radio* (the smaller the better) will give you a good idea of what programming is enjoyed in the country you are visiting. You can frequently tune in the Armed Forces network and maybe pick up a bit of the news. A fascinating pastime is to listen to the local music; if some of it is Americanized, it's amazing how soon you'll pick up a little of the local language.

A *tape recorder* will bring back the sounds of the country, from the time you awaken to the time you go to bed. Don't forget to bring extra tapes; they too are more expensive than at home.

Flashlight (and a few extra batteries), *Candle* (just in case everything fails), *Tweezers,* small *Medicine Kit,* plus medicine and prescriptions in generic terms, *Rubber Bands, Small Scissors, Swiss Knife,* (one with everything will solve problems of scissors, bottle opener and others), small *Sewing Kit* and a few buttons. A small kit with toilet paper, soap, small plastic container of powdered detergent and your favorite cosmetics, just in case no refills are available. Remember only one small extra of anything is usually sufficient.

Extra Eyeglasses (sun and regular), plus a copy of your eyeglass prescriptions. If you have any serious medical problem, like diabetes, wear a *Medic-Alert Tag* or *Bracelet.* Do not forget some medication for diarrhea. (*Lomotil* can usually be bought without a prescription in some areas; but bring a supply—it will solve many problems.)

A few *Plastic Bags* will carry dirty laundry—different colors for different loads —for example, one color for items that didn't get dry just before take off. The more you color-code what you pack, the less time you'll have to spend searching.

A Berlitz *World Wide Phrase Book* frequently does wonders. You can use a favorite trick when lost or seeking a not-to-be-missed site. Buy a local postcard of the spot you want to go to, or a card of a monument, etc. near your destination, and show it to someone. This seldom fails to get results and most often you'll have a guide who will take you where you want to go at no cost. It's usually the hospitality of the South Pacific, Australia and New Zealand. People respond to a smile, a friendly attitude, or to someone who is lost. Thus, the first words to learn are "please" and "thank you."

 BEAUTY HINTS FOR MEN AND WOMEN. Hair: The humidity in the South Pacific will play an extremely important role when it comes to people who take special care of their hair. If your hair is straight, it will probably droop like a limp rag, but if you happen to have curly hair, it will most probably turn into the latest bush style. Without knowledge of how to attractively solve that problem, you may wish to have lessons before you leave home.

Several weeks before your trip, let your hair stylist know where you'll be traveling, the temperature and the humidity problem. (Refer to section on "Climate.") Wavy hair can be cut short enough to solve the bushy swelling. Long, straight hair may be cut in a short simple style easy enough to handle wherever you may travel.

Eyes: If you wear glasses, take along an extra pair or a prescription. Sunglasses are extremely important in the tropical area—it is wise to have a pair even if you don't usually wear them. The reflection of sky, water or white sandy beaches can create big problems. If you plan on relaxing under that palm tree reading, it may be worth the investment of purchasing a pair of sunglass-reading spectacles.

Skin: It is important to take care of your skin in this tropical land. For protection you'll need a sunscreen. If your skin is fair, take the sun a little at a time and keep it lubricated. A sun hat will help keep your face from turning to leather (it will also keep your hair healthy). Keep in mind reflection problems. If you are unprotected, it can cause serious sunburns. If your skin is oily, it is best to keep it clean. The more you perspire, the more you may wish to rinse your face to keep your oil glands and perspiration from completely clogging your pores. Those small disposable towelettes are ideal for purse or pocket—but remember, fresh cool water will also do the same job.

PHOTOGRAPHER'S HINTS. Best advice is to be sure to carry sufficient color film. Several of the smaller islands still do not stock fresh color film in all sizes, and to avoid disappointment, carry more color film than you plan to use. You'll probably end up using it all on your first stop if you don't take a good supply. And colored film is expensive away from home.

Black and white film is usually available in the capital cities. It can often be processed overnight and rates are generally comparable to those at home.

A good filter for bright sunlight is a must on your photo checklist, as well as mailing containers for sending color film home. While it may be a nuisance to trek off to the post office, another good hint is to airmail your exposed film for processing as often as possible. If possible, your unused film should be stored in plastic bags in a refrigerator.

In taking snaps, you should do the polite thing and ask if you may photograph people.

Hint: Shooting pictures in the Pacific region—green will overtake most other colors in your photo. If you overexpose by one-half stop you may help solve this problem in places such as the Cook Islands, Tahiti and other tropical islands.

When photographing people be sure they pose in the shade and try for back-lighting for more natural poses.

TRAVELING WITH CHILDREN. Traveling with children is always full of surprises, but the biggest one, for parents who haven't tried it, is that trips abroad with children are more enjoyable than those without. The peculiar curiosity of children, their enthusiasm about new lands and people and the special way they have of melting the reserve of strangers add a rewarding new dimension to travel.

Preparing the children should begin about two months prior to departure. Check the planned itinerary with their doctor to see what inoculations may be necessary. The physician can also advise what special prescriptions or feeding formulas should be taken along. Each child should have a thorough physical and dental exam.

Minor medical problems can easily be handled with a good first aid kit. Include the standard contents as recommended by the Red Cross, any special prescriptions required, spare glasses, a cough syrup, a stomach-ache remedy, a laxative, children's aspirin, an ophthalmic ointment and antidiarrheal tablets (they go down easier than the liquid). One of the greatest triumphs of medical science, as far as traveling children are concerned, is the individually packaged gauze pad. These are ideal for cleaning up the scrapes and scratches children collect the world over. A tube of zinc-oxide is a versatile aid for sun and wind burn, diaper rash and minor abrasions. The dosage and directions for all medicines should be checked with the physician before departure. Pack the kit in a small shoulder bag so it can easily be kept handy.

The itinerary itself should take the children into consideration. Because children's "biological clocks" are more finely tuned than adults', long trips should be divided into segments as short as possible to allow the children to adjust to time zone changes. This also decreases the period of time in which children can repeat the age-old question, "Are we there yet?"

Packing for children requires little extra effort. Clothing should be as simple, comfortable and versatile as possible. Wash-and-wear and stain-resistant fabrics will make life easier for parents. One of the handiest items will be a box of the small pre-moistened towelettes for impromptu cleaning of hands and faces. If a child is not yet a good walker, it is a good idea to pack him or her in a back carrier which allows a parent to carry a child while keeping their own hands free.

The times which try parents' souls (and their progeny's) do not usually occur at some major juncture of a trip, as one would expect, but at the scores of times when the family is waiting for a plane, waiting for a meal to be served, waiting for everyone else to get ready to leave for an outing. The solution is deceptively simple: toys. A few small cars such as the Corgi and Matchbox toys, a mini-doll a few inches high, small notebooks and pencils, small puzzles and games, should be kept on reserve in pocket or purse. If, when boredom rears its ugly head, the parent can produce a pastime, it is like a bridge over troubled waters. Easily portable collections of stamps, coins, jacket emblems, seashells or minerals also can be called into the breach when needed.

Hunger pangs have a way of striking children at the exact time when food isn't available. Carrying a small snack the children like will keep their sunny dispositions from suddenly clouding. Cereal products such as granola bars are nutritionally balanced and convenient.

Another continuing need of itinerant children is for what the Greeks call *to meros,* "the place" (lavatory), and it is indeed the place for anyone traveling with children. If you learn no other word of the language of the country in which you are traveling, you should know the one for "the place." It will save anxious moments of sign language when you have a very fidgety youngster in tow.

The languages themselves today prove little problem in all but the most out-of-the-way areas. Children have an innate ability to pick up foreign languages. It is not at all uncommon to see youngsters on tour acting as translators for their monolingual parents.

Most children adapt to foreign food more easily than their parents. However, spicy, rich foods and restaurants which appear unsavory should be avoided. Fresh milk, the child's staff of life, should be "almost universally suspect abroad," a widely-traveled physician has written. The same goes for ice cream. Drinking water in large hotels and restaurants is usually reliable, but bottled water is best for baby formulas.

SPECIAL NOTE: The people on the islands of the South Pacific love children —yours, theirs and their neighbors'. You will find this one of the delightful experiences in travelling through these countries with your children. Don't be surprised if you are invited to visit with a perfect stranger you may meet on a local bus. Your newfound friend will want you to share the joy of family life. If you have room in your suitcases for some frisbees, you will soon find yourself one of the most popular tourists on the island. Remember to leave one behind as a memento—if you take your whole supply with you the first visit, you'll have none to share elsewhere. Simple gifts such as frisbees are a small price to pay for the tremendous amount of hospitality you will receive wherever you go.

 HOW TO GET THERE. There are three possibilities: by air, sea or a combination of these. *From North America:* you should look into the possibility of 1) using the maximum stopover privileges and side trips at little or no extra cost on your airline ticket; (note that all carriers do not offer the same routing to or through the South Pacific); 2) going around the Pacific in a circle-type tour, picking up local airlines but not retracing the same route when you head back; 3) taking advantage of various combinations of plane and ship tours that will give you an exciting itinerary; and 4) making side trips by local airlines or shipping companies within your destination, if you have time and can go with an open schedule.

From Europe: You can travel by air over the North Pole through Moscow and Siberia to Tokyo, then south to your Pacific destination. You can also go through New York, San Francisco/Seattle/Los Angeles, to the Pacific. Another routing could be London, Bahrain, Singapore, Sydney then to the island destinations. There are also many other routings, so consult your travel agent.

If you have an economy or first-class ticket, you can have a number of stopovers included at no extra cost. If you are traveling by excursion or package, your stopovers will be limited.

In 1985 many changes took place with Pacific carriers. International and regional routings changed. Air fares became bargains again, especially for those heading to the South Pacific.

Consider buying a tour package from your travel agent who works with specialty Pacific tour operators and air carriers. *Air New Zealand, Continental, Pan American, Qantas* and *UTA French Airlines* all offer air/drive, air/special interest, air/South Seas or similar bargain combinations. (You will have to check cancellation policy on package tours carefully, however.)

Except for carriers traveling to and from Australia and New Zealand, there are only 5 direct international carriers that fly to the South Pacific from North America: *Air New Zealand, Continental Airlines, Pan American Airways, Qantas,* and *UTA French Airlines.* Travel throughout the South Pacific, once you get to Samoa, Fiji, or Tahiti, is mostly by regional carriers. *Air New Zealand* simplified its fare structure to 4 levels: first-class, business, full-fare economy, and 30-day advance purchase economy—all with unlimited stopover privileges. Tickets are good for one year.

Listed below are the destinations covered in this guide and the international and regional carriers that will get you there. Note: at presstime, *United Airlines* has made a bid to purchase *Pan Am's* Pacific business, but nothing has been finalized.

American Samoa (Pago Pago). From Apia (W. Samoa): *Polynesian Airlines, South Pacific Island Airways*. Auckland (via Western Samoa): *Air New Zealand/ South Pacific Island Airways (SPIA), Polynesian Airlines*. Cook Islands: *Air Nauru*. Nauru: *Air Nauru*. Suva (Fiji): *Air Pacific*. Tonga: *SPIA, Hawaiian Airlines*.

Australia. From North America: *Air New Zealand, Continental Airlines, Air Pacific, Pan American, Qantas, UTA.* Regional carriers: From Apia: *Polynesian Airlines*. Port Moresby (Papua New Guinea): *Air Niugini, Qantas.* Port Vila (Vanuatu): *Air Vanuatu, Ansett, Polynesian Airlines.* Tahiti: *Qantas, UTA, Air New Zealand.* Nadi: *Air Pacific, Polynesian Airlines.* Nouméa (New Caledonia): *Qantas, UTA.*

Cook Islands (Rarotonga). From Aitutaki (Cook Islands): *Cook Islands Airways*. Apia: *Polynesian Airlines*. Auckland, Christchurch, Wellington: *Air New Zealand*. Nadi: *Air New Zealand*. Nauru: *Air Nauru*. Papeete: *Air New Zealand, UTA.* Sydney, Brisbane, Melbourne: *Air New Zealand, Ansett, Trans Australian Airlines.* Pago Pago (American Samoa): *Air Nauru, Polynesian Airlines.*

Fiji (Nadi). From North America: *Air New Zealand, Continental Airlines. Qantas.* Regional carriers: From Apia: *Polynesian Airlines*. Auckland: *Air Pacific, Air New Zealand*. Brisbane: *Air Pacific*. Honiara, Guadalcanal (Solomon Islands): *Air Pacific*. Nauru: *Air Nauru*. Nouméa: *Air Caledonie*. Papeete: *Air Pacific, Air Nauru*. Sydney: *Air Pacific, Air New Zealand, Continental, CP Air, Qantas.* Tonga: *Air Pacific.*

Kiribati (Tarawa). From Honolulu via Christmas Island: *Air Tungaru*. Nauru: *Air Nauru*. Funifuti (Tuvalu): *Ar Turgaru*. Nadi: *Air Tungaru.*

New Caledonia (Nouméa). Auckland: *Air New Zealand, UTA*. Brisbane: *Air Caledonie*. Hobart (Tasmania): *Air Caledonie, Ansett*. Honolulu: *Continental* with *Air Caledonie*. Melbourne: *Air Caledonie, Qantas*. Nauru: *Air Nauru*. Papeete: *UTA*. Perth: *Ansett*. Sydney: *Qantas, UTA*. Wallis & Futuna: *Air Caledonie:* Port Vila (Vanuatu): *Air Caledonie.*

New Zealand (Auckland). From North America: *Air New Zealand, Continental Airlines, Pan American, Qantas* (via Australia). From Apia: *Air New Zealand, Polynesian Airlines.* Nadi: *Air New Zealand, Air Pacific.* Papeete: *Air New Zealand, UTA.* Pago Pago: *Air Nauru, Air New Zealand, Polynesian Airlines, SPIA.* Rarotonga: *Air New Zealand.* Suva: *Air Nauru, Air New Zealand, Air Pacific.* Tonga: *Air New Zealand, Polynesian Airlines.* Honiara: *Air Nauru.*

Papua New Guinea (Port Moresby). From North America: *American Airlines, United Airlines,* both with *SPIA* from Los Angeles via Honolulu, *United Airlines* with *SPIA* and *Qantas* from San Francisco. Auckland: *Air Niugini.* Brisbane: *Air Niugini, Qantas.* Cairns (Queensland): *Air Niugini.* Melbourne: *Ansett, Air Niugini.* Sydney: *Qantas, SPIA.* Honolulu: *Qantas, SPIA.* Honiara: *Air Niugini.*

Solomon Islands (Honiara, Guadalcanal). Adelaide: *Air Pacific* with *Solomon Island Airways, Ansett.* Brisbane: *Air Pacific* with *Solomon Island Airways.* Espiritu Santo (Vanuatu): *Solomon Island Airways.* Kieta (Papua New Guinea): *Solomon Island Airways, Air Niugini.* Melbourne: *Air Pacific* with *Solomon Island Airways, Ansett.* Nadi/Suva: *Air Pacific.* Nauru: *Air Nauru.* Port Moresby: *Air Niugini.* Port Vila: *Air Pacific, Solomon Island Airways.*

Tahiti (Papeete). From North America: *Air New Zealand, Qantas, UTA.* From Adelaide (Australia): *Air New Zealand, Ansett, Qantas.* Apia: *Polynesian Airlines.* Auckland: *Air New Zealand, UTA.* Brisbane: *Air New Zealand, Qantas.* Easter Island: *Lan Chile.* Hobart (Tasmania): *Air New Zealand, Qantas.* Honolulu: *Air New Zealand, Continental, Qantas, SPIA, UTA.* Melbourne: *Qantas.* Noumea: *UTA.* Pago Pago: *Polynesian Island Airways.* Rarotonga: *Air New Zealand, UTA.* Sydney: *Air New Zealand, Qantas, UTA.* Wellington: *Air New Zealand.*

Tonga (Tongatapu). From Apia: *Air New Zealand, Polynesian Airlines.* Auckland: *Air New Zealand, Air Pacific, Polynesian Airlines.* Honolulu: *Hawaiian Airlines, Polynesian Airlines.* Pago Pago: *Hawaiian Airlines, Polynesian Airlines.* Nadi/Suva: *Air Pacific.* Wellington: *Air New Zealand.*

Vanautu (Port Vila). Apia: *Polynesian Airlines.* Australia: *Air Pacific, Air Vanuatu, Ansett.* Honiara: *Air Pacific, Solomon Island Airways.* Nadi/Suva: *Air Pacific.* Nauru: *Air Nauru.*

Wallis and Futuna: From Nadi and Nouméa: *Air Caledonie.*

Western Samoa (Apia): From Auckland, Christchurch, Wellington: *Air New Zealand, Polynesian.* Honolulu: *SPIA, Polynesian Airlines.* Nadi/Suva: *Air Pacific, Polynesian.* Pago Pago: *Polynesian, SPIA.* Papeete: *Polynesian Airlines.* Rarotonga: *Polynesian.* Sydney: *Polynesian Airlines.* Tonga: *Air New Zealand, Polynesian, SPIA.*

STOPOVERS. Air carriers have opened many Pacific doors with their new on-line stopover privileges. You must work with your travel agent, but to give you an idea of how this works investigate "circle" fares. Low season is always the best bargain dollarwise, and circle fares mean multi-destinations for you. Remember these are special fares; you cannot change carriers. Stopover or multi-destination examples: *Air New Zealand's* low-season fare of $1000 from Los Angeles include stopovers in Honolulu/Fiji/New Zealand (Auckland) with return via Cook Islands and Tahiti/Los Angeles. For $100 more you can add Wellington and Christchurch (New Zealand) and continue to Sydney or Brisbane with a return to Auckland, Cook Islands, and Tahiti/Los Angeles. Your travel agent can also give you other routings on *Qantas, Pan American World Airways,* and *UTA French Airlines.*

BY SEA. The main reason to cruise the Pacific is to cruise. The leisurely pace, the meals, the entertainment and activities, the elegance, the beauty of the royal-blue water combine to make a cruise a very special kind of vacation. Having your floating "home" carry you in the dark of night from one port to the next is certainly travel with maximum convenience and comfort.

Ships have been sailing the Pacific for hundreds of years. Today's fleet includes luxury ships on round-the-world cruises, and a few bargain cruises with luxuries (and cost) cut to the minimum.

The number and variety of cruises grow each year. If you are single, dieting, want to stop smoking, interested in theater, or would like to meet people living in the ports of call, special-interest cruises may be your choice. If you can put together a group of about 15 passengers, you will be given, from many lines, a free trip yourself. And any group, large or small, may travel as a party on almost any scheduled cruise, arrange meeting rooms for seminars, screen special films, or set up whatever convention facility it needs.

After you've done some of your own research (the Sunday newspapers are one source, then the library, your friends, and the cruise lines listed below), see your travel agent for specific advice and booking—but remember that your agent cannot predict your fellow passengers (although he should be able to advise you about types of people on certain lines and cruises), and that can make a big difference for your holiday plans.

Ship accommodations, all meals (maybe five a day!), the voyage itself, entertainment, cruise staff services, and landing and embarkation facilities such as tender service, are included in the price. Figure about $150 per day for a cruise. Not included in your fare are transportation to and from port of embarkation (unless it is a fly/cruise package); wines and liquors consumed on board; laundry, shore excursions, port taxes, personal services such as beauty shop or barber appointments, and tips. As to shore costs, excursions are optional. You can spend a whole day on almost any island, swim, have lunch ashore, for $50 or so, if you wish.

How to Choose Cabins. If price is important, consider that you will spend very little time in your cabin and while the inside, smaller ones are the lowest price, you have full run of the ship and all the facilities just like those staying in the most luxurious suites. (If you can afford it, though, there's nothing like the pampering in the luxury accommodations). Almost every cabin available on all ships has a toilet and a shower. You pay extra for a bathtub. And note that many "single" cabins, especially on older ships, have an upper berth as well as the lower, available for a second person in the room, at minimum cost, so you can take a "better" cabin—i.e., a larger one—and pay minimum for the extra person, averaging out close to minimum rates for both.

Agents may book you with a "guarantee." No ship line queried would give a written definition of the term, but one travel agency defined it thus: "By a guarantee, they mean that the passenger is guaranteed a space on board at a certain rate. The room will be assigned at a later date, possibly even on the day of sailing. It does not mean necessarily an upgrade to a more expensive cabin, though chances are that you will be upgraded, but this is only implied." If the line has your commitment, it assumes that you have spent all you are willing to spend for the voyage, and if it can sell lower cost space again, it may do so. Higher price cabins sell more slowly, however, so you may be moved into one.

Tipping. Most ship's personnel who serve you directly depend on tips for their livelihood. Tipping is not all that expensive or troublesome. The following rules of thumb are suggestions:

Cabin steward—$5–$5.50 per person/per day (he shares with cabin boy, etc.).

Dining room steward—same (he shares with busboy).

Deck steward—$6 per person per trip.

Head dining room steward (maitre d'hotel)—$40, half on departure. Some may refuse a tip.

Table captain (if any)—$20 per couple for the trip, maybe more if he prepares many special dishes at your table.

Wine steward—15% of the wine bill.

Night steward—75¢ to $2 per service, or proportionately for the whole trip if you use his services frequently.

Bartender—15% to 20% of the bar bill each time.

Most tips should be given on the last evening of your trip, with two exceptions: the bartender and the maitre d'. If you are concerned about a "good" table, the maitre d' can be of service to you only at the beginning of the trip.

Tipping on a ship is a little different from other places; you will be seeing your stewards each day and often develop a personal kind of relationship with them. As a matter of fact, you ought to, because you find out a lot that way.

If the cruise is longer than about 14 days, the daily tip average may be a little less, and half might be given after one week; the crew can use the money in port.

Seating Arrangements and People in General. Some lines accept table reservations and assign seats when you book passage; others want you to make arrangements when you are aboard. Table size varies from two to about eight or ten. If you like to sit alone, say so right away. If you are traveling in a group, be sure that the maitre d'hotel or others making the assignments know your preference. If you don't like your table companions, with whom you will be eating at least two meals a day every day, let the maitre d' know right away so you can be moved—with a polite "I just found some old friends aboard" excuse. If you wait too long, it will be embarrassing.

One of the good reasons for cruising is to meet people. The ship is a very special kind of place, and all those stories about shipboard romances have a strong basis in fact. Beautiful clothes, dim lights, continuing dance music, soft air, champagne corks popping, the sound of water slipping past, work a kind of magic.

Even for less romantic souls, something happens. When you are with people on a ship for a week or two, their personalities become clear, and the shipboard characters emerge quickly. Everyone gets to know the best dancer, the clown, the seasoned traveler. And the usual social inhibitions which keep people apart, often unwillingly, in a hotel, dissolve in shipboard conviviality. After all, you're there in the middle of the great sea together—there is possible an unusual kind of closeness which no hotel, anchored as it is on solid land, can provide. But in communion with the sea there is also possible a quiet privacy, usually found on land only if you retreat behind a closed door. Shipboard life can provide as close, or as impersonal, an encounter as you like.

Weather and Health. If you are worried about seasickness, stop worrying. Most ships have excellent stabilizers, and medicines are available to stop the green death before it begins. The older remedies, such as Dramamine, often have side effects, such as making people sleepy, but the newer ones, chiefly meclizine, marketed over the counter under trade names like Bonine, don't do that. Check with your doctor. If you're really doubtful, take one (following directions) before you even board the ship, and continue during the cruise, before you feel anything. If you somehow wait too long and start to feel queasy, get to the ship's doctor right away; some of the newer shots are almost miraculous in their effectiveness.

One warning: when the weather is warmer than you're used to, you may lose a lot of body moisture. Be careful not to become dehydrated—drink plenty of liquids.

Departure Ports and Shore Excursions. More and more ships leave for the Pacific from San Francisco, Los Angeles and Seattle on the West Coast of the U.S. However, now that air/sea cruises are becoming more popular with those who cannot take lengthy voyages, cruises can start in Australia, New Zealand, or other ports on a ship's itinerary.

Almost all cruise ships maintain a shore excursion booking office on board; the shipping line either gets a commission from the provider on shore or sets up the excursions itself. These are optional and are usually sold individually. If you are the kind of person who wants minimal responsibility for arrangements, but still wants to see the islands, consider such excursions. If you are handicapped or have trouble physically getting around, certainly use an excursion. But if you like freedom, or want to interact with the people on the island rather than the other passengers, write to car rental agencies and reserve a car (well in advance; at least a month) or ask your travel agent to book your car for the days you want. Pay in advance if you can; several rental outfits habitually overbook without a thought about the hapless passengers with only one day to spend on an island. Or, hire a car and driver for the day, but be sure to fix the price, itinerary and hours before you enter a car. And don't believe a driver who tries to sell you his services and says that there are no rental cars available. Get that information only from a local tourist office (usually located near your landing point) or from a uniformed tourist guide.

If driving, be sure to read up on the island first. Don't worry about getting lost; most islands are small, and if you find the water and keep going around, you'll eventually get back to "Go."

What to Wear. Clothing aboard ship is like that seen at any elegant landbound resort. Even with the trend toward informality, bring a dinner jacket or several long dresses. Dressing up is part of the fun of cruising, especially for the Captain's Dinner and the Captain's Cocktail Party. Even on less formal evenings, passengers change for dinner. Suits or sports jackets (with shirts and ties) are expected on men, and while turtlenecks may be generally accepted, there is a tendency for maitre d's to grimace.

During the day, resortwear is fine. Sports shirts, shorts, slacks, sweaters, sandals and sneakers are all acceptable (but no bathing suits in the public rooms!). You will need comfortable clothes for shore visits. Very brief clothing worn on public streets is not considered proper, even though on beaches less-than-minimum may be acceptable.

Daily Schedule and Available Services. The daily activities are usually announced the night before, by a printed schedule; these include lectures by experts in such fields as law, psychology and finance; descriptive lectures about the islands by the cruise director; arts and crafts; scheduled and unscheduled bridge games; dance lessons (free daily in a group, available privately for a fee); a library; games at poolside; shuffleboard; ping-pong; a gym; a sauna; language lessons (depending on the nationality of the ships's crew); movies (features, often first-run, sometimes non-English).

There is usually a photographer on board. The ship's drug store is stocked with such sundries as toothpaste, shoelaces, etc., but, of course, bring your own prescription medications. Usually there are facilities for religious observances. Ships' gift shops (and liquor stores) often can compete with land shops in price. Beauty and barber shops are on board. Make your appointments early in the cruise, and consider bringing a wig, even if you don't like them. Also, don't bring electric hair dryers or similar appliances, as most ships don't have adequate electric power for them in the cabins, and they are not permitted. Laundry and dry cleaning facilities are often available, but try to stick to wash-and-wear when you can.

Suggestions. Bring an extra pair of eyeglasses if you wear them.

Don't let one bad experience—a slow steward, a slightly cold opening-night meal, or something equally unimportant—spoil your whole experience. Relax a little. If you look for defects, you'll find them. Nothing is "like it used to be."

Use your cruise director as a source of information, but rely on what you read in good guidebooks, descriptive material sent out by governments, and your own instincts as well.

Shop on shore in the afternoons; lots of your fellow passengers will have gone back to the ship, the stores will be less crowded, and the sales help, if tired, will not be so rushed. There's no danger of their running out of merchandise!

Consider cruises with fewer ports and more days at sea. Getting there is more than half the fun!

Take the ship's tour. See the kitchen, "behind the walls," where passengers normally don't go. The ship is a self-contained city afloat, usually making its own fresh water, running its own bakeries, photo labs, print shop. See the bridge, where ultimate control of this city is centered.

 CRUISES. *Royal Viking Line,* One Embarcadero Center, San Francisco, CA 94111. (800) 422–8000. The line made a major shift in 1984 to Pacific destinations. Now four 14-day *South Pacific Cruises* are offered, commencing in either Auckland or Sydney. They vary east and west bound so 2 14-day cruises can be combined into a 28-day cruise without repeating ports. Also offered: *Oceania* Christmas and New Year 24-day cruise, and a 24-day *Pacific/Orient* cruise. RVL's *Pacific Plus* program has 9 cruise combinations from 17 to 49 days, which include free round-trip air fare and a 3- or 4-day land package. Some of the *Royal Viking Star's* exotic ports of call: Opua (NZ), Nuku'alofa (Tonga), Pago Pago (American Samoa), Apia (Western Samoa), Vila (Vanuatu), and Suva (Fiji), with many new destinations to be added.

Society Expeditions Cruises, 723 Broadway East, Seattle, WA 98102. (800) 426–7794. The line purchased the *Lindblad Explorer* in 1984 and will be offering cruises on the new *MS Society Explorer.* 1986 cruises will include "Project Lost Islands of the Pacific" following the path of Captain Bligh of the *Bounty,* and "Halley's Comet Expeditions."

Cunard Line, 555 5th Ave., New York, NY 10017. (800) 327–9501. *Queen Elizabeth 2* (QE2) Circle Pacific and Orient cruises with segmented or full cruises. Ports of call: Easter Island, Papeete, Pitcairn Island, Moorea, Bora Bora, Torres Straits, Bali, Jakarta, Singapore, Bangkok, Hong Kong, Shanghai, Pusan, Kobe, Yokohama, Maui, San Francisco/Los Angeles.

P & O Cruises, 2029 Century Park East, Los Angeles, CA 90067; *P & O Cruises Australasia,* 6P0546, Sydney 2001, Australia. *P & O* offers air/sea cruises aboard the liner *Oriana.* Price of cruise includes round-trip transportation from major U.S. gateway cities and Sydney. Cruises from 6 to 15 nights. Ports of call, depending on length of trip: Hobart, Brisbane, Melbourne, Newcastle, Auckland,

Fiji Islands, Solomon Islands, New Caledonia, Tonga, Vila, and Santo (Vanuatu), Pago Pago.

Exploration Holidays and Cruises. 1500 Metropolitan Park Bldg., Olive Way at Boren Ave., Seattle, WA 98101. Cruises aboard the ship *Majestic Tahiti Explorer.* Sample 8-day/7-night itinerary: Opunohu Bay, Raiatea, Uturoa, Bora Bora, and Moorea. Also possible to segment this cruise for 4 nights or 3 nights. Ask cruise line or your travel agent about *air/sea* packages.

Sitmar Cruises Australasia, 47 Elizabeth St., Sydney, NSW 2000, Australia. Offers one- to three-week cruises year-round from Sydney aboard the ship *Fairstar.* For other *Sitmar Cruises* write: 10100 Santa Monica Blvd., Los Angeles, CA 90067.

Blue Funnel Cruises, 4th floor, Ocean Bldg., Collyer Quay, Singapore 0104. Offers 14–19-day South Pacific cruises between December and April from Sydney to Singapore.

Princess Cruises, 2029 Century Park East, Los Angeles, CA 90067. (800) 252–0158, California; (800) 421–0522 nationwide. Offers South Pacific/Orient and Tahiti/Hawaii cruises aboard the *Pacific Princess.*

Farrell Lines, 1 Whitehall St., New York, N.Y. 10004. Offers cargo/passenger service from New York to Australia and New Zealand. This American flag line operates 2 monthly 21-day trips from New York to the east coast of Australia via the Panama Canal.

American Hawaii Cruises, 550 Kearny St., San Francisco, CA 94108. (415) 392-9400. 7-day cruises through the islands of Tahiti year round. Stops will be made in Rangiroa Atoll, Huahine, Raiatea, Tahaa, Bora Bora, and Moorea. Prices will range from $1195 to 2495. Special rates on airfare and some free hotels in Tahiti before and after cruise.

INTER-ISLAND SHIPS

You may be able to schedule a number of unusual and adventurous trips by checking out the ships that travel from port to port in the list below. Many ships that travel between small islands carry everything from chickens to light freight, mail, and hearty, adventurous passengers. Write: *Bank Line Pty Ltd.,* 18th floor, One York St., Sydney, NSW 2000, Australia; *Chandris Lines,* Chandris House, 135 King St., Sydney, NSW 2000, Australia; *Lloyd Triestino,* 8 Spring St., Sydney, NSW; *Nauru Pacific Line,* 80 Collins St. Melbourne, Victoria 3000, Australia. Comparing shipping companies on a regional basis, it is possible to travel for months on end by arranging your trip between local shipping lines and regional air carriers. This type of travel is not for those in a hurry as much of the shipping schedule of these boats depends on the loading and unloading of goods/cargo.

American Samoa: An inter-island boat runs from Pago Pago to Apia in Western Samoa and to Manu'a Islands in American Samoa. The Manu'a trip takes from six to eight hours one way, once weekly. Cost: US$20 double, round trip. For further details: *Government of American Samoa, Office of Tourism,* Pago Pago, American Samoa 96799.

Australia: The *Elizabeth E* has 4-day cruises in and around the Whitsunday Islands and the outer Barrier Reef. The 112-foot cruiser can accommodate 24 passengers in two single and 11 two-berth air-conditioned cabins. Facilities include dining room, bar. The ship visits islands of Brampton, Lindeman, Long, Hayman, South Molle, Dent, Hook and Daydream. Cruises every Monday (except during February and March) from Mackay Outer Harbour, returning on Thursday. Write to *Elizabeth E Cruises,* 102 Goldsmith St., Mackay, Qld. 4740.

Roylen Cruises offers a 5-day cruise to the Great Barrier Reef through the Whitsunday Islands. Three 112-foot ships are available: *Roylen,* carrying 25 passengers in one three-berth and 11 twin cabins (all with share facilities); *Roylen Vianne,* identical to the *Roylen,* but air-conditioned; and *Roylen Petaj,* carrying 16 in one single and seven twin cabins (all with private facilities). Cruises depart every Monday from Mackay Outer Harbour, return on Friday. Operator is the principal booking agent for Brampton Island resort. Bookings: McLean's Roylen Cruises, River St., East Mackay, Queensland 4740, Australia. *M. V. Coonawarra P/L,* 289 Flinders St., Adelaide, South Australia 5033. Offers 42-passenger diesel-engine paddlewheeler *Coonawarra* making 5-day trip on Murray River. Travels 260 miles through open country, ties up along bank at night. Cabins have hot and cold water, some with private shower and toilet. Vessel has 3 decks, sun lounge, bar. Booking agent: South Australia Government Tourist Bureau, 18 King William Street, Adelaide, South Australia. *Murray River Queen,* c/o South Australian Government Tourist Bureau, 151 Franklin St., Adelaide, South Australia 5000. Paddle wheeler makes a 5-day cruise from Goolwa to Swan Reach and back. The vessel has 36 air-conditioned cabins, with shower and toilet in each. Four decks, dining room, bar, promenade areas and sun deck. *M. V. Kurrukajarra,* P.O. Box 1901, Townsville, Queensland, Australia 4810. Offers 5-day cruises from Townsville through the Hinchinbrook Channel visiting the Palm Islands Group, Family Islands Group, Dunk Island, Bedarra Island and the Great Barrier Reef. Leaves Tuesday 9 A.M. and returns 5 P.M. Saturday. Accommodations for 12 in four 2-berth and one 4-berth cabin.

Cook Islands: *Silk and Boyd Ltd.,* Box 131, Rarotonga, operate cargo vessels between the islands of the Cook Group on the 400-ton *Manuvai* 17-passenger ship. Two and four berth cabins. Price is approximately NZ$10 per day Cook Island Group. Other ships make calls at: Aitutaki, Atiu, Mangala, Manihikl, Mauke, Mitiaro, Pago Pago (American Samoa), Palmerston, Penrhyn, Pukapuka, Rakahanga, Rarotonga, Suva (Fiji). Service varies from one call weekly to one call every six weeks. Travel is at night, with days spent on the islands.

Fiji: *Islands in the Sun Fiji,* c/o John Holmes, P.O. Box 126, Ross, Ca. 94957. (415) 457-7222 or 3. Operates 3-day/night cruises (Wed./Sun.) from Lautoka. Sails via Treasure, Beachcomber and Mana Island Resorts, then cruises the Mamanuca group and the Yasawas, visiting Fijian villages and island caves. All 39 cabin suites air-conditioned with private facilities. Meals and entertainment included in the US$275 and up price. The *Tui Tai,* a 3-masted 80-passenger, 140-ft. schooner offers a 7-day/night cruise for the 18–35 age group. 1985 price US$370 per person. Write *Holmes* (see address above). *Blue Lagoon Cruises, Ltd.,* P.O. Box 54, Lautoka, Fiji. Offers cruises on 5 ships through the Yasawa Island Group. Fares include all meals, activities and entertainment. Cabins are self-contained; approximately F$230–300 (1985) for 3-day cruises. *Ferry Service:* Operates daily between Vanua Levu and Taveuni. Departs from Buca Bay, a taxi ride from Savusavu; a small boat carrying Fijians, Indians, copra and maybe a rooster tied into a coconut frond basket. Sails across Somosomo Strait to Taveuni. Fare: F$1.50.

Kiribati (formerly Gilbert Islands): There is no scheduled passenger service. Local transport would be questionable for the average tourist. However, the Gilbert Islands Shipping Corp., offers occasional service according to cargo requirements. One-way fare: A$53 deck; A$159 A-class; A$106 B-class. There is also service between Tarawa and Washington Island/Fanning Island/Christmas Island every three months. Fares one-way Tarawa/Washington Island: A$63.90 deck; A$191 A-class; to Fanning: A$65 one-way; $A195 A-class; to Christmas: $A69.60; A$208.80 A-class. For details, write to *Kiribati Tourist Bureau,* P.O. Box 77, Bairiki, Tarawa, Kiribati, Central Pacific.

Tuvalu Government (Ellice Islands): *Ministry of Communications & Transport Vaiaku,* Funafuti, Tuvalu, Central Pacific. Service between Tuvalu Islands (Ellice), Kiribati and Fiji. Ports of call: Niulakita, Nukulaelae, Funafuti, Nukufetau, Vaitupu, Nui, Niutao, Nanumanga, Nanumea, Tarawa, Suva. Fares range from

A$5 to A$38. Accommodations are available only on deck. Be sure to have food and soft drinks, inflatable cushion and mat. This trip for the very adventurous.

New Caledonia: Cruises to the coral reef and nearby islands; a scheduled passenger service between Noumea and the Isle of Pines and the Ile Ouen. Write *Office of Tourism of New Caledonia,* 27 rue de Sebastopol, Noumea, New Caledonia.

New Zealand: Wellington to Picton service (52 miles across the Cook Strait) is operated by New Zealand Railways aboard four ferries for passengers, automobiles and railway freight cars. Daily sailings from Wellington are at 10 A.M. and 4 P.M. daily, and 6:40 P.M. Monday through Saturday; 8 A.M. Wednesday through Sunday, with somewhat similar departures from Picton. Crossing takes 3 hours 20 minutes. Lounges, cocktail bars on board. Cabin berths available on some ships at extra charge. One-way passenger fare NZ$16.70. The voyage is scenic: the first 40 minutes are in Wellington Harbour, followed by a two-hour traverse of the lower end of the North Island thru Cook Strait, after which the ship enters the narrow gap of Tory Channel and steams for an hour down the sheltered deep-blue waters of Queen Charlotte Sound to Picton.

Papua New Guinea: Cargo/passenger serivce between Madang and Lae is offered by *Lutheran Shipping M.V. Totol,* Box 789, Madang, PNG. Fares one-way K$18. There are two air-conditioned 4-berth cabins available. Rate includes accommodation and all meals. If service is disrupted, airplanes are provided at no extra cost. A medical officer travels with the vessel. Alcohol is not served and passengers are requested not to bring it aboard.

Melanesian Tourist Services Pty. Ltd: (P.O. Box 707, Madang, Papua New Guinea, or UNIREP through your travel agent. Offers cruises on the *Melanesian Explorer,* 3–16 days and accommodating 36 passengers. Includes: Trobriand Island, Upper Sepik River, Milne Bay Islands. Library, a/c, TV, lecturer.

Solomon Islands: Local companies operate scheduled services to a number of islands and several other companies provide non-scheduled services. The Government Marine Department runs scheduled and non-scheduled services and, like the commercial operators mentioned, can carry a limited number of passengers. The most regular services run from Honiara to the Western Solomons and Malaita.

Prices listed below are approximate and schedules subject to change. Write the company for your specific sailing date.

Solomon Islands Government, Ministry of Transport & Communications, Marine Division, P.O. Box G22, Honiara, Solomon Islands, has inter-island services to a number of ports: Fares from Honiara (Guadalcanal) one-way, deck (in Solomon Islands $): Kira Kira $12.50; Graciosa Bay $19.50; Auki $7; Sikaiana $16.50; Ontong Java $18.00; Rennell $15.00; Bellona $14. The ships *Bilikiki* and *Bona* sail about once a month. Write to Solomon Islands Government, *Central Co-Operative Association,* Commonwealth St., P.O. Box 151, Honiara, Solomon Islands. The *Atawa* leaves first week for Honiara on Monday to Maringe Coast (Santa Ysabel) returning on Friday. Second week, leaves Honiara on Monday calling at nine North Malaita ports and returning on Friday. Third week, leaves Honiara on Monday calling at 11 Makira and Santa Ana ports, returning on Saturday. Fourth week, leaves Honiara on Monday for Auki and West Malaita calling at 11 ports and returning on Friday. Fares subject to change.

The *Tinapili* first week, trips to Makira and Ulawa returning the following day on each occasion. Second week, leaves Honiara for 15 ports on the Hograno Coast (Santa Ysabel) on Monday returning on Saturday. Third week, leaves Honiara for Auki and South Malaita calling at 10 ports and returning on Friday.

Ysabel Development Company, Commonwealth St., P.O. Box 92, Honiara. The *Ligomo* leaves Honiara for Santa Ysabel northeast coast ports at 10 P.M. on the first and third Tuesdays in each month, returning to Honiara on Saturday. The *Ligomo* leaves Honiara for Santa Ysabel south coast ports at 10 P.M. on the second and fourth Tuesday in each month, arriving back in Honiara on Saturday. The *Libaka* leaves Honiara on Mondays and Thursdays at 10 P.M. for Buala and Santa Ysabel and intermediate ports, returning to Honiara on Wednesday and Saturday mornings. Honiara/Santa Ysabel (northeast coast); Honiara/Santa Ysabel (south coast); Honiara/Buala (Santa Ysabel).

Melan-Chine Shipping Co., PO Box 71, Honiara. Operates *Thomas E* to and from Honiara/Tulagi on a regular schedule. Other ships sail to San Cristobal, Savo, Santa Ysabel, and Ontong Java.

Coral Seas Limited, Commonwealth Street, P.O. Box 9, Honiara. The *Compass Rose II* leaves Honiara for Auki on Malaita every Friday. Fare from $10. *Lu Mi Nao* sails every Sunday for Western Provinces. Fares $12–25. *Compass Rose* sails fortnightly for South Malaita and the East. Fares from $15.

Saratoga Shipping Company, off Commonwealth St., P.O. Box 611, Honiara, Solomon Islands. The *Saratoga* leaves Honiara every Monday at mid-day for all ports west of Gizo arriving at Gizo at 6:30 P.M. on Tuesdays; departing Gizo mid-day Wednesday; arriving Honiara 6 A.M. Fridays. It leaves Honiara every Friday at 10:30 P.M. for Auki arriving at 6 A.M. Saturdays; departing Auki 10:30 A.M. Sundays, arriving Honiara 5:30 P.M.

Tahiti: Daily boat service departs Papeete Mondays-Sundays at 9:15 A.M. Departs Moorea at 4 P.M. Takes about 50 min. on the *Keke III.* Other Moorea boats are car ferries. The *Raromatai Ferry* connects Tahiti with Huahine, Raiatea, Tahaa, Bora Bora. The *Temehani II,* operated by Société de Navigation Temehani, B.P. 9015, Papeete (Mota Uta) Tahiti, travels between Tahiti and Huahina, Rauatea, Bora Bora, Tahaa, Raiatea, Huahine, and Papeete.

Tahiti Yachting. Arue Nautical Center, P.O. Box 363, Papeete. Offers 28- to 65-foot sailboats for rental on daily or weekly basis. Write for information and rates.

Compagnie Française Maritime De Tahiti, B.P. 368, Papeete, Tahiti, Society Islands operates the *Taporo III* from Papeete (Tahiti) to Huahine Island, Raiatea, and Bora Bora Islands. Fare (excluding meals) is US$15.

The *Taporo V* sails from Papeete to: the atolls in the Tuamotus and the Marquesas Islands.

Ocean Voyages, 1709 Bridgeway, Sausalito, CA 94965. Offers 8-day cruises aboard 46-foot ketch *Roscop.* Trips begin in Huahine and end in Bora Bora. Prices in 1985 were $925 a person. *Vanessa,* 38-foot sloop, offers 7-, 10- and 14-day cruises to Huahine, Raiatea, Tahaa, Bora Bora, and Maupiti for 2–3 participants. Prices start at $795 a person (1985). Ocean Voyages has a variety of vessels available throughout French Polynesia and the South Pacific. Call for details: (415) 332-4681.

Tonga: *The Pacific Navigation Company* operates a local shipping service which connects Nuku'alofa with 'Eua, Ha'apai, Vava'u and the Niuas. The Nuku'alofa, Ha'apai, Vava'u run is generally one round trip per week and is operated by the inter-islands ferry *Olovaha.* The ship is one class and has two berth cabins and 30 reclining seats in the observation lounge. Sailing time Nuku'alofa/Ha'apai is 8 hours; Ha'apai/Vava'u is 7 hours. There is daily service, except Sundays, between Nuku'alofa and 'Eua. Takes approximately 3 hours. There is no advance bookings on the inter-island ferry due to frequent changes in service due to local commitments and weather. Write to *Tonga Visitors Bureau,* 37, Nuku'alofa, Tonga.

Western Samoa. Passenger/vehicle ferry service between *Upolu* and *Savaii* islands daily. Takes 1½ hrs. on scheduled services. WS$1/person. WS$12/car.

The *Apia/Pago ferry* (passenger/car) leaves *Apia* Sundays, Tuesdays, Thursdays at 10 P.M. and returns from *Pago Pago* on Mondays, Wednesdays, and Fridays at 4 P.M. Takes approximately 6 hrs; WS$12/person. Bookings through *Western Samoa Shipping,* Matafele, Apia. There are several Savaii/Apia/Pago sailings each day. Make arrangements only after arrival in Samoa and confirm well in advance.

 LANGUAGES. English is widely understood throughout the South Pacific and especially in the larger cities. English speaking visitors will have little language difficulty in the leading hotels, restaurants, travel agencies, airports, and shops.

For general information, listed below are the official languages for each country.

American Samoa. Samoan; English understood and spoken by 85% of the population.

Australia. English.

Cook Islands. Maori and English.

Fiji. English.

Kiribati (formerly Gilbert Islands). Gilbertese and English.

New Caledonia. French.

New Zealand. English and Maori.

Papua New Guinea. Pidgin and Motu. There are over 700 dialects throughout Papua New Guinea. English is used in business and government circles.

Solomon Islands. English and over 60 island dialects.

Tahiti. French and Tahitian. English is understood in Papeete.

Tonga. Tongan and English.

Vanuatu (formerly New Hebrides). Both French and English.

Western Samoa. Samoan and English.

 HOTELS. Variety is the spice of life in the South Pacific. There's a place for every pocketbook. There are thousands of hotels, motels and resorts in Australia, New Zealand and the South Pacific. But you may discover a fine distinction between the sophisticated hotels of the major cities of Australia and New Zealand and the accommodations on many of the small islands, some of which are just beginning to invest in hotels of the better class. While we do not pretend to know every nook and cranny on all the islands, there are some hotels and resorts listed in the Practical Information section for each destination in this book. Those mentioned as resorts will usually have most of the activities available at any international resort (such as golf course, swimming pool, tennis courts, lawn bowling, fishing boats, snorkling, scuba diving, glass bottom boats, and water skiing equipment).

The larger the hotel, the more facilities. Many of the hotels on the small islands, while not considered resorts, will have some sport activities or access to clubs nearby.

However, on many of the small islands in the South Pacific, you can rent self-contained cottages where you can do as you please and find out just what "getting away from it all" really means. Just so you are not completely out of touch, there are usually other facilities nearby—restaurants, mini-grocery stores, swimming pools, and the ever present white, sandy beach.

SPECIAL NOTE: One important hint to remember in the tropics is that service will vary with the climate. Learn to relax and not to expect the type of service you might receive in the United States. Enjoy the slow pace—take advantage of the company you are with—whether at the dining table or awaiting room service for that refreshing drink. The climate and humidity throughout the Pacific will slowly catch up with you and then it will be easy to understand why service, regardless of how plush the hotel, takes just a little longer than in cooler destinations.

 **ROUGHING IT.** The Pacific has some youth hostels and camping facilities, providing an inexpensive and in a sense the most intimate way of getting to know various countries. Recommended for the young in body and spirit. For information write to the following:

U.S.A.: *American Youth Hostels, Inc.,* 1332 Eye St. N.W., Washington, D.C. 20005; *Campgrounds Unlimited,* Blue Rapids, Kansas 66411; *National Campers & Hikers Association,* 7172 Transit Road, Buffalo, N.Y. 14221.

Canada: *Canadian Youth Hostels Association,* National Office, 333 River Road, Vanier City, Ottawa, Ontario K1L 8B9.

Great Britain: *Camping Club of Great Britain and Ireland,* 11 Lower Grosvenor Place, London S.W.1.; *The Youth Hostels Association,* 14 Southhampton Street, Strand, London W.C.2; *Worldwide Student Travel,* 37 Store Street, London, W.C.1.

New Zealand: *Youth Hostel Association,* 36 Customs Street East, Auckland. For camping in New Zealand, come during the summer months (December through Easter). There are two kinds of camps: "motor" or "camping" sites.

Motor camp: Provides additional and/or superior equipment and amenities.

Camping site: Provides lesser standard of equipment, and is usually in remote area.

A directory, issued by the Camp and Cabin Association, is obtainable from the National Tourist Office. Reservations advisable during the December to Easter season.

For further information, write to the nearest *National Tourist Bureau* (see section "Tourist Information"), or *Automobile Association* offices: 33 Wyndham Street. Post to P.O. Box 5, Auckland; 166 Willis Street. Post to P.O. Box 1053, Wellington; 210 Hereford Street. Post to P.O. Box 994, Christchurch.

Australia: There are over 90 Youth Hostels, each state with its own association. Members of other hostels which are affiliated with the *International Y.H.A.* are welcome to join the Australian Association.

Inquiries concerning Youth Hostels in Australia should be directed to: *Australian Youth Hostels Association,* 26 King Street, Sydney, NSW 2000.

Campmobiles are for hire and accommodate up to five persons. They are self-contained. Rates range about A$300 per week plus mileage.

Caravan (Trailer) Hire & Camping Equipment: Equipment that can be towed behind cars and camping equipment are for hire or purchase. Camping sites have independent water supply, sewerage, hot showers, laundry facilities, and electricity supply.

For further information, check with your travel agent, nearest *Australian Travel Information Bureau,* or write directly to *Campmobile Rentals Department,* Volkswagen Australia Pty Ltd., 27 Waterloo Road, North Ryde, New South Wales 2113.

 FOOD. There is such a variety of food, it would be impossible to describe specialties for all the countries in this book in a paragraph or two. Listed below, however, are some of the kinds of food that can be expected and the type of restaurant facilities available. Check each country's "Practical Information" section for particular ideas of where to dine.

It is strongly suggested that you recheck both the "Health" and the "Water" sections for advice on each country.

As for alcohol, each destination has its own rule on regulated drinking hours. Some bars and restaurants are quite relaxed about their hours of business; some even ignore what is known as the official closing hours. (See "Customs" section for what spirits may legally be brought into the country.)

American Samoa. Don't expect gourmet food here, although there are plenty of different types of dining establishments. Probably the best solution is to eat at your hotel. The Rainmaker Hotel offers American and Samoan food. Most enjoyable is a "fia fia"—or Samoan feast where you will eat roast pig, breadfruit, taro, "pulusami"—a Samoan delicacy—and all the fruits of the islands.

Australia. Hotels in major centers of the country have some of the best international cuisine. Prices range according to taste and Australia now has restaurants to match every pocketbook. Specialties to look for would be seafood, meat, and tropical fruit. International restaurants are popular. Most cities have special sophisticated dining and dancing establishments.

Cook Islands. Restaurants and dining facilities on Rarotonga are limited. Most tourists eat at the hotels where they are staying; however, there are some small restaurants and cafes around the town.

Fiji. It used to be that good food was available only at the few major hotels. Today, however, Fiji is opening up more quality resorts in nearby islands. A few have dining alfresco, entertainment; some have a band.

New Caledonia. You might suspect you are in some French province when you taste some of the outstanding food in Noumea. You may also wonder if you are in Paris at the best of the gourmet restaurants. No matter where you travel in New Caledonia you'll be able to enjoy excellent French cuisine. But there is a great variety of other foods too, such as Indonesian, Chinese, Indian, Spanish, Vietnamese. Take your pick. You'll never starve, nor be disappointed in most any dining establishment, deluxe or moderate. One point—there are few modest type eateries. The French enjoy their food and want the best. Just remember, don't hurry—relax and take time to savor every bite.

New Zealand. This country is a world leader in meat and dairy products. It is probably the greatest consumer of lamb, beef and pork—venison and gamebirds also are a part of a daily diet somewhere on the North and South Islands. Fish and shellfish are plentiful too. It will keep you busy just trying to make up your mind what you'll want to devour each evening. Auckland, Wellington, Christchurch and Dunedin have the greatest selection of restaurants considered "excellent."

Papua New Guinea. Beef and poultry from the Highlands, plus fresh vegetables and fruit are the choices you have in the hotels and restaurants around the country. Seafood is delicious and you can dine on crab, prawns, crayfish and barramundi. Papua New Guineans claim their local fruit such as strawberries, pineapples, pawpaws, mangoes, passionfruit and bananas served fresh and available daily are as good as any other.

Solomons. Except for the Hotel Mendana and Hotel Honiara there are few restaurants of anything to write home about. However, 28 miles west of Honiara is the Tambea Village Resort that serves both western and Chinese food. If you've rented a self-contained cottage, all your cooking utilities will be furnished and there is usually fresh tinned goods, fresh vegetables and fresh fish available.

Tahiti. You can dine in the most elegant atmosphere at the Restaurant Gauguin at the Hotel Maeva Beach. Pink table cloths and fresh flowers plus gourmet food—some people claim this is sufficient reason to get them to Tahiti. To go along with the excellent dishes on Tues., Thurs., and Sat. there is Tahitian entertainment. Chateaubriand for two is about $25, fresh lobster with brandy sauce and curried rice is under $20. Along with all this there is an orchestra and you can dance nightly. While most of the restaurants serve excellent food, the costs are not all in the $20 range; you can dine for less at La Petite Auberge on the foods of Normandy and Brittany—such as frog legs or smoked salmon for much less. Cheaper still, just for a very few francs, you can buy the long, slender, delicious, crusty French bread—as fresh as the loaves you buy in Paris. With it, and a little cheese and some wine, you can sit along the waterfront and watch the life of French Polynesia pass by. One reminder: your food budget in Tahiti can go "out of sight" if you don't plan carefully.

Tonga. In addition to the dining rooms at the various hotels, the main street of Nuku'alofa has several small restaurants featuring Tongan food such as 'ufi (a large white yam) and taro, or lu pulu (meat and onions, marinated in coconut milk and baked in taro leaves in an underground oven). Other specialties include poultry, breadfruit, sweet potatoes, and tapioca. But if you want to enjoy an evening out with music, dancing and special entertainment, try a Tongan feast with roast suckling pigs, crayfish, chicken and local fruits and vegetables, also cooked in the underground oven.

Vanuatu (formerly New Hebrides). While this island group was the world's only condominium (half French/half English), the best restaurants are French and are located in the hotels (mostly in Vila) or on the island resorts. All hotels in Santo have restaurants. In the cafe category in Vila you'll find French, Chinese, Vietnamese, European and in the Solaise Motel you'll even find pizza and spaghetti.

Western Samoa. Aggie Grey's Hotel, the Samoan Hideaway Beach Resort, and the Hotel Tusitala serve the best of Samoan and western meals. The fia fia (Samoan feast) in Western Samoa is the same as those served in American Samoa. Seafood and pork, and the canned corned beef are Samoan favorites, along with taro, breadfruit and tapioca. It's best to stick to the hotels for western style food. One of the best restaurants in Apia is Pancho's. Very popular with business people and local Samoans. Excellent seafood. Any taxi driver knows how to get there.

 GUIDE SERVICES. Almost every local Government Tourist Bureau can recommend reliable guides, as well as your local travel agent if you choose to select an agent on arrival. It is best not to hire the services of someone who approaches you on the street—the rates may turn out to be more expensive than those of bona fide or government licensed operators.

In a few places like Samoa, the Cook Islands or other small islands you may find children offering their services just because they like you, or want to practice their English. If they offer to lead you to a certain store or market place, they will most probably do it just for the pleasure of showing their hospitality to a visitor to their country. Children do not expect to be paid. The hired guide is another matter and will want his pay as bargained for before the tour. Most tour agents and guides have set prices; be sure to confirm these rates.

 SHOPPING. American Samoa. Tapa cloth, shell beads, purses, wood carvings, woven laufala table and floor mats. U.S. citizens can bring home $800 duty free, including one gallon of liquor from duty free shop.

Australia. Opals, aboriginal art, handbeaten copper and silver, leather goods, toy koalas and kangaroos. Store hours: M-F 9–5:30, Sat. 9–12.

Cook Islands. Wood carvings, traditional patterns, pearl shells, woven products, embroidery, Panama hats, baskets, hand-made ukeleles. Coins and stamps are good collector's items. Duty free shops: M-F 7:30–3:30, Sat. 7:30–11:30.

Fiji. Tortoiseshell work, filigree jewelry, wooden carvings, kava bowls. Clothing from local cloth can be made in a few days at moderate prices. (No bargaining.) M-F 8–5; closed 1–2 P.M. Sat. 8–1. Duty free shops.

Gilbert Islands. Baskets, table mats, fans in all sizes and shapes plus a variety of other handicrafts made from pandanus leaves, coconut leaves. Shells are a big items from turtle shells to sea shells. Sea shell necklaces are popular local items. Tourists usually snatch up the models of Gilbertese canoes, houses and swords. (The swords are made from shark's teeth.) Items are available at the Handicraft Store in Beito. Hours: M-F 8–5. Closed from noon to 1 P.M. Sat. 8–noon.

New Caledonia. Items of shell, coral, wood carvings and handpainted materials, aloha shirts, tapa cloth, Polynesian music records. French best buys: lingerie, shoes, fabrics and clothing for women. Ties and continental shoes for men. Boutiques with Italian shoes, sportswear from London. Store hours: M-F 7:30–5:30, closed 11–2; Sat. 7:30–11.

New Zealand. Greenstone items (jade) such as brooches, earrings, tie pins and tikis; shell items, wood items: bowls, cribbage boards, Maori gods, walking sticks, war clubs, woolen car robes, lambswool rugs and sweaters.

Papua New Guinea. Carvings, statuettes, ceremonial masks from Angoram and Sepik, crocodile carvings from Trobriands, Buka basketware, arrows, bows and decorated axes from the highlands. Carvings and artifacts can be bought in most towns and settlements at reasonable prices. Some stores ship purchases. In Port Moresby, *Trobriand Crafts* on Douglas Street and *Paua Agencies* offer packing, shipping and air freight services. (Note: The Health Authority at the port of embarkation probably will require certificates of fumigation for most artifacts.) *Girl Guides Handicraft Shop* is a museum for the crafts of Papua New Guinea, and has excellent small gifts such as Buka trays or carvings. It has one of the largest selections in Port Moresby; Lakatoi artifacts near Koki has simple to valuable crafts, including Chambri Lakes pots and wood carvings from the Trobriands. Other shops include: *South Pacific Artifacts, Higoadi's* for collection of handwoven ponchos, blankets, rugs and embroidered table linens. Hours: 9–5 daily except Sunday.

Solomon Islands. Walking sticks, mother-of-pearl work, war clubs and other curios in carved and inlaid wood. Conch shells and rare varieties of cowrie. *New Georgia* (western district) has carved fish, turtles and birds. Carvings in ebony, inlaid shell are unique. Tailors in Chinatown have bargain rates. Note: Replicas of artifacts may be freely exported. The genuine ones, including shell money, dress ornaments and weapons may not be taken from the Solomons without special permission. Hours: M-F 8–5, closed 12:30–2; Sat. 8–12:30. Chinese stores have extended hours.

Tahiti. Wooden tikis, war clubs, carved shells, costume jewelry of mother-of-pearl, baskets and woven hats. Tahitian fashions (from bikinis to ball gowns) in hand-blocked materials. French perfume is lower than in Paris, as are crystalware and French liquors. Duty free shop at Tahiti-Faaa International Airport.

Tonga. Tapa cloth and woven goods, considered among the finest in the South Pacific. Baskets and mats, grass skirts, fans, model wood carvings, tortoise shell ornaments, brooches, earrings, rings and silver inlaid knives. *Langa Fonua,* the women's organization of Tonga, sells fine inexpensive handicrafts at Langa Fonua House. Arrangements can also be made to have lunch or tea in the society's attractive old house. Hours: M-F 8:30–5; Sat. 9–12.

Vanuatu (formerly New Hebrides). Grass shirts and baskets from Futuna and Tanna. *Pentecost:* Carved ferns and masks from Ambrym and Malekula; woodwork from Tongoa and Santo; pig's tusks (rare and expensive), necklaces made of shells or colorful seeds from villages near Vila. Hours: M-F 7:30–5, closed 11:30–2; Sat. 7:30–11:30.

Western Samoa. Woven baskets, trays, tortoise shells and carved wooden items, tapa cloth. *Western Samoa Handicrafts Corp.* in Apia has authentic handicrafts and is sponsored by the government to preserve Samoan culture. Hours: M-F 8–4, closed noon–1:30; Sat. 8–12:30.

CONVERSION TABLES

Basic

Simplified: 1 inch = 2.54 centimeters; 1 foot = 12 inches = 30.48 centimeters; 1 yard = 3 feet = 0.9144 meters.

Simplified: 1 ounce = 28.35 grams; 1 pound = 453.5924 grams. 2.2 pounds = 1 kilo.

Simplified: 1 U.S. gallon = 3¾ liters; 1 English gallon = 4½ liters.

Centimeters	Length Inches	Gram(mè)s	Weights Ounces
5	2	100	3.33
10	4 (under)	200	6.67
20	8 (under)	250	8.03
30	11¾	500	16.07
40	15¾	1 kilogram (kilo)=	2.2046 lbs.
50	19¾		

1 meter = 39.37 inches

Clothing

Although you may see several charts with comparative U.S.-British-Continental sizings, in our experience these are not truly standardized. Best take along a tape measure, or rely on the shop assistant's assessment (in the first place) of your sizing. Always try on a garment before purchasing: an apparently correct sizing may prove to have arm-holes too wide or too narrow, sleeves too long or too short. After all, each country sizes according to the average measurements of its nationals, just as in the United States and Great Britain. Dress fabrics are usually one meter (100 cm.) wide.

Kilometers Into Miles

This simple chart will help you to convert to both miles and kilometers. If you want to *convert from miles into kilometers* read from the center column to the right, if *from kilometers into miles,* from the center column to the left. Example: 5 miles = 8.046 Kilometers, 5 kilometers = 3.106 miles.

Miles		Kilometers	Miles		Kilometers
0.621	1	1.609	37.282	60	96.560
1.242	2	3.218	43.496	70	112.265
1.864	3	4.828	49.710	80	128.747
2.485	4	6.347	55.924	90	144.840
3.106	5	8.046	62.138	100	160.934
3.728	6	9.656	124.276	200	321.868
4.349	7	11.265	186.414	300	482.803
4.971	8	12.874	248.552	400	643.737
5.592	9	14.484	310.690	500	804.672
6.213	10	16.093	372.828	600	965.606
12.427	20	32.186	434.967	700	1,126.540
18.641	30	42.280	497.106	800	1,287.475
24.855	40	64.373	559.243	900	1,448.409
31.069	50	80.467	621.381	1,000	1,609.344

Tire Pressure Converter

Pounds per Square Inch	16	18	20	22	24	26	28	30	32
Kilogrammes per Square Centimeter	1.12	1.26	1.40	1.54	1.68	1.82	1.96	2.10	2.24

Gallons Into Liters

U.S. Gallon	Liters	Imperial (British) Gallon	Liters
1	3.78	1	4.54
2	7.57	2	9.09

3	11.36	3	13.63
4	15.14	4	18.18
5	18.93	5	22.73
6	22.71	6	27.27
7	26.50	7	31.82
8	30.28	8	36.36
9	34.07	9	40.91
10	37.85	10	45.46

There are five Imperial (British) gallons to six U.S. gallons.

 SPORTS. It is obvious that with all that water and beach in the South Pacific, any sport remotely connected with the two is extremely popular—and there are many experts to help you swim, water ski, surf, snorkel, skin and scuba dive, sail and fish.

However, sports activities are by no means limited to water contact. The climate is most conducive to play and in Australia, New Zealand and the South Pacific islands you will find much action—whether participant or spectator—all the way from skin-diving in Fiji to snow skiing in Australia and New Zealand (during the Northern Hemisphere's summer months).

Golf, yachting, tennis, fishing, horseback riding, lawn bowling, polo clubs—members of any of these overseas organizations are usually given honorary membership rights, social and club facilities.

We recommend a letter from your home secretary written a month or so in advance to the club secretary which will perhaps bring you a calendar of coming events and should guide you ahead of time of club rules. Write to local Government Tourist office for club addresses.

Here is a thumbnail sketch of activities. For more details, see country chapters.

American Samoa. Fishing, snorkeling, surfing, swimming, tennis, golf, skin diving, scuba diving, yachting, cricket.

Australia. Cricket, football, fishing, hunting, golf, greyhound racing, horse racing, lawn bowling, motor racing, polo, skiing, skin diving, target shooting, tennis, trail riding, trotting, yachting.

Cook Islands. Fishing, golf, horse racing and riding, lawn bowls, sailing, skin diving.

Fiji. Fishing, golf, lawn bowling, scuba and skin diving.

Kiribati. Lobster and big-game fishing, swimming.

New Caledonia. Cricket, horseback riding, snorkeling, spear fishing, swimming, tennis.

New Zealand. Fishing, golf, hiking and bush walking, horseracing, hunting, lawn bowls, skiing, tennis, rugby football, cricket, yachting and rowing.

Papua New Guinea. Bush walking, game fishing, golf, horseback riding, polocrosse, sailing, scuba diving, squash, water skiing.

Solomon Islands. Fishing, golf, skin diving, swimming, tennis, yachting, water skiing.

Tahiti. Fishing, golf, horseback riding and racing, scuba diving, swimming, tennis, yachting.

Tonga. Boating, fishing, horseback riding, skin diving, surfing, swimming.

Vanuatu (formerly New Hebrides). Sailing, fishing, skin diving and tennis.

Western Samoa. Boating, cricket, fishing, golf, horseracing, lawn bowling, longboat races, skin diving, swimming, tennis, track and field.

MEET THE PEOPLE. A home visit may consist of a meal with a host family, at no cost to the guest, or a longer stay whereby the visitor lives with the family as a paying guest. The time involved can be a few hours to a few days and gives the tourist an opportunity to talk fairly intimately and cast aside the "stranger" image in a foreign land, and become a member of the family. Following are three countries that promote "meeting the people."

Australia: By writing well in advance you can arrange to meet Australian families through the following organizations. To assist in matching of personalities the letter should include some information about yourself, interests, etc., also details of arrival date, length of stay. These are nonprofit organizations and hosts do not provide accommodation: *International Friendship Foundation,* Box 4248, GPO, Sydney 2001, N.S.W., Australia; Chairman, Hospitality Committee, Australian-American Association, 39 Lower Fort St., Sydney, 2000 N.S.W. Australia; *Queensland Government Tourist Bureau,* Adelaide and Edward St., Brisbane, 4000 Qld., Australia; *Tasmanian Government Tourist Bureau,* 80 Elizabeth St., Hobart, 7000, Tasmania, Australia.

Friendship Clubs: The following clubs keep their members up-to-date on developments in travel to Australia. USA: *Australian Kangaroo Club, Inc.,* P.O. Box 4230 Irvine, Ca. 92716. Tel. (714) 957–0292. *Australian-New Zealand Society of New York Inc.,* 41 E. 42nd St., Room 822, New York, N.Y. 10017. Tel. (212) 986–1457; Southern Cross Club, P.O. Box 19243, Washington, D.C. 20036. Tel. (202)659–3560 A. H. (202) 232–8375. *Down Under Club, W.T.S.* 5669 Duluth St. Minneapolis, Minn. 55422. Tel. (612) 546–8822. *Friends of the Koala and Kiwi Association,* Rockefeller Center, Suite 612, 610 5th Ave., New York, N.Y. 10020; *British Social and Athletic Club,* P.O. Box 25429, Los Angeles, Ca. 90025. Tel. (213) 478–0994.

New Zealand: A number of families all through the country offer friendly hospitality to visitors from overseas. Farm and town houses. Locations: Auckland, Christchurch, Wellington, Nelson, Rotorua and farming areas throughout the country. Reservations required one to two months in advance. Rates vary according to standards of accommodations and whether or not meals are included, but are lower than hotel rates.

New Zealand farm holidays give visitors the choice of staying overnight with local families on farms which specialize in sheep, in cattle or in raising crops. The cottage holiday gives visitors their own house on farm property—with linens and food supplied. Accommodations range from basic shearers' quarters to modern houses, and all have electricity, hot water, bathroom, stove and refrigerator.

The live-in program is just that: In the main house with the farm family. With both programs, visitors participate in the daily routine of farm life, pitching in with the work. Most farms have recreational facilities that include trout fishing, deer and pig hunting and hiking and riding. These are normal working farms and not hotels.

For brochures and further information write: New Zealand Farm Holidays, PO Box 1436, Wellington; Hospitality Haere Mai, P.O. Box 56-175, Auckland; Homestay Limited, P.O. Box 630, Rotorua; New Zealand Hospitality Limited, P.O. Box 309, Nelson; or the Tourist Office.

Fisherman Live-In Home Holidays is offered by Club Pacific's Angler-to-Angler program. A dozen itineraries for 17–30 days, ranging in price from NZ$2,420 to NZ$3,192, including air fare from Los Angeles via Air New Zealand or Pan American. Write Mel Krieger, Club Pacific, 790-27th Av. San Francisco, Ca 94121.

Tonga: While overnights are not encouraged, day visits to guest houses run by local families can be arranged. Visitors can also stop at villages to meet families and see handicraft demonstrations, preparations for a feast, dancing and religious ceremonies. Meetings with farmers and teachers can be arranged. Cost depends on transportation used and whether a meal is provided. Write: Tonga Visitors Bureau P.O. Box 37, Nuku'alofa, Tonga.

Other countries: *People of the Pacific's Special Odysseys,* 3430 Evergreen Point Road, P.O. Box 37, Medina, WA 98039, (206) 455-1960, offer special-interest tours to the South Pacific. Off-the-beaten-track locations in which small, unregimented groups learn about the culture of the South Pacific. Trips are unusual and far from layer cake hotels and the beaches of Waikiki. Destinations: Fiji, Tonga, Western Samoa, and the Cook Islands. These are not physically demanding trips but require an adventuresome spirit.

Also, write directly to the local government tourist bureau for information on possible in-home programs.

TIME ZONES. There are a great number of time zones in the South Pacific region. Using GMT (Greenwich Mean Time) as the standard guideline, listed below are zones for the major cities.

American Samoa. GMT−11 Pago Pago

Australia. There are three time zones: Eastern Standard Time (EST) is 10 hours ahead of GMT; Central Standard Time (CST) is 9½ hours ahead; and Western Standard Time (WST) is 8 hours ahead. During the summer months most States introduce daylight saving. Major area time zones are: Eastern (EST): Brisbane, Cairns, Canberra, Hobart, Melbourne, Sydney; Central (CST): Adelaide, Alice Springs, Broken Hill, Darwin; Western (WST): Perth.

Cook Islands. GMT−10½
Fiji. GMT+12 Suva
New Caledonia. GMT+11
New Zealand. GMT+12
Papua New Guinea. GMT+10
Solomon Islands. GMT+10
Tahiti. GMT−10
Tonga. GMT+13
Vanuatu (formerly New Hebrides). GMT+11
Western Samoa. GMT−11 Apia

TIPPING. Tipping is a very touchy subject in the South Pacific, Australia and New Zealand. It is one place in the world where you can usually keep your hand in your pocket for services rendered, except for exceptional requests.

American Samoa. No tipping. Visitors are asked to honor this custom.

Australia. Tipping is not obligatory in hotels or restaurants, and service charges are not added to your bill. Hotel porters are usually tipped 20¢, and waiters and waitresses in deluxe hotels and restaurants receive 10% for good service. Taxi drivers and porters at shipping and railway stations have set charges.

Cook Islands. No tipping. Visitors are asked to honor this custom.

Fiji. Hotel porters receive 10¢ for each bag. Otherwise, tipping is very light and then only for special services.

Kiribati. Tipping not encouraged.

New Caledonia. No tipping. Visitors are asked to honor this custom.

New Zealand. Not a tipping country, but porters do receive 20¢ a bag.

Papua New Guinea. Tipping is not customary nor encouraged. Tourists are asked to honor this custom.

Solomon Islands. No tipping. Visitors are asked to honor this custom.

Tahiti. Positively no tipping. It is contrary to the Tahitian tradition and idea of hospitality.

Tonga. Tipping is not expected nor encouraged. It is only acceptable for very special services.

Vanuatu (formerly New Hebrides). No tipping. Visitors are asked to honor this custom.

Western Samoa. No tipping. Visitors are asked to honor this custom.

 DRINKING WATER. Generally speaking, the water in most of the South Pacific Islands, Australia, and New Zealand is safe to drink in the major areas and capital cities. If there is a question about the local water, you will usually find bottled water in your hotel rooms and in the dining rooms. In the outlying areas of American Samoa, Western Samoa, and Tonga, drink bottled water. Drink only bottled water in the Cook Islands and Papua New Guinea.

In Tahiti the water is not all safe to drink; tourists will be safer buying bottled water.

Special note: If you are heading for remote areas, you might take a supply of "Halazone," a small pill available in most drug stores. It may make the water taste peculiar, but it renders it potable.

If you plan on driving long distances, it is wise to take bottled water, no matter what country you visit.

 ELECTRICAL CURRENT. The electric current varies to such a degree in the South Pacific that it is wise to carry a mini-converter. This device converts 220V foreign current into 110V domestic. The Franzus Co. (see below for address) Number 18/21 converter handles all portable appliances up to 1000 watts. Their F-11 model works with equipment up to 50 watts.

Most foreign wall outlets usually require *round* pins. In some areas you may have to use a 3-pronged plug. Australia and New Zealand have *blades* similar to those of the U.S., but they are not easily available. A plug adapter is required to fit American appliances to foreign wall outlets but remember that adapters *do not convert voltage.* For complete information and a list of the type of equipment you may need, write to the *Franzus Co., 352 Park Avenue South, New York, New York 10010.*

The following is an up-to-date guide for the South Pacific.

American Samoa. 110V/60 cycles (same as U.S.).

Australia. 220V/240V/50 cycles. 110V converters in most hotels.

Cook Islands. 230V/50 cycles. Most hotels have 3-pronged pin plugs. (Some have 110V current.)

Fiji. 240AC/50 cycles.

Kiribati. 230–240V/50 cycles everywhere except Christmas Island, where it is the same as in the U.S.

New Caledonia. 220V,AC/50 cycles.

New Zealand. 230/240V/50 cycles.

Papua New Guinea. 240AC/415V/50 cycles. Some areas have DC. There are no 110V converters. Generators in outlying areas shut off at 11:00 P.M. In other areas some close down their generators from 11:00 A.M. until early afternoon.

Solomon Islands. 240V/50 cycles AC.

Tahiti. Old hotels still have 110V/60 cycles. Newer hotels have 220V/50 cycles with 110V outlets.

Tonga. 230V/50 cycles AC. Most hotels have 110V outlets for razors.

Vanuatu (formerly New Hebrides). 240V, AC/50 cycles.

Western Samoa. 110V/60 cycles.

Before plugging in any electric appliances, be sure to check the outlet as to whether it is 110V or 220V. A converter does not work in a 110V outlet, and your appliance could be ruined if used incorrectly. It is also wise to check the type of current before using converters, as some will not work with direct current (DC).

Note: While American appliances work on 60 cycles and foreign systems use 50 cycles, do not be alarmed. There may be a slight slowdown but no harm to your equipment. (Exceptions are clocks and hi-fi equipment, which should not be used with converters.)

 MEDICAL TREATMENT. You will never be far from medical attention, although it will vary from place to place.

American Samoa. The main hospital is in Pago Pago. Dispensaries are located in the outer islands.

Australia. Modern hospital facilities located throughout the country.

Cook Islands. The main hospital is in Rarotonga. Cottage hospitals are located in the smaller islands.

Fiji. Medical attention available throughout the islands.

Kiribati. Small hospitals on Tarawa and Christmas Islands. Simple medical facilities elsewhere.

New Caledonia. Hospital facilities available in Noumea. Services limited elsewhere.

New Zealand. Modern hospital facilities located throughout the country.

Papua New Guinea. Hospitals in major centers. Medical attention close at hand in all other instances.

Solomon Islands. The main hospital is located on Guadalcanal. Church missions have medical facilities on other islands.

Tahiti. Government hospitals and private clinics available on Tahiti. Infirmaries and dispensaries available on Moorea, Raiatea, and Huahine.

Tonga. Medical facilities available throughout the main centers of the kingdom.

Vanuatu (formerly New Hebrides). Hospital in main centers. Small clinics in outlying areas.

Western Samoa. Main hospital is in Apia. Medical attention available in all other areas of the country.

Note: The *International Association for Medical Assistance to Travelers* is a worldwide association of physicians whose sole purpose is to help travelers. Write to IAMAT, 736 Center St., Lewiston, N.Y. 14092, for information. A similar service is available from *Intermedic,* 777 Third Avenue, New York, N.Y. 10017.

 DRY CLEANING AND LAUNDRY. Remember, you will be traveling in tropical and sub-tropical countries once you reach the South Pacific region. Woolens are seldom needed.

Dry cleaning services are not available in all areas, so it is wise to pack wash and wear or cotton type clothing. (See section on "What to Wear.")

Australia and New Zealand have some coin operated facilities in larger cities. For fast and efficient service it is best to have all laundry services handled through your hotel.

 READING MATTER AND NEWS. Except for Australia and New Zealand, don't expect to pick up a daily American or English language newspaper or magazine. New Caledonia and Tahiti have French langugage newspapers —Tahiti also produces one English edition.

Try to forget what is going on at home while you are on vacation. However, while traveling through the islands, if you must find out what is going on in the world, you can usually find at least one daily press publication, not necessarily newspaper style.

RADIO AND TELEVISION. Limited radio programs (2–8 hours) on smaller islands. Most programs are in the local languages. Except for Australia and New Zealand, television is very limited, even if it is available.

TOURS. Traveling by a package or group tour, you are free of all the petty, everyday financial problems. All expenses, including hotels, transportation, meals, sightseeing, taxis and guides are paid in advance. This is an ideal situation for those who cannot take much money out their country. (Meals are not included in all tours so make certain you check with your agent as to exactly what is included in the tour you purchase.)

It assures you of companionship and saves you the trouble of coping with strange language and moneys. Your tour or package takes in all the important points of interest and has the advantage of leaving you free to enjoy them with never a care about the irksome details of travel. Someone else worries about train and bus connections, someone else looks after your luggage and someone else pays the bills for you as you go along. Finally, you are able to anticipate every expense.

For first-time travelers to the South Pacific, Australia or New Zealand, it is probably advisable you handle all your arrangements with your travel agent. (Except for small details more easily arranged after arrival.) This is where you can save considerable money on accommodations and other pleasures of the islands. Tours come under many names: Circle Pacific, Excursion; Fly/Drive, etc. You save on special rates when it comes to "high" or "low" season flights. Many large tour operators have packages with airlines and hotels where they can order blocks of rooms, set up interesting sightseeing events, thus saving you a considerable amount of money over the regular economy or first-class ticket.

On tours or packages, you will usually find you can fairly well relax and do as you please if you do not want to take a coach tour the day one is arranged. The coach will just go off without you and you will be able to do as you please. (Just be sure you advise your tour guide ahead of time.)

In instances where the tour will move on to another island for overnight stays, you will have to pay your own accommodation for staying behind plus any meals involved. (This is the decision you must make before you buy your package or group tour—when you occasionally want to individualize, you will want to be prepared and make certain you'll have enough funds to cover the extra expenses.) When your group returns from their overnight elsewhere, your costs go back to the original arrangement.

Traveling to the Pacific is an adventure in itself because you will be crossing the largest and deepest body of water in the world—more than one-third of the world's surface. (Geographers say you can put all the continents in the world in the Pacific and still have room left over for another Asia—the largest continent). Therefore, because of the distances involved, you do not hop from one country to another as simply as you do in Europe, or as you travel the different states in the U.S.

Air transportation is the most convenient form for getting around if time is a factor. And this is where your travel agent will be your best friend since islands have air transportation only once or twice a week. (Refer to sections "Regional Transportation" and "Domestic Airlines"). There is little information available to the consumer, and not all travel agents are aware of some of the smaller regional or domestic airlines or schedules in the Pacific. Therefore, in the regional and domestic airline sections, there is a list of all lines now flying the South Pacific, along with sample fares. But because of the complexity of routing—use a knowledgeable travel agent when booking.

Listed in each chapter are some tours offered by responsible and reliable operators. Their packages are arranged so you can sample what you want. Some of the tours are adventurous, others for sun worshippers who just want to sit and relax, some are special interest. The listings are only samplings of the vast number of the exciting South Pacific, Australia, and New Zealand trips available.

GETTING AROUND

 BUS SERVICE. On some of the small islands a local bus trip can turn out to be one of the truly delightful experiences of your travels. Some buses are the open-air type with usually enough room to squeeze in everyone on the island. Most people will want to talk to you, know where you are from and "Why you come Samoa?"

While some buses have unscheduled routes—and the routes rather irregular—you'll reach your destination eventually and make many friends along the way. Buses such as the ones on American Samoa start early in the morning and stop about 5 P.M. They do not run on Sundays or holidays.

In Tahiti a small bus is called "le truck." Like the buses in Samoa, you can't help but have fun. They are decoratively painted, fares are cheap and you meet loads of locals with the same spirit mentioned above.

Some territories have scheduled services, many do not. Just be prepared to wait—take photos, make notes, write those post cards you keep promising to send home. Most probably, you'll have just as much fun watching the passing parade.

The major cities or main tourist cities have guided tour buses (some buses holding up to 40-45 passengers) that travel between capital cities or make tours of special interest. Local agents can arrange these tours from one to as many days required for your particular project. (See individual cities for tour details.)

Smaller eight to twelve passenger buses are also available, usually for one to three-hour sightseeing tours of the major highlights.

Buses arranged by travel agents have guides to point out the sites of interest.

 TRAINS. Australia. There are 45,000 km of national and state-owned and operated railroads connecting all state capitals (except Hobart and Darwin) and many other urban and centers. The principal services follow the coast from the main terminals; an east to west line provides unbroken rail link from Sydney to Perth (via Broken Hill and the Nullabor Plain). All trains on the main trunk lines are air conditioned, have first- and second-class seats and sleeping cars. Dining cars are available on most trains. Some of the cabins and roomettes on the express trains have private toilet facilities and showers with hot and cold water. Overseas passengers are entitled to carry 80 kg. of luggage.

Accommodations. There is little difference between first and second class (economy), except that economy seating may not have reclining seats. First-class sleeping compartments have their own facilities, while those for economy class are located at the end of the particular car. Some trains have motorail facilities for transporting cars.

Bookings. Reservations must be made in advance, even months ahead of time for such popular expresses as the Indian-Pacific and other long-distance trains. Peak travel periods for Australians are the summer months from December through February; the school holidays in May and from August through September; and Easter week.

Rail and Motorcoach Passes: These are great bargains but must be purchased before arrival. Allow unlimited first-class travel.

Austrailpass. (Sample 1985 rates) 14 days for US$300; 3 weeks for US$375; 1 month for US$465; 2 months for US$645; 3 months for US$743. First-class travel offers reserved seats. Must be purchased before arrival. Available through Australian Travel Service/Tour Pacific, P.O. Box 2078, 116 S. Louise St., Glendale, CA 91205. Phone: (800) 423–2880; in California, call (800) 232–2121.

Also available (before arrival) through ATS: *Budget Austrailpass.* Economy seats; economy berths only available on a limited number of services. In 1985: 14 days US$220; 21 days US$278; 1 month US$340; 2 months US$475, 3 months US$550.

Fiji. The South Pacific Sugar Mills offers a free service during crushing season (May-December) through 400 miles of sugar cane fields. Tourists usually take a one hour ride out of Lautoka and then take a taxi back to town.

New Zealand. *New Zealand Government Railways,* Railways Private Bag, Wellington. Offers rail service throughout both North and South islands. The "Silver Fern," an air-conditioned and hostess-served, scenic daylight service, runs each way Monday through Saturday between Auckland and Wellington. The 11-hour trip costs NZ$63. The "Northerner" overnight express between Auckland and Wellington runs both ways nightly and is made up mainly of seat cars with a limited number of sleeping cars, has licensed dining car. There is rail/ferry service between Wellington and Picton with a number of round trips daily. In the South Island, the "Southerner" train service runs Monday through Saturday between Christchurch, Dunedin, and Invercargill.

Off Season Railways Tourist Pass: Good for travel from February 1 to mid-December. Rates 8 days for NZ$145; 15 days for NZ$190; 22 days for NZ$255. Maximum extension is 6 days at NZ$10 per day. 8-day pass must be purchased from New Zealand Tourist office before arrival, as must railway passes for high season (mid-December through January), when prices are somewhat higher. All other passes can be purchased in New Zealand.

 TAXIS. Taxi services are available throughout the South Pacific territory. However, rates and services vary to such a degree, it is best to refer to the guide listed below to judge whether or not you should use taxi services or hire a car with driver. All prices are approximate.

American Samoa. Rates are approximate. $1.00 for short ride; $16 for circle island tour, or $6 per hour. Confirm rates before journey.

Australia. Readily available throughout the country. Rates vary from place to place.

Cook Islands. Taxis operate 7:00 A.M. to midnight. Rate NZ .30 flag fall, NZ .40 first mile and NZ .35 additional mile.

Fiji. Rates are by car, not per person. Plentiful and reasonable. Local trips about $.30 first mile. Journey out of town: agree on fare in advance.

New Caledonia. Rates Fr 20 per km or Fr 12 per mile.

New Zealand. Available in all major centers. Rates vary according to distance. Meters in all cabs.

Papua New Guinea. In district centers at $.20 per mile. Considered best means of public transportation.

Solomon Islands. In Honiara and Auki. Negotiate before riding as taxis have no meters.

Tahiti. Flag fall Fr 60 plus 45 per km, with minimum of Fr 100, in Papeete limits; Fr 90 outside city. Fares double after 11:00 P.M. Circle trip around Tahiti Island, with stops at restaurants and points of interest, approximately Fr 4,000 (1-4 passengers).

Tonga. Open air 3-wheel taxis called "Ve'etolu." Fix price beforehand.

Vanuatu (formerly New Hebrides). Rates fixed by law. No bargaining.

Western Samoa. 20-30 Sene for trips in Apia. Agree on fare out of town in advance.

MOTOR SCOOTERS AND BICYCLES are available in Australia, Cook Islands, New Zealand, American Samoa, and Tahiti. They are relatively inexpensive and are an easy way to explore the South Pacific. Some of the other smaller islands may have invested in motor scooter rentals by the time this book goes to press. Check with the local tourist bureau on arrival.

Check with your hotel for bicycle rental services.

CAR RENTAL

Car hire is possible in every country, with *Budget, Avis,* and *Hertz* usually available. There are also many local firms which may offer self-drive holiday packages. New Zealand Tourist Office offers a free, general information auto guidebook that includes information on geography, climate, and road signs, and maps showing principal arteries and distance between major cities. Prices below are for economy cars only. (Rates are approximate.)

Your travel agent should have a list of international firms and rates.

COUNTRY	INT'L. DRIVER'S LICENSE	LEFT OR RIGHT DRIVE	1985 RATES (US$ PER DAY)	ROAD CONSTRUCTION
American Samoa	U.S. or Int'l.	Right	$25[1]	paved primary
Australia	Preferred	Left	$25[1]	good roads
Cook Islands	Local license required	Left	$27[1]	adequate
Fiji	No	Left	$35[3]	all-weather roads
New Caledonia	U.S. or Int'l.	Right	$33[3]	excellent, problems in rainy season
New Zealand[3]	Yes	Left	$27[3]	excellent roads
Papua New Guinea	Yes	Left	$11[2]	paved/ graded; mostly
Solomon Islands	No	Left	$36[1]	rough roads
Tahiti	No	Right	$30[3]	asphalt/ stone-surfaced
Tonga	Yes	Left	$29[1]	blacktop/ gravel roads
Vanuatu	U.S. or Int'l.	Right	$38[3]	4-wheel drive best
Western Samoa	Yes	Right	$24[2]	surfaced/ secondary roads

[1]Unlimited mileage
[2]Plus mileage
[3]Minimum number of days required. Note: advance booking necessary on smaller islands.

AIRPORT TAXES. Many countries charge an airport departure tax in order to help maintain and upgrade airport facilities.

Listed here are the countries that have airport taxes and their charges:
Australia: A$20; *Fiji:* $5; *New Zealand:* NZ$2; *Papua New Guinea:* Kina 10; *Western Samoa:* WS$20; *Solomon Islands:* SBD5; *Tuvalu:* A$2.50; *Tonga:* T$5; *Vanuatu:* Vatu 1000.

AUSTRALIA

AUSTRALIA: Continent or Island?

by
EMERY BARCS

Whether one calls Australia the world's smallest continent or the largest island, it is a land of fascinating contrasts. Almost the size of the United States (excluding Alaska and Hawaii) and one and a half times the land area of Europe (excluding the Soviet Union), Australia had 15,400,100 people in September 1983. Australia is also the only continent inhabited by a single nation, although 1 in 5 Australians was born overseas. Australia's tropical north is a short jet hop from the equator; yet, from its southernmost point, one-day trips by plane are organised for tourists to the frozen reaches of Antarctica. While the major resort areas of the big cities provide maximum creature comforts for the most demanding visitor, trips off the beaten track or to the sparsely populated hinterland, called the outback, need careful preparation. For there, the traveller will be left very much alone.

In Australia, untamed nature is never far afield from the amenities of technological civilisation. While this proximity is a major attraction to the visitor, it also poses risks which may not be obvious. Let's suppose you are driving along one of the thousands of golden sand beaches studding the Australian coast. The day may be hot and the water inviting. But sharks may occasionally lurk in those blue waters, especially if the sea happens to be flat that day. The calm waters around Australia may also turn into rip currents that can drag the swimmer far out to sea or churn up giant waves that sweep cliff-climbers or rock fishermen into the seething water from seemingly safe ledges.

On land, that innocent looking Australian bush stretching from the roadside may, in fact, be a treacherous thicket. Hardly a weekend goes by without search parties seeking bush walkers—often allegedly experienced—who have become lost in the maze. Most times they are found; sometimes they are not. But these are sensible warnings only. They are not intended to dampen the traveller's interest in surfing, swimming, fishing, or exploring the bush. On the contrary, by using common sense, prudence, and readily available advice, the visitor will enjoy a safe Australian vacation, mixing adventure with a pleasant holiday schedule.

The overseas visitor should also be prepared to look at the Australian scenery with fresh eyes in order to appreciate it. For there is great beauty in the Australian landscape. Sydney's harbour, for example, with its flamboyant opera house, has been favourably compared with Rio de Janeiro's; the huge canyons of the Blue Mountains in New South Wales rank among the world's finest sights; and the riot of colour in suburban gardens is a lasting inspiration to horticulturists.

But the Australian countryside rarely radiates mellow serenity. More often it appears harsh and alien at first sight. Indeed, one's first encounter with nature in Australia is perhaps akin to the experience of looking at abstract paintings or listening to atonal music for the first time—an experience of puzzlement, even dismay. Even the first Europeans who landed in Australia were shocked when they surveyed their surroundings. One may therefore need time to discover for oneself the often austere and melancholy beauty of much of the continent.

The Land

There are a number of reasons why Australia is vastly different from the other continents. The first is its age. It is one of the oldest of the earth's land masses—older than Europe or America. Second, it has been physically isolated from the rest of the world for some 50 million years, perhaps even longer. Third, this isolation assured the survival of unique strains of flora and fauna. And last, Australia's remoteness, coupled with its uninviting shoreline, discouraged western explorers from colonising the continent until about two centuries ago.

Bounded by the Arafura Sea on the north, the Coral and Tasman Seas of the South Pacific Ocean on the east, and the Indian Ocean on the west and south, Australia's coastline runs 12,446 miles (19,914 kms.)—about equal to the distance between Sydney and London via Suez. It is surrounded by a rather shallow continental shelf averaging 100 fathoms (600 ft.) deep and ranging between 20 and upwards of 150 miles (32-240 kms.) wide. One of the coast's unsurpassed glories is the Great Barrier Reef, a wonderland of coral reefs and coral islands extending more than 1,250 miles (2,000 kms.) north of Brisbane, capital of Queensland, to the island of New Guinea.

Varying greatly in size, the six States and two Territories which make up the Commonwealth of Australia occupy the continent's 2,967,909 square miles (7,716,563 sq. kms.) of land. The largest is Western Australia, 975,920 square miles (2,537,392 sq. kms.)—four times larger than Texas and 11 times the size of Great Britain, followed by Queensland, 667,000 square miles (1,734,200 sq. kms.), South Australia, 380,070 square miles (988,182 sq. kms.), New South Wales, 309,433 square miles (804,525 sq. kms.), Victoria, 87,884 square miles (227,620 sq. kms.), and the island State of Tasmania, 26,383 square miles (68,595 sq. kms.). The sparsely populated Northern Territory sprawls over 520,280 square miles (1,352,728 sq. kms.) while the Australian Capital Territory, which includes the federal capital of Canberra, is hemmed into 939 square miles (2,441 sq. kms.) and is fast becoming too small for its rapidly growing population.

Although Australia has often been described as an empty bowl as parts of its edges are higher than its centre, it is in fact, the flattest of the continents mainly because of its age. Here, the elements have had more time to plane the protuberances. The continent has an average height of only 1,000 ft. above sea level compared with a world mean of 2,300 ft. The enormous plateau which rises in the west spreads over about three-quarters of the total area and occupies almost the whole of Western Australia, the greater part of the Northern Territory, a sizable chunk of South Australia, and parts of Western Queensland. East of the Great Western Plateau are the Central Eastern Lowlands, mostly a dry belt crossing Australia from north to south which at one point—Lake Eyre in South Australia—drop to some 36 ft. below sea level. In prehistoric times, roughly 60 million years ago, the Lowlands were part of the sea floor. East of them rise the Eastern Highlands, otherwise known as the Great Dividing Range, which follow the contours of the coast from the top of Australia to the bottom of Tasmania. Although the average altitude of the Highlands is a mere 2,700 feet, its highest peak, Mount Kosciusko, in the picturesque Australian Alps in New South Wales, rises to 7,316 ft. The great majority of Australians live in the 30-250 mile wide coastal strip east of the "Great Divide."

Climate and Weather

While the relatively small Australian nation owns a huge amount of land, much of it remains uninhabited. The reason is that almost all of the unsettled land—about 70% of Australia's total territory—is so arid as to be unfit for civilised habitation in its undeveloped state. In recent years, the discovery of impressive mineral wealth in the deserts has led to the establishment of mining towns provided with all modern conveniences, including airconditioned homes and offices. But water for these settlements has had to be piped long distances, and everything people need for survival must be brought from far away. Even in the somewhat more habitable areas on the fringe of the arid "dead heart" of Australia, water is so scarce and vegetation so sparse that several square miles of land are needed to keep one sheep alive.

The total annual average run-off of all Australian rivers is only a fraction of that carried by some of the world's mighty waterways—about two-thirds that of the St. Lawrence in North America and half that of the Amazon in South America. Australia's largest river, the 1,600 mile (2,560 km.) long Murray, is one of the continent's most important

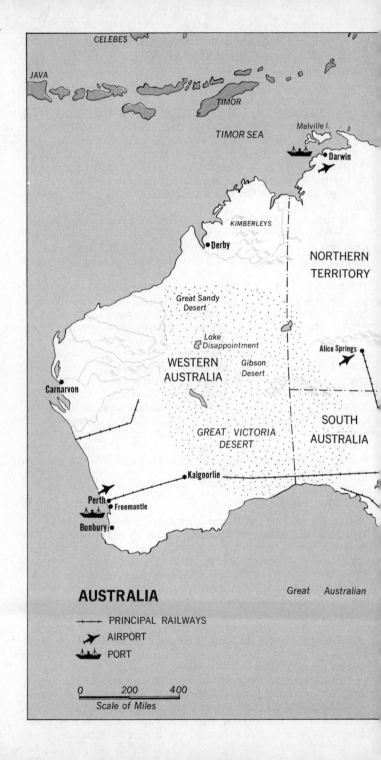

CELEBES

JAVA

TIMOR

TIMOR SEA

Melville I.

Darwin

KIMBERLEYS

Derby

NORTHERN
TERRITORY

Great Sandy
Desert

Lake
Disappointment

WESTERN
AUSTRALIA

Gibson
Desert

Alice Springs

Carnarvon

SOUTH
AUSTRALIA

GREAT VICTORIA
DESERT

Kalgoorlie

Perth
Freemantle

Bunbury

Great   Australian

AUSTRALIA

—•—•— PRINCIPAL RAILWAYS

✈ AIRPORT

⚓ PORT

0   200   400
Scale of Miles

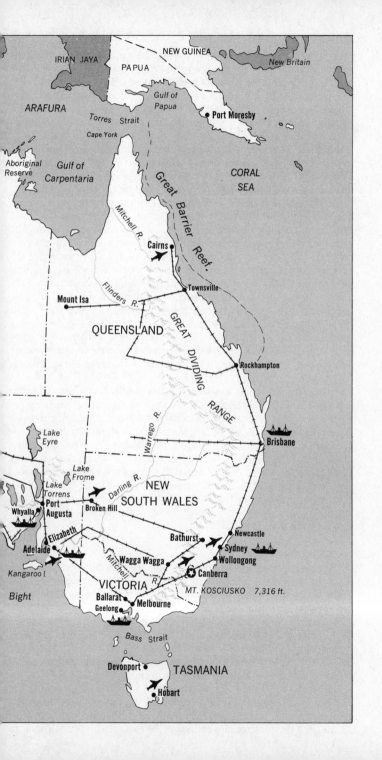

streams. With the Darling, it forms Australia's most wide ranging river system, draining an area of more than 400,000 square miles (1,036,000 sq. kms.). But most of Australia's rivers are small and coastal, flowing into the sea. Maps may show various internal river systems but these "rivers" are usually little more than dry sandy beds or a series of rapidly evaporating water holes, some flowing into great salt "lakes" as dry as the river beds, such as Lake Eyre in South Australia.

But while Australia is the world's driest continent, this information will be of negligible interest to the majority of travellers who will want to visit only the more closely settled regions where the action takes place. Only a few will journey into the desert lands in the remote outback.

As for water—it continues to be a problem in all parts of Australia but scientists have utilized the most advanced technology in the world to harness available resources. Except for occasional severe droughts, which may entail some restrictions on water use, visitors will suffer no privations. In fact, they may never become aware of the situation for the reason that Australians themselves are among the world's most spend-thrift water-users. The average Australian would feel deprived to miss a daily shower—even to limit the use of a garden hose.

Sometimes the problem is too much rather than too little water—and in the wrong place. When the rains come, dry river beds become raging torrents, flooding the countryside and isolating townships by making roads impassable. Motorists would therefore be wise to read weather information, including reports on the state of roads, whenever there is heavy rainfall.

Australians are great sun-worshippers—hardly surprising in a sun drenched land. The average daily sunshine in the capital cities ranges from 5.9 hours in Hobart to 8.4 hours in Darwin. Inland, the average is even higher. Years ago, one of Australia's most popular humourists, the late Lennie Lower, reported from Marble Bar (Western Australia): "I am now in that part of the British Empire on which the sun never sets." Still, only about 39% of Australia (half of Queensland, a bit more than one-third of Western Australia, and four-fifth of the Northern Territory) lies within the hot, tropical zone. The remaining areas, includ-ing the whole of New South Wales, Victoria, South Australia, and Tas-mania, are in the temperate zone.

The Seasons

"I could never get used to that," said the legendary English schoolboy when his geography teacher explained that in Australia everything is "upside down." Winter in Australia arrives when the northern hem-isphere swelters in summer heat, and Sydneysiders prepare for bed when it is midday in London. But, while visitors have little difficulty in adjust-ing to a reversal of seasons, Australia's close observance of northern hemisphere traditions at Christmas time is somewhat incongruous when one sees posters of Santa Claus in arctic garb against a background of reindeer and snow, while the mercury is climbing to 100° F (38° C).

Except in the high mountains, where plenty of snow falls in winter and the heath is fragrant with alpine flowers in summer, the seasons in Australia are not as marked as they are in the northern hemisphere. Most plants keep their foliage all year round. In general, the summer months are December, January and February; autumn includes March, April and May; winter comes in June, July and August; spring runs through September, October, and November. The rainy season in the tropical north is during the summer months.

Australia has three time zones: Eastern Standard Time is 10 hours ahead of Greenwhich Mean Time; Central Australian Time is 9½ hours ahead, and Western Time is 8 hours ahead. Therefore, when it is noon in Perth, it is 1:30 P.M. in Adelaide and 2 P.M. in Sydney, Melbourne, Canberra, Brisbane, and Hobart. During the summer months, most States introduce daylight saving of an hour.

Only in a few regions, such as the Alps and other high mountain ranges in southern Tasmania and at night in some of the deserts, does the thermometer dip below freezing, though cold snaps, mostly at night, may occur elsewhere. Summer can be very warm; temperatures of around 100°F (38°C) are not exceptional even in the temperate zone, but they rarely continue for more than a day or two. Maximum summer averages in the capital cities vary between 90°F (32.2°C) in Darwin and 70°F (21°C) in Hobart. Minimum summer averages range from Darwin, 77°F (25°C) to Hobart 52°F (11.1°C). The maximum average winter temperatures range from 87°F (30.5°C) in Darwin and 53°F (11.6°C) in Canberra, while minimums range from 69°F (20.5°C) in Darwin to 33°F (0.5°C) in Canberra.

Throughout the year, one can always find some region in Australia where the climate is excellent for touring. But some months are better than others for visiting certain parts of the continent. Three of the State capitals—Sydney, Melbourne, and Perth—are really all-season cities. Brisbane and Darwin are rather hot in summer. Adelaide, Hobart, and Canberra, on the other hand, are on the cold side in winter. The best months for exploring the Great Barrier Reef are between April and November; for the Northern Territory and Central Australia (Alice Springs, Ayers Rock) between April and October; and for the Gold Coast of Queensland, between April and November. The skiing season usually begins at the end of May or early June and lasts until September.

Plants and Animals

Fossil evidence indicates that in the Cretacious period (from Latin *creta,* meaning chalk) some 65 million years ago, when dinosaurs reached the peak of their development and birds and possum-like mammals proliferated, Australia was still connected by land with Asia. But dating from perhaps 50 million years ago, when the sea cut off Australia and turned it into a separate land mass, plant and animal life there developed almost independent of the rest of the world until the arrival of the white man a couple of centuries ago. We say "almost" because some migratory birds kept coming and going to and from other continents.

Hence all plants and animals stranded in Australia had to adapt themselves to the continent's special conditions. The most impressive plants are the 450 species of eucalyptus or "gum" trees which thrive practically in every soil and in every climate—the tropical north, the freezing Alps, the deserts, and the rain-soaked forests. One of its species, the mountain ash (to be found in Victoria and Tasmania), is the tallest hardwood in the world, growing to 300 ft. and more. There are 600 species of acacias; the most common of them is the *wattle*—so called because early settlers found its saplings useful for constructing hut walls and roofs of interlaced (wattled) branches and mud, known as "wattle and daub." Thousands of species of wildflowers thrive all over Australia. Western Australia has the largest number of species, about 2,000.

While Australia has neither indigenous hoofed beasts nor primates, some unique animals live there. The oldest of them is probably the platypus which, although a mammal, lays eggs, suckles its young from enlarged pores, has webbed feet and a duck-like bill, lives on river banks but is not really an aquatic creature and cannot stay under water for more than about a minute. Some zoologists believe that it is a "living fossil," a surviving example of the transition from reptiles to mammals.

Another strange fellow is the echidna or spiny anteater, which looks like a kind of hedgehog but isn't. While it is difficult to find platypus and echidnas in their natural habitat (both are protected animals and cannot be hunted or captured without authorisation), every major Australian zoo has a few of them.

About half of Australia's 230 species of native mammals consists of a wide variety of marsupials—from giant 8-foot-tall kangaroos to tiny mouse-like creatures. Their one common characteristic is that they carry and feed their young in pouches. The best known Australian marsupials belong to the family of kangaroos which abound on the continent. The name is aboriginal but its meaning is uncertain. (The story that it means "don't know"—because when the first white settlers asked aboriginals what they called the strange animal, they muttered "kanguru", meaning that they did not understand the question—is a fiction.) Kangaroos, using their powerful hind legs and their strong tails, can clear 27 ft. or more in a single leap and can hop along at speeds of 25 miles an hour for short distances. They breed fast and, because they live mainly on grass, sheep and cattle breeders consider them nuisances.

No one knows the size of the kangaroo population but there are millions in Australia. A recent survey has estimated their number in New South Wales alone at some 3.5 million. For a while, conservationists, fearing their extinction, fought for a total prohibition on hunting them and, in 1973, the federal government forbade the export of kangaroo skins. The hunting prohibition, however, led to such an increase in the number of kangaroos that it has been withdrawn and replaced with regulations limiting the number of animals allowed to be shot in the whole of Australia—1.26 million in 1977. A small fee is charged for a hunting licence. But whether pest or not, the kangaroo has become a symbol of Australia. It figures in the national coat of arms together with that other exclusively Australian creature, the flightless but fast-running bird, the emu.

The most endearing Australian indigenous animal is undoubtedly that sleepy, bearlike, harmless tree-dweller, the cuddly koala. The aboriginal name means "one who doesn't drink" which is more or less true, for the koala seems to obtain most of the liquid it needs from the leaves of certain eucalypt trees which seem to make him permanently drowsy. The koala is also a protected animal and the Australian prohibition on hunting koalas since the early 1930's may have come just in time to prevent the extinction of the inoffensive, defenseless, and charming animals which had been killed by the millions for their skins.

Australia's only large predatory mammal, the dog-like dingo, is not indigenous to the continent. Some zoologists now believe that its ancestor was the Indian plains wolf. It is generally accepted, however, that the dingo was brought to Australia by the Aborigines 7,000 to 10,000 years ago as a semi-wild hunting dog.

Another predatory mammal, the Tasmanian tiger, was thought to have become extinct but some naturalists now believe it may have survived in the impenetrable and unexplored forests of western and southwestern Tasmania.

Australian mammals include 70 species of rats, water rats, and mice, 50 species of bats, more than 20 species of whale, several species of seals, and the seacow or dugong, which lives in the warm northern seas.

Australia is a veritable paradise for ornithologists and bird watchers. There are some 720 kinds of birds, 530 of them exclusively Australian. They include 60 species of parrots and 70 species of honey eaters. Other distinguished Australian birds are the aristocratic black swan, the Cape Barren goose, the dancing and singing lyrebird, and the slightly sinister looking kookaburra whose sepulchral laughter has earned it the name of "laughing jackass." The widespread belief that Australian birds don't sing is nonsense; some of them perform veritable arias.

Someone once wrote "Name anything that jumps, slithers, or crawls and Australia has it." An exaggeration, of course, but it is true that the continent is the home of a considerable variety of insects, spiders, and 6.6 percent of the world's reptiles. Yet, one can live years, even a lifetime, in Australia without ever confronting any of the nastier species. Indeed, it takes considerable expense and effort to see the large estuarine crocodile which lives in northern salt waters. None of the 240 species of lizards is dangerous though some of them—such as the dramatic frilled lizard—may look threatening. Some 20 of the 140 species of land and freshwater snakes are dangerous to man but there is only minimal chance of encountering them on the usual tourist itinerary. (The story may be different if one ventures into the bush.)

There are some 54,000 known species of insects and probably 100,000 or more species in all. Insects include about 1,000 species of ants. Some are almost two inches in length; others move with a six-inch jump. Only two of the 1,500 species of spiders are venomous—the redback, of the same family as the American black widow, and the funnel-web, related to the American tarantula. The large hairy so-called "tarantula" of Australia is the huntsman, which is non-poisonous though it can give a painful bite. At any rate, a few sensible don'ts will greatly lessen the risks of being bitten or stung: don't walk in tall grass; don't disturb old timber; lift stones carefully, and look before you sit down.

Minerals and Metals

Australia is very rich in minerals and metals. During the past 30 years or so new discoveries have considerably raised the estimates of known reserves. For example, Western Australia alone has an estimated 24,500 million tons of iron ore containing more than 54 percent of iron. Australia is well provided with an important energy resource: coal. Eastern

Australia has at least 200,000 million tons of black coal; Victoria has 66,700 million tons of brown coal. The continent is also the largest bauxite producer with 5,500 million tons of reserves. There are large deposits of lead, zinc, copper, nickel, mineral sands, uranium, and natural gas. The country produces about two-thirds of its crude oil requirements. Australia's world famous opals are the most important semi-precious stone mined.

AN AUSTRALIAN CHRONOLOGY

First Aboriginal settlers arrive in Australia.	c. 28,000 B.C.
Ptolemy's theory of a Southern Terra Incognita.	c. 150 A.D.
Luis de Torres sails through the strait between Australia and New Guinea.	1606
Willem Jansz sails into the Gulf of Carpentaria.	1606
Dirk Hartog examines the west coast of Australia.	1612
Abel Tasman discovers Van Diemen's land (Tasmania).	1642
William Dampier lands on the northwest coast.	1688
James Cook lands at Botany Bay.	1770
The first British convict fleet arrives.	1788
Capt. Arthur Phillip formally takes possession of eastern Australia, including Tasmania, and establishes colony of New South Wales.	Jan.26, 1788
Sheep breeding begins.	1796
Crossing of the Blue Mountains opens up new regions for settlement.	1813
Establishment of five additional colonies:	
Tasmania	1825
Western Australia	1829
South Australia	1834
Victoria	1851
Queensland	1859
Transportation of convicts ends, Eastern colonies	1840
Tasmania	1853
Western Australia	1868
Australian Colonies Government Act paves way for responsible government.	1850
Discovery of gold.	1851
Commonwealth of Australia, a federation of six former colonies (now States), comes into being.	Jan.1, 1901

Australia's Past

There are many theories about when and how the first humans—the ancestors of the present Aboriginals—reached Australia. Estimates have varied between 10,000 and 30,000 years ago but at least 30,000 years now seems to be accepted as reasonable. Some scientists argue that those ancient dark-skinned hunters and food-gatherers wandered into Australia when it still formed a continuous land mass with Asia. Others assert that the Aboriginals came by rafts and canoes. Whatever the fact, once they reached Australia they developed in the same kind of isolation as the animals and plants. During the thousands of years between their arrival and the landing of white explorers no record has survived of any contact with outsiders.

A remarkable feature of the Aboriginals' isolated evolution is that while they created a complex social order, fascinating expressions of art, and a mythology, their technology—except for the aerodynamically complicated boomerang—stagnated in the Stone Age. They had no agriculture and no domesticated animals except the dingo. They also did not know how to work metals.

One may assume that at some time Asian seafarers ventured as far south as Australia. But, if they landed, they left no mark. As for the Europeans, Ptolemy, the Greek mathematician, astronomer, and geographer (A.D. 126-161) suspected the existence of a Terra Incognita (Unknown Land) in what is now the Southern Indian Ocean; but it took another 15 centuries before the first Europeans sailed within sight of that mysterious southern land. A ship under the command of the Spaniard Luis de Torres sailed through the strait (named after him) between Australia and New Guinea in 1606, but whether he actually sighted Australia is not known. Willem Jansz, a captain of the Dutch East India Company, arrived in the same year. His pinnace *Duyfken* sailed into the Gulf of Carpentaria and he charted 200 miles (320 kms.) of the coastline, although Jansz mistook it for a part of New Guinea.

Thirst for knowledge and adventure played only a minor part in these and subsequent voyages to the antipodes. Their main purpose, like those of the great explorations in previous centuries, was the furthering of trade and the acquisition of new resources. On both counts, Australia disappointed the early sailors, many of them Dutch, as Dutch navigators had learned from experience that after rounding the Cape of Good Hope they could reach the Dutch East Indies faster if they took a straight eastern course as far as Australia before turning north. In this way, they were able to use the prevailing winds, the mariners' "brave west winds," for the longest time. These navigators included Dirk Hartog, probably the first European to land on Australian soil—an island (now carrying his name) off the Western Australian coast which his ship, *Eeendracht,* reached on October 25, 1616. The pewter plate, which Hartog left on the island to record the event, is now in the National Museum of Amsterdam. In 1642 another Hollander, Abel Tasman, discovered what is now Tasmania. Rather modestly, he gave it the name of Van Diemen's Land in honour of the Governor-General of the Dutch East Indies. Although Tasman raised the Dutch flag and declared that the island was henceforth a possession of Holland, his fellow countrymen were not interested when they heard of the event. Neither did they show much enthusiasm for Willem de Flaming's report in 1697 that he had reached the Swan River. Today, Perth—the Western Australian capital—stands on its banks.

William Dampier, an English buccaneer, was the first Briton to land in New Holland (as Australia was then called). The date was 1688 and the place King Sound in the northwest. He thought it a desolate place and gave us the first description of the Aborigines "the miserablest people in the world." Eleven years later, he returned in a Royal Navy ship and explored a bit more of the inhospitable northwest coast. During the next decades, Britons, Dutch, and essentially everyone else forgot New Holland which became a sort of fantasy land. Here, Jonathan Swift located "the country of the Yahoos," degraded, brutish creatures, visited by Gulliver.

The misconception that Captain James Cook discovered Australia still lingers on. He did not, nor did he claim to have done so. It is true, however, that discovery and exploration of the east coast of Australia during the voyage of Cook's ship, the *Endeavour,* became one of the most important of all the early voyages of discovery. Cook's instructions from the British Admiralty were, first, to make certain astronomical observations from Tahiti; then to sail southwards; and then, if necessary, westwards, to look for a "continent or land of great extent." On April 20, 1770, Cook sighted the southeastern corner of Australia at Point Hicks. On the 29th, he landed in a large bay in what is today south Sydney and called it Botany Bay because of the variety of hitherto unknown plants which the English botanist Joseph Banks and his Swedish colleague, the naturalist Daniel Carl Solander, found there. A week later, Cook continued his voyage north, charted the coast and, eventually, on the small Possession Island off Cape York in the north, took possession of eastern Australia for Britain. Upon reaching home, Cook gave an enthusiastic report about the economic possibilities of eastern Australia which he named New South Wales. Although his book *The Voyages of Captain Cook* became a best seller and was translated into several languages, Britons were only mildly interested in the newest extension of their possessions.

Early Colonizers

It took the American Revolutionary War to provide the British Government with the necessary impetus to pay attention to Australia. Loss of the American colonies meant that there was no longer a viable place to ship law breakers sentenced to transportation. Australia looked like a suitable alternative. It was sufficiently remote and, as Prime Minister William Pitt declared in Parliament, it offered the cheapest way to reduce the prison population which was overcrowding Britain's jails. So Australia became the new repository for convicts and on May 13, 1787, the First Fleet of 11 ships sailed from England with approximately 1,030 people including roughly 760 convicts under the Command of Capt. Arthur Phillip who was to be the first Governor of the new colony. After a voyage lasting eight months, the fleet reached Botany Bay on January 18, 1788.

Capt. Phillip, however, regarded the bay as unsuitable for a settlement. But a few miles north, he found "the finest harbour in the world, in which a thousand sail of the line may ride in the most perfect security" and transferred the operation to that site. He named the place Sydney (after Lord Sydney, Secretary of State for the Colonies) and that's where Australia's premier city with a population in excess of three million now stands. The date of the landing in Sydney Harbour at Sydney Cove was January 26, 1788, now celebrated as Australia Day.

At the time it was a miserable settlement, in physical and human terms. Some of the convicts were political offenders and petty rascals; but the majority consisted of hardened criminals. Only a few had learned any trade or knew anything about agriculture. In addition, most of the European plants and the cattle transported by the fleet soon died in the new surroundings. During the early years, the colonists had to rely upon food supplies imported from overseas and there were many times when the venture appeared doomed. In due course, however, land with better soil for farming was found further inland and new settlements were established. By 1792, when Governor Phillip retired for health reasons and returned to England the colony was almost self-sufficient in staple foods.

For the next 20 years or so, the newcomers still occupied only a small coastal strip. A few exploratory voyages were made, the most important being the expedition of Capt. Matthew Flinders who circumnavigated the continent for the first time in 1802-1803. Flinders is credited with having first used the name "Australia"; previously, the continent had been called New Holland, New South Wales, or Botany Bay. For some time, the early settlers could not move much further inland because of the "impassable" barrier of the Blue Mountains. But in 1813 Gregory Blaxland, a farmer, Lieutenant William Lawson, a former member of the New South Wales Corps, and acting Provost Marshal William Charles Wentworth found a way across the mountains, following the ridges instead of gullies and ravines. The successful crossing eventually led to the opening of the country for settlement farther afield from Sydney. Exploration continued throughout the 19th century and, although almost the whole of Australia has now been surveyed and mapped, some little known areas still remain. Later explorers had the advantage of setting out on expeditions from newly established settlements, five of which became capitals of new colonies: Hobart, Tasmania, established in 1804; Brisbane, Queensland, 1824; Perth, Western Australia, 1829; Melbourne, Victoria, 1835; and Adelaide, South Australia, 1836. In 1839, the harbour of Darwin was discovered by H.M.S. Beagle and named in honour of Charles Darwin who had been a naturalist with an earlier expedition of the Beagle. It is now the site of the capital of the Northern Territory.

Gold and Fleece

Two factors have been of the utmost importance in the relatively fast development of Australia. One was the successful breeding of sheep; the other, the discovery of gold.

Although the saying that "Australia rides on the sheep's back" is no longer quite valid, without the establishment of a large wool growing industry at an early date, the continent's development would have been a great deal slower and probably quite different. At the start, Australia produced nothing that could be sold to the rest of the world to create sufficient income and encourage outside investment in development. The "father" of Australian sheep breeding was Capt. John McArthur who, with others, began to breed Spanish merinos—some imported from the Cape Province (South Africa) and others from the Royal Merino stud at Kew, England. The experiments were extremely successful and, by the beginning of the 19th century, New South Wales produced the world's finest wool. In 1810 the colony had 25,000 sheep. Three years earlier the first wool (245 lbs.) had been sent to London. In 1975, Australia had 153.1 million sheep and exported about 1,700 million lbs. of wool.

The early settlers—immigrants, freed convicts, marines, and discharged military personnel who chose to stay in Australia—received land free of charge. After the crossing of the Blue Mountains, some people took possession of land on the western plains simply by "squatting" on it. The only condition for obtaining official approval of ownership was the obligation to employ convicts, which really meant cheap labour for minimal costs of feeding and clothing them. Still, for the growing number of free settlers, the system of transportation of criminals and attendant problems became intolerable and the demand for abolition grew. Regular transportation to the eastern colonies ceased in 1840 and to Tasmania in 1853. Western Australia, on the other hand, continued to receive transported convicts to overcome an acute labour shortage but the system finally was terminated in 1868. During 80 years of transportation, approximately 168,000 convicts were sent from Britain to Australia.

The discovery of gold in 1851 gave a big boost to Australia's population. Between 1850 and 1870, it more than quadrupled—from 405,000 to almost 1,650,000. When the gold boom for the individual prospector petered out in the 1870's, many "diggers" decided to stay in the country as tradesmen, merchants, and farmers. In 1854, gold caused Australia's only bloody uprising against government authority, the Eureka Stockade, resulting in the deaths of about 30 men. The miners' chief grievance was a decision of the Government of Victoria to licence gold mining and the refusal of some miners to pay the licence fee. The trouble, which originally started over a broken window in the Eureka Hotel in the town of Ballarat, has been transformed into a legend of social rebellion of the underdog against authority.

Evolution of a Commonwealth

The present six Australian states evolved from the same number of colonies established at different dates: Tasmania, in 1825; Western Australia, 1829; South Australia, 1834; Victoria, 1851; and Queensland, 1859. The Australian Colonies Government Act of 1850 bestowed considerable rights of self-government on them. They developed independently from each other, even without much consideration for their mutual interests. They introduced different laws and built railways with different gauges. Today, however, a standard gauge main line runs between the east and west coasts, providing an unbroken connection between Perth, Sydney, and Brisbane. A standard gauge line also connects Brisbane, Sydney, and Melbourne.

From 1891 onwards negotiations began to develop for federation, and were finally crowned with success on January 1, 1901, when the Commonwealth of Australia came into being. The Earl of Hopetown became its first Governor-General and Sir Edmund Barton, a former speaker of the New South Wales Legislative Assembly, its first Prime Minister.

In both World Wars, Australia fought with the Allies. In World War I (1914-1918), when the population was fewer than five million, 417,000 Australians served in the armed forces—322,000 of them overseas in Gallipoli, Europe, and Palestine. Some 60,000 were killed. In World War II (1939-1945), about one million persons—eight out of ten males between 18 and 35 years of age—enlisted in the forces. About 550,000 served overseas; 34,300 died on active service. Australian contingents also fought in the Korean and Vietnam wars. While no enemy force has ever landed in Australia, Japanese planes bombed Darwin heavily in World War II; two Japanese submarines fired a few shells at Sydney and Newcastle; and three of their midget two-men submarines penetrated

Sydney Harbour. The Japanese sank a depot ship killing 19, but two of the midget submarines were sunk.

Government

Australia, a self-governing parliamentary democracy, has dominion status in the British Commonwealth of Nations. Also called a commonwealth herself, she is similar in political structure to Britain and, to a lesser extent, the United States, with its elected Senate and House of Representatives (Parliament). With a strong central government headed by the Prime Minister, leader of the ruling party, Australia is a federation of six States (New South Wales, Victoria, Queensland, South Australia, Western Australia, and Tasmania), each with its own government enjoying limited authority. The central government is also directly responsible for the two internal territories—the Northern Territory and the Australian Capital Territory—as well as for Australia's external territories. As a step toward self-government, a Northern Territory Government with restricted powers was established in July 1978. There are also roughly 900 local government bodies at city, town, municipality, or county levels.

The basic law of Australia is the country's federal constitution. The States also have their constitutions and there are some who believe that with 7 governments, 7 public services, and 900 local government organisations, the nation is expensively over-governed and over-administered. Movements to abolish the States and retain only the federal structure, however, have failed to attract large scale support among Australians, who are always suspicious of attempts to concentrate power in fewer hands.

Australians were the world's first people to introduce voting by secret ballot in parliamentary elections. Now all citizens, 18 years of age and over not only have the right but the legal duty to vote in all federal and state parliamentary elections. Failure to do so draws a fine unless one has a valid excuse.

Australia though an independent nation, maintains a close official relationship with Britain. The British monarch, Queen Elizabeth II, is also formally Queen of Australia and, as such, is Head of State. She is represented in the country by a governor-general and six State governors. All are designated by the elected (Federal or State) governments and appointed by the monarch on their recommendation. Except in extraordinary circumstances, the governors act on the advice of the elected ministers but they have so-called "reserve powers" which enable them to act independently in cases of extreme crisis.

Members of all Australian governments must also be members of their respective parliaments to which they are responsible. At present, four parties are represented in the Australian (Federal) parliament: The Liberal Party, a moderately conservative group, founded in 1944; the National Country Party, with mainly rural backing, established in 1918; the Australian Labour Party, which is akin to the British Labour Party and dates back to 1891; and the Australian Democrats, a small middle-of-the-road party. Federal elections in December 1984 returned a 16-seat majority for Labor in the 148-seat House of Representatives.

Following the British tradition, the Australian House of Representatives is the more important of the two chambers in Parliament. The Prime Minister has always been one of its members, although this is not a constitutional requirement.

A number of political parties are not represented in the federal and state parliaments. They include the Democratic Labour Party (established after a split in the Labour Party) and three Communist Parties (two pro-Moscow, one pro-Peking). To date, the overwhelming majority of the Australian electorate has favoured moderate political parties and shied away from extremes.

The present Governor-General is Sir Ninian Stephen, a former High Court Judge. The Prime Minister is Bob Hawke (Labor), a former president of the Australian Trade Union Council (ACTU). The leader of the opposition is the Liberal Party's Andrew Peacock, a lawyer.

The Judiciary

One of Australia's most cherished and respected institutions is its independent judiciary. Each State has its own structure of civil, criminal, and children's courts, and industrial tribunals. The highest judicial authority is the High Court of Australia, established by the Constitution and consisting of a Chief Justice and six Justices appointed for life. The High Court deals with all matters arising from the Constitution as well as with appeals against the decisions of any of the six State Supreme Courts.

Social Security and Health

Australia was one of the first "social welfare states" in the world. Some of its initiatives in this field have been considered almost revolutionary. For instance, old age pensions were introduced in 1909; invalid pensions a year later; and maternity allowances in 1912. At present, social security payments represent the largest single item in the federal government's budget. In addition, the States are still responsible for a number of social welfare services including housing, public health, and maternal and child welfare.

Women are eligible for old age pensions at their 60th birthday and men at their 65th. But these payments depend on an assessment of income. Old age pensions are usually paid to people who have lived in Australia for more than 10 years. As Australia has reciprocal pension arrangements with several countries, immigrants from those countries who decide to retire to their native land will receive their Australian pension there. Invalids, widows, and child supporting mothers receive benefits similar to old age pensions. Since World War I, veterans from every war in which Australia has been engaged have been entitled to a number of "repatriation" benefits which (depending on certain conditions) include pensions as well as medical and hospital treatment.

Australia's medical services hold to a very high standard. Most Australian universities have medical schools offering five- or six-year training courses, after which graduate doctors must serve at least a year in an approved hospital before they are registered. Only registered doctors may practise. Five Australian universities have dental schools. In April 1983 there were 18,577 medical practitioners (13% of them women) and 5,300 dentists. About 70% of the 1,112 hospitals are government owned. There is a government-run medical insurance plan, "Medicare," financed by a 1% levy on taxable income. Everyone must belong to it. But in addition to Medicare one may also insure oneself privately for supplementary benefits. There is no "free medicine" in Australia except for pensioners.

Visitors needing medical attention may be sure of excellent care once they have contacted a doctor. The problem could be to find a doctor, especially on weekends and holidays or at night when even Australians may encounter difficulties in summoning one. However, the better hotels and larger motels in the urban centres have one or more doctors and dentists on whom they can call in a medical emergency. You can also go to the Casualty Department of a public hospital. In normal circumstances, ambulance services in urban areas are good and, if necessary, they will transport a sick person to the Casualty Department of the nearest public hospital.

A unique Australian institution is the Royal Flying Doctor Service which provides medical attention and care for people in the vast and isolated regions of Australia's inland. The doctors operate by aircraft from a number of centralised bases and keep in touch with their patients by two-way radios. There is a separate Australian Government operated aerial medical service in the Northern Territory and aerial ambulance services function in New South Wales and South Australia.

The Economy

A wealthy country by any standards, Australia is self-sufficient in most raw materials except for crude oil, sulphur, and phosphate. It is among the world's major producers of wool, grains, and a long list of metals and minerals, especially iron ore. Australia's high standard of living and her prosperity depend on the export of her farm and mineral products which make up 76% of all goods sold overseas. Manufactured products account for only 20% of the total.

Before World War II, Britain was Australia's best customer, buying about half of all exports. Now she takes only 7% of the total. Since the late 1960's Japan has emerged as Australia's number one customer.

Until the end of the 1940's, Australia imported between 40%-50% of all goods—mainly industrial products—from Britain. The British share is now down to less than 15% as the United States has become Australia's largest supplier with American goods now a third of all imports. Japan has also stepped up sales to Australia. Other important trading partners include the People's Republic of China, Southeast Asia and European Common Market countries.

At present, Australia's main socio-economic problems are low international commodity prices, inflation and unemployment.

Foreign Affairs and Defense

Australia's foreign policy is committed to its own territorial security and to peaceful coexistence in the family of nations. Aid to less fortunate countries totals roughly about A$500,000,000 a year or about A$33.3 for every Australian man, woman, and child. Traditionally and emotionally Australia has closer and friendlier ties with some countries than with others. Britain, Canada, New Zealand and, to a lesser extent, the United States are considered members of the same family. Despite the recent tensions between New Zealand and the U.S. (caused by New Zealand's strong antinuclear policy, which has meant the barring of U.S. warships), ANZUS, the alliance concluded between Australia, New Zealand, and the U.S. in 1951, remains the cornerstone of the country's defence planning. There are also close contacts with the Association of South East Asian Nations (ASEAN), a group which comprises Indonesia, Singapore, Malaysia, Thailand, and the Philippines. Australia was also a founding member of the United Nations and has been involved in many of its activities.

The task of designing an efficient defence system for a country as huge as Australia with a coastline almost equal to the distance between Sydney and London has focused on the creation of a highly trained, combat-ready nucleus for each of the country's three services: Army, Navy, and Air Force. While Australians are justly proud of their war records, they are reluctant to impose stringent military regulations in peacetime. As a result, there is no peacetime compulsory military service. All fighting forces are volunteers who sign contracts for various periods of time. Many make soldiering their lifelong careers. At present, some 70,000 Australians are on active defence service—17,000 in the Navy, 31,500 in the Army, and 24,000 in the Air Force. In addition, 22,000 reservists have training obligations, and in excess of 31,000 civilians are employed in related non-combatant jobs.

PEOPLES OF AUSTRALIA

White Majority and Aborigines

Out of a total population of more than 15 million, the overwhelming majority of Australians belong to the Caucasian race. Some 30 or 40 years ago, one could have added that, except for a small minority, the major population came from Anglo-Saxon and Irish stock. To a lesser extent, this is still true. Since the end of World War II, however, there has been an influx of about 4,000,000 immigrants from more than 60 countries—the majority from the British Isles. The large-scale immigration has been a major factor in changing a people with an insular mentality into an outward-looking and cosmopolitan nation. As one would expect, the change is most marked among the nation's youth.

Old, ingrained attitudes have not, of course, completely disappeared in the last two generations but only traces of the once prevalent xenophobia have remained. For example, until the late 1940's many Australians reacted with raised eyebrows at the very least when people talked in a foreign language in a public place. Today, one may speak Swahili or Tagalog, Russian or Chinese without causing the slightest stir.

Since the abandonment of the so-called "White Australia" policy—which never existed officially but created difficulties for non-white immigration to the country—Australia has become a melting pot of races. According to the last published census (1971), major immigrant groups were: English, Welsh, and Scots, 1,024,000; Irish, 66,000; Germans, 110,700; Greeks, 160,200; Italians, 289,400; Dutch, 99,200; Polish, 59,-700; Yugoslavs, 129,800. Some 30,000 were born in the U.S.A. and 12,800 in Canada. Asian-born immigrants numbered 167,200, and Africans 61,700. Between 1971 and 1976, a further 350,000 immigrants have permanently settled in Australia.

To these figures should be added the unknown number of second and even third generation immigrants who, although born in Australia, still retain close cultural ties with their parents' homelands. The present policy of all Australian governments (federal and state) encourages "New Australians" (the term bestowed on immigrants in the early 1950's and now increasingly replaced with "Ethnics") to become naturalised citizens, retaining the cultural heritage of their native countries and sharing their inheritance with "old Australians." It is inevitable that it will be some time before difficulties—learning of English and adoption of a new lifestyle—are overcome and the immigrant fully adjusts to Australian conditions. But despite islands of discontent among certain immigrant groups, the process of adaptation has been astonishingly fast and successful in Australia. A large number of New Australians occupy distinguished positions in the economic, artistic, scientific, and cultural life of the country. Two post-World-War-II refugees have already reached the citadels of political power: Misha Lajovic, a Slovene, is a member of the Federal Parliament's Senate, while Dr. Andrew Mensaros, a Hungarian, was a minister in the West Australian State Government. The New South Wales Supreme Court—the highest court in the State—has a Hungarian among its judges.

The Aboriginals

It is a sad paradox that the aborigines, who lived in Australia many thousands of years before the first white man ever saw the continent, today represent a problem to the Australian majority. In 1976, the Aboriginal population was 160,915, 1.2% of the total population.

As mentioned earlier, their ancestors came to Australia from Asia perhaps 60,000 years ago. But they do not look like any other Asians though their limbs are somewhat similar to those of Indians. The shape of their heads and their features are quite unique. They have a wide face with a large flat nose, deep-set eyes to protect them from the sun, bushy eyebrows, and a strong protruding jaw. The colour of a full-blooded Aboriginal is dark brown. That of mixed bloods—now the great majority —varies from a deep sun tan to almost white. Very few Aboriginals still roam the vast expanses of the continents arid centre as nomadic hunters and food gatherers. Of the statistically ascertained Aboriginals in 1971, 60,000 lived in rural areas including mission stations and on Aboriginal reserves, and 46,000 lived in urban areas. Yet as recently as 1962, an expedition that entered the Woomera Rocket Range area in Central Australia discovered 71 Aborigines who had never been in contact with white people.

The Aboriginals' experience under white rule in the past is not an attractive story. When the First Fleet arrived, perhaps 300,000 of them roamed the wide expanses of Australia. They lived in some 450 tribes of various sizes but even the largest contained only a few scores of families. Each tribe had its own territory for hunting and food gathering and clashes between them over border transgressions and other infringements are supposed to have been rare. Except for those in Tasmania, they boomerangs, stone axes, sticks for making fire, and grass bags. They wore no clothes; the dog was their only domesticated animal.

Whether they lived the lives of miserable Stone Age savages or were a happy breed in a paradisaical environment, saved for so long from destructive civilisation, may be open to argument. But it is hardly surprising that the newly arrived whites stood uncomprehendingly before the Aboriginal enigma. They did not understand the deeper meaning of what appeared to them a near animal existence which filled them with revulsion and horror. After all, most of the early newcomers found themselves in Australia very much against their wish. Even the free settlers had come only with the aim of getting rich and getting out as fast as possible. Because Aboriginals were useless as exploitable slave labourers and a nuisance as occupiers of the land, they were brushed aside—peacefully, if possible; brutally, if necessary. As a result, whatever their original number might have been, within a century only a small fraction survived.

On the mainland, the Aboriginals gave up the struggle for their ancient land almost without resistance. In due course, most of them became state wards—fed, clothed, and housed sparingly from the public purse, and looked after by religious missionaries or public servants. Others drifted to urban areas where they lived on the peripheries as despised outsiders. Only very few chose to continue their old primitive lifestyle in the wilderness. Not premeditated genocide but a clash between Stone Age survivors and some of the seamiest manifestations of civilisation (such as disease and alcoholism) was the main reason for the Aboriginals' tragic fate.

The record was different on the island of Tasmania, where the Aboriginals resisted and where hunting parties were organised to exterminate them. By 1835, only 203 of the estimated 5,000 Tasmanian Aboriginals survived and they were deported to the small and barren Flinders Island between Tasmania and the mainland. The Tasmanian race became extinct in 1888.

Towards the end of the last century it was believed that the Australian Aboriginal was doomed to die out in a few decades at most. Yet the contrary has happened. With more enlightened government policies, the Aborigines have not only survived but their numbers are fast increasing. Past wrongs inflicted on them cannot be undone but they are being compensated, to some extent, with specific efforts to assist their economic, social, and cultural development. Since the referendum of 1967, which endorsed the abolition of all discriminatory laws, Aborigines have become fully fledged Australian citizens. One of them, Sir Douglas Nicholls, became Governor of South Australia and another, Mr. Neville Bonner, has been elected to the Federal Parliament's Senate.

Education and industrial training of Aboriginals as well as land ownership procedures have been stepped up. In the past, official policy has been to attempt assimilation of the Aborigines with the white body politic. Now the emphasis is on what most Aboriginal leaders seem to demand: full citizenship and equal rights, with the right to maintain a separate cultural and social identity. Without question, the lot of the Aboriginal in Australian society made great strides in recent years. But there is plenty of room for further improvement. Even the most inveterate optimists believe that it will be a long time before the legally equal Aboriginal becomes a fully accepted member of Australian society.

But how long Aboriginal culture will survive as a separate, living force when full acceptance is achieved is anybody's guess. At any rate, great effort is being taken to save what has survived in Aboriginal culture and art. As they had no written language, their laws, myths, and lore were passed from generation to generation by word of mouth. Their often enchanting stories explaining life's phenomena from the creation *(Dreamtime)* of the world as well as their bark paintings, tribal customs, and taboos are carefully collected. Wall paintings, when discovered, become protected by law in order to save them from the ravages of man and nature. There are wall paintings in the Northern Territory which may be 5,000 years old (coach tours from Darwin are organised to inspect them). A number of works, including landscapes, bark-paintings, and boomerangs, are on sale in Darwin, Alice Springs, and in souvenir shops in the capital cities. Aboriginal reserves located all over Australia are now governed by their own elected councils; one must request their permission to visit. As a rule, Aborigines do not mind visitors but they dislike being gaped at as if they were exhibits in some human zoo.

The Australian Way of Life

Australians are easy to live with. This may be too sweeping a generalisation and many Australians, who criticise their own nationals for petty bourgeois attitudes, may energetically refute this statement. Yet, compared with the people of many other nations, Australians are more helpful, more tolerant, and more resistant to injustice than most.

These traits are not unmitigated blessings in every situation. For instance, the tendency of so many Australians to side with the real or imagined underdog in all circumstances has led them to believe that "authority is always wrong." Some analysts of the Australian scene have explained this phenomenon as an inheritance from the country's early colonial period when forebears of the present Australians had often misused authority in their effort to survive.

This distrust of authority, a basic feature of Australian life, is expressed on many levels. The Commonwealth Constitution, for example, provides that people must be asked by referendum whether they will agree to changing certain laws. During the past 76 years, only a few of these referendums have ended with an affirmative vote. But latent suspicion of power is manifested in more pedestrian ways. Police in a chase can count on very little help from passersby, not so much because Australians are afraid of becoming involved as because so many of them instinctively bestow the benefit of the doubt on the chased.

The popular Australian practice of "cutting down tall poppies to size" has nothing to do with gardening but is another form of the anti-authority phenomenon, an attempt to cut down people who have climbed too high in their respective fields.

Australians, as a whole, seem to be immune to hero worship in politics or government. In its two centuries of history, Australia has never had anyone approaching the status of a charismatic leader even for a brief period. Internationally successful sportsmen and women become temporary heroes as long as they don't appear to think that they are "better" than others. The same may be true for those who have achieved international recognition as artists, scientists, musicians, or writers. It is the talented rather than the humble or the average who must "know their place" to live happily ever after.

This attitude has given rise to the legend that Australian society is classless and egalitarian. It is neither. It is true, however, that class is far less important in Australia than in most Western countries; also, on a personal level, the feeling of equality is more genuine than it is elsewhere. Australia has no homebred aristocracy, and titled immigrants (including British) play an unimportant part in social life. Nor is money the necessary rope for climbing to the top of the social pyramid. There are a few clubs in Australia where not even third generation multi-millionaires will be accepted as members unless they have the "right kind" of family background, are "on the land," work in acceptable professions, and belong to the "old boy" network by birth, by adoption, or mainly by marriage. Whatever political or economic influence they may have had in the past is of little import. Upward social mobility is nevertheless fairly widespread and, except for a few ultra-conservative strongholds, it matters more what persons are than what social stratum they come from.

Public opinion polls have consistently shown that most Australians consider themselves middle class. The population includes a large proportion of trade union members who represent about 55% of the total work force. This is not surprising. While pockets of poverty exist mainly among the uneducated and untrained, the old and the Aborigines, Australia is hardly a country of paupers. Some 60% of all dwellings, for example, are occupied by people who own them or are paying them off in installments. Thousands more are saving for a deposit on a home. There are few families without a motor car, a refrigerator, radio, and TV. In a population of 15.25 million, there are more than 3.5 million telephone subscribers. Middle class *is* a rather flexible concept and it consists of a number of economic strata; most Australians will fit into one of them between the thin layer of have nots at the bottom and the even thinner ceiling of the very rich on top.

The ambition of most Australians to own a home surrounded by a plot of land has largely created the environment in which they live—the sprawling dormitory garden suburb with all its merits and disadvantages. Few Australians will live in a rented flat if they can help it, even an apartment of one's own or "home unit" is considered second rate except when it is in the luxury class. Despite its vast expanses, Australia is one of the world's most urbanised countries. About 85% of the population live in city and town conglomerates while only 15% live in rural areas. Still, that small garden plot is important because Australians are genuinely fond of being outdoors.

What do Australians look like? No answer is satisfactory. The variety of types in Australia defies any general description. They may be tall or short; fair haired or dark, blue or brown eyed. Well fed and well dressed? Yes. But certainly the image of the average Australian as a tall, muscular, bronzed outdoor type is a fiction.

If it is difficult to generalise about the outward appearance of Australians, it is even harder to find common denominators in their character. As mentioned before, they are easy to live with. They are also a gregari-

ous people—a likeable lot, happy to invite strangers with suitable intro-
ductions or credentials to their clubs, their outings, even to their homes.
But it may take a long time before a close friendship develops.

Australians are supposed to be among the world's most inveterate
gamblers and drinkers. While there are surely millions of Australians
who never gamble and hardly ever touch alcohol, this generalisation may
be rather near the mark.

There are four legalized gambling casinos in Australia: one each in
Hobart, Launceston, Alice Springs, and Darwin. But there are plenty of
illegal gambling places in every capital city. Most are said to be fairly
well run; the main risk in visiting them is a police raid which will
inevitably land the tourist in a court and result in a fine. Sydney is
especially rich in underground gambling casinos—"underground" is
used figuratively, as they are usually upstairs in main shopping areas.
The government of New South Wales would like to legalise some of the
better ones in order to collect taxes. But the plans have run into heavy
opposition from churches and other groups on moral grounds and from
casino operators who are afraid of having to forfeit considerable profits
in taxes.

The absence of legal casinos does not mean that the Australian is
deprived of approved gambling. Far from it. The main outlets are horse
and dog racing, lotteries and, in New South Wales and Canberra, poker
machines. According to recent calculations, Australians gamble $1 for
every $3 they pay in Federal taxes. Poker machines in New South Wales
consumed between A$3,500,000 and A$5,000,000 in 1979–80. In the
same year, people in the State of Victoria "invested" (an Australian
euphemism for legal betting) A$400,000 every hour of the day and night.
In the calendar year 1979 (the latest available figure), an estimated
A$700 was spent on gambling by every Australian man, woman and
child. Of course, some of this amount was returned to the "investors"
in winnings, and the governments also reaped large sums in taxes.

Alcoholism is also a problem. According to the Foundation for Research and Treatment of Alcoholism and Drug Dependence, in 1976 the
estimated 258,000 alcoholics in the work force of more than 6,200,000
cost the economy about A$532,000,000. Drug addiction is as much a
curse in Australia as in most western countries.

The Australian Language

One of the obstacles to an acquaintance between foreign visitors and
Australians may be language. Australians speak English. But Australian
English is spoken even by the educated with an accent which is quite
noticeable and, in its extreme form, is sometimes unintelligible to the
untrained ear. Lengthy and rather inconclusive arguments have been
going on for many years about the origins, reasons for, nature and
aesthetics of this accent. Some like it; others are outraged by it. Long ago,
a poem appeared in the *Bulletin,* Sydney, January 13, 1894, which ended "Twere better if thou never sang/Than voiced it in Australian
twang." Australians can be quite touchy on this subject and it may be
wiser to accept their perfectly valid argument that it is their sweet right
to pronounce their language as they want. There is one consolation,
however. The ear becomes accustomed to equating something that

sounds like "oi" with "i" and "aye" with "a" ("aye noice daye todaye"). One need not worry about regional variations; surprisingly enough, considering the enormous size of the country, there are no regional dialects though some people assert that there are slight differences between Sydney and Melbournean pronunciations.

Besides a distinct accent of debatable felicity, Australians have also developed a large number of superb slang words. Take the word "wowser," which the late Sidney J. Baker defined in his *Dictionary of Australian Slang* as "a puritanical enthusiast, a blue-stocking, a drab-souled philistine haunted by the mockery of others' happiness." And Baker rightly quotes the *Daily Telegraph* (of Sydney) which commented on July 31, 1937; "If Australia had given nothing more to civilisation than that magnified label for one of its most melancholy products—the word wowser—it would not have been discovered in vain." Now, 40 years later, the average Australian would still agree with this judgment.

Here are a few examples of Australian contributions to colourful English. An "Abo" means, of course, an Aboriginal. Originally an "Anzac" meant a member of the Australian and New Zealand Army Corps who fought on Gallipoli in World War I; now the term includes all who served in any subsequent wars. "Aussie" can mean Australia or an Australian. "Back of beyond" is the remote inland. To "barrack for" is to shout encouragement to one's side. "Battlers" are persons who struggle for an existence; they are usually spoken of with compassion. A "black-tracker" is an Aboriginal employed mostly by police to find a lost or wanted person. An idler or a loafer who imposes on others is a "bludger." A red haired person is nicknamed "Bluey." A "bloke" is a chap or a fellow and "bonzer" means good or excellent, hence a "bonzer bloke" is a very nice chap. "Bullsh" is a contemptuous term for nonsense or a baseless statement but, because of its derivation, it is not used in polite society.

To be on "compo" is to receive worker's compensation for an accident on the job. "Cooee" is a penetrating cry used especially in wild country to make contact with a person some distance away. Not to be in cooeeing distance means to be fairly far away from someone. To "feel crook" is to be ill or off colour. A "digger" is an Australian soldier. "Dinkum" or "fair dinkum" means genuine, true, or honest. A dinkum Aussie is an Australian in every sense of the word. "I'm easy" expresses indifference in a friendly way; one doesn't really care one way or another. To plead for "a fair go" is to plead for reasonableness or for the giving or receiving a fair chance. To "get stuck into" something is to do a job with zest.

"Goodoh" is a loose statement which, depending on the way it is said, can mean different degrees of approval from excellent to a sceptical perhaps. On the other hand, "my oath" is a very strong affirmation. To be "on the outer" means to be broke. "Plonk" is poor quality wine. A "squatter" is not necessarily someone who settles on property he doesn't own; the term can also mean a large landowner. Hence, squattocracy is the nearest thing to an Australian landed aristocracy. The poetic sounding "sundowner" really means a work-shy tramp who arrives at a property to ask for food and shelter at sundown in order to dodge work in return. "Tucker" is food and "yabber" is chatter.

The same words can have several meanings. An invitation to dinner is usually for an evening meal, except on Sunday when it means lunch. "Tea" can be afternoon tea or (evening) dinner except on Sundays and holidays, when it is always the evening meal.

Women

One of the most widely held beliefs about Australia is that it is a man's world. The implication is that in Australia women are permitted to play an important role only in the home and, to be tolerably happy, must know their greatly restricted place everywhere else. If notions of this kind have ever been valid, which is rather doubtful, they are certainly antiquated now. Australian women were among the first to obtain the right to vote at parliamentary elections. The first Australian state to introduce female suffrage was South Australia in 1894 (a year after New Zealand, which pioneered that reform in the British Commonwealth). Women obtained the vote in Australian Commonwealth elections at the time of federation. By 1908, all states had passed similar legislation and, by 1923, women had the right not only to vote but also to sit in any of the nation's seven parliaments (federal and state).

At present, a woman senator, Margaret Guilfoyle, is the Minister of Finance, and many women occupy distinguished positions in the professions, the arts, the judiciary, science, and journalism. Of course, many more are members of the "work force" in which the rule is equal pay for both sexes for equal work. Except as fighting members of the armed forces and as ministers of religion, there are practically no positions from which women are barred. It is true, however, that some trade unions still refuse to admit women as members, thereby preventing them from obtaining employment in that field. As *Australia Handbook,* an official publication, states: "The majority of women is still concentrated in the eight traditional female occupations—clerk, saleswoman, typist, stenographer, domestic, process worker, nurse, and teacher."

The proportion of women in the work force has steeply increased in recent years. In 1961, only 30% of women over the age of 15 were working; by 1975, this figure had risen to 41.9%. Nearly two-thirds of working women are married; most have children. The proportion of working women among immigrants is especially high—about 36% of the total female work force was born outside Australia. The main reason is that a single wage rarely enables a person with a family to save money for a house, a motor car, and the other amenities of the Australian standard of living. Among immigrants, it is very often the woman's salary which makes the quick attainment of this standard possible.

Another exploded myth about male social dominance in Australia is that at social gatherings men and women group separately because men dislike discussing serious matters with women. The truth is that men and women mix—or separate—in Australia much as they do in any other western society. The sexes are also as equal.

THE ARTS IN AUSTRALIA

More than Matilda

Within a short two centuries Australians have not only succeeded in establishing a flourishing economy, and one of the world's most advanced social organisations; they have also created a culture, based on British-Western traditions which has taken on an increasingly national character.

One of the important features of Australian culture is its geographical dispersal. Each of the six state capitals, as well as the federal capital of Canberra, is a cultural centre well provided with universities, libraries, art galleries, museums, theatres, symphony orchestras, and cultural and scientific associations. To live in Perth in the "Far West" or in Hobart in the "Deep South" imposes no cultural deprivation on Australians.

Literature

The first poets of note dealing specifically with Australian themes and emotions were Adam Lindsay Gordon (1833-70), A.B. (Banjo) Paterson (1864-1941), whose "Waltzing Matilda" has become the country's best known song, and Henry Lawson (1867-1922), followed by C.J. Brennan, R.D. Fitzgerald, Kenneth Slessor, Douglas Stewart, A.D. Hope, James McAuley, Judith Wright, and Nancy Keesing.

The convict James R. Tucker (1808-1886) was the first Australian author who received international attention with his autobiographical novel *Ralph Rashleigh* in which he describes the arrest of a bank robber in London, his deportation, and his life in the penal colony of New South Wales. Other noteworthy authors of this epoch were Marcus Clarke (1846-81), who also wrote about the life of a convict in *For the Term of*

His Natural Life, and Thomas Alexander Browne (1826-1915) who, under the name of "Rolf Boldrewood," wrote *Robbery Under Arms,* a saga of cattle thieves. Between the two World Wars, Norman Lindsay, Katharine Susannah Pritchard, Kylie Tennant, Brian Penton, and Henry Handel Richardson (Mrs. J. G. Robertson) became internationally known. A number of distinguished contemporary writers include Patrick White, Nobel Prize winner (1973), and the best-selling author Morris West, as well as Xavier Herbert, Hal Porter. Christina Stead, Alan Moorehead, Thomas Keneally, Russel Braddon, Donald Horne, Ronald McKie, and John O'Grady.

Colleen McCullough's *Thorn Birds,* a compelling saga of three generations of Australians, remained on all best seller lists in the United States throughout much of 1977.

Ross Campbell was an outstanding humorist, and Ray Lawler and David Williamson are among the more popular Australian playwrights.

Painting and Sculpture

There has been an explosion in the output and appreciation of art during the past 30 years. Only since World War II can one speak of a truly Australian school of painters. Their predecessors, distinguished and talented as they were, imitated European models and trends. While the earliest Australian painters were mainly convicts whose portraits and landscapes had historical significance but little artistic value, the first Australian painters of artistic importance were German-born Conrad Martens and Swiss-born Abram Buvelot (second half of the last century). At the turn of the century, the "Heidelberg School" (Heidelberg is a suburb of Melbourne) tried to add some Australian content to French impressionist spirit. Practitioners Eliot Gruner and Hans Heysen have a secure place in the history of Australian art. But the Australian school begins only with the rise to prominence of such painters as William Dobell, Russell Drysdale, Sidney Nolan, and Arthur Boyd whose works can be found in the art galleries of many countries. A number of foreign-born artists, mainly refugees from totalitarian countries, have also enriched Australia's art world. They include Hungarian-born Desiderius Orban, and Judy Cassab and Sali Hermann of Swiss origin.

In this connection, one should again mention Aboriginal art. Rock and cave paintings, some of them centuries old, and the bark paintings, mainly in Arnhem Land in the north and other parts of the Northern Territory, are expressions of considerable natural artistic talent. Among Aboriginal artists who adopted the western idiom, Albert Namatjira, painter of Australia's "dead heart" was a highly gifted craftsman.

Music

It is a rare day in the Australian capital cities—except perhaps in mid-summer—when music loving tourists from abroad cannot find a concert, or even an opera performance, worth attending. Every State capital has at least one symphony orchestra, maintained by the Australian Broadcasting Commission (ABC). Some have a second or third supported by private associations. While the ABC is the largest musical entrepreneur in the country, organising some 800 concerts a year, there are a large number of musical societies which provide the means for local and overseas artists to present themselves to Australian audiences. The most important is Musica Viva of Australia, a chamber music association with headquarters in Sydney and branches in all capitals, including Canberra. Symphony concerts have been so much in demand that the ABC has had to organise three subscription series of 20 concerts each in Sydney alone. Each is attended by about 2,800 people. Musica Viva's chamber music concerts have some 10,000 subscribers.

Rock and roll from Australia is also making its mark on the rest of the world. The band Men at Work, in particular, has had huge success in the U.S. with their first two albums.

Among the many Australian singers and instrumentalists who have achieved international fame are Dame Nellie Melba, Peter Dawson, Harold Williams, Florence Austral, Eileen Joyce, Joan Sutherland, John Brownlee, Dame Joan Hammond, Geofrey Parsons, June Bronhill, and Marie Collier. Well known composers include Richard Meale, Peter Schulthorpe, Malcolm Williams, George Dreyfus, Felix Werder, Colin Brumby, and Nigel Butterley. The country's major opera company is the Australian Opera which performs in most capital cities. The more recent additions to buildings for music, opera and ballet performances are the world famous Sydney Opera House on the harbour, the Festival Theatre in Adelaide, the concert hall in Perth, and the Seymour Centre in Sydney.

The Media

Australians rank among the world's most avid newspaper readers, radio listeners, and television viewers. Altogether there are some 600 newspapers, ranging from small four- or six-page local sheets published once or twice weekly to mass circulation metropolitan dailies. Neither the government nor any political party owns a newspaper. The 17 dailies published in the capital cities are controlled by three publishing groups which also hold shares or controlling interests in the radio and TV stations. The 17 capital city newspapers have an average daily circulation of one copy for every two people. Large, high quality newspapers (all morning) include *The Age,* of Melbourne; *The Sydney Morning Herald,* of Sydney; *The Advertiser,* of Adelaide; and *The West Australian,* of Perth. *The Sun News-Pictorial,* a morning paper in Melbourne, has the largest circulation of all; it had a net paid circulation of 649,133 copies daily in September 1979. Except for *The Australian,* a morning daily paper printed in Sydney, Melbourne and Brisbane, all others are sold in the cities and states in which they are published.

Australia has a lively and extensive periodical press. The *Australian Women's Weekly* (actually a monthly now) sells almost 1,000,000 copies a month while the weekly *Woman's Day*'s circulation hovers around the half million mark. Among the weeklies, the 103-year-old *Bulletin* of Sydney maintains a high standard of reporting and comment on politics, social issues, economics, and the arts. There are also innumerable specialised magazines including some published in foreign languages for the immigrant communities.

While neither federal nor state governments have any special rights enabling them to interfere with print media, the story is rather different with broadcasting. Ownership of Australian broadcasting is part public and part private. The Australian Broadcasting Commission, a statutory body similar to the BBC, runs the national radio and television stations. Private companies operate commercial radio and TV stations under licence from the Minister for Posts and Telecommunications. The transmitters are operated by the Australian Telecommunications Commission. A 3-person radio and television Tribunal monitors standards. To date, no government, Conservative or Labour, has attempted to interfere with programming. At present there are 93 national and 118 commercial radio stations and 84 national and 48 commercial TV stations. The ABC maintains a special "rock radio" station (2JJ Sydney) targeted at youth between the ages of about 18 to 25. There are also radio transmissions in the languages of immigrants (ethnic radio). Probably the most popular foreign broadcasts in the whole of South East Asia are the transmissions of Radio Australia in Melbourne which include 51 news bulletins a day, in nine languages: English, Indonesian, Mandarin, Cantonese, Japanese, Vietnamese, Thai, French, and Pidgin English.

Some 8,000 journalists are employed by the Australian media. With the exception of a few top men in executive jobs, practically all journalists belong to the Australian Journalists' Association (AJA), which is registered as a trade union. In general, journalistic standards are high. But Humbert Wolfe's oft quoted lines about the British journalist can also be applied to the Australian species:

> You cannot hope to bribe or twist
> (Thank God) the British journalist,
> But seeing what the man will do
> Unbribed, there's no occasion to.

Science

Australian science has been one of the greatest beneficiaries of the enormous advance in international communications. Australian scientists no longer work in isolation; scores of them visit overseas countries to keep abreast of the latest developments in their fields and many of their foreign colleagues come to Australia to lecture and to learn. More than 200 Australian societies are engaged in scientific pursuits, the best known being the Australian Academy of Science and the Australian and New Zealand Association for the Advancement of Science. The first Royal Society established outside of Britain was in Tasmania. Two Australian scientists working in Australia have received Nobel prizes: the virologist Sir Frank Macfarlane Burnet (1960), and the neurologist Sir John Carew Eccles (1963). Australians have also been prominent in many branches of science including radio-astronomy in which they have done considerable pioneering work. The Commonwealth Scientific and Industrial Research Organisation (CSIRO), one of the world's outstanding organisations of its kind, maintains some 100 laboratories and field stations. It is engaged in all areas of scientific research except for defence technology and atomic energy, which are covered by the Australian Atomic Energy Commission and the Defence Science and Technology Organisation.

Education

In Australia, education is compulsory up to the age of 15 (except for Tasmania, where it is 16) and, at all three levels (primary, secondary, and tertiary), it is free except for non-governmental schools. While the Constitution mandates education to be a responsibility of each state, the federal government, which has complete responsibility for education in the Territories, grants huge subsidies to the states to enable them to meet the soaring costs of maintaining and expanding their educational institutions. A dispute has been going on for years between those who want to nationalise all education and others who wish to maintain the present two-tier system with the corollary that private schools (called "public schools" as in England) would continue to receive financial support from the governments. There are about 7,400 government schools; "public" schools total 2,200, mostly run by churches. Some 2.5 million children attend government schools; 638,000 go to private schools. For children who live in the outback, or who are handicapped by illness or physical disability, the states maintain correspondence schools supplemented by Schools of the Air. These use two-way radios enabling teachers to give the same lessons to children hundreds of miles apart. Teachers are also able to talk to their pupils who, in turn, can talk to each other.

Australia has 19 universities with a total student body of about 160,-000. There are also 78 colleges of advanced education which place greater emphasis on practical than on theoretical training and research, and 167 technical colleges. Whether Australia gets its money's worth from the spiralling amounts spent on education is hotly debated. At present, it appears that educational opportunities will continue to expand. Every year, thousands of foreign students, partly through Australian scholarships and partly with private support, study at Australian schools and universities. Most are from Asian countries.

FACTS AT YOUR FINGERTIPS
FOR AUSTRALIA

 PLANNING YOUR TRIP. Until the jet age, Australia was rarely considered by tourists as a destination. Until the end of World War II, travel time from Europe by passenger boat was eight weeks, and about a month from the west coast of North America. Today, Australia can be reached from either point in 24 hours or less. Although Australia has been unable to compete with the more traditional tourist targets, it has become firmly established as a major international tourist attraction. By 1973-74, overseas visitors had spent an estimated 19 million nights and about A$162 million in Australia. The influx since that time has transformed Australian tourism into a major industry. Many tourists include Australia in a South Pacific or Far East and South East Asia round trip. When planning such a tour, remember that Australia itself is a very large area and distances are vast. Hence, if time in Australia is limited to a week or ten days, one should not try to crowd too much into the visit as transportation can become a time-consuming factor. But even allowing only a short period, one can comfortably visit some of the main cities and make excursions to the countryside to enjoy the scenery and the unique Australian flora and fauna. But if one wants to visit the Great Barrier Reef, at least a week should be set aside solely for this purpose. For, while actual travelling time from Sydney or Melbourne to one of the Reef islands may be only a few hours, the total trip from a big city hotel until one is settled at an island location will take the best part of a day. The same is true for the return trip.

To give an idea about distance and travel time by jet, rail, and coach, here is a table prepared by the Australian Tourist Commission. Starting point is Sydney.

Journey from Sydney to	Road Miles / kms.		Jet time	Rail time hours	Coach time
Adelaide	885	1416	1.50	25.15	23.40

Alice Springs	1844	2950	5.20	64.30	56.25
Brisbane	630	1014	1.10	15.30	17.45
Canberra	192	307	0.30	5.00	4.45
Darwin	2533	4053	6.30	-	92.50
Hobart	717	1147	2.30	18.00	14.30
Perth	2717	4347	5.20	65.45	72.15

 TOURIST OFFICES. *USA.* New York: 489 Fifth Avenue, 31st Floor, New York, NY 10017. Tel: (212) 687-6300.

Los Angeles: 3550 Wilshire Boulevard, Los Angeles, CA 90010. Tel: (213) 380-6060.

United Kingdom. London: Qantas House, 49 Old Bond Street, London W1X 4PL Tel: (01) 499-2247.

Canada: 120 Eglinton East, Suite 220, Toronto, Ontario M4P 1E2. Tel: (416) 487-2126.

Europe. Federal Republic of Germany: Neue Mainzerstrasse 22 D6000/Frankfurt am Main 1. Tel: (0 611) 235071.

New Zealand. 29 Customs Street West, Auckland 1. Tel: (09) 79-9594.

Japan. Sankaido Building, 7th Floor, 9–13 Akasaka, 1-Chome, Minato-ku, Tokyo 107. Tel: (03) 585-0705.

Singapore: 400 Orchard Road, Singapore 0923. Tel: 235-2295.

Travellers from Malaysia, Indonesia, Philippines, Thailand, India, Middle East, Nouméa, Papua New Guinea, Africa, or any other place, can write directly to the Australian Tourist Commission Head Office, 324 St. Kilda Road, Melbourne 3004, Victoria, Australia.

 HOW TO GET THERE. While Australia's lifeline is the sea which completely surrounds it, the most convenient way of getting there is by air. No ship lines currently operate regularly scheduled passenger services between America or Europe and Australia, but several cruise lines call at Australian ports as part of longer itineraries. If you're determined to travel to Australia by ship, ask your travel agent which cruise lines call there as part of Orient, South Pacific, or around-the-world itineraries. Most passenger ships sail from Europe through the Suez Canal on the outward journey and return via the Panama Canal—or the other way around. The sea voyages take about six weeks and fares vary.

In contrast to the paucity of passenger ships, there is a near glut in air services. Two dozen international airlines connect Australia with the outside world; among them, they provide several flights daily in every direction of the compass to and from the international airports of Sydney, Melbourne, Perth, Brisbane, Darwin and Cairns. The airlines include: Qantas, Air New Zealand, Air Niugini, Continental Airlines, Air Pacific, CP Air, UTA French Airlines, British Airways, Lufthansa, Thai Airways, and Pan Am. Note: At press time it looks as if United Airlines may be replacing Pan Am on Pacific flights, though details are not yet finalized.

People who visit Australia from practically any part of the world and buy a normal return ticket from their starting point to Hobart (Tasmania) can stop over at no extra cost in most (in certain circumstances all) Australian capital cities, plus a few other urban centres. Airlines and travel agents can suggest a number of variations for such flights around Australia on an international ticket.

The year 1982 saw many changes in air fares to all parts of the world. One could travel by budget, economy, super-apex and other types of special tickets.

Then came the gas crunch and increased costs. Some new airlines entered the Pacific picture. All in all competition seems to be the game in air fares now and it will be the wise shopper who checks and double checks prices.

There are money-saving fares to Australia but please remember that the lower the fare, or the bigger the bargain, the more time must be given to reserving space.

The airlines and tour operators have many special price packages, too, such as fly/drive. Be sure to check these with your travel agent.

It is now also possible to travel to Australia by a combination of coaches, four wheel drive vehicles, railways, ships, and planes. The more adventurous tourist can choose among itineraries that are partly overland to Australia via the Middle East and India, or through Siberia, Africa, or even South America. On most of these trips participants live in accommodated coaches, or camp somewhere on the roadside at night. Such trips are mainly for the hale and hearty young. The main operators of these adventure tours are *Capricorn Overland Travel and Tours,* 21 Ebury Bridge Road, London SW1W 8QX; *Hughes Overland Ltd.,* 25 Battersea Bridge Road, London SW 11 3BA; *Intourist* (Soviet Agency for Foreign Travel), London, 292 Regent Street W1R6QL; *Penn Overland Tours Ltd.,* Broad Street Hereford, HR 4 9 AG; *The Sundowners Ltd.,* 8 Hogarth Place, London SW5 OQT.

 WHAT WILL IT COST? For two reasons, Australia is not inexpensive for either its inhabitants or for visitors. First, Australians enjoy one of the highest standards of living in the world: wages and salaries are high and this is reflected in costs and prices. Second, while the air age has reduced travel time, it cannot cut the huge distances over which people and goods must be transported to and from Australia and within the country. And mileage costs money. As travel conscious Australians ruefully say: "Europe is not 19,200 kms. but A$1,500 away." Still, an Australian holiday need not be exorbitantly expensive. Bargains and combined round trips reduce the cost of fares considerably as we shall try to indicate. A note of caution: inflation also erodes the value of the Australian dollar and therefore prices may change considerably—invariably upward. At press time (mid-1985) the exchange rate is A$1-US$0.68.

Unless visitors are determined to "rough it," or can afford luxury treatment all the way, two people with moderate tastes may not be wide of the mark to budget for A$100 to A$135 for their daily expenses as follows:

Room in medium class hotel or motel	A$50
Breakfast	4
Lunch in self-service restaurant	6
Dinner at a top restaurant	35
Sightseeing bus tour, full-day	20
An evening drink	3
Tips	3
City bus fare	.60–$2
	A$123

As can be seen, this budget does not include expensive extras such as theatre, and concert or movie tickets. There are also a few ways to cut expenses further. A roadside picnic while on a motoring tour will cost less than lunch even in a modest self-service cafe. In recent years there has been a substantial increase in the number of high-quality serviced apartments available in Melbourne, Sydney, Gold Coast and Perth. Many inner city apartments have been converted for this purpose. These apartments are self-contained and fully serviced and permit the traveller a flexibility at a cost well below normal hotel rates. In major cities they generally cost about US$200 a week. Building, health and maintenance standards throughout Australia are stringent and these apartments, like the better hotels, meet such requirements. Many can be rented on a *daily* or *weekly* basis. Service

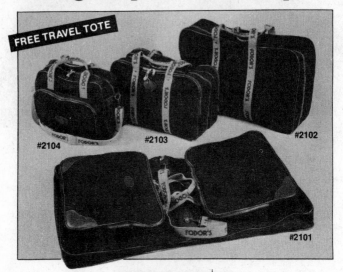

apartments, however, usually provide everything for reasonable housekeeping from blankets and linen to cooking utensils so one can live as the natives live—well, almost. But the most popular way to see Australia at relatively low cost is to join one of the dozens of inclusive tours organised by expert operators.

 TIPPING. The belief that tipping is not the general custom in Australia is no longer valid. Today, tipping is expected, especially from foreign tourists. It need not be extravagant —30–40 cents added to the set charge for a porter at a railway station or a shipping terminal is sufficient. Small change is usually left for a taxi driver. If, for instance, the fare is $1.60 give the driver $2. As hotels and restaurants do not add service charges to the accounts, a tip of 10% of the bill is appropriate. As a general rule in Australia, tipping is expected for all those services for which one would tip in America or Europe. The danger of refusal is minimal although there is no tipping in some of the exclusive social or sporting clubs (members contribute to a pool); one may avoid embarrassment simply by asking a member about the practice. But—when in doubt—tip.

 WHAT TO TAKE. Because of the difference in seasons in the northern and southern hemispheres, travellers from Europe and North America to Australia may depart in extreme heat and arrive in cool to cold temperatures or vice versa. Although one experiences "real" winter only in the highlands of eastern and southern Australia, mornings and evenings—and occasionally mid-day hours—may be quite chilly elsewhere as well. Therefore, between May and October, visitors would be well advised to pack medium-weight clothing.

Light weight dresses and suits are worn in Australia in summer. But the Australian climate is rather unpredictable and in some places—Sydney, for instance—extreme heat can be suddenly followed by a cool snap. Hence, at least a light-weight pullover or cardigan should be taken. The safari suit for men and pantsuits for women have been accepted in Australia for all except the most formal occasions. Certain restaurants, however, will not admit men unless they are wearing a jacket and a shirt with tie, or a coat with a turtle neck shirt. But in Australia, as elsewhere, the tendency is to dress rather casually: formal dress is required less and less frequently.

Although the majority of Australians still dress conservatively, they have become as accustomed to the denim revolution as other westerners. Not even a jeans and tails combination or a heavily embroidered evening frock worn at midday in a busy street will raise more than a good natured chuckle.

As manpower is expensive so is laundering, especially in hotels and motels. Most motels—even some of the most expensive—have laundries with coin-operated washing machines installed for their guests. Today, washing one's drip-dry shirt or underwear in the bathtub of one's private bathroom in a better hotel is the rule rather than the exception. Nevertheless, if one is in a great hurry, garments can be dry cleaned or laundered within hours. But it is safer to count on 24 hours.

If one forgets to pack an essential item, it is hardly a problem to replace it in Australia. Although Australian manufacturing industries have developed considerably since World War II, the country still relies heavily on imports, especially for certain luxury goods. The cosmetics section of any large department store carries most of the better known overseas brands of toiletries for women and men. Voltage in Australia is 220–250 volts and 50 cycles AC. Three-pronged plugs are used throughout the country, so a converter and travel adapter are needed for small appliances. 110-volt outlets are usually found at leading hotels.

Australian clothing sizes (socks, stockings, gloves included) used to be the same as in Britain or America, but since the switch to the decimal system are now marked in the European way. Most salespeople, however, know the "old" sizes.

Average Temperature (°Fahrenheit) and Humidity

Perth	Jan	Feb	Mar	Apr	May	June	July	Aug	Sept	Oct	Nov	Dec
Average max. day temperature	84°	85°	81°	76°	69°	64°	62°	63°	66°	69°	76°	81°
Days of Rain	3	3	4	8	14	17	18	18	14	12	6	4
Humidity, Percent	51	51	57	61	70	75	76	71	66	60	52	51

Sydney												
Average max. day temperature	78°	78°	76°	72°	67°	62°	61°	64°	68°	71°	74°	76°
Days of Rain	13	13	13	14	13	12	11	11	11	12	12	13
Humidity, Percent	65	68	71	73	75	76	74	68	62	60	60	63

Tasmania												
Average max. day temperature	69°	70°	67°	62°	57°	52°	52°	55°	59°	62°	65°	67°
Days of Rain	11	10	11	12	14	15	15	16	15	17	14	13
Humidity, Percent	59	63	67	72	78	80	80	76	67	63	60	58

General hints: Important about Australia is that the seasons are reversed from the Northern Hemisphere. Temperatures are in the 80s in Adelaide, Brisbane and Perth in January. Hobart runs in the high 60s. Sydney and Melbourne will average in the high 70s. Alice Springs runs a high 95. February, March, and April are pleasant months, as is the beginning of autumn. Winter starts in June and opens the ski season. While summer comes in December, many consider October and November ideal. Rain is seldom a problem in Australia. Try to avoid Brisbane in February and March during its hot and humid period.

HOW TO GET AROUND. Travel in Australia offers tourists a wide range of choices according to their tastes and/or their pocketbooks.

Australia is well provided with regular internal *air routes*. Most places of any importance can be reached by plane or are within reasonable distance of an airport or airstrip. The two major Australian airlines are Ansett and Trans Australian Airlines (TAA), but a "brash newcomer," East-West, began offering cut-price fares on the major routes in June 1983. The resulting price war was a bonanza for travellers, but it pays to shop around before buying a ticket; if possible, book in advance. All three operators have excellent safety records. Special discounts and package tours are available to international travelers. Tour tickets are valid for 90 days and you can usually stay in one place or region as long as you choose. Both major companies offer combination tours by plane, coach, and drive yourself car.

Ansett and TAA also offer weekend package tours—economy class travel and accommodation for two nights in first class hotels—and package holidays of seven days or more (except in peak holiday periods) to practically every important resort area in Australia including the Great Barrier Reef, the Gold Coast, and the snowfields—with rebates of 30% on normal prices. These are not "group" tours but prepaid individual holidays.

Travellers who prefer *bus* to air travel may buy concession tickets from the two largest coach operators: Ansett Pioneer Express, and Greyhound Australia. There are passes for unlimited travel for 14, 21 and 30 days, or even two months.

Some of these entitle passengers to a discount on accommodations and on tickets for sightseeing tours in capital cities. All major Australian cities are linked by express bus services with air-conditioned vehicles. Buses on overnight non-stop routes are equipped with washrooms and toilets.

Rent-a-car companies operate all over Australia; many of them offer a variety of money-saving arrangements. Motorists may want to get in touch with the National Roads and Motorists Association (NRMA).

Railways of Australia is also in the concession-fare business. Austrailpass, valid for unlimited travel on Railways of Australia for specified time periods, can only be purchased outside Australia. It is priced at A$400 for 14 days, A$500 for 21 days, A$620 for 1 month, A$860 for 2 months, and A$990 for 3 months. A 7-day extension may be purchased with a 14-day Austrailpass for A$200. All travel is first class and there are no further concessions for children. Any travel agent can sell Austrailpass or Budget Austrailpass, a less expensive ticket valid for economy-class rail travel.

TOURS. Dozens of tour wholesalers and virtually all the airlines that fly to Australia market a variety of tours Down Under through your hometown travel agent. Generally speaking, tour wholesalers do not sell their products directly to the public. You'll have to consult an airline or travel agent if you wish to visit Australia as part of an organized or "pre-packaged" tour. *Qantas,* for example, works with a number of tour wholesalers in North America, Europe, and Asia in marketing all sorts of tours—fly/drive, fly/rail, fly/camper, Outback safaris, luxury 'round Australia motorcoach programs, and vacations at the resorts along the Great Barrier Reef, to name a few.

Although most tour wholesalers won't sell you a tour directly, they will gladly send you brochures about group and independent tours they are operating this year. These contain such information as price, departure dates, airlines, and even the number of meals included in the tour package. Ask for brochures about tours to Australia from *Adventure Center,* 5540 College Ave., Oakland, CA 94618 (camping safaris, Great Barrier Reef resorts, sailing and yacht charters); *tour-Pacific,* 116 South Louise St., Glendale, CA 91205 (motorcoach tours, camping tours, fly/drive, fly/rail); *Bali Hai Holidays,* 433 Brookes Ave., San Diego, CA 92103 (city tours, motorcoach tours); *Australian Explorers,* Professional Building, Parlin, NJ 08859 (Outback sightseeing tours).

Several tour operators concentrate on what are known in the travel industry as special-interest tours. These tours explore a particular aspect of Australian life. For example, there are wildlife tours that visit game reserves, mining tours that visit opal and gold fields, ornithology tours that birdwatch their way through Australia, and tours that visit the aboriginal areas of the great Australian Outback. Some of the major wholesalers with special-interest tours are *Voyages of Discovery,* 737 Pearl St., La Jolla, CA 92037 (astronomy tours); *World of Oz,* 3 E. 54th St., New York, NY 10022 (complete range of special-interest tours, including Halley's Comet-watching tours); *Wilderness Travel,* 1760 Solano Ave., Berkeley, CA 94707 (bush camping expeditions); *Sobek Expeditions,* Angels Camp, CA 95222 (scuba diving tours); *Thru the Lens Tours,* 5855 Green Valley Circle, Culver City, CA 90203 (photography tours); *Evergreen Travel Service,* 19505 "L" 44th Ave., Lynnwood, WA 98036 (tours for the disabled); *AT Reef Adventures,* 292 S.W. 34th St., Ft. Lauderdale, FL 33315 (scuba diving tours); *Nature Expeditions International,* P.O. Box 11496, Eugene, OR 97440 (natural history tours); *Veterans Tours International,* P.O. Box 633, Brunswick, ME 04011 (tours of interest to World War II veterans); *Gold Discovery Tours,* P.O. Box 4660, Sylmar, CA 91342 (gold and gem prospecting tours).

Still other tour operators offer luxurious escorted tours with tour managers to handle all the details of travel and guides to point out all the places of interest. They include *Maupintour,* 1515 St. Andrews Dr., Lawrence, KS 66044; *Olson*

Travelworld, 5855 Green Valley Circle, Culver City, CA 90230; *Percival Tours,* 1 Tandy Center Plaza, Ft. Worth, TX 76102; *Travcoa,* 4000 MacArthur Blvd., Newport Beach, CA 92660; *Four Winds,* 175 Fifth Ave., New York, NY 10010; *Globus-Gateway,* P.O. Box 482, Forest Hills, NY 11375.

Station Tours: There are a number of tours to sheep and cattle properties. Some are within easy reach of major centers; others are deep in the outback. In many cases overnight accommodations are offered to the visitor. In addition to observation of station life, there is swimming, fishing, wildlife observation, tennis and horseback riding.

Visitors can embark on an adventurous outback camping tour with *Bill King's Australian Adventure Tours,* c/o Australian Travel Service, 116 South Louise, Glendale, Ca. 91205. *Koala Tours,* 2930 Honolulu Ave., La Crescenta, CA 91214, also markets farmstay vacations in Australia.

For tours from Brisbane: Dagworth Sheep and Cattle Station, via Winton, Queensland 4735. Offers wildlife, tours to historic sites, daily routine, tennis, swimming and horseback riding. Road transportation from Winton by arrangement.

For tours from Sydney: Ansett Airlines, 510 West 6th St., Los Angeles, Ca. 90014. Pelican sheep station, 136 miles from Sydney, offers demonstrations of sheep mustering and shearing, opportunity to attend sheep and cattle sales. Sapphire-hunting safaris can also be arranged. "Jolly Swagman" tour includes travel by air to Dubbo, a country town in New South Wales, where visitors are shown and participate in a wide variety of rural activities including sheep mustering and shearing, boomerang throwing demonstrations and visiting a wildlife sanctuary.

 MOTORING IN AUSTRALIA. On a population basis, Australia ranks among the most highly motorised nations in the world with about one vehicle for every three persons. Hence, facilities for motorists—such as petrol (gasoline) stations, repair shops, and motor inns (motels)—along the main roads and in the towns and cities are plentiful and range from good to excellent. The roads, even some of the major and most travelled highways, are of mixed quality but few meet the high standards of American or European expressways. On the whole, Australian roads are not made for driving at high speeds. While signs along some highways indicate safe maximum speeds for normal weather conditions, motorists should always obtain information about the conditions of roads (especially secondary roads and tracks) before setting out on a lengthy trip. This is especially important after heavy rains when even main highways can be flooded and impassable for days.

Opinions about the ability and manners of Australian drivers differ a great deal but a few suggestions are in order: if you are involved in an accident, even a minor one, insist on calling a policemen, note the other car's registration number and do not argue about who has been at fault. Also be aware that in Australia it is a serious offence, punishable by law, not to stop after an accident or to refuse assistance to a person injured in an accident regardless of whether or not one was involved in the accident. In other words, assistance is obligatory.

Traffic in Australia keeps to the left side of the road; in most instances, those approaching from the right have the right of way at an intersection. Stop signs mean just what they say; it is not enough to slow down—you must stop completely. And "give way" signs mean you must give way to all other traffic whether you are on another driver's right or not. On zebra-crossings, pedestrians have absolute right of way as soon as they have stepped on them. Therefore, motorists must halt in front of the crossing and wait until the pedestrian has passed them before proceeding. It's the law in Australia that all occupants in a car wear seat belts. Penalties for contravening regulations are severe and include minimum fines of A\$20, loss of licence and, if the offence is very serious, jail.

International Driving Permits are recognised throughout Australia and driving licences, issued by competent authorities, are accepted from bona fide foreign visitors. However, to avoid possible complications, it is wise to carry International Permits rather than rely on your locally issued driving license, especially if it is not in English. Tourists who bring their cars to Australia must obtain third party insurance, covering financial responsibility to third parties. A compulsory third party insurance charge is automatically added to car-hire charges. Comprehensive insurance coverage is also available. Visiting motorists should be aware that foreign insurance policies are *not* valid in Australia.

Foreign motorists who are members of organisations affiliated with the Alliance Internationale de Tourisme or the Federation Internationale de l'Automobile are entitled to services by Australian motorists' organisations which provide assistance on the road, issue maps and information, and help the motorist in every other way. Most of these Australian bodies are well organised and their staffs, including patrolmen, are efficient and helpful. Tipping them is neither necessary nor expected; an attempt to do so may even be considered an affront.

BUSHFIRE. Motorists, hikers, and campers should be especially conscious of fire—the greatest hazard in the Australian bush. A carelessly thrown away cigarette, a fire lit in a spot which has not been carefully prepared and cleared of all inflammable materials (including leaves and branches) may start an inferno, devastate huge areas, and threaten lives. Along the main highways and in most national parks there are many prepared fireplaces. Use them if possible. If there is none, the utmost care should be taken when lighting a fire anywhere in the open at any time—especially in summer. A fire must be watched continuously and completely extinguished when no longer needed. Fires in the open are permitted most of the time but on days when hot weather and winds greatly increase the fire hazard, a prohibition is imposed. These prohibitions, well advertised in the media, should be meticulously observed, not only because transgressors are heavily fined but because they may cause widespread disaster.

WEIGHTS AND MEASUREMENTS. Because the decimal system has been introduced in Australia only in the past decade, everybody will understand if one talks about yards instead of metres, miles instead of kilometres, pints instead of litres and Fahrenheit instead of Celsius or centigrade. Still, as instruments (scales, petrol-pumps, thermometers) have been converted to decimals, it is necessary to know a few examples:

Temperature: Water boils at 100° Celsius or Centigrade, which is 212° Fahrenheit, and freezes at 0° C. and 32° F.

Length: 1 inch = 25.4 millimetres; 1 foot = 30.5 centimetres; 1 mile = 1.61 kilometres. Conversely, 1 centimetre = 0.394 in., 1 metre = 3.28 ft. or 39 in., and 1 kilometre = 0.621 (or ⅝) mile.

Weight: 1 oz. = 28.3 grams; 1 lb. = 454 g.; 1 stone = 6.35 kilograms. Conversely, 1 g. = 0.0353 oz.; 1 kg. = 2.20 lb.; 1 kg. = 0.157 stone.

POST, TELEPHONE AND TELEGRAPH. Australia is well equipped with all postal facilities. Stamps can be bought not only at post offices but usually at the front desks of hotels and motels. To send telegrams or cables, it is not necessary to go to the post office; they can be sent by telephone, though not from public telephone booths, and the cost will be charged to the subscriber.

Local telephone calls throughout Australia cost 20 cents. in a public booth. Instructions for "trunk" or long distance calls are clearly set out in telephone booths and in the front of telephone books. Charges are made on the basis of a three minute call. The operator will indicate when three minutes have expired and more coins are required if additional time is needed. If you have no coins, you can request the operator to reverse the charge. Subscriber Dialling (STD), available from private numbers, allows uninterrupted long distance calls to be made to most places in Australia. The STD prefix number for a particular location can be found in the front of telephone books.

TOBACCO. Australian manufacturers produce a large variety of cigarettes, cigars, and pipe tobacco. They are sold in the hundreds of small tobacconists in the city centres while, in the suburbs, main distributors are hairdressers, news agents, supermarkets, and some grocery shops. British, American, and several French brands of cigarettes are also available in the tobacco shops of the larger cities. These shops, as well as the tobacco sections of the larger department stores also carry a wide range of imported cigars and pipe tobacco.

DUTY FREE SHOPS. Australian trade practice laws deal severely with false advertising and fraudulent trading. Hence, duty free shops at international airports and in the cities are just what they claim to be: they sell goods without charging duty.

BUSINESS HOURS. Most Australian shops open at 9 A.M. and close at 5:30 P.M., Monday to Friday, and trade from 9 A.M. to noon on Saturday. Late shopping day (9 P.M.) is Thursday in Sydney and Canberra, and Friday in Melbourne and Darwin. Banks are open from 10 A.M. to 3 P.M., Monday to Thursday, and until 5 P.M. on Friday. They are closed on Saturday. Post offices are open from 9 A.M. to 5 P.M., Monday to Friday. Office hours are usually 9 A.M. to 5 P.M., Monday to Friday.

HOLIDAYS. Australians are keen holidaymakers. Whenever possible, they try to take extra holidays on a Monday to stretch the weekend. After arranging these "long weekends," the real reason for the holiday is forgotten. For instance, Queen Elizabeth II (also Queen of Australia) was born on April 21, 1926. But in 1978, five Australian States celebrated her birthday on Monday, June 12, while the sixth, Western Australia, celebrated it on Monday, October 9. If a religious holiday or a national holiday happens to fall on a Saturday or a Sunday, the following Monday is usually declared a holiday to compensate workers for the "loss." Banks, shops and offices are often closed.

Anzac Day, April 25, is such a holiday. Now commemorating Australians (and New Zealanders) who died in service in the two World Wars, it remains a testimonial to the Australian and New Zealand Army Corps (ANZAC) which, in 1915, exhibited great heroism in the ill-fated landing on the Gallipoli Peninsula.

Main holiday periods in Australia coincide with the two great religious holidays —Christmas and Easter—and with school holidays. The Christmas school holidays begin in December and last until the beginning of February. A shorter school holiday is in May. A third falls between the end of August and the beginning of September. Tourist accommodations for these periods are heavily booked months in advance.

SEASONAL EVENTS. In recent years, Australia has followed the international trend toward officially sponsored festivals to attract native and foreign tourists. To date, some events are of great interest to the visitor from abroad; others are, at best, only a valiant effort. A list of the major recurring events follows:

January: Ocean beach surf carnivals in all States. Really worth seeing. Held on weekends, they include surf swimming competitions, races between life-savers' boats, surfboard races, and rescue competitions. These are traditional and characteristic Australian events.

Marksmen's competition (Schuetzenfest) at Hahndorf, near Adelaide (South Australia). The main festival of Australia's large ethnic group of German origin, with much shooting, wine and beer drinking, dancing, and music. A pleasant event for those who enjoy German "Gemütlichkeit."

February: Royal Hobart Regatta with a two day aquatic carnival. Mildly interesting.

Festival of Perth. A month long festival of culture.

March: Adelaide Festival of Arts. Held every even numbered year and lasting 21 days, it is the most successful Australian cultural event of its kind, drawing large numbers of visitors from other States. Performances of opera, theatre, ballet, music, light entertainment, and poetry reading. A good opportunity to become acquainted with Australian culture.

Canberra Week. A week long celebration to commemorate the founding of the national capital. Main emphasis on popular entertainments such as fairs, pop-concerts, and barbecues.

Moomba. The 10-day festival of Melbourne, including street parades with imaginative floats decorated by all kinds of organisations.

March/April: Sydney Royal Easter Show. A must for visitors who want to learn something about Australia's economy in an easy way. It is the annual exhibition of the country's primary and secondary industries, with side-shows providing additional entertainment, mainly for young people. Standards of the exhibits are very high.

April: Barossa Valley Vintage Festival. Another South Australian happening in the Germanic style. Held every odd year—to alternate with the Adelaide Festival—it offers a chance to taste some of the country's best wines.

"Rocks" Argyle Celebrations. A rather *arty* week long happening in one of the oldest and most picturesque districts of Sydney.

May: Bangtail Muster, Alice Springs (Northern Territory). A rodeo with related events.

June: Townsville (Queensland) Pacific Festival. Lasts three days and offers samples of the culture of South Pacific peoples.

July: Three major horse races—The Doomben Ten Thousand and the Doomben Cup in Brisbane, and the Grand National Steeplechase in Melbourne.

August: Ballarat (Victoria). Beginning of the Royal South Street Competitions (cultural) which last until October. They include the Grand National Eisteddfod.

September: Melbourne Royal Agricultural Show. The main competitor of the Sydney Royal Easter Show.

October: Australian Open Golf Tournament. Bathurst 1000-km. motor race, growing in prominence as one of the great endurance races in the world, with U.S. drivers and commentators making appearances.

November: The famous Melbourne Cup, Australia's main horse racing event of the year, takes place in Melbourne on the first Tuesday of the month.

December: Sydney to Hobart Yacht race. Starts on Boxing Day over a 621 miles (994 kms) course.

Australian Open Tennis Tournament (December-January) at various capitals.

SPORTS. Australia is for people who care about sports and there are few sports—indoor or outdoor—played in Western countries which have no adherents in Australia. Sports clubs are mushrooming. As a rule, an introductory letter from an overseas visitor's home club of similar standing will be sufficient for the tourist to gain admission. The proviso of "similar standing," though never expressed in so many words, is important. Some Australian sports clubs are affiliated with parallel organisations abroad (this is especially true for the larger golf clubs) and they welcome each other's members.

If, however, one seeks a game of golf, tennis, bowls, cricket or whatever and has no contact, one can always consult the yellow pages of the telephone directories. Under the main heading "Clubs" one will find a list of sports clubs from archery to yachting. A phone call should produce a satisfactory result.

Here is a short guide to some of Australia's main spectator or participant sports:

Cricket. The season is between October and March. Most years see the visit of an overseas team either from England, West Indies, Pakistan, India, or New Zealand with Test matches usually played over five days in the five mainland capitals. Every season, interstate matches are played for the Sheffield Shield, and every city and town down to the smallest community has at least a concrete pitch and some sort of competition cricket.

Fishing. Australia offers some of the best fishing in the world. For fresh water angling, a licence costing between A$2 and A$6, depending on the State, is necessary. The States also regulate closed seasons and bag limits. The best trout streams and lakes are in the Snowy Mountains (New South Wales) and in Tasmania. In Victoria, trout may be fished all year round and in New South Wales between September and April. The Great Barrier Reef off the Queensland coast offers excellent opportunities for game fishing. Marlin, tuna, Spanish mackerel, sailfish, sea pile, and giant grouper abound in those waters. The main game fishing ports for the Great Barrier Reef are Cairns and Dunk Island. Other good fishing centres are to be found in New South Wales at Port Stephen, Sydney, and Bermagui; in Tasmania, at Ealehawk Neck and St. Helens; and in South Australia, at Port Lincoln, American River, and Ceduna. One may charter a fishing boat from A$80 to several hundred dollars a day.

Football. Besides horse racing, it is the most popular spectator sport in Australia. Four codes are played. Australian Football (Victoria, South Australia, Western Australia, and Tasmania), Rugby League (mainly New South Wales and Queensland), Rugby Union (New South Wales, Queensland, Victoria) and Soccer. Matches, prominently announced in the sporting pages of newspapers, are usually held on Saturday and Sunday afternoons.

Golf. There are dozens of golf courses around Sydney and Melbourne and several in other capital cities. But a great number of provincial towns—even small ones—have golf clubs and golf links. Many of them welcome visitors. There are also public (municipal and a few privately owned) golf courses. Compared with other countries, green fees are very modest. It is usual for the local professional to rent clubs to the visitor.

Horse racing. The most prominent Australian spectator sport takes place on Saturday and on some holiday afternoons and also in some places midweek. The Melbourne Cup, on the first Tuesday in November, is a national event. Large amounts of money are bet with bookmakers and on the totalisator every weekend.

Lawn bowls. This sport is played throughout the year by women and men. There are many bowling clubs, and visitors are welcome.

Skiing: Skiing in Australia became a mass sport only after World War II. The season usually begins in May or June and lasts until September or October. During the past 30 years or so, new ski villages with first class accommodation and ski lifts have come into being. The best ski centres in New South Wales are Thredbo Village, Perisher Valley, and Smiggin Holes—all in the Snowy Mountains; in Victoria, Mt. Buller, Falls Creek, and Mt. Buffalo are ski centres.

Skin diving. The Australian Tourist Council says, "Scuba diving and snorkelling are popular pastimes. Adventurous scuba divers search for wrecks, which are quite numerous around King and Flinders Islands off Tasmania and, to a lesser extent, off the coast of Western Australia and South Australia. But the most popular diving area is the Great Barrier Reef. Heron and Daydream Islands have compressors and air bottles for hire but your own regulator and demand valves are needed. Air bottles may also be hired in capital city sports stores."

Target shooting. Clubs receive visitors and usually provide equipment.

Tennis. Tennis is immensely popular in Australia; there is hardly a settlement of any size without a tennis court—or scores of them—for rent. The Australian championships in January are one of the four major world tournaments. The State championships are held in January and February.

Water sports. The great season for Australian water sports is between September and April. There are many sailing clubs which extend hospitality (honorary membership) to overseas club members. The main sailing centres are: Sydney Harbour, Derwent River in Hobart, Gulf of St. Vincent at Adelaide, Perth's Swan River, Melbourne's Port Phillip, and Brisbane's Moreton Bay and Brisbane River. The easiest sport for the visitor to join in is surfing. Sydney's beaches, such as Bondi and Manly, are world famous and there is also good surfing in most States. But a warning is necessary: it is wise to surf only on beaches which have regular surf lifesaving club patrols; also be careful to bathe in zones marked out by flags.

A spectacular summer sight is the regular surf carnival conducted by most major surf clubs.

 MEETING THE PEOPLE. To meet Australians on a superficial basis is fairly easy. There are no organisations such as exist in some other countries, which bring together tourists with locals usually of similar standing and interests to introduce the visitor to the indigenous lifestyle. Hence, an introduction from a mutual friend, acquaintance or an institution can be very useful. But—if you simply wish to talk to people at random, take the opportunity on Saturday afternoon when thousands flock to spectator sports—horse racing, football, cricket, or whatever is on at the moment—and join them at any of these events. In no time, you will find yourself in animated conversation with people nearby; soon, explanations and advice will be flowing from all directions, especially if word gets about that you are an overseas tourist, without a clue about what cricket or Rugby football is all about. Such chance meetings may be followed by an invitation to join your new friends in some pub for a drink.

At this point, a warning may be useful. Tourists ought to be aware that more often than not an invitation to the pub means joining a "school," in which each participant orders a round of drinks for all. To fail to order a round is bad form. Hence, if one does not want to drink too much and wishes to "stay out" of a round without offending, it is wise to "shout" (pay for) one of the early rounds and stay out of those which follow.

 CHILDREN AND YOUNG PEOPLE. Almost all Australian hotels and motels have concession rates for children, provided they do not occupy a separate room. On all ordinary trains, trams, and buses, children under 4 travel free; between 4 and 16, they pay half fare. International airlines charge half fare for children up to 12; up to the age of 2 an additional child travelling with a family pays 10% of the normal fare, provided the child does not occupy a separate seat.

Internal Australian airlines offer concession fares not only to children but also to certain categories of youth. Under 3, children fly free, provided they do not occupy separate seats. Between 3 and 15, they pay half fare. Children under 5 are not allowed to fly alone but arrangements can be made for a hostess to fly with a child. There will be a charge.

Overseas university and college students under the age of 26, flying on Australian airlines, receive a 25% concession by producing their passports and either an International Students' Identification Card or a New Zealand University Students' Registration Certificate as well as an overseas airline ticket issued at the students' concession rate of 75% of the normal fare.

HOTELS AND MOTELS. Australian capital cities and major resorts have both first class and deluxe hotels, as well as less expensive budget and moderately priced accommodations. On the whole, the Australian hotel-motel industry is well organised, efficient, and well run. In top class hotels, service is usually good though high manpower costs, including stiff rates for overtime, weekend, and holiday work, make it difficult for management to provide instant and lavish service round the clock, except in the most expensive big-city hotels, all of which have 24-hour room service.

Most of the top grade hotels and motels are in the capital cities. The cost of manpower has led to the development of motels which provide most of the usual hotel facilities including garage space—but less personal service than one might expect. Hotels and motels in summer and winter resort areas range from modest to very good. Most motels are less than 10 to 15 years old and are comfortably up-to-date. Few motel rooms are without a private bathroom (shower, toilet, washbasin, hot and cold water) and practically all are equipped with a refrigerator and tea and coffee making facilities. Frequently, they have a swimming pool, restaurant, and bar. The motel suite with kitchenette where all meals can be prepared is gaining popularity, especially for families with children. These units can take up to six people and there are concession rates for children.

There are more than 90 youth hostels in Australia. The Australian Youth Hostel Association is affiliated with the International Youth Hostel Federation. Enquiries should be directed to: Australian Youth Hostels Association, 26 King Street, Sydney, NSW 2000.

FOOD AND DRINK. The influx of immigrants to Australia since the end of World War II and the rocketing tourist trade since the advent of the jet age have produced several side effects. One has been a thorough change in Australian eating and drinking habits. Until about 30 years ago, the menu of the average Australian restaurant (including those of all but the very best hotels) offered little better than a roast, a grill, and "three vegs." In country towns, there was the usual Greek restaurant and/or a fish cafe which added fried fish and chips to the usual fare. Some of these have survived and the motorist cannot count on eating in the establishment of a Brillat Savarin in the outback.

But much has changed. Capital cities and tourist resorts are well provided with eateries which serve the food of a great many nationalities: Italian, Greek, French, German, Yugoslav, and the almost indispensable Chinese. Sydney and Melbourne have excellent restaurants that serve food to please the most demanding palate. Prices in these establishments are not modest—dinner for two with a cocktail and some reasonable wine can cost A$50 or more. Of course, one may eat quite well for half that price at many restaurants, cafés, and bistros in most Australian cities.

Australia has no national dish except the meat pie (minced steak with gravy in pastry) which some Australians adore and others dislike, and the kangaroo-tail soup which few Australians have ever tasted. But the foodstuffs which the country produces are among the best in the world. Sydney rock oysters are probably unsurpassed. Excellent fish include the john dory and the barramundi. Australia's beef, pork, mutton, and lamb are world famous. The continent also produces a wide variety of tropical and temperate zone fruits and vegetables. Food prices are rather high—not at the farm level but in the markets because of the high cost of transportation. In general, it is quite safe to eat raw fruit and salads. Tap water is safe to drink throughout Australia.

Immigration has also created that strange phenomenon—the Australian delicatessen shop which, in the past 30 years or so, has developed from a modest grocery and small goods store into an international gourmet's mart. Most are owned by "migrants" (the usual Australian term for immigrants), and even the smallest delicatessen is likely to carry a wide range of imported (mostly tinned) foodstuffs from dozens of countries. Recently, when the Australian federal government banned the import of certain cheeses as a health precaution, the outcry that ensued may have caused the innocent traveller to suspect that slow starvation was in order for the people. Cuisine in Australia has certainly ceased to be merely the French word for kitchen!

Drinking habits have also changed. The favourite Australian alcoholic beverage is still beer, brewed with a high alcoholic content. Sticking to a certain brand of beer—usually the one or two produced in the drinker's home State—amounts to something like an act of faith. Australians like their beer icy cold and that's how it is served in the "pubs," local slang for bars. (See section on Where To Meet Australians.)

During the last decade, however, wine consumption has increased about fourfold (now 11 litres or 19 pints per person a year is the average) and it is still on the upswing. There are 15 main wine producing areas in Australia: one in Western Australia, six in South Australia, two in Victoria, five in New South Wales, and one in Queensland. Tourists are welcome in all of them. As for quality, Australian red or white table wines compare favourably with the best in other countries and Australian wine makers take great pride in their products. Names such as Penfold's Stoneyfell, Woodley, Kaiser Stuhl, Yalumba, Hamilton, Orlando, Hardy's, Mildara, Wynn's, Lindeman's, and McWilliams have won international recognition.

Until a few years ago, the sale and consumption of liquor in pubs and restaurants were permitted from 10 A.M. to 6 P.M. in most Australian States. Present liquor laws, however, now permit sale until 11 P.M. or midnight. Bona fide hotel guests may now obtain a drink at almost any hour, but pubs are open at different times in the States and Territories.

CUSTOMS. Tourists can bring in duty-free personal goods to the value of A$200, 200 cigarettes, 250 grams of tobacco or cigars, 1 litre of alcohol.

NEW SOUTH WALES

The Oldest of the Six States

by
EMERY BARCS

If you have comparatively little time to spend in Australia yet want to get the feel of the immense country you would be wise to concentrate on the oldest of the six States: New South Wales. For while there is no substitute in the rest of Australia for such unique places as Queensland's Great Barrier Reef, or the ochre-coloured lonely charm of the central desert, New South Wales can offer most of what the rest of the country has. As New South Wales people assert—it has more, and what it has is better. There is at least some truth in this chauvinistic assertion. Though New South Wales, with over 5,360,400 inhabitants, is Australia's most populous State, it ranks only fourth in area. Yet it is still so large that it could accommodate the combined territories of the United Kingdom, Germany, Austria, Holland, Denmark and Switzerland. Within its boundaries, New South Wales offers a great variety of tourist attractions, from the near-tropical north, to the Snowy Mountains of the Australian Alps in the south. Its 1,300 km. of coastline is studded with golden beaches, and it has picturesque waterways, including a 1930 km. stretch of Australia's main river, the Murray, plus other major rivers the Darling (2560 km.), the Murrumbidgee (1500 km.), the Lachlan (1480 km.), the Macquarie (860 km.) and the Namoi (850 km.). Scenic coastal rivers with good fishing opportunities include the Hawkesbury, the Hunter, Macleay, Clarence and Shoalhaven. Climatically the whole state is in the temperate zone.

Getting around New South Wales is no problem, for the state is well equipped with all means of transport and has an extensive road network ranging from expressways to dirt tracks. There are plenty of opportunities to participate in organised tours, or to set out on your own by hiring almost anything that moves, from bicycles, motor boats, automobiles (with or without caravans) to aeroplanes. Besides sightseeing you may inspect activities of special interest. New South Wales is Australia's richest and economically most developed state where you can not only pay a quick visit to some of the world's most advanced farms, but also spend a holiday in the country as a paying guest in some of them. Connoisseurs may spend pleasurable hours tasting some of Australia's best wines in the Hunter Valley vineyards. Those interested in heavy industry may wish to see Australia's largest iron and steel works at Port Kembla, near Wollongong, south of the city, which use the vast deposits of high quality black coal of the region for energy. Or you may venture further afield to the silver-lead-zinc mining centre of Broken Hill, about 1,100 km. from Sydney, which is almost a state within a state with its highly developed trade union organisation.

Should the visitor be confronted with any special problem he or she may get expert advice from the staff of the travel centers which the Government of New South Wales maintain in Sydney (16 Spring Street), in Melbourne (353 Little Collins Street), in Brisbane (corner Queen and Edward Streets) as well as in tourist information centers in the New South Wales country towns of Albury and Tweed Heads.

Like all Australian States, New South Wales has its own parliament and government. The parliament consists of two chambers: Legislative Assembly elected by popular vote, and the Legislative Council, whose members were elected by the two chambers sitting together. But a referendum held on June 17, 1978 decided the members of the Council should also be elected by popular vote. The State Premier (in Australia the Head of the Federal Government is called Prime Minister while the leaders of state governments have the title Premier) and his ministers are all members of parliament. They look after such issues as education, transport, health, social welfare, justice and police (although the Federal Government is also involved with some of them). At present three parties are represented in the New South Wales parliament. Labor is in power (1981) led by Premier Neville Wran. The Crown's representative in the State is Air Marshal Sir James Rowland, KBE, DFC, AFC.

PRACTICAL INFORMATION FOR NEW SOUTH WALES

HOW TO GET THERE. Sydney, the capital of New South Wales, is the main gateway of eastern Australia. Passenger ships from overseas call at Sydney Harbour, and scheduled international passenger aircraft land at the city's Kingsford Smith airport. Sydney is also well provided with transport to and from other capital cities by rail, air and road. You can sometimes book a berth on some ship which happens to be sailing between Sydney and another Australian port.

By rail: Two overnight trains run between Sydney and Melbourne seven days a week. They are the Southern Aurora (sleeper only) and the Spirit of Progress. The day-time Intercapital Daylight runs from Monday to Saturday. The best trains between Sydney and other capital cities are: Brisbane, the Brisbane Limited; Canberra, Canberra-Monaro Express—both daily. Perth, Indian Pacific—Sunday, Thursday, and Saturday.

By air: Both Trans-Australia Airlines (TAA) and Ansett operate frequent flights daily between Sydney and all other state capitals. *By bus:* Pioneer, Greyhound, and VIP Coaches run express coach services from Adelaide, Brisbane, Canberra, Melbourne and Perth to Sydney.

 HOW TO GET AROUND. The state has very extensive air, rail and road transport services.

By air: East West Airlines carries passengers to Albury-Wodonga, Falls Creek (Victoria), Forster, Glen Innes, Grafton and the Gold Coast (Queensland). *Air New South Wales* covers the towns of Wagga, Mudgee, Coffs Harbour and Casino. Commuter Airline Service travels between Young, Moruya, Cootamundra, Nowra, Scone, Newcastle, Tumut, and many other towns.

By rail: Government railroads operate throughout the state, and the State Rail Authority of New South Wales offers well organized and economically priced day-long conducted combined railcoach and launch tours from Sydney, and even three to seven day holidays further afield. The dates of these excursions and holidays vary but the shorter tours are usually on Sundays and public holidays. The NSW Government Travel Center (16 Spring Street, Sydney, Tel: 231-4444) will provide further information. Recommended shorter tours include separate trips to: the Blue Mountains, Jenolan Caves, Hawkesbury River; Old Sydney Town; Bowral; Canberra (Mondays to Saturdays); South Coast (Tuesdays). Longer holidays include 3 days in the Alps; 4 days in the Snowy River country and in Canberra; 5 or 7 days on a sheep station where one can become acquainted with life on an Australian property (including horse riding, sheep mustering and shearing etc.) but with all comforts provided; 6 days at the northern New South Wales seaside towns of Port Macquarie and Coffs Harbour.

By bus: Several companies run half-day and full-day sightseeing tours around Sydney and its vicinity. A similar tour to Canberra (7:30 A.M.–9:00 P.M.) costs A$33 for an adult and A$20 for a child; the two-day sheep station holiday cost is A$131 for an adult and A$102 for a child. The price of a "Sydney in a Day" bus and launch tour with lunch was A$36 for an adult and A$20 for a child.

 INDEPENDENT TRAVEL. The independently minded who wish to move around by themselves and camp may rent all they need for that purpose. Some of the main operators in this field are:

Cars: Avis Rent-a-Car, 140 Pacific Highway, North Sydney, Tel 922–8161. Budget Rent-a-Car, 93 William St., Sydney, Tel 339–8888. Hertz Rent-a-Car, 65 William St., Sydney, Tel 357–6621.

Campervans: John Terry, Hill St. and Parramatta Rd., Homebush. Tel 764–3444. *Caravans:* Parravans, Curtis and Mulgrave Rds., Mulgrave 2750, Tel 77–5577. Meridian Holidays, PO Box 90, Mosman. Tel 27–6179. Adventure Caravans, 144 Stoney Creek Rd. Bexley, Tel 50-8043. Holiday Motor Home, 31H Princes Hwy., Banksia. Tel. 597–2533.

Houseboats: Aquapark Holidays, River Rd., Wisemans Ferry. Tel (045) 664308. Holiday Afloat, 65 Brooklyn Rd., Brooklyn. Tel 455–1368.

Boats: Halvorsen Hire Cruisers, Kuringai Chase Park, Box 21, Turramurra. Tel 457-9011.

Light aircraft: Overseas visitors licence authorisation by the Commonwealth Department of Transport.

An important reminder: the localities which follow the street names in the above lists (for instance, Epping or Bexley etc.) are all in the Sydney region and the telephone numbers can be dialled directly.

Camping: Sydney region prepared camping sites: Lane Cove, North Ryde, Bass Hill, Carlton, Castle Hill, and Narrabeen.

Seaside Camping: Terrigal, Avoca, Port Macquarie, Coffs Harbour, Forster, Ballina, Tweed Heads, Nambucca Heads, Narooma, Bateman's Bay, Merimbula, Kiama, Lake Conjola. *Lake sites:* Burrinjuck Dam, Hume Weir, Lake Eucumbene, Lake Jindabyne, Burrendong Dam, Menindee Lakes, Wyangala Dam. *Country towns:* Katoomba, Cooma, Dorrigo, Gundagai, Bathurst, Dubbo, Albury, Wagga, Armidale, Wellington, Cowra.

Roadside Rest Areas: For motorists the New South Wales Department of Main Roads has provided 93 rest areas on the major highways. They are established near a particularly attractive spot, such as a river, lake, waterfall or a lookout, which provide panoramic views of the surrounding countryside. The rest areas are provided with shelters, tables, seats, fireplaces, firewood, drinking water and litter bins. At all sites, the Department's maintenance teams call regularly. The use of the properly constructed fireplaces and rest areas assists in the prevention of disastrous bushfires which sometimes result from the attempts of motorists to build barbecues beside the road.

 FARM HOLIDAYS. The demand for experience of the outback has been big enough to persuade some farmers and graziers to open their homesteads (and add new facilities) for tourists. There are quite a few country properties where people can spend their holidays. The quality of accommodations varies a great deal. In some of them people must bring their own sleeping bags, in others all modern conveniences (including hot shower and toilet) are attached to the room. They don't take in more than a dozen people at most and it can be great fun if you like a civilized introduction to bucolic life for a week or two. The better of these farms include San Michele (M. & K.G. Shanley, tel. 0648 4-2229) and Reynella (R. & J.Rudd, tel. 0648 4-2386) in the foothills of the Snowy Mountains. The owners of Reynella organise seven-day horseback safaris into the Kosciusko National Park between December and February. It's a good way to lose weight (if you can stand the exercise) and to enjoy the season when the Alpine heaths are at their fragrant best. Details concerning tariffs, are available from Travel Centre of N.S.W., 16 Spring St., Sydney, tel 2314444.

SYDNEY

Sydney, capital of the state of New South Wales, is not only Australia's oldest, largest and liveliest city where about 22% of all Australians live, but also one of the few cities of the world which tourists find easily manageable. This may sound paradoxical, because what is generally known as "Sydney"—a conglomerate of seven separately administered cities (Sydney, Parramatta, Liverpool, Penrith, Campbelltown, Blacktow and Bankstown), four shires (Sutherland, Baulkham Hills, Hornsby and Warringah) and 33 municipalities—occupies a larger area (12,061 square kilometres) than Greater London or New York. Still, the tourist can effortlessly cope with Sydney because the main attractions are so close together; many of them within easy walking distance of the city center, Martin Plaza. It takes only 10 minutes to saunter from there to Circular Quay, the birthplace of Australia as we know it today, and the terminal of the ferry boats which ply one of the world's largest and most enchanting harbors. From the Quay, or from the many stops in the city en route, one can reach any of several ocean and harbor beaches for surfing or swimming in less than 30 minutes by bus. A few minutes bus or train ride will take the visitor to King's Cross, Sydney's nightclub and entertainment centre so fondly remembered by thousands of visitors, including mariners from dozens of nations and American soldiers, sailors and airmen who spent quite some time (and money) there while on leave during World War II, the Korean, and the Vietnam wars.

To be in Sydney and not take a boat trip on the harbor would be as strange and unthinkable as to be in Venice and not hire a gondola. For unless you have seen the city from the water you have not really seen it at all. There are several choices; you may simply board a commuter ferry like thousands of Sydneysiders do, or take part in one of several daily harbor cruises lasting two or three hours or hire a motor launch and explore many of the arms and bays which border the harbor's 240 km. of foreshores. The most rewarding way, however, is to get an invitation on a sailing boat. It is from the water that one can fully appreciate the lofty elegance of the Harbor Bridge, the largest single-span bridge in the world—affectionately called "The Coathanger." It connects the city proper with the north shore and has been as much a symbol of Sydney as the Eiffel Tower is of Paris.

It is also from the water that one experiences the most thrilling views of another world-famous landmark: the masterpiece of the Danish architect Joern Utzon, the Sydney Opera House. Situated at Bennelong point, between Sydney Cove and Farm Cove, the mighty building gives the impression of being about to break its moorings and glide over the water with the help of the billowing glazed concrete "sails" of its roof. The Opera House has now challenged the Harbor Bridge as the tourist symbol of Sydney. Behind the Opera, and also on the opposite shore, "mini-Manhattan" office towers look down on the busiest port of the South Pacific, and on the cradle of the Australian nation.

Growth of a Metropolis

In two centuries that "cradle"—once a lonely camp site at the bottom of the world—has grown into the fourth most populous city of the Commonwealth—after London, Bombay and Calcutta. This rapid growth has not been an unmitigated blessing, for much that could have turned Sydney into an incomparably more beautiful place has been lost in the hasty process. For instance, there is no drive around the harbor; except for a few short stretches of public parks and beaches the foreshores are occupied by private gardens, or are used for commercial purposes. Or another example: after World War II when building activities were resumed on a large scale, the authorities could have made the widening of the narrow streets—originally footpaths or ox cart tracks—a

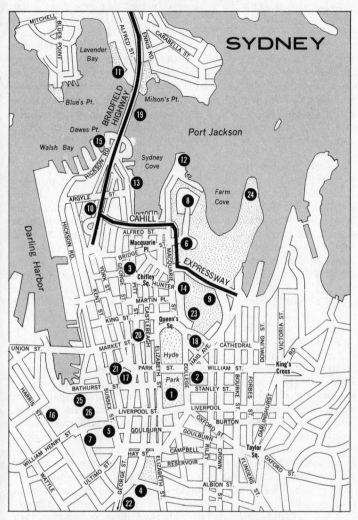

Points of Interest

1) Anzac War Memorial
2) Australian Museum
3) Australia Tower
4) Central Railway Station
5) Museum of Applied Arts
6) Conservatorium of Music
7) Sydney Technical College
8) Government House
9) National Art Gallery
10) Observatory
11) Olympic Swimming Pool
12) Opera House
13) Overseas Passenger Terminal
14) Parliament
15) Pier One
16) Power House Museum
17) St. Andrew's Cathedral
18) St. Mary's Cathedral
19) Sydney Harbor Bridge
20) Sydney Tower
21) Sydney Town Hall
22) University of Sydney
23) The Mint Museum
24) Mrs. Macquarie's Point
25) Entertainment Centre
26) Chinatown

condition for issuing building permits. Instead they acquiesced in the creation of concrete canyons of skyscrapers, which have dramatized the city skyline but made traffic congestion worse. Traditionally, Sydney's trouble has been its builders' assertion that what was good for them was also good for the public. Another reason for the slapdash development of the inner city was a lack of civic pride. In any contest between the aesthetic and the profitable the latter was sure to win. Lately this attitude has changed. The few surviving mementos of Sydney's past, such as the Rocks area with its century-old houses, are being carefully restored, and once dreary business thoroughfares such as Martin Place—now rebaptised Martin Plaza—are being transformed into places for public enjoyment, including free concerts for lunch hour crowds.

Sydney undoubtedly shares the woes of many other cities. Traffic congestion and overcrowding of public transport at peak hours are as bad as anywhere. But smog has not become a serious problem yet. The sun still shines 342 days out of every 365. And while Sydney suffers from housing problems, and substandard dwellings are not unknown, it has no wretched slums of the kind one finds in Europe or North America. On the other hand, it has no super-luxury district either. A few grand homes situated in large grounds—survivors of an age when domestic help was not such a problem as it is today—still exist, but most of them are marked for demolition and will soon be replaced by homes of more modest proportions and much better design. Rich Sydneysiders may live lavishly but not ostentatiously. The reputedly "posh" districts of Sydney —Bellevue Hill, Darling Point, Vaucluse in the eastern suburbs, the upper North Shore between Roseville and Wahroonga, and Palm Beach and its surroundings further out at the seaside—are no more than upper middle class precincts, even if a Rolls or a Mercedes stands next to a more modestly priced second or third car in the garage, and a barbecue and swimming pool (which has become so commonplace that no one would think of it as a status symbol) have been built in the backyard.

Sydney has shared with other Australian cities the misfortune that its adolescence and early adulthood coincided with a rather poor period of Western architecture. This has left its mark not only on its many Victorian public buildings but also on many of the older suburbs with their acres of red or liver colored cottages with tiled roofs of the same hue. Thousands of them were built by speculators, frequently to the plans of some London architectural firm and designed for English climatic conditions. The Anglo/Irish immigrants obviously liked these reminders of their origins. A change in architectural styles and tastes came only after World War II when local and immigrant architects began to build homes in harmony with Sydney needs and environment. To carry out their ideas they often had to fight the ultra-conservative tastes of building authorities, but now there is little opposition to their work and, whatever other drawbacks they may have, Sydney's newer suburbs look all the better for the change. Compared with the rest of the world's, housing standards have remained high and the aim of most Sydneysiders is still to own a home in which each member of the family has their own room.

Changes in Sydney during the past 30 years or so have not been restricted to physical appearance. The mentality of its people has also changed. The old jibe that Sydney is "the world's smallest big city"—

originally directed at the narrow-minded insularity of its citizens and not at the size of the place—is no longer valid. Sydneysiders may not be as suave and sophisticated as Parisians, Londoners or New Yorkers, but neither are they clumsy colonial oafs, suspicious of all outsiders. This is hardly surprising, since Sydney has become one of the most polyglot and cosmopolitan cities in the world. But then, what are the people of Sydney like? Of course generalisations must always be taken with a grain of salt, but the "typical" Sydney male may be described as a rather quick-witted, smooth-mannered and well turned out individual, with a fair idea about which side his bread is buttered on. He is not exactly lazy but will not over-exert himself with work if he can help it. He will not intentionally mislead or deceive others (unless he makes a career of it, when he can be deadly persuasive), but it is his nature to appear helpful and obliging and therefore he has a dislike for saying no to a request for help. Hence, his assurance that he would do something for you "first thing in the morning" can be a polite suggestion that you should forget all about it. The female of the Sydney species is genuinely more interested in things cultural than her mate. Hence in theaters, concerts, and art exhibitions, women usually outnumber men by two to one. Frequently they form a successful team, because they share a highly materialistic attitude towards the problems of getting on in the world. The pleasures of keeping up with the Joneses attract them and the heartaches connected with it don't seem to bother them a great deal. They try to elbow themselves into whatever place they wish to reach in business or society with rather refreshing frankness and without being unpleasantly brash. On the whole they are friendly, approachable, and hospitable to an almost American degree (but who can compete with Americans in this respect?) and Sydneysiders are less provincial than many other Australians.

Sydney is not only the oldest civilised settlement in Australia and New Zealand, but in the whole south-western Pacific. A few physical mementos—some churches and public buildings—which date back to the first decades of its founding in January 1788, have survived as witnesses to the city's early history. However, considering the sordid beginnings of the place as a penal colony, what is surprising is not that so little has remained, but that there has been anything worth preserving. The founder of the City was Captain Arthur Phillip, commander of the First Fleet, who realised that the place to establish a settlement was not Botany Bay, discovered by Captain Cook, but "the finest harbor in the world" which Phillip found a few miles further north, and where Sydney stands today. The early history of Sydney is, in fact, the early history of the whole of Australia and we have dealt with it there. Here is a short chronological list of some of the events in the city's development from the establishment of a miserable camp at the edge of the continent to a mighty metropolis.

1788	Settlement at Farm Cove
1789	James Ruse granted land at Rose Hill (now Parramatta) and became the first settler there.
1792	First foreign trading vessel "Philadelphia" arrived.

1793	First church built (in Hunter Street).
1802	First book ("General Standing Orders") printed in Sydney.
1803	First newspaper *Sydney Gazette and N.S.W. Advertiser* published.
1809	First post office opened.
1810	First race track opened (Hyde Park).
1823	Legislative Council appointed to assist the Governor in colonial affairs.
1831	First immigrant ship arrives and the first steamer, *Sophia Jane,* reaches Sydney.
1838	David Jones (now Australia-wide chain department store) opened first shop.
1841	Gas used for street lighting.
1842	First omnibus licensed.
1844	Exports exceed imports for the first time.
1849	The last convict ship arrives.
1850	University of Sydney founded.
1856	Registration of births, deaths and marriages inaugurated.
1858	First electric telegraph line opened.
1871	National Art Gallery founded.
1883	Railroad from Sydney to Melbourne established.
1898	Sydney and Newcastle connected by phone.
1910	Saturday half-holiday established.
1915	Conservatorium of Music opened, and first policewoman appointed.
1932	Harbour Bridge opened.

Sydney is now governed by an elected City Council, which consists of the Lord Mayor and 20 aldermen. The head of the city's administrative services is the Town Clerk.

EXPLORING SYDNEY

If you are in a hurry, or don't like treading the sidewalk for hours, then the best way to see Sydney is to join a conducted coach or coach-and-ferry-boat tour. Or you may view the city from the Sydney Tower, in the heart of the city. Sydney Tower opened in 1981 and is the tallest building south of the Equator, rising 324.8 m. above sea level. Double-decker lifts transport visitors (ticket: $3.50) up to the nine-story Turret at the peak of the Tower in around 40 seconds. The Turret has two restaurants with rotating floors and two observation levels, from which you can see horizons some 70 km. away.

More energetic visitors will probably enjoy exploring the city on foot; the mildly undulating terrain will hardly strain people in reasonable physical shape, and the rewards of seeing the town and the people at a leisurely pace make the effort worth while. One can of course decide on innumerable variations for this sort of exploration, but here are a few easy half-day itineraries.

Circular Quay, The Rocks, Opera House

By bus to Circular Quay, where at one of the ferry wharves you may get timetables for ordinary ferry runs and Harbor cruises. Turning left (towards the Bridge) a few minutes' walk brings you to Sydney's oldest quarter, The Rocks. It was here, after landing on January 26, 1788, that Captain Arthur Phillip established the first settlement, and where the nation was born. The Rocks was the site of Australia's first prison, barracks, store and hospital. However, a few decades later the district became the roughest, toughest and most miserable slum of the new city. These conditions were mainly responsible for the outbreak of bubonic plague there at the end of the last century. After the disease was eradicated, the Rocks remained a slum, though situated in what was potentially one of the city's most valuable sites. Fears that The Rocks would completely disappear if it were allowed to become another concrete jungle, led to the establishment in 1968 of the Sydney Cove Redevelopment Authority, with a charter to restore, renovate and redevelop the area. Much of this has already been done with loving care, and today The Rocks appears more or less as it looked at the beginning of the 19th century. It has no buildings of outstanding architectural value but it has atmosphere. Erected in 1815, Cadman's Cottage, close by the Overseas Passenger Shipping Terminal, is Sydney's oldest building. John Cadman, governor Lachlan Macquarie's superintendent of boats, lived there. It is now a museum and visitor center. The Argyle Centre (open 10 A.M. –5:30 P.M. seven days a week), where artists and craftsmen exhibit and sell their ware, is a large convict-built brick building dating from the 1820s. Originally a bond store in which convicts were housed in the cellars, it is now a major tourist attraction. Proceeding through the Argyle Cut, hewn from the rocky hillside by convicts in 1843, one reaches Argyle Place with its early terrace houses, and the Garrison Church designed by architect Henry Ginn, begun in 1840. The insignia of the regiments which worshipped there are displayed in the church. Nearby is Sydney Observatory (1858) on Observatory Hill with fine views of the harbor. Lower Fort Street has a number of fine colonial houses, and at Dawes Point, cannons, which were once supposed to defend Sydney, are exhibited. Walking back around Circular Quay you reach the Sydney Opera House, where conducted tours of the complex lasting about one hour are held daily between 9 A.M. and 4 P.M. The dramatic design of the building by Danish architect Joern Utzon was selected in 1957 from entries in an international competition. It took about 14 years (1959-1973) to build it. The cost of $A102 million was mainly provided by state lotteries. The Concert Hall seats 2700 people, the Opera Theatre 1550, the Drama Theater 550, and the Cinema and Chamber Music Hall 420. After visiting the Opera House you can lunch in one of the two restaurants in the complex: the formal and rather expensive *Bennelong,* or the self-service *Harbor Restaurant* which has an open air terrace. Provided the weather is suitable, it is pleasant to sit and watch the ships and ferries glide by.

Royal Botanic Gardens, Art Gallery, N.S.W. State Library

From the Opera House, stroll through the Royal Botanic Gardens on the shores of Farm Cove. The Gardens are open from 8 A.M. to sunset every day. Here Australia's first farm was established. There are wide expanses of lawns, Australian and overseas plants, and its special attractions include azaleas (September), roses (early spring and autumn) lots of fountains, and statues. Adjoining the Botanic Gardens are Government House, the residence of the Governor of New South Wales (not open for visits), and the Conservatorium of Music, originally built in 1817 as the Government House stables. Leaving the Gardens at Shakespeare Place, a short walk across the Domain—a grassy expanse where speakers on all kinds of topics harangue the crowd on Sunday afternoons —takes you to the Art Gallery of New South Wales. (Open 10 A.M.–5 P.M. Monday–Saturday; 12 noon–5 P.M. Sundays; 10 A.M.–5 P.M. public holidays. Closed Good Friday and Christmas Day.) The Gallery has a fine collection of Australian Art. From the gallery retrace your steps to Shakespeare Place. There stands The State Library of New South Wales, a fine yellow sandstone building in the classical museum style which also houses the Mitchell and Dixson Libraries and Galleries. It contains the world's greatest collection of Australiana, developed from the nucleus of some 61,000 books, manuscripts, maps, views and portraits left to the nation by David Scott Mitchell, a wealthy non-practising lawyer, and collector, on his death in 1907. Sir William Dixson (1870-1952) gave the library a further fine collection of Australiana and Pacific artifacts. Among the library's treasures are a 1623 First Folio Shakespeare and a first edition of *Julius Caesar.* After that you will probably feel like returning to your hotel.

The Inner City, Hyde Park, Australian Museum

Park Street is a good starting point for a walk in the inner city. The street has become a dividing line between the city's smarter part (down to Circular Quay) and more modest section (up to Central Station), where the many Chinese restaurants in Dixon and Campbell Streets are the main tourist attractions. At the junction of Park Street and George Street stands the Town Hall, a massive building erected between 1868 and 1889 and designed by eight or more architects who seemed unable to agree on the Italian or French Renaissance style. At its opening it was claimed to be the largest in the world. The modern office tower which the City Council has erected behind it has not helped to improve the appearance of the older edifice. The Town Hall auditorium, which seats 2500 people, is equipped with a large organ of 6 keyboards, 127 stops and 8,672 pipes. A small plaza separates the Town Hall from St. Andrew's Anglican church, the oldest cathedral in Australia. It is a pleasant neo-Gothic church opened in 1868 after many delays. It seats some 850 people. Opposite the Town Hall towards Circular Quay, the Queen Victoria Building, an architectural curiosity, occupies a whole city block. Designed in 1893 for the City Council by architect George McRae to accommodate shops and a fruit and vegetable market (but never used as such) it used to house the municipal library. Now it is under renovation. Continuing along George Street towards the Quay one reaches Martin Plaza with its well proportioned General Post Office (built 1866 to 1886) and impressive bank and office buildings on both sides. In front of the G.P.O. is the Cenotaph, a memorial to Australian soldiers killed in wars, where a changing of the guard takes place every Thursday between 12:30 and 12:50 P.M. Until 1973 Martin Place (as it was known until recently) was a busy traffic thoroughfare. Since then it has been gradually transformed into a pedestrian plaza and public entertainment area with sunken level amphitheater, where musicians of varying quality entertain the lunchtime crowd between noon and about 2 P.M. The atmosphere is cheerful and the sight is serene despite an excess of concrete (some of it colored). Between Martin Plaza and Circular Quay is the territory of Sydney's (and indeed much of Australia's) big business. Here are most of the international airlines and multinational enterprises, the two most exclusive clubs (Union and Australian), the Commonwealth and New South Wales Government buildings, the Stock Exchange and the head offices of Australian and overseas (mainly British) insurance companies. A short distance from Martin Plaza (in George Street) is Wynyard, Sydney's busiest suburban railroad station, which also has an entrance in York Street.

The tourist who has already seen Circular Quay can then walk up Bridge Street to find himself in Macquarie Street, opposite the Botanic Gardens and the Conservatorium. On the left corner is the Treasury Building (1849-94), and on the right the Department of Services (formerly known as the Chief Secretary's Department), built in 1878. The tall modern State Government Office, nicknamed "the black stump", is situated further to the right towards Hyde Park at the corner of Bent Street. Macquarie Street is probably the only street in the city of Sydney which one could justifiably call "elegant." Many professionals, especially doctors, have their offices there. No. 133, now headquarters of the Royal

Australian Historical Society, is one of the few surviving witnesses of the early 19th century when the street was one of Sydney's choicest residential areas.

Continuing up the left-hand side of Macquarie Street away from Circular Quay we pass the State Library and come to the early 19th century area now occupied by the New South Wales State Parliament House, Sydney Hospital, The Old Mint building and Law Courts. This was the site of the Rum Hospital, so called because in 1810 Governor Lachlan Macquarie gave a licence to import 45,000 gallons of rum to two businessmen, Garnham Blaxcell and Alexander Riley, and to the colony's chief surgeon, D'Arcy Wentworth, in return for financing the badly needed hospital. The hospital, a two-storied building with two surgeons' barracks, was finished by 1816 and it must have been a terrible place even by the standards of those times. The hospital section was demolished to make way for the Victorian bulk of Sydney Hospital (opened 1894) but the surgeons' barracks have survived. One part of the surgeons' quarters now forms a section of the State Parliament House and the other, known as the Old Mint building, is now a museum. These surviving sections of the old Rum Hospital suggest that with its colonnaded facade it must have looked quite attractive. Although Parliament House has become quite inadequate (a new building has been discussed for almost a century) inside it has a lot of quaint charm. It can be visited between 9:30 A.M. and 4 P.M., when the Houses are not sitting. At the end of Macquarie Street stands Hyde Park Barracks, the work of Francis Howard Greenway, the most important architect of Sydney's convict period. Himself a convict, transported to Australia for 14 years for concealing his assets at a bankruptcy trial in 1814, Greenway designed several of early Sydney's best buildings. Hyde Park Barracks was originally built for convicts doing public works, such as road-making. It was also a place of punishment. However, by the middle of the 19th century, after transportation of convicts to New South Wales had ceased, the Barracks were transformed into a reception centre for English, Scottish and Irish immigrants, where they received food and shelter until they found jobs. In 1878 the building was reconstructed to house the District Law Court of New South Wales. It is now a museum open daily. The clock that decorates the façade was made in Sydney and carries the inscription: "L. Macquarie Es., Governor, 1817". Opposite the Barracks, on the other side of Queen's Square, is the handsome St. James Church, another work of Greenway. It was dedicated in February 1824, and contains memorials to distinguished families of Australia's early days. In the centre of Queen's Square (now a plaza) stands a rather commonplace statue of Queen Victoria (unveiled in 1888).

Hyde Park extends from Queen's Square to Liverpool Street, between Elizabeth and College Streets. It is one of the inner city's open spaces, with well kept paths, trees and flower beds. However, complaints are mounting about the encroachment of statues, fountains and rest rooms on the green space. Originally established by that great town planner and builder, Governor Macquarie, as a town common, and named by him after London's Hyde Park, the expanse was first used for military drill, cricket and horse racing. Park Street, which (with its continuation William Street) connects the city with the eastern suburbs via Kings Cross, bisects Hyde Park. In the middle of the northern half of the Park stands one of Sydney's best known landmarks, the Archibald Fountain, the work of the French sculptor Francois Sicard. The fountain, completed in 1933, was a gift to the city by the late J.F. Archibald, one of the founders in 1880 of Australia's top-ranking weekly quality magazine, the *Bulletin*, to commemorate the French-Australian alliance in World War I. Apollo stands in the middle of the fountain, surrounded by other mythological figures. The Anzac War Memorial dominates the southern section of Hyde Park. The 33 m. concrete construction faced with red granite on the outside and white marble inside, and decorated with statues of World War I soldiers by Rayner Hoff, was opened in 1934. Opposite the eastern side of the park rises the brown stone neo-Gothic St. Mary's (Roman Catholic) Cathedral built by William Wardell from 1866 to 1886, with further additions in 1900 and 1928. At the corner of College Street and William Street is the Australian Museum (Sunday and Monday, 12 noon–5 P.M.; Tuesday–Saturday and holidays, 10–5; closed Christmas Day and Good Friday). A visit, even if only a short one, is highly recommended, for the Museum, founded in 1827, has the world's best collection of Aboriginal art and a permanent exhibition of the art of the South Seas.

Kings Cross and the Harborside Suburbs

A bus from Park Street or from Hyde Park corner of Elizabeth and Park Streets follows William Street—Sydney's new car sales center—to Kings Cross. The "Cross", as Sydneysiders call it, is strictly speaking the junction of William Street, Victoria Street, Darlinghurst Road and Bayswater Road. But in Sydney parlance, living "at the Cross" can mean anything from the junction proper to Potts Point, Elizabeth Bay or Woolloomooloo. Although this is where most of Sydney's nightspots are concentrated it is nothing like London's Soho, Hamburg's Reeperbahn or the Pigalle area of Paris. For it is not really a red-lamp district but a rather odd mixture of sleazy and smart, rough and bohemian. It has strip joints and elegant restaurants which come to life in the evening, while during the late morning and early afternoon its main streets, Darlinghurst Road and Macleay Street, teem with all kinds of show-people who do their shopping in the supermarkets and food stores or meet in the cafés. Elizabeth Bay House in Onslow Avenue, designed in 1832 by John Verge and built for the Colonial Secretary Alexander Macleay, has been declared a historic building and is now administered by the Historic Houses Trust of New South Wales. Originally it stood in large grounds full of Australian and South Sea plants but it is now surrounded by high rise buildings. It is open Tuesday-Friday 10A.M.-4 P.M., Saturday 10 A.M.-5 P.M., Sunday 12 noon-5 P.M. At the end of Macleay Street, the short winding Wylde Street (nicknamed the Burma Road) leads down to Woolloomooloo Bay. The name is Aboriginal and the area is supposed to have been an Aboriginal burial ground. In recent years the district has been a bone of contention between conservationists who want to improve the slum, but retain its present character, and developers who wish to turn it into a modern business and residential quarter. As a result of a compromise, redevelopment is in progress. A large part of the shore of Woolloomooloo Bay is occupied by wharves, and on the Bay's eastern side the Royal Australian Navy has a large establishment which dates back to 1788. The tip of the Navy complex, called Garden Island, was indeed an island until World War II when the Captain Cook Graving Dock was built and the narrow channel dividing it from the mainland was filled in. But the old name has stuck. From Woolloomooloo you may take a bus to the city, or walk there in 15 or 20 minutes. Or you can return to the Cross, which is a good starting point for inspecting Sydney's harborside eastern suburbs, which are the city's most expensive residential districts. The Main Harbor Cruises, which depart 7 times daily from #6 Wharf Circular Quay, touch most eastern suburb harborside bays. But, of course, they must be seen from the land to appreciate them thoroughly. Distances between the bays are too big for comfortable walks. Use a bus (or taxi) for parts of that tour.

Take a Darling Point bus at the Cross (in Bayswater Rd.) and alight at St. Mark's church (Anglican). It was designed by Edmund Blacket, Australia's most prolific church-builder—50 of them in New South Wales—and consecrated in 1852. It is Sydney society's favourite church for weddings. Walking down Greenoaks Avenue next to the church you reach Ocean Avenue, which leads to a small park on Double Bay. The Double Bay shopping centre, a short way from the Harbor, is one of the smartest in Sydney. (Note: in Australia "shopping centre" means one or more streets where most of the shops of a suburb are situated.) Although the charge that wealthy European immigrants have appropriated Double Bay for themselves is exaggerated, the suburb is certainly one of the city's most cosmopolitan and polyglot areas. It is no mere coincidence that Cosmopolitan is the name of the hotel in Knox Street, Double Bay's geographical heart. You may feel like having a rest and a snack before boarding another bus in New South Head Rd. for Rose Bay. En route you pass by Point Piper (named after a customs collector of the early days) with its elegant villas. Getting off the bus at Rose Bay police station, stroll along the few hundred yards of one of the rare harbourside walks left in Sydney and enjoy the view across Rose Bay itself, the largest bay in the Harbor. Another possibility is to take bus 324 (from the Quay), or 327 (from Central Railway) and travel via Rose Bay to a stop near Vaucluse House in Wentworth Road. Vaucluse House was owned by William Charles Wentworth, one of the most important and wealthiest Australian politicians of the first half of the 19th century. He was the son of D'Arcy Wentworth (one of the partners in the Rum Hospital deal) and a convict girl. Vaucluse House, surrounded by a beautiful garden, is interesting for its historic memories (the Constitution of New South Wales was drawn up there) and for its furniture and paintings, which reflect the lifestyle of a prominent Sydney family some 150 years ago. Nearby Nielsen Park includes one of the pleasant Harbour beaches, Shark Bay—but don't be nervous, it has shark netting. From there one may take a bus to Watson's Bay, near the entrance to Sydney Harbour. It is an enchanting place with beautiful views of the Harbour which can be enjoyed while lunching at Doyles seafood restaurant on the water's edge. A little further on is small sheltered Camp Cove, where Captain (later Governor) Phillip and his party came ashore and rested on January 22, 1788, when they discovered the magnificent harbor on the shore of which Sydney now stands. Between Camp Cove and the Heads is out-of-the-way Lady Jane Beach, one of Sydney's two "official" nudist beaches.

On the high cliffs above Watson's Bay looking out over the Pacific Ocean, stands a copy of Australia's first lighthouse, named after Governor Macquarie, designed by Francis Greenway, and completed in 1818. It was replaced in 1883 with the present building which resembles Greenway's design.

Seeing the Harbour

During his voyage in 1770 Captain James Cook sailed past the Heads of Sydney Harbour. He marked them on his chart as the entrance of a "safe anchorage", which he called Port Jackson after George Jackson, a Secretary of the British Admiralty. But Cook did not have time to find out what lay beyond those Heads; the discovery was left to Captain Phillip, who unfurled the British flag at Sydney Cove on Monday, January 26, 1788. January 26 is now celebrated as Australia Day, provided it falls on a Monday. If not, it is held on the following Monday. Sydney Harbour—or Port Jackson as it is still officially called—is about 26 km. long, and its average width is 1.5 km. But, as we have said before, its foreshores meander along many arms and sheltered bays and total about 240 km. The Harbour has been created over thousands of years by the confluence of two freshwater rivers, the Parramatta and Lane Cove, which meet between the suburbs of Greenwich and Drummoyne. At 2 P.M. on Sundays and public holidays a ferry leaves # 5 Jetty at Circular Quay for a two-hour cruise. Before their confluence the two rivers form the peninsula of Hunters Hill, one of Sydney's most charming suburbs, where a number of well-to-do French immigrants settled in the mid-19th century. They built the attractive stone houses with cast iron railings and decorations which stand in leafy gardens. Many of them have pleasant views of the river and of Sydney's skyline. By the end of World War 2 many of these old buildings had fallen into disrepair and could be bought for a song. However, their new owners have restored most of them, modernizing the interiors while keeping the old architectural appearance. Today Hunters Hill is one of Sydney's most coveted residential areas. Other noteworthy sights on this cruise include St. Ignatius College, a Jesuit school known as Riverview, which overlooks the Lane Cove River, and has a famous observatory founded in 1909; the 330 m. long single-span concrete arch Gladesville Bridge, the longest of its kind in the world; and four small islands in the mouth of the Parramatta River. The largest of them, Cockatoo, which now houses a dockyard, was until the last quarter of the 19th century Sydney's most horrible prison for reconvicted criminals. Goat Island, now headquarters of the marine fire brigade, served a similar purpose. Spectacle and Schnapper Islands are used by the Navy. None of the four islands is open to visitors. Opposite Cockatoo Island is Balmain, named after William Balmain who served as a surgeon with the First Fleet. In recent years Balmain has become an artists' and intellectuals' colony despite its industrial character.

Several regular daily harbor cruises by ferries and hydrofoil leave Circular Quay (for details see *Practical Information*). Most of them offer refreshments and running commentaries about the most notable sights. They include Fort Denison (off Mrs. Macquarie's Point, nicknamed Pinchgut, probably because in the early days recalcitrant convicts were sent to the barren little island with bread and water). But stories of terrible sufferings inflicted on prisoners in the Fort's dungeons are false. There have never been dungeons there. Fortification of the little island was first planned to guard Sydney from an invasion after two United States cruisers had managed to slip into Port Jackson undetected on a dark night in 1839, without any hostile intentions. The project was later dropped, then revived to protect the colony from a feared Russian attack after the Crimean War. A Martello tower with thick walls was completed in 1875. The Fort was named after the State Governor of the time, Sir William Denison. Pinchgut with its old cannons, 3½ m. thick walls and beautiful views of the city, is undoubtedly worth a visit. Tuesday–Saturday three tours leave # 2 Jetty Circular Quay: 10:15 A.M., 12:45 P.M., and 2:15 P.M. Book at the Maritime Services Board Public Relations section, room N26, Circular Quay. Tel. 240-2111.

Off Point Piper are two other small islands—Clark and Shark—which are open for visits or picnics from dawn to dusk. For details contact the National Parks and Wildlife Service, 189 Kent St., Sydney. Tel. 237-6500.

On the north side of the Harbour in the pleasant inner suburb of Kirribilli are Admiralty House and Kirribilli House, both owned by the Commonwealth Government. The former is used by the Governor-General and the latter by the Prime Minister when they are in Sydney. But the main attraction of this area is Taronga Park Zoo, open every day 9:30 A.M.-5 P.M. The most pleasant way to get there is by ferry from #5 Jetty, Circular Quay. Sydney had a zoo in the 1870s at Moore Park, which was transferred to its present harbor-side site in 1916. With its unique collection of Australian and 5,000 other animals, Taronga is one of the world's great zoos. It is also the most beautifully situated, with its enchanting views of the harbor. The Aboriginal name Taronga means "lovely seaviews". The section for Australian animals is near the main gate on Bradley's Head Road, where visitors arrive. Further around the northern side of the Harbour is Balmoral Beach, a pleasant place for a swim, protected by shark-netting. Much of the land in this area is occupied by military reserves. Past Balmoral is Middle Harbor with the Spit Bridge, and farther on Roseville Bridge which leads to the northern ocean beaches through French's Forest. Middle Harbor, which reminds one of the dreamy charm of some northern Italian lakes, is one of the most picturesque areas of Sydney, despite the densely settled shores of its many bays and arms. It is worth while paddling in a canoe to the upper reaches which abound in water birds. However, don't swim in the quiet waters of Middle Harbor. That's the sort of environment which sharks favor.

Manly is the last (or if one enters the Heads by ship, the first) of the northern harborside suburbs. It was Governor Phillip who gave it the name when, during a visit to the area in May 1788, he found that the Aborigines there had qualities "that gave me a much higher opinion of them than I had formed from the behavior of those seen in Captain Cook's voyage, and their confidence and manly behavior made me give the name Manly Cove to this place." Manly was separated from the other Sydney settlements for many years; the first ferry service between it and the city began in 1847 and a road link was established only in 1924. Now there are regular ferry, hydrofoil and bus services. An enjoyable way of seeing the sights of Manly is riding in a horse-drawn cart, which operates mainly on weekends. Manly has one of Sydney's finest ocean beaches and a swimming pool in the harbor near the ferry wharf. Australia's great sport, surfing, began at Manly back in 1902 as an act of rebellion. The more or less authenticated story has it that a Manly journalist, William Gocher, entered the water in defiance of the law which forbade daylight surf bathing.

Darlinghurst Jail and Court House, Victoria Barracks and Paddington

All buses which connect the city with the suburbs of Bondi, Watsons Bay, Bronte, Clovelly, Coogee, Maroubra and the districts around Botany Bay, stop at Taylor Square in front of the iron fence which separates the street from the interesting buildings of Darlinghurst Jail and Court House. When they were built in the 1840s this was the limit of closely settled Sydney. The great stone Court House, designed in neo-Greek style by Mortimer Lewis, still serves its original purpose. But the jail has been converted from a place for punishing criminals into one for educating youth; since 1921 it has housed the East Sydney Technical College and its Art School. One building, the women's prison, has been reconstructed as an auditorium called the Cell Block Theatre, with mementos of its grim past still visible. The Court House and the Jail have been built from the beautiful yellow sandstone found near Sydney Harbour which gives a special character to many surviving buildings of the city's early period.

About 15 minutes walk along Oxford Street from the Darlinghurst Court House is Sydney's most impressive military building complex: Victoria Barracks. They are open to the public on Tuesday at 10:30 A.M., when there is a changing of the guard. Conducted tours are also arranged. (For information ring 339-3496.) The Barracks, designed by Colonel George Barney, an architect who also worked on the construction of Circular Quay and Fort Denison, were commenced in 1841 and finished seven years later. "Finished" is perhaps not the right word because new buildings have been frequently added to the old ones. Paddington is now considered a part of the city itself. The British-colonial style buildings, with their airy verandas, are of considerable architectural value. The buildings are arranged around a spacious, grassy paradeground with the 225 m. Main Block, originally designed to house the soldiers and their families, parallel to Oxford Street. Until 1870 Victoria Barracks housed British troops. Now only a few soldiers actually live there; the buildings are used as army offices.

Until the 1950s Paddington, the district which developed around Victoria Barracks, was one of Sydney's worst slums. Then journalists, writers, theatre people and the like settled there because they found that they could buy an old house near the city. These new settlers were followed by a second generation of developers who carried the rejuvenation of the area further. Today Paddington is no longer cheap or neglected. It has chic restaurants, bars and art galleries, boutiques and shops which sell objets d'art, including costume jewellery—some of it made on the premises. The district has been likened to London's Chelsea. The atmosphere is genuinely Victorian and if its inhabitants have their way it will remain so, whatever changes progress threatens in future.

Universities

Sydney has three universities. The oldest of them—and the oldest in Australia—is the University of Sydney, situated past Central Railway Station in Parramatta Road. Like all universities in the country it is owned by the State and is run with financial support from the Commonwealth. Inaugurated in 1852, its original home was the building which now houses part of Sydney Grammar School in College Street. The main sections of the university, in neo-Gothic style, were designed by Edmund Blacket, an English architect who came to Australia in 1842. They were begun in 1854 and finished six years later. Blacket's work, inspired by medieval English architecture, is tasteful and elegant. The same cannot be said of many other buildings which now cover the university grounds. It seems that no effort has been made to harmonize the complex. Of interest to visitors are: the Main Quadrangle, the Fisher Library (named after a shoe and boot merchant who bequeathed a large sum to the university), the Nicholson Museum of Antiquities, and the Great Hall where university ceremonies and concerts are held. Several residential colleges are attached to the university, the oldest of them St. Paul's, also designed by Blacket. Sydney's second university is the University of New South Wales in Anzac Parade, Kensington, a southern suburb. Established in 1949 on the old Kensington racecourse, it has won academic distinction since, but no admiration for the architectural excellence of its buildings, erected on a stringent budget in utilitarian modern styles. The third university, Macquarie, in Balaclava Road, North Ryde, was opened in 1967 on a site next to Lane Cove River Park. Without a car it is rather difficult to get there, but private buses run from the suburban electric train stations of Chatswood, Eastwood and Ryde, and the Epping buses (288 and 289) from Wynyard station in the city pass nearby. The all-concrete buildings, which look as if they had been designed as settings for a science-fiction movie, are worth seeing. An excursion there may be combined with a visit to Lane Cove River Park or to the concerts held in the transparent-roofed courtyard of the main building. Performances are announced in the *Sydney Morning Herald.*

Botany Bay

No visit to Sydney would be complete without a trip to Botany Bay, where Captain Cook's *Endeavour* dropped anchor on April 29, 1770. It can be reached by taking a bus from the city to the suburb of La Perouse. The Comte de La Pérouse, commander of two ships, *L' Astrolabe* and *La Boussole,* arrived off Botany Bay in January 1788, three days after the First Fleet under Governor Phillip. Whether Phillip and La Pérouse ever met is doubtful, but it is certain that the French officers dined and wined their British fellow officers on board their ships. The French made no attempt to dispute British ownership of the place, although they stayed in Botany Bay for some six weeks. Some time after that both French ships disappeared, probably perishing in a storm near the New Hebrides. Today there are two reminders of the short French visit to Botany Bay: a column erected in 1829 by the French explorer H.Y.P. de Bougainville, and next to it the grave of Father Louis Receveur, a Franciscan priest who travelled with La Pérouse and who died in Botany Bay on February 17, 1788.

The ships of the First Fleet were at first anchored at the entrance of Botany Bay near Bare Island, named after an entry in Captain Cook's journal which spoke of "a small bare island which lies close to the north shore" within Botany Bay. Bare Island—just off La Perouse—is now linked to the mainland by a causeway. In 1885 the Government of New South Wales built a fort there following the Russian invasion scare. Today it is a protected historic site with a small museum which is open to visitors every day. Opposite La Perouse, on the southern shore of Botany Bay, is the suburb of Kurnell and the spot where Captain Cook landed. The Captain Cook's Landing Place Museum, containing displays featuring the famous seafarer's voyages, was opened in 1967.

The Beaches

It is no exaggeration to say that Sydney's beaches range from excellent to magnificent. From about the middle or the end of October until the end of April the water is usually pleasantly warm—although there are hardy "icebergs" who swim the whole year round. In addition to their excellence Sydney's main beaches can all be reached by public transport, and all are patrolled (from October till Easter) by volunteer members of the Surf Life Saving Association of Australia. They are expert in saving people from drowning. The Association was founded in 1907 and since then has been credited with rescuing more than 100,000 people. But you get into trouble only if you don't follow the rules. Surf only between the flags placed on the beach by lifeguards, who know where currents can be dangerous. They are also on the lookout for sharks and ring a warning bell when they spot one, before going out in a surf boat to chase it away. Lifesavers also treat people stung by bluebottles (Portuguese men-o'-war), nasty creatures with stinging tentacles.

Sydney has two groups of ocean beaches—one north, the other south of the harbor. Surfing is free except if one wants to use the dressing shed and a locker, when a small fee is charged. The northern beaches are Manly (Manly, North Steyne, Queenscliff) 16 km from the city, followed by (with their distances from the city in kilometers) Freshwater (19), Curl Curl (21), Dee Why (22), Collaroy (23), Narrabeen (23), Warriewood (28), Mona Vale (30), Newport (34), Bilgola (36), Avalon (37), Whale Beach (38) and Palm Beach (43). The southern beaches are Bondi (8), Tamarama (8), Bronte (8), Clovelly (no surf, 8), Coogee (8), Maroubra (11), Malabar (no surf, 13), Wanda, Elouera, Cronulla (30). There are beaches on both northern and southern harbor foreshores: some have protected swimming enclosures.

When at the beach, remember these two warnings: Don't dive into the calm water of the harbor—that's where the sharks like to lurk. Sydney sunshine, especially in summer, is very powerful, and dangerous for those with delicate skins.

National Parks and Nature Reserves

The Sydney region has two large national parks: Royal National Park to the south and Ku-ring-gai Chase National Park to the north. There is also the Lane Cove River Park which is nearest to the city center— about 10 minutes drive from the northern side of the Harbor Bridge.

The Royal National Park, established in 1878, covers an area of 14,000 hectares. It can be reached by car by turning off Princes Highway at Loftus or Waterfall (32 km from the city). The electric train stops at Royal National Park station from which a road leads to the entrance to the park at Audley (1 km) Here a causeway separates the fresh and tidal waters of the Hacking River. It is a pleasant spot for picnicking, boating or even staying overnight in the local motel. The park has sealed roads for motoring and many well kept paths for exploring on foot. The place is loveliest in spring and early summer when most of the 700 species of wild flowers are in bloom.

Ku-ring-gai Chase National Park is 24 km from Sydney. Access is by car, bus and ferry. Drive along Pacific Highway through some of Sydney's choicest northern suburbs and turn off either (a) at Pymble or Mt. Colah for Bobbin Head or (b) past Gordon into Mona Vale Road and follow it as far as Terrey Hills, then turn to Coal and Candle Creek and Commodore Heights until reaching the end of the road at West Head. The views from here over wide sweeps of river and ocean are among the most spectacular in Australia. Ku-ring-gai Chase National Park may also be reached by the ferry, which runs from Palm Beach (connected by bus with Sydney) to The Basin (inquiries, tel 918–2747), or the Palm Beach-Patonga-Bobbin Head ferry (leaves 11:30 A.M., and takes about 4 hours 20 minutes. Inquiries, tel. 918–2742).

Lane Cove River Park is 12 km from the city. Access is by car turning off Pacific Highway at Chatswood into Fullers Bridge Road. It is a popular picnic place, crowded on weekends and holidays. The river is rather polluted and swimming is discouraged. A paddlewheeler plies the Lane Cove River on scenic cruises.

A pleasant place for an outing is Koala Park, on Castle Hill Rd. in Pennant Hills. By car, access is via Pacific Highway to Waitara, turning into Pennant Hills Road to West Pennant Hills. Koala Park is about 1 km. from there along Castle Hill Rd. On public transport, access is by electric train to Pennant Hills station, and from there by # 184 bus which runs every half hour to Koala Park. There are koalas, kangaroos and emus in the Park. A milk bar sells snacks. The Park is open daily, including public holidays, from 9 A.M. to 5 P.M. Fee.

PRACTICAL INFORMATION FOR SYDNEY

HOW TO GET AROUND. From airport to the city (hotel) or suburb (Sydney): The cheapest transport to and from the airport is via the Urban Transport Authority buses, which run every 20 to 30 minutes between Circular Quay (Jetty 2) and the International Air Terminal, stopping at 5 points en route. A$2 for adults. Kingsford Airport Bus Service runs smaller coaches on request between 6 A.M. and 10 P.M. A$2.80 for adults, A$1.40 for children. Bookings must be made at least an hour before pick-up time; tel. (02) 667-3221. Taxis are available at the airport; most airlines accept bookings in flight for chauffeur-driven cars. The taxi fare from airport to city center is between A$10 and A$12. Hired cars are somewhat more expensive.

Sydney's transport system of Government buses, electric trains and ferries suffers from an ailment common to most fast-growing cities: it is over-taxed in peak hours and insufficiently used in between. In addition, it is organised in such a way that most traffic-lines radiate from the city, to groups of suburbs in more or less straight lines without adequate connections between suburbs either side of those lines. Only electric trains run from one end of Sydney to the other, bus trips start and terminate in the city. Ferries run from Circular Quay. There are no trams. Sydney's electric trains are part of the State railway system and they are fairly fast and reliable. The city proper is serviced by an underground loop—the City Circle, from Central Railway Station to Town Hall, Wynyard, Circular Quay, St. James and Museum and back to Central. It is an economical way to travel in the city. A second recent and very convenient rail extension goes from Central Railway Station to Town Hall, Martin Place, Kings Cross, Edgecliff, Bondi Junction and back. The Government bus service is being modernised and is adequate except at peak hours. Most bus lines connect the city with the suburbs though there are a few shuttle services to suburban railroad stations, and a few inter-suburb private buses.

The minimum bus and train fare is 50¢, increasing by 40¢ per "section." Train tickets *must* be bought at the station where the trip begins. (Mounting a train without a ticket may result in a fine of A$200.) Bus fares are usually paid on the bus and having the exact fare ready is appreciated but not mandatory. Maps of the transportation system are not readily available, but an excellent street directory—*Gregory's*—is on sale in bookshops and at many newsagents. (In Australia, a newsagent is a seller of newspapers, magazines, and cheaper books, as well as stationery.)

There are plenty of taxis, which may be hailed, hired from official ranks, or booked by phone for a small added charge. Main city taxi ranks are at St. James Station, Circular Quay, Carrington Street and Foveaux Street (near Central Station). Radio-cab services include: De Luxe Red and Yellow, tel. 339–0488; Legion 2–0918. You can also order air conditioned chauffeur-driven limousines for short city trips or for long tours. These cars are usually excellent and their drivers are careful and competent.

Ferries and combined ferry and bus trips: In good weather the most pleasant, though not the fastest means of transport, is the ferry. Even if the temperature is fairly high you get the benefit of an ocean breeze on the harbor. There are ways to combine a ferry from Circular Quay and bus to reach one's destination.

Motoring: Parking is very difficult in the city. Street parking is controlled by meters accepting only 10 cent coins. Space is usually difficult to find, especially between 8 A.M. and 7 P.M. After 6 P.M. no street parking fees are charged. Motorists who disregard advisory signs, overstay meters, or park in loading zones and other restricted areas are liable to fines. The traffic police (male and female "grey ghosts") place tickets under a windscreen wiper, and while the motorist has the right to explain why he or she contravened regulations, dispensation from paying the fine is rarely if even given. It is cheaper and safer to park in one of the 40 privately owned parking stations in the city (see Parking Stations in the Yellow Pages of the telephone directory) although they are by no means cheap. Fees are lower at the three parking stations operated by the Sydney City Council, but it is difficult to find a space in them between 8:30 A.M. and 1:30 P.M.

 TOURS. A wide range of half-day and one-day tours around Sydney and its environs in comfortable, air conditioned coaches are organised by 6 main operators, AAT, Pioneer, Australian Pacific, Clipper, and Murray. Competition between them is keen and consequently the services are good. Most tours depart from Circular Quay West, opposite the Maritime Services Board building, but coaches will pick up passengers—if arrangements are made when booking—from city and Kings Cross hotels and motels.

An especially good value is the "Sydney Explorer"—a 17-kilometer bus trip around Sydney's top tourist spots. One can step off at any of 20 stops, walk as much as one likes, then climb aboard again at the same or any other stop. "Sydney Explorer" buses run every 25 minutes from 9:30 A.M. to 5 P.M. seven days a week.

A pamphlet explaining the tour and what can be seen near each stop is available from the New South Wales Government Travel Centre (corner Pitt and Spring Streets, City). All-day ticket A$7 for adults, A$3.50 for children. Family rates are available.

Harbour and Ocean Cruises: Captain Cook Cruises (all cruises depart No. 6 Jetty Circular Quay; tel 27–9408). "Coffee Cruise" daily all year at 10 A.M. and 2 P.M.; 2½ hours. Harbour and Middle Harbour. Adults A$13.00, children A$8, coffee included. "Luncheon River Cruise," Harbour, Parramatta and Lane Cover rivers. Daily all year at 12:30 P.M. Adults A$9; children A$6.50; buffet luncheon A$9 extra. "Sydney Harbour Budget Cruise," at 9:30 A.M., 11 A.M., 2:30 P.M. Main harbour points. "Harbourside Sydney in a Day." Full day tour: reservations essential. Monday to Friday. Departs 9 A.M. Harbourside highlights: guided rocks-quarter walk; visit of Opera House where luncheon is served. Adult A$27. "Candlelight Dinner Cruise," August 1–May 31, Tuesday–Saturday; June and July, Friday and Saturday only. Departs 7 P.M., returns 9:30 P.M. and 11 P.M. Dinner and dancing. A$34.

Sailing cruise on board ketch Tahi Waitangi with Denis and Jann Pilkington. An all day excursion from Palm Beach (a Sydney seaside suburb) departs at 10 A.M., returns at about 4 P.M. A delightful outing for sailing fans. Tel 919–5555.

 THEATRE AND ENTERTAINMENT. Live theatre in Sydney has not as large a following as one would expect in a city of more than three million people. Yet there is nothing "provincial" about Sydney's theatrical life, and performances range from professional to excellent. In addition to the Drama Theatre of the Opera House, the main live theatres are *Royal* (MLC Centre, King Street); and the three theatres at *The Seymour Centre for the Performing Arts* (corner Cleveland St. and City Rd.). Smaller theatres—with high quality experimental performances—include the *Ensemble* (78 McDougall St., Milson's Point); *Genesian* (420 Kent St); *Northside Theatre Co.* (Marian St., Killara), about 25 minutes by electric train from Wynyard or Town Hall stations; *New Nimrod,* (Elizabeth St.—Entrance Goodlet St).

Theatre Restaurants—nightclubs which maintain a high level of style and decorum, include *Bull'n Bush* (113 William St.); *Dirty Dick's* (313 Pacific Highway, Crows Nest); *Les Girls* (female impersonators, Roslyn St., Kings Cross); *Bunratty Castle* (The Rocks); *Golden Garter* (Crown St., Sydney); and *The Music Loft* (The Corso, Manly). Jazz-fans can listen to the best jazz in Sydney at the *Soup Plus Restaurant* (282 George Street), where some excellent musicians including Dick Hughes, Judy Bailey and the Jim Coburn Quartet perform regularly.

For daily theatre programs—including movies—consult the advertisement section of the *Sydney Morning Herald.*

 GALLERIES. Art in Australia is booming and a large number of Australians buy Australian paintings and sculptures. As a result, the number of art galleries has increased and many are of high quality. The numerous commercial art galleries include the *Argyle Centre,* 18 Argyle St.; *Artarmon Galleries,* 479 Pacific Highway, Artarmon; *Barry Stern,* 19–21 Glenmore Rd., Paddington; *David Jones,* David Jones Store, Elizabeth St.; *Hogarth Galleries,* 7 Walker Lane, Paddington; *Holdsworth Gallery,* 86 Holdsworth Street, Woollahra; *Macquarie Galleries,* 204 Clarence St.; *Rudy Komon,* 124 Jersey Rd., Woollahra. The hours in which these and other galleries are open vary a great deal.

SHOPPING. In Sydney you can buy practically anything that the wide world can offer—provided you are ready to pay the price. Candidly, Sydney is not a bargain hunter's paradise. Except for a few products like kangaroo-skin or opals, there is nothing that can be bought here more cheaply.

However, one should be careful about where one buys opals. The wisest thing is to go to one of the city's several well established jewelers. They will charge the fair price. The visitor will overpay for gems if he or she falls for the sales-talk of an unknown dealer. Beware of bargains—not only in opals but in other goods, especially watches—offered by a chance acquaintance met in a bar or some other public place.

HOTELS AND MOTELS. Hotels are categorized as follows: *Expensive:* A$80 and up; *Moderate:* A$60–79; *Inexpensive:* below A$60. Rates are for double rooms.

Boulevard. *Expensive.* 90 William St. 270 rooms, 15 suites. A very good hotel in an up and coming environment. Midway between city and the Kings Cross nightclub district.

Hyatt Kingsgate. *Expensive.* Kings Cross Rd. Off Sydney's night club area. Good international standard. 395 rooms, 5 suites. Decor somewhat bleak but spectacular views of the city and the harbour from upper floor rooms. Front desk service unreliable in handling reservations and messages.

Inter-Continental. 117 Macquarie St. Completed late 1985. Luxury hotel in the colonial treasury building. Harbor views; gourmet dining.

Menzies. *Expensive.* 14 Carrington St. City centre. 441 rooms, 15 suites. Frequented mainly by business people. First-class international standard. Wide choice of restaurants: grill, Spanish, smorgasbord, Japanese. Air conditioned.

Regent of Sydney. *Expensive.* 199 George St. 620 rooms, 47 suites. International class. Close to Circular Quay for rail, bus, or ferry travel. Swimming pool, sun lounges, boutiques, health club; all business facilities available. Restaurants, bars, cafeterias. Air conditioning; parking.

Sebel Town House. *Expensive.* 23 Elizabeth Bay Rd. Smaller hotel with attentive service; popular with celebrities. Harbor views.

Sheraton-Wentworth. *Expensive.* 61–101 Phillip St. 415 rooms, 33 suites. Main banking, insurance, and big-business district. Government offices nearby. All first-rate international hotel services. A very good restaurant on the 5th floor. Shopping arcade, beauty and barber shops, and car rental. A Western International hotel. Air conditioned.

Sydney Hilton. *Expensive.* 259 Pitt St. 582 rooms, 37 suites. Mid-city, center of main theater and shopping areas. All first-rate international hotel services including swimming pool, restaurants, bars, cafeterias, parking.

Wynyard TraveLodge. *Expensive.* 7–9 York St., 210 rooms. Top-class hotel/motel services, plus restaurant, bar and pool. Air conditioned.

Cosmopolitan. *Moderate.* Knox Street, Double Bay. 81 units, 4 suits. Top-class motel accommodation, good service. Situated in the center of one of Sydney's smartest areas with expensive boutiques and restaurants nearby.

Koala Park Regis. *Moderate.* Park and Castlereagh Streets. 126 rooms, 6 suites. Near Town Hall in main business and theater center. Good motel-type accommodation.

Manly Pacific International. *Moderate.* 55 North Steyne, Manly. 156 rooms, 24 suites. Luxury hotel on the beach at Manly. Short trip to the city by hydrofoil, or a leisurely trip by bus or ferry. Restaurants, swimming pool, parking facilities, boutiques, cafeterias.

Imperial. *Inexpensive.* 221 Darlinghurst Road, Kings Cross. 150 rooms, most with bath. Essential services.

Killara Motor Inn. *Inexpensive.* 480 Pacific Highway, Killara. About 16 km. from city center. 41 units all with bath. Comfortable, handy to golf clubs. Swimming pool, convention facilities, good restaurant.

 DINING OUT. Sydney has a large number of very good eating places ranging from grand-hotel international to small "ethnic" family-run establishments. If you are in a hurry, or trying to be economical, the *Cahill* chain of self-service restaurants, with more than a dozen establishments in the city, can be recommended.

Among the big hotel restaurants (on the expensive side), perhaps the most pleasant is that on the fifth floor of the *Wentworth.* Food and service are excellent. Tables must be reserved, for the place is very much in demand. Other commendable restaurants in the same category are the *San Francisco Grill* of the *Sydney Hilton* and *Kables* at the *Regent.*

In downtown Sydney one of the great attractions is the *Summit Restaurant* on the 47th floor of the Australia Tower in Australia Square. It has a rotating platform which turns slowly so that in a couple of hours one can see all the city and far beyond. The Summit serves smorgasbord luncheons and à la carte dinners (expensive) and is open seven days a week.

While the Summit is high up, another attraction, the self-service restaurant of the *Opera House,* is almost at water level. It is not expensive and the food is only fair. But to eat on its Harborside terrace on a mild, sunny winter day or on a warm summer night with the wide expanse of Port Jackson before you and the ships gliding past is an experience you will not easily forget.

A third city restaurant where one can enjoy the view is the *New Hellas* on the third floor at 287 Elizabeth Street, which overlooks Hyde Park. The food is Greek, the service is good and the prices are modest. It is open on Sundays.

A very good French restaurant in the heart of the city is *Le Provencale* at 142 King Street, though it tends to be a bit noisy and is certainly not cheap. Tables must be reserved.

Among the number of good Chinese restaurants in the Haymarket area the *Dixon,* at 51 Dixon St., deserves a mention.

A good place for a quick snack (including a very good curry) is the *Ceylon Tea Centre* at 64 Castlereagh St., just off Martin Plaza. It is open for lunch only and it is advisable to be there before 12:30 because later it becomes crowded.

While few of the intimate restaurants (such as *Le Provencale*) are in the city itself, there is a wide choice in the eastern suburbs. Among the well established restaurants outside the inner city, the most expensive is perhaps the *Chelsea* (119

Macleay St., Potts Point) where you dine—it is open for dinner only—in old-style splendour. Another good restaurant in the same area is *Primo's Lafayette* at 76 Elizabeth Bay Rd. The expensive but excellent eastern suburb restaurants include *Eliza's* at 29 Bay Street, Double Bay; Prunier's *Chiswick Gardens,* 65 Ocean Street, Woollahra (dinner only); *D'Arcy's,* 92 Hargrave Street, Paddington; *Pegrums,* Gurner Street, Paddington, and *The Yellow Book,* 1 Kellett Way, Potts Point. *Beppi's,* at the corner of Yurong and Stanley Streets, East Sydney, is a favourite for Italian food, while those who want to eat Japanese may visit the *Nagoya Sukiyaki House* at 188 Victoria Rd., Kings Cross (dinner only, closed Sunday), or *Santory* (expensive) 529 Kent St.

Just across the Harbour Bridge a number of good to high quality restaurants have opened for business in recent years. Many of them have a special national character and as a rule they are somewhat less expensive than those in the same class in the eastern suburbs. Their main drawback is, of course, that they are not as easy to reach from downtown as the restaurants on the eastern side of the harbour. Restaurants in the area with a French accent include *La Potiniere,* 178 Blues Point Rd., *Breheny's Restaurant,* 123 Blues Point Rd., and *L'Orangerie,* 1 Young St., Neutral Bay., *Stuyvesants House,* 45 Alexander St., Crows Nest, has Dutch food, and *Restaurant Malaya,* 73 Mount St., North Sydney, specializes in Chinese, Indonesian and Malaysian dishes.

ENVIRONS OF SYDNEY

Blue Mountains

The City of the Blue Mountains, a favourite holiday resort near Sydney, is not a city at all, but a collection of 24 separate townships dispersed over an area of 1,350 square km. of mountainous bushland traversed by the Great Western Highway. The largest of the townships, Katoomba, centre of the "city", is 106 km. by road or rail from Sydney. You can easily "do" the Blue Mountains in a day, but if possible, spend a few days there. Besides lovely bush walks and excursions on horseback, the area offers scenically attractive golf courses to the visitor. They are interesting to low handicap golfers, but not too challenging for the weekend player. The courses at Blackheath and at Leura are exceptionally attractive, with spectacular views of the Blue Mountains across deep valleys from some of the greens at Leura. There are a number of easy walks around the localities, such as the attractive 40 minute stroll from the Blackheath swimming pool to Govetts Leap, where the wild landscape looks as if prehistoric monsters could rise at any moment from the depth of the green forests. There are more arduous walks, but don't forget the first rule of the inexperienced bushwalker—never wander away from the beaten track.

Popular walks include the 6 km. Federal Pass Walk which takes about 2½ hours and skirts the foot of the cliffs between Leura and Katoomba Falls. One descends near Leura Falls by way of 1330 graded steps between lush vegetation—mountain ash, cedar, bloodwoods, and all kinds of gums—and follows the track which passes Linda Falls, Leura Falls, Weeping Rock and one of Katoomba's great sights, the Three Sisters rocks, before arriving at the foot of the 245 m. Katoomba Falls, from where the Scenic Railway can take the wayfarer back to the top. The Scenic Railway, only 415 m. long, is reputedly the steepest in the world, and it's quite a thrill to travel on it down into Jamieson Valley, a drop of 230 m. The Scenic Skyway—taking passengers from one cliff-top to another over a void of 275 m.—is another tourist attraction in Katoomba. If driving to the Blue Mountains it is worth stopping at the Norman Lindsay Gallery and Museum at Springwood (opened 1973) which exhibits works by one of Australia's best known artists, who lived there from 1912 until his death in 1969 at the age of 91.

PRACTICAL INFORMATION FOR THE BLUE MOUNTAINS

The Blue Mountains Tourist Association, Echo Point Rd., Katoomba, (047) 82-1348, provides free information and accepts bookings for accommodations and coach tours.

HOTELS AND MOTELS

Leura: *Everglades,* 54 units, all with private shower. Well appointed interiors, telephone, central heating, TV, heated pool and sauna. Reasonable restaurant. Near golf course.

Leura Gardens, opposite golf course, 78 units, 2 suites, all with shower. Heated pool, sauna, games room. Good restaurant.

Katoomba: *Alpine Motor Inn,* 21 units, 4 suites, all with shower. Central heating, air conditioning in 15 units, heated pool, sauna.

St. Elmo, 15 units all with shower. Air conditioning.

Blackheath: *Redleaf,* 42 units, 4 suites, all with shower. Heated pool.

The Central Coast

The Central Coast between about 50 km. and 120 km. north of Sydney —midway between Sydney and Newcastle—is aptly known as "the playground of two cities". The township of Gosford at its heart can be reached by electric train. The road includes a 40 km. stretch of express turnpike—one of the few in Australia. (Instead of the turnpike you can drive along the less comfortable but scenically more rewarding old Pacific Highway which has been maintained in good repair.) The Central Coast's greatest attractions are connected with watersports, fishing and surfing, but the area also has large tracts of unspoiled bushland for quiet walks along lakes and rivers. In vacation periods the main resorts are rather noisy and overcrowded, for the area has been developed into one of Sydney's main school-holiday areas. It has an equable climate, and is sheltered from the winds. The area's proximity to Sydney (about an hour by electric train from Gosford) has also persuaded an increasing number of people to retire there, or to buy or build a weekend house. The main townships are Gosford, (which serves as a distribution point for the area), Woy Woy and Ettalong off Brisbane Water, and Terrigal. An interesting tourist attraction is Old Sydney Town, near Gosford—a recreation of Sydney Cove and its surroundings as they were in the early 19th century. The Visitors Information Centre, 200 Mann St., Gosford, tel. (043) 25-2835, is open from 9 A.M.–5 P.M. from Mondays to Fridays, and from 9 A.M.–12 on Saturdays.

HOTELS AND MOTELS

Gosford: *Gosford,* 28 units, all with shower. Air conditioning, heated pool.

Woy Woy: *Glades Colonial,* 14 units, all with shower. Air conditioned.

Terrigal: *Cobb and Co. Motor Inn,* near beach, golf course and bowling club. 30 units, all with shower. Air conditioning, pool, room service.

The Entrance: *El Lago Commodore,* 37 units, 1 suite, all with shower. Air conditioned, playground, sauna, restaurant.

Upper Hawkesbury

This attractive river area on the northwestern outskirts of Sydney was discovered by a rowing expedition under the command of Governor Arthur Phillip in 1789. 21 years later, in 1810, Governor Macquarie established five towns—Windsor, Richmond, Castlereagh, Pitt Town and Wilberforce (the Five Macquarie Towns) in the area. Castlereagh has almost disappeared but the other four are still expanding; it won't be very long before the Sydney suburban sprawl swallows them. There are several early 19th century buildings in the area which are worth seeing. They include St. Matthew's Church of England, Windsor, designed by Francis Greenway; the restored Court House at Windsor, and the Anglican Church of St. Peter at Richmond. At Richmond the Royal Australian Air Force maintains an air-base. The Hawkesbury itself offers scenic beauty and excellent water-skiing from Windsor Bridge to Wiseman's Ferry. A one day excursion from Sydney by car to Windsor—with a 10 km. drive from Windsor to the Hawkesbury at Wiseman's Ferry—may also take in on the return trip the City of Parramatta. Although Sydneysiders consider Parramatta an outer suburb, not a separate city, this view is not shared by the people of the place, who think that its founder, Governor Phillip, should have stuck to his original idea and made Parramatta the capital of the young colony. Today the city is mainly industrial and has little charm, although it has retained a number of good buildings from the early days. They include the carefully restored Old Government House, the oldest surviving public building in Australia, completed in 1816 and now surrounded by Parramatta Park; Experiment Farm Cottage (1820) in Ruse Street, which stands on the site of James Ruse's farm, memorable as the first land grant given in New South Wales (1792); Elizabeth Farm House, built by John Macarthur in 1793, the oldest existing building in Australia; and Hambledon (1824), built by John Macarthur for Miss Penelope Lucas, the governess of his children. Two other buildings worth a visit are the Lancer Barracks in Smith Street (1820), which contains a military museum, and St. John's Church, founded in 1799 but twice rebuilt since.

Water Supplies and Lions

Sydney's domestic and industrial water supply comes from six major storage dams. Assuring adequate supplies for the fast expanding Sydney region even during periods of major drought, is the huge task of the Metropolitan Water Sewerage and Drainage Board. London stores 16,-000 liters of water per person, Los Angeles 182,000 liters and Sydney nearly 863,000. When full, the six major storage dams contain 2,612,450,000,000 liters of water—sufficient to supply the city and its adjacent regions through a drought lasting longer than any yet experienced. But recently a new catchment area of some 5,620 square km. at the Shoalhaven River, south of Sydney, has been added to the existing works. The Shoalhaven scheme should be in full service by 1984. The Water Board welcomes visitors to the storage dam sites, which are within easy driving distance of Sydney. They are large, picturesque, manmade lakes and the Board has erected picnic areas with fireplaces on the shores of all of them. Visitors need no permit.

Near Warragamba dam is the African Lion Safari, where some 50 lions roam over 90 acres of land surrounded by a high fence. Visitors must stay in their cars (no convertibles, please) and are not permitted to lower the windows.

EXPLORING NEW SOUTH WALES

The Hunter Region

If you believe that coal-mining regions must look drab and bleak, you should see the verdant Hunter region of New South Wales. Here the god of coal must share his power, and influence, with a more cheerful deity—Bacchus. For, after coal, wine is a most important product of this rich and beautiful part of the State. It begins about 100 km. north of Sydney at Catherine Hill Bay and extends 145 km. north, just past Taree and 275 km. west to the Great Dividing Range, covering an area of some 30,000 square km. Comparing places is rarely a rewarding exercise, but in the Hunter region one is often tempted because the scenery changes so rapidly, reviving memories of past travels. You may be looking down on the blue waters of some Mediterranean shoreline, or faced with an Italian lake, or a vineyard which could be in France. And all this without leaving the region named after its main river, the 470 km. Hunter, which rises in the Mount Royal Range and flows into the Pacific Ocean at Newcastle, Australia's sixth largest city. But lovely and extremely useful as the Hunter is, it can also be dangerous; hardly a year goes by without the river breaking its banks and inundating the countryside.

The Hunter region's modern history begins with that permanently present character of early Australian history—the convict. In 1797, when Lieutenant John Shortland, commander of a Royal Navy whale-boat stationed at Sydney, received orders to sail north, he wasn't entrusted with the task of discovering anything but of finding some runaway convicts. Instead he found the mouth of a large river about 105 km. north of Sydney, which he named Hunter after John Hunter, who had succeeded Phillip as Governor. A settlement for twice convicted criminals was established there in 1801 and three years later—it was a very English epoch in Australian history—the place was named Newcastle and the surrounding district Northumberland. Gradually, however, the newly founded settlement followed the usual Australian pattern. With the influx of immigrants, the jail became transformed into a thriving colony. By the 1820s the settling and opening of the Hunter region was well under way. The discovery of huge reserves of high quality coal—which in turn encouraged the establishment of industry—greatly helped the region's development. Nowadays the Hunter region produces about 16 million tons of coal a year, of which some 7 million tons are exported.

The Hunter region is easily accessible from Sydney by various means of transport. Its most important urban centre, Newcastle, is only 167 km. from Sydney along the Pacific Highway (a stretch of it is an express turnpike)—a comfortable drive of 2½ hours or less depending upon the traffic, which can be rather heavy. At Hexham, just outside Newcastle, the New England Highway—an inland route to Brisbane—branches off the Pacific Highway, which continues to meander along the sea up to Queensland. There are several daily rail services between Sydney and

Newcastle, including the Newcastle Express, which takes about 2½ hours. Daily air services also operate between the two cities.

Although Newcastle (pop. 270,000) is looked upon as being an industrial centre and is proud of its reputation as Australia's "City of Enterprise", it can also be a pleasant holiday resort. Downtown Newcastle is not very pretty, although the gradual replacement of the strictly utilitarian and unimaginative office buildings and trading premises with architecturally more interesting structures is improving the city's appearance. Most Australian urban settlements—large or small—are trying to find something which they can claim as a national, regional, or international record. Newcastle has produced two of them: its 3 km. Hunter Street is claimed to be Australia's longest main street, and the Newcastle Public School, which took in its first scholars in 1816, is said to be the oldest school in Australia still operating on its original site. The city's pride is the War Memorial Cultural Centre, established from the donations of business firms and private citizens, which houses a good library, and serves as a venue for cultural activities including concerts, art exhibitions, lectures and the like. Some of Newcastle's most pleasant beaches are at the end of the streets in the city centre. For instance, Newcastle Beach is only 180 m. from Hunter Street. Between August and May, eight Newcastle beaches are patrolled daily by life-savers. One of them, Bar Beach, is floodlit at night.

Lake Macquarie and the Seashore

About 18 km. south of Newcastle is Australia's largest seaside lake, Lake Macquarie, with an area of 110 square km. and 150 km. of foreshores. The lake is one of Australia's most delightful watersport centres; excellent for fishing, sailing, yachting and water-skiing. Because of its sheltered situation it is very pleasant in winter, and receives enough sea-breezes to be agreeably ventilated in summer. The little lakeside townships and villages have a large population of retired people. One of Australia's most distinguished artists, the painter Sir William Dobell, lived in Wangi Wangi, which is one of the attractive resorts. His home is now a museum dedicated to his memory.

About 50 km. north of Newcastle is Port Stephens, which takes in a number of resorts such as Nelson Bay, Shoal Bay, Fingal Bay, Tea Gardens, Lemon Tree Passage, Karuah and Soldiers Point. The area has been aptly described as "a blue-water wonderland" which offers the visitor a wide range of sports and entertainments. You may fish in the morning and play golf and tennis, bowls or squash in the afternoon. Port Stephens can be reached by road (bus services run from Newcastle to Nelson Bay). A regular air-service operates from Sydney to Williamtown, 16 km. from Newcastle and a short distance from Port Stephens by car or bus. In the Port Stephens area are the twin towns of Tea Gardens and Hawks Nest, situated on the picturesque Myall River which joins the Myall Lakes. A large National Park surrounds them. Suggestions that the sands of the lake area should be mined have caused a stormy controversy, and mining has now ceased. Still further north, 325 km. from Sydney and 147 km. from Newcastle, is yet another excellent holiday centre in the town of Forster. There are some 20 ocean beaches in its immediate vicinity and the township has a long frontage on Wallis Lake, the water of which is rarely less than 20°C—even in winter. Access to Forster is by a scenic road—the turn off from the Pacific Highway is near Bulahdelah—which leads past small lakes and resorts. You can also fly from Sydney to Taree and proceed from there to Forster by bus, or travel from Sydney by train to Taree or to Newcastle and from there take a bus to Forster.

About Coal, Wine, and Brick Throwing

The centres of the Hunter region's coal mining industry are the towns of Maitland (pop. 38,863) and Cessnock (pop. 17,000). But neither resembles the sooty coal towns of Britain, Belgium, France, or Germany. They have managed to look like any other Australian working-class suburb, with neat houses and well-tended gardens. Although both Maitland and Cessnock are built on coal they are also the centers of prosperous farming districts, for they have some of the most fertile soil in New South Wales. Several farm homesteads near the two towns built in the first half of the last century are still in use. They are not open for inspection, but the Maitland City Council has issued a booklet titled "Historical Buildings of Maitland and District" which describes them. Cessnock has Australia's most modern geriatric hospital, the Allandale Hospital, which cares for between 600 and 700 patients and carries out research on the problems of aging. Near Cessnock are the famous vineyards of Pokolbin, which produce some of the country's best wine. Well-known vineyards include Drayton's Bellevue and Happy Valley, Tyrrells' Ashmans, Lindemans' Ben Ean and McWilliams' Mt. Pleasant. Conducted tours are available and visitors have plenty of opportunity to sample the final product.

Stroud is not one of the larger settlements of the Hunter region (its population is only about 570), but besides having a few early 19th century buildings such as the Anglican Church of St. John (1833) and a well designed court house, its international fame rests on the brick-throwing ability of its citizens. Every year there is a brick-throwing and rollingpin-throwing contest among four towns called Stroud in different parts of the world—the U.S.A., Canada, England, and Australia. In this competition six men from each Stroud compete at throwing housebricks, and the results from each centre are collated to decide the international winner. The ladies of the four Strouds compete in the rollingpin-throwing competition.

PRACTICAL INFORMATION FOR THE HUNTER REGION

TOURIST INFORMATION. Centers are maintained by several communities in the Hunter region. Some are able to make travel and/or accommodation bookings. They include: Newcastle, City Hall, King St. Monday to Friday 8:30 A.M.–5 P.M., tel (049) 26-2323, Nelson Bay, Victoria Pde., daily 9 A.M.–5 P.M., tel (049) 81-1579; Forster, Tourist Information Centre, Monday to Friday 8:30 A.M.–4:30 P.M., tel (065) 54-8541.

Hexham Tourist Information Centre, Pacific and New England Highway, 9 A.M.–4 P.M. Monday–Friday, 10 A.M.–2 P.M. Saturday and Sunday, tel. (049) 64-8006.

The NRMA maintains more than a dozen depots in the Hunter region where motorists in trouble can obtain help on the road. If not in possession of an NRMA list of depots call the association's Newcastle branch (8 Auckland St. tel. (049) 2-4821) for information.

 SEASONAL EVENTS. Festivals are staged by several communities, usually in the same months every year, but the exact dates vary and should be checked. Visitors may be especially interested in the Murrurundi and District Sheep Dog Trials (February), the Hunter Valley Vintage Festival in Cessnock (March, every second year), the Thoroughbred Week—with sales and races—in Scone (May), the International Brickthrowing Contest in Stroud (July), Gloucester Rodeo in November, and the Myall Mardi Gras at Tea Gardens, Hawks Nest (December).

 HOTELS AND MOTELS. There are no luxury-class hotels or motels in the Hunter region, and only a few are in the expensive (A$47 single, A$48 double) category. As a rule the motels in the region are newer and more modern than the hotels and most of them belong to the moderate price category (A$37–46 single, A$38–47 double).

Cessnock: *Hunter Valley Motel,* 20 units, 1 suite, all with shower, heating, fans.

Maitland East: *Molly Morgan,* 36 units, all with shower. Air conditioning, pool, restaurant.

Newcastle: *Telford,* situated on beach front. 90 units, 1 suite, all with shower. Air conditioning, colour TV, restaurant (closed on Sunday).

TraveLodge, overlooking Newcastle beach. 72 units, all with shower; pool, restaurant.

NOTE: The Tourist Authority of the Hunter Valley has published a handy pamphlet with lists of accommodation, estate agents, car hire, taxi and air charter firms in the Hunter region. Available from the New South Wales Government Travel Centre, corner of Pitt and Spring Streets, Sydney.

The North Coast Region

Overseas visitors to Australia, or even Australians, who set out from Sydney to drive north—perhaps to Surfers Paradise in Queensland—may never arrive there. Not because they face any serious dangers en route, but because they may succumb to the attractions of places on the way. The Pacific Ocean coast north and south of Sydney is among the world's most beautiful and pleasant seashores. In addition, while most holiday resorts along it are provided with the amenities of modern civilisation, few are overcrowded even during the peak holiday season.

Nowhere is this more true than on the North Coast of New South Wales, which is studded with holiday spots whose existence is not primarily based on the tourist business. Most of them are centers of thriving agricultural areas, attractive places where people go about their business in a leisurely way and where courtesy and service are still not merely memories of the past. The North Coast region (adjacent to the Hunter Valley region) is about 560 km. long, with the Wang Wauk River at its southern and Queensland at its northern border. Its average width between the Pacific Ocean and the Great Dividing Range is 80 km. There are few secondary industries in this narrow strip of land (some people wish there were more) and not many factory chimneys to spoil the idyllic landscape of undulating farmland with herds of grazing cows, green fields of sugarcane and maize, extensive tropical fruit gardens with their fine pineapples, bananas, melons, mangos, pawpaws, avocados, peanuts and macadamia nuts. There are picturesque fishing villages in sheltered bays and mountains rising to more than 1,000 m. broken by deep ravines with cascading creeks. North Coast local patriots even assert—with some justification—that the sun rises in Australia in their territory, because Cape Byron is the most easterly point of the mainland.

Access to the North Coast either from Sydney or Brisbane is no problem. The Pacific Highway runs through it, and good and scenically beautiful roads, including the Bruxner, Gwydir and Oxley Highways, branch off it and lead to the New England region. There are several daily plane connections from Sydney to some of the major towns of the area, and trains and express coaches run frequently every day between the New South Wales and Queensland State capitals, stopping on the way at North Coast localities.

Traveling north along the Pacific Highway, the first larger town is Taree (pop. 14,696) on the banks of the Manning River. 13 km. farther is Wingham, with a Vampire Jet aircraft in its park, placed there to commemorate the 50th anniversary of the Royal Australian Air Force in August 1971. There are several pleasant fishing villages in the district and motel accommodation is available. But the first larger resort place on the way north is Port Macquarie, which can be highly recommended for a vacation. Established in 1821 as a convict settlement on the banks of the Hastings River "the Port", as it is affectionately known, is a favourite long-weekend target of Sydneysiders. It has 40 motels including some very good ones, a couple of licensed hotels and two restaurants of respectable quality—one German, the other French. Port Macquarie's St. Thomas Church of England is the third oldest church in Australia (built between 1824 and 1828) and there is an interesting collection of convict relics in the local museum. There are the usual watersport facilities and an interesting and fairly flat golf course which will tax your skill but not your stamina. Two cruisers operate along the placid Hastings River. Situated up the river 19 km. away is Wauchope, an important timber centre, and railhead for Port Macquarie. Timbertown, 3 km. west of Wauchope, is the re-creation of a typical Australian timber town of the 1880s, and is well worth a visit; activities include travelling on an old steam train, taking a waggon ride, seeing a bullock team working and watching craftspeople in period dress demonstrating their skills. The Wauchope district also claims an international record: it has the biggest blackbutt forest in the world. Another worth-while excursion from Port Macquarie is by car or coach to the Comboyne Plateau, a largely inaccessible wilderness of dense forest, waterfalls and cascades, including the spectacular 150 m. Ellenborough Falls near the little township of Comboyne. From one spot the view—from Forster to Port Macquarie—is simply breathtaking. There is a difficult motor road to the world's largest blackbutt tree, a 300 year old, 70 m. giant with a girth of 11 m. It is advisable to join an organised tour to the Plateau.

North of Port Macquarie is Kempsey, a pretty town and headquarters for the Macleay River, with nine motels, six hotels and five caravan parks with "on site" vans and cabins. In the vicinity are a number of popular resorts: South West Rocks, Stuarts Point, Crescent Head and Grassy Heads. They have excellent beaches for surfing and are patrolled by lifeguards during the season. There are two tourist attractions near South West Rocks—the old Trial Bay Jail with a museum, and the Smoky Cape Lighthouse (open for inspection on Tuesday and Thursday) with beautiful views of long stretches of beaches and surf. A drive from Kempsey upstream along the Macleay River is well worth while. Nambucca Heads, 526 km. from Sydney, is another popular resort, and Shelley Beach, one of its beauty spots, has been favoured by Australian and overseas painters. The next important town is Coffs Harbour, center of the largest banana producing district in Australia (587 km. from Sydney). Among popular attractions there is the Pet Porpoise Pool situated at Park Beach, where porpoises and Australian seals perform twice daily. Coffs Harbour has a championship 18-hole golfcourse and several very well appointed caravan parks. About 80 km. from Coffs Harbour is Grafton, situated on both sides of the Clarence River and famous for its Jacaranda Festival in the first week of November, when thousands of jacaranda trees are in full bloom.

The largest center on the New South Wales North Coast north of Newcastle is Lismore on the Richmond River—the longest navigable coastal river in the State. 31 km. from there is Ballina, one of the main fishing ports of the North Coast and a good place for fishing, surfing and sun-bathing. Cape Byron, 47 km. from Lismore, is the spot "where the sun first greets Australia". Australia's most powerful lighthouse (claimed to be the second most powerful in the world, with a light of 3,000,000 candle-power) stands there. Incidentally, Cape Byron was named by Captain Cook in May 1770 after John Byron, grandfather of the poet Lord Byron, who commanded a round-the-world voyage in 1764-1766. Near the Queensland border is one of the region's most attractive areas, the Tweed Valley, where the Tweed River meanders through its rich farmlands. The Tweed's source is in the rain forests of the McPherson Ranges, and it ends at Tweed Heads, the most northerly town in New South Wales. The valley itself is dominated by the 1,157 m. Mt. Warning, which is accessible from the town of Murwillumbah. There is a marvellous vista from its peak—a rather arduous ascent for untrained climbers.

PRACTICAL INFORMATION FOR THE NORTH COAST REGION

TOURIST INFORMATION. There are several Regional Tourist Associations with headquarters at important centers and knowledgeable staff. Coffs Harbour: Park Ave. Tel (066) 52-1522. Grafton: Duke and Victoria sts. Tel (066) 42-4677. Lismore: Tourist Information Centre, Ballina St. Tel. (066) 21-1518. Muwillumbah: Pacific Highway, Tel. (066) 72-1340. Port Macquarie: Horton St. Tel. 1-9657. Taree: 250 Victoria St. Tel. (065) 52-1801. The headquarters are open 9 A.M.-5 P.M., Mondays to Fridays; and 9 A.M. to noon on Saturdays.

CARAVAN PARKS AND CAMPING GROUNDS.
There are a very large number of both in the region,
including smaller resorts. However, it is advisable to book
well ahead especially during the holiday season. Bookings
by telephone can be made either directly to the caravan parks or through the
Regional Tourist Centres. Lists are available from the New South Wales Government Travel Centers in Sydney, Melbourne, Brisbane. (But the Travel Centers do
not provide a booking service for caravan parks.)

HOTELS AND MOTELS

Taree: *El Greco,* 16 units, all with shower. Air conditioning, pool, playground,
baby sitting.

Port Macquarie: *Sand Castle,* 45 units, 10 suites, all with shower, restaurant
and room service. 10 suites have cooking facilities. Pool, covered parking.

Beachfront, 37 units, all with shower. Air conditioning in 10 units, cooking
facilities in 33 units. Pool, sauna, restaurant (closed Saturday and Sunday).

Bermuda Breezes, somewhat out of town (6 km. from post office) but handy
to main beach and golf club. 6 units, 10 suites, all with shower, cooking facilities.
Pool, tennis court, baby sitters.

Coffs Harbour: *Coff Harbour Holiday Village,* 28 units, all with shower. TV,
heated pool, sauna, billiard room.

Zebra, 46 units, all with shower. Air conditioned, TV, pool, restaurant with
room service.

Grafton: *Camden Lodge,* 29 units, 3 suites, all with shower. Air conditioning
in 20 rooms. Telephone, TV, 2 pools, convention facilities, restaurant.

Lismore: *Karinga,* 31 units, all with shower. Air conditioned, telephone, TV,
restaurant with room service.

Benelong, 25 units all with shower. Air conditioned, telephone, TV, cooking
facilities.

Ballina: *All Seasons,* 40 units, all with shower. Air conditioned, telephone, TV,
heated pool, restaurant.

Murwillumbah: *Murwillumbah Motor Inn,* 31 units with shower. TV, telephone, pool.

Tweed Heads: *Fairlight,* near several beaches, ½ km from shops. 20 units all
with shower. Telephone, TV, pool.

Australia's New England Region

Tourists who have had their fill of surf and beaches may find a pleasant
change by driving from the ocean westwards over one of the three
highways to the New England region, the hinterland of the North Coast.
(Actually, some consider parts of the region categorized here as the
North Coast region to be part of the New England region.) The highways
are the Oxley from Port Macquarie; the Gwydir from Grafton; and the
Bruxner from Lismore.

The name New England has a nostalgic air—and not by chance. The
region, discovered by the explorer John Oxley in 1818, has an "English
atmosphere", especially in autumn (April, May) on the Tablelands,
which are situated at an average altitude of 900 m. above sea level with
peaks up to 1,610 m. (Round Mountain). Here the thousands of trees
imported from England and planted by English settlers shed their golden
leaves in autumn. Winter is *really* winter with snow and frost. However,
only the mountains and the higher slopes of New England remind one
of the northern hemisphere. Further to the west, where the region's rich

black soil plains spread out endlessly, you are in the "real Australia" again.

Although New England can offer much to the traveler, its tourist attractions are rather for the leisurely wayfarer than for the tourist with limited time. One of the unusual pastimes in the region is "fossicking" for gemstones. Looking for them has become so popular that a special reserve has been set aside in the Glen Innes district for amateur fossickers. It is unlikely that a find will make you rich, but it is good fun and needs neither great effort nor expensive equipment. The latter can be bought or hired from hardware stores in the township nearest to the localities where gemstones are found. These include beryl, aquamarine, emerald, topaz, sapphire, zircon, spinel and diamonds. (New England is not opal country.) The best localities for fossicking are: Emmaville, Torrington, Glen Innes, Inverell, Copeton, Tingha, Kingsgate, Oban, Uralla, Bendemeer, Hall Creek (in the Moonbi Range), Nundle and Bingara. A fossicker must obtain a licence (A$2.50 single, A$5.00 for families) to fossick on Crown land. No license is necessary on private land available for fossicking. The Crown land licence can be obtained either from the Department of Mineral Resources, CAGA Centre, Bent St., Sydney, from the Mining Registrar in Armidale or the Inverell Tourist Information Centre.

Traveling north on the New England Highway (which branches off the Pacific Highway outside Newcastle) the first important town is Tamworth, 449 km. from Sydney. It is a pleasant and prosperous agricultural center (pop. 29,656) and it claims to have been the first Australian city to use electricity for street lighting. Tamworth is also the "Country Music Capital" of Australia. Some 94 km. farther is Uralla, which offers good angling in the downstream waters of the Macdonald River. "Thunderbolt," one of Australia's most notorious bushrangers (an euphemism for bandit), is buried in Uralla cemetery. He was shot dead by a policeman in May 1870.

A short drive (23 km.) from there is Armidale (pop. 19,000), the largest centre of the New England Tablelands. It is 1,000 m. above sea level. The numerous educational institutions—including the University of New England, the Armidale Teachers' College, and the Armidale Technical College—have stamped their mark on the city. With a large population of academics and students, Armidale has a lively cultural life. Its Hinton Benefaction Art Gallery, housed in the Teachers' College, contains what is probably the best collection of Australian paintings outside Sydney.

As Armidale is about half way between Sydney and Brisbane on the New England Highway, it is a favourite resting place. However, it is well worth staying there not only overnight but for a full day. There are many beauty spots, and the city's Development Center in Rusden St. (tel 72-3771) will provide detailed information.

Glen Innes, 99 km. from Armidale, is located at the intersection of the New England and Gwydir Highways, 1073 m. above sea level. It is another good resting place with comfortable hotel and motel accommodation and several caravan parks open from late spring to early autumn. Winter snowfalls can be rather severe there, as all along the Tablelands section of the New England Highway.

The last large town on the highway before reaching Queensland is Tenterfield at the junction of the New England, Bruxner and Mt. Lindesay Highways. Tenterfield considers itself the birthplace of Australian Federation because it was in its School of Arts on October 24, 1889 that Sir Henry Parkes, then Premier of New South Wales, delivered a speech which started the movement that some 11 years later brought about the Australian Commonwealth (the union of the six Australian states into one nation). Incidentally, in Australian usage a School of Arts may be but is usually not a place where the arts (painting, sculpture, etc.) are taught. It is a cultural center with a public library, lecture room or hall and similar amenities. The Tenterfield School of Arts is now a national monument. The Boonoo Boonoo Falls (pronounce Bunnabernoo), where a stream cascades 210 m. to the valley below, is some 30 km. along a rough road from the town.

Australia's best known spa for rheumatic complaints, Moree, is situated on the North Central Plain of New England. The water is obtained from an artesian well more than 900 m. deep. Moree can be reached by regular rail, air and coach services from Sydney, Brisbane, and several New England centres.

The New England region has magnificent National Parks including New England National Park, 72 km. east of Armidale, with its rain forest, fascinating bird life and impressive lookouts. Another, Gibraltar Range National Park, is about half way between Glen Innes and Grafton along the Gwydir Highway. A third, Mt. Kaputar National Park, can be reached by a fairly good gravel road from Narrabri. There are tourist cabins for up to six persons in all three National Parks, but visitors must take their own provisions.

PRACTICAL INFORMATION FOR THE NEW ENGLAND REGION

TOURIST INFORMATION. There are 19 information centres and 23 NRMA Depots throughout the New England region.

HOW TO GET THERE. *By train:* Regular daily services from and to Sydney are provided by the Northern Tableland Express and North Mail. For timetables, fares and bookings contact the New South Wales Government Travel Centre in Sydney, Melbourne, Brisbane, or the State Rail Authority on York Street, Sydney.

By air: Airlines of NSW from Sydney to Moree and Narrabri. East-West Airlines from Sydney to Armidale, Glen Innes, Inverell, Tamworth; from Brisbane to Armidale, Coolangatta, Tamworth. East Coast Airlines from Brisbane to Armidale and Tamworth via the Queensland Gold Coast; from Newcastle, and from Canberra, to Armidale and Tamworth.

By bus: Ansett-Pioneer, McCafferty's Coaches, Deluxe Coaches, and Greyhound run regular express coaches from Brisbane to Melbourne via the New England Highway. There is an express coach (Kirklands) from Tenterfield to Lismore via the Bruxner Highway. There are many bus services within the New England region (see local tourist information centers for timetables, fares and bookings).

HOTELS AND MOTELS

Armidale: *Moore Park Inn,* near golf courses, trout fishing gorges, mountain views. 21 units, 1 suite, all with shower and air conditioned. Swimming pool, hot spa. Convention facilities, restaurant.

Glen Innes: *Alpha,* 16 units, all with shower, heating, electric blankets, telephone, TV. Restaurant.

Gunnedah: *Gunnedah,* 21 units, all with shower, air conditioned, telephone, TV. Restaurant.

Narrabri: *Nandewar,* 44 units, all with shower, air conditioned, telephone, TV. Pool.

Tenterfield: *Henry Parkes,* 18 units, all with shower, central heating. Restaurant, pool.

Tenterfield Motor Inn, 22 units, all with shower, 16 units centrally heated; electric blankets, telephone, TV.

The North-west Country Region

The North-west region is not conventional tourist country, but those who like wide horizons and a sort of "prairie" atmosphere will be attracted to the seemingly unending expanses of the rich sheep and cattle raising and wheat growing part of Australia. The region is especially pleasant in spring and autumn when the days are mild and the nights are cool. It has a number of picturesque rivers—the Macquarie, Bogan, Castlereagh, Namoi, Gwydir and Macintyre—where fishing is good. They flow northwards and north-westwards into the Darling, which empties into the Murray, which, in turn, ends in the Southern Ocean some 3,000 km. away. Most of the time they are friendly, useful waterways, but when rains swell them they become broad seas inundating hundreds of square kilometers of the countryside, drowning beasts and devastating property.

Dubbo, the main center of the North-west region (412 km. by road from Sydney), is a pleasant town of 23,986. But if you want to obtain the real "feel" of the region, travel all the way to Bourke, called "the gateway to the Outback." Situated on the Darling, 789 km. by road from Sydney, the town is the hub of the world's richest wool producing area. There is a plane service from Sydney to Bourke, and a daily train runs as far as Dubbo, with a road coach connection to Bourke Monday, Wednesday, and Friday. There are some 300 sheep and cattle properties in the Bourke area, which produces an average of 50,000 bales of wool a year. A rodeo held at Bourke late in winter (July, August) is good fun if you like a spectacular show.

Besides sheep, cattle and wheat the most famous products of the region are opals, and the best place to find them is around Lightning Ridge, 766 km. by road from Sydney. The nearest town and railhead to "the Ridge" is Walgett. One can stay either at Walgett, or in the hotel or motels in the middle of the opal fields, which also have an 80-site all-amenities caravan park. However, perhaps the most attractive proposition for the tourist is to stay at the Pineopal Lodge, 48 km. from Walgett, which offers a farm holiday combined with opal fossicking in motel-type accommodation.

The Lightning Ridge fields are the only source of the famous black opals. There, as well as in the nearby Glengarry and Grawin fields, you may find, in addition to opals, other semi-precious stones including agate, jasper and topaz.

HOTELS AND MOTELS

Dubbo: *Country Comfort,* adjoining golf course. 39 units, all with shower, air conditioned, telephone, TV. Pool, sauna, restaurant with room service.

Homestead, 25 units, all with shower, air conditioned, central heating, telephone, TV. Pool, playground, restaurant.

Lightning Ridge: *Lightning Ridge Hotel/Motel,* 24 units, all with shower, air conditioned. Near opal mining.

The Outback Region

There could hardly be a better introduction to the Outback region than the warning of the NRMA to motorists intending to travel in the outback:

"1. The vehicle should be in first-class mechanical order and the driver, or some member of the party, should have a reasonable knowledge of running repairs. In addition to the normal spare, an extra wheel with tyre and tube should be carried. 2. In addition to the normal tool kit, which should include a good jack, tyre pump, shovel, axe and tow rope a dozen other items should be carried. [For full list ask for an NRMA pamphlet.] 3. A well equipped first aid kit, 4½ liters of drinking water per person, food and a reserve drum of petrol are essentials. 4. Advice should be sought from police or other responsible persons regarding road and weather conditions ahead. The advice should be rechecked at each opportunity en route. Your proposed itinerary should be known so that, if necessary, a search could be made more easily. If in need of assistance stay with your vehicle. Do not over-exert yourself and conserve your water supply."

That is the sort of advice you need in the region "back o' Bourke" if you venture off the highways and sealed roads. It's a big place—more than 12,000,000 hectares, and it is inhabited only by some 2,000,000 sheep, who produce an average of 60,000 bales of wool annually. It is an arid place, and for hundreds of kilometers its borders with Queensland in the north and South Australia in the west are fenced against dingos (a sort of wild dog). Yet, forbidding as most of the region is, it also has a strange wild beauty which attracts many tourists who like to face a challenge. This goes only for visitors who decide to organise their own expedition off the beaten track. Users of the regular transport systems are not exposed to any greater risks than commuters travelling between their suburbs and the city.

The main destination of the regular transport systems is the Outback region's only important urban centre: Broken Hill, or the "Silver City" as it is nicknamed. Broken Hill, a city of 26,913 inhabitants, owes its existence to the world's richest known silver-lead, and zinc deposits, on top of which it stands. Discovered by chance in 1883 by Charles Rasp, a German-born boundary rider (horsemen who check that fences of sheep and cattle paddocks are intact), the deposits are now mined by several big companies.

Although almost everything that humans and industry needs must be brought to Broken Hill from considerable distances—the main water supply is pumped from the Darling River some 110 km. away—the city today is a very pretty place with well kept gardens surrounding substantial dwellings and public buildings, including a modern Civic Centre which would be the pride of much larger cities.

One of the most interesting peculiarities of Broken Hill is that for all practical purposes it is run by the Barrier Trades and Labour Council, the central body of the local trade unions. Together with the employers, it has worked out such an effective mechanism for negotiating issues between the two sides that Broken Hill has had no serious industrial trouble for half a century.

Another unusual feature of Broken Hill is its very low crime rate and its thriving cultural activities. There are, for instance, several art galleries; one of Australia's most prominent painters who turned to art from mining, Pro Hart, lives there. It is the center of the Royal Flying Doctor Service and of the School of the Air (see main introduction to Australia). Its tourist attractions include organised inspections of some of the mines.

Outside Broken Hill, visitors to the Outback region may also enjoy a swim in the 16,200-hectare man-made Menindee Lake, 110 km. east of the city, where there are other water sports including water-skiing. There is a caravan park at the lake which is connected to Broken Hill by a good road. The Kinchega National Park, 113 km. south-east of Broken Hill, is the home of the emu and the red kangaroo. Mootwingee, meaning "green grass", 132 km. north of Broken Hill, is a sacred Aboriginal tribal ground rich in rock engravings, cave paintings and stencils of kangaroos, lizards, emu and dingo tracks, some dating back 2000 or 3000 years. White Cliffs, northeast of Broken Hill, is worth a visit for opals.

PRACTICAL INFORMATION FOR THE OUTBACK REGION

HOW TO GET THERE. Regular *rail* services are provided by the Silver City Comet and the Indian Pacific from Sydney to Broken Hill.

By air: Air NSW from Sydney to Broken Hill and Ansett Airlines from Adelaide to Broken Hill.

By bus: Ansett from Sydney and Greyhound from Adelaide to Broken Hill.

TOURIST INFORMATION. Broken Hill: Information Center at the corner of Bromide and Blend Sts., Broken Hill. Tel. (080) 6077.

ACCOMMODATION: Several properties cater for paying guests. For further information write to the Broken Hill Information Center or call (Broken Hill) (080) 6077 or 6078.

HOTELS AND MOTELS. Broken Hill: *Hilltop,* 29 units all with shower, air conditioned, electric blankets, telephone, TV. Pool, restaurant.

Crystal, 36 units all with shower, air conditioned, telephone, TV. Convention facilities, restaurant.

The Murray Region

If you wish to spend a holiday in relaxing rather than scenically spectacular surroundings, somewhat off the main tourist track, one of a number of serene little towns along the New South Wales section of the mighty Murray River may be the place to go. The river, which rises in the Australian Alps and after a course of 2,600 km. empties its waters into the sea at Lake Alexandrina in South Australia, is a fisherman's paradise. It also teems with bird life. A special attraction of the Murray region is the properties which take in paying guests for farm holidays. As they may do so one season but not in another, it is wise to obtain details from the information center in Albury, the most important town in the Murray region. The address is: NSW Government Tourist Information Center, Hume Highway, telephone 21-2655.

The Murray was discovered by the explorers Hume and Hovell during their overland trip from Sydney to Port Phillip (Melbourne) in 1824. They called it the Hume. But six years later, in 1830, Captain Charles Sturt "discovered" it again and named it Murray after the British Colonial Secretary of that time. For about a quarter of a century between the early 1850s and the late 1870s the Murray and its tributaries were important trading and transportation channels, with some 100 paddle-steamers and 200 barges plying them. But with the development of the faster rail and road transport, shipping on the Murray began to decline and finally ceased after World War 2. However, in recent years several of the rusting old paddle-wheel river boats have been reconditioned and new ones built, and they are now being used as pleasure boats taking tourists on half-day excursions or week-long trips on several stretches of Australia's "Ol' Man River".

Albury (pop. 35,107), with its twin town of Wodonga across the Murray River in Victoria, was chosen as one of Australia's main "growth centres" in the Australian Government's master plan, now suspended, to divert people from the state capitals on the coast. The choice was a good one. For Albury has many of the requirements of a potentially large urban centre. It is situated along the main railway line and on one of the two main highways which connect Sydney (581 km. away to the north) with Melbourne (308 km. to the south). The national capital of Canberra is 357 km. by road. 3 km. from the city of Albury is the airport with connections to all State capitals and many other places within and outside New South Wales. The Murray provides almost inexhaustible water supplies. The mainly agricultural hinterland is prosperous, and for pleasure and relaxation Albury itself is well provided with cultural and sporting amenities. In addition it is close to the playgrounds of the Australian Alps.

Those pleasant little townships along the Murray River include Corowa, with a first class airfield and a fine 18-hole golf course; Mulwala (on a lake near Corowa) with a "boatel," where guests can moor their boats underneath their units; Tocumwal, with good river beaches nearby; and Moama, Barham and Wentworth, the last-named town being situated near the junction of the Murray and the Darling, Australia's second largest and second most important river.

PRACTICAL INFORMATION FOR THE MURRAY REGION

HOW TO GET THERE. *By train:* Regular services to Albury from Sydney and Melbourne by Inter-Capital Daylight, Southern Aurora and Spirit of Progress.
By air: East-West Airlines from Sydney and Melbourne to Albury.

By bus: Ansett-Pioneer Express, Cobb & Co., and Greyhound provide services from and to Sydney, Melbourne, Adelaide and Brisbane via Albury and other Murray Region towns, including Deniliquin, Holbrook, Tocumwal and Balranald. There are restrictions, however, on bus services, so check with the New South Wales Government Tourist Commission (NSWGTC), in Sydney, Melbourne, or Brisbane before travelling.

HOTELS AND MOTELS. Albury: *TraveLodge,* 140 units, 3 suites, all with shower/bath, air conditioned, telephone, TV. Restaurant, room service including liquor.

Commodore, near swimming pool, Hume Weir (with fishing and skiing) and golf course. 40 units, all with shower, air conditioned. Restaurant.

Corowa: *Corowa Motor Inn,* 36 units, 15 with shower, air conditioned, TV. Cooking facilities in 8 units.

Tocumwal: *Kelly's Thomas Lodge,* 14 units, all with shower, air conditioned, TV. Restaurant (closed on Sunday).

Wentworth: *Two Rivers,* 24 units, 12 suites, restaurant.

The Snowy Canberra/South-east Region

The Snowy Canberra/South-east Region of New South Wales has one of the most varied concentrations of tourist attractions in Australia. The enchantingly beautiful South East Coast is world famous among big game fishermen. It has 250 km. of dreamy bays, inlets and friendly little towns where visitors can stay at modern and well run hotels, motels or caravan parks. And a couple of hundred kilometers away the towering peaks of the Snowy Mountains and of the Kosciusko National Park gaze down on slopes that are snow covered in winter, and bedecked with fragrant wild flowers in spring and summer. Here in the mountains is one of the world's greatest hydro-electric schemes with its picturesque artificial lakes and fast-flowing streams which abound in trout and fish.

Until after World War II it was not easy to reach either the South East Coast or the Snowy Mountains from Sydney or Melbourne. Today travel is very good. From Sydney one may travel to the South East Coast either by train as far as Nowra, then by coach; or alternatively all the way by coach or car along the Princes Highway, which is a fine sealed road connecting Sydney and Melbourne. (Turn off the Federal Highway near Goulburn.) There are also regular passenger flights from Sydney to the fishing center and resort of Merimbula, with connecting buses to other localities. Regular daily coaches run from Melbourne to the area. Visitors to the Snowy Mountains may go by rail or fly from Sydney to Cooma and proceed from there by car or coach, or drive all the way to the snowfields. Tourists from Melbourne can choose between going by road all the way, by plane to Cooma, or by express coach to Canberra with connection to Cooma.

The Princes Highway is a scenically charming road which meanders through lengthy stretches of timbered country near quiet inlets and bays. Motorists are advised not to drive very fast and to overtake with great care on the winding, narrow road. The South East Coast begins some 280 km. south of Sydney near Durras Lake, and 14 km. further one reaches the resort of Batemans Bay on the estuary of the Clyde River. Batemans Bay and the other South Coast localities mentioned are excellent for fishing and for water sports. Fishing villages include Narooma (Aboriginal for "clear blue water") and Bermagui ("canoe-like"), which became internationally famous after the American novelist Zane Grey wrote about their exceptional big game fishing qualities. Two other popular resorts are beautifully situated Merimbula (473 km. from Sydney) and about 50 km. further to the south, Eden, a tuna fishing center.

There are two good roads from the South East Coast to Cooma, the gateway to the Snowy Mountains. One leads from Batemans Bay through Braidwood and Canberra, and another, the Snowy Mountains Highway (branching off Bermagui and Merimbula) through Nimmitabel. Cooma is the most cosmopolitan town in Australia; its 8,000 inhabitants were born in 50 different countries. People of 27 nationalities helped build the Snowy Mountains Hydro-Electric Scheme and their national colours are displayed on high poles in the Avenue of Flags in the town's Centennial Park. Every year thousands of visitors descend on Cooma—mainly skiers in winter and a good many trout fishermen in summer—and many spend a night in the town before dispersing to their destinations in the mountains the following morning.

Mountains and Skiing

The Snowy Mountains cover an area of hundreds of square kilometers and have Australia's highest peaks, including the tallest of them all, the 2230 m. Mount Kosciusko. Why Kosciusko? Because the Polish explorer Paul Edmund de Strzelecki, who found it in 1840, named it after his country's national hero. The national park of the same name, with an area of 6,143 square km., is the largest national park in the New South Wales and contains all of the state's snowfields. In Australia skiing has become a popular sport only since World War 2. Before the war there was only a state-owned hotel and two chalets in the whole vast snow country. Now there are dozens of hotels, motels, and lodges for the general public and many clubs have built "huts," some quite substantial, for their members. One of the main ski-centers is Thredbo Village on the Alpine Way at the foot of Mt. Crackenback (1936 m.), a wilderness some 25 years ago and now a lively playground with ski-lifts and tows on the slopes, and shops and nightclubs for after-ski in the village. It was Charles Anton, an Austrian refugee from Hitler and a ski enthusiast, who saw the potential of the area in the late 1940s and started the movement for a ski-village at Thredbo. The Ramshead Range divides Thredbo from the other two main ski centers of the Kosciusko National Park: Smiggin Holes and Perisher Valley. The old chalet at Charlotte's Pass, near the top of Mt. Kosciusko, is open in the ski season and in the summer holidays. It has been recently refurbished, has excellent ski slopes nearby and is the best starting point for day-long excursions into the silent white world of the Main Range. If you want to spend a few days in the snow country, but have no gear, you need not worry. Practically everything can be hired either in Sydney, Melbourne or on the spot.

Electricity and Trout Fishing

How to use water instead of letting it run to waste in the sea is an old preoccupation of Australians. It was in 1884 that the New South Wales Surveyor-General of that time, P.F. Adams, made a revolutionary proposal. He suggested that the waters of the Snowy River, which rises on the eastern slopes of the Snowy Mountains near Mt. Kosciusko and enters the Tasman sea after winding southwards for about 435 km., should be turned inland and used for irrigation. It took another 65 years before work on the scheme was started, in August 1949, by the newly created Snowy Mountains Hydro-Electric Authority. But then the work was executed on a truly grand scale. Since then the waters of the Snowy Mountains have been diverted into the Murray-Murrumbidgee river system and used not only for irrigation but also for the generation of electric power. Sixteen large dams and many smaller ones, seven power stations, about 130 km. of roads, and 80 km. of aqueducts have been built. The last generator began production in 1974. Total generating capacity of electric power is four million kilowatts, and 2,500 million cubic meters of water are available annually for irrigation.

The man-made lakes and dams and the opening of the rugged Snowy Mountains by roads have enabled the Snowy Mountains Hydro-Electric Authority to create a large trout fishing region which is surely the best in Australia, and a very good one by world standards. The anglers who flock there have added to the development of the mountains as a winter-summer resort paradise which is growing year by year. But it is a controlled growth which is not allowed to threaten the environment or the scenery. Many establishments are now open all the year except for a few weeks around May, a mid-season period when the weather in the area is least favourable for holidaying.

There is a wide variety of trout fishing sites from fast, cascading streams in the high mountains, to the more placid waters of lakes and dams. The best way to approach the trout waters, like the snowfields, is via Cooma. The 188 km. stretch of the Snowy Mountains Highway between Cooma and Tumut—which runs partly through Kosciusko National Park—is studded with excellent trout fishing places. Many of them can offer good accommodation with or without full board.

The main lakes and dams, well stocked with rainbow trout, brown trout, and some Atlantic salmon, are: Jindabyne, Lake Eucumbene (the largest of them all, containing nine times as much water as Sydney Harbour), the Tantangara, Talbingo, and Jounama Dams, and Lake Blowering. The best trout streams can be approached from the centres of Cooma, Dalgety, Jindabyne, Thredbo Alpine Village, Khancoban, Adaminaby, Kiandra, Bombala and Nimmitabel.

PRACTICAL INFORMATION FOR THE SNOWY CANBERRA/SOUTH-EAST REGION

As this region really consists of two different tourist areas, we have divided this section accordingly into two parts. "Seacoast" gives information for the South East Coast, "Mountains" for the Snowy-Kosciusko area.

SEACOAST

HOW TO GET THERE. *By car:* along the Princes Highway. *By train:* to Nowra, then by bus. *By air:* Air NSW to Merimbula. Other regular air-services: Melbourne by Executive Airlines and Kendell Aviation to Merimbula. *By bus:* Ansett-Pioneer Express from Sydney or Melbourne. Check for restrictions concerning bus travel.

One day and half-day *tours:* Batemans Bay: Clyde River Cruises, Mariners Lodge. Eden: Charter Craft and Marine Services, 8 Weecon Street.

 HOTELS AND MOTELS. Batemans Bay: *Mariners Lodge,* water frontage, near golf course. 17 rooms all with shower, air conditioned, telephone, TV. Convention facilities, restaurant. Additional 25 motel units with shower in each.

Clyderiver Lodge, 30 units, 5 suites, all with shower, central heating, fans, telephone, TV. Boat hire.

Bermagui: *Beachview Motel,* 18 units, all with shower, telephone.

Eden: *Halfway,* 30 units, all with shower, TV. Restaurant.

Merimbula: *Black Dolphin,* near surfing beach and golf course. 49 units, all with shower, air conditioned, telephone, TV. Pool, restaurant.

Moruya: *Moruya,* near surf beach and race course. 8 units all with shower, telephone available. Barbecue.

Narooma: *Highway,* near beach, golf course, bowling greens, tennis, fishing and riding. 55 units all with shower, telephone, TV. Cooking facilities in 8 units. Lounge, pool, restaurant.

Whale, 4 units, 8 suites, all with shower, telephone in 10 rooms, cooking facilities in the suites. 2 pools, restaurant.

MOUNTAINS

 TOURIST INFORMATION. Cooma Visitors' Centre, open daily. Films about the area are screened at the Center every day. Kosciusko National Park Visitor Center, Sawpit Creek (just inside the entrance to the Park on Mt. Kosciusko Road). New South Wales Government Travel Centers at Sydney. NSW Government Tourist Information Centres at Albury, Tweed Heads.

 HOW TO GET THERE. From Sydney: *By car:* Via Hume Highway to Goulburn, thence via Federal Highway to Canberra and Monaro Highway to Cooma. Via Princes Highway to Batemans Bay, then Braidwood–Canberra–Cooma. Princes Highway to Bega, then Nimmitabel–Cooma via Snowy Mountains Highway.

By train: via Goulburn to Cooma, then by coach, taxi or rental car.

By air: Cooma airport, then coach, taxi or rental car. **From Melbourne:** *by car:* Via Hume Highway and Corryong–Cabramurra–Kiandra–Cooma. Via Hume Highway, Corryong, Khancoban, Murray One Power Station, Scammel's Spur Lookout, Thredbo, Jindabyne on Alpine Way, Cooma. Via Princes Highway, Cann River, Bombala, Cooma (on Monaro Highway).

By air: Cooma Aerodrome.

By bus: Express coach to Canberra, with connection to Cooma. Weekend coach tours run from Sydney to the snowfields between June and October. The coaches leave Sydney between 6 P.M. and 9 P.M. on Fridays, arrive on the snowfields early Saturday morning, leave again for Sydney on Sunday afternoon, and arrive in Sydney between 1:30 A.M. and 2:30 A.M. on Monday. As the schedule reveals, this is for the young and hardy.

 HOTELS AND MOTELS. Jindabyne: *Alpine Gables,* 42 units all with shower, central heating, air cooling, telephone, TV. Restaurant, spa, sauna.

Siesta Villa, 34 units all with shower, central heating. Restaurant (closed on Wednesday in summer).

Smiggin Holes: *Smiggins Hotel,* good ski hotel/motel with all modern conveniences in the heart of the Kosciusko National Park.

Perisher: *The Man from Snowy River,* 50 rooms, all with shower, central heating, pool, lounge, restaurant.

Marritz Chalet, smallish but excellent establishment with very comfortable rooms (all with bathroom), heated internal pool and very good Austrian cuisine. Rather expensive.

Thredbo Village: *Thredbo Alpine Hotel,* largest hotel in the Australian Alps, 63 rooms, all with shower. Central heating, heated pool, sauna, bar and restaurant.

The Riverina Region

The Riverina region will fascinate those interested in agricultural activities and irrigation schemes. Except for its mountainous southeastern part, the Riverina consists of a succession of sprawling plains with sheep and cattle pastures, wheat fields and, on the irrigated land, orchards and vineyards. The 1690 km. Murrumbidgee (an Aboriginal word for "big river"), one of Australia's largest waterways, rolls through it, supplying the irrigation channels of the Murrumbidgee Irrigation Area (MIA)—1300 square km. of verdant oasis in an otherwise dry countryside.

Tourists driving from Sydney to Melbourne who wish to visit the MIA may stop at Wagga Wagga, "capital" of the Riverina (485 km. southwest of Sydney), a thriving and developing town on the Murrumbidgee River with a population of about 36,832. A tour of Wagga Wagga and of the three main centers of the MIA, Narrandera, Leeton and Griffith, can be fitted into a day's outing. The MIA maintains a Tourist Information Center at Narrandera Park, open Mondays to Fridays and Saturday mornings.

PRACTICAL INFORMATION FOR THE RIVERINA REGION

HOW TO GET THERE. *By rail:* Regular rail services are provided by the Inter-Capital Daylight Express, Riverina Express, Southern Aurora, South Mail and Spirit of Progress.

By air: From Sydney: Air NSW to Wagga, Narrandera. From Melbourne: Kendell Aviation to Griffith and Wagga. *By bus:* Ansett-Pioneer: Melbourne–Sydney via Gundagai, Melbourne–Brisbane via Griffith, Adelaide–Sydney via Hay, Darlington Point, Griffith, Barellan, Ardlethan, Temora, Cootamundra. Melbourne–Brisbane via Wagga, Cootamundra. Adelaide–Sydney via Hay, Ardlethan. Greyhound: Melbourne–Sydney via Wagga, Gundagai. Melbourne–Brisbane via Hay. Check regarding restrictions on bus travel.

HOTELS AND MOTELS. Cootamundra: *Cootamundra Gardens,* 23 units with shower, air conditioned. Pool, restaurant (closed on Sunday).

Griffith: *Acacia,* 59 units, 4 suites with shower, air conditioned, telephone, TV.

Gundagai: *Sheridan,* 17 units with shower.

Hay: *Inlander,* 41 units with shower, air conditioned. Pool, convention facilities, restaurant.

Leeton: *Leeton Gardens,* 24 units with shower, air conditioned, telephone, TV. Restaurant.

Riverina, 38 units with shower, air conditioned. Barbecue, TV lounge, pool.

Narrandera: *Fig Tree,* 22 units with shower, air conditioned, telephone, TV. Pool, sauna, restaurant and room service.

Tumut: *The Creel,* 15 units with shower, air conditioned. Telephone available, TV, pool.

Wagga Wagga: *Carriage House,* 37 units with shower, air conditioned, restaurant and room service.

Koala Welcome Inn, 50 units with shower, air conditioned, telephone, TV. Pool, restaurant.

Wagga Town House, 38 units with shower. Central heating. restaurant (closed on Sunday).

Greater Sydney Outer Region

Like the Snowy Canberra/South-east region, the adjoining Outer region has a double personality. Its 242 km. of coastline, skirted by the Princes Highway, is the dream-come-true of people who love water sports, don't want to be crowded, but wish to enjoy the comforts of our technological age. But if you leave the Princes Highway, say at Oak Flats, and drive for less than an hour along the Illawarra Highway, you will be in the heart of the Southern Highlands, where the atmosphere recalls the countryside of England. The Southern Highlands have none of the majesty of the Australian Alps or the mild beauty of certain parts of the Blue Mountains. But they are mellow, lovely and charming. Although winter days can be cold and summer days hot, the climate is pleasant in spring, and in autumn simply wonderful. Small wonder that many people settle there after retirement.

The Coast

Illawarra is an Aboriginal term meaning "high place near the sea", and indeed, for lengthy stretches the Princes Highway runs through hills which advance to the sea shores, offering spectacular vistas of the coastline.

Setting out from Sydney, the first and last big city on the Princes Highway is Wollongong, with a population of about 208,601. Wollongong is now the third-largest city in New South Wales. It is a bustling industrial city with a large percentage of "New Australians" who give the place a distinctly cosmopolitan character. Port Kembla—which is part of Wollongong—is the site of one of the world's largest steelworks, established in 1928. Between Port Kembla and Shellharbour is Lake Illawarra, a 42 square km. "pool" with popular camping sites and a reputation for excellent prawns. Shellharbour itself is an attractive secluded spot which got its name from the many shells once found on its shores.

Kiama, 120 km. from Sydney, is the next important resort. Cattle breeders know it as the place where the famous Australian Illawarra Shorthorn (AIS) cattle were developed.

One of Kiama's main tourist attractions is the Blowhole, a few minutes' walk from the main shopping centre. When strong southeasterly seas are running, as they often do, a large volume of water surges high into the air and falls back into the sea. At night the Blowhole is illuminated with multi-colored flood lights.

Visitors to Kiama should not miss the Minnamura Falls Reserve, a natural rainforest area only 15 km. from the sea.

Another 45 km. on is Nowra/Bomaderry, where the South Coast railway terminates and buses take over passengers heading further south. Nowra is a busy tourist center with all kinds of sporting facilities on water and land—including a beautifully laid out 18-hole golf course on the Shoalhaven River. It is also the focal point of nine smaller resorts nearby and a starting point for a large number of scenic attractions within a radius of 40 km. A Tourist Center at Bomaderry near the bridge which connects it with Nowra will provide detailed information to visitors.

The seaside between Nowra and Durras Lake at the southern border of the Outer region is studded with bays and lakes with well developed holiday amenities. Jervis Bay (172 km. south of Sydney), which is partly Commonwealth of Australia territory and is the site of the Royal Australian Naval College and other naval establishments, is one of them. Others include Sussex Inlet at the mouth of the St. Georges Basin; Lake Conjola, Burrill Lake, Tabourie Lake and Durras Lake. Just off Princes Highway, north of Ulladulla, is a lovely little spot called Mollymook with some of the South Coast's finest beaches and a pleasant little golf course near the surf.

The Marlin Hotel, in neighbouring Ulladulla, is well known among Australian and international big-game fishermen for its service, accommodation and cuisine. Fishing is the most important local industry, most of the fishermen being Italians or of Italian descent. Their Blessing of the Fleet festival, stretching over four days at Easter, includes the colourful ceremony of blessing the fishing boats by Catholic priests.

The Southern Highlands

Staying at one of the hotels or motels in the favourite tourist resorts of the Southern Highlands—Mittagong, Bowral, Moss Vale and Bundanoon—you will find a large proportion of New Australians of Central European origin among the guests, especially in spring and in autumn when the trees in bloom or rust coloured foliage awake memories of their native lands. In addition, the four townships are relatively near to Sydney and communications between them and the city by road and rail are good. The main railway line from Sydney to the south-west and to Melbourne traverses the area, as does the Hume Highway, although only Mittagong—now connected with Sydney by a new 80 km. expressway— is situated directly on the Highway. There are many easy bushwalks, and short drives lead to scenic lookouts over hundreds of square km. of wildlife reserves and parks.

Early in Australia's history, in 1798, John Wilson, an ex-convict turned explorer who lived for some time with Aborigines, penetrated the Southern Highlands. In 1803, John Macarthur received the grant of land at Camden where he carried out the wool-growing experiments which played such an important part in Australia's economic development. The well-kept farms and properties, and the beautifully tended gardens surrounded by hawthorn hedges, give the area an especially neat and friendly appearance.

There are several popular festivals in the area: in February Mittagong stages the Dahlia Festival; in March Moss Vale holds a Bush Week in conjunction with the annual Agricultural Show; and in October Bowral's

Tulip Festival takes place. Every second year at Easter the Australian *Musica Viva Society* turns Mittagong into a music-center for four days with lectures and chamber-music performances, usually by at least one ensemble of international renown. The Morton National Park, with headquarters at Fitzroy Falls near Moss Vale on the Nowra Road, has spectacular lookouts and pleasant picnic grounds. So are the Wombeyan limestone caves in the Mittagong area.

Four km. from Mittagong along the Hume Highway a road turns off and runs for 65 km. through breathtaking mountain scenery to Wombeyan. Five of the caves are fully developed for inspection, and tours accompanied by expert guides start from the Kui Kiosk at Wombeyan five times a day. The road between Mittagong and the Wombeyan Caves is only partly sealed but quite good, though careful driving is necessary. A longer road (162 km.) to the Caves from Mittagong via Moss Vale, Goulburn, and Taralga is easier going, especially for cars towing caravans. Accommodation is available at Goulburn, about 80 km. from Wombeyan.

PRACTICAL INFORMATION FOR THE GREATER SYDNEY OUTER REGION

HOW TO GET THERE. *By rail:* To Nowra (Bomaderry) and from there by bus. There are several trains daily from Sydney to Mittagong, Bowral, Moss Vale and Bundanoon. *By bus:* Ansett-Pioneer runs express coach services from Melbourne to Sydney via Nowra, Berry and Wollongong. Greyhound Express from Melbourne to Sydney via Mittagong. *By car:* Along the Princes Highway. To the Southern Highlands via Hume Highway.

HOTELS AND MOTELS. Berrima: *Berrima Bakehouse,* 18 units with shower, central heating, heated indoor pool.
Bowral: *Golf View,* 23 units with shower. Restaurant (closed on Sunday).

The Ivy Tudor Village, 22 units with shower, central heating, air cooling. Restaurant.

Craigieburn, 66 rooms (62 with shower/bath). TV lounge, pool, golf course.

Links House, recently modernized. Old-world charm. Opposite golf links. Good cuisine. Very personal attention by owners Mary and Barry Gray.

Bundanoon: *Holiday Motel,* 21 units with shower, TV. Heated pool, restaurant.

Kiama: *Briggdale Seaside,* 7 units with shower, telephone, TV. Barbecue.

Gibson's, 17 units with shower, fans in some units. Barbecue.

Motel 617, 19 units with shower. Telephone available, TV, pool, playground.

Mittagong: *Melrose,* 16 units with shower. Central heating, fans, TV.

Poplars, 15 units with shower, TV. Restaurant (closed on Sunday).

Moss Vale: *Dormie House,* private hotel, adjoins golf course. 31 rooms, 3 suites, with shower/bath. TV available (fee).

Bong Bong Motel, 10 units with shower, fans available, heating.

Nowra: *Parkhaven,* 30 units with shower, air conditioned, telephone, TV, restaurant and room service, pool, convention facilities, baby sitting.

Valdemere, 25 units with shower, air conditioned, TV, restaurant.

Ulladulla: *Windmill,* 9 units, all with shower, fans, telephone, TV.

Town Motel, 10 units with shower, air conditioned.

Mollymook: *Surfside,* near surf and golf course. 15 units with shower.

Mollymook, 10 units with shower, TV.

Wollongong: Boat Harbour, 44 units with shower, telephone, TV. Restaurant (closed Sunday), room service.

Downtown, near beaches, golf, bowling clubs and shopping centre. 31 units with shower, air conditioning in 9 units, restaurant (closed on Sunday), room service including liquor.

The Golden West Region

The Golden West region is a vast, prosperous, mainly pastoral area of New South Wales with one main tourist attraction: the Jenolan Caves. Yet if you want to spend a few days or even weeks relaxing in a rural atmosphere, living the life of the people on the land, this is an excellent area in which to do it. Several homesteads take in paying guests, giving the visitor a sheep-station holiday where he or she can watch or participate in work on the property. Most of these places are near the towns of Bathurst, Orange, Cowra and Parkes.

The region is full of places closely connected with Australia's early history. Bathurst, for instance, is Australia's oldest inland city, founded by Governor Lachlan Macquarie in 1815, two years after the crossing of the Blue Mountains by Blaxland, Wentworth and Lawson. It was near this town that gold was discovered, starting Australia's colourful gold rush days. This was also one of the most notorious bushranger areas, where outlaws made life insecure until well into the second half of the last century.

It was Cowra, a town of the Golden West region, which saw one of the most dramatic, behind-the-front-line episodes of the Pacific zone in World War II. On August 4, 1944 Japanese prisoners-of-war in the Cowra camp attempted a mass break for freedom. It was a suicidal venture in which some 250 Japanese and four Australian soldiers died. They are buried in separate well-tended cemeteries adjacent to each other.

There are several ways to visit the region's most interesting tourist attraction, the Jenolan Caves. They are situated 183 km. by road from Sydney and can be seen in one day's return trip. But it is advisable to spend at least one night at Jenolan Caves House a pleasant old-fashioned hotel built in 1898 (and several times extended and renovated since) where accommodation is comfortable and the tariff reasonable. (Book through Travel Centre of N.S.W.) Another, and perhaps even more pleasant way, is to combine a visit to the caves with a holiday in the Blue Mountains near Sydney, for the caves are only 77 km. from Katoomba.

The discovery of the Jenolan Caves is connected with an episode in the "romantic" history—as it is now regarded—of the bushranger era. In the 1830s an escaped convict called James McKeown was the terror of travelers along the Western Road in the Blue Mountains. In 1838, one of his victims, James Whalan, decided to take revenge by hunting down the bushranger in his hideout. He found McKeown's tracks and followed them on horseback through unexplored country until—after riding through a huge natural archway which he called the Devil's Coachhouse —he looked down on a peaceful valley with a small farm at the bottom. He concluded that it must be the bushranger's refuge, and next day returned with his brother Charles and a couple of troopers. They captured McKeown in a big cave in the mountainside—now known as McKeown's Hole—and found that the place was full of similar "holes".

After delivering McKeown to the authorities, the brothers returned and explored more of the caves.

In 1866 the New South Wales Government declared the caves and their environment a reserve. A lot of work has been done on both over the year, and now the caves can be comfortably inspected.

Jenolan has two types of caves: great natural archways which can be inspected independently, and underground "dark" caves which can be visited only in the company of a guide. Cave tours depart several times daily. They last about an hour and a half. No special clothing is necessary, but well-soled shoes are advisable.

Another group of caves is at Abercrombie, some 76 km. from Bathurst. They are not as spectacular as the Jenolan Caves but have a Grand Arch claimed to be the greatest natural tunnel in the world. It is 221 m. long, 60 m. wide and in places more than 30 m. high.

PRACTICAL INFORMATION FOR THE GOLDEN WEST

TOURIST INFORMATION. There are some two-dozen tourist information centers in the region, with the major ones at Bathurst, Cowra, Forbes, Lithgow, Orange and Parkes. Some will make travel and/or accommodation bookings, including bookings for farm holidays.

HOW TO GET THERE. *By train:* Regular rail services are provided by the Central West Express, and the Western Mail.

    By air: From Sydney: Hazelton to Orange, East Coast to Cowra. Hazelton Airlines to Coandobolin. From Canberra: Hazelton Air Services to Orange.

By bus: Ansett-Pioneer, and Greyhound run express coaches through the region in their Melbourne-Brisbane services. Check about restrictions on bus travel.

Jenolan Caves: *By train and bus:* Electric trains run from Sydney daily to Katoomba, where passengers transfer to the local rail company (the trip takes less than four hours). *By bus:* Coaches run from Sydney (7½ hours) as well as from Katoomba and Blackheath and in summer from Bathurst. *By car:* Motorists setting out from Sydney take the Great Western Highway to Mount Victoria (124 km.). From there the Highway descends through Mitchell's Pass to Hartley and the Lett River Bridge (135 km.). Immediately beyond this bridge the Jenolan Caves Road branches to the left of the Great Western Highway, running for 39 km. to the Caves.

HOTELS AND MOTELS. Bathurst: *Telford Bathurst,* 70 units, 3 suites, all with shower, air conditioned, telephone, TV. Restaurant (closed on Sunday), pool, playground, convention facilities.

    Forbes: *Telford Plainsman, Motor Inn,* 44 units with shower, air conditioned, telephone, TV. Pool, restaurant.

    Orange: *Oriana,* 47 units with shower, central heating, fans, telephone, TV. Pool, restaurant.

    Parkes: *Bushman's Motor Inn,* 35 units with shower, air conditioned, telephone, TV. Pool, restaurant (closed on Sunday).

    West Wyalong: *Charles Sturt,* 34 units with shower, air conditioned, telephone, TV. Pool, sauna, restaurant.

Lord Howe Island

The tiny—11 km. long, 2 km. wide—Lord Howe Island is a heavily forested green speck 702 km. east of Sydney in the Pacific Ocean. What it can offer to tourists is pleasant climate the year round, relaxing holidays with such unsophisticated pastimes as fishing, bush-walking or bicycling, and accommodation in simple guest houses. The island has a permanent population of some 250. Many of its visitors are "regulars" who return for a holiday year after year. There is a golf course.

Transport from the Mainland to "Lord Howe" (which is a dependency of New South Wales) is by air.

From Sydney: Daily service by Norfolk Island Airlines. **From Brisbane:** Services Wednesday and Saturday by Norfolk Island Airways. **From Port Macquarie:** Services Wednesday and Saturday by Oxley Airlines.

Tourist Information: Lord Howe Island Tourist Center, Suite 31, 310 George St. Sydney 2000, tel(02)233-2111.

Norfolk Island

Norfolk Island, 1449 km. off the east coast of Australia, is a beautiful little (8 km. long, 4 km. wide) spot of volcanic origin in the Pacific Ocean. Since 1914 it has been a territory of the Australian Commonwealth. (Before that it belonged to New South Wales.)

Every year some 10,000 people spend their holidays on the island; fishing, swimming, walking, playing golf (on a nine-hole course) and bowls—or simply lazing in the mellow sunshine.

Despite its tiny size, Norfolk Island has an interesting history. Sighted by Captain Cook in 1774, it became a penal colony in 1788. Until 1855, when it was closed, the most intractable prisoners were sent there. Some of the buildings which they erected are still in use; they form the nucleus of Kingston, the administrative headquarters of the island.

In 1856, the year after the last convict had been taken from the island, the place was voluntarily settled by the 194 residents of Pitcairn Island. They were the descendants of the mutineers of the *Bounty* who, in 1789, had cast adrift in an open boat their captain, William Bligh, with 18 of the men who wished to go with him. The mutineers, commanded by Fletcher Christian, then settled on Pitcairn Island with some Polynesian (Tahitian) women. Today half of Norfolk Island's permanent population of about 1,000 have a *"Bounty* ancestry".

The best way to get to Norfolk Island is by air: With Air N.S.W. and East-West Airlines. Some small ships call on the island but they are unreliable because landing is allowed in good weather only and therefore cannot be guaranteed. Hotel and guest house accommodation is reasonable and holiday flats and cottages are available.

Information: Norfolk Island Tourist Board, PO Box 211, Norfolk Island 2889, Pacific Ocean.

AUSTRALIAN CAPITAL TERRITORY

Canberra and Environs

In 1901 when the federation of Australia became established the new country had a proper government—without a proper home. For Australia had no capital; it was governed mainly from Melbourne where parliament also sat. Certainly, the Constitution provided that a capital should be built. It had to be somewhere within the area of New South Wales at least 160 km from Sydney. On selection of the site it would be transferred from State to Commonwealth jurisdiction. Many communities, wanting to become the future centre of Australian political and administrative life, had offered themselves for the role. None was accepted. It was eight years before, in 1908, a suitable site was chosen on the western slopes of the Great Dividing Range, about 310 km from Sydney and 660 km from Melbourne. The area of 2,359 square km was transferred from New South Wales to the Commonwealth. It consisted mainly of cleared grazing land with two tiny villages (Hall and Tharwa), five mountain peaks above 1,500 meters, and the narrow Molongolo River, a tributary of the Murrumbidgee, running through it. But what should the new capital be called? Suggestions poured in but it was not until 1913—when the first buildings were begun—that the choice was made. Australia's capital was to be called Canberra, an Aboriginal word meaning "meeting place."

An international competition to select the design of the new capital was won by the distinguished American architect Walter Burley Griffin in 1909. But more than 40 years passed before Canberra's development really got under way. Earlier, because of the two World Wars and the depression in between, there was no money available for the ambitious project. Besides, few people wanted to live in a place which was nominally a city, but in reality a huge building site with empty spaces between the few houses standing in forlorn isolation. A temporary parliament building was finished in 1927—with extensions it is still in use; a small shopping centre was erected—it is still there; comparatively modest homes for the Governor-General and for the Prime Minister were constructed—they still live in them; and a few government departments, including the Prime Minister's, managed to function from crowded quarters in Canberra. But as soon as parliament was adjourned on Fridays for the weekend the great scramble home began and for a while after World War II a roster system had to be introduced so that at least one Minister, in addition to the Prime Minister, stayed in the capital on Saturdays and Sundays. In the 1950s, when the Federal Government began to insist that diplomatic representatives should move from Sydney to Canberra, a veil of gloom descended on the illustrious ambassadors and their staffs.

Seeing Canberra today one would hardly believe that this was the situation only about two decades ago. For, whatever its shortcomings may be, the national capital is one of the world's most beautiful modern planned cities. Some 12 million trees and shrubs planted in its open spaces have transformed the former grazing paddocks into continuous parklands. Damming of the Molonglo has created Lake Burley Griffin, a peaceful expanse of water with 36 km of park shores including the Commonwealth Gardens. The architectural style of the public building ranges from good to excellent and many of the new embassies, built by some of the 61 foreign diplomatic representations in the national capital, are show pieces. Occasionally some of them open their doors for public inspection—at a small charge, which goes to charity.

Canberra's rate of growth has outstripped that of any other place in Australia. In 1957 only some 36,000 people lived here, 20 years later more than 200,000, and by today the population is in excess of 240,000 people. A large proportion of the population consists of New Australians and many of them work in the service industries, including tourism. More than two-and-a-half million tourists a year now flock to Canberra merely to see the country's capital. They can stay in numerous hotels or motels—some of the best in the country. The best season to visit Canberra is spring, when the thousands of Australian and exotic trees and bushes are in bloom, or in autumn when the mellow sun shines on rusty foliage. Summer, on the other hand, can be hot and winter rather cold.

Although politics and government provide most of the jobs in Canberra—about 60% of the population is in the public service—the capital is fast developing into an artistic and intellectual centre. The National University is here and so are the headquarters of several scientific institutions, including the Commonwealth Scientific and Industrial Research Organisation (CSIRO) and the Academy of Science. The attractive Civic Centre provides theatre and concerts. For those who wish to spend their holidays in Canberra, the city offers a wide choice of sporting activities including rowing, swimming, horse riding and golf, and even a nude bathing beach on the banks of the Murrumbidgee River. Certainly, Canberra has many critics who bewail the social stratification which

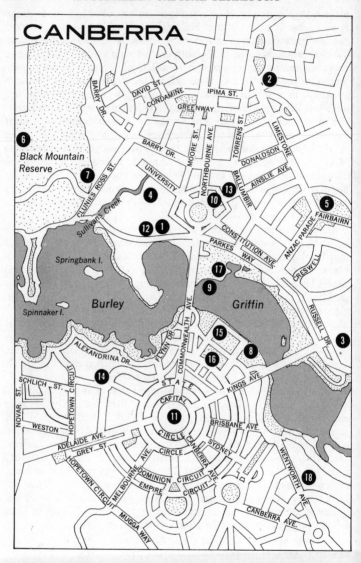

CANBERRA

Points of Interest

1) Academy of Science
2) All Saints Church
3) Australian American Memorial
4) Australian National University
5) Australian War Memorial
6) Black Mountain Lookout and Telecom Tower
7) Botanic Garden
8) National Gallery and High Court
9) Capt. Cook Memorial Water Jet
10) Civic Square and Theater Center
11) Capital Hill
12) Institute of Anatomy
13) Monaro Mall
14) Mosque
15) National Library
16) Parliament House
17) Planning Exhibition
18) Railway Station

automatically puts one into a niche according to his or her political pecking order or public service rank; the loneliness, especially of young wives and mothers who had to move to Canberra leaving behind their close relations and friends; the boredom, such as felt by some foreign diplomats used to pulsating urban life and unable to become reconciled to the slow-motion provincialism of Australia's national capital. Still, the advantages of living in a beautiful city away from the hectic bustle, pollution and traffic problems of the major cities obviously outstrip the drawbacks.

Canberra proper occupies only the northern part of the Australian Capital Territory (ACT)—the area acquired by the Commonwealth—and three new townships, Woden, Belconnen and Tuggeranong have been developed to cope with the swelling population, for Canberra is tearing at its seams. The ACT has a fully elected 18-member House of Assembly but is primarily administered by a Federal Minister for the Capital Territory. The people of Canberra elect two members to the House of Representatives and two to the Senate of the Federal Parliament.

Exploring Canberra

Parliament House is the obvious place to begin an inspection of Canberra's important buildings. It was erected as a transitional solution—"something more than provisional and less than permanent"—between 1923 and 1927. The Founding Fathers of Federation dreamed of something more grandiose. But by 1923 the parliamentarians who had assembled in Melbourne since Federation in 1901, realised that if they insisted on carrying out the founder's plans they would have to wait longer before they could move to the national capital. Hence they decided to make do with something more modest for the next 50 years or so. At that time (1923) the Federal Parliament had only 36 Senators and 74 members of the House of Representatives, so the building to which they moved in 1927 was at least adequate for their needs. Today the Senate has 76 members and the House of Representatives has 148. With additions during the past half-century the number of rooms stands now at 638 and even this is insufficient, so construction of a new Parliament House, planned for completion in 1989, has begun on Capital Hill.

But the old building will probably be maintained, and rightly so. Admittedly, its architecture is not memorable, but it is quite a pleasant building. And, after all, it is an historical relic which will be better appreciated with the passing of time. The interior of Parliament House, though not spectacular, is in muted good taste. The main entrance leads to the colonnaded King's Hall, decorated with portraits of the Queen, by Australian artists, past Governors-General, Prime Ministers, Presidents of the Senate and Speakers of the House of Representatives. The most interesting exhibit in King's Hall is one of the three surviving copies of Magna Carta in its 1297 version. On the right of King's Hall (looking into it from the entrance) is the chamber of the Senate and to the left is that of the House of Representatives.

Visitors may sit in the galleries and listen to the proceedings of either the Senate or the House of Representatives. Tickets of admission may be obtained on application to the Principal Attendant personally, or by mail. There are no tours of inspection when both Houses are sitting.

However, when only one House is in session, public tours of the other Chamber are provided. When sittings commence in the afternoon, tours operate in the morning. The house is open daily.

The National Library, designed by the Sydney architects, Bunning, Madden and O'Mahoney, stands on the southern shore of Lake Burley Griffin. It was built between 1964 and 1968 at a cost of about A$8 million. It is a building of classical simplicity, and its perfect proportions make it look smaller than it really is (110 meters long and 52 meters wide). Many fine Australian materials, including timber, have been used in its interior decoration. There are several exhibition areas, a theatre seating 300 people and a main reading room seating 150. There are other reading rooms for special studies and for newspapers and periodicals. Altogether the library has more than three million volumes but it can be extended to store many more. Artistic features of the National Library include a copper relief above the entrance door by Australian sculptor Tom Bass; on the lake side of the building a bronze casting by Henry Moore; in the foyer three tapestries designed by Mathieu Mategot and woven of Australian wool at Aubusson, France. The library also exhibits relics of Captain Cook's voyages. Guided tours of the library start at 11:15 A.M. and 2:15 P.M. Monday to Friday. It is open seven days a week. The High Court building, opposite the library, was completed in 1980 and is another of the attractions in the Parliamentary Triangle. Next to it stands the new National Gallery, opened in October 1982. Visiting hours are 10 A.M.–5 P.M. Monday through Saturday; 12 noon to 5 P.M. Sunday.

Some Memorials

Erected to commemorate the men and women of Australia who gave their lives in their country's wars, the War Memorial is one of the world's most important military museums. It was originally started to commemorate Australian servicemen and women of World War I but when it was opened on November 11, 1941, World War II was well on its way. The exhibition galleries contain an enormous wealth of war equipment and pictures. The Library and Records section has a collection of more than 12,000 paintings, sketches and sculptures, more than 250,000 photographic negatives and prints, and in excess of 1,200,000 metres of historic film. The library also holds 75,000 books, 5,000 volumes of bound periodicals, 150,000 diaries and memoirs. The Australian War Memorial is open to visitors every day except Christmas Day.

Canberra has paid tribute to the memory of Captain Cook by installing a powerful water jet in the Central Basin of Lake Burley Griffin in the cove below Regatta Point, some 180 metres from the shoreline. The jet can spout a column of water weighing some six tons about 150 metres into the air. The sight is as beautiful as it is impressive. A mechanism automatically turns off the jet when the wind reaches a velocity of 19.2 km per hour and turns it on again when the windspeed drops below that figure. A globe on the shore, three metres in diameter, shows the routes taken by Captain Cook and they are described on the handrail surrounding it. The Captain Cook Memorial operates daily from 10 A.M. to noon, from 2 P.M. to 4 P.M.; from 8:30 P.M. to 9:30 P.M. (with floodlights) during daylight saving time (end of October to the beginning of March) and other special occasions as directed by the Department of Capital Territory.

The Canberra Carillon, which stands on Aspen Island near Kings Avenue Bridge in Lake Burley Griffin, is a gift from the United Kingdom Government to mark Canberra's 50th birthday. It is one of the largest of its kind in the world and has 53 bells. The biggest of them weighs six tons and the smallest 7 kgs. The three-column tower was built by the British Ministry of Buildings and Public Works; the bells were cast and the "clavier" (playing keyboard and frame) was constructed by John Taylor and Sons, Loughborough, England. Recitals are given regularly and the Westminster chimes, which sound every quarter of an hour between 8 A.M. and 9 P.M., are relayed by landline to the city centre.

The Australian-American Memorial, a 79-metre aluminium shaft surmounted by an eagle, commemorates America's help in the defence of Australia in World War II. It stands in the centre of a building complex housing the Defence departments at Russell. The Australian National University's grounds are open to the public. Tours may be arranged for interested groups through the University Information Office in Balmain Crescent. The headquarters of the Australian Academy of Science is one of Canberra's landmarks: a copper-covered shell concrete dome, 46 m. in diameter. Opposite, in the Institute of Anatomy buildings, there is an interesting exhibition of Aboriginal history and culture. The Civic Square and Theatre Centre are on a rather small scale. The Centre consists of two buildings: the larger Canberra Theatre, really an auditorium, seating 1,200 people, and the smaller Playhouse seating 312. Outside the city proper on the Murrumbidgee River within the limits of the Tuggeranong new town development, stands Lanyon homestead, owned by the Australian Government. Nearby is a gallery which houses an exhibition of Sidney Nolan paintings, a gift of the famous artist to the nation. The Royal Military College, Duntroon, can be seen by joining a conducted tour held every day at 2:30 P.M. from Monday to Friday between April and October. People interested in Australian flora should visit the National Botanic Gardens (entry from Clunies Ross Street) which are devoted entirely to Australian native plants. The gardens are laid out on the slopes of Black Mountain, on the summit of which rises the Telecom Tower.

PRACTICAL INFORMATION FOR CANBERRA

HOW TO GET THERE. *By air:* Canberra is connected by direct flights to Adelaide, Brisbane, Sydney, Melbourne, Newcastle, Wagga, Griffith, Orange, and Dubbo. Six flights operate daily from Sydney and six from Melbourne. *By rail:* Canberra has a direct rail link with Sydney. From Melbourne passengers disembark at Yass Junction and connect by motorcoach. *By bus:* Direct passenger coaches run between Canberra and Sydney, Melbourne, Sale, Adelaide, Narooma, Wollongong, Bega, Orange, and Cooma. From other mainland capitals there are connections through Sydney and Melbourne.

Motorists may contact the NRMA centre at Northbourne Avenue, tel. 433-777 for information and 474-444 for 24-hour emergency road service. Gas is available in Braddon (24-hour supply) from stations on the inner city perimeter. Parking: a red-painted curb indicates a no-parking area.

MEDICAL EMERGENCIES. Canberra Hospital, Acton Peninsula, 432-111; Woden Valley Hospital, Yamba Dr., Garran, tel. 81-0433; Calvary Hospital, Haydon Dr., Bruce, tel. 52911. Emergency calls for ambulance, police and fire free of charge, 000.

ENTERTAINMENT. A free booklet, "This Week in Canberra," containing current theatre, concert and movie listings is available from hotel desks, travel bureaus etc.

HOTELS AND MOTELS. Rates, for double rooms, are classified as follows: *Expensive:* A$70 and up; *Moderate:* A$50–69; *Inexpensive:* below A$50.

Canberra International Motor Inn. *Expensive.* Northbourne Ave. City's newest; opened March 1981. First-class facilities, including 115 units (9 are luxury suites), and unusual central court with pool, bar, restaurant. Coffee shop, gift shop, 24-hour service, courtesy limousine. 2 km. from town center.

Hotel Canberra Rex. *Expensive.* Northbourne Ave., Braddon. First-class hotel about 1.5 km. from city centre. 158 rooms with private facilities and 18 suites. All facilities in this class of hotel—including restaurants, guest lounges, bars, swimming pool, tour arrangements. 24 hour service, entertainment some nights.

Noahs Lakeside International Hotel. *Expensive.* London Circuit. 16-story first-class hotel beside Lake Burley Griffin. 215 units including luxury suites. All premises are air conditioned. Two restaurants, four lounge bars, a coffee shop, two cocktail bars and a heated swimming pool. 24-hour room service.

Parkroyal Motor Inn. *Expensive.* Northbourne Ave. One km. from town center. First class with 77 units, restaurant, bar, pool, sauna, 24-hour service.

TraveLodge Canberra City. *Expensive.* Northbourne Ave. and Cooyong St., Braddon. Five minutes' walk from city centre. 72 units with private facilities. Very comfortable. Amenities include restaurant, swimming pool, 24-hour room service.

Embassy Motel. *Moderate.* Adelaide Avenue and Hopetoun Circuit, Deakin, about 3 km. from city centre. 84 units with private facilities. Air conditioned, swimming pool, a reasonable restaurant, nearby shopping centre.

Nineteenth Hole. *Inexpensive.* Adjacent to Gloucester golf course. 22 units, all with private bathrooms, TVs, radios, telephones. Laundry, pool.

Noahs Town House Motor Inn. *Inexpensive.* 12 Rudd St., Canberra City. In the centre of the national capital. 68 units with private facilities. Very good restaurant on the premises.

 DINING OUT. There are some 200 eating spots in Canberra and its immediate environment. Many of them serve the special tastes of certain ethnic communities. The Canberra Consumers Inc. (a non-profit making body) publishes a small booklet on them. Five Canberra restaurants received 1984 Golden Plates Awards, given every two years to restaurants judged on menu, catering, decor, and value for money. The winners are: *Peaches; Nobb's; Hill Station; Jean-Pierre Le Carousel;* and *The Hermitage.*

Canberra Tourist Bureau, corner London Circuit and West Row, Canberra City, provides information and brochures for visitors.

VICTORIA

A Pioneering State

by
ANTHONY BERRY

While all other Australian states long ago had labels attached which came about as a natural development of some singular attribute or ambiance (Queensland, "the Sunshine State", Tasmania, "the Apple Isle"), Victoria had to wait for government action as recently as 1977 before it was officially tagged "the Garden State."

Not surprisingly, it was a label that Victorians themselves were slow to adopt, for such descriptions cannot be applied by official decree. Decrees are subject to change and following a State election in 1982 the new Labor Government let it be known that it did not favor this title.

So Victoria—although admittedly well-endowed with gardens—may have to wait some time for an alternative "tourist tag".

Where History Lives

Better, we feel, to think of Victoria as the historical state, for few others can better it for its wealth of outstanding memorials to the country's pioneering past. History lives in more lively and more frequent fashion throughout Victoria than anywhere else in the Commonwealth.

The word "museum" has been almost completely done away with; instead we have "historical park" or "pioneer settlement"—places where one steps back a hundred years or more to walk the streets and visit the homes of the people responsible for turning a penal settlement into a colony of some substance.

The person who tours throughout Victoria can see at first hand how the river trade developed to make major ports out of towns hundreds of miles from the sea; how gold miners lived, worked and played; how farmers fanned out from the coastal fringe to tame what is even today a still fairly inhospitable landscape for straying city-dwellers unversed in country skills. In Victoria there is a historical park devoted to the now-dead, once-lively, coal industry; and another which re-creates the days of the tall ships which plied a rugged coastline to get the farmers' produce to the markets in the cities of the world.

The accusation has been made that Victoria is over-endowed with museums, that even the smallest township now seems to have a collection of implements, bric-a-brac and household items which duplicate the ones the visitor has already seen several times before on his journey.

An itinerary that includes Moe (early explorers), Korumburra (coal), Beechworth (bushrangers), Echuca (the river trade), Swan Hill (rural pioneers), Bendigo (the Chinese immigrants), Ballarat (gold rush days) and Warrnambool (the tall ships) will provide a deep insight into a history which, although recent, is unique in the world due to the life-styles forced upon its participants by a terrain and climate the like of which few of them had previously experienced.

Today, that ruggedness is still there, though the visitor tackles it in comfort.

Victoria's Turbulent Past

Although the coastline of what is now known as Victoria was first sighted by Lieutenant Hicks from Captain Cook's "Endeavour" in 1770, it was not until 1797 that a much closer look was taken at this part of Australia. It was then that Matthew Flinders and George Bass discovered the strait (now called Bass Strait) dividing Tasmania from the mainland mass of Australia and began a more detailed survey of the coastline.

The authorities in Sydney sent a Lieutenant Collins to settle the area in 1803—a year after Lieutenant Grant had sailed into Port Phillip Bay—for a close investigation of the area. Mr. Collins was not the most enterprising of people, choosing as he did a poor sandy site for a settlement and then reporting back unfavourably with a request for transfer to Van Diemen's Land (now Tasmania).

It was 30 years later before the first true settlement began, when immigrants examined the grazing potential of the state's southwestern corner. The leading figures in this settlement were the Henty family, still greatly honoured in the thriving town of Portland, which owes much to their early endeavours. Until the Hentys came, this part of the coast had been largely the preserve of whalers and sealers—itinerants rather than settlers.

About the same time as the Hentys were opening up the southwest, John Batman and John Pascoe Fawkner were exploring the shores of Port Phillip Bay and the valleys around the Yarra and Maribynong Rivers. Batman coerced an aboriginal tribe into selling him 600,000 acres

The most spectacular views of Sydney's world-famous Opera House are to be had from the water. The sail-like roof makes the building itself look as if it will glide out over the harbor. *(Photo: Australian Tourist Commission)*

The beauty of Tasmania is easily explored by car. Pictured here is New Norfolk, Derwent River Valley. *(Photo: Australian Tourist Commission)*

Ayers Rock in Australia's Northern Territory continually changes color throughout a day—a particularly vivid show at sunset. *(Photo: Australian Tourist Commission)*

Australia's second largest city, Melbourne combines sophistication and small-town charm. *(Photo: Victorian Arts Center, courtesy Australian Tourist Commission)*

A breathtaking similarity to Switzerland is obvious in Queenstown, New Zealand. Here the steamer *Earnslaw* is arriving at Queenstown Bay, Otago. *(Photo: New Zealand Tourist Office)*

The stereotype of Fiji—as an ideal spot for the traveler looking to escape civilization—is remarkably accurate. Pictured is the Fiji Cultural Center. *(Photo: Brett)*

The Samoas are the heartland of Polynesia. Here is Rain-maker Mountain on Pago Pago, the capital of American Samoa. *(Photo: Brett)*

In contrast to the people of American Samoa, many of those in Western Samoa can be seen living their lives in traditional native fashion. Pictured is a village in Western Samoa. *(Photo: Western Samoa Visitors Bureau)*

in return for a supply of goods and trinkets worth £200, a pittance even in those days. Batman declared the site an ideal place for the building of a village, and the development of Melbourne began.

The squatters moved in, the Governor paid a visit, a survey was ordered to plan the new town, and the first mayor and councillors took office in 1842. Meanwhile, other immigrants were pushing north towards the River Murray and, from over the Snowy Mountains, into the rich farming lands of Gippsland in the western half of the State.

A New Breed

These were the new breed of Australians, wishing to be known and recognised as separate from the convict-based origins of New South Wales. Landing was refused to convict ships arriving from England and the separatist movement grew in strength until, in 1851, what until then had been "the Port Phillip District of New South Wales" was constituted as the colony of Victoria. (Victoria still comprises the same 87,884 square miles, making it the smallest state on the Australian mainland and taking up just three per cent of the country's total land mass. Yet its population accounts for nearly a third of the country's inhabitants and it contributes similarly to the national wealth.)

Within a year of being declared a separate colony, Victoria became the scene of a gold rush which contributed much to the opening up of its inland regions. The precious metal was discovered in many parts of the state and led to the establishment of several substantial country towns, many of which still survive and prosper while others indicate their one-time existence only by deserted churches, rusting machinery, garbage-filled mine shafts and piles of rubble that once formed a house, shop or hotel.

It was on the goldfields that Australia experienced the one and only revolution in its history. Miners seeking gold at Ballarat revolted against conditions imposed upon them by the authorities, demanded the abolition of the licensing system and of the ownership of property as a qualification for voting rights. They burned their licences, built a stockade at Eureka and rallied around a new Australian flag. The "revolution" occurred on December 3, 1854, and resulted in the deaths of five policemen and 22 rebels. The leaders were eventually found not guilty and many of the miners' more pressing demands were met.

Today, a park and diorama commemorate the Eureka Stockade incident and the timber head of the mineshaft is a landmark for an historical park where visitors can participate in the life of miners in the 1850s. In the park you can hire a gold pan and "fossick" (pick over old claims) for gold; but travel a few miles further and you can stand alone amid the scattered remnants of once thriving settlements and more vividly recapture those rumbustious days of not so long ago.

Older residents claim there is still plenty of gold to be extracted from the ground in this part of Victoria though it seems unlikely there will be a repeat of the days when 319,000 ounces of gold were being won in a single year from just one small corner of the state.

The gold rushes and development of a thriving rural industry contributed much to the development of Victoria in general and to Mel-

bourne in particular. Few incidents of major historical importance occurred but the state and its capital steadily prospered.

The Keynote Is Diversity

In a state that is almost the size of Western Germany and more than
half as big again as Greece, it is not surprising to find a huge diversity
of terrain, climate and vegetation. There are rain forests and deserts,
snowfields and tobacco plantations, vineyards and potato fields, vast
wheat prairies and frost-protected market gardens. Yet it is all reasonably compact when viewed in the overall Australian context. It is possible
to drive from a cold and wet Melbourne winter into the sunshine and
desert dryness of Mildura in one day. In two hours' drive, you can be
on the snowfields. In summer, escaping the high humidity and soaring
temperatures of Melbourne you can soon be amid the mountain freshness
of the alpine region.

Once outside Melbourne, there are few built-up areas to negotiate.
Thus the driver can proceed easily at the permitted maximum speed of
100 kmh (63 mph) for hour upon hour and encounter little traffic or
delays. Not only are all main roads paved, but so are the majority of
minor roads. Dirt roads are encountered only when diverting into more
remote regions—perhaps exploring the Grampians or taking some of the
rain forest tracks of Gippsland. For such expeditions, a four-wheel-drive
vehicle is the best form of transport in all but the driest time of year.

The climate varies greatly over the state. The weather in Melbourne
will often be vastly different from what towns a few miles away on the
other side of the Great Dividing Range are experiencing. It has been said
that Melbourne can experience all four seasons in one day, so greatly and
rapidly does its weather change. However, extremes are rare apart from
a few summer days when the temperature rises to about 100°F. Equally
rare are temperatures below freezing point.

Travellers are likely to be delayed by fog only on an average of 20 days
a year, and this will generally turn out to be a mere morning mist that
disappears within a few hours. Rainfall is just under 660 mm (27 inches)
a year, falling an average of 143 days. The north of the state is far drier
than the south; and the eastern half is much, much wetter than the
western half. Officially, the weather is described as "mild in the main but
disconcertingly changeable." The most stable, pleasant months seem to
be March to June, and October and November.

Such mixed weather leads to mixed vegetation growing amid a highly
varied terrain; volcanic in part, arid and flat for thousands of acres, seven
mountain peaks rising above 6,000 feet and a coastline that varies from
gaunt, wreck-strewn cliffs to tranquil lakelands. A third of the state is
covered by mountain wilderness and bushland—ideal for bushwalkers
but dangerous country for the unwary and inexperienced.

The waters offshore present many opportunities for boating, fishing,
surfing and simple swimming. Sharks are a hazard only occasionally and
undercurrents can be dangerous on certain beaches. It is essential, therefore, to use only those beaches which are patrolled by life-saving clubs
or which are clearly designated as safe in all respects.

Victorians tend to flock to the beaches and lakes throughout the high
summer, leaving the inland roads almost deserted. They show a great

fondness for power-boating, water-skiing and fishing so that piers, jetties and launching ramps are forever busy throughout the summer weekends. The climate makes outdoor living by tent or caravan a pleasant pastime.

Access to Victoria tends to be direct into Melbourne for anyone coming by rail or air. Interstate express coach services terminate in Melbourne, too. Motorists will cross the border from the neighbouring states of South Australia and New South Wales at any of a number of points on major highways. But they should be prepared for confiscation of any fruit they are carrying—a measure designed to eradicate the fruit-fly menace.

Exploration of the state has been made easy by the creation of 12 distinctly separate and well-defined tourism regions. One of these comprises Melbourne; the remainder cover the country areas. Each has its own visitor information centre in addition to the information centres to be found in the larger towns. But before starting any exploration of the inland regions one first needs to come to grips with Melbourne.

MELBOURNE

Certain quotations and incidents from the past will arise in any description of the state's capital city, the sprawling, secretive, partially gracious, slightly pompous and far from egalitarian Melbourne.

When first buying the land on which it stands from the Aborigines for little more than a string of beads, explorer John Batman declared the site to be an ideal place for a village. Such understatement! Today, no more than 148 years later, that "village" contains almost three million people and covers an area of 520,000 acres. In addition to being one of Australia's two most important commercial and financial centers, Melbourne is the headquarters of the two main domestic airlines (Ansett and TAA) and the home of several Federal government departments and statutory bodies. The place where Batman is believed to have stepped ashore from the Yarra River and completed his land purchase is today commemorated by a single flagstone, trodden unobserved by millions of footsteps hurrying to and from rush hour trains, and by a mosaic mural in the foyer of the Commercial Union Assurance premises.

Completely uncommemorated but never forgotten in Melbourne folklore is the remark made by film star Ava Gardner during the filming in Melbourne of the cataclysmic movie *On the Beach.* Melbourne, declared Miss Gardner, had proved itself to her to be the ideal place in which to make a film about the end of the world. The city had already died!

More recently, English model Jean Shrimpton set the entire city back on its heels by daring to appear at the Melbourne Cup horse race (the year's sporting and social highspot) not only wearing a mini-skirt but also bare-legged, hatless and gloveless. The matriarchs who rule Melbourne society are still recovering from this affront, although the summertime streets are filled with women of all ages still following the fashion launched by Miss Shrimpton.

Put these anecdotes together and you have a summation of the Melbourne of today: still very much a village in many ways, definitely prone to give outsiders the appearance of dying the moment the shops close and, despite being outwardly as modern as any other city, still liable to flutter its eyebrows, give a maidenly blush and express its displeasure if one oversteps an unstated but well-marked line.

But it's a lovely, lively city nonetheless, and much of the pleasure it affords lies in its discovery bit by secret bit.

Exploring Melbourne

Its central square mile business and commercial area is a grid of main streets interlaced with a network of arcades that entail plenty of walking if they are to be explored to the full. Here you will find elegant boutiques, many extremely small and very specialised one-person businesses, and innumerable bistros and restaurants. Redevelopment has been rapid over the past decades and appears certain to continue for some time yet. High office blocks are changing the skyline from its previously fairly low profile, and work is progressing on the city's standing joke—an underground railway system that has been talked about for half a century and only now is nearing completion.

One city block of the main shopping area, Bourke Street, has been experimentally turned into a pedestrian mall which may later be extended another block. Grandiose plans for a city square eventually reached fruition when the Queen performed the opening ceremony in May 1980.

In past years, residents and visitors could take a lift to the top of one of the many high-rise buildings for a fine overall view of the city. Now, due to increasingly strict safety regulations, such opportunities are greatly restricted. The uppermost suites of such hotels as the Southern Cross, Regent of Melbourne, and Hilton provide the visitor with the most accessible vantage points.

Further exploration can be done by tram (streetcar), a transportation system that is the subject of frequent debate but which seems destined to remain. Tram routes cover most of the main city streets and spread for many miles out into the surrounding suburbs.

Within the city centre are several superb parks and gardens, some of which are considered by authorities to be the best of their type anywhere in the world. The white "Christmas cake" edifice of Government House is set in one of these gardens and, in another, is the cottage in which Australia's discoverer, Captain Cook, spent his English childhood.

The Royal Park houses the zoological gardens—the place in which to walk among Australian animals in their natural setting amid native flora.

Because Melbourne hosted the 1956 Olympic Games it is well endowed with near-city sports arenas. Most impressive of these, however, is the Melbourne Cricket Ground which dates back many decades before the Olympics. To watch a cricket match (in summer) or a football match (in winter) in this gladiatorial setting is to see the Victorian in his true clothing. The big sporting occasions are rumbustious, noisy, emotional events in which the crowd of 120,000 is rarely silent and the wisecracks flow like water.

Lie Down and Look Up

Also on the city fringe is the imposing new arts centre, gaunt, grey and windowless from the outside but a sheer delight inside where garden courtyards display sculpture and admit natural light. Lie down on the carpeted floor of the great hall for the best view of the world's largest stained glass ceiling, a magnificent achievement by local artist Leonard French.

A further insight into the Victorian (and Australian) character is gained by visiting Tattersalls in Flinders Street. This is the local lottery centre. Public drawings are held at regular intervals, although the gambling high spot of the week is at 9:30 every Saturday night when seven out of 40 numbered balls decide who has won close to $1 million in the newest pastime of Tattslotto. Millions of dollars are invested each week on just this one form of gambling. Much more is spent on horse-racing (Melbourne has several tracks and almost daily racing), dog-racing and trotting.

Melbourne is unquestionably a cosmopolitan city. Migration has ensured this. One statistic of note is that it is now the world's third largest Greek city.

It also has an extremely large Italian population plus substantial numbers of Yugoslav, Turkish, Dutch, Maltese, Chinese and, of course, British immigrants. Twenty per cent of the people living in Victoria were born outside Australia and a third of all children born in the state come from immigrant families. Thus there has developed a rich melange of cultures which the visitor experiences most of all in the choice of cuisines available in innumerable restaurants. It is experienced, too, in the big markets—the Victoria, the South Melbourne and the Prahran—which always exhibit lively and colourful vignettes of the Melbournians and their way of life.

Once a year, Melbourne lets its hair down and stages a festival called "Moomba"—allegedly Aboriginal for "Let's get together and have fun." Slow to develop, it is now a mammoth open air event of music, dancing, art shows and concerts. There is water-skiing on the river, parades in the streets, paintings in the parks and concerts in the gardens. It attracts artistes from other parts of the world and is recommended as a good time to be in Melbourne. It takes place over 10 days at the end of February and the first week of March.

The city is the centre of the country's "rag trade" and boasts many elegant dress shops. There is quality (and expensive) shopping to be had at "the Paris end" of Collins Street (that's the bit where there are a few trees and a couple of pavement cafes) and in the chic suburb of Toorak. Although Melbourne contains the largest department store in the southern hemisphere (Myer) it also has by contrast a wealth of small shops which provide the goods and services not available from the large concerns. The small family-run retailer is a prominent feature of Melbourne life which ensures that the shopper can find virtually any item or service required. Free enterprise at its best is seen on the Esplanade at the bayside suburb of St. Kilda every Sunday morning when, on payment of a small fee, anyone can set up their pavement stall to sell their wares. Craftwork of all descriptions dominates the scene here.

Highspots of the Melbourne year, apart from Moomba, are the Melbourne Show (a funfair and agricultural gathering) in September and the Melbourne spring racing carnival with the running of the Melbourne

Cup (the first Tuesday in November), bringing the entire nation, including Parliament, to a halt.

PRACTICAL INFORMATION FOR MELBOURNE

HOW TO GET THERE. *By air:* Most international passengers arrive through the international Melbourne Airport at Tullamarine; in the same complex are the major Australian domestic airlines, Ansett, East-West, and TAA. International airlines serving Melbourne are Air Nauru, Air New Zealand (which has direct flights from New Zealand ports), Alitalia, British Airways, Continental, Garuda, KLM, Cathay Pacific, Malaysian Airlines System, Lufthansa, Philippine Air Lines, Qantas, Thai International, Singapore Airlines and, at press time, Pan Am, though United may pick up Pan Am's Pacific destinations.

By rail: Main trunk routes are Albury from New South Wales and Sydney and from Western Australia (Perth) through South Australia (Adelaide). The train runs overnight, nightly between Melbourne and Adelaide and nightly and daily between Melbourne and Sydney. There is also a service between Melbourne and the Federal capital, Canberra, via Yass, Mondays to Saturdays.

By sea: Sea passengers arrive at Station Pier, Port Melbourne, but services from overseas are now almost non-existent. Cruise ships, too, make only rare calls and all major companies now operate out of Sydney. P & O, Sitmar and CTC Lines are the main providers of cruises and line voyages.

HOW TO GET AROUND. *By air:* Ansett and TAA have regular services between Melbourne and all state capitals plus Canberra and Alice Springs and Darwin, linking with intrastate airlines at each place for onward travel to smaller towns. East-West flies between Melbourne and Sydney and from Melbourne to other cities in the country. Tullamarine, 10 miles northwest of the city, is the International and domestic airport, and is equipped to take any commercial aircraft now flying in the world, including the Concorde which has long been promised but has yet to arrive other than on proving flights. The second, and former major airport, Essendon, six miles northwest of Melbourne, and is mainly used by commuter and charter airlines and executive aircraft.

By road: Modern express coaches link Melbourne with all other mainland states, the main operators being Ansett Pioneer, Greyhound, Olympic East-West and Deluxe Coachlines. These and other companies also offer coach tours, while car-hire firms include Avis, Hertz and Budget.

By rail: Apart from major trunk routes interstate, Victorian Railways operates suburban rail services fanning out from the city, in some cases connected by bus to outer suburbs from the rail terminus.

STAGE AND REVUES. On the theatre scene, Melbourne has experienced a strong revival of interest in repertory and experimental theatre in recent years. The *Theatres Building* in the *Victorian Arts Centre* is a new spot for stage performances. Other major productions staged in Melbourne are still housed in the city's main venues, *Her Majesty's Theatre* at 219 Exhibition Street; the *Princess* in Spring Street, the *Atheneum* in Collins Street, the *Playbox* in Russell Street and the *Comedy Theatre* at 240 Exhibition Street. Playwrights such as David Williamson, Jack Hibberd and John Romeril have brought Australia into the limelight overseas and seen a new national pride emerge in the local culture. And smaller theatre companies have sprung up in the inner suburbs. The first of these was *La Mama* in Carlton, and this was followed closeby by the *Pram Factory,* now the home of the Australian Performing Group.

MELBOURNE

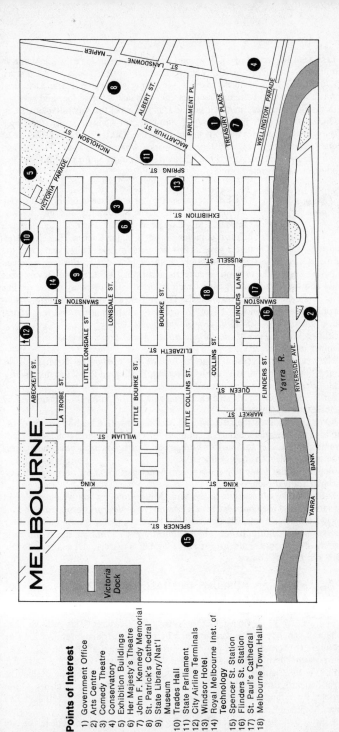

Points of Interest

1) Government Office
2) Arts Centre
3) Comedy Theatre
4) Conservatory
5) Exhibition Buildings
6) Her Majesty's Theatre
7) John F. Kennedy Memorial
8) St. Patrick's Cathedral
9) State Library/Nat'l Museum
10) Trades Hall
11) State Parliament
12) City Airline Terminals
13) Windsor Hotel
14) Royal Melbourne Inst. of Technology
15) Spencer St. Station
16) Flinders St. Station
17) St. Paul's Cathedral
18) Melbourne Town Hall

Less than ten years ago, a new kind of theatre began here, at La Mama in Faraday Street, a rough, earthy, abrasive, radical theatre. You sit on hard seats, sip coffee in a compact little space in the corner and watch a new Australian drama come to life. A drama that bites, that gets below the surface and grapples with the aggressiveness, materialism and frustrations of the Australian character.

Out in Richmond, the *Pumpkin Theatre* at 314 Church Street, the *Union Theatre* at the Melbourne University in Parkville, and the *Alexander Theatre* at Monash University regularly stage new works, while the *National Theatre* and *Polais Theatre* in St. Kilda and the *Fitzroy Regent Palace* in Fitzroy also offer live productions from time to time.

MUSIC occupies an important place in the life of a strong section of the Melbourne community and has done so since the early days of settlement. The new *Victorian Arts Centre* complex houses a major *Concert Hall*. The *Melbourne Symphony Orchestra* gave its first concerts in 1906. Thirty years later the Australian Broadcasting Commission, financed by radio license fees, assumed responsibility for the orchestra's concerts and from 1949 the State Government made additional monetary grants which financed visits by many of the world's finest conductors and instrumentalists. The orchestra now gives about forty subscription celebrity concerts a year, 12 celebrity youth concerts and four choral concerts with the *Royal Melbourne Philharmonic Society*.

Musica Viva, Soirees Musicales and *Allegri Music* present regular evenings of chamber music.

The venues for orchestral concerts include the Melbourne Town Hall, the Robert Blackwood Hall at Monash University, Wellington Road, Clayton and the Dallas Brooks Hall in East Melbourne.

An opera season is presented each year both by the national company and by Victoria's own State opera.

Ballet also finds a strong following in Melbourne with a healthy section of the public. The *Australian Ballet,* a company of world standard which has made several highly successful tours of Europe and North America, has headquarters at Mt. Alexander Road, Flemington.

Melbourne has many fine musical and ballet performances during its *March Moomba* festival each year.

There are *open air concerts* in the Myer Music Bowl on Sunday afternoons in the summer and Melbourne's *Free Entertainment in the Parks* programme begins early October each year. Classical and jazz concerts, plays, variety shows, ethnic entertainment, cultural dances are on almost every day during lunch and early evening in Melbourne gardens: Fitzroy, Flagstaff, Treasury, Alexandra, The Domain and the city square.

MUSEUMS AND GALLERIES. Melbourne's cultural life attained an exciting new dimension in August, 1968 when the first unit of the *Victorian Arts Centre* was built to house Victoria's early art treasures. This massive bluestone and concrete edifice was designed by noted Australian architect Sir Roy Grounds. It encloses three open courtyards and covers an area of eight acres incorporating both parklands and pools. The National Gallery's outstanding feature, is the *Great Hall* with its dramatic stained glass ceiling by Melbourne artist Leonard French. Housed here are works by Memling, Rubens, Goya, Tiepolo, Rembrandt, Brueghel, Cezanne and Picasso. Located at 180 St. Kilda Road, Melbourne, the Gallery is open seven days a week.

A host of smaller, individually owned galleries can be found both in the city and surrounding suburbs. Exhibitions change regularly and the Saturday morning newspaper carries a comprehensive list of what is currently showing and where. Among the more established of these are the *Young Originals Gallery* at 380 Punt Road, South Yarra, *Realities* in Jackson Street, Toorak; *Manyung Gallery,* 1408 Nepean Highway, Mt. Eliza; *Avant Galleries,* 579 Punt Road, South Yarra and *Impressions* at 283 Toorak Road, South Yarra.

Montsalvat at Hillcrest Avenue, Eltham is an artists colony set in a rustic atmosphere of 23 acres some 20 miles out of Melbourne. The grounds are open all the time with the gallery houses (a collection of quite remarkable buildings devised and constructed by the Jorgensen family) open weekends and public holidays.

The *Victorian Artists Society* at 430 Albert Street, East Melbourne and the *Malvern Artists Society* at 1299 High Street, Malvern are both worth a visit.

 SHOPPING. Melbourne is the fashion centre of Australia and is also noted for its totally stocked department stores; ethnic food shops; haute couture boutiques and quality woollen goods.

The largest store is the *Myer Emporium* in downtown Bourke Street. This street, with arcades fanning from it, is the city's main shopping centre. Collins Street, running parallel (Melbourne's city roads are laid out in grid fashion) has fashions one end (the east) and finance and travel and big business houses running through to the other end.

Australian and Papua New Guinea artifacts, and opals from central Australia are widely sold, and there are duty-free shops stocking all these in Collins Street and Queen Street crossing Collins, in Melbourne's centre.

Victoria's craftsmen are little publicised and hard to find. But ask around if you are visiting a particular area and you will often find a local potter (Melbourne's Dandenong Ranges, little towns such as Eltham, have many potters) woodworkers and even in one or two western towns, boomerang carvers.

If you can't get out to them, go to southern suburb of St. Kilda and to the esplanade there on Sunday mornings, and these craftspeople will come to you. Painters, jewellery workers, woodworkers, leatherworkers, potters display their goods on the pavements to strollers-by.

If you do go out into the country, visit the re-created towns at Ballarat, Echuca, Swan Hill, Beechworth and Korumburra and you should be able to buy locally made souvenirs there.

 CLOSING HOURS. Department stores in all Victorian cities and major provincial centres open from 9 A.M. until 5:30 P.M. Monday to Thursday; 9 A.M. to 9 P.M. Fridays; 9 A.M. to noon Saturdays. Most smaller shops follow this fashion, but delicatessens and milk bars (candy stores) and fast food (takeaway) stores open at night also.

Banking hours: most city banks operate from 8 A.M. to 6 P.M. for savings account; 10 A.M. to 3 P.M. for other business and the latter hours also apply in suburban and country banks with a closing time extended to 5 P.M. on Fridays. Banks are closed on Saturdays.

 PARKS AND GARDENS. Victoria's recreational parks are one of the first impressions that visitors get when they start their tours of Melbourne, and later the State.

One of the first and most beautiful parks of all is the *Royal Botanical Gardens* in the middle of the huge Domain Park which also houses Government House. Nearby are the *Alexandra Gardens* along the Yarra River banks. Across the river surrounding the north and east of the business and retail centre are the *Treasury Gardens, Fitzroy Gardens, Exhibition Gardens and Flagstaff Gardens.*

In each suburb special reserves are set on many street and avenue corners as recreation reserves or botanical gardens.

Melbourne has many natural and man-made parks in the Dandenong Ranges, nearby and in the You Yangs to the west. Special amenities and facilities are blended into the countryside and the forests to allow people to enjoy their beautiful surroundings and to conserve the countryside. Picnic facilities are scattered throughout in cleared areas and are constantly patrolled.

Coach trips and rail provide access for visitors to many of these areas and all are accessible by motor car.

 WHAT TO DO WITH THE CHILDREN. *Luna Park* has the usual amusement park attractions—scenic railway, Big Dipper. In the outer suburbs, *Lower Eltham Park* has the Diamond Valley Railway open Sundays and public holidays, where kids can watch working models of steam trains and go for 10-minute rides on the two mile track. They can take another train journey, speed boat rides and visit a paddle steamer at the picnic and recreation area, *Carribbean Gardens* at Scoresby, or just ride one of Melbourne's trams, the only ones still operating in Australia on a commercial basis. For older children, the sound and light show at *Captain Cook's Cottage* in Melbourne's Fitzroy Gardens is interesting and so may be a visit to the *National Gallery* to lie on the floor (the done thing) and gaze up at the beautiful ceiling in the Great Hall. In one of the city's shopping arcades, *Royal Arcade,* look up at the entrance arch and see Gog and Magog's huge figures. In good weather hire a bicycle in Alexandra Avenue, along the southern banks of the Yarra, and ride along the bicycle track.

 HOTELS AND MOTELS. Heaviest bookings for hotels in Melbourne are late September–November. The Melbourne Cup race is held in November, and it would be wise to skip Melbourne during that time if you do not have reservations. The price ranges for 2 people in a double room are: *Deluxe:* A$75 and up; *Expensive:* A$60–75; *Moderate:* A$40–60; *Inexpensive:* A$25–40.

Chateau Commodore. *Deluxe.* 131 Lonsdale St. Licensed restaurant. Liquor room service. 24 hr food service. Pool. In heart of city.

Commodore Old Melbourne Hotel. *Deluxe.* 5–17 Flemington Rd., North Melbourne. Licensed restaurant. Liquor room service. 24 hr food service. Pool. Built round courtyard all styled after old world village. Close city en route to airport. Member Commodore chain.

Melbourne Hilton. *Deluxe.* Wellington Parade, City East. Licensed restaurant. Liquor room service. 24 hr food service. Pool. Member Hilton chain.

Regency Hotel. *Deluxe.* Lonsdale and Exhibition sts. Complete amenities. Restaurant. City's newest hotel.

Regent of Melbourne. *Deluxe.* Collins St. Every amenity. Wide selection of restaurants, shops. 24-hr. room service. In-room bars.

Southern Cross. *Deluxe.* 131 Exhibition St., City. Licensed restaurant. Liquor room service. 24 hr food service, air conditioned. Centre theatre, commercial area.

Windsor Hotel. *Deluxe.* 103 Spring St., City. Licensed restaurant. Liquor room service. 24 hr food service. Old fashioned atmosphere, decor and service.

Commodore Exhibition Motor Inn. *Expensive.* 293 Exhibition St. No dining facilities but rate includes light breakfast. Kitchen facilities in rooms. Close theatre, shops, exhibition buildings, convention hall. Member Commodore chain.

Commodore Queens Road. *Expensive.* 4 Queens Rd. Licensed restaurant. Liquor room service. Near city, beach, golf, badminton, squash, table tennis. Member Commodore chain.

Crossley Lodge Motel. *Expensive.* 51 Little Bourke St. Licensed restaurant. Liquor room service. In heart of city.

Downtowner Motel. *Expensive.* Cnr. Lygon & Queensberry Sts., City North. Licensed restaurant. Rates include light breakfast.

Hotel Australia. *Expensive.* 266 Collins St., City. Licensed restaurant. Liquor room service. 24 hr food service, entertainment, air conditioned. In heart of city. Off-season rates available.

Melbourne Parkroyal. *Expensive.* 441 Royal Parade, City North. Kitchen facilities in rooms. Licensed restaurant. Liquor room service. 24 hr room service. Pool. Nr golf and other sporting facilities. Member Southern Pacific chain.

Noahs Hotel Melbourne. *Expensive.* Cnr Exhibition/Little Bourke Sts., City. Licensed restaurant. Liquor room service. 24 hr room service. Pool.

Palm Lake Motor Inn. *Expensive.* 52 Queens Rd., City outskirts. Licensed restaurant. Liquor room service. 24 hr room service. Pool. Opposite golf course and lake.

President Motor Inn. *Expensive.* 63 Queens Rd., City outskirts. Off season rates available. Licensed restaurant. Liquor room service. 24 hr food service. Nr beach, lake, golf course, tennis courts.

Sheraton Hotel. *Expensive.* 13 Spring St., City. Licensed restaurant. Liquor room service. 24 hr food service. Opposite Parliament buildings, gardens. Member Flag chain.

St. Kilda Road TraveLodge Motel. *Expensive.* Cnr Albert Rd/Park St. Licensed restaurant. Liquor room service. 24 hr food service. Pool. Overlooks parklands, war memorial, shrine. Member Southern Pacific chain.

Victoria of Melbourne. *Expensive.* 215 Little Collins St., City. Licensed restaurant, bar, beauty shop, air conditioned. Heart of city.

Hosies Hotel. *Moderate.* 1 Elizabeth St., City. Licensed restaurant. Liquor room service. Opposite main railway station. Heart of city.

Innkeepers Ramada Inn. *Moderate.* 539 Royal Parade, Parkville. Opposite parks, nr golf course, football oval, games and recreation areas.

Koala Queenslodge. *Moderate.* 81 Queens Rd., near city. Kitchen facilities in rooms. Licensed restaurant. Liquor room service. 24 hr room service. Pool. Nr recreational park and lake. Views across bay. Member Koala chain.

Lennons Parkview Motel. *Moderate.* 303 Royal Parade, Parkville. Kitchen facilities in rooms. Licensed restaurant. Liquor room service. Opposite parkland, close university.

Motel Marco Polo. *Moderate.* Cnr. Harker St./Flemington Rd., City outskirts. Licensed restaurant. Liquor room service. Pool. Nr race course (Flemington), showgrounds, en route out of city to airport.

Park Avenue Motel. *Moderate.* 461 Royal Parade, Parkville. Nr zoo, golf course and other sports.

Park Squire Motor Inn. *Moderate.* 94 Flemington Rd., Parkville. Nr parks, zoo, hospitals, Flemington race course, showgrounds.

Parkville Motel. *Moderate.* Weekly tariff available. No restaurant, but kitchen facilities in rooms.

Princes Park Motel. *Moderate.* 2 Sydney Rd., Brunswick. Kitchen facilities in rooms. Nr Flemington and Moonee Valley race courses, showgrounds and freeway to city and airport.

Travel Inn Motel. *Moderate.* Cnr Grattan/Drummond Sts. Licensed restaurant. Liquor room service. 24 hr food service. Pool. 10 mins city, close university, museum, Flemington race course, cricket ground. Member Flag chain.

Glensborough Private Hotel. *Inexpensive.* 48 Wellington Parade, City East. Room without private facilities. No dining facilities but rate includes light breakfast. Opposite cricket ground and public gardens in eastern edge of city.

Magnolia Court. *Inexpensive.* 101 Powlett St., City East. Rates include light breakfast. Rooms have kitchen facilities. No restaurant.

MELBOURNE ENVIRONS

Airport West
Hotel International. *Moderate.* Lancefield Rd. Liquor room service. Licensed restaurant. Nr Melbourne International Airport. Rate includes hot breakfast.

Aspendale
Aspendale Shore Motel. *Moderate.* 31 Nepean Highway. Liquor room service. No restaurant. Nr beach, golf course.

Bayswater
Bayswater Hotel Motel. *Moderate.* Mountain Highway. Includes light breakfast. Liquor room service. Licensed restaurant. Mountain views.

Beaumaris
Beaumaris Bay Motelodge, *Moderate.* 31 Bodley St. Liquor room service. Licensed restaurant. Nr beach, fishing, golf course.
Beaumaris Hotel. *Inexpensive.* Liquor room service. Licensed restaurant. 24 hr food service. Overlooking bay, near golf club.

Brighton
Brighton Savoy. *Moderate.* 150 The Esplanade. Nr beach, shops, yacht club.

Brunswick
Moreland Motor Hotel. *Moderate.* 888 Sydney Rd. Licensed restaurant. Liquor room service. On main road between Sydney and Melbourne. Nr transport, shops.

Bulleen
Sentimental Bloke Motor Hotel. *Moderate.* 1 Thompsons Rd. Liquor room service, licensed restaurant. Nr golf course.

Carlton
Innkeepers Lygon Lodge. *Moderate.* 204 Lygon St. Liquor room service. Licensed restaurant. Five mins city centre, opposite bowling rink, parklands. Member Flag chain.

Chadstone
Matthew Flinders Hotel. *Moderate.* Cnr. Batesford/Warrigal Rds. Liquor room service. Licensed restaurant. 24 hr food service. Nr golf course, shopping complex, swimming pool, beach, railway station. Member MFA Homestead chain.

Clayton
Monash Hotel Motel. *Inexpensive.* 2077 Dandenong Rd. Liquor room service. Licensed restaurant. Walking distance Monash University.

Coburg
Barham Motel. *Moderate.* 726 Sydney Rd. Liquor room service. Licensed restaurant. Pool. On main road between Sydney and Melbourne. Nr Melbourne International Airport and zoo. Member Flag chain.
Coach House Motel. *Moderate.* 844 Sydney Rd. Liquor room service. Licensed restaurant. Pool. On main Sydney-Melbourne road. Nr golf course, Melbourne International Airport and zoo.

Croydon
Dorset Gardens Hotel/Motel. *Expensive.* 335 Dorset Rd. Rate includes hot breakfast. Liquor room service. Licensed restaurant. 24 hr food service. Heated pool. Mountain views. Nr golf course, Healesville wild life sanctuary, heliport, sauna and tennis courts.

Croydon Hotel Motel. *Moderate.* Maroondah Highway. Rate includes light breakfast. Liquor room service. Licensed restaurant.

Dandenong

Dandenong Motel. *Moderate.* 147 Princes Highway. Liquor room service. No restaurant. Nr beach, golf course, racetrack.

Doveton

Prince Mark Motel/Hotel. *Inexpensive.* Cnr Power Rd./Princes Hwy. Liquor room service. No restaurant. Nr golf course. Mountain views.

Essendon

Alexander Motor Inn. *Moderate.* 982 Mt Alexander Rd. Licensed restaurant. Liquor room service. Close train, tram, bus. Adjacent freeway, both Melbourne international and Essendon light aircraft airports. Member Flag chain.

Footscray

Palms Motel. *Moderate.* Geelong Rd. Includes hot breakfast. Liquor room service. No restaurant. Nr golf and race courses.

Frankston

Ambassador Centre. *Expensive.* 325 Nepean Hwy. Licensed restaurant, swimming pool, all meals available.

Hawthorn

California Motel. *Moderate.* 138 Barkers Rd. Air conditioned; laundry; all meals available. Pool. Member Flag chain.
Whitehorse Inn. *Moderate.* 5 Burwood Rd. Includes hot breakfast. Licensed restaurant.

Keilor

Keilor Motor Inn. *Moderate.* 765 Calder Hwy. Restaurant and liquor service.

Keysborough

Keysborough Hotel/Motel. *Moderate.* Cnr. Cheltenham/Corrigan Rds. Includes light breakfast. Liquor room service. Licensed restaurant. Nr golf course, large shopping complex, swimming pool, beach, railway station. Member MFA Homestead chain.

Lower Templestowe

Templestowe Hotel. *Moderate.* Parker St. Rate includes hot breakfast. Nr beach, golf course.

Mentone

Mentone Hub Motel. *Moderate.* 200 Nepean Highway. Breakfast only. Nr beach, golf course, light aircraft airport. Member Flag chain.

Moorabbin

Southside Six Motor Hotel. *Moderate.* Cnr. South/Bignell Rds. Liquor room service. Licensed restaurant. 24 hr food service. Nr transport, shops.

Noble Park

Sandown Park Motel. *Moderate.* 433 Princes Highway. No restaurant. Nr racecourse. Member MFA Homestead chain.

Nunawading

Hotel Burvale. *Moderate.* Cnr. Springvale Rd./Burwood Highway. Liquor room service. Licensed restaurant.

Oakleigh
Red Carpet Inn. *Moderate.* 1330 Dandenong Rd. Liquor room service. Licensed restaurant. Opposite large shopping centre.

Preston
Council Club Motor Hotel. *Moderate.* 1 Cramer St. Liquor room service. Licensed restaurant.

Rowville
Stamford Hotel. *Moderate.* Cnr. Wellington/Stud Rds. Includes light breakfast. Liquor room service. Licensed restaurant. Nr golf course. Mountain views.

Sandringham
Commodore Sandringham Hotel. *Moderate.* 118 Beach Rd. Liquor room service. Licensed restaurant. Opposite beach. Nr golf course.

South Yarra
Avon Motor Hotel. *Moderate.* 126 Toorak Rd. Rate includes hot breakfast. No restaurant.
Motel Domain. *Moderate.* 52 Darling St. Rate includes hot breakfast. Nr park, swimming pool, botanical gardens.
St. James Motel. *Moderate.* 35 Darling St. Rate includes light breakfast. No restaurant. 24 hr food service.

St. Kilda
Cabana Court Motel. *Moderate.* 46 Park St. Includes light breakfast. Kitchen facilities in rooms. Nr beach. Member MFA Homestead chain.
Car-O-Tel. *Moderate.* 4-6 Carlisle St. Kitchen facilities in room. Nr beach, amusement park, shopping centre. Member MFA Homestead chain.
Executive Motel. *Inexpensive.* 239 Canterbury Rd. Liquor room service. No restaurant. Nr beach, transport.
Linden Court Private Hotel. *Inexpensive* 26 Acland St. Some cheaper rooms without private facilities. Rate includes light breakfast. Nr beach.
Montmartre Hotel. *Moderate.* 92 Grey St. Nr beach, shopping centre, park, golf course. Member Flag chain.

Tullamarine
Tullamarine TraveLodge. *Expensive.* At Melbourne international airport. Liquor room service. Licensed restaurant. 24 hr food service. Pool. Free airport bus service (five mins). Member Southern Pacific chain.
Gladstone Park Hotel. *Moderate.* Mickleham Rd. Includes hot breakfast. Liquor room service. Licensed restaurant. Nr Melbourne international airport.

DINING OUT
Melbourne's cosmopolitan nature means that the city offers variety for diners. Price ranges for a 3-course meal (excluding wine) are: *Expensive:* A$30 and up; *Moderate:* A$15–30; *Inexpensive:* A$7–15.
Clichy's. *Expensive.* Nouvelle cuisine. Reservations essential.
Fanny's Restaurant. *Expensive.* French cuisine. Operating 17 years under same ownership. Reservations suggested.
Florentino. *Expensive.* Italian and French cuisine. First class.
Empress of China. *Expensive.* In Melbourne's Chinatown. Bring your own wine.
Lazar Restaurant. *Expensive.* Antique décor, silver service.
Pamplemousse. *Expensive.* French cuisine. Dancing, live music.
Fountains. *Expensive.* Predominantly French cuisine. Bring your own wine.
Bacchus Restaurant Bistro. *Moderate.* Greek and International.
Beppi's Bistro. *Moderate.* Italian dishes a specialty.
Cafe de Paris. *Moderate.* French cuisine. Garden setting.

Charley Brown's. *Moderate.* Piano and violin entertainment.
Dirty Dick's Elizabethan Rooms. *Moderate.* Grand Elizabethan manner—food, entertainment and costumed waitresses.
Istana Indonesian Restaurant. *Moderate.* Indonesian music weekends.
Society Restaurant. *Moderate.* French and Italian.
Xenia Restaurant. *Moderate.* Specializing in Greek cuisine. No credit cards.
Pancake Parlour. *Inexpensive.* Colonial décor and atmosphere.

EXPLORING VICTORIA

When the Victorian government started taking an interest in tourism as a means of decentralising industry, it offered grants to improve visitor facilities and divided the state into tourism regions.

Imagine Victoria, then, as a vast fan, with Melbourne its center region. Spreading out from there are the geographical regions easily reached by good highways. Bordering Melbourne on the east is the Melbourne Leisure region incorporating the Dandenong Ranges towns. The Gippsland region centers on Morwell, Moe, Yarram and Leongatha, and the East Gippsland region stretches to the border with New South Wales.

The Maroondah Highway running east of Melbourne turns northeast and is the road to take for the North East region of the Victorian Alps towns of Beechworth and Bright and the river towns of Yarrawonga and Wangaratta.

North and northwest of Melbourne is the North West region focusing on Mildura and Swan Hill, towns on the Murray River, forming the border between Victoria and New South Wales.

On the western borders of Melbourne region are Otway-Geelong, reached by the Princes Highway running west. Keep on this highway and you'll reach the South West region with the magnificent Ocean Road scenery. The Western Highway, which is the main and shortest highway between Melbourne and Adelaide, takes in the North Central region and gold rush towns like Ballarat, and further west goes through the wheat district of the Wimmera region. Due north of Melbourne is the Central Highland area which includes Bendigo—take the Calder Highway for this region.

South Gippsland

Highway One leads east and west from the city, going around the coast to Sydney and Adelaide on its journey around virtually all the Australian coastline. The Hume Highway—the fast way to Sydney—comes in from the north and splits the state in two. Travelling is faster in the flatter, more open western half than in the mountainous winding roads of much of the eastern half.

Setting out from Melbourne eastward down Highway One, it's worth diverting to the fishing community of San Remo and Phillip Island in order to see the nightly parade of fairy penguins as they come ashore to their homes in the dunes. The island is a producer of chicory, and is the home of colonies of seals which sport themselves on rocks at the tip of the island.

To continue the detour down the South Gippsland Highway leads to the National Park at Wilson's Promontory, more than 100,000 acres of unique bushland and superbly rugged coastal scenery.

To get back onto Highway One entails traversing the rolling green hills of South Gippsland to reach the source of much of the State's power supplies: the huge brown coal deposits around Yallourn, Morwell and Moe.

Stop for a while at the Gippsland Folk Museum at Moe to obtain an insight into the life of the early settlers. It has a main street that has been reconstructed with old buildings brought in from all over the nearby region.

Lakes and Timber

Further down the highway at Sale (134 miles from Melbourne) is the beginning of the coastal lake district and the first signs of activity associated with offshore drilling for oil and gas. Twenty miles to the south is the aptly named Ninety Mile Beach, a wild, unspoilt paradise for surfers and beach fishermen.

Forty-three miles further on is Bairnsdale, commercial centre of the East Gippsland region. It owes much of its prosperity to the surrounding dairy and timber industries as well as to the year-round flow of tourists to the nearby Gippsland Lakes. An interesting sight is the painted ceiling of St. Mary's Church where a local Italian migrant tried to outdo Michelangelo.

East of Bairnsdale, 23 miles down the highway, is the resort and fishing township of Lakes Entrance. It sits at the centre of a chain of inland waterways that extend for 50 miles inland of the Ninety Mile Beach. Ferries operate to other townships around the lakes and it is possible to hire cruisers. Nearby is the Aboriginal settlement of Lake Tyers.

At the timber town of Orbost (234 miles from Melbourne), or 47 miles further on at Cann River, there is the choice of continuing along Highway One or heading off into the mountains and tall timber country.

Continue and the road leads to the tranquil far south-east corner of Victoria, the mild and balmy resort of Mallacoota with its 11,000 acre national park and a huge expanse of sheltered lakes. Abalone divers go out from Mallacoota, setting their fragile craft to leap the rip that divides the lakes from the ocean.

Gold Country

Take one of the inland highways, and the country changes drastically. The roads wind their way up mountainsides among some of the world's tallest trees and into the high open plains where wild horses ("the brumbies") still roam free and where the remains of yet another gold rush (in 1851) can be seen scarring the hillside at Omeo. This small township has had an unequal share of disasters: it was ruined by earthquakes in 1885 and 1892 and almost completely wiped out by a bushfire in 1939.

Omeo is the jumping off point for a journey through the high plains of cattle ranches and trout streams. Traversing the mountains leads down through the foothills into the Murray Valley at Corryong, Tallangatta or the twin towns of Albury-Wodonga.

Close by is yet another gold mining area and the country where bushranger Ned Kelly built his notoriety. Mementoes of Kelly and his gang are numerous but little remains of his home or the hotel where he was captured after a gunfight with the police.

The township of Beechworth holds a Golden Horseshoes Festival every year to commemorate the member of parliament who once rode through the town on a horse shod with golden shoes. Beechworth then had a population of 8,000, 61 hotels and a theatre which attracted performers from all over the world. Today, it has 3,500 inhabitants and is noteworthy for the excellence of its trees, parks and gardens. Several buildings remain from the gold rush days. They include a fine powder magazine, Chinese funeral ovens and the honey-coloured government buildings of the 1850s.

Thirty miles from Beechworth is the tobacco growing centre of Bright which plays an important role as a staging post for visitors to the ski resorts in winter. Gold mining continued here well into the present century.

Wine and Bluestone

Wine production has come back into importance in this part of Victoria and the region holds a Winery Walkabout every June when the vintage is ready. The vine disease, phylloxera, killed the industry at the turn of the century but it has become reestablished in recent years and is now once more the home of several important wineries which open their doors to the public. Especially noteworthy are the cellars of All Saints which have been classified by the National Trust.

From Rutherglen it is an easy run back down the Hume Highway through Wangaratta, Benalla (a popular centre for gliding) and Seymour to Melbourne.

Head off westward down Highway One from Melbourne and the road leads into the wealthy Western District of vast pasturelands and huge family properties. It leads, too, to a rugged coastline where there is scant shelter for shipping and many a wreck has occurred. The Great Ocean Road skirts the shore for much of the way and provides a superbly scenic drive. Inland, the plains are flat and open for many miles but at Tower Hill, near Warrnambool, the country is volcanic and a nature reserve has been created in the caldera (an enlarged crater) of an extinct volcano.

One of the most interesting towns of the region is Port Fairy, the second oldest town in Victoria and a sheer delight for its wealth of old bluestone buildings set close to the banks of the River Moyne. Originally a whaling station, it still thrives as the base for a fishing fleet which keeps local hotels well supplied with fresh crays and lobsters. There are strong Irish overtones about Port Fairy (it was originally called Belfast) and the area surrounding it. Bluestone is still being quarried on the outskirts of town and its innumerable stately and gracious old buildings are being restored and preserved. Open days are held regularly so that the interiors can be seen.

Head inland for Casterton and Hamilton and the route passes along the Glenelg River and across rolling gum-tree studded country to Warrock Farm—a complete township remaining as it was when first built and settled more than 100 years ago. All the buildings are classified by the National Trust and are still in daily use by the fourth generation of the same family that first settled there.

Through Hamilton (notable for its art gallery) the road leads back down the Hamilton Highway to Melbourne.

River Country

To see the wheatlands and the big river country take the Calder Highway running northwest out of Melbourne, through the old market town of Castlemaine (see the beautifully restored market) to Bendigo. Here is the Chinese stronghold of Victoria, complete with joss house, temple and an annual festival when a dragon dances down the main street. From Bendigo (via the revived and busy pottery) it is an easy drive to the River Murray at Echuca, the river's nearest point to Melbourne, 128 miles from the city.

Echuca is at the junction of the Murray, Campaspe and Goulburn Rivers. Today it is at the centre of a thriving irrigation area growing rice, cotton and linseed. Once, however, it was a bustling inland port with wharves handling 100,000 bales of wool a year and controlling the floating downstream of the output of a busy logging industry. Those days are now recalled in restored wharves and hotels, paddle-steamers plying for pleasure rather than trade and several museums containing mementoes of the river trade's main personalities. Chief of these was Henry Hopwood, an eccentric who took control of the punt which crossed the river at Echuca to link Victoria with New South Wales.

Take the Murray Valley Highway westwards out of Echuca and the route goes through Kerang to Swan Hill, site of a Pioneer Settlement noteworthy for an excellent sound and light presentation in which the audience moves among the exhibits in rubber-wheeled carriages. This village faithfully recreates the early lives of the pioneers and recounts many stories of the treks into the Outback, their encounters with natives and their problems in victualling, receiving medical aid and growing crops.

From Swan Hill the road follows the banks of the Murray all the way to the far corner of Victoria at Mildura, centre of the citrus, wine and dried fruit industry. This is a broad-avenued town first settled by the Chaffey Brothers from California and still owing much to their foresight and planning. It attracts sun-seekers all year round and has built up a major tourism industry thanks mainly to its equable climate.

Because the Chaffeys were strong prohibitionists, liquor licences were unobtainable in Mildura for many years. This led to the setting up of licenced clubs to which most of the local population belongs, one of them boasting the longest bar in the southern hemisphere, and which, in April 1980, admitted women for the first time.

From Mildura there is a choice of the Calder or the North-Western Highway for a fast run back to Melbourne. Take the North-Western for a new route and come back through Ballarat—scene of the Eureka Stockade "revolution" in the 1850s and noteworthy now for its Sovereign Hill project, which successfully recreates the town as it was in the gold mining era. It is possible to fossick (picking over abandoned workings) for gold, dine by candlelight amid crinolines and top hats and pass beneath a hillside along a miner's tunnel. From Ballarat it is a fast 70 mile drive back into Melbourne via expressway.

PRACTICAL INFORMATION FOR VICTORIA

 HOW TO GET THERE. Before mentioning the various means of transport, it should be emphasized that Victoria is very strict on the import of fruit, flowers, vegetables, birds, insects and animals. The dreaded fruit fly is a threat to the big fruit growing industry. Thus at airports, railway stations, seaports and at the main roads into Victoria there will be fruit fly inspectors and/or signs.

By air: Most international passengers arrive through the international Melbourne Airport at Tullamarine; in the same complex are the major Australian domestic airlines, Ansett, East-West, and TAA. Low-cost carrier East-West Airlines offers bargain fares from Sydney to Melbourne. International airlines serving Melbourne include Air Nauru, Air New Zealand (which has direct flights from New Zealand ports), Pan American, (though its Pacific route may be taken over by United) British Airways, Alitalia, Singapore Airlines, and Qantas.

By rail: Main trunk routes are via Albury from New South Wales and Sydney and from Western Australia (Perth) through South Australia (Adelaide). The train runs overnight, nightly between Melbourne and Adelaide and nightly and daily between Melbourne and Sydney. There is also a service between Melbourne and the Federal capital, Canberra, via Yass where a bus connects to Canberra.

By road: Modern express coaches link Melbourne with all other mainland states, the main operators being Ansett Pioneer, Greyhound, Olympic East-West, and Deluxe Coachlines. Visitors with valid driver's licenses (see "Facts At Your Fingertips") may hire cars from firms such as Avis, Hertz and Budget.

 HOW TO GET AROUND. *By air:* Ansett and TAA have regular services between Melborne and all state capitals plus Canberra and Alice Springs and Darwin, linking with intrastate airlines at each place for onward travel to smaller towns. East-West flies between Sydney and Melbourne and from Melbourne to other cities in Australia. Tullamarine, 10 miles northwest of the city, is the international and domestic airport, and is equipped to take any commercial aircraft now flying in the world. The second, and former major airport, Essendon, six miles northwest of Melbourne, can take all aircraft up to Boeing 727 and DC 9s and is mainly used by commuter and charter airlines. Such are Executive Airlines, Merimbula/Melbourne and Melbourne/Launceston/Devonport; Kendell Airlines, operating between the New South Wales towns of Cooma, Wagga and Griffith to Melbourne and from the coastal towns of Merimbula (NSW) and Mallacoota (Victoria) to Melbourne.

Skybus, a private concern, operates buses between the airport and several locations in the city every 30 minutes. Price is A$4–5. There are good reliable taxis costing 80 cents flagfall, 35 cents per km.

By rail: Apart from major trunk routes interstate, Victorian Railways operates suburban rail services fanning out from the city, in some cases connected by bus to outer suburbs from the rail terminus. It also operates trains on a less frequent basis into the southeast area of the State (Gippsland) and northward to the Murray River town of Mildura and to country towns in the Western district.

By car: Road travel is the most popular form of travel for holiday-makers in Australia. Victoria gets more than its share of vacationers because of the top class road system within the state. The rules are the same as those for the interstate: keep to the left; give way to oncoming traffic on your right. This latter rule is superseded in Victoria when the road you are on has a priority road sign—broad upward arrow crossed by a narrow line. Traffic entering your road on your right has to give way. However, a "major road takes priority" rule predominates.

In the city look out for overhead lane signals, usually operating at peak traffic

Sounding of horns is forbidden except in an emergency or when overtaking. You can drive in any lane marked with a green or white light regardless of its position on the road.

Two unusual road rules apply to the city of Melbourne, which has trams operating on its main roads. Always pass a tram on the *left;* but when a tram has stopped you must stop also unless there is a railed safety zone for tram passengers. Then you may overtake with care—again on the left.

At the intersection of Flinders, Collins and Bourke Streets with Elizabeth and Swanston Streets, drivers wishing to turn *right* must keep well in the *left* lane, drive forward, keep on the left until the forward moving traffic has finished and then turn right, across the whole intersection. This is so that you do not impede a tram driving down the centre of the road while waiting to turn right.

In built-up areas where there are traffic lights the speed limit is 37 mph (60 kmh). Outside this area, the limit is 60 mph (100 kmh). If you see a P plate on a car this means the driver is new, having passed the driving test but still on probation.

Leading car rental companies in Victoria are Astoria, Avis, Budget, Hertz, Letz, all of whom require the driver to be 21 years of age. Special reference is required if under 25.

The RACV (Royal Automobile Club of Victoria) is the major source of information on all aspects of road travel and transport in Victoria.

Melbourne's most noted form of transport is the tram, the last in Australia. Brisbane took its trams out a few years ago to improve traffic flow. In came more cars and made it worse!

At the time of writing, concession cards offering eight trips within metropolitan Melbourne for $2 were available; a city trip is the same price all the time, 30 cents regardless of number of stops. "Travel Cards" (bought from the conductor) are valid for the entire network but only for the day of issue. The trams service not only the city, but radiate out to the suburbs.

Express coach companies Ansett Pioneer Express, Cobb & Co. and Greyhound operate interstate services from Melbourne and there are several local bus lines.

 TRAILER TIPS. Victorians love to go camping and caravanning (trailer camping). This State has, per square mile, probably the best road system of all and plenty of parks to cater for holidaying families. Thus, beware of Victorian coastal parks at peak seasons—December, January and Easter holidays.

Many parks are then crowded or untidy, or both, with vacationers living cheek by jowl in crowded conditions they would not tolerate in their own homes. Inland, during these times, and everywhere during the rest of the year, parks are of a high standard with laundry, barbecues and hot showers. A deposit for a key to the facilities is usually requested.

Because there are so many parks, and for very detailed information on attractions, facilities and how and where to book, consult the RACV Australian Outdoor Guide which you can buy from this motoring organisation, 123 Queen Street, Melbourne.

Most parks will garage your caravan for you; they have minimum stay periods over the peak holiday season. Most have also on-site caravans but the price quoted is for two to four people for a site without power. LPG means bottled gas available.

SPORTS. All the major sports enjoyed by Australians and overseas visitors are found in Victoria.

Pride of place throughout the winter is *Australian rules football,* played on a large oval-shaped field in stadiums (in Victoria) which seat up to 100,000 people and normally attract crowds up to 60,000 and 70,000 during major games mid-season. The game is most popular in Victoria and is an adaptation of Gaelic and rugby football.

Racing is popular throughout the year, and Melbourne has the distinction of being the only city in the world which has a public holiday for a horse race—the Melbourne Cup, which has been raced on the first Tuesday in November since 1867. For three minutes (the average duration of the race) virtually the whole population of Australia stops to listen to the race on radio. The Melbourne Cup is the highlight of what is known as the Spring Carnival in Melbourne, with picnic races in outer metropolitan resort centres, run midweek between major races.

WINTER SPORTS. The major winter sports are: Australian rules *football, soccer, rugby,* men's and women's *hockey, basketball, netball, baseball, softball, lacrosse, skiing, skating.*

SUMMER SPORTS. In summer *cricket, tennis, track and field, swimming, surfing, sailing, hiking,* and *archery* are popular.

Year-round sports include *horse racing, trotting, road running, greyhound racing, motor racing, cycle racing, hillclimbs* and *rallies.*

Golf, squash, 10-pin bowling, skating, rowing, water-skiing, angling and *shooting* all claim large followings. *Jogging* is now widely enjoyed and the Big M Marathon from suburban Frankston to the city centre (September or October) has become a major event with 8,000 runners taking part. Cycle tracks have been laid down along the banks of the River Yarra and in some suburbs.

Pride of place for spectator sports is the *Melbourne Cricket Ground,* less than a mile from the centre of Melbourne. This stadium, site of the 1956 Olympic Games, holds 130,000 spectators for Victorian Football League (Australian Rules) Grand Finals and records of 80,000 and more for international cricket tests.

The *VFL Park,* headquarters for the league is at suburban Waverley, about 17 km from Melbourne, and other major grounds are spread through the suburbs and at Geelong. Major district cricket matches are played at these grounds and at the Albert Ground, next to Albert Park off St. Kilda Road.

Kooyong Tennis Courts in suburban Hawthorn (Kooyong is a suburb of Hawthorn) is the scene of many Davis Cup tussles and one of the great grass courts of the world.

Swimming and *track and field* are performed in facilities built for the 1956 Olympic Games, in Swan Street, less than a mile by tram, bus or taxi from the centre of the City.

Racing is at Flemington—Australia's premier racecourse; 6 km from Melbourne; Caulfield—second to Flemington in Victoria and 10 km from Melbourne; Moonee Valley—a small and beautiful course, 6 km from the City; and Sandown—a larger racecourse and motor circuit, 18 km from the City.

Greyhound racing is run at several tracks around Victoria, but the main metropolitan track is at one of the former Olympic Park grounds, now headquarters of Victorian Rugby Union.

Golf is played on many public and private courses around Melbourne and in the country. The leading courses are southeast of Melbourne and are the scene of Australian Opens and other major events which annually attract such major players as Jack Nicklaus, Gary Player, Johnny Miller, and internationals from

Australia and all over the world. Leaders include Royal Melbourne, Commonwealth, Yarra Yarra and Metropolitan.

 GARDENS. Central Highlands region: *Bacchus Marsh* lion and tiger safari park. Turn off the Western Highway. Exotic animals, adventure playgrounds, picnic and barbecue facilities. *Werribee Gorge State Park,* spectacular scenery, picnics, walking. *Naringal,* a magnificent Western District sheep property, admits day visitors. Has airstrip, swimming pool, tennis courts and feeds visitors right royally, wine and all. Overnight accommodation.

Gippsland region: *Moss Vale Park,* along the coast road from Leongatha. Stands as a memorial to its founder, Francis Moss. He came to Gippsland from Ballarat in 1888 after the first gold rush had ended and later established a nursery here. *Turtons Creek* 10 miles north of Foster, scene of early gold discoveries, is well known for its fern gullies and as a haunt by lyre birds. *Won Wron Forest* via Yarram is a foothill forest of messmate, peppermints and stringbark with orchids, wildflowers, birds, wallabies and kangaroos.

Goulburn region: *Lake Mokoan,* via Benalla and Winton, is Victoria's fourth largest reservoir. It is built on the former Winton swamp and bird life abounds. *Kyabram Fowl and Fauna Park* is 130 acres with five lakes and variety of birds including a 40-acre enclosure for kangaroos and emus.

North Central region: *Dawson's Cactus Gardens* at Bendigo also contains a large collection of historic bottles. Parking, picnic areas, barbecue. *Hanging Rock Reserve* at Woodend features horse racing on New Years Day and Australia Day. Visitors can try their hand. Barbecue and picnic facilities. *McIvor Range Reserve* at Heathcote is a recreational park with timber and apiary displays, powder magazine and log cabin. *Mt. Alexander Koala Park* reserve at Harcourt. Picnic area, barbecue facilities. North East region: *Dargo High Plains,* south of Mt Hotham, a beautiful spectacle in spring, with wildflowers.

Northwest region: *Kulkyna State Forest,* wildlife sanctuary at Colignan via Red Cliffs. *Golden River Fauna Gardens,* Mildura, by the Murray River. Has abundance of native animals and birds. *King's Billabong* off Cureton Avenue, Nicholls Point, has an abundance of bird life.

Otway-Geelong: *Fairy Park* at Anakie. Animated and stone figures depicting fairy tales, somewhat the worse for weather. *Koombahla Park,* Ocean Grove. Bush setting for picnics, barbecues, trail rides. $5 each including barbecue.

Westernport-Healesville region: *Emerald Lake,* Emerald, via Belgrave. Four acre lake with recreational facilities. Pool with dressing shed, toilets. National *Rhododendron Gardens* at Olinda—extensive complex is within Olinda state forest. Open daily. Toilet/barbecue facilities. *Nicholas Memorial Gardens,* Sherbrooke—flowering shrubs and alpine plants. Mountain scenery walks, public restaurant. *Peninsula Gardens,* Rosebud. Picnic and barbecue park covering 350 acres with pool, golf course, zoo. Closed winter, open daily Oct–Feb. *William Ricketts Sanctuary,* Olinda. Ricketts carved aboriginal and animal heads out of stone and tree trunks all over the sanctuary. Open daily. *Tesselaar's Tulip Farm,* Silvan, a tulip and hyacinth farm. Flowers for sale.

Wimmera: *Lions Park,* Warracknabeal. Collection of birds and animals in picturesque land of the Yarriambiack Creek. *Wathe Fauna Reserve,* north of Lascelles. Breeding area of the mallee fowl.

 TOURS. Victoria is just made for touring by bus or car. Ansett and TAA have fly-drive exploring tours of the State which include flights from interstate capital cities. Within Victoria, operators Ansett Pioneer, Victour (tour name of the Victorian Government Travel Authority) Australian Pacific Coaches (APC), AAT, Greyhound Trans Otway and Victorian Railways (Vicrail) offer weekend to two-week tours.

Ansett Pioneer, AAT and APC also operate half and full day tours in Melbourne and out to the surrounding area. Such tours visit the *Dandenong Ranges* and *Healesville Sanctuary* to the east, where the rare duckbilled platypus can be seen and emus eat out of your hand; to *Eildon Reservoir* lakes and the trout hatchery to the northeast; the gold mining historic area of *Castlemaine* and the working *Wattle Gully* gold mine; the mineral springs area of *Daylesford* and *Hepburn* to the northwest; *Mitchelton Winery* in the north; down southeast to *Walhalla*, a ghost town; south to scenic *Phillip Island* and the fairy penguin parade at dusk, or the spectacular coastal and mountain scenery of *Wilsons Promontory National Park;* the *Acheron Way* and *Warburton* forest and mountain area eastward; and the recreated gold mining town of Ballarat's *Sovereign Hill* to the west, plus *Bendigo,* another gold town, with a famous pottery.

All these attractions are naturally included on longer tours which go to the *Grampian Mountains* in the west for wonderful wildflowers in spring; further on to the *Little Desert;* up north to *Swan Hill* and its working, growing, pioneer settlement and the citrus-growing town of *Mildura.*

Vicrail has two discovery tours, one of the eastern, one of the western half of the state. The latter goes by coach to Ballarat, Geelong and along the scenic Great Ocean Road to Warrnambool, up to the country centre of Horsham and across to the river town of Mildura, with a train journey back to Melbourne. The eastern tour starts with train to Mildura and coach back to Melbourne via Swan Hill, Shepparton, Bright, Beechworth and Benalla.

 SPECIAL INTEREST TOURS. For a small state, Victoria has a diversity of special interest tours. Apart from the Melbourne Cup tour aimed at interstate visitors and offered by TAA and Ansett, Victour (the State Government tourist bureau) is the office to see for special interest trips.

Samples are a horse stud tour to see studs, visit the Totalisator Agency Board (TAB) to inspect the modern computerised betting operation and to see Flemington Racecourse and other notable courses.

There's a farming tour to see sheep and wheat properties, to visit an agricultural museum and a pastoral research farm. There are also dairyfarming and mixed farming tours.

The Golden Victoria tour takes travellers into the gold mining area west of Melbourne, historic remains of gold mines, and *Dunolly* and *Moliagul* where the Welcome Stranger, the largest single mass of gold found in the world (210 pounds) was discovered just eight inches under the ground. The tour finishes with a visit to *Sovereign Hill,* Ballarat's recreated gold rush town.

In the Murray River country on the north border of Victoria lie the vineyards of the state and a six day tour visits these and the NSW wineries, sampling and seeing.

There's an ornithologists' tour to study native birds out west and north of the city and right down south to Phillip Island where the fairy penguin wades ashore at dusk.

There are three golf tours, one going south of the city down the Mornington Peninsula, one going north into river and winery country and one west to Geelong for the magnificent scenery of the Great Ocean Road. All include games on good and scenic courses.

Finally, there's a flora and fauna trip lasting 12 days—most comprehensive since it goes south and east and south and west of the state—and a Discover Victoria tour of seven days. This incorporates the main attractions of the recreated coal mining town at *Kurrumburra,* limestone caves, trout farms, wine areas, the historic river port of *Echuca, Swan Hill* with its pioneer settlement and the gold area of *Ballarat.*

All these tours are based on a minimum of 25 people travelling.

INDUSTRIAL TOURS. Besides specific inclusive tours, many public and private enterprises are open to casual callers or individuals who make a booking or telephone call before arrival. The northeast region is where these are concentrated.

Central highlands region: *Chateau Remy* winery at Avoca at the foot of the Pyrenees Ranges, open Monday to Friday, cellar door sales: *Great Western Cellars and Winery,* one of the most famous, about 16 miles west of Ararat at Great Western. Owned by Seppelt, four tours daily weekdays and Saturday morning. Bottle shop open 9-6 P.M. Numerous other vineyards have been established and have built traditional-style cellars to welcome visitors.

Gippsland region: Australian Paper Manufacturers, *Maryvale Mill,* between Morwell and Traralgon, where the manufacturing process can be seen. (Telephone to arrange visit.) Morwell, *open cut mine,* also at Yallourn. Open daily. Go to reception centre at Yallourn or No. 1 gate at Morwell's Hazelwood station.

Goulburn region: *Baileys Vineyard* five miles north of Glenrowan, founded 1870. Open weekdays and Saturday. Picnic tables, barbecue. *Chateau Tahbilk,* just past Seymour, one of the most beautiful and historic properties in Victoria. Underground cellars. Closed Sundays. *Girgarre Cheese Factory*—Victoria's largest, specialising in fancy cheeses. Inspection by arrangement between April and September. *Shepparton-Ibis Milk Products*—tours Monday-Friday 10 A.M. Butter and powdered milk products. *Mitchelton Vineyard,* north of Seymour, imaginative concept incorporates both vineyard and tourist complex on banks of Goulburn river. Swimming and wading pools, playground, restaurant, wine tasting facilities.

At Shepparton, *Ibis Milk Products* operate tours weekdays 10 A.M.; *Shepparton Preserving Co.* also has weekday tours at 10 A.M. and 2 P.M.—it is the largest canning factory in the southern hemisphere.

North Central region: *Wattle Gully Gold Mine* has daily tours through mining tunnel by train and then by foot to see battery and winding room. (Excellent little tour.) *Whipstick Eucalyptus Factory* shows how oil of eucalypt and other products are extracted from these trees. Sundays only. *Charlie's Hope* gold mineworking, vintage machinery. Open daily. Restaurant near. Parking, picnic area.

North East region: *All Saints Winery,* Wahgunyah, built about 1880, classified by the National Trust. Museum of wine-making and vineyard equipment. Open Mon-Sat. Picnic and barbecue facilities. *Brown Bros Winery,* Milawa—one of the best of its kind.

North West region: Near Lake Boga is *Bests Winery,* where the ancient art of winemaking is coupled with modern techniques. Cellars classified by National Trust. Tour weekdays four times a day. *Bonnonee Winery,* near Irymple, is open for visitors Mon-Sat 10 A.M. to 6 P.M. *Lindeman's Winery* at Keradoc is open for inspection only weekdays, no sales or wine tasting.

Mildura has a variety of factories and vineyards open to the public. These include *Dried Fruit and District Packing House,* packers of oranges, grapefruit, raisins—call any time weekdays; *Urban Water Trust,* filtration plant, Mon, Wed, Fri morning and afternoon; *Mildura Vineyard Winery,* Mon-Sat 10 A.M. to 6 P.M., tastings available; *Sunup Citrus* juice extraction plant, weekdays. At Swan Hill, the pheasant farm and aviaries have a large display of Australian and overseas birds, daily from 10 A.M.

Westernport-Healesville: *Badger Creek Gardens,* a plant nursery are specialist growers of ferns and indoor plants; weekends and public holidays daily; other times by appointment. *General Motors Holden* car assembly plant at Dandenong, eight miles south east of Melbourne, inspection by appointment Mon, Tues, Wed, Fri, 2 P.M. Similarly appointment-only visits to HMAS *Cerberus,* Royal Australian Navy training establishment at Crib Point.

MUSEUMS. Central Highlands region: *Creswick Historical Museum* in gold country shows a magnificent record of early colonial history and district; *Daylesford Museum* has a large wide-ranging collection of mining, dioramas, records, aboriginal artifacts; *Langi Morgala Museum* is a folk museum of early Ararat—aboriginal weapons and effects; steam locomotive and machinery.

East Gippsland region: Genuine aboriginal artifacts in the *Aboriginal Art Museum* at Lakes Entrances and at the same town, the *Antique Car Museum,* claimed to be the state's leading collection of cars and motorcycles. Bairnsdale has an interesting collection of memorabilia in its *Historical Museum,* and the *Sea Shell Museum,* Lakes Entrance, has more than 30,000 shells and the number is continually growing.

Gippsland region: Moe has *Gippsland Folk Museum,* a tangible memorial to the discovery of the rich Gippsland region, with everything on display from slab kitchen to livery stable. At Warragul, the *Old Shire Hall* has become the historical museum showing the history of the area.

Goulburn region: Euroa and district historical society *Farmers' Arms Museum* is a delightful seven-room museum staged in an 100-years-old inn. Benalla—the *Kelly Museum,* Victoria's most famous Bushranger has many folk relics plus the authentic witness box in which Kelly stood, from the old Benalla courthouse. Also at Benalla is the *Pioneer Museum.*

North Central Region: Bendigo—*Dai Gum San Wax Museum* has lifesize wax models depicting Chinese life over several centuries, a tribute to the Chinese who flocked to the Victorian goldfields in the boom days. Wedderburn's *General Store* is also its museum, with coachbuilder and blacksmiths shop. Dunolly has replicas of the largest nugget of gold ever to be found—the 'Welcome Stranger' plus historical items in the *Goldfields* and *Arts Society* museum. There are *Folk* and *Pioneer Museums* at Pyramid Hill, Kyneton, Maldon (itself a historical town) and at Eaglehawk which also has a log lock-up.

North East region: *Yackandandah Bank* of Victoria once housed gold won from local goldfields; now restored as a museum to house historical items. *Millfield Riding School and Carriage Museum* here has a collection of horse-drawn carriages and farm animals for children. At Wodonga many old aircraft are shown at the *Drage's Aircraft Museum* while gold is the theme of the *Eldorado Museum,* situated on Reid's Creek goldfield at Eldorado. Rutherglen's *Wine and Gold Museum* has gold relics and a general collection in an old barber's shop still used today. The owner, Jack O'Keefe keeps visitors absorbed with stories of the past.

Beechworth's *Burke's Memorial Museum* is one of the finest country museums in Victoria. It commemorates Robert O'Hara Burke, the eccentric explorer who, in 1856, was superintendent of police here. The *Carriage and Harness Museum* at Beechworth has an outstanding collection of carriages used during the late 1800's. Corryong—*Man from the Snowy River Museum* includes many unique exhibits such as the oldest ski collection in Australia. It is named after the poem written by Banjo Paterson.

North-west region: *Historical Museums* at Kerang and Wentworth—latter has fine collection of relics, photos and exhibits. Also at Wentworth is a *Motorcycle Museum.* Swan Hill's *Military Museum* has a unique display of more than 2,000 items of human interest; the collection is based on the personal stories of men and women of all nations caught up in the World War. Another war museum is at Mildura, the *War Birds Museum,* with wartime aircraft on the site of the former fighter training base which operated during World War II.

Otway-Geelong region: *Historical Museum* at Apollo Bay, *Maritime Museum,* relics of maritime significance to the area, at Queenscliff. At Geelong, see the unique *Museum of Vintage Steam Trains,* Belmont Common Railway.

South-west region: *Agricultural Museums* at Hamilton, records of early German settlers, and at Marino, machinery and antiques of the 1900's. *Historical Museums* at Portland, Casterton, and a *Gem Museum* (opals, fossils etc.) at

Warrnambool. Also at Warrnambool, *Flagstaff Hill Maritime Museum* in course of creation.

Westernport-Healesville region: Rosebud—*Aquarium* and *Museum* housing 4,000 exhibits from butterflies to aboriginal artifacts. Mornington—*Old Post Office Museum; Historical Museum* at Sorrento.

Wimmera region: *Historical Museum* at Kaniva, Naracoorte *(Old Mill Museum)*. Jeparit's *Wimmera-Mallee Pioneers' Museum* is a 10-acre complex with many historic buildings, period furnishings and countless antiques. The *North Western Agricultural Machinery Museum* at Warracknabeal depicts the history of the wheat industry with giant steampowered chaff cutters, combine harvesters and tractors.

SEASONAL EVENTS. *January:* Corryong, *Folk Festival:* Rutherglen, *Rowing Regatta.*

February: Colac, *Rowing Regatta.*

March: Melbourne's biggest carnival, *Moomba,* street processions, open air theatre, dancing, art displays, water skiing on river, fairs, competitions. Whole city swings. Maffra, *Mardi Gras* on Labour Day weekend, usually second Monday in March. Monbulk *Mountain Festival:* this small town is set in heart of Dandenong Ranges east of Melbourne; Wedderburn (heart of gold rush country), *Gold Dig* competitions, gold panning. Benalla, *Rose Festival;* Numurkah, *Rose Festival.*

April: Mildura *Rowing Regatta. Bright,* autumn festival. *ANZAC Day,* dawn service remembering the war dead, with procession to the Shrine, Melbourne.

August: Maryborough, *Golden Wattle Festival,* when this western country town is ablaze with the yellow blossoms on this native gum tree.

September: Daffodil Festivals at Leongatha and Kyneton.

October: Echuca, *Rich River Festival,* re-enacting the old days when this river city was an important centre of the paddle steamer trade. Dunolly, *Gold Dig* commemorating the day when the "Welcome Stranger," largest nugget of gold ever found in Australia, was discovered.

November: Melbourne Cup. This city is only one in the world which has a public holiday for a horse race. All Australia listens to the radio while it runs. Dimboola, *Rowing Regatta.* Geelong, *Gala Day;* Horsham, *Rowing Regatta.*

December: Melbourne's Christmas Eve—the community gathers at the open air Myer Music Bowl to sing carols by candlelight. *Myrtleford Rodeo* on Boxing Day attracts the best riders from all over Australia.

SHOPPING. There has been a considerable exodus into country regions where people are active in the fields of arts and crafts. Numerous small potteries, art galleries, craft shops and the like produce highly individualized items which make a good buying alternative to mass-produced souvenirs. What follows is only a small selection. Central Highlands region: *William Barkell Arts and Crafts Centre* at Clunes sells pottery and *Clunes Cottage Crafts* features goods made by local artists. Another craft shop is at Ararat—*The Spiders Web.*

East Gippsland: *The Jolly Jumbuck Craft Centre* has leather work and pottery but also shows the only greasy wool being spun commercially in Australia.

Gippsland region: Alan Boucher's *Blue Gum Gallery* has a variety of oils, water colours and sketches.

Goulburn region: *Benalla Regional Art Gallery* has potters, spinners and weavers working on the premises.

North Central region: *Bendigo Pottery*—potters throwing and decorating pots —handmade pottery for sale; *Whipstick Eucalyptus Factory* sells oil of eucalypt and associated products.

North East region: Buy strawberry wine and fresh strawberries from *Allans Flat Strawberry Farm* at Yackandandah. At same town, visit *The Workshop,* where spinning wheels, cane craft, crochet work and knitting can be bought and the art gallery where Frank La Compte still paints. Beechworth—*Cottage Craft* shop has pottery, leather goods, sheepskins for sale; *Gallery* has crafts and painting on display which can also be bought. *The Anvil* at Kergunyah is a popular haven for art enthusiasts and paintings and ceramics are sold here. *Eldorado Curiosity Shop* sells antiques, handcrafts. Buy fresh trout from *Golden Hills Trout Farm,* Silver Creek Road, Beechworth only privately owned trout farm in the area.

North west region: *Aggies Antiques* at Merbein include extensive range of furniture, crockery and china; *Busy Hands Cottage Industries* at Wentworth for hand made goods of every kind; *Craftsmens Market*—cottage industries and handcrafts at Mildura where also are *Granny's Antiques.*

Westernport-Healesville region: *Badger Creek Pottery*—stoneware displays, working pottery kiln firing demonstrations, paintings, opals, jewellery; *Hand Craft Gallery* at Flinders collects and sells stuff from all over Australia.

 HISTORIC SITES. Central Highlands: *Adam Lindsay Gordon's Cottage,* Ballarat, in the botanic gardens. Original timber cottage filled with the personal papers and effects of the famous Australian poet and his contemporaries. Open most days. *Eureka Stockade Park,* Ballarat, on the site of the pitched battle—Australia's only rebellion, in 1854. Stone monument, diorama. *Montrose Cottage*—goldfields period, Ballarat. *Killarney,* Warrenheip, 19th century brick mansion extensive grounds. Open weekends and holiday periods.

East Gippsland region: *Angus McMillan Cottage,* Metung. Home of discoverer of the Gippsland Lakes. *St. Mary's Church,* Bairnsdale—murals, painted ceilings.

Goulburn region: *Brookfield Homestead,* Numurkah. Old property with old machinery, etc; *Faithful Creek Homestead,* which the Kelly gang used as a base for their robbery of the Euroa bank. Ruins only remain after the 1939 bushfires.

North Central: *Castlemaine Market,* beautiful restoration of gracious building now containing audiovisuals of early goldmining days and explorers. *Dudley House,* Bendigo, stately old home and garden containing Bendigo historical display. *Miners' Right Gallery and Store,* Bowenvale-Timor via Maryborough. This is a 127-year-old store which has never closed its doors for trading. Open daily.

North East region: *Beechworth Cemetery,* where Chinese burning towers still stand. Many Chinese gold seekers are buried here and their headstones are still readable. *Beechworth Court House,* scene of bushranger Ned Kelly's final trial. Open by appointment. Also at Beechworth, Ned Kelly's cell beneath the town hall where Kelly was imprisoned at the age of 16.

Westernport-Healesville: *McCrae Homestead,* McCrae, first homestead built on the Mornington Peninsula (1844). Open daily December until Easter, then school/public holidays. *Henty's Cottage,* Olinda, is the home of Victoria's first settler, first man to grow and shear sheep, to plant grapes. Open daily except Friday.

Wimmera region: *John Shaw Neilson Cottage,* Nhill. Memorial to the poet who wrote much of his early poetry while working in the country round Nhill. He was born in 1872. Open weekdays.

 NATIONAL PARKS. Dense rain forest in the south east, red sandy stretches in the north, desert scrub and bush in the west—Victoria has a wide variety of scenery in its national parks and reserves.

All are easily accessible by road, along which are motels and hotels. So parks do not have great accommodation facilities, apart from camping areas, maybe a caravan site or two, or not even that, since they are unnecessary.

Eastern Gippsland region: *Captain James Cook Park,* via Cann River, covers 7,000 acres, is rich in birds, and the waters teem with fish. *Glenaladale Park* between Sale and Bairnsdale is a dry forest of red box, yellow box, intersected by deep rain forest gullies. Walking tracks, picnic shelters and water, fireplaces provided. *Lind Park* between Orbost and Cann River has the Gippsland waratah, mainly dry sclerophyll forest. Fireplaces, picnic tables etc., on the highway. The *Lakes National Park* between Lake Victoria and Reeve in the Lakes Entrance area has varied and rich birdlife, kangaroos, emus, sand plain flowers. Picnic shelters, toilets, fireplaces at Point Wilson. *Wingan Inlet Park,* via Cann River, has excellent fishing, jungle-like subtropical vegetation. Water, fireplaces available. This is the landing place of explorer Bass in his whaleboat Tom Thumb on a coastal survey in 1797.

Gippsland region: *Tarra Valley-Bulga National Park,* near Yarram. Fern gullies, mountain ash and myrtle, beech trees, and home of the lyre bird. Picnic shelters, fireplaces and toilet, parking areas provided. *Wilson's Promontory National Park* is about 140,000 acres with camping and cabins at Tidal River. Very popular holiday area for Victorians. It is the southern extremity of the Australian mainland where kangaroos, wallabies, wombats and koalas abound. The park is named after a London merchant who provided explorers Bass and Flinders with their provisions for their journeys. Toilets, store and kiosk in the Tidal River area.

Goulburn region: *Barmah Forest,* west of Nathalia, is not a national park but worth mentioning as the world's largest forest of red river gum. It stretches along both banks of the River Murray. Breeding ground for waterfowl and emus. Camping facilities, fishing and shooting. *Fraser National Park,* near Alexandra, is ideal for boating, fishing and water sports as it borders the Eildon lakes. Grey kangaroos and black wallabies inhabit this 7,500 acre caravan park and "boatel."

Kinglake National Park covers about 12,000 acres and is characterised by tall temperate forest of mossmate and peppermint. Waterfalls, wombats, lyrebirds can be seen. Car parking, toilets, barbecue facilities at Mason's Falls, kiosk (but no meals). *Kyabram Fowl and Fauna Park* on the southern extremity of the town has a 40-acre enclosure within the 130 acre park for kangaroos and emus. There are five lakes with duck, ibis, swan and pelican. Daily bus service to and from Melbourne, via Heathcote; rail from Melbourne twice daily weekdays, once Saturdays.

North Central region: *Barringo Wildlife Reserve* at Gisborne commercial deer farm; kangaroos, wallabies, koalas as well.

North East region: *Dargo High Plains Area*—a beautiful spectacle in spring with its colourful wildflowers. South of Mt Hotham. *Mt. Buffalo National Park* comprises 26,000 acres, has magnificent alpine scenery. Popular for horseriding, skiing, walking, fishing. Camping is permitted. Huge chalet providing full-board accommodations; bookings through Victour offices. Shelters, fireplaces, parking, refreshments. *Warby Ranges* at Wangaratta is attractive bush country with koalas and blackboy trees.

Northwest region: *Hattah Lakes National Park* 43,000 acres, noted for mallee scrub, grey and red kangaroos, waterbirds and bush birds. Fireplaces and toilets available.

Otway-Geelong region: *Alan Noble Sanctuary,* Anglesea. One acre with miniature lake, water birds.

Southwest region: *Mt. Eccles National Park,* a volcanic crater and small crater lake, open mannagum forest. Fireplaces, picnic shelter and tables, toilets. *Port Campbell Park*—coastal scenery and rock shapes including "London Bridge," "The Arch," "Twelve Apostles" and offshore islands where mutton birds breed. Caravan sites with/without power, hot water, showers.

Westernport-Healesville region: *Churchill National Park,* eight miles north of Dandenong. Open forest area of eucalypt forest especially suited to family picnics. Varied bird population. Fireplaces, water, toilets. *Ferntree Gully National Park* covering 1,300 acres of tree fern, eucalypt forest, peppermint, grey gum. Car parking, barbecue facilities, tables, shelters, toilets, private kiosk. *Sherbrooke Forest Park* via Belgrave, a beautiful area of trees and ferns. Barbecue, tables, seats, kiosk at Kallista. *Steavenson Falls,* Victoria's highest, floodlit at night, half a mile from Marysville, camping ground.

Wimmera region: *Little Desert National Park,* 100,000 acres. Great variety of flowers and birds, especially in spring. Mallee fowl mounds can always be seen. Fireplaces and drinking water. Near Kiata. The Little Desert is technically a desert because there is not enough rainfall to raise crops. Tiny marsupials scamper, kangaroos and lorikeets and honeyeaters come hundreds of miles to feed on the spring blossoms. Four wheel drives are available from Kaniva and Nhill to explore the desert, see the waterhole and the track where the Gold Escort route wound through the desert from South Australia to the Victorian goldfields. This desert is the home of the rare mound-building lowan (or mallee) bird. *Wyperfield National Park,* 150,000 acres, is Victoria's largest. Reached via Rainbow. The landscape varies from virgin mallee (a scrub-like bush after which the whole area around here is named) to red sandhills capped with native pine and tea tree. The rare Regent parrot is easily seen here. Kangaroos and emus are plentiful and relics of old station properties can be seen.

HOT SPRINGS. In the early part of this century, the *Daylesford-Hepburn Springs* area about 80 miles northwest of Melbourne saw its heyday. Tourists, especially Europeans, would flock there to taste the varied waters and take a hot bath. Then popularity died and the place became neglected; however, it is now being revived and smartened up and at Hepburn Springs today mineral baths and waters and rest rooms are available.

GAMBLING. Victorian law does not allow casinos or gambling in the form of slot machines, etc. Those seeking these diversions usually stay in one of the River Murray towns and cross the border into New South Wales to enjoy the poker machines at one of the licensed clubs. Huge amounts are, however, wagered each week in Victoria on horse and dog racing, football pools, the Tattslotto numbers game and Tattersalls lottery.

WHAT TO DO WITH THE CHILDREN. Central Highlands region: For animals go to the Bacchus Marsh *Lion and Tiger Safari Park.* Take a ride on an original Ballarat tram round the shores of Lake Wendouree. *Kryal Castle* at Warrenheip near Ballarat is a replica of a medieval English castle and at Ballarat, *Golda's World of Dolls* houses one of the largest collection of dolls in the world. Pan for gold at *Sovereign Hill* recreated gold mining town in Ballarat.

East Gippsland region: *Buchan Caves;* Collins *Wooden Toy Factory* at Bairnsdale, open weekdays, solid toys made from local wood.

Goulburn region: Horse-minded kids might like to see the quarter horse and Appaloosa stud at *Running N Ranch,* at Nathalia and those with a bent for nature could find interest in the Snobs Creek *Fish Hatchery. Kinglake House of Bottles,* at the entrance to Jehosaphat Valley National Park, is made of 13,569 bottles and inside has a display of bottles from all over the world.

North Central region: *Barringo Wildlife Reserve* is a commercial deer farm (also kangaroos, koalas) open weekends and public holidays. The *Vintage Talking Tram* at Bendigo takes passengers through the heart of Bendigo with tape-recorded commentary on points of interest.

North East region: Beechworth's *Silver Creek Tunnels,* series of mining tunnels, one of which it is possible to walk through; look for gold in Woolshed Creek goldfields.

Otway-Geelong region *Freshwater Creek Big Bottle,* made out of thousands of bottles and includes slides and collection of old bottles. Open during school holidays. Same place, go to *D'Oro Homestead* and join in activities—donkey rides, etc. Four hundred acres of farmland and 80 acres natural bush. Visit the largest volcanic caves in Victoria at *Mt. Widderin Station.*

Westernport-Healesville region: Ride *Puffing Billy* through fern forests in the Dandenong Ranges—a 77-year old steam engine.

Wimmera region: Put a coin in the slot and hear the history of the horse and its contribution to the development of Australia at the *Draught Horse Memorial,* Main Street, Nhill; go rock climbing at *Mt. Arapiles,* Natimuk; visit *Naracoorte Caves* and the snake pit in the same town; at Stawell, see a world in miniature showing man's social and technological evolution.

HOTELS AND MOTELS. Price ranges for double rooms are: *Expensive:* A$50 and up; *Moderate:* A$35–50; *Inexpensive:* A$25–35.

Alexandra

Redgate Motel. *Moderate.* Near Lake Eildon—water sports.

Anglesea

The Cabins Motel. *Moderate.* Pool. Near beach, shops.

Ararat

Chalambar Motel. *Moderate.* Rate includes light breakfast. Pool. Near Grampians mountains, golf course.

Golden Gate Motel. *Moderate.* Liquor room service. Licensed restaurant. Pool. Near mountain climbing facilities, golf, tennis, bowls. Member Flag chain.

Axedale

Brolga Hotel/Motel. *Moderate.* Liquor room service. Licensed restaurant. Sun balconies overlook lake. Boating, fishing, swimming, waterskiing. Indoor bowls, pool tables. Golf course, 9 km.

Bairnsdale

Bairnsdale Motor Inn. *Moderate.* Pool. Near beach, golf, sporting facilities. Mountain views. Member Flag chain.

Motel Main. *Moderate.* Pool. Near lakes, golf, tennis, squash courts.

Motel Marlin Motor Inn. *Moderate.* Near all water sports, fishing.

Town Central Motel. *Moderate.* Includes light breakfast. In heart of lakes region, near ocean.

Wander Inn. *Moderate.* Rate includes cooked breakfast. No restaurant. Near lakes, fishing, golf, squash courts. Member Zebra chain.

Travelana Motel. *Inexpensive.* Off-season rates available. Near beach, golf course. Member MFA Homestead chain.

Ballarat

Ambassador Motel. *Moderate.* Licensed restaurant. Pool. Near golf course. Sovereign Hill recreated gold mining village.

Avenue Motel. *Moderate.* Pool. No restaurant. Near golf course, lawn bowling. Member MFA Homestead chain.

Balwaren Hotel. *Moderate.* Light breakfast included. Near Eureka Stockade, Sovereign Hill, Kryal Castle.

Begonia City Motel/Hotel. *Moderate.* Includes hot breakfast. Liquor room service. Licensed restaurant. Near Sovereign Hill, Eureka Stockade, Kryal Castle.

City Oval Motel/Hotel. *Moderate.* Includes light breakfast. Liquor room service. Licensed restaurant. Walking distance to town. Near lake, parkland.

Eureka Lodge Motel. *Moderate.* Includes light breakfast. No restaurant. Near Eureka Stockade, swimming pool.

Old Ballarat Travel Inn. *Moderate.* No restaurant. Opposite Sovereign Hill. Member MFA Homestead chain.

Park View Motor Inn. *Moderate.* Licensed restaurant. Near lake, golf course, gardens. Member Flag chain.

Peppinella Motel. *Moderate.* No restaurant. Near three golf courses, lake. Member Flag chain.

Balook

Grand Ridge Motel. *Moderate.* Rate includes hot breakfast. Licensed restaurant. Bush walking, trout fishing. Near beach.

Beechworth

Beechworth Motor Inn. *Moderate.* No restaurant. Pool. Near snow country (1 hr.), golf, bowls, tennis, horseriding. Mountain views.

Golden Heritage Motor Inn. *Moderate.* No restaurant. Near snowfields (1 hr.), water skiing. Mountain scenery.

Benalla

Motel Black and White. *Moderate.* No restaurant. 24 hr. food service. Near golf course, bowls and swimming. Restaurant next door.

Bendigo

Captain Cook Hotel/Motel. *Moderate.* Liquor room service. Licensed restaurant. Near lake, golf course, race course.

Golden Hills Motel. *Moderate.* Liquor room service. Licensed restaurant. 24 hr. room service. Pool. Near golf course. Has large garden. Dinner dances. Floor shows. Member Flag chain.

Welcome Stranger Motel. *Moderate.* Includes cooked breakfast. Liquor room service. Licensed restaurant. Near lake (waterskiing), golf courses, tennis, bowls. Member Flag chain.

Bright

Bogong View Motor Inn. *Moderate.* Licensed restaurant. Pool. Near golf, bowls. Scenic walks. Mountain views. Member Flag chain.

Pinewood Motel/Hotel. *Moderate.* Includes light breakfast. Off-season rates available. Licensed restaurant. Town centre.

Red Carpet Inn. *Moderate.* No restaurant. Pool. Mountain views. Member Flag chain.

Alpine Hotel/Motel. *Inexpensive.* Includes light breakfast. Kitchen facilities in rooms. Licensed restaurant. Near golf course.

Buchan

Forest Lodge Motel. *Inexpensive.* Includes cooked breakfast. Mountain views. Bush walks. Caves. Trout fishing, golf, tennis.

Cohuna

Garby's Hotel/Motel. *Moderate.* Liquor room service. Licensed restaurant. Near golf course, fishing, shooting.

Colac

Commercial Hotel/Motel. *Moderate.* Liquor room service. Licensed restaurant. In city centre. Near golf course.

Colac Lake Motel. *Inexpensive.* Overlooking lake.

Corryong
Pinnibar Motel. *Moderate.* No restaurant. Pool. Mountain views.

Creswick
Rhodeside Motel. *Moderate.* Includes light breakfast. Liquor room service. No restaurant. Near bowls, golf, fishing and koala park.

Dromana
Blue Dolphin Motor Lodge. *Moderate.* Rate includes cooked breakfast. No restaurant. Near beach, golf.

Gazebo Lodge. *Moderate.* Licensed restaurant. 24 hr. food service. Near beach.

Drouin
Casa Blanca Motor Inn. *Moderate.* Licensed restaurant. Near golf, bowls, river.

Echuca
Caledonian Hotel/Motel. *Moderate.* Some cheaper rooms without private facilities. Hot breakfast included in rate. Liquor room service. Licensed restaurant. Kitchen facilities in rooms.

Echuca Motel. *Moderate.* No restaurant. Pool. Member Flag chain.

High Street Motel. *Moderate.* No restaurant. Near historic points of interest.

Euroa
Castle Creek Motel. *Inexpensive.* No restaurant. Near swimming, golf, tennis. Mountain views.

Falls Creek
Pretty Valley Ski Lodge. Limited number of rooms. Open June–September during snow season. Own ski hire service. Games room.

Fish Creek
Promontory Gate Motel/Hotel. *Moderate.* Includes cooked breakfast. Licensed restaurant. Mountain views. Nearest hotel to Wilsons Promontory national park.

Foster
Foster Motel. *Moderate.* Pool. Nr Wilsons Promontory, golf, bowls. Member Flag chain.

Wilsons Promontory Motel. *Moderate.* Licensed restaurant. 24 hr. food service. Near beaches. Fishing.

Geelong
Commodore Geelong. *Expensive.* Liquor room service. Licensed restaurant. Near beach, golf. Member Commodore chain.

Innkeepers, Geelong. *Expensive.* Liquor room service. Licensed restaurant. Near beaches, golf. Short distance post office. Member Flag chain.

Geelong TraveLodge. *Expensive.* Liquor room service. Licensed restaurant. 24 hr. food service. Central location overlooking city to bay. Member Southern Pacific chain.

Buena Vista Motor Inn. *Moderate.* Licensed restaurant. Pool. Near beaches, tennis, bowls and croquet. Member Flag chain.

Dinosaur Hotel/Motel. *Moderate.* Liquor room service. Licensed restaurant. Near beach, golf, next squash courts. Mountain views.

Sundowner Hotel/Motel. *Moderate.* Rate includes hot breakfast. Liquor room service. Licensed restaurant. Near leading surf beaches.

Glenrowan

Kelly Country Motel. *Inexpensive.* Rate includes light breakfast. Near wineries, lake. No restaurant.

Hamilton

Newark Homestead. *Moderate.* Near art gallery, gardens. Member MFA Homestead chain.

Harcourt

Castlemaine Motel. *Moderate.* Near bowls, swimming pool. Member Flag chain.

Healesville

Maroondah View Motel. *Moderate.* Rate includes hot breakfast.

Sovereign Hotel. *Moderate.* Some cheaper rooms without private facilities. Includes hot breakfast. Liquor room service. Licensed restaurant. Near golf, horseriding.

Horsham

Commodore Major Mitchell Motor Inn. *Moderate.* Liquor room service. Licensed restaurant. Near swimming pool. In main shopping area. Member Commodore chain.

Galaxy Motel. *Moderate.* Includes light breakfast. No restaurant. Pool. Near golf course. Member MFA Homestead chain.

Jamieson

Lakeside Hotel Motel. *Inexpensive.* Includes hot breakfast. Liquor room service. Licensed restaurant. Fishing, boating, swimming near.

Kyneton

Central Highland Motor Inn. *Moderate.* No restaurant. Near golf course, historical buildings, museum, racecourse, bowls, fishing.

Lake Boga

Lake Boga Motor Inn. *Moderate.* Liquor room service. Licensed restaurant. Pool. On edge of Lake Boga. Member MFA Homestead chain.

Lakes Entrance

Abel Tasman Motor Lodge. *Moderate.* Includes light breakfast. No restaurant. Pool. Water sports, fishing, golf nearby.

Glenara Motel. *Moderate.* Off-season rates available. Liquor room service. Licensed restaurant. Pool. On beach front. Near golf course.

Sherwood Lodge Motor Inn. *Moderate.* Off-season rates available. Near beach, lakes, caves. Member Flag chain.

Sparkle Motel. *Moderate.* Includes light breakfast. Near shops, surf beach. Member MFA Homestead chain.

Learmonth

Loura Motor Inn. *Moderate.* Edge of Lake Learmonth. Member Flag chain.

Lorne

Motel Kalimna. *Moderate.* Includes hot breakfast. Licensed restaurant. Tennis court, croquet lawn. Overlooks ocean.

The Lorne Hotel-Motel. *Moderate.* Some cheaper rooms without private facilities. Includes hot breakfast. Liquor room service. Licensed restaurant. Table tennis. Near beach, golf course.

Mallacoota

Mallacoota Inlet Hotel/Motel. *Moderate.* Includes light breakfast. Off-season rates available. Liquor room service. Licensed restaurant. Pool. Near beach, lake, golf course. Member Flag chain.

Marysville

The Cumberland. *Moderate.* Liquor room service. Licensed restaurant. Pool. Own bowling green, croquet green, tennis court. Resort hotel in mountain setting. Golf course, horseriding near. Own putting green.

Marysville Hotel/Motel. *Moderate.* Liquor room service. Licensed restaurant. Near golf, bowls, horseriding.

Mildura

Mildura Grand Hotel. *Expensive,* Rate includes hot breakfast. Liquor room service. Licensed restaurant. 24 hr. food service. Near river, golf course. Indoor games facilities. Heated swimming pool.

Central Motel. *Moderate.* Pool. Near river. Member Flag chain.

Commodore Mildura. *Moderate.* Liquor room service. Licensed restaurant. Pool. In main shopping area. Near river, golf course. Member Commodore chain.

Innkeepers Mildura Country Club. *Moderate.* Licensed restaurant. Pool. On golf course. Member Flag chain.

Mildura Inlander Motor Inn. *Moderate.* Liquor room service. Licensed restaurant. Pool. Bowling green, two lawn tennis courts, golf putting course, sauna. Member Flag chain.

Northaven TraveLodge. *Moderate.* Licensed restaurant. Pool. On main Melbourne-Adelaide highway. Member Southern Pacific chain.

Sunset Deakin Motel. *Moderate.* Rate includes light breakfast. Off-season rates available. Licensed restaurant. Pool. Set in parklands. Member Sunset chain.

Mornington

Ranch Motel. *Moderate.* Liquor room service. Licensed restaurant. Pool. Near beach, sporting facilities.

Morwell

Del Spana Motor Inn. *Moderate.* Licensed restaurant. Member Flag chain.

Latrobe Valley Motel/Hotel. *Moderate.* Some cheaper rooms without private facilities. Hot breakfast included. Licensed restaurant.

Mount Beauty

Allamar Ranch Motor Inn. *Moderate.* Rate includes light breakfast. No restaurant.

Meriki Motel. *Moderate.* Rate includes hot breakfast. Golf course.

Mount Buffalo

Government Chalet. *Expensive* but all meals included. Off-season rates available and some cheaper rooms without private facilities. Pool.

Tatra Inn Motel. *Expensive/deluxe* range but dinner and breakfast included. Off-season rates available. Some cheaper rooms without private facilities. Liquor room service. Licensed restaurant. Pool. Year-round mountain holiday resort. Skiing in season.

Mount Buller

Aarlberg. *Expensive/deluxe.* Off-season rates available. Liquor room service. Licensed restaurant. Pool. Near Lake Eildon, golf course, horseriding. Snow skiing in season.

Kooroora Chalet. Light breakfast included. Licensed restaurant. Pool. Horseriding. Snow skiing in season.

Pension Grimus. Off-season rates available. Licensed restaurant. Open only during winter skiing season.

Nathalia

Motel Nathalia. *Moderate.* Kitchen facilities in rooms. No restaurant. Pool. Bowls, tennis, swimming, fishing, golf, nearby. Member Golden Inn chain.

Peterborough

Schombers Inn. *Moderate.* Includes light breakfast. Licensed restaurant. Near beach, golf course, tennis courts.

Phillip Island

Continental Motel. *Expensive.* Includes light breakfast. Off-season rates available. Liquor room service. Licensed restaurant. Pool. Opposite beach, squash court.

Isle of Wight Hotel/Motel. *Expensive.* Cheaper rooms without private facilities. Rate includes light breakfast. Off-season rates available. Licensed restaurant. Pool. Near beach, golf, shops. Private tennis courts.

Erehwon Point Motel. *Moderate.* Includes hot breakfast. Off-season rates available. Kitchen facilities in rooms. Near main beach.

Koala Park Holiday & Tennis Resort. *Moderate.* Rate includes light breakfast. Pool. Near koalas, penguins. Tennis courts with first class coaching available.

Sunseeker Motor Inn. *Moderate.* Off-season rates available. Kitchen facilities in room. Pool. Near beach, own tennis court, children's play area, gas barbecues. Member Flag chain.

Yackatoon Holiday Lodge. *Moderate.* Some cheaper rooms without private facilities. Rate includes light breakfast. Pool. Near beach, golf course, yacht club.

Porepunkah

Buffalo Motel. *Moderate.* Trout fishing. Member MFA Homestead.

Port Campbell

Lochard Motor Inn. *Moderate.* Off-season rates available. Near beach.

Port Fairy

Motel Tatra. *Moderate.* Includes light breakfast. Liquor room service. Licensed restaurant. Near beach, golf course, tennis courts, bowling club, fishing, boating. National Trust building.

Seacombe House Motel. *Moderate.* Some cheaper rooms without private facilities. Includes light breakfast. Licensed restaurant. Near beach, golf course. Table tennis, billiards room.

Portland

Grosvenor Hotel. *Moderate.* Rate includes light breakfast. Licensed restaurant. Near beach. Member, MFA Homestead chain.

Janroy Motel. *Moderate.* Rate includes light breakfast. No restaurant. Near squash courts, harbour.

Motel Siesta. *Moderate.* Off-season rates available. Pool. Near beach, town centre. Member Flag chain.

Portland Motel. *Moderate.* Liquor room service. Licensed restaurant. Overlooking bay.

Richmond Henty Hotel/Motel. *Moderate.* Liquor room service. Licensed restaurant. Pool. Near beach, Member Flag chain.

Queenscliff

Queenscliff Hotel. *Expensive.* Renovated old hostelry run by renowned Melbourne restaurateur. Excellent gourmet weekends.

Rutherglen

Red Carpet Inn. *Moderate.* Pool. Opposite vineyards, wineries.

Sale

Commodore Hacienda. *Moderate.* Liquor room service. Licensed restaurant. Pool. Near golf, fishing, shops. Member Commodore chain.

Thomson River Motel. *Moderate.* Licensed restaurant. Pool. Member Flag chain.

Shepparton

Overland Hotel Motel. *Moderate.* Liquor room service. Licensed restaurant.· Near swimming pool, golf, tennis, skiing. Member MFA Homestead.

Parklake Motor Inn. *Moderate.* Liquor room service. Licensed restaurant. Pool. Opposite lake, heated swimming pool, tennis courts, park. Member Flag chain.

Shepparton Inlander Motor Hotel. *Moderate.* Liquor room service. Licensed restaurant. Near shops, swimming, fishing.

Victoria Hotel. *Moderate.* Some cheaper rooms without private facilities.

Koala Village Welcome Inn. *Inexpensive.* Licensed restaurant. Pool.

Sorrento

Oceanic Motel. *Moderate.* Rate includes hot breakfast. Surfing, golf, bowls, bay fishing.

Stawell

Gift Motel. *Moderate.* Rate includes light breakfast. Golf course.

Hi-way Eight Motor Inn. *Moderate.* Includes light breakfast. Pool. Near winery. Member MFA Homestead chain.

London Motel. *Moderate.* Licensed restaurant. Pool. Near golf course, swimming pool. Member Flag chain.

Thornton

The New Rubicon Motor Hotel. *Moderate.* Liquor room service. Licensed restaurant. Pool. Near water sports Lake Eildon, fishing, golf, bowls.

Traralgon

Airport Motel. *Moderate.* Rate includes light breakfast. Pool. No restaurant.

Trans Eastern Motel. *Moderate.* Licensed restaurant. Pool. Near golf course. Member Flag chain.

Motel Traralgon. *Inexpensive.* Weekly rates available. Adjacent golf course. Member MFA Homestead chain.

Tyabb

Peninsula Motor Inn. *Moderate.* Liquor room service. Licensed restaurant. Near beach, golf, sailing, horseriding, surfing. Member Flag chain.

Wangaratta

Maximum Motel. *Moderate.* Liquor room service. Licensed restaurant. Near mountains, lake, golf course. Member Flag chain.

Meriwa Park. *Moderate.* Licensed restaurant. Near mountains, golf, lakes. Member Flag chain.

Suncourt Motel. *Moderate.* Includes light breakfast. Pool. Golf putting green.

Warburton

Motel Won Wondah. *Moderate.* Includes hot breakfast. Set in one hectare (2½ acre) gardens. Near swimming pool, golf, tennis courts.

Mount Victoria Motel. *Moderate.* Some cheaper rooms without private facilities. Includes light breakfast. Kitchen facilities in rooms. Near golf course, Olympic swimming pool. Set in one hectare (2½ acre) garden.

Warrnambool

Downtown Motel. *Moderate.* Licensed restaurant. Near surf beach.

Timbertop Motel. *Moderate.* Licensed restaurant. Member Flag chain.

Turn Inn Motel. *Moderate.* Tariff includes cooked breakfast. Weekly and off-season rates available. Kitchen facilities in rooms. Near beach.

Warrnambool Motor Inn. *Moderate.* Near highway from Melbourne. Near beach, racecourse. Member Flag chain.

Western Hotel/Motel. *Moderate.* Liquor room service. Licensed restaurant. Near beach.

Wedderburn

Goldseeker Motel. *Moderate.* Licensed restaurant. Pool. Member Flag chain.

Wodonga

Provincial Motels. *Moderate.* Liquor room service. Licensed restaurant. Pool. Near golf course, squash courts, bowls, tennis courts, boating. Member Flag chain.

Stagecoach Motel. *Moderate.* Includes hot breakfast. No restaurant. Near Hume Weir, tennis courts, wineries. On main Melbourne/Sydney highway.

Sunset Motel. *Moderate.* Licensed restaurant. Near tennis courts, boating, drive-in theatre. On main Melbourne/Sydney highway.

Warrina Motor Inn. *Moderate.* Liquor room service. Licensed restaurant. Near golf course, gardens, Hume Weir, wineries, historic attractions. Member Flag chain.

Wellington Wodonga Motel. *Moderate.* Includes hot breakfast. No restaurant. Pool. Near golf course.

Yarram

Tarra Motor Inn. *Moderate.* Licensed restaurant. Near Tarra Valley and Bulga national parks. Near beach, golf, bowls. Member Flag chain.

Yarrawonga

Cypress Gardens. *Moderate.* Licensed restaurant. Pool. Situated on lake and near sporting facilities.

Garners Bridge Motor Inn. *Moderate.* Includes light breakfast. No restaurant. Near lake, golf course.

Yarrawonga Highway Motel. *Moderate.* Pool. No restaurant. Near sporting facilities, lake. Member MFA Homestead chain.

 DINING OUT. More than any other State, Victoria is known as the home of BYO—Bring Your Own (wine). This started when people discovered there was no law against taking wine into an *unlicensed* restaurant if the proprietor allowed it. Now more than 1100 such restaurants exist in this State, bringing wining and dining within the reach of thousands more people. Be warned, however, that there are frequent changes of ownership and staff. Restaurants come quickly into prominence and just as quickly go.

Licensed restaurants are bound by law to provide more facilities and furnishing for guests and these facilities show up in the higher prices. Thus it is common to see elegantly dressed women and men walking into BYO restaurants carrying bags or baskets of bottles. The proprietors of BYO restaurants will serve the wine and cool it if necessary for guests.

In recent years, exceptionally good restaurants have been springing up in the suburbs of Melbourne, where entrepreneurs have discovered that residents will eat out if they don't have far to go. These restaurants are especially popular on Sundays, when most city restaurants are closed.

Prices in Australian restaurants change so much it is impossible to give a rating for each, but expect to pay from $6 to $10 for the main course at places mentioned and from $15 to $40 for a three course meal without wine or tips, depending on type of restaurant. *Expensive* range would be more than $40; *moderate* $15 to $40; *inexpensive* less than $15.

Assume a restaurant is licensed unless stated otherwise.

Abbotsford
La Seine. *Moderate.* BYO. French cuisine.

Airport West
Hotel International. *Moderate.* Floor show three nights a week.

Albert Park
Phillip De Marco's. *Moderate.* BYO. Tiny restaurant, once public toilets! Overlooks bay.
Le Postillion. *Moderate.* Very French.

Armadale
The Batavia. *Moderate.* BYO. Indonesia.

Aspendale
Hong Kong Kitchen. *Moderate.* BYO. Chinese. Offers nine course Mandarin dinner. Closed Tues.

Bayswater
Bayswater Hotel-Motel. *Moderate.* Disco Thurs-Sat. Closed Sun.

Brighton
Alexander's Restaurant. *Expensive.* Licensed, dancing.
Froggies. *Expensive.* French cuisine.
Le Guillotine. *Expensive.* Small and French.
Copper Pan Restaurant. *Moderate.* BYO. Danish-German specialties.
Khyat's Hotel. *Moderate.* Bistro and gourmet restaurant.

Camberwell
C.J.'s. *Expensive.* BYO. Italian food. Candlelit atmosphere. Closed Sun.
Viking Restaurant. *Inexpensive.* BYO. Scandinavian, Italian dishes.

Carnegie
Ruffin's Restaurant. *Moderate.* BYO. Swiss chef. Variety main courses.

Carlton
Fives Restaurant. *Expensive.* BYO. Serving Australian dishes. Closed Tues.
Nickelby's *Expensive.* French cuisine, licensed.
El Calamaro. *Moderate.* BYO. Italian seafood. Lunches only.
Johnny's Green Room. *Moderate.* Open 24 hours day. Italian dishes. Billiard room. Mixed clientele.

Caulfield
La Croisette. *Moderate.* BYO. French cooking.

Chelsea

Settlers Tavern. *Moderate.* BYO. Steak, pizza, pancakes. Closed Tues.

Croydon

Hunter's Lodge Restaurant. *Expensive.* Licensed, dancing, reservation recommended.

Dandenong

Hamlet. *Moderate.* French and Italian cuisine.

The Dandenongs

Kenloch. *Moderate.* In Olinda. Set in beautiful gardens, views across bay. Band Sat.

Coonara Springs Restaurant. *Inexpensive.* In Olinda. Licensed, reservation recommended.

Kallista Tea Rooms. *Inexpensive.* Unlicensed. Panoramic views Dandenong Ranges. Salads and Devonshire teas. Seashell museum, art gallery, gift section.

Sherbrooke Forest Restaurant and Kiosk. *Inexpensive.* In Kallista. Steaks, salads.

The Stag. *Inexpensive.* In Monbulk. BYO. Closed Tues.

Doncaster

Five Crowns Restaurant. *Expensive.* Shoppintown Inn Hotel. Licensed, reservations recommended.

East Melbourne

Chopsticks. *Moderate.* Chinese style banquets (up to 15 courses), Expensive. Cantonese, Shanghai dishes. Other meals.

Bims Restaurant. *Moderate.* BYO. Danish sauces and specialties.

Eltham

Eltham Barrel. *Moderate.* Austrian-German. International smorgasbord.

Fitzroy

Au Chateaubriand. *Moderate.* A la carte or set menus.

Flying Trapeze Cafe. *Moderate.* BYO. Australian meals. Young local talent perform own comedy material. Closed Sun.

Glen Waverley

Squires Cellar. *Expensive.* Village Green Hotel. Licensed, band, reservation recommended.

Hampton

Troika. *Moderate.* Russian and Hungarian specialties. Gypsy music. Two good floor shows each night. Open to 3 A.M.

Hawthorn

Leonda. *Expensive.* Three piece band. International cuisine. Set in beautiful parkland overlooking river.

Nat's Steak & Seafood Restaurant. *Expensive.* BYO. French food.

Naughty Nineties Music Hall. *Expensive.* BYO. Four course dinner. Old Time Music Variety Show. Closed Sun-Mon.

Miramare Sea Food Restaurant. *Moderate.* BYO. Italian food. Closed Sun.

Moustache. *Moderate.* BYO. French food.

Rabelais. *Moderate.* BYO. French food. Closed Sun.

Heidelberg

Edelweiss. *Moderate.* Austrian and Australian food. Austrian band and dancing nightly.

Ivanhoe

Golden Mango. *Moderate.* BYO. Indian cuisine.

Jolimont

Frenchy's. *Moderate.* French food. Closed Sun.

Kew

La Brochette. *Moderate.* French, Greek food. Greek music weekends.
La Bretagne. *Moderate.* French dishes.

Laverton

Shell Laverton Restaurant. *Moderate.* Unlicensed. Quick wholesome meals for travellers.
Westgate. *Moderate.* French, Continental dishes. Closed Sun.

Malvern

Vienna Schnitzel Bar. *Moderate.* BYO. Austrian dishes. Live music three nights a week.

Mornington

The Courtyard. *Moderate.* BYO. French food. Dancing Fri-Sat. Closed Sun.
The Overlander. *Moderate.* Extensive varied smorgasbord. Band, dancers, guest singer nightly.
Ranch Motel. *Moderate.*

Narrewarren East

Muddy Creek Restaurant. *Moderate.* BYO. Home cooking. Set in 26 acres near Cardinia Dam.

North Melbourne

The Great Australian Bite. *Expensive.* Restaurant set in old terrace house where casual elegance prevails. Closed Sun/Mon.
Smacka's Place. *Expensive.* Cosmopolitan dishes. Dixieland jazz and floor show Thurs-Sun.
Bogart's Disco-Restaurant. *Moderate.* Nostalgic décor. Reservation necessary.

Northcote

E & G Beker Charcoal Grill. *Moderate.* BYO. Closed Sun.

Prahran

Bernadi's. *Expensive.* French and Italian.
Scandinavian. *Moderate.* BYO with intimate atmosphere. Closed Sun.

Richmond

La Bastille. *Expensive.* French dishes.
Enris. *Moderate.* BYO. Argentine cuisine.

Sandringham

Le Petit Parisienne. *Expensive.* French cuisine.
The Lighthouse. *Moderate.* Seafood specialties.
Ausonia Pizza. *Inexpensive.* BYO. Open till 1 A.M.

South Yarra

The Love Machine. *Expensive.* Mod. decor. French cuisine. Dancing all evening. Closed Sun-Mon.

Maxim's. *Expensive.* International standard French cuisine.

Pickwick. *Expensive.* Elegant décor. Continental cuisine. Dancing.

The Two Faces. *Expensive.* French specialties. Member International Relais de Campagne Chateaux-Hotels Relais Gourmands.

Angies. *Moderate.* BYO. French food.

Edouard. *Moderate.* French food and grills.

Golden Ox Cave. *Moderate.* BYO. Steaks and grills. Intimate atmosphere. Open fireplaces.

Omar Khayyam. *Moderate.* BYO. Lebanese food. Closed Sun.

Percy Pringles. *Moderate.* Wide variety menu. BYO. Closed Sun-Mon.

The Prime Rib. *Moderate.* Botanical Hotel. Closed Sun.

Syndal

Le Gallois. *Moderate.* BYO. French dishes.

Toorak

Glo Glo's. *Expensive.* French cuisine in superb atmosphere.

Ginis. *Moderate.* Closed Sun.

Katies Tavern. *Moderate.* BYO. Charcoal grills. Home style pies.

Silvers. *Moderate.* Open 8 P.M.-3 A.M.

Topo Gigio Bistro. *Moderate.* Casual atmosphere. Italian cuisine.

Woodchoppers Cabin. *Moderate.* Log cabin with relaxed atmosphere. BYO. Closed Sun.

West Melbourne

La Chaumiere. *Expensive.* BYO. French food. Closed weekends.

Williamstown

Craigantina. *Moderate,* BYO.

Windsor

Allisons Restaurant. *Moderate.* Restaurant is large Victorian terrace house full of antiques. French cuisine.

Taj Mahal. *Moderate.* Indian food. Recorded music.

SOUTH AUSTRALIA

In the Desert, an Oasis of Wine and Food

by
MAXWELL WHITING

Maxwell Whiting is a former travel editor of the Adelaide morning newspaper, The Advertiser.

Land of "crow-eaters", driest State in the driest Continent: South Australia has such huge expanses of almost uninhabited semi-desert that most people have seen only a fraction of its 984,200 square kilometres of sunburnt country.

It is a State still searching for pioneers; a State where a journey into the "Outback" by camel, car, train or plane is an adventure.

Yet South Australia, in many respects, is the most "civilised" Australian State—famed for its wines, opals, arts festival, food and hospitality.

The State's stark horizons stretch upwards to the Northern Territory and eastward to Queensland, New South Wales and Victoria. The setting sun goes down in flames behind the desert border of Western Australia.

Most of South Australia's 1,300,000 people—who are white except for 6,000 black Aborigines and a few non-Caucasian settlers from other countries—live within 200 miles of the same vast ocean that laps the shores of Antarctica, some 32° of latitude further south.

In this rich and productive coastal strip lies Adelaide, the state's lively capital and principal city.

ADELAIDE

Adelaide—once the "City of Churches"—is now much more. It's the nation's Festival City, with one of the world's best multi-purpose performing arts complexes.

You can ride down the main street in a free bus, enjoy oysters and champagne in a restaurant, watch professional horse races on the city parklands without charge, and play 18 holes of golf on a course only a few minutes drive from the office.

It's a green-belted city. The southern business centre is buffered by parks and the River Torrens from the elevated, largely residential precincts on the north side. Stroll away from the main city office and shopping area—down leafy King William Road and across the river past Adelaide's Test Match cricket oval. A few minutes more and you're at the little knoll reserve called "Light's Vision", looking down upon acres of recreation lawn, where Davis Cup tennis is played, and where Australia's most famous cricket players have hit for centuries.

The tall-spired church to the left is St. Peter's Anglican Cathedral, where Queen Elizabeth has worshipped and the Archbishop of Canterbury has preached. The building in the other direction—its smokestack painted in the colors of an Adelaide football team—was the city's main brewery. In the distance, though only about five miles beyond the parklands and the cluster of tall office buildings, is Adelaide's distinctive backdrop of "everlasting hills".

Everlasting? A big chunk of the hills' face is being quarried out for grinding into stones for making roads, exposing raw quartzite rock faces to the view of people in residential areas below. Nowadays, the worked-out faces are camouflaged with dark bituminous paint. From upper windows of the city's office buildings you can see the line of hills pointing down to the coast less than 10 miles away. There, on calm blue waters, spinnakers billow from a hundred trailer-transported yachts on sunny Saturdays.

Tucked away in the hills are Italian market gardens, small villages with German traditions, little farmlets looking as though they have been plucked from the English countryside, magnificent old villas, cheese factories, orchards and vineyards.

There is also a thriving handicraft industry, with galleries displaying painting, pottery, leatherwork and weaving.

Up here you will find at Hahndorf the scene of the annual *Schuetzenfest* and German beer festival, a gallery specialising in the works of Australia's greatest landscape artist, Sir Hans Heysen, picnic spots, and walking trails. In season you can pick wild blackberries, or buy some Devonshire tea.

The Adelaide Hills wind 800 kilometers from their southern tip, where they meet the sea, to their northern-most meeting place with the Flinders Ranges. It is one experience to enjoy an "orchestra-pit" view of the Hills from the city or its beaches, but quite another thing to marvel at the reverse view, looking down from the gallery of Mount Lofty summit upon the tree-filled metropolis and its sweep of coastline below.

It is a quick easy drive to Mount Lofty. It takes less than 30 minutes from the city centre to the 2,300 ft. (700 m.) lookout, where the air is fresh and scented with acacia and eucalyptus forest flowers, where rainbow-coloured parrots fly, and small lizards sun themselves on strips of fallen bark and boulders.

Adelaide was well-planned, thanks to its founder—Colonel William Light, the State's first Surveyor-General. Because of his foresight, you can picnic or have a barbecue (with firewood supplied free by the City Council) in the parklands five minutes from major stores and office buildings—or stroll in wide streets and find shade in a garden square. And Adelaide is a capital city where the old colonial architecture and the new buildings are good neighbors.

Arts Centre

As a multi-purpose complex for the arts, the $20-million Adelaide Festival Centre has few equals. Built overlooking the River Torrens, in Elder Park, the centre is the envy of the rest of Australia—even of Sydney with its monumental Opera House building.

It has a 2000-seat concert theatre, a more intimate 650-seat drama theatre, an exciting 350-seat experimental theatre, and an outdoor amphitheatre for 1200.

The Festival Centre has been hailed as the most versatile and functional building for the performing arts anywhere.

Almost 1000 performances are staged at the centre each year.

The centre is the main base for the most widely publicised of South Australia's festivals, the Adelaide Festival of Arts, held every two years (even numbers) in March.

The Festival attracts musicians, performers and audiences from around the world—like Yehudi Menuhin, Rudolph Nureyev, Yevtushenko, Zurich's *Collegium Musicum* and the Royal Shakespeare Company.

The final stage of the Festival Centre, opened by Queen Elizabeth in March 1977, completes the huge plaza surrounding the complex of buildings, and has exposed for public appreciation the largest outdoor work of art in Australia—a spectacular and controversial collection of environmental sculpture by West German artist Otto Hajek.

Beneath Hajek's concrete garden, which includes an art work camouflaging the Festival Centre's exhaust stack, is an underground park for more than 300 cars. Some critics say the multi-colored concrete figures Hajek designed for the plaza look more like tank traps.

The Festival Theatre is the busy hub of Adelaide's performing arts activities. Since its opening in mid-1973, this modern concert hall and lyric theatre has presented a great range of events including orchestral concerts and recitals, grand opera, ballet and drama, films, musical comedy, variety, folk, rock and jazz concerts, conventions and conferences.

A pipe organ of unusual engineering design was paid for by monies raised from public appeal. The tons of pipework and mechanism float on an air cushion so it can be easily pushed off stage.

The Playhouse in the Festival Centre is the permanent home of the South Australian Theatre Company which presents a repertoire of at least 10 major productions annually, covering the classics, the best of contemporary overseas drama, and the latest works of Australian playwrights. This very intimate theatre was designed for both proscenium arch and thrust stage productions.

The Space is the most unorthodox of Australia's new performing venues. This enclosed box-like auditorium has been designed for complete flexibility of production. It has been used in many different actor-audience configurations for avant-garde drama and dance performances, for musical comedy, one-man shows, puppetry, recitals, opera, music theatre and folk.

When the architects for the Festival Centre drew up the first sketch plans for the drama theatres, they were attracted to the fall of the site where it slopes down Elder Park towards the River Torrens. The resulting valley between the main theatre buildings provided a bonus for the centre in the form of an open air amphitheatre.

This performing area is used mostly in the warmer months for rock, folk and variety concerts, and is suitable for drama, dance and music theatre performances.

Surrounding the performing areas of the Festival Centre are several hectares of open plaza and terrace which provide ideal venues for outdoor happenings. The centre organises poetry readings, story telling for children, folk song recitals, puppet shows and street theatre.

The plaza and terrace has an orangery—the orange trees were becoming well established by mid-1978—which will provide shade and color for people relaxing on benches outside the lounge bar and other gathering points.

The Festival Theatre Restaurant offers *à la carte* and *table d'hôte* menus for up to 100 diners. An outdoor terrace cafe at the Elder Park end of the theatre is for less formal eating with bar service. The Playhouse Bistro, seating up to 80, overlooks the River Torrens and is an ideal place for lunch or pre-performance dinner.

Public tours of the Festival Centre are conducted on the hour every hour, between 10 A.M. and 4 P.M., Mondays to Saturdays.

Visitors can enjoy the centre's permanent collection of art works, worth well over $250,000, and see stimulating exhibitions which are staged regularly at the Playhouse gallery.

A two-monthly diary giving details of forthcoming attractions at the Festival Centre is available free from the South Australian Government Travel Centre in Adelaide, Melbourne and Sydney, or by writing direct to the Adelaide Festival Centre Trust, King William Road, Adelaide, South Australia 5000.

Food and Drink

Through the influence of high class Continental and Oriental chefs, there is a new sophistication in dining in Adelaide's 200 restaurants (most of which serve South Australian wines).

World standards are attained in many, and several have won awards for food and service.

There are restaurants and cafes catering for French, German, Greek, Hungarian, Italian and Spanish tastes in food; others have Dutch and Indonesian, Indian, Chinese, Japanese and Lebanese fare. There are theatre restaurants, pizza houses, pancake and seafood specialists, and many places that provide the best in English and Australian dishes.

Culinary choices range from Adelaide's famous "piecart floaters" (a meat pie in vivid green soup) to American blueberry pancakes served day and night.

Many restaurants have liquor licences enabling them to serve the full range of drinks with meals. Others retain the South Australian "wine" licence. This permits them to serve all types of wine, including fortified wines. They carry very comprehensive wine stocks and are well worth a visit.

PRACTICAL INFORMATION FOR ADELAIDE

 HOW TO GET THERE. *By air:* Domestic airlines Ansett and TAA operate direct flights to Adelaide from Sydney, Melbourne, Perth, and Darwin; some international flights also land here. *By car:* From Melbourne, Sydney, Perth and Darwin. *By bus:* Ansett Pioneer, Greyhound and Deluxe coaches. *By train:* From Melbourne in "The Overland" daily overnight express and from Perth and Sydney by the "Trans-Australia Express" and the "Indian-Pacific". From Melbourne direct, and from Perth and Sydney by transfer to connecting trains in South Australia, where rail gauges differ.

 SPECIAL INTEREST TOURS. Cleland Wildlife Reserve at Mount Lofty, overlooking Adelaide Plains, where Australian native animals can be seen at close quarters and sometimes handled—including kangaroos, koalas and wombats.

One of the easiest ways to see Adelaide and the city's surroundings, is to take the day or half-day tours available from the South Australian Government Travel Centre.

Wineries, the mouth of Australia's longest river, the Murray, a wildlife reserve and a recreation park in the Hills, are some of the attractions visited on these short tours.

The Adelaide area half-day coach tours cost up to A$12; full-day up to A$23. One combines a visit to waterfalls in the foothills a few miles east of the city and to a foothills winery.

Another is an evening coach trip to Windy Point, a vantage point above the metropolitan area to view the thousands of lights gleaming from streets and buildings spreading about 41 kilometres north and south, and about eight km. west to the Adelaide coastline.

There is a tour to the mouth of the River Murray that passes through the historic old river port of Goolwa, on Lake Alexandrina, from where Australia's largest paddleboat operates tours up river.

The Barossa Valley, 72 km. north-east of Adelaide, is the most famous of South Australia's vineyards. South Australia produces about 65% of Australia's wines and about 83% of its brandy. A vintage festival is held every two years in March or April. Tourists can visit the winery chateaux, sip the fine wines, buy at cellar-door prices, and sample German gourmet food. Further north is the Clare Valley wine district. Southern Vales wineries are less than one hour's drive south of Adelaide. Wineries can be visited at centres along the River Murray between Renmark and Morgan. The State's most southerly vineyards are at Coonawarra, about 10 km. from Penola, near the border of Victoria.

MUSEUMS AND GALLERIES. The South Australian Museum, Adelaide, has an outstanding collection of Australian birds and animals and an astronomy annex. The Art Gallery of South Australia has an international collection and is particularly rich in examples of Australian art. Trotting Hall of Fame, Bolivar, has a wide range of exhibits on history of trotting in Australia. Transport Museum, St. Kilda, provides nostalgic rides on restored trams. The Constitutional Museum in the old Legislative Council Chambers has been described as the finest political museum in the world.

SEASONAL EVENTS. *Adelaide Festival of Arts.* Held every two years in March (even-number years). It assembles internationally famous performers in all branches of the arts. *Barossa Valley Vintage Festival.* Held every two years (odd-number years) in late March or April. A seven-day festival in Australia's most famous and productive vineyard country, 72 km. (45 miles) northeast of Adelaide. Festival includes wine auctions and tastings and entertainments. *Hahndorf Schuetzenfest.* Traditional German shooting festival, held annually in January at Hahndorf Village, 29 km. (18 miles) east of Adelaide. Each Easter at Oakbank in the Adelaide Hills, the Onkaparinga Racing Club stages Australia's biggest picnic race meeting.

GARDENS. Adelaide's main parks and gardens are only a short walk or drive from the city centre, which is surrounded by hundreds of acres of public parkland.

In the city's Botanic Garden, children can feed ducks. In the Veale Gardens there are rose beds, a creek, grottoes, fountains and conservatory. Rymill Park has a boating lake, playground and barbecues.

Bonython Park, on the banks of the River Torrens, has a lake for sailing model boats on, barbecue areas and an excellent adventure playground.

There is a representative collection of Australia's unique flora in the Mt. Lofty Botanic Garden in the Adelaide Hills. Blackhill Conservation Park overlooks the Torrens Valley.

Wittunga Botanic Gardens are noted for their exotic South African plants.

SPORTS. South Australia's sunny summer climate makes water sport enjoyable anywhere along its vast coastline, which is deeply indented by two gulfs. One of the biggest man-made sailing boat havens in the world has been formed at the Adelaide suburb of North Haven on the Saint Vincent Gulf coastline.

There are more than 33 km. of safe family swimming beaches in a strip near Adelaide—some 20 minutes drive from the city centre. The home of fresh-water boating is the South Australian section of the River Murray, house-boats being most popular. Berri, Mannum and Renmark are the main hiring centres. Boats with 5 to 10-berth accommodation may be hired for weekends or longer periods. There are 6-day cruises on a River Murray paddlewheel boat and a Rhine-style cruise ship.

St. Vincent Gulf and Spencer Gulf are especially interesting for skin diving, because of their numerous reefs and old wrecks.

In fresh water, Mount Gambier's Little Blue Lake, where dives of up to 46 m. may be made, is popular in winter. Scuba equipment can be hired from Adelaide Skindiving Centre, 7 Compton Street, Adelaide 5000. Tel. (08) 516144.

There is surfing at Victor Harbor, Robe and Port Macdonnell. A 600-metre "sweat track" has been laid down by the National Fitness Council at East Parklands, starting from the eastern end of Halifax Street. Night baseball is played every Wednesday during summer at Norwood Oval.

The River Murray, between a one- and three-hours' drive from Adelaide, is ideal for water skiing. Favorite spots there are Barmera on Lake Bonney, Murray Bridge, Loxton and Goolwa.

Further afield are Wallaroo and Port Lincoln.

Details of all facilities are available from the South Australian Government Travel Centre, King William Street, Adelaide 5000. Tel (08) 2121644.

Adelaide's grass lawn tennis courts are said to be among the best in the world. The Memorial Drive Courts, in Adelaide's central parklands, may be hired for about $20 a day during the week and $26 on Sundays. All of South Australia's lawn bowls clubs are open to visitors. Arrangements can be made for visitors to play together, with local members, or in tournaments. For further details contact the Secretary, Royal South Australian Bowling Association, 310 South Terrace, Adelaide 5000. Tel. (08) 2233613.

There are many golf courses in Adelaide including a public one in the city's central parklands. For further details contact the Assistant Secretary, South Australian Golf Association, War Memorial Drive, Adelaide 5000. Tel. (08) 514371. Adelaide, because of its long dry summer, is one of the principal homes of cricket in Australia. The world's most famous cricketer, Sir Donald Bradman, lives here. Major interstate and international Test matches are played at the Adelaide Oval, on the central parklands beside the War Memorial Drive, North Adelaide.

Among the championship golf courses open to visitors is the Kooyonga Golf Club, May Terrace, Lockleys, near Adelaide Airport. For enquiries, Tel. (08) 436163.

Night trotting and motor racing attract big audiences at tracks a few miles from Adelaide. Many minor spectator sports are played at week-ends on Adelaide's central parklands. Netball is popular with women.

Adelaide has several racecourses, including one in the city's central parklands where admission to the "flat" is free, and there is off-street car parking for a small charge. Many winners of Australia's major races have been trained on properties near Adelaide, some of which have been visited by the Queen and the Duke of Edinburgh.

Football in South Australia is mainly played according to Australian Rules. In Adelaide it is the main spectator sport in winter and is played on the Adelaide Oval and at Football Park, West Lakes. Often the ground is turned to a quagmire, but because of the quality of the turf and skill of the curator, it is always restored in time for cricket in summer.

WHAT TO DO WITH THE CHILDREN. Adelaide's long almost-rainless summer, and mild winters, mean that young people can enjoy outdoor recreation most of the year. In summer holidays and on hot week-ends, many children are swimming and sun-bathing along Adelaide's 33 km. of white sand beaches or at other beach resorts in the State—enjoying recreations like tennis, cycling, picnicking in the Adelaide Hills.

The Adelaide Zoo with its collection of docile and friendly animals such as wallabies and kangaroos, amusing monkeys and an Indian elephant to ride upon, is sure to make any child happy.

Located in the city's central parklands, the zoo is bordered by the River Torrens. A river launch takes you right to the front door. The launch leaves from Elder Park, immediately below the Adelaide Festival Centre, a pleasant strolling distance from principal hotels, airline and coach offices, and the railroad station.

The Cleland Wildlife Reserve at Mount Lofty, open daily and served by coach tours from the city, gives children an opportunity to come face to face with kangaroos, koalas and wombats, some of which can be hand-fed and cuddled. There is a Marineland at West Beach.

SHOPPING. Champagne flowed from an ornamental 19th century fountain when South Australia's former Premier (Mr. Don Dunstan) pressed a button to open Adelaide's first pedestrian shopping mall late in 1976.

Not quite what was expected, even in South Australia, the principal wine state. But it symbolised the bubbly new atmosphere that has come to Adelaide's most important shopping centre since Rundle Street was closed to cars, buses and commercial traffic, and given over entirely to people.

Bordering the brick-paved mall, with its shady trees and casual benches, its fruit and flower stalls, are scores of big department stores and small specialty retailers stocking everything from raspberries to refrigerators.

On Sundays, puppeteers, circus performers, story tellers entertain hundreds of people. As a commercial and community venture, the success of the Rundle Mall is already assured.

Adelaide's shopping arcades are crammed with interesting businesses. Take John Ferwerda's violin shop for instance—on the upper level of Adelaide Arcade, where Mr. Ferwerda makes hand-crafted violins.

British, European and Asian goods are to be found in Adelaide shops, but of special interest to the visitor are the several shops around town stocking authentic and traditional Aboriginal arts and crafts. If it's a didgeridoo you want, or simply a kangaroo skin or picture painted on bark, you can expect to find it in Adelaide.

In the Rundle Mall is a flower stall selling unique and beautiful blooms cut from Australian native plants that flourish so far from cities that most people have never seen them growing in the wild.

Visit Adelaide's Central Market and you could imagine yourself in the heart of Europe instead of walking through the biggest produce market in the Southern Hemisphere.

The market, which began in the latter 1800s, has scores of stores selling vegetables, cheeses, fruit, meats and delicacies such as roll mops, caviar, snails, Greek confectionery and German wursts. At least 60,000 visitors a week stroll from city offices or drive in from home to savor the aroma of fresh fruit and vegetables, or fresh-ground coffee, and bump their way happily through crowds of shoppers laden with bags of produce.

The market, situated near Victoria Square, trades Tuesdays, Fridays and Saturdays from 7 A.M. until well after other city shops have shut.

There is a car park for 500 vehicles above the market, and the stalls below may be reached by escalators.

The produce is displayed in 76 stalls. Nearby is the meat hall where butchers offer sides of lamb, beef and veal. And there is a fish market stocked with snapper, whiting, freshwater Murray cod, oysters and squid. Arcade shops adjoining the markets sell a host of products ranging from clothing to wines and second-hand books and records. Whatever you buy, be careful not to throw the wrapping down, as there are fines of $20 for littering in Adelaide.

TOURIST INFORMATION SERVICES. South Australian Government Travel Centre, 18 King William Street, Adelaide, 5001. Tel. (08) 212-1644 Cables, Govtourist. Telex 82487.

 HOTELS. Adelaide has many comfortable and conveniently located hotels and motels but is short on lavish accommodation of top international standard. Most of the newer establishments are in the coastal and suburban areas. The price ranges for 2 people in a double room are: *Expensive:* A$60 and up; *Moderate:* A$40–60; and *Inexpensive:* A$20–A$40.

Adelaide TraveLodge. *Expensive.* One of two in South Terrace operated by same company. Full range of hotel facilities. TV, licensed restaurant, swimming pool.

Gateway Inn. *Expensive.* North Terrace. The city's newest hotel, located in prestige area opposite Parliament House with spacious views from upper floors over Festival Centre and beyond to the parklands. Rooftop swimming pool. 226 rooms. Ansett airline terminal, bus terminal and carpark in same complex.

Grosvenor. *Expensive.* North Terrace. South Australia's largest residential hotel. Opposite railway station. Restaurant, bar, beauty and gift shops, air conditioned.

Hilton International. *Expensive.* On Victoria Square with excellent views and all features expected of a Hilton hotel.

Oberoi Adelaide. *Expensive.* Brougham Place, North Adelaide. 147 rooms, has elevated location overlooking parks, St. Peter's Cathedral, city buildings and Adelaide Hills beyond.

Park Royal. *Expensive.* South Terrace. Opposite south parklands away from the central business district. Has sauna and baby-sitting facilities.

South Terrace TraveLodge. *Expensive.* In South Terrace opposite parkland. 140 rooms. Restaurant, pool, air conditioned.

Town House. *Expensive.* In Hindley Street in the heart of the entertainment and restaurant area.

Arkaba Court. *Moderate.* Glen Osmond Road. 4 kms. from downtown. Air conditioned. Licensed. Kitchen facilities in rooms. Swimming pool.

Regal Park. *Moderate.* Barton Terrace, North Adelaide. Pleasant views across north parkland; close to main road to city centre.

Royal Coach. *Moderate.* Dequetteville Terrace, Kent Town, On edge of city parklands; 42 modern units, sauna, pool.

Ambassadors. *Inexpensive.* King William St. Three blocks from city center, 28 rooms.

Earl of Zetland. *Inexpensive.* Flinders St. 30 rooms. Three blocks from city centre.

Newmarket. *Inexpensive.* North Terrace. Renovated building with magnificent spiral staircase; overlooks parklands on city's west side about 8 km. from airport and beaches.

Sands. *Inexpensive.* Glen Osmond Road, Fullarton. A suburban near-city motel of 21 rooms on main route to Adelaide Hills. Swimming pool and baby-sitting.

 RESTAURANTS. Dining out in Adelaide and South Australia is informal, but you would not be overdressed in city restaurants if you wore a jacket and tie.

Most restaurants are open six days a week, the usual hours being lunch from noon to 2:30 P.M.; dinner from 6 P.M. to midnight.

A three-course meal for two with wine should cost about A$45.

Benjamin's. Tasteful restaurant overlooking Torrens Lake. Excellent seafood. Recommended entrees: seafood omelet, prawns *diable,* half-tails of lobster filled with chunks of white meat and rich port wine sauce, whole tender baked prawns and mushrooms served in twin shells with light cream sauce. South Australian Rhine riesling wines go well with the dishes.

The Barn. At McLaren Vale in the Adelaide Hills. Originally an overnight stage for bullock teams hauling wheat. It is a meeting place for wine connoisseurs and has an art gallery.

Decca's Place. Located in trendy Melbourne Street, North Adelaide, among shops and hotels restored to old-time elegance. This vine-wreathed restaurant serves a wide range of local and international seafood dishes. Recommended: a seafood-for-two dish, bedded on lettuce, covered with crumbed prawns, scallops, whiting fillets, with medallions of crayfish in a lush white sauce.

Drumminor. Located in Modbury, about 20 km. from the city, in a converted mansion. Fairly expensive. Among the specialties: spaghetti marinara, with crayfish meat, prawns and oysters; duckling in a tomato sauce, with rice and parmesan cheese; king crab cocktail with a mayonnaise sauce topped with stuffed olives. For dessert, try the pears *zabaglione,* prepared and simmered at the table.

Da Ettore. Real Italian delicacies served in delightful surroundings—though the restaurant is located in the comparatively poor, industry-blighted suburb of Hindmarsh, 3 km. from the city centre, on the busy highway to Port Adelaide. Specialties include *trippe alla parmigiana* (tripe with tomato sauce and parmesan cheese) and *fegato alla griglia* (grilled liver and onions).

Festival Theatre Restaurant. Ideal for theatergoers but also worthy of patronage in its own right. Has peaceful view over River Torrens.

Henry Ayers. In a marvellous, stately old Adelaide home. Considered Australia's most expensive restaurant. Elegant surroundings, silver service, superb cuisine.

Maximilian's Farmhouse. At Verdun, in the Adelaide Hills. A sprawling 15-room old-fashioned rural home has been converted into a farmhouse restaurant. The menu features beef dishes served with various sauces, as well as excellent appetisers, entrees and a selection of grills. A good start is a bowl of farm-style soup crowded with vegetables and topped with parmesan cheese and parsley.

Olivet House. Located high in the Adelaide Hills at Stirling. Excellent French food. Try veal kidneys in red wine, onion and mushroom sauce, simmered until very tender and served with rice. Or veal cutlets on the bone, swimming in mushrooms, cream and parsley and spiked with black peppercorns.

Old Mill Restaurant. At Hahndorf in the Adelaide Hills. 140-year-old converted flour mill. Hearty German food, old stone walls and heavy exposed beams. Famous for its Hofbrauhaus nights, when a whole pig is carried in, carved in front of the diners, and served by waitresses in Bavarian costumes to the accompaniment of accordion music.

Once a Jolly Swagman. At Littlehampton in the Adelaide Hills. Converted meat packing plant. Meals are delivered by "Matilda the Cow". She hangs from chains attached to a running rail and is wheeled between the customers by a "swagman" to the centre of the dance floor. Here, a panel is removed and out of her belly comes the beef course. The restaurant is three stories high, in a garden setting depicting the 1920's era. There's an "early Austalian" orchestra.

Swains, in Glen Osmond Rd (6 km from the city center), claims the best seafood in town and specializes in locally caught whiting, crayfish and prawns.

Vanessa's. Converted Methodist church more than 100 years old boasting stained-glass windows, silverware and lace tablecloths. At Willunga, 45 km. south of Adelaide.

Exploring South Australia

The Barossa Valley

The Barossa Valley, only one hour's drive from Adelaide, is Australia's premier wine producing district. It is the place to go to sample red and white wines, ports, brandies, sherries and champagnes that are among the world's best.

Settled by German immigrants last century, Barossa has a distinctive charm. The greenery of its 32 kilometres of vineyards, dotted with old wineries and villages, contrasts with sunburnt farmlands bordering the Valley. The Barossa's popularity reaches a peak every two years when the Vintage Festival is held during seven days in March or April.

Thousands of people, many from other States hundreds of kilometres away, come to the valley to celebrate the putting down of the vintage with dancing, feasting, street processions, auctions of rare wines, music and singing. Fine old German traditions characterise life in the Barossa.

There are squelchy grape-treading contests, a tug of war between rival wineries, maypole dancing, grape picking contests, and brass bands. The wine flows generously from bottles of claret, burgundy, hock, riesling and tingling cold champagne.

Throughout the year all wineries welcome tourists, but week-days are best for visits. Wineries have the option to trade on Sundays. However, due to high labor costs, only a few have decided to extend their hours. A range of wines can be bought at cellar doors, and sampled at free wine-tastings. Guided tours are available at most major wineries, on weekdays only.

Nuriootpa, the Barossa's commercial centre, grew around a primitive hotel used in the 1840s by bullock-waggon drivers travelling north to the Burra copper mines.

The Barossa was named in 1837 by Colonel William Light. He called it Barrosa (Hill of Roses) after a mountainous ridge in Southern Spain. It was wrongly spelled on an early map and the existing name was allowed to stand.

Members of a Lutheran community seeking to escape religious persecution in the old German provinces of Silesia and Prussia laid the foundation for today's thriving wine industry. Their migration to South Australia in 1838 was aided by a wealthy Scottish merchant, George Fife Angas, one of the forces behind the South Australia Company which was formed to settle the new colony.

The first 200 Lutherans to arrive made their way to the Barossa and settled first at Bethany and then at Langmeil, from which Tanunda, in the heart of the Barossa, has grown.

Pioneer wine-growers like Johann Gramp, who in 1850 bottled a hock similar to those produced back in Germany, found the Barossa's climate and soil ideally suited to grape growing. Their success paved the way for the future. The German influence continued to dominate the Valley's progress and development, giving it a lifestyle and culture unlike the rest of South Australia.

By the early 1900s the district was sprinkled with towns and hamlets with German-sounding names such as Schoenborn, Langmeil, Krondorf, Siegersdorf and Gnadenfrei.

The Valley is famous for German foods like *Stinkerkaese* (cottage cheese), *honigkuchen* (honey biscuits) and *streuselkuchen* (crumbletop cake). Tempting meats like *mettwurst, fritz* and *blutwurst* make novel picnic ingredients, washed down with a smooth Barossa red wine.

Barossa restaurants like *Die Galerie, Die Weinstube* and *Weinkeller* serve *Schweinefleisch* (smoked pork), *Sauerbraten* (marinated beef) and *Apfelstrudel* (an apple sweet) against a gay background of rowdy Bavarian bands playing foot-stomping music and stirring drinking songs.

At Tanunda, where there is a rich musical heritage, brass bands come hundreds of kilometres to meet in annual competition. The town's pride is the German *Liedertafel,* a male choral society started by early settlers. At *Tanzfest* time, local spray painter-musician Neville Alderslade is apt to put aside his trumpet and blow a tune out of a garden hose for fun.

Other notable wine-producing districts to visit are Clare Valley and Southern Vales—both within 90 minutes driving distance of Adelaide. Travelers receive the same friendly welcome as at the Barossa. Further afield are the wine-growing districts of Coonawarra, in the cooler southeast of South Australia, and the Riverland, a low-rainfall area where hundreds of acres of vines are irrigated from the River Murray.

The foothills of Adelaide, only a few minutes' drive or bus-ride from the city centre, are still producing luscious ports, white table wines and sparkling wines despite the expansion of new housing.

The Outback

South Australia is so dry that in all its vast area of 380,000 square miles (984,200 sq. km.) there is scarcely one permanent running stream. South Australia is the driest State in the world's driest continent.

South Australia's "Outback", stretching hundreds of miles to the north of Adelaide, is a little-known wilderness where ill-prepared travelers can die of thirst in the fierce summer heat—and where a whole year's rain can fall overnight, turning a vast flat area into a quagmire.

This is where nature put Australia's biggest lake (Lake Eyre)—in the "Dead Heart" of a huge inland drainage system that is below sea-level. Evaporation is so great that the lake is mostly a dry salt-pan—yet in rare flood times it becomes a hazardous inland sea one-third the size of Switzerland.

Lake Eyre held water for several years from 1973 thanks to timely replenishment from often-dry rivers such as the Cooper, that came roaring down from Queensland. In places the lake was up to 70 km. wide and more than 130 km. long, and as deep as seven metres—but saltier than the sea and useless for irrigating the desert. By mid-1979 the lake had dwindled to being a small puddle only visible from the air.

Only a handful of hardy cattle station people live within 50 km. of the lake, but the novelty of the water's great expanse has attracted adventurers from down south to sail yachts and water-ski on it. Boating can become hazardous when breezes chop up the surface.

All this water—yet in 1954 the lake's salt bed was so dry and hard that the late Donald Campbell was able to race over it and set a land speed record.

Between Adelaide and Lake Eyre are Australia's two richest opal mining settlements—Coober Pedy and Andamooka—where many residents carve underground homes to protect themselves from the fierce heat of summer. There is even an underground church.

Aborigines

The Aboriginal people of South Australia form only a small proportion of the State's population. Of the 6,000, about one-third live around Adelaide and others are scattered around the country and River Murray districts.

Some 2,000 tribal Aborigines live outback in a semi-traditional situation, remote from Europeanised population centres, in the far north-west of South Australia near the borders of Western Australia and the Northern Territory.

Here, in the Musgrave Ranges area, is an Aboriginal Reserve of about 40,000 square miles with adjacent pastoral properties and Presbyterian Church land on which they live a nomadic life.

This is the homeland of the Pitjantjatjara Tribe. Settlements include Ernabella (about 800 miles from Adelaide), Fregon, Indulkina, Mimili and Armata, each having varying populations depending on Aboriginals' movements and ceremonial activities.

Most of the Aborigines in the north-west have jobs or receive Federal Government payments. Many have abandoned hunting.

At Ernabella, which can be visited by whites who first contact the Department of Aboriginal Affairs in Adelaide, there is an experimental irrigation project for growing dates and vegetables and developing a nursery for Australian native plants.

It is not general practice to allow unrestricted tourism on Aboriginal reserve lands. In and around the main north-west reserve, the Aborigines are encouraged to make artifacts and craftwork. Ernabella women are noted for their weaving.

The Murray River

Australia's greatest river, the Murray, flows for its last 650 km. to the sea through South Australia. It's the grandest, most beautiful section of all—meandering lazily from Renmark through vineyard and orchard country around Berri, Loxton and Barmera and dairying flats around Murray Bridge and Tailem Bend, until it discharges into Lake Alexandrina and loses itself in the Southern Ocean surf near Goolwa.

For most of this last journey it falls only about one inch a mile—giving it a tranquil, lake-like surface that's ideal for boating, water skiing and swimming. Backwaters and billabongs, filled by occasional floods and high rivers, are teeming with birdlife—ducks, pelicans, water fowl and ibis.

It's perfect for a close-to-nature holiday: cruising along the river in a houseboat, waking at sunrise, plunging from your sundeck into cold and invigorating waters, then clambering aboard for a sizzling breakfast of bacon and eggs (or Murray Cod or Callop). Followed day after day by swimming, sunning, eating and fishing, before drifting into a secluded lagoon and tying up to a willow for the night.

You can take a five-day cruise on a brand new Rhine-style cruise ship, the *Murray Explorer,* or the big paddlewheeler *Murray River Queen,* as an alternative to hiring your own houseboat.

The *Murray River Queen,* with modern hotel-type accommodation on her four decks for 70 passengers, was the largest vessel ever to ply an Australian river until its owners launched the *Explorer* in mid-1979. Outwardly, this majestic paddlewheeler resembles many of the old river vessels which traded up and down the Murray last century before the introduction of railways made them obsolete.

But the Queen was nostalgically designed purely for the tourist. She cruises from Goolwa across Lake Alexandrina and upstream to Swan Reach. All cabins have private facilities and air-conditioning. Amenities include a liquor licence, writing and TV lounge, and large sun deck. The 5½-day trip, leaving Goolwa on Mondays, costs about A$450 per person.

The *Explorer* has 71 cabins on its three decks—one four-berth, one six-berth and the rest two-berth, all of them with own shower and toilet. There is a sauna, spa bath and sundeck. The ship cruises from Renmark through the wine country, downstream to Berri, Loxton and Waikerie. It traverses locks and is notable for its extremely shallow draught and special equipment to enable it to navigate sandbanks and other typical Murray obstacles. The 5½-day cruise costs from A$350 per person.

The paddlewheelers head a fleet of houseboats and pleasure craft which allow visitors to spend hours or weeks watching Murray vistas glide by. The houseboats have become very popular since their introduction in 1963 and it is advisable to book well in advance.

Capable of six to eight knots, the houseboats are easy to steer and carry most of the comforts of home. *Liba Liba* houseboats sleeping five, seven and eight, may be hired at Renmark. All have two-way radio, hot water, refrigerators, gas stove, shower and toilet, and are virtually unsinkable. The rates for hiring a five-berth boat are from A$400 a week, plus a 14 percent surcharge during school holidays. Similar boats operate from Berri, Loxton, Blanchetown, Kooringal Park and Mannum in South Australia. Bookings for Murray River cruises and houseboats can be made through the South Australian Government Travel Centre.

Cabin cruisers, motor boats and speedboats add variety to the river fleet. At most towns in the Riverland district and the Lower Murray, boats are available for hire or charter, for sightseeing, fishing and water skiing.

On the Murray at Mannum, which is about 80 km. east of Adelaide, one of the true original paddle-wheelers, *Marion,* lies at rest in a special dock after 60 years work as a reminder of the glorious days of steam, when tons of *mallee* roots were carried on board as fuel. *Mallee* is a name for several species of low-growing Eucalyptus trees that are native to dryer parts of the State, especially around the River Murray, and the slow-burning roots, generating great heat, were a favorite fuel—not only for steam engines, but for domestic hearths in Adelaide—until oil, gas and electricity supplanted them.

Fires of *mallee* roots, or the sawn boughs of *mallee* trees, are still kindled in the grates of some South Australian homes and country accommodation places as a reminder of "the good old days", when folks had time to gaze for hours, half-hypnotised, into the radiating red-hot mass until their limbs were warm enough to defy the chill of winter bedsheets.

Although the Murray Cod (to six feet long and weighing to 182 pounds) is Australia's most important freshwater edible fish, a small (eight inches) lobster-like crustacean known as a *yabbie* has become the most popular river delicacy in restaurants and hotels. Until recent years people, especially children, have caught yabbies only for fun, not commerce, using a hookless piece of string baited with a lump of red meat. When the yabbie claws the bait, a long-handled net or sieve is used to lift it ashore. Another method is to punch holes in a bucket, fix a lump of bait to the bottom, and lower it down on the end of a rope. Pull up the bucket when you think a yabbie may be in it.

Today there is such demand for yabbies that they are deliberately farmed. Henry Jones, a storekeeper turned yabbie farmer, runs *Yabbie City,* a restaurant at Clayton, a small township near Lake Alexandrina about two hours drive from Adelaide by way of Strathalbyn. About 40 diners at a time can sit down to a meal washed down with local district white or red wine.

The Peninsula

The rolling Adelaide Hills extend southward down Fleurieu Peninsula through vineyard country to the sea. Few South Australians get their tongue around the name Fleurieu—a reminder of the French explorer Baudin who was busily naming our landmarks until he encountered British navigator Matthew Flinders at sea, not far from the mouth of the Murray River, in 1802.

On Fleurieu the names of the towns tell the story of the way of life in the earliest days of settlement more than 30 years after that encounter —names like Victor Harbor and Port Elliot, which once sheltered trading ships from other lands. There are many reminders of the days of whaling and windjammers in these towns.

The peninsula coastline has rugged rocks, charming little bays and secluded nooks. From Cape Jervis, where Kangaroo Island sweeps across Backstairs Passage, the coast faces the Southern Ocean. Here dense sea mists can suddenly roll in to cover steep cliffs, untamed scrub and secluded valleys where small streams wind to the sea. This is a haven for the bushwalker and the naturalist, brought within reach by the scenic road between Cape Jervis and Victor Harbor.

At Victor Harbor, where no ship has called for years, but memories are all around in the solid breakwaters and causeway to Granite Island, there is a modern and an old-style hotel, a motel, guest house, and caravan park accommodation close to the long crescent of beach.

South Australia's first railway linked nearby Port Elliot with Goolwa, main port for the River Murray steamers and barges in the 1850s. Today it is a popular resort set between ocean, river and lakes.

At Moana, Southport and Seaford on the Saint Vincent Gulf coast, and at Parsons, Chiton, Middleton and Boomer beaches on the ocean side of the peninsula, surfers can ride the waves all year through. The fishing is good on Fleurieu Peninsula, all the way round from Christies Beach to the Murray mouth.

Inland, Fleurieu Peninsula supports vineyards, orchards, forests and farms.

McLaren Vale is the centre of the Southern Vales wine-growing region stretching from Reynella to Langhorne Creek. There are more than 40 wineries in the Southern Vales which welcome visitors and offer sales wines, which are cheapest at the cellar door. The Barn, at McLaren Vale, is a gallery and museum, as well as a restaurant specializing in the food and wine of the district.

At Willunga, fine old buildings, many roofed by locally quarried slate, have a delightful surrounding of almond orchards.

Further south, at Hindmarsh Falls, water tumbles down over massive rocks set in eucalyptus trees. The 1870 Pioneer Village at Morphett Vale, on Fleurieu Peninsula, contains one of the country's finest collections of Australiana.

On the main road from Adelaide to the Southern Vales wineries or Victor Harbor, the village is a good place to break your journey for an hour or so.

The village has 11 buildings; comprising a settler's cottage, general store, Cobb and Co. coaching depot, blacksmith and clockmakers' shops, a saddlery and a pub—all furnished authentically in period style. The village is a stopover during one-day coach tours from Adelaide operated by the South Australian Government Travel Centre.

Kangaroo Island, off the tip of Fleurieu Peninsula, is Australia's third largest island after Tasmania and Melville. It's quiet and seemingly remote from the mainland, though only 112 kilometres south of Adelaide.

In the city you must go to a zoo or marine park to see a seal. On KI, as it is generally abbreviated, the seals sun themselves on the white beach sand. And in the bushland behind the calm bays you can hear slithering goannas and scuttling echidnas.

Kingscote, the island's business centre, is only 30 minutes' flight from Adelaide Airport, and in the holiday season it is one of Australia's busiest rural centers. From beach, rock or boat, Kangaroo Island provides some of the world's best fishing spots—with everything from big sharks in the deep water to tiddlers hooked from the end of a pier.

You can journey to Kangaroo Island at a more leisurely pace by sea from Port Adelaide in the car ferry *Troubridge*. Any of the island's three towns—Kingscote, American River and Penneshaw—are a base for exploration of the island, which has a coastline of 451 km. There's accommodation in hotels, motels, lodges and caravan parks. Pennington Bay is a spectacular surfing beach.

Vivonne Bay shelters a crayfishing fleet. At Seal Bay, seals breed and play in a protected haven.

Flinders Chase, covering much of the western end of the island, is Australia's largest fauna and flora reserve. Here you can share lunch with a sooty kangaroo and look for wedgetail eagles and wild orchids.

The formations of stalactites and stalagmites at Kelly Hill Caves were discovered when a horse fell through the ground in the 1880s. Public tours of the caves are conducted daily.

Outdoor Life

South Australia is great recreational vehicle and camping country. There are more than 170 good campervan parks and hundreds of other attractive bushland and riverside places where people who love the outdoors can stop.

About 80% of tourist activity here involves travel by private car, and about 25% of holiday accommodation is campervans and tents.

The State's lack of high mountains and its hundreds of miles of straight roads mean that holiday trips are easy on vans and trailers, and driving can be a relaxation. The most rewarding time to travel in the South Australian countryside is spring (September to November) and autumn (March to May). Especially popular at these times are the resorts in the Flinders Ranges, where wildflowers carpet the rugged mountains in spring.

Summer (December to February) attracts visitors to the southern parts of the State, to the beach resorts near Adelaide, to Eyre Peninsula and to Mount Gambier. With the exception of the northern Flinders Ranges, parts of Kangaroo Island and the Outback, all driving in South Australia is on sealed roads.

People driving vans from the eastern States can motor through South Australia's riverland and enjoy the community atmosphere of the Murray River towns such as Renmark, Berri, Loxton, Barmera and Waikerie. At many centres along the hundreds of miles of lazily flowing river they can stop for a glass of Riverland wine or citrus fruit juice.

Visitors coming towards Adelaide through the New South Wales border city of Broken Hill pass by the majestic Flinders Ranges. The ranges' vivid colors, native eucalypts and craggy peaks make them a favorite subject for landscape painters.

In the heart of the ranges is Wilpena Pound, a popular resort with modern motel accommodation. It is a base for tours of the old mining town of Blinman and the peaks, valleys and gorges. Arkaroola, in the northern Flinders Ranges, is a sheep station and fauna sanctuary. It is a gemstone area of great interest to geologists. Roads give access to spectacular gorge and dry river-bed scenery.

Accommodation is available at Arkaroola village. There are motels, bunkhouses, shearers' quarters and caravan and camping facilities. Package tours are available to the area from Adelaide.

From the Flinders Ranges the route to Adelaide passes south through the wineries of Clare and the Barossa Valley.

Another good region for recreational vehicles is Eyre Peninsula, across which extends the 2,700-km. Eyre Highway linking Adelaide and Perth (Western Australia). Although it passes through hundreds of kilometres of semi-desert and treeless plains, the Eyre Highway no longer holds many fears for motorists and caravaning enthusiasts since it was bitumen-sealed in 1976.

Before the Eyre Highway was tamed there were long stretches of rough primitive road that resembled a dirt track in summer and a quagmire in winter. The highway had a reputation as one of Australia's worst. It became the graveyard of many cars that were abandoned by their owners, and caused tyre blow-outs, broken axles and shattered windshields.

Though the highway is now a smooth black ribbon, a car trip from Adelaide to Perth still requires planning. Drivers should check that their vehicles are in good mechanical condition, and should carry basic spares such as radiator hoses, fanbelts and spare tyre—and, most important, adequate drinking water in summer. There is a driving distance of several hours between settlements that can provide comprehensive road service. However, there are refuelling stations at least every 90 km.

There is access to Eyre Peninsula by air and boat as well as by road. Planes fly regularly to Port Lincoln and Whyalla. Port Lincoln, on Southern Eyre Peninsula, is the home of South Australia's tuna fishing fleet and one of the State's many quiet holiday retreats. Sunshine, seals, sailing and swimming are the main attractions for visitors.

Holiday fishing is very good along the whole Eyre Peninsula coast, which also has a reputation among big-game fishermen. The largest catch, a white pointer shark brought in on 39 thread, set an all-tackle world record. It weighed 1179 kilos.

The port and steel-making town of Whyalla is on the Peninsula caravan route. Thousands of visitors are shown over the steelworks each year.

On Yorke Peninsula, which is shaped like a foot but lacks Italy's elegant heel, are the old copper mining towns of Moonta, Kadina and Wallaroo, where descendents of Cornish miners keep up a Cornish festival (Kernewek Lowender) during the second or third week of May of each odd-numbered year.

Entering the State through the southeast means calling at Mount Gambier, Australia's "Blue Lake" city. The mount itself is an extinct volcano and inside the cone is a lake which makes a mysterious color change from sombre grey to brilliant blue every year about the end of November—reverting to normal color in June.

The Mount Gambier district has Australia's largest commercial pine forests. Travelers can taste locally produced cheeses and wine from the nearby Coonawarra district, wander through the Naracoorte Caves, or sit down to a picnic lunch of lobster from one of the region's fishing villages.

There are regular air services to Mount Gambier, operated by Ansett Airlines of South Australia and O'Connor Airlines.

Closer to Adelaide, one can spend pleasant days driving through the Mount Lofty Ranges down Fleurieu Peninsula, stopping by at old fishing and sailing villages such as Port Elliott, Victor Harbor and Goolwa.

PRACTICAL INFORMATION FOR SOUTH AUSTRALIA

FACTS AND FIGURES. South Australians are nick-named "crow-eaters", because of the large number of crows, and the vast area of dry unproductive land only fit for them. The state bird, however, is not the crow but the magpie or piping shrike. The floral emblem is Sturt's desert pea. The wombat is the fauna emblem. Adelaide is the capital. The state population is about 1,300,000.

HOW TO GET AROUND. *By air:* Local flights are provided by Airlines of South Australia to Kangaroo Island, Eyre Peninsula, Mount Gambier, Renmark and Broken Hill. Light planes available as air taxis. Regular light plane flights made by Opal Air, Emu, Commodore, Eyre Charter, and other operators.

By car: Highways from Adelaide to all four State borders. Car rentals: Avis, Budget, Hertz. *By bus:* Ansett Pioneer, Greyhound and Deluxe. *By train:* State Transport Authority.

Tour Operators: Ansett Airlines of South Australia, Ansett Briscoe, South Australian Government Travel Centre, and Premier Roadlines.

SPECIAL INTEREST TOURS. At Andamooka and Coober Pedy, more than 700 km. north of Adelaide and accessible by car, coach and light plane, visitors may search for the world's best opal provided they buy a miner's right. Miners live underground as protection against extreme summer heat. Visitors can camp cheaply underground in converted opal mines.

 MUSEUMS. Birdwood Mill Museum, about 46 km. from Adelaide has a collection of old cars and motorcycles which is the nucleus of an Australian automotive museum. Australia's motor vehicle industry and motor sport originated in South Australia.

 NATIONAL PARKS AND FORESTS. Australia's unique fauna and rare plants are features of a number of national parks within South Australia. They include Flinders Ranges National Park (access via Hawker), Lincoln National Park (access via Port Lincoln), Coorong National Park (access via Princes Highway from Adelaide), and Flinders Chase National Park (on Kangaroo Island). State Parks near Adelaide are Para Wirra and Belair Recreation Parks.

 SPORTS. Gliding and hang-gliding are established sports, though membership is small. World gliding records have been established at Waikerie, on the River Murray. Big game fishing is centred on the ports of Eyre Peninsula and Kangaroo Island. Record catches of the giant white pointer shark have been made.

 TOURIST INFORMATION SERVICES. For details of all tourist areas in South Australia, the South Australian Government Travel Centre, 18 King William Street, Adelaide, 5001. Tel. (08) 513281 and 2121644. Cables, Govtourist. Telex 82487.

 HOTELS AND MOTELS. Since many areas of South Australia are sparsely settled, accommodations can be hard to find in some places. There are, however, some good hotels in the major population centres. Rates for 2 people sharing a room are: *Expensive:* A$50 and up; *Moderate:* A$30–50; *Inexpensive:* under A$30.

Barossa Valley

Tanunda: Tanuda Hotel. *(Moderate).* Air conditioned. Liquor license. Private facilities. *Weintal. (Moderate).* Modern 40-unit hotel set in old town of 2500 people. Air conditioned. Colour TV and refrigerators in units. Dining room, lounge, park and pool.

Angaston: Vineyards Motel. *(Moderate).* About 80 km. from Adelaide in beautiful vineland. Located on Stockwell Road. 20 units on ground floor. Most comforts.

Lyndoch: Barossa Motel. *(Moderate).* Air conditioned. Swimming pool. TV, refrigerators and coffee-makers in room. Licensed restaurant. *Lyndoch Hotel. (Inexpensive).* 34 units. Town population only 421. 52 km. from Adelaide, on Sturt Highway.

SOUTH AUSTRALIA

Eyre Peninsula
Port Lincoln: *Blue Seas Motel. (Moderate).* 13 units. Heating, electric blankets, refrigerators. *Hilton Motor Inn. (Moderate).* 34 units. Air conditioned, room service, licensed dining room. *Tasman Hotel. (Moderate).* 33 rooms. Air conditioned, electric blankets, TV, room service. *Kingscourt Motel. (Inexpensive).* 36 rooms. In Tasman Terrace near ocean. Cooking facilities, room service, licensed dining room, air conditioning. *Sorrento Motel. (Inexpensive).* 12 units. On Lincoln Highway. Cooking facilities.

Ceduna: *East West Motel.* (Moderate). Air conditioned. Private facilities. Licensed restaurant. Pool. TV. *Highway One Motel.* (Moderate). Air conditioned. Private facilities. Licensed restaurant. Refrigerator, TV.

Whyalla: *Alexander Motor Inn.* (Moderate). Air conditioned. Private facilities. Coffee-makers, refrigerators, TV in rooms. Licensed restaurant. Pool.

River Murray Area
Renmark: *Ventura Motel. (Moderate).* 11 rooms. Located in main street. Air conditioned, refrigerator, electric blankets, covered parking. *Fountain Motel. (Moderate).* 20 units. All usual facilities plus ski boat hire. *Renmark Country Club. (Moderate).* 40 units. Situated on Renmark Golf Course. Private patio. All usual facilities. Swimming pool, licensed restaurant, children's game room. *Renmark Hotel. (Inexpensive).* 63 rooms. Overlooks River Murray. Nearby golf course and bowls, tennis, water-skiing, boating, fishing, swimming, picnic sites. Dinner-dance Saturdays. *Citrus Valley Motel. (Inexpensive).* 20 units. On Sturt Highway route to Sydney. Air conditioning and electric blankets, refrigerator, TV, under-cover parking.

Berri: *Berri Hotel. (Moderate).* 43 units; and *Berri Motel. (Moderate).* Both in Riverside Avenue, and both with all facilities and comforts and a licensed restaurant. *Berri Lodge Motel. (Inexpensive).* 9 units. Room service.

Barmera: *Barmera Hotel. (Moderate).* 47 rooms. Motel section has 14 units with facilities. Room service, dining room, pool, refrigerators. *Lake Bonney Motel. (Moderate).* 30 units. Licensed dining, room service, air conditioning.

Loxton: *Loxton Motel. (Moderate).* 18 rooms. Air conditioned, pool, TV, licensed dining room.

Waikerie: *Waikerie Hotel-Motel. (Moderate).* 35 rooms. Air conditioning, refrigerator, room service, dining.

Southeast Areas
Mt. Gambier: *Commodore. (Expensive).* Air conditioned. Private facilities, coffee-makers, TV, refrigerators, electric blankets. Licensed restaurant. *Travelodge. (Expensive).* Air conditioned. Private facilities, coffee-makers, refrigerators, TV in rooms. Pool. Licensed restaurant. *Federal Hotel. (Moderate).* 16 rooms. Air conditioned, electric blankets, dining room. *Jens Hotel. (Moderate).* 25 rooms. Older style with comfort of log fires. Well-situated in city centre opposite cave gardens. Electric blankets, refrigerators, room service. *Blue Lake Motel. (Moderate).* 34 units with refrigerators, tea and coffee-making facilities. Overlooks Mt. Gambier from hillside vantage point. *Grandview Motel. (Moderate).* 36 units with views of the lakes and the city. TV, refrigerators, electric blankets, billiards, table tennis. *Grand Central Motel. (Moderate).* 27 units. Near shopping, lakes, Olympic pool, tennis and bowls. *Highway Village Motel. (Moderate).* 41 units. Most facilities, including room service and dining room. Pool. *Mount Gambier Motel. (Inexpensive).* 33 units. On road to Penola. TV, heating, laundry. *Tower Motor Inn. (Inexpensive).* 18 units. TV, electric blankets, tea-making facilities. *Baldorney Guest House. (Inexpensive).* 19 rooms. Room service and dining room, TV, tea-making, electric blankets, refrigerators.

WESTERN AUSTRALIA

Home of "the Most Fortunate People"

by
ANTHONY BERRY

When English seafaring buccaneer William Dampier stumbled across the far western edges of the Australian continent he described the inhabitants he found there as "the miserablest people in the world." He informed the British government that the land seemed unsuitable for agriculture; it was barren and useless so far as this 17th century navigator was concerned.

Dampier's comments provoke a good-natured smile from today's inhabitants of Western Australia, for they consider themselves the most fortunate people of all who live on this vast continent.

Not for nothing was Western Australia officially called "the State of Excitement." Now the state's title is "Home of the America's Cup."

A State on the Move

It is here, in a region about the size of Western Europe and accounting for a third of the entire country, that many of Australia's greatest developments are taking place. Within its million square miles lies one of the world's richest storehouses of mineral wealth—deposits of iron, bauxite, nickel, natural gas, oil and gold. It has vast wheatlands, abundant forests, seas rich with all manner of fish as well as even more oil and gas.

It has a pleasant, equable climate and its capital, Perth, has more sunny hours, even temperatures and clear days than any other Australian city. It is closer to Asia than to the rest of the nation and its inhabitants set themselves apart from much that the rest of Australia thinks and does, seeing secession as a real and feasible possibility.

One rich and free-thinking grazier has, in fact, already done just that. The self-titled "Prince Leonard" of the Hutt River Province actually declared his property as having seceded from the Commonwealth of Australia and has developed a thriving tourism industry as a result. The secession was not taken seriously by authorities and the State's Department of Tourism has described it as a gimmick and refused any promotional assistance to "Prince Leonard." Visitors must take the "Prince" and his Province as they find it.

Not all West Australians would go quite as far as "Prince Leonard" has gone; but there is definitely an air of vibrancy about the West and its people that is less readily detected in the rest of the country. Its people walk tall and *are* tall. (Exotic cabarets around the world derive many of their long-legged chorus boys and girls from the suburban homes of Perth.) There is a spring in the step of the rush hour crowds. This is the luckiest state in what has been termed "The Lucky Country"—and the people who live there know it only too well.

It looks west out over the Indian Ocean toward Africa, south to the controversial whaling waters of Antarctica, northeast toward India and Southeast Asia and, from its northern coast, is separated from Indonesia by only three hundred miles of water. It measures some 2,000 miles from north to south and 1,000 miles from east to west. Yet its inhabitants total about a million, with most of them living in the South West.

About half the population is under 24 years of age; a third of them are teenagers. They marry young and have their children early. It all adds to the general air of go-go youthfulness that is an inescapable facet of life in the west. Yet hardly more than a decade ago, Western Australia was a quiet, sleepy and almost neglected backwater of the country. It took a mineral boom, a vast inflow of capital to foster the boom, and an inrush of migrants to transform the state into its present exciting condition.

Iron Ore and Wildflowers

Lying beneath the stark ochre-red rocks of the Hamersley Ranges is enough high-grade iron ore to meet all the world's needs for many years to come. Some of the ore is so rich in mineral content that it is possible to weld two pieces together prior to any refining process.

Mountains are being moved—and new ones created—by mechanical shovels that can shift up to 24,000 tons of ore a day. A visitor to the huge mining projects of the Hamersley region moves in a world of Goliaths, dwarfed by giant machines and the vast landscape. New towns, ports and railways have sprung up to provide the support services for the mining projects. Places once remote and inaccessible have come within reach of all.

In the far north, on the border with the Northern Territory, is the far-sighted Ord River irrigation scheme designed to change grazing lands into fertile crop-growing country. From this has come the creation of a 286 square-mile reservoir containing nine times the amount of water in Sydney's impressive harbour. Old homesteads of early settlers now lie beneath the waters of Lake Argyle, which has become a holiday centre for anyone wanting to see the grandeur and fauna of the tropical north.

But not everything is modern, mechanised development, extracting ton after ton from the earth. Pearling luggers still set out from the coast which once drew divers from all over the East to make Broome one of the busiest ports along the entire Western Australia coast. Until 1978, whalers set out from Albany on a strictly controlled search for the great sperm whales of the southern oceans. Now, whaling has stopped but the station remains as a tourist attraction. The sea also provides good living for exporters of tuna and crayfish tails.

Once a year, much of the state bursts into colour as the wildflowers bloom. Areas north and south of Perth bring coachloads of sightseers to see the brilliant kaleidoscope that covers the ground from Geraldton to Albany. From August through November is the time to go.

The true traveler who wants to see Western Australia in its entirety will probably enter the state in the northeast on the route out of Darwin, tour right down the coastline (with an occasional detour inland), stop awhile in Perth and then continue on around the southwest and across the Nullarbor Plain into South Australia. For some of the year, such a journey would be impractical. Western Australia has a wet season and a dry season in its more northerly regions. And when it's wet, it really is just that. Monsoonal rains teem down and roads can become impassable. Total annual rainfall is generally less than received in Perth, but it tends to come all at once with the summer months (November through February), having high humidity and travel by road not recommended.

Distances between towns are often great. National Highway Route One now is almost fully paved within Western Australia, although a stretch of unpaved road still exists between Fitzroy Crossing and Halls Creek. The Great Northern Highway is paved from Perth through to Newman.

Due to the distances involved, a recommended alternative to road travel is to tour the northern region by air, using Perth as a starting point.

PERTH

When the first manned spacecraft was orbiting the earth it was the middle of the night as the crew tracked across Australia. As they passed over Perth, the city turned on all its lights. It was then that the spacemen knew that, somewhere far below, there were people thinking of them.

Such a gesture is typical of the gregarious, expansive people who live in Perth. Maybe it is the isolation, maybe the feeling of space; but whatever the reason, the Sandgropers—as they are jibingly called by other Australians—tend to be the most open, relaxed and easy-going of all Australians. One could also attribute to the equable climate and clear air the tendency of West Australians to be bigger, taller and bonier than their fellows in other parts of the country.

Geography, terrain and climate have set Perthians aside from the rest of Australia. The city they live in is unique for its isolation: a million people living on the fringe of a continent, 1,750 miles from their nearest city neighbour (Adelaide) and staring across an ocean where the next landfall (Mauritius) is 3,600 miles away.

The city hugs the banks of the Swan River, climbs a hill to the beautiful King's Park and closes off some of its city streets so that pedestrians can stroll unhindered by a vehicular population that rivals Los Angeles for the world's highest per capita level of car ownership.

A Mellow, Sun-Blessed City

Although often referred to as a planned city, Perth has none of the sterile orderliness of other places, notably Canberra, which come into this category. Its early designers set about blending the city with the benefits already bestowed by nature. The site was originally selected by Captain James Stirling in 1827 on orders from the same Governor Darling who had also ordered the setting up of a military post farther down the coast at Albany. Early British government reluctance to assist in the creation of another settlement was overcome when Thomas Peel formed a group willing to underwrite the migration of 10,000 people. Stirling named the city after the Scottish birthplace of the then secretary of state for war and the colonies, Sir George Murray. Thomas Peel proved to be a poor organiser and could not even create work for the 300 emigrants he brought out from England in 1829. Growth was slow. It took the gold rush of 1892 to spark progress. Suddenly the pace quickened, a port was established at Fremantle and the coming of the railway from the other side of the continent in 1915 put the final seal on the establishment of modern-day Perth. It is now a mellow, sun-blessed city, spacious, green and floral. Its crowning glory is the King's Park, a thousand acres of mostly natural bushland spreading out over a hill looking down into the city's business and commercial heart. Few would argue with the claim by Perth citizens that this is the best city parkland in Australia. For this, they thank Governor Sir Frederick Weld who first proposed preservation of the area as far back as 1871.

The city's oldest surviving building is the old court house in Stirling Gardens. The Old Mill in South Perth was built a year earlier (1835) and has undergone restoration work to take it back to its original appearance. Inside are relics from pioneer days. Convict labour was used to build the Town Hall in the style of an English Jacobean marketplace. It stands on the corner of two of the city's main streets, Hay and Barrack. Further reminders of England are to be found on a walk along London Court, a Tudor-style shopping arcade linking Hay Street Mall with St. George's Terrace.

A popular excursion from Perth is to Rottnest Island. This is said to be a corruption of the words "rat's nest." Such was the description given to it by early Dutch explorers. They mistook the strange and rare marsupials, "quokkas," which infest the island for a large breed of rat. Once a penal settlement, Rottnest is now a popular retreat for city-dwellers. The island's only form of transportation is the bicycle; accommodation options include hotels, cottages, lodges, and tents; there are dozens of deserted sheltered coves and beaches.

Tour, too, the 82 miles north of Perth to New Norcia. Here, the Benedictine order of monks still runs a mission first set up in 1846 to help aborigines. At one stage in its history the monastery was separated from the Perth diocese and became responsible directly to the Vatican. Later it gained status as a diocese in its own right. Now it is a self-supporting property, farming some 20,000 acres.

South of Perth are coastal resorts that provide good surfing, swimming and fishing. Rockingham is 28 miles away and Mandurah involves a 50 mile drive. Twenty-five miles to the northeast and set among hills is Mundaring Weir, and at Yanchep (32 miles north from Perth) there is a pleasant holiday and picnic complex complete with native fauna and limestone caves. Eight miles from Yanchep is the new tourist complex of Yanchep Sun City.

PRACTICAL INFORMATION FOR PERTH

HOW TO GET THERE. *By air:* Perth is served by the following international airlines: *Qantas,* from the U.K. and Singapore, from Bali and Bangkok; *British Airways* from London, Singapore, and Bombay; *Cathay Pacific Airways* from Hong Kong; *Malaysian Airlines System* from Kuala Lumpur; *Singapore Airlines* from Singapore; *South African Airways* from Mauritius and Johannesburg; *Air India* from Bombay; *Garuda* from Jakarta and Bali. All except the Asian airlines carry on the service from Perth to Sydney, and some also to Melbourne, to connect with Pacific and North American destinations.

By sea: The only passenger ship service into Fremantle (the port for Perth) is an occasional P&O ship and CTC cruises to Southeast Asia.

By bus: A number of companies operate express coach services linking Perth with the eastern states. Some continue to Port Hedland, and 3 companies operate all the way to Darwin during the "dry" season and also in the "wet" season when weather permits.

By car: Drivers can follow the same routes as buses and also, except in the wet (Dec.–Feb.) rainy season in the tropical north, drive down the west coast of the state from Darwin. Some of the roads can be flooded in the wet season.

TOURS. Several companies operate daily tours around the city, beaches, hills, riverside and other points of interest. A variety of ferry cruises, south to Fremantle or north to the vineyards, are also available. Extended tours by coach, using both "established" and "safari" accommodation, are offered, and air tours cover all parts of the state.

MUSEUMS AND GALLERIES. A modern day rush to preserve the past before it is too late has led to the opening up of several private collections in many towns. The main museum and galleries of any note are in Perth and Fremantle.

Old Mill, South Perth, built in 1835 and still complete with its sails, is part of a folk museum. Mon., Wed., Thurs. & Sun. 13:00 to 17:00; Sat. 13:00 to 16:00. *Western Australia Museum,* Perth, displays traditional and contemporary Australian paintings. Small section of bark paintings. Blue whale skeletons, meteorites, comprehensive collection of history and culture on Aborigines. Monday through Thursday 10:30 A.M.–5 P.M.; Friday to Sunday 1–5 P.M.

The *Western Australian Art Gallery* houses traditional and contemporary exhibitions. Open daily 10 A.M.– 5 P.M.

MUSIC. Regular concerts at Perth Concert Hall. Parkerville Amphitheatre has open-air concerts in natural bush setting. Classical recitals, ballet and opera at the Octagon Theatre. The Perth Entertainment Centre offers a variety of performing arts, touring bands, and other attractions. Some trendy discos can be found. Free open-air concerts at Supreme Court Gardens in summer.

NIGHT LIFE. Perth offers a wide selection of night-time attractions to locals and visitors alike. There's sophisticated wining and dining, bawdy theater-restaurants, live theatre, nightclubs and cabarets. A variety of large and small restaurants offer dishes to suit all tastes. Wine taverns are popular evening entertainment places, while the Parmelia Hilton's Garden Restaurant and the Sheraton's River Room offer sophistication.

DRINKING LAWS. The general Australian phenomenon of "bring-your-own" is as prevalent in Western Australia as elsewhere. Licensed restaurants operate from noon to 3 P.M. and from 5:30 P.M. to 12:30 A.M. weekdays and 5:30 P.M.–10 P.M. Sundays. Hotels and taverns generally are licensed to open from 10 A.M. until 10 P.M. from Monday to Saturday. On Sundays they are restricted to 11 A.M. until 1 P.M. and from 4:30–7:30 P.M. Perth has several nightclubs open Monday through Saturday, 8 P.M.–3:30 A.M.

SHOPPING. The center of Perth is now a pleasant pedestrian area with big department stores and many smart boutiques. There are several arcades full of the smaller specialty shops. Tudor-looking London Court is most popular with souvenir hunters. Normal shopping hours are 8:35 A.M. to 5:30 P.M. Monday through Friday; 8:35 A.M. to midday on Saturday, with late-night shopping on Thursdays to 9 P.M. Specialty shops trading in local products and catering mainly to the tourist trade are permitted to trade 24 hours a day if they wish.

SPORTS. Perth's climate is ideal for outdoor living, and the city offers all popular sports to its residents and visitors. The Western Australian Walking Club welcomes visitors on its regular walks within a 50-mile radius of the city.

HOTELS AND MOTELS. Like other Australian cities, Perth and its environs offer a variety of accommodations. *Expensive:* A$60 and up; *Moderate:* A$45–60; *Inexpensive:* A$20–45.

Perth and Suburbs

Chateau Commodore. *Expensive.* Cnr. Hay St/Victoria Ave. Liquor room service. Licensed restaurant. 24 hr food service. Pool.

Gateway Inn. *Expensive.* 10 Irwin St. Liquor room service. Licensed restaurant. 24 hr food service. Pool. Located in Ansett Airlines city terminal complex.

The Kings. *Expensive.* 517 Hay St. Liquor room service. Licensed restaurant. 24 hr. food service. Pool.

Parmelia Hilton Hotel. *Expensive.* Operated by Hilton International. Mill St. Liquor room service. Licensed restaurant. 24 hr food service. Pool. Air conditioned. Nr golf, beaches, park, overlooking river.

Perth TraveLodge. *Expensive.* 54 Terrace Rd. Liquor room service. Licensed restaurant. Pool. Overlooks river.

Riverside Hotel. *Expensive.* 150 Mounts Bay Rd. Liquor room service. Licensed restaurant. Pool.

Sheraton-Perth Hotel. *Expensive.* 207 Adelaide Terrace. Liquor room service. Licensed restaurant. 24 hr food service. Pool. River views from all rooms.

Merlin-Perth Hotel. *Expensive.* Cnr. Adelaide Terrace and Plain St. 24-hr room service, including liquor room service. Pool. River views.

Orchard Perth Hotel. *Expensive.* 707 Wellington St. Japanese, Italian, Chinese, French, and Indonesian restaurants. 24-hr room service with liquor room service.

Parmelia Hilton. *Expensive.* Mill St. Liquor room service and 24-hr food service. Pool. River views.

Perth Ambassadors. *Expensive.* 196 Adelaide Terrace. 24-hr food service and liquor room service. Pleasant accommodations.

Perth Park Royal. *Expensive.* 54 Terrace Rd. 24-hr room service. Pool. Overlooks park and Swan River.

Transit Inn. *Expensive.* 37 Pier St. Liquor room service. Licensed restaurant. 24 hr food service. Pool.

Crestwood Inntown. *Moderate.* 70 Pier St. 24 hr food service.

Freeway Hotel. *Moderate.* 55 Mill Point Rd., S. Perth. Liquor room service. Licensed restaurant. 24 hr food service. Pool.

Highways Town House. *Moderate.* 788 Hay St. Liquor room service. Licensed restaurant. 24 hr food service. Pool.

Mounts Bay Lodge. *Moderate.* 166 Mounts Bay Rd. Liquor room service. Licensed restaurant. Pool. Next Kings Park. River Views. 0.4 km from city.

The New Esplanade. *Moderate.* 18 Esplanade. Liquor room service. Licensed restaurant. 24 hr food service. Overlooking river.

Town Lodge. *Moderate.* 134 Mill Point Rd., South Perth. Kitchen facilities in room. No restaurants. Pool. Nr golf, bowls, zoo, park. Weekly rates available.

Imperial Hotel. *Inexpensive.* 411 Wellington St. Liquor room service. Licensed restaurant.

Bentley

Hospitality Inn. *Moderate.* Liquor room service. Licensed restaurant. Pool.

Como

Swanview Motel. *Inexpensive.* On riverfront. Pool.

Floreat Park

Hotel Floreat. *Inexpensive.* Licensed restaurant. Nr beach, golf.

Inglewood

Civic Hotel. *Moderate.* Includes hot breakfast. Licensed restaurant.

Innaloo

Nookenburra Motor Hotel. *Moderate.* Kitchen facilities in rooms. Liquor room service. Licensed restaurant. Nr beach.

Maylands

Maylands Hotel. *Moderate.* Includes cooked breakfast. Liquor room service.

North Cottesloe

Ocean Beach Hotel. *Inexpensive.* Liquor room service. Licensed restaurant. Restaurant. Beach front, nr golf, tennis.

Rivervale

Arkaba Inn. *Inexpensive.* Pool

Flag Lodge. *Inexpensive.* Pool. Member Flag chain.

DINING OUT. Perth offers a large variety of restaurants, both in cuisine and atmosphere. As in the rest of the State, there are both licensed and Bring-Your-Own bottle (BYO) restaurants. Prices tend to be reasonable in Perth, with the following categories: *Expensive:* A$15 and up; *Moderate:* A$10–15; *Inexpensive:* less than A$10.

Emperor's Court. *Expensive.* Lake St. Chinese dishes. Licensed.

Room with a View. *Expensive.* The Esplanade, Perth. Licensed.

Ruby's. *Expensive.* Pier St. Victorian elegance. Licensed.

Casa Latina. *Moderate.* William/Francis Streets. Italian, French, Spanish cuisine. Winehouse license.

Le Coq d'Or. *Moderate.* Hay St. Very chic, ideal for a quiet lunch. BYO.

Costa Brava. *Moderate.* James St. Elegant but informal Spanish restaurant. BYO.

Kings Park Garden Restaurant. *Moderate.* Kings Park. Good food, magnificent views. Licensed.

Mamma Maria's. *Moderate.* Aberdeen St. Good food, ethnic decor. Licensed.

Oyster Bar. *Moderate.* James St. Local and other specialites. BYO.

Roman Forum. *Moderate.* Oxford St. Perth's largest steakhouse. BYO.

Silver Swan at Gateway Inn. *Moderate* Irwin St. Superior grill. Licensed.

Sorrento. *Moderate.* James St. Italian. BYO.

Canton. *Inexpensive.* Hay St. Old established, ideal for pre-theatre dining. BYO.

Golden Eagle. *Inexpensive.* James St. Reservations imperative. Licensed.

Ming Palace. *Inexpensive.* City Arcade. Extensive menu. BYO.

Also recommended are *Foxy Lady* (Allendale Square), *Fid's Restaurant* (Aberdeen Street), *La Chaumiere* (Stirling Highway), *Lautrec's* (Hay Street), *Room with a View* (in the new Esplanade Hotel) and *Prideau's* (Rockton Rd. and Stirling Highway).

EXPLORING WESTERN AUSTRALIA

The fact that much of this state is so sparsely populated means that distances between towns are often great. Improvements to major road links have opened up many areas to the visitor, but some of Western Australia's most rugged and beautiful attractions are best reached by air.

Although Perth is the state capital, with far the largest concentration of population, it was 250 miles to the south, in the former whaling port of Albany, that the first settlement of Western Australia took place. The town spreads around Princess Royal Harbor and is protected from the stormy southern oceans on three sides.

Forty-four soldiers and convicts, sent by the Governor to thwart French attempts to colonise the area, were the first to settle in Albany in 1826. They landed on Boxing Day, December 26. Development was slow until the whaling fleet moved in during the 1840s. There was a period of growth right through to the present century but when Fremantle became established as the port for Perth, Albany's development slowed. Today, it is a town of historical interest, the starting point for travel into the wildflower regions of the southwest and for tours to see the south coastal areas.

The State's oldest residence, Old Farm, can be seen on Strawberry Hill. Orchards, wheatlands and fields of clover are the hallmark of the Albany region. So, too, are its thriving herds of cattle, its tuna fleet and the acres of potatoes.

Snow is sometimes an unexpected sight on the bluffs of the Stirling Ranges and there are some incredibly weird coastal rock formations where the ocean hammers incessantly against the shores.

Butting on to the eastern boundary of the Albany region is the area known as Esperance, running right along the shores of the Great Australian Bight as far as the South Australian border. As recently as 1954 there were only 36 farmers in these 57,000 square miles of mostly open country; today there are more than 600 farming in excess of a million acres. It is a land that is only now beginning to blossom and develop, experiencing its first real prosperity since gold was discovered in the 1890s.

The only town of any size is also called Esperance, after the frigate that brought Huon de Kermadec into the bay in 1792. John Eyre passed by in 1841 but permanent settlement did not take place until Andrew Dempster obtained a lease over 100,000 acres in 1866. It was the gold rush of 1893 that brought the first real increase in population. Prosperity came to Esperance as it became a seaside resort and an outlet for the frustrations and fortunes of the Goldfields miners.

A burgeoning wheat-growing project was killed off by the Depression and the farmers left the land. Modern research has shown how the land can be improved and the farmers have returned. One American investor, Allen Chase, decided to ignore the research findings, however, and went his own way about developing 1,500,000 acres. His project failed but has since been taken up by other investors, notably the American television personality, Art Linkletter. Now the farmers are returning and the land is realising its potential of becoming one of Australia's biggest producers of beef, fat lambs, wool, wheat, oats, barley and linseed.

The southern seaboard of seemingly endless rolling plains presents a wild and windswept scenery not to be found anywhere else in Australia. There are three million acres of rolling heath with a rainfall of 16 to 24 inches. Further inland is the dryer, harsher mallee scrub country—another three million acres of it—where the rainfall is a mere 13 to 16 inches.

Nevertheless, the Esperance area is expanding rapidly as a trading and business centre and is one of the best examples of the vitality that is so typical of Western Australia. It remains a popular holiday centre, for it boasts some of the best unspoilt coastal scenery anywhere on the Australian seaboard.

On the western side of the Albany region, taking up the southwest corner of the state, is the South West Region, centered on the town of that name, the third largest in Western Australia. This was another early sighting by French mariners, explored by Captain Freycinet in 1803 but first occupied from the land by an expedition which set up a military post in 1829. The oldest stone church in Western Australia is at Busselton. A workman's cottage that became a church in 1848 is at Australind, and the well-lit Yallingup Caves are worth an inspection.

Central Hinterland: A Tidal Wave in Granite

Inland from the Bunbury and Albany regions is the area designated as the Central Hinterland. Here, grain and wool provide the economic backbone. More grain is grown and more wool is clipped here than anywhere else in the state. It covers an area roughly equal in size to the whole of the North Island of New Zealand. Farms here comprise millions of acres and account for more than a third of all the cleared land in Western Australia. The main centre is the Avon Valley township of Northam, 66 miles by road northeast of Perth, although one of the oldest rural settlements in the state is the smaller centre of York. York is named after the English city, and has now been preserved and restored as a historical attraction.

The railways play a vital role in the Central Hinterland's daily life. Tracks and sidings fan out from Northam to provide the link by which the grain is sent after harvest from the wheatfields to the ships waiting alongside the wharves in Fremantle. The prairie country comes to life at each harvest and then sleeps for the rest of the year. Huge silos dot the landscape, storehouses for grain awaiting the next train.

This is one of the regions where road travel by private car is quite feasible. Good roads enable you to drive the 218 miles to the eastern wheatlands township of Hyden to see the extraordinary granite overhang quite accurately named Wave Rock. Estimated to have been formed 2,700 million years ago, the rock appears like a huge tidal wave, several hundred yards long, about to break over the dry, flat country that surrounds it. To make the journey worthwhile stop, too, to see other nearby weird and wonderful rocky formations such as The Humps and Hippo's Yawn. In Bates Cave there are aboriginal rock paintings.

Taking up more than 307,000 square miles inland from these three regions is the ore-rich desert of the Kalgoorlie region. Bigger than Texas, it is home to less than 50,000 people. Yet, at the height of the gold rush in 1905, there were 200,000 people on the goldfields. New fortunes are being created today by the discovery of nickel, mined now not by the small-time prospectors of the type who first opened up the area, but by giant corporations who are building completely new treed and landscaped towns in the midst of a previously barren and inhospitable land.

The Lure of Gold

Alluvial gold was first discovered at Coolgardie in 1892 by prospectors William Ford and Arthur Bayley. A year later, Irishman Patrick Hannan made a strike which was reported around the world. With Thomas Flanagan and Dan Shea he made a strike which simply involved collecting nuggets from the surface of the sandy gullies. In a few days they collected 200 ounces of gold and the boom began. The town of Kalgoorlie grew from this boom and sits on what is considered the richest square mile of rock ever known. To date it has given up close to 40 million ounces of fine gold, and the locals still maintain there is much more to come.

Life on the goldfields was rugged. Living conditions were primitive and unsanitary. Intense heat with little shade added to the miners' discomfort. Many died. It was only when a water supply was piped through the 350 miles from the Darling Ranges in 1903 that many of the problems of disease and drought were relieved. Just how pitifully men were prepared to live in the expectation of making a fortune is depicted in a highly graphic museum in the main street of the pioneer town Coolgardie. Here are the tents, the utensils, tools, mementoes and records of the pioneers. It is a moving portrayal of an era when, according to one reporter, one half of Coolgardie was busy burying the other half, so high was the mortality rate. Burial was a primitive business. Anything would be used as a coffin. Miners went to their graves encased in coffins that bore the names of tinned foods or liquor. One carried the inscription "Stow away from boilers," obviously in the belief that he had made his peace with his Maker.

Today Coolgardie bustles with tourists and the local inhabitants have turned to less bloodthirsty pastimes. The town has three motels, a hotel, a safari village, guest house, and caravan park—still a little short of the 23 hotels and three breweries of its heyday. Legend has it that in those times, water was more expensive than whiskey!

The town then had two stock exchanges, two daily and four weekly newspapers and was second only in size to Perth and Fremantle. But today, a genuine atmosphere of ghostliness pervades the shimmering air. The town has been left to die but the echoes of its tough, rumbustious founders work easily on the imagination.

Kalgoorlie survived the gold rush. Twenty four miles to the east of Coolgardie, it is still a town of grandiose boom-time buildings, wide streets and pioneering spirit. It owes its modern prosperity as much to the gold which is still being won as to the more recent discovery of nickel.

The name of Paddy Hannan has been preserved in street names, a statue and a tree. The tree is said to mark the spot where the fortunate Irishman made his first strike. As a relic from the more permissive gold rush days, Kalgoorlie boasts one of the few red light districts tolerated by the authorities, although it's not featured in the tourist brochures.

Southeast of Kalgoorlie, 35 miles down the highway, is the model town of Kambalda, built by the Western Mining Corporation for workers at Australia's first commercial nickel mining venture. Kambalda is living proof that the desert can bloom and flower. You drive through a well-wooded but harsh plain, not unlike that of the old goldfields of South-eastern Australia, to be greeted by tree-lined streets, green lawns and gardens full of flowering shrubs. There are saltpans to be visited at Lake Lefroy and it is possible to go down a former gold mine specially set up to show visitors old and new methods used in the extraction of the precious metal.

Reminiscent of the pioneering days are the covered wagons and camels to be seen around Coolgardie. They are no longer used but are preserved as a reminder of an era only a couple of generations away.

Geraldton: Shipwrecks and Copperfields

Move coastwards and northwards from the Kalgoorlie region and you arrive in the area of Geraldton. This sprawls over 113,000 square miles and boasts some of the best year-round Mediterranean-style climate in the whole state.

It is an area rich in reminders of the state's early history. The coastline is littered with wrecks from the first exploration attempts. Best known is that of the Batavia, which sank in 1629 and from which relics are slowly being recovered and restored for public display. The Zuytdorp (wrecked in 1712) and the Zeewyck (1727) are two other vessels among the many which provide sport and excitement for divers. Offshore are the Abrolhos Islands, charted and named by the 16th century Portuguese navigators. The islands are renowned for the excellent fishing grounds. Cray-fishing is a thriving export industry that has attracted millions of dollars of investment money into the main town, Geraldton. The size of the commercial fishing fleet is strictly controlled and there is a closed season from August 15 to November 15.

While the rest of the country was undergoing gold fever, the area around Geraldton was experiencing the first flush of being the centre of major copper deposits. The Wanerenooka copper lode was discovered as early as 1842. Lead mining began at Northampton in 1848. Copper has been successfully mined since 1940. Worthwhile excavations of barytes, beryl, ochre and tantocolumbite ores have also been made. A field of natural gas was discovered at Dongara in 1970 and a pipeline now leads from there to supply consumers in Perth.

North of the Geraldton region is the sparsely populated 76,000 square miles of the Carnarvon region. Most of the inhabitants live in Carnarvon or Exmouth. Much controversy has centred on Exmouth for it is the site of the North West Cape communications centre, built by the commonwealth government for the American navy. The base contains one of the biggest very low frequency radio transmitters anywhere in the world and protesters against its existence claim that this has helped make Australia a prime target for possible future global warfare. At Carnarvon is another space-age contraption, the former NASA tracking station now used by Radio Australia following Darwin's devastating cyclones of 1975. Guided tours of the station can be arranged at the tourist bureau in Carnarvon.

Close by is where the Dutch explorer Dirk Hartog made one of the first landings and explorations of the Australian coast. That was in 1606. Ninety-three years later came William Dampier with his findings that he had discovered a country which appeared to be useless, barren and peopled by the most miserable beings. The streets of Carnarvon were planned with a width of 44 yards so that camel trains, which proved the mainstay of communications until the 1920s, could easily turn around.

The Gascoyne Agricultural Station, six miles from town, gives an insight into the research and development taking place in an area which has far into reached its full farming potential. There are blowholes on Quobba Station (42 miles from Carnarvon) and, 15 miles further on, Cape Cuvier presents the unusual sight of multi-coloured cliffs, 400-feet high, being pounded by the Indian Ocean.

The Pilbara: Bursting at the Seams

Travel north from Carnarvon and you reach the most exciting pioneering region of all Western Australia: The Pilbara. It is one of the most highly mineralised regions on earth. It is bursting at the seams with ore of all types and grades. It is a vast, scarred and ancient land, sunburnt and brooding. The predominant colour is rust-red ochre. It is an awe-inspiring, terrifying land of gorges, gullies, rifts and valleys that stretch to a very far horizon. Cavernous holes are being gouged out of the ground, mountains are being blasted aside and new mountains being created from the resultant rubble. It is a frontier land; pioneering country of the first order. The mining companies have built entire new towns, constructed hundreds of miles of railways and created ports capable of taking the world's biggest ships.

The region's main outlet for its products, Port Hedland, is one of Australia's fastest growing towns. First founded by pearl fishers in 1857 it now handles massive bulk ore carriers of 100,000 tons or more. Its an unlovely, untidy rambling town which still needs to be seen by anyone wanting to grasp the enormity of the mineral boom which has brought rapid civilisation to a land where, until very recently, only a few Aboriginal tribes and hardy Outback graziers were prepared to settle and live. Port Hedland is today what Cossack used to be: the most important port on the coast.

Much of Cossack had disappeared beneath the dunes until a determined restoration program was undertaken. Today the courthouse is perhaps the best example of this work. Cossack can be found five miles off the highway between Roeburne and Port Sampson, south of Port Hedland. At its height, it boasted a population of about 400, with an additional 1,000 people living there when the pearling fleet was "laid up" between May and September.

Inland from Port Hedland is the town which has the reputation of being the hottest place in Australia. Other settlements in the area might, however, dispute Marble Bar's dubious claim to fame. But many of them were not in existence when it recorded, in 1923-24, the longest known heat wave. For 160 consecutive days the temperature exceeded 100°F. It is quite common for the thermometer to register over 120°F on many days between October and March. Yet in winter, frosts are not unknown. Marble Bar has been described by reputable commentators as "a grim, lonely little settlement" and they say it is typical of much of the Western Australian Outback. So it is a place for visiting by those seeking out the unique aspects of this often weird and wonderful land.

Many of the names which appear on a present-day map of the Pilbara would not have been there even a quarter of a century ago. And most of the landmarks that then were named had little significance to anyone but land surveyors and geographers.

Kimberley: "Overlanders" Country

Much the same can be said for the final and most northerly of the distinctly different regions of Western Australia: the 162,000 square miles of the Kimberley. It is sparsely populated, monsoonal and three times the size of England. The rains fall in the summer (November to March), a wet season with varying intensity measuring from 15 to 50 inches. However drought broke this cycle in 1982–83.

In the winter "dry," however, there are seven months of almost endless blue skies and warm days. Then the great rivers slow to a trickle and the rich soil of the estuary flats cries out for irrigation. The great hope of the Kimberley is the Ord River Scheme. This is intended to bring a controlled water supply to 178,000 acres of open plains which have traditionally been used only for grazing. On land that has been the sole preserve of cattlemen since the 1880s, crops of all kinds are now being successfully grown. The scope of the research and development can best be seen at the Research Station just a few miles out of Kununurra, the administrative centre of the Ord River Scheme. After soaking up the technical data on growing maize and other crops, take a catamaran trip among the teeming bird and water life of Lake Argyle.

On the coast, 1,255 miles away from Perth, is what remains of a once thriving and tempestuous pearling industry. Pearling grounds discovered off the coast near Broome led to its establishment in 1883. Rapid expansion, plus oppressive conditions for the workers, followed soon after. Despite frequent damage from cyclones and numerous deaths brought about by hazardous working conditions, the trade flourished. A polyglot population developed. Japanese, Filipinos and Koepangers (from Indonesia) migrated to Broome. One of the most lasting memorials of a trade that went into quick decline with the advent of plastic and other synthetics is the Japanese cemetery where many a pearler is buried. The cemetery has a column dedicated to 40 Japanese drowned in a 1908 cyclone which claimed a total of 150 lives.

Long before Tasman, Dampier, King, Forrest and other explorers came to this coast it was visited by carnivorous dinosaurs. Proof of this is to be found in tracks made by these prehistoric beasts at the foot of sandstone cliffs close to Broome. The tracks have been verified as genuine. Generally they are covered by the tides, but a cast of the originals can be seen above highwater mark. There is an enormous rise and fall in tides all around the Kimberley coast. Port developments have, to some extent, overcome these difficulties, especially for the shipment of minerals, and beef is shipped out through Broome and Wyndham. In some places the fall is as much as 40 feet.

Anyone who has seen pictures of the tall, gaunt, Australian stockman droving cattle across thousands of miles of dusty plains should pay a call on Derby, administrative centre of the Kimberley. The country around here will revive memories of the movie "The Overlanders" and take you back to the days of the Durack family which herded its beasts all the way from Western Queensland into the Kimberley. The town makes a feature of the strange-shaped boab tree, a curvaceous, bottle-shaped piece of timber found in generous numbers in this region. Five miles south of the town is a boab tree which once had its hollow centre used as a prison for native wrongdoers.

Two hundred yards from the tree is Myalls Bore. The Bore is the water supply for a cattle trough claimed to be one of the world's longest in order to cope with the thousands of beasts mustered here on their way to the abattoirs and the great "road trains" which hurtle down the highways to southern cities.

Because of the need for a reliable surface transportation system, fine weather "beef roads" now run across the Kimberley, making touring by car a much more feasible proposition than it was a few years back. However, the inexperienced would always be well advised to leave the driving to someone else; keep your car in the garage and take a seat on a coach, safari vehicle or aircraft instead. To do this, head first of all to Perth.

PRACTICAL INFORMATION FOR WESTERN AUSTRALIA

HOW TO GET THERE. *By air:* Western Australia is served by *Qantas* from the U.K. and Singapore, from Bali and Bangkok; *British Airways* from London, Singapore, and Bombay; *Cathay Pacific Airways* from Hong Kong; *Malaysian Airlines System* from Kuala Lumpur; *Singapore Airlines* from Singapore; *South African Airways* from Mauritius and Johannesburg; *Air India* from Bombay; *Garuda* from Jakarta and Bali; *Air New Zealand* from Auckland. All except the Asian airlines and *Air New Zealand* carry on the service from Perth to Sydney, and some also to Melbourne, to connect with Pacific and North American destinations. Domestic airlines *TAA, East-West,* and *Ansett* link Perth with other State capitals, Ansett WA and East-West serve northern towns en route to Darwin.

By bus: A number of companies operate express coach services linking Perth with the eastern states. Some serve the northwest and link the capital with Darwin.

By car: Drivers can follow the same routes as buses and also drive down the west coast of the state from Darwin. Some of this road is flooded in the wet season.

By rail: The *Indian Pacific* runs from Perth to Sydney on Sunday, Tuesday and Thursday evenings and from Sydney to Perth on Monday, Thursday, and Saturday afternoons. The *Trans Australian* runs Perth-Port Pirie-Adelaide-Melbourne on Monday, Wednesday, and Saturday evenings and from Port Pirie to Perth on Monday, Wednesday and Saturday afternoons. Both trains offer sleeping berths and the journey takes three full days.

HOW TO GET AROUND. Western Australia's size means the visitor must have plenty of time to attempt crossing it by car. Major road links have been upgraded in recent years, but secondary roads are not recommended to those unfamiliar with outback conditions. Weather forecasts should be carefully monitored by travelers in the north of the state. Express coaches, tours and air and road services offer choices to the traveler.

It is natural in so vast a state and so comparatively new a country that air travel plays a tremendous part in getting around. Thus, besides the two major Australian airlines, Ansett and TAA that serve all major airports, Airlines of Western Australia services Kalgoorlie and northern towns, and commuter airlines such as Avior, Skywest, and others fly into small settlements.

As most visitors to Perth also want to see the rest of Australia, this state can be seen on the Discover Australia air fares with Ansett and TAA which give, at one fare, a routing of unlimited travel within 90 days in four travel patterns. Greyhound and Ansett Pioneer have similar unlimited travel passes.

Airport car rental desks at Perth are operated by Budget, Hertz and Thrifty. Other companies operating in the city include Avis, Letz, Avaca, Bayswater Car Hire, Drive-A Dollar, Kalamunda Rental Cars, Lo Rate Car Rentals, National Rent A Car System, Ryans Rent A Car, Sydney Anderson Rent A Car, Houghton Hire Cars.

Motorised caravans (campervans) can be hired from Fleetwood which claims to be the largest firm of its type in Australia. Westland and Funabouts also have fleets of campers for hire. For hire of cars and campervans, minimum driver age is 21. Perth and suburbs and country towns have a plentiful supply of caravan hire firms. Trail Bike Hire WA is in suburban Subiaco. Tents and camping gear can be hired from Open Road Rentals, Trend Tent Rentals, and Ava Tent.

SPORTS. The state is home of *Australia II,* winner of the America's Cup. Elimination races for the 1987 Cup challenge will be sailed throughout 1986. Sandhills between Fremantle Harbor and Scarborough Beach, 8 miles to the north, will serve as grandstands for viewers. Races can also be viewed on foot from three boat harbors within walking distance of Fremantle Harbor, one-half mile from the heart of colorful Fremantle. Western Australia is renowned for big-game fishing, and offers facilities for all the more conventional sports. Gloucester Park, Perth, is considered the best trotting track in the southern hemisphere. There are plenty of good public *golf courses* plus several excellent private clubs which usually welcome visitors. *Tennis* is played at night as well as in the daytime.

Surfing is superb down most the hundreds of miles of coast but is best done on patrolled beaches. Even quite small country towns have their own swimming pool. *Canoeing* is good on the upper reaches of the Swan River. *Land yacht racing* takes place on Lake Lefroy.

WHAT TO DO WITH THE CHILDREN. Parks, gardens and beaches are plentiful and provide the mainstay of juvenile diversions. Take children to see the black swans and wild ducks on Lake Monger or to the South Perth Zoo's collection, which includes several species unique to the State. The dancing horses at Bodeguero are something unusual, and youngsters will have fun pedalling a bike on traffic-free Rottnest Island. Horse riding on open country trails is readily available. The caves at Yanchep and the penguins on Penguin Island National Park should also interest and amuse the kids. River cruises are popular.

SEASONAL EVENTS. *January:* Mandurah/Kanyana *Carnival Aquatic Sports,* street parades; Busselton *Festival,* sports, dancing; *Hyde Park Holiday,* Perth, arts and culture festival. Perth *Festival,* January to March: concerts, opera, yachting, bathtub championships, regatta, films.

March: Vintage Festival, Middle Swan. Grape picking, wine tasting, auctions.

June: Northern Festival. Folk songs, pottery, art, silverwork.

July: Boab Festival Derby. Novelty events, golf parade.

August: Sunshine Festival, Geraldton. Water skiing, cycle races, rodeo, parade. *Shinju Matsuri Festival,* Broome. Great crab race, corroborees (nocturnal Aboriginal festival), Pearl Queen, lugger race all tied in with the Japanese pearling industry. *Fe Na Cl Festival,* Dampier-named, derived from chemical formulas for iron and salt. *Spinifex Spree,* Port Hedland. Bierfest, horseracing, local drama. *Top of the West,* Kununurra. *Mardi Gras,* Cotton Queen. *Nameless Festival,* Tom Price, after Mt. Nameless. Sporting contests. *State drama festival,* Crawley, Perth. *Isles Festival,* Aug-Sept, Esperance Bay. bierfest, bare foot waterskiing, motor bike scrambles. *Tropical Festival,* Carnarvon. *Kwinana Festival,* Kwinana.

September: Perth Royal Show, largest in Western Australia. *Fortescue Festival,* sports contests, parade. *Pagala Festival* Paraburdoo.

October: Kalamunda Week, Kalamunda. *Perth Bierfest. Fremantle festival.*

December: Christmas-New Year's Ascot Horse Racing Carnival, Perth, including Perth Cup.

NATIONAL PARKS. Most of the designated reserves are to be found reasonably close to Perth: the rest of the State is just one great big wide open space. The *Penguin Island Reserve National Park,* 30 miles south of Perth and half a mile offshore from Safety Bay, justifies its name by being a sanctuary for penguins. Canoeing is good at the *Walyunga National Park,* where the Swan River pours out through the Darling Ranges. Caves are a feature of the *Yanchep*

National Park, 30 miles north of Perth. The Yonderup Cave was an aboriginal burial ground. The park contains boating facilities, a golf course, wildlife reserves and picnicking amenities. The *John Forrest National Park* is 3,500 acres of natural bushland in the Darling Ranges. It is 20 miles from Perth, off the Great Eastern Highway. Historic buildings and bird life are the main interest in the *Yalgorup National Park,* situated between Bunbury and Mandurah and about 60 miles south of Perth. Giant karri, jarrah and red gum trees are seen at their best in the *Walpole-Nornalup National Park,* some 260 miles southeast of Perth. Go to *Hamelin Bay Park,* close to Augusta (200 miles south of Perth) for fishing and swimming. You need a four-wheel-drive vehicle to gain access to the limestone pinnacles and white-sand drifts of the *Painted Desert, Pinnacles, Nambung National Park* 110 miles north of Perth. For extremely rugged coastal scenery there is the *Cape Le Grand National Park,* 20 miles out of Esperance on the state's most southerly shores.

HOT SPRINGS. The only known hot springs in Western Australia are at *Mount Winn,* on Liveringa Station in the Kimberley region.

 HISTORIC SITES. Most of Western Australia's history is of very recent vintage and is centred on the coast and the goldfields. The earliest prehistoric remains are dinosaur footprints on the cliffs by Broome. Then come the occasional Aboriginal etchings to be found in the more remote regions. You need to be an expert diver to see the earliest mementoes of the State's discoverers for these are the wrecks that lie beneath the ocean off the coast. The State's oldest building is in Albany.

Albany: Old Farm, Strawberry Hill, is oldest dwelling in the state. *St John Evangelist Church,* consecrated 1848, is oldest church. *Busselton:* site of first timber mill (1854). *Broome:* Japanese cemetery and pioneer cemetery provide interesting record of pearling industry. *Cossack* is a windswept ghost town with several still quite imposing and beautiful buildings. *Coolgardie* vividly recalls the gold rush days and reeks with atmosphere recalling those hard and boisterous times. *Derby: Prison Tree* shows how recalcitrant natives were treated at the turn of the century. *Kalgoorlie:* several memorials to Paddy Hannan help create a personality behind the gold rush. *Meekatharra* is where the School of the Air educational programmes for Outback children first began in 1959. *New Norcia,* 80 miles from Perth, is a Benedictine mission settlement founded in 1846. *Hall's Creek* has mud-brick ruins of an old town founded in the state's first gold rush in 1885. *Pinjarria* is one of the oldest rural settlements and the scene, in 1834, of a battle between soldiers and natives.

 MUSEUMS AND GALLERIES A modern day rush to preserve the past before it is too late has led to the opening up of several private collections in many towns. They are not all well documented or displayed but do reflect the enthusiasm and special interests of their owners. The main museums and galleries of note are in Perth and Fremantle.

Maritime Museum, Fremantle, originally built as asylum, contains notable displays on whaling, pearling and maritime history. Relics of old wrecks.

 TOURS. Albany has tours to the more rugged parts of the coast and to the disused whaling station. From Geraldton there are tours out into the gorges of the Murchison River and from Kununurra it is easy to trip out to Lake Argyle for a cruise. Wittenoom is another centre for gorge tours. Amesz Adventure Tours provide off-the-track safaris of 7 and 14 days. Ghost Town Safari Tours cover the triangle of gold towns with short and very interesting tours.

TRAILER TIPS. Buy the Australia Outdoor Guide from the Melbourne-based RACV (motoring organisation), 123 Queen St., Melbourne.

HOTELS AND MOTELS Prices can be a little unpredictable in some Outback centers, but as a guide: *Expensive:* A$50 and up; *Moderate:* A$40–50; *Inexpensive:* A$20–40.

Albany

Esplanade Motor Hotel. *Moderate.* Licensed restaurant. Liquor room service.
Travel Inn Motel. *Moderate.* Mountain and city views. Flag chain.
Ace Motel. *Inexpensive.* Hot breakfast included. Nr beach, golf, town.

Augusta

Augusta Motor Hotel. *Moderate.* Licensed restaurant. Nr golf, mountains, swimming pool, local attractions.
Leeuwin Motel, *Moderate.* Licensed restaurant. Nr beach, caves.

Balladonia (Eyre Highway)

Balladonia Hotel/Motel. *Moderate.* Pastoral area, wildflowers.

Bunbury

Bussell Motor Hotel. *Moderate.* Liquor room service. Licensed restaurant. Pool. Nr beach, golf.
Chateau La Mer Motor Lodge. *Moderate.* Kitchen facilities in room. Licensed restaurant. Pool.
Clifton Beach Motel. *Moderate.* Pool. Nr beach, golf.
Hospitality Inn–Ocean Drive. *Moderate.* Pool, Tea and coffee making facilities.
Captain Bunbury Hotel. *Inexpensive.*

Busselton

Amaroo Motor Lodge. *Moderate.* Kitchen facilities in room. Nr beach, town centre.
Geographe Bay Motor Inn. *Moderate.* Kitchen facilities in room. Liquor room service. Licensed restaurant. Pool, beach front, barbecue, playground, boat launching, gardens.

Carnarvon

Carnarvon. *Moderate.* Licensed restaurant. Pool, opposite inlet.
Hospitality Inn. *Moderate.* Liquor service to rooms. Pool.
Tuckeys Port Hotel. *Inexpensive.* Licensed restaurant. Pool.

Cloverdale

Cloverdale Hotel. *Moderate.* Liquor service to rooms. Licensed restaurant. Close public transport. Nr racecourse.

Coolgardie

Golden Flag Motor Inn. *Moderate.* Licensed restaurant. Pool. Playground.

Dampier

Mermaid Motor Hotel. *Moderate.* Licensed restaurant. Pool. Nr beach, views Dampier, Archipelago Islands.

Denham

Shark Bay Hotel/Motel. *Moderate.* Licensed restaurant. On waterfront.

Denmark

Denmark Motel. *Moderate.* Licensed restaurant. Liquor room service.
Denmark Unit Hotel. *Moderate.* Fishing.

Derby

Spinifex Hotel. *Moderate.* Licensed restaurant. Liquor room service. Also inexpensive rooms without shower or toilet.

Emu Point

Emu Point Motel. *Inexpensive.* Kitchen facilities in room.

Esperance

Esperance Motor Hotel. *Moderate.* Licensed restaurant. Some inexpensive rooms without shower and toilet. Nr main street and beach. Opposite Post Office.
Esperance Travellers Inn. *Moderate.* Licensed restaurant.
Highway Motel. *Moderate.* Pool, opposite beach. Nr all amenities.

Exmouth

Norcape Lodge. *Expensive.* Liquor service rooms. 24 hour room service. Licensed restaurant. Pool. Nr beach, squash courts.
Potshot Inn. *Moderate.* Liquor service to rooms. Licensed restaurant. Pool.

Fremantle

Captain Fremantle Motor Lodge. *Moderate.* Liquor room service. Licensed restaurant. 24 hour food service. Pool, nr beaches, sportsgrounds.

Kalbarri

La Grange Motel. *Expensive.* Pool. Kitchen in each unit.
Kalbarri Hotel/Motel. *Moderate.* Nr beach, fishing.

Kalgoorlie

Hospitality Inn. *Moderate.* Pool, nr airport, racecourse.
Palace Hotel. *Moderate.* Hot breakfast included. Licensed restaurant.
Sandalwood Motel. *Moderate.* Near airport. Licensed restaurant. Pool. Two units for paraplegic or disabled persons are available.
Tower Motor Hotel. *Moderate.* Liquor room service. Licensed restaurant. Pool.

Kambalda West

Kambalda Motor Hotel. *Moderate.* Liquor room service. Licensed restaurant. Pool. Nr salt lakes, golf.

Karratha

Walkabout Hotel. *Expensive.* Liquor room service. Licensed restaurant. Pool.

Kununurra

Hotel Kununurra. *Expensive.* Liquor room service. Licensed restaurant. Pool.
Lake Argyle Inn. *Moderate.* Licensed restaurant. Pool. Part of tourist village with inn, caravan and camping park, store, boat cruises on lake.
Swagman Inn. *Expensive.* Licensed restaurant, pool, liquor room service.

Mandurah

Atrium. *Expensive.* Resort hotel with pool.
Hotel Peninsula. *Moderate.* Some inexpensive rooms without shower or toilet.

Manjimup

Kingsley Motel. *Moderate.* Licensed restaurant. Situated in heavy karri and jarrah forest.

Manjimup Hotel. *Inexpensive.* Some rooms without shower and toilet. Licensed restaurant.

Newman

Walkabout Hotel. *Expensive.* Liquor service to room. Licensed restaurant. Pool.

Paraburdoo

Paraburdoo Hotel. *Moderate.* Limited room service. Licensed restaurant. Pool. Former mining town.

Rockingham

Rockingham Hotel. *Moderate.* Licensed restaurant.

Rottnest Island

Rottnest Lodge Resort. *Expensive.* All meals included. Lesser charge for rooms without shower or toilet. Restaurant. Licensed premises.

Hotel Rottnest. *Moderate.* Includes all meals. Licensed restaurant. 19 km off WA west coast, colony of quokkas (small marsupials).

Scarborough

Contacio International Motor Hotel. *Moderate.* Liquor room service. Licensed restaurant. Pool. On beach front.

Sands Motel. *Moderate.* Off-season and weekly rates avail. Liquor room service. Licensed restaurant. Pool.

Subiaco.

Victoria Hotel. *Inexpensive.* Very central.

Tom Price

Mt. Tom Price Motor Hotel. *Moderate.* Liquor room service. Licensed restaurant. Nr golf, bowls, squash, tennis, swimming pool.

Walpole

Walpole Hotel/Motel. *Moderate.* Licensed restaurant. Wildflowers, fishing, coastal scenery, national park.

Warwick

Warwick Hotel. *Moderate.* Perth suburb. Liquor room service. Licensed restaurant. Nr beach, golf, tennis.

Wattle Grove

Wattle Grove Motel. *Moderate.* Licensed Restaurant. Outer suburb. Pool.

Wickham

Wickham Hotel. *Moderate.* Liquor room service. Licensed restaurant. Pool. Heart of Pilbara mining centre. 6 km (4 miles) from ghost town of Cossack.

Wittenoom

Fortescue Hotel. *Moderate.* Licensed restaurant. Pool. Scenic gorge country.

Wyndham

Wyndham Town Hotel. *Moderate.* Licensed restaurant. 45 m from Cambridge Gulf.

Yallingup

Caves House Hotel. *Moderate.* Includes hot breakfast. Weekly rates available. Lower prices for rooms without shower or toilet. Licensed restaurant. Garden setting. Nr beach, wildlife park, tennis, bowls.

DINING OUT For a 3-course meal (wine not included), prices range from: *Expensive:* A$20 and up; *Moderate:* A$15–20; *Inexpensive:* A$8–15.

Applecross

Hunting Horn. *Moderate.* Ardross Street. Licensed.

Cannington

Bacchus. *Moderate.* Albany Highway. Singing chef, music and entertainment. Licensed.

Como

Frenchy's. *Moderate.* Melville Parade. Authentic French. BYO.

Chelsea Village

Elegant Sufficiency. *Expensive.* Stirling Highway. Specialises in personal attention and silver service. BYO.

Claremont

La French Taverne. *Expensive.* Stirling Highway. Classical French provincial decor and cooking. Licensed.

Crawley

Matilda Bay. *Expensive.* Waterfront setting with magnificent views of Perth across the river. Licensed, dancing.

Corrida Beefhouse. *Moderate.* Crawley Bay. Excellent grill room in parkland. BYO.

Fremantle

Tumtum Tree. *Moderate.* High Street. Cozy and informal, specialises steaks, grilled fish. Log fires in winter. Unlicensed.

Mosman Park

Peppercorn. *Moderate.* Clyde St. Another warm and casual restaurant in the tradition of a French bistro. Loge seating. BYO.

Nedlands

Maggie's Restaurant. *Moderate.* Broadway. Home style cooking. Popular. BYO.

South Perth

Hindquarters. *Moderate.* Canning Highway. Popular, licensed steakhouse.

Subiaco

Mediterranean Restaurant. *Expensive.* Rokeby Road. Indoor and outdoor dining in warm, casual atmosphere. Licensed.

THE NORTHERN TERRITORY

Two bored young men sunning themselves on a rock in Darwin Harbour decided to ask the local radio station to play a request tune for one of their friends. The request, they said, came from the Rocksitters Club, Darwin Harbour.

Inquisitive listeners to the program enquired about the club. Some set out to find it. A number succeeded and were welcomed as members. The joke had become reality. But the membership list soon closed as the rock could only seat 30 or so bodies plus their supply of refreshments.

Rocksitters and Dry Regattas

And so the Rocksitters Club came into being and one more crazy dimension was added to the already oddball way of life to be found in the Northern Territory. Maybe it is the climate; perhaps the isolation and loneliness. But certainly this vast, tropical, unpeopled 523,000 square miles of Australia seems to have more than the average number of eccentric and unusual happenings.

The Territorians are almost aggressive in their eccentricity, determined to set themselves aside from the rest of Australia by fostering a laconic, rough and ready image of themselves that comes as close as anyone is likely to get to the popular idea of the tall, gaunt, leathery tough Australian bushman of the imagination.

The Territorians swagger and boast. Their talk matches the size and vastness of the land to which they cling. They are used to extremes of sun, rain and distance, and they emphasise this familiarity in their conversations with strangers. But beneath it all they are still by and large suburbanites. They swagger off home to their air-conditioned suburban villas, dig the garden, check the freezer and settle down to an evening's television. It is an intensely social and sociable life they lead for they have most of the comforts of their big city brethren thousands of miles to the south but few of the distractions.

Thus the Rocksitters Club was a welcome newcomer. It fitted in with a pattern formed by such notable occurrences as the Beer Can Regatta (which creates work and entertainment from the territory's most used commodity), the Bangtail Muster and—highspot of them all—the Henley-on-Todd Regatta.

The Todd is the river which flows intermittently through the centre of Alice Springs. More often than not it is simply a sandy indentation straggling between the gum trees. It is in this dried-up creek bed that the residents of Alice Springs hold their annual version of the august international rowing regatta that occurs each year on England's River Thames.

There are a few slight differences between the two events. Due to lack of water, the Territorians depend on footpower to propel their craft. The rowing eights and yachts have no bottoms; the crews have to pick up their craft and run. It is a slapstick, raucous, hearty carnival and typifies the Northern Territory. Spectators watch safe in the knowledge that the Alice Springs Surf Life Saving Club (so it is a thousand miles to the nearest beach!) is on hand to rescue any capsized craft.

Darwin and a Town Called "Alice"

Alice Springs, a desert city, is one of two main centres of population in the Northern Territory; the other, a thousand miles "up the track" to the North is Darwin, a city rebuilt after being almost completely destroyed by a cyclone that struck on Christmas Day, 1974.

The two are completely dissimilar. "The Alice"—as it will always be known—is now a far cry from the bush shanty town depicted in Nevil Shute's *A Town Like Alice* but remains a cattleman's town nonetheless. Darwin, however, is a port and administrative centre. The majority of its population are public servants living there on detachment rather than with any view towards permanent residency.

Darwin receives heavy monsoonal rain from November to March and humidity is extremely high. Alice Springs escapes the monsoons but has high summer heat. Darwin is surrounded by lagoons, thickly-wooded swamplands with buffalo, crocodile and an exotic bird population. Around Alice Springs are the rich red hills of the desert ranges and limitless deserts stretching hundreds of miles in all directions.

Pioneers of the 1800s

The first land exploration of the area now occupied by the Territory came when Charles Sturt ventured into the desert regions to the south of Alice Springs in the 1840s. Nothing much more was discovered about the region until John McDougall Stuart made three expeditions between 1860 and 1862. On one of these, in 1860, he became the first white man to cross the Macdonnell Ranges. His route took him some 30 miles to the west of Alice Springs. Settlement only began when work started eleven years later on building an overland telegraph line from Adelaide to Darwin. John Ross then selected Heavitree Gap (still the main approach to the town) as the best way to bring the telegraph through the ranges. Discovery of the actual springs was made soon afterwards. They were named after the wife of the man responsible for construction of the telegraph line, Sir Charles Todd.

Alice Springs thus happened due to its usefulness as a staging post. Darwin, however, received more urgent and earlier attention because of its importance as a strategic link between Great Britain and Australia. The coastline thereabouts was first properly explored in 1802 by Mathew Flinders. Between 1824 and 1849 three attempts were made to establish permanent settlements. All three—at Raffles Bay, Port Essington and Melville Island—failed. It was probably as true then as it is today that the optimists of the dry season soon become the pessimists of the wet season; the monsoons have killed off many high hopes, and development has always been slow.

Naturalist Charles Darwin, who made several scientific expeditions on board the Beagle, is the man after whom the town is named. The Beagle was the ship sailed by Captain J. Stokes when he discovered the port in 1839.

This event was followed by a further period of inaction until a shipful of settlers arrived from South Australia in 1869 to populate a townsite that had been selected three years earlier. At that stage the town was named Palmerston and it was only in 1911 that Darwin was given his accolade.

Farms of a Million Acres

The overland telegraph reached the town in 1872, a gold rush seduced thousands into heading north for a short-lived period of hope, and farmers seeking cheap labour opened up million-acre properties for their cattle. All this resulted in Darwin quickly achieving a population of 10,000. Alice Springs, meanwhile, languished and still only had 27 white residents as recently as 1927.

It was the coming of the railway, north across the desert from Adelaide in 1929, that set in motion the first real settlement in The Alice. The train is known as the Ghan: a tribute to the many Afghan camel drivers who formed the mainstay of overland trade and communication until quite recent times. Camels still roam the Outback areas and race annually in the Alice Springs "Camel Cup." There is also a thriving export trade to Middle East countries. Visitors have several chances close to Alice Springs of taking a short ride on these snarling, bumpy beasts.

In more recent times Alice Springs has leapt ahead, largely due to its popularity as a staging post for touring into Central Australia but also in part due to the location of a mysterious American communications centre on the outskirts at Pine Gap.

Darwin: Wet or Dry, It's Hot

Darwin's progress has been less steady. Setbacks have been many. The early enthusiasm for its pastoral potential waned under the hardships of tropical living, due largely to the inability of settlers from temperate zones to adapt either their way of life or their methods of farming to a climate made up of just two distinctly different seasons. It was either wet or dry—and always hot.

Nowhere is this better described than in the classic of Australian folklore, *We of the Never Never,* Mrs. Aneas Gunn's story of settlement of a Northern Territory cattle station at the turn of the century. It is a touching story of hardship and heroics, of dismay and determination, that needs to be read by anyone wishing to come to grips with the character of the Northern Territory.

Darwin boomed briefly thanks to gold. Then died. Then boomed again as pastoralists set up huge cattle stations based on the exploitation of cheap native labour. But the optimism petered out and the city's growth slowed again. World War II turned Darwin into an important military base. The northern outpost of the country, it was closest to any invading forces. It suffered the only air raid ever experienced in Australia, a traumatic experience for a country that has always been so far removed from the areas of battle. A post-war slump set in and it took the discovery of uranium at nearby Rum Jungle, plus an ill-fated scheme to develop rice plantations at Humpty Doo, to bring back a sense of purpose to the area. In recent times the city's growth has been due as much to the influx of public servants as to any other factor. The cyclone devastated the city but reconstruction work brought it back to its previous level of development and a flourishing new city has arisen from the rubble.

Exploring the Northern Territory

Highways lead in from Western Australia (to Katherine), from Queensland (to Tennant Creek) and from South Australia (to Alice Springs). There will always be a certain amount of back-tracking no matter which route travellers follow—unless they take the unwise step of venturing out across the desert. The best scheme is to enter from the south, tour up the track to Darwin with occasional diversions and then backtrack into Western Australia or Queensland. From Alice Springs there are roads (mostly unpaved) out to the gorges of the Macdonnell Ranges, to Ayers Rock and to the Olgas. It is a 250 mile drive across the desert to reach the great sandstone monolith of Ayers Rock. Its great hump rises 1143 feet from the desert. Its base measures five and a half miles.

The rock is notable for its significance as an Aboriginal shrine and for the way it continually changes colour. Much of its base is covered in vegetation and just to drive around it is to witness scenes of great variety and rapid change. Be there at sunset and you will see the colours shift through the spectrum until darkness descends and there is nothing left but a huge brooding elongated dome that defies explanation or description. Just 20 miles further on is an equally inexplicable phenomenon: the cone-shaped domes of the Olgas. Less famous than Ayers Rock, they are just as unusual and just as fascinating.

Take the road out of The Alice to the Jay Creek Native Settlement and you pass the boulder that marks the grave of John Flynn, the man who set up the Flying Doctor Service, now headquartered in Alice Springs. Travel on to Standley Chasm but be sure to get there at noon. The overhead sun pours down into this narrow defile and turns the sandstone walls into every shade of gold, ochre, orange, russet and red.

Going north up the Track (it's never given its proper name of Stuart Highway) the first settlement reached is Tennant Creek—313 miles away. This is one of the oldest gold and copper mining centres in the Territory. It has become an important staging post on the journey north as it is just 16 miles south of the junction with the Barclay Highway coming in from the east through Queensland. On the approach to Tennant Creek, 60 miles out of town, you pass the Devil's Marbles. This group of huge granite boulders were believed by Aboriginals to be eggs laid by the mythical rainbow snake.

Continue up the track through Renner Springs, Elliott and Newcastle Waters to reach the settlement of Daly Waters. It is a good place to take a break for fishing and boating. Rivers from here on abound with fish of an extremely succulent and meaty variety. Cooked fresh over an open fire in the clear, clean air of this unindustrialised vastness, they take on a flavour known to only a few among modern day man.

Sunny Beaches and Sheer Cliffs

When you reach the next outpost of civilisation at Larrimah you are still about 320 miles from Darwin. This township is the end of the railway line that runs south from Darwin, with no link on to the southern states. It was built primarily to serve the needs of the cattle stations so that they could move their beasts more quickly to market. Forty miles further on, and five miles off the highway, is the Mataranka cattle station which provides limited accommodation for tourists. Set amid palm groves and warm springs it is notable for the Elsey Memorial Cemetery which contains the graves of the hardy settlers mentioned in "We of the Never Never."

Drive on for 64 miles and you reach the busy, prosperous small community of Katherine at the junction of the road north and the route in from Western Australia. It is at the heart of inland Australia's best network of rivers, gorges and places of significance in Aboriginal mythology. Kintore Caves, 17 miles to the northwest, are of great anthropological importance. The Katherine Gorge, 22 miles to the northeast, is a magnificent waterway of calm waters, sheer cliffs, secluded sandy beaches, abundant wildlife and, in its upper reaches, complete solitude. Crocodiles can be seen sunning themselves and gliding into the water. The fishing is excellent. Boat cruise passengers are entranced by the perfect reflections of trees and cliffs in the blue-green water. Early morning or late afternoon are the ideal times to visit.

Thirty-two miles north of Katherine is the chain of waterfalls cascading into deep rock pools at Edith Falls. The fresh water crocodiles that make their homes in the rock pools are a protected species. To travel through the tropical greenery to the higher falls and pools usually entails use of a four-wheel-drive vehicle plus some walking.

From Katherine the route north goes through the historic mining centre of Pine Creek to Adelaide River, 72 miles south of Darwin. Here is the cemetery in which are buried the civilians and members of the armed forces killed during the 1942–43 Japanese air raids on Darwin. To see the actual river, take the only form of access, the cruiser *Daniella II,* which departs from the Adelaide River bridge on the Arnhem Highway about 100 miles north of the actual township. It will take you into the domain of buffalo, kangaroos, crocodiles, brolgas and wild pig undisturbed by human presence.

On the final run into Darwin, through Batchelor and Rum Jungle, you will see roads off to left and right. These are the routes to take to the great Aboriginal reserve of Arnhemland, to the falls and hot springs of Knuckey's Lagoons, Tumbling Waters, Berry Springs and Robin Falls. But first establish your base in Darwin.

Exploring Darwin

The city of Darwin sits on a peninsula with its commercial and business heart overlooking the harbour and much of its residential area concentrated in the suburbs of Parap and Fannie Bay looking out over Fannie Bay.

There is no mistaking its role as a port and administrative centre. This is reflected in the number of four-square, imposing public buildings and the numbers of ships lying at anchor. It is short on sights for visitors to see. Most interest lies in coming into contact with the people and their way of life. The city is an ideal base from which to explore the tropical coastland rather than being of great interest in its own right. It is the base and starting point for operators of tours and safaris, many using four-wheel-drive vehicles, into the plains, forests and swamplands that enfold the city on all but its seaward side. Its botanical gardens, however, are an unrivalled reserve of tropical luxuriants. At East Point reserve, four miles from downtown, there is an artillery museum and the guns which defended the city during World War II.

Exploring Alice Springs

The Stuart Highway becomes Todd Street for the couple of miles or so that it slices through The Alice. This is the main shopping street, the site of many hotels and restaurants and the place from which to get your bearings to all other points of interest. Todd Street is a rich melange of smart suburban housewives, high-booted cattlemen, often brawling Aborigines, rubbernecking tourists and the weather-beaten roughnecks who sample the high life in town for a few days then head off back to the solitude of the desert. For all its spruce new homes and sparkling supermarkets, The Alice is still a frontier town. You can sense it in the air, see it in the people.

Travel not more than a couple of miles in any direction and you are on the border of a seemingly limitless desert, hot and inhospitable. One of the most noticeable buildings on Todd Street is the John Flynn Memorial Church. The service he founded, the Flying Doctor, has its base nearby (between the hospital and the gaol!) and can be visited. Stop, too, to attend a lesson at the School of the Air, a unique service by which the children hundreds of miles away on isolated cattle stations gain their education. A mile out of town, close by the actual Alice Springs, are the restored remains of the original telegraph station which led to the founding of the town. It contains a graphic portrayal of the laying of the line from Adelaide to Darwin. Alice Springs boasts Australia's only commercial date farm and the Pitchi Richi sanctuary two miles from town has a comprehensive collection of Aboriginal artifacts.

Alice Springs has developed a strong reputation as a centre for artists. For such a small town it contains quite a number of galleries. Many concentrate on Aboriginal artists while others are outlets for the creations of their owners.

You will see Alice and its surroundings at their best from April to October. But August is the highspot. This is when carnival follows carnival and there are picnic races such as the three-day event at Hartz Ranges. It is these occasions that one sees the Territorian in his true colours. And it's a sight not to be missed!

PRACTICAL INFORMATION FOR THE NORTHERN TERRITORY

HOW TO GET THERE. *By air:* Alice Springs and Darwin are served by the two main domestic airlines, Ansett and TAA from most southern cities. East-West flies Perth –Yulara (Ayers Rock)–Sydney. International services tend to fluctuate and it would be wise to check the current situation. *By rail:* There is a rail link from Adelaide to Alice Springs that connects with the trans-continental service between Sydney and Perth. *By bus:* Coach companies have routes in from the south, east and west all the way to Darwin.

HOW TO GET AROUND. *By air: TAA, Ansett* and *Airlines of Northern Australia* link all main towns and settlements and even some quite remote places. Charter operators Tillair have a mail run stopping at Outback stations on which passengers can fly.

By bus: Services run basically north and south up the Stuart Highway on a scheduled express basis. Extended tours operate out of Darwin and Alice Springs to all points of interest.

By car: Stick to the main highways if you must drive yourself. The roads take an immense toll of vehicles and drivers and it is best to leave the driving to someone else unless you are experienced in driving over such terrain and long distances. Main highways are paved but any extensive touring will entail considerable amount of driving over unpaved roads. Always stock up with ample water, food and spares before setting out away from main highways and let someone know where you intend traveling.

MUSEUMS. A few small private collections but little of any status yet established other than the incredible Guth Panorama which gives a vivid 360-degree view of the terrain for many miles beyond the Alice. Alice Springs: Old *Telegraph Station Museum* tells incredible story behind establishing communications between Adelaide and Darwin. Open daily. Pitchi Richi: collection of Aboriginal artifacts. Open daily. *East Point Reserve Artillery Museum,* Darwin.

HISTORIC SITES. A young country where the weather and time have ensured little preservation of the past. The *Ryans Well Historical Reserve* 80 miles north of Alice Springs has a well and homestead built before the turn of the century. The *Elsey Memorial Cemetery,* Mataranka, commemorates the pioneers of the north's cattle industry. *Aboriginal legends* are told in rock paintings at Mt Olga, Ayers Rock, Mount Sonder, around Katherine and in Arnhemland.

TOURS. *By bus:* Operators offer day and half-day sightseeing tours in Darwin and Alice Springs. They also run extended tours into Arnhemland and out as far as Ayers Rock. Several companies based in southern cities provide tours which get well off the main highways, follow stock routes and cross the major deserts. Chief among these are *Australian Pacific, Centralian Staff, Greyhound and AAT-King's.* Based in Alice Springs is the *Central Australian Tours Association* which covers the entire area around Alice Springs with everything from half-day to extended tours.

TOURIST INFORMATION. The Northern Territory Tourist Commission has offices in Alice Springs and Darwin to provide a comprehensive information service to visitors. For pre-trip planning, visit their offices in Sydney, Melbourne, Adelaide, Brisbane and Perth. Overseas, visitors should call on the Australian Tourist Commission.

SEASONAL EVENTS. For climatic reasons, most of the special events take place between April and November. Highlights of the year tend to emphasise the zany or sporting life of the Territory rather than any cultural facet. Darwin Festival is usually held over the Queen's Birthday long weekend in June. It offers a rodeo, skin diving, power boat and sailing events plus an aquatic carnival. The beer-can regatta was first held on a trial basis in June, 1975, and has become an annual event. Darwinians celebrate the Tennant Creek gold rush with a street carnival in August and have a Schutzenfest in June.

Alice Springs has the Bangtail Muster (a parade of satiric floats) in May and then saves itself up for the crazy Henley-on-Todd Regatta on the last Saturday in August, hoping that no rain will fall so that the creek bed will remain dry enough for "rowers" and "yachtsmen" to pick up their craft and run. Leading rodeo riders are in town in late August for the Apex Rodeo and around about the same time there is an exciting and unpredictable afternoon assured with the running of the annual camel races. Slightly higher up the cultural scale is the Alice Springs Festival Week scheduled for the first week each November. This concentrates on art, craft and Aboriginal music and dancing.

 NATIONAL PARKS. The Northern Territory Conservation Commission controls many of the open spaces in the area but there are two designated national parks—Kakadu and Ayers Rock-Mt. Olga. Greater control is being sought over important areas such as Ayers Rock and Mt. Olga reserves in order to stem decay through weather and vandalism. Rangers are based in these areas and provide interpretative information as well as policing the crowds. Main parks around the Darwin area are *Berry Springs* (40 miles south), *Mataranka Pool* (280 miles south) and *Howard Springs* (22 miles southeast). Around Alice Springs there is *Kings Canyon* (140 miles west), *Ormiston Gorge* (80 miles west), *Palm Valley* (90 miles west), *Trephina Gorge* (50 miles east) and *Henbury Meteorites* (90 miles southwest).

 CAMPING OUT. Main sites outside of Darwin and Alice Springs are at Mataranka, Howard Springs, Daly River, Glen Helen Gorge, Ayers Rock-Mt Olga National Park, Ormiston Gorge, Jim Jim (in Arnhemland), East Alligator River and Katherine Gorge. Expect to pay around $1 a night.

 CAMPERS. If you wish to get off the beaten track, it's best to take a fully-equipped campervan. Unpowered sites cost between $8 to $10 for two persons a night; powered sites run out around $20.

Alice Springs: *Wintersun Gardens,* Stuart Highway, has town water, showers, laundry, playground, gas. *Carmichael Tourist Park* is on Larapinta Drive and is part of the Coast-to-Coast network of parks. Carwash, kiosk, lounge, laundry and hot showers available. *Green Leaves Tourist Camp,* Burke Street, offers barbecue area, hot showers, laundry and kiosk. There is a service station attached to *Stuart Caravan Park* on Larapinta Drive. Carwash, laundry, hot showers, gas and ice available. At *Ayers Rock* you pay the national park entry fee of $1.50 on top of the camp site charge of $7 for two and are not allowed a stay of more than two weeks. The camp has 240 sites, bore water, laundry, barbecue, kiosk and hot showers.

Camper parks in Darwin were used after the cyclone to provide accommodation for those made homeless. The situation has improved but the parks still contain many permanent residents and advance booking is recommended. Choose from *Shady Glen* (240 powered sites in Farrell Crescent), the *Overlander* in McMillans Road (120 sites, 50 with power) *Bloodwood Caravan Park* (full facilities), *Coolalinga Caravan Park,* Stuart Highway (all facilities), *Howard Springs Caravan Park* (full facilities), all within 32 km from GPO.

Other parks in the territory are at Elliott: *Midland Caravan Park,* playground, kiosk, laundry, showers; Katherine: *Stuart Caravan Park;* Larrimah: *Larrimah Caravan Park*—all facilities, 40 sites, 20 with power; Mataranka: *Homestead Tourist Resort*—thermal bathing pool, playground, kiosk, restaurant and recreation room; Tennant Creek: *Tennant Creek Caravan Park*—130 sites, toilets, hot showers, laundry and barbecue.

HOT SPRINGS. There is a fairly extensive thermal area within fairly close proximity of Darwin. *Howard Springs,* 20 miles south, are the nearest. There are also *Berry Springs* (40 miles south) and *Douglas Hot Springs* (130 miles south). But the best and most extensive are amid the palms and tropical foliage of *Mataranka Pool,* 280 miles down the track from Darwin.

MUSIC. The best you will be offered in this field will come from the occasional name band, group or personality making a quick tour around the Territory. Otherwise rely on local folk, pop and instrumental groups playing in clubs and cabarets. There is a disco and theatre restaurant at the Desert Inn Hotel in Alice Springs and the *Central Australian Folk Society* meets every Sunday night in Alice Springs.

ART GALLERIES. A great number are to be found in Alice Springs. Seek local help to pick the Aboriginal artists of merit if you cannot rely on your own judgment. General impression is of fairly high prices. *Guth Galleries* is long established and recommended.

DRINKING LAWS. From Monday through Saturday hotels are open from 10 A.M. until 11.30 P.M. On Sundays they are limited to trading from noon until 10 P.M. Most accommodation houses have bar facilities.

NIGHT LIFE. This is centred on the hotels and restaurants. Mainly of the music-for-dancing variety at a fairly unsophisticated level. There is a cabaret at the *Old Riverside* Hotel in Alice Springs and Darwin has several places of the discotheque/cabaret type. *Diamond Beach Casino* operates at Mindil Beach. A casino and hotel resort operates in Alice Springs.

SPORTS. A very prominent feature of life in the Territory, especially in Darwin which is well endowed with a wide range of facilities. There is *tennis, golf, speedway racing, horseracing, squash* and *gliding* in Alice Springs. Darwin has most of these plus the asset of being on the coast. It offers good *swimming, sailing* and *surfing.* Keep clear of the sea water during the wet season as this brings in the venomous sea wasp with its painful sting. The weather is no deterrent to even the most active sports being played with considerable vigor by the people of Darwin. An annual 16-mile *road walk* attracts hundreds of competitors.

HOTELS AND MOTELS. In the Northern Territory these tend to charge more for the same trappings and inferior service to that given by similar establishments down south. Higher wages, an itinerant workforce and the cost of freighting in supplies are all part of the reason. In Darwin, much of the accommodation has been rebuilt since the cyclone but is still in short supply. Early reservations are essential. Accommodations are listed according to price categories based on double occupancy, room only unless otherwise stated. *Expensive:* A$50 and up; *Moderate:* A$35–50; *Inexpensive:* A$25–35.

Alice Springs

Diamond Spring Casino Country Club. *Expensive.* Casino, pool, tennis courts, disco, silver-service dining, 24-hour coffee shop.

Alice Flag Motel. *Moderate.* Pool, mountain views, kitchen in room, free in-rm coffee.

Desert Sands. *Moderate.* Restaurant. Liquor service. Breakfast inc. Free in-rm. coffee.

Elkira Motel. *Moderate.* Pool. Restaurant. Free in-rm coffee.

Midland Motel. *Moderate.* Pool, lic. restaurant, free in-rm coffee. Near golf, bowls, squash. Tours arranged.

Oasis Motel. *Moderate.* Pool, lic. restaurant, in-rm. coffee. Playgd.

Ross River Homestead. *Moderate.* Resort 80 km from town with cattle station atmosphere. Horse riding. Witchetty grub hunts. Boomerang demonstrations. Evening fireside talks on Outback life. Lic. restaurant, pool.

Telford Alice Hotel. *Moderate.* Pool, scenic view of MacDonnell Ranges from lookout tower. Licensed restaurant.

Territory. *Moderate.* Overlooks Todd River. Pool, licensed restaurant, free in-rm coffee.

White Gums Motel. *Inexpensive.* Pool, self-contained units.

Ayers Rock

Yulara Tourist Resort. Contains **Sheraton** Hotel with rooms priced A$100–120; **Four Seasons Hotel** with rooms priced from A$95; camping facilities; pool; licensed restaurant; shops. It offers the only noncamping facilities for tourists at Ayers Rock.

Darwin

Darwin Hotel. *Expensive.* Focal point of social life. Licensed restaurant and a pool.

Diamond Beach Casino–Mindil Beach. *Expensive.* All facilities. Minimum two nights.

Don Motor Hotel. *Expensive.* Downtown location, pool, licensed restaurant, free in-rm. coffee.

Telford Top Inn. *Expensive.* Near beaches. Two restaurants. Room service. Free in-rm coffee. Pool.

TraveLodge. *Expensive.* Central, overlooking waterfront. Pool, 24-hr room service, licensed restaurant.

Telford International. *Moderate.* Licensed restaurant, pool. Central.

Tiwi Lodge. *Inexpensive.* In-rm coffee. No restaurant.

Katherine

Corroboree Motel. *Expensive.* Licensed. Swimming pool.

Crossways. *Moderate.* Breakfast inc. Pool, licensed restaurant.

Katherine Hotel/Motel. *Moderate.* Licensed restaurant.

Mataranka Homestead Resort. *Moderate* (no rooms with private facilities). Thermal swimming pool, air strip, licensed restaurant.

Riverview Motel. *Inexpensive.* Breakfast included. Free in-rm coffee.

Tennant Creek

Tennant Creek Motor Hotel. *Moderate to deluxe.* Breakfast included. Licensed restaurant. Free in-rm coffee.

QUEENSLAND

The Sunshine State

by
EMERY BARCS

Many Australians talk about their fellow Queenslanders as Americans talk about Texans—in a tone of slightly puzzled benevolence, frequently accompanied by a tolerant smile. The suggestion, more implied than stated, is that the people of the "Sunshine State," as they call their home, are somehow different from other Australians. The difference, if it exists at all, may be one of degree not substance. Perhaps Queenslanders are friendlier, more expansive, more hospitable and, at the same time more conservative than their countrymen. Perhaps more of them have preserved the frontier spirit in their sprawling State—the second largest in Australia and three times the size of France plus Holland and Belgium, but with a population of only about two million.

There is little difference, however, among Australians. Five-sixths of Queenslanders live in urban centres, almost half of them in the Brisbane area. Most of the remaining one-sixth are farming families. Those who live on one of the huge cattle stations really know what isolation means; they may talk to their "next door" neighbour over the telephone or two-way radio but, to see them, they may have to drive for long hours over some of the roughest roads in the world or use a light aircraft, if they can afford one.

The area of Queensland is 1,727,530 square kilometres representing 22.5 per cent of the continent and 31 per cent of its settled territory. It stretches 2,100 kms. from the New South Wales border in the south to

Cape York in the north, and 1,450 kms. from Sandy Cape in the east to the Northern Territory. More than half of the State is situated in the tropics. Within its borders are endless plains, forest-covered mountains, and one of the world's wonders—the 2,000 kilometre long Great Barrier Reef which, as one travel writer has put it would alone be worth a trip to Australia.

Tourism a Major Industry

Tourism is one of Queensland's main industries and a great many spots along the State's 5,100 km. coastline, as well as several of the 750 islands between the Great Barrier Reef and the mainland, have been turned into holiday resorts. But Queensland is much more than a huge playground. It is also a potential economic giant.

Already it provides almost one-quarter of Australia's export income from such items as sugar, tropical fruits, grains, beef cattle, metals, wool, and minerals. But still only a quarter of the eight million hectares of potentially cultivable land is used for crops.

The State has major reserves of copper, bauxite (the world's single largest alumina plant is at Gladstone), lead, zinc, silver, rutile, nickel, uranium, phosphate, vanadium, and commercial deposits of gold, tin, zircon, silica, lime, and salt. But while it might be instructive to visit the bauxite mines in the Weipa region of Cape York Peninsula or the mining town of Mount Isa near the Northern Territory border, not many visitors are likely to spend their time and money travelling there—except perhaps when these places are included in the itinerary of one of the many organised (and mostly very well organised) coach tours to the Queensland "outback" which even few Australians have ever seen.

The Convict in History

The establishment of Queensland was closely connected with the convict, the main architect of early Australian history. From the 1820s onward, resentment at the deportation of convicts to the colony of New South Wales had become widespread among the free settlers; at about the same time, the need arose for a separate place for intractable prisoners. In 1821, when Sir Thomas Brisbane took over as Governor of New South Wales, he instructed the masters of some of the colonial cutters to explore the coast around Moreton Bay, some 800 kms. north of Sydney. It was another three years, however, before the first settlement north of Brisbane—on what is today the Redcliffe Peninsula—was established in September 1824 with a group of convicts and a small detachment of guards as the first inhabitants.

The site was unhealthy, anchorage unsafe, and the Aborigines in the vicinity hostile. So, by early 1825, the settlement was moved to a new position some 32 kms. upstream from the mouth of the Brisbane River which enters the sea in Moreton Bay. It did not take very long to discover the area was "too good" to be reserved for a mere penal station. In 1839, the convicts were withdrawn from what then became known as Brisbane and, three years later, in 1842, free settlers were officially permitted to move in.

Britain abolished the transportation of convicts to New South Wales in 1840. But this only increased Britain's seemingly insoluble problem of what to do with the growing number of criminals sentenced to imprisonment as well as those who had already served their term. Ex-convicts had practically no chance of employment in Britain. By 1845, the problem had become so acute that the British Government decided to establish a new place under the sun for former convicts and for the "exiles"—prisoners who were released from prison under the condition that they serve the rest of their sentence as deportees in a penal colony.

The choice for the new colony fell on the northern part of New South Wales, north of latitude 26 degrees, to be called New Australia. But, in 1846, three months after the first party of ex-convicts and "exiles" landed some 500 kms. north of Brisbane, the scheme was abandoned. However, while the officials and guards withdrew, some of the involuntary settlers stayed put and opened up the country around today's Gladstone area. More settlers arrived but while their demand grew louder for establishment of their own colony—instead of being governed from Sydney, hundreds of kilometres away—their numbers grew slowly. In 1859 when, at last, the British Government agreed to create Queensland from New South Wales north of the 29th parallel, the new colony still had a population of only 23,520. The shortage was a major impediment to the new colony's development; the problem escalated, however, when the labour needs for pastoral and agricultural industries (mainly sugar cane growing), were multiplied by the discovery of metals and minerals.

A Chapter of Barbarism

This scarcity of labour, especially cheap labour, was the cause of one of the most sinister episodes in Australia's economic and social history— the "importation" of Kanakas (a Polynesian word for "man") from the South Sea islands to work on the Queensland sugar cane fields. Camouflaged as a respectable search for labour, this recruitment of workers was, in fact, no better than slave-trading.

It was carried out by owners of luggers who sometimes induced young and strong islanders with small gifts to enter into a contract to work in Australia for a specified time after which they were to be taken home. Frequently, however, Kanakas were forced at gunpoint onto the boats and into virtual captivity. To the increasingly loud protests in the rest of Australia against the barbaric practice—called "blackbirding" by Australians and "man-stealing" in their own language by islanders—the Queensland Government, in 1868, introduced the first laws to regulate the working conditions of the islanders, although the cane growers said that they would be ruined if recruitment of Kanakas were prohibited.

Subsequent government actions improved the system to some extent until, in 1904—after Federation—recruitment of Kanakas was finally banned, and 3,600 natives were repatriated. Predictions that the Australian sugar industry would die if cheap island labour were prohibited has proved to be quite wrong. In 1897–98, Australia produced 1,073,883 tons of cane; in 1979–80 she produced 20 million tons.

Politics and Government

In addition to sending representatives to the Federal Parliament and participating in the Federal Government, Queensland, like all other Australian States, has its own parliament and government. However, while the other States have bicameral legislatures, the Sunshine State, which likes to be a bit different, has only a single chamber legislative assembly. All over the age of 18 who are British subjects, have lived in Australia for at least six months, and in a Queensland electorate for three, have the right—and duty (for voting is compulsory)—to vote at legislative assembly elections which normally occur every third year. In 1983 a conservative National Party government was elected.

Australians are certainly not the only people who expect the "government" to look after their manifold needs, but they must be rather high on the list of those who do. And Queenslanders, despite their penchant for individualism, are no exception. Their government is confronted with huge problems; it administers a State which has more than seven times the land area of Britain but only one-thirtieth of her population. No matter whether they live in closely settled urban areas or in the outback, Queenslanders expect their government to provide them with many services for their needs—from transport to education, cultural activities to health care. By and large, Queenslanders, like other Australians, *are* reasonably well looked after.

More than one-fifth of the State's 2.5 million people are at school—some 54,000 children in kindergartens and State pre-school centers; 469,800 in primary, secondary and special schools; there are 22,400 students at universities; a total of 123,200 attend technical colleges and other colleges of advanced education. Formal education is compulsory between the ages of 6 and 15 and, while 1,250 of the schools are owned and run by the State, 265 primary and 70 secondary schools are maintained by private organisations, mainly by the churches. "Schools of the Air" for children in remote areas conduct classes over two-way radio networks from three bases: Mount Isa, Charleville, and Cairns; an efficient and successful Adult Education Board has expanded its work to some 300 urban and rural areas.

Culture, Sports and Airplanes

Not so many years ago—certainly well into the post-World War II era—many Australians interested in the arts and sciences regarded Queensland as a hopeless cultural desert. They have been quite wrong. During the past 20-25 years, Queensland has literally soaked up culture. The development of the creative and performing arts during this period has been impressive and by no means limited to the state capital of Brisbane which is the headquarters of cultural activities. Queensland now has its own Brisbane-based symphony orchestra, ballet company, and opera company. But some 20 youth orchestras are spread throughout the State. New cultural centres, each with its own modern theatre, are mushrooming everywhere, including Mount Isa, Cairns, Townsville and Toowoomba.

Sports, however, still have a considerable edge in popularity over cultural pursuits. Except for winter sports—Queensland has no snow-fields—the tourist can participate in practically any sport played in the western world. Indeed, in a country where sports are considered vital to existence, Queenslanders—of all Australians—are perhaps the greatest devotees.

Queenslanders claim to be the healthiest of Australians with an average life expectancy of 71 years and a low infant mortality. State-operated health services are certainly competent. For example, the Queensland Radium Institute in Brisbane is one of the most advanced cancer treatment centres in the world. In addition, medical-surgical services through the Royal Flying Doctor, Flying Surgeons, and Aerial Ambulance organisations are routinely provided to the State's most remote areas.

Flying also plays a major role in Queensland's transport and communications systems—the only way to cope with the State's huge distances. There are 20 nationally controlled airports, 100 odd authority and privately controlled aerodromes, and four island-resort heliports apart from mainland heliports, plus dozens of airstrips on outlying cattle stations. The aeroplane is, of course, no answer to the problems of bulk transport over hundreds of kilometres. The Queensland Railways operate over 9,741 kms. of tracks, and new lines are being opened to connect inland mining and rural centres with seaports which now handle more than 50 million tons of goods a year. The total length of all roads in the State is about 170,000 kms. of which more than 44,000 kms. are bitumen sealed.

BRISBANE

Lots of tags have been attached to Brisbane, capital of Queensland, including "Australia's New Orleans," "the branch office town," or "the only Australian State capital built on the banks of a river which really looks like a river." All of these tags fit to some extent. Differences of opinion begin when people discuss Brisbane's spirit and culture. Some assert that its spirit is boorish and its culture nonexistent. Others insist that nowhere else in the country will one find so much good natured tolerance, friendliness, and hospitality as well as a steadily growing interest in the creative and performing arts as in that semi-tropical city.

How one feels about Brisbane may largely depend upon the time of year one becomes acquainted with it. In summer, when the city broils beneath an eiderdown of grey clouds, only the most inveterate chauvinist will find it tolerable. But during the cool months, say from May to October, few other spots in and out of Australia can match Brisbane's weather. The air is mellow, yet invigorating. One wants to stay there forever.

The city and the river which meanders through it were named after the Scottish soldier and astronomer, Sir Thomas Makdougall Brisbane (1773–1860), Governor of New South Wales from 1821 to 1825. The waterway was discovered by two escaped convicts in 1823 and the penal settlement was established the following year on its banks, 32 kms. upstream from its entry into Moreton Bay. Thirty-five years later, Queensland, named after Queen Victoria at her suggestion, became a separate colony. Brisbane, its capital, was still a primitive town.

In 1864, a huge fire destroyed practically the whole city centre; some of the better buildings, which might have been worth preserving as historic documents, perished in the disaster. Brisbane is therefore rather poor in landmarks of the city's early period. One of the survivors is the Observatory, a massive tower standing in Wickham Terrace. Built in

1829 by gangs of convicts when the infamous Captain Logan commanded the penal colony, it was originally designed as a windmill to crush
corn. But the contraption did not work. To make use of the building,
Captain Logan had a treadmill installed. Convicts worked 14 hour shifts
and few survived the horror to hear the good news that:

> "Like the Egyptians and ancient Hebrews
> We were sorely oppressed by Logan's yoke,
> Till kind providence came to our assistance
> And gave this tyrant his fatal stroke."

A Treadless Treadmill

In the 1920s, the treadmill was removed and used as a movie prop for
a film about the convict era; it then disappeared. The Observatory (windmill) building itself, however, served some useful purpose between 1935
and 1939 when it was used as a transmission station for television experiments. Since then, it has been closed and visitors are not allowed inside.

The list of other buildings of note is short: City Hall is the seat of
Brisbane's municipal administration. There is also an interesting concert
hall with an organ reputed to be one of the best in Australia. A lift-ride
to the tower costs a few cents (worth spending because of the extensive
view from the top). Parliament House, opposite the Botanic Gardens,
was opened in 1868. It is a fair example of imitation French Renaissance.

The University of Queensland, on the banks of the Brisbane River, is
one of Australia's most pleasant campuses. Note its landscaped park.
The city's second university, Griffith, is also remarkable for its greeneries
including 300 year old stumpy grass-trees called blackboys. (Incidentally, Brisbane has also been called a "multi-coloured city" because of the
variety of its flowering trees, including jacarandas, tulip trees, coral trees,
flame of the forests, oleanders, poincianas, bougainvillea, frangipanis,
and bauhinias. The city is rarely without one or another in flower.) There
are a fair number of churches of which St. John's (Anglican) Cathedral
in Ann Street is perhaps the most impressive. Brisbanites claim it is the
world's last cathedral still being built in the Gothic style.

Sanctuaries for Beasts and Birds

There are several sanctuaries not far from the city centre. Lone Pine
Koala Sanctuary is a half hour drive west of City Hall. Its animal
population includes koalas, kangaroos, wombats, and emus. A platypus
can be seen between 3-4 P.M. It is open from 9.30 A.M. to 5 P.M. Bunya Park,
24 kms. north of the city, surrounds an artificial lake and features a
mystery maze to "The Bunyip." The African Lion Safari at Yatala on
the Pacific Highway has lions, tigers, leopards, bears and other animal
species including Australia's only liger (a cross between a lion and a
tiger).

There are a few spots near the city centre where one can obtain
impressive bird's eye views of Brisbane, and beyond. From Bartleys Hill,
5 kms. away, one can see the city, the port, the Taylor Range and, in the
distance, the Great Dividing Range. Mt. Coot-tha (286 metres, 8 kms.
from the city centre) commands similar views. It has a restaurant which
serves reasonable meals and, at dinner, offers an unforgettable view of

the city's sea of lights. Mount Gravatt (194 metres, 10 kms. from the city centre) presents panoramic views as far away as the Glasshouse Mountains (72 kms.) and the border ranges of New South Wales. The Sir Thomas Brisbane Planetarium and a tropical plant dome are housed in the Mt. Coot-tha Botanic Gardens.

Brisbane is, of course, a young city where anything dating back more than a century is "antique" and deemed worth preserving. Most of it—such as Newstead House in Newstead Park, the oldest preserved home in Queensland where the State's Royal Historical Society has its headquarters—is pleasant enough but will hardly arouse rapturous enthusiasm in the visitor. Although many who knew Brisbane before World War II now lament the disappearance of its quiet provincial life and its early-to-bed, early-to-rise schedule, the visitor (unaware of any change) may enjoy the city's present tempo—vibrant without being hectic.

In summer because of the heat and in winter because of habit, Brisbane begins moving about an hour earlier than the southern cities, such as Sydney or Melbourne. But it doesn't go to sleep after sunset any longer. While it would be misleading to claim that Brisbane has a night life, there are theatre-restaurants where one can spend a pleasant evening, and restaurants with good fare. If certain trends continue, Brisbane may become Australia's most amusing city.

At any rate, it is no longer a mere transit centre for tourists heading for Queensland's main attractions—the Sunshine Coast and the Great Barrier Reef to the north, and the Gold Coast to the south. It has become a tourist attraction in itself where the visitor in not too great a hurry would be wise to spend a few days.

Moreton Bay, Stradbroke, Tangalooma

About a 20 minutes drive from Brisbane is the vast and sheltered expanse of Moreton Bay, Brisbane's marine playground. Its area of 1,903 square kilometres is strewn with islands. Three of them—Stradbroke, Moreton, and Bribie—are quite large and inhabited, but several smaller ones are also inhabited and cultivated, yielding considerable crops of vegetables and tropical fruits. The mainland shores are studded with holiday resorts, well equipped for all kinds of water sports—swimming, sailing, and fishing.

South Stradbroke Island resort is reached by launch or seaplane from the Gold Coast: launches leave from Surfers Paradise and Southport and the seaplane departs from Paradise Waters.

Stradbroke, the southernmost of the three large islands in the Bay, is 61 kms. long. In 1896, huge waves driven by a wild cyclone gouged a channel across it so that now the island is cut in two. Named after the Earl of Stradbroke, who discovered it in 1823, it is an important sand-mining centre and large amounts of titanium, zircon, and rutile are extracted from its beaches. Air and launch services operate from Brisbane to North Stradbroke, and ferry boats for motorists ply between the coastal villages of Redland Bay and Cleveland. There are good swimming beaches on the bayside, such as Dunwich and Amity Point, and several surfing beaches facing the ocean. A small national park, with

Lake Kaboora in its centre, offers pleasant, easy bush-walks amid a riot of wildflowers.

North of Stradbroke is 39 kms. long Moreton Island which is connected to Brisbane by a launch and air to the island's main centre, Tangalooma. The unique feature of the island named by Matthew Flinders in 1799 is the huge sand hills—reputedly the biggest in the world—which rise up to 279 metres (Mount Tempest). The main sports are swimming, fishing, and surfing.

Bribie Island (27 kms. long) is at the northern end of Moreton Bay and 63 kms. from Brisbane. It is one of the few spots in Australia where the colonisers met with fierce resistance from the Aborigines who practised cannibalism. Bribie is connected by a concrete bridge with the mainland at Toorbul Point at the southern end of Pumicestone Passage. There is also a daily coach service to and from Brisbane. The island is a wildlife sanctuary with large numbers of native animals and plants; wild boronia which flowers between August and December is a special attraction. There are two small settlements at the southern end of the island, Bongaree and Woorim. A golf course, bowling greens, and water sports are provided for visitors.

PRACTICAL INFORMATION FOR BRISBANE

HOW TO GET AROUND. *By bus:* The Brisbane City Council provides the bus service. For all kinds of information (routes, stops, departure times) tel. 225-4444 Monday to Saturday, 6.15 A.M.–11.15 P.M., Saturday, 6.30 A.M.–11.30 P.M. Sunday 9.30 A.M.–6 P.M. For A$3, one may buy a ticket which entitles its holder to any number of journeys on the day of purchase, after 8:45 A.M. Family A Fare ticket, A$3.50, is available after 6.30 P.M., Monday to Friday; after 12.30 P.M., Saturday, Sunday and public holidays for any number of journeys on the day of issue. One person or a family group of no more than six persons (with only two adults) may use it.

By ferry: Services operate across the Brisbane River at several points: West End bus terminal-St. Lucia; Edward St. and the Customs House-Kangaroo Point; New Farm Park-Norman Park; Hamilton-Bulimba; Customs House-East Brisbane-New Farm; Commercial Road, Valley-Oxford St., Bulimba; Hawthorne-New Farm. For information, call: tel. 399–4768.

By rent-a-car: Several firms are in business. They include: Budget Rent a Car, tel. 52-0151; Manx Auto Rentals, tel. 52-7288; Letz Rent a Car, tel. 262-3222; Scotty Rent a Car, tel. 52-7400; Hertz of Australia, tel. 221-6166; Avis Rent-a-Car, tel. 52-7111.

TOURIST INFORMATION SERVICES. Queensland Government Tourist Bureau, corner of Adelaide and Edward Streets, tel. 31-2211. For advice of a confidential nature, the Citizen's Advice Bureau, 168 Ann St., tel. 221-4343; or the Brisbane Visitors and Convention Centre, City Hall, tel. 221-8411. Also Royal Automobile Club of Queensland, 190 Edward St., tel. 221-1511.

TOURS. *By coach:* Ansett Pioneer, Boomerang, Journey to Happiness, and Happy Hours offer half-day and whole-day coach tours of the city and day long tours of the surrounding districts as far north as the Sunshine Coast and as far south as the Gold Coast. Typical fares in mid-1984 were: half-day tours: A$7; day tours: Brisbane City Sights A$20; Gold Coast, A$13–24; Tamborine Mountain, A$22; Lamington National Park, A$28; Stradbroke Island (coach and launch), A$18–21. Children half fare.

By bay and river launches: To Moreton Bay. A 5 hour round trip cruise to Tangalooma on Moreton Island on Wednesday, Friday, Saturday, and Sunday, including lunch, A$25, with children (3 to 13 years) half price. Down River, Tuesday and Thursday (half day), adults, $6, children $3. St. Helena Island, from Manly; includes conducted tour of the ruins of convict settlement; adults A$10, children A$5.

Brisbane River. Three hour round trip to Moreton Bay on Sunday and public holidays. Departs from Botanic Gardens, $5, children A$2. Lone Pine Koala Sanctuary, daily. Round trips may also be made by travelling there by launch and returning by bus. Fare by launch both ways (about 3½ hours), A$14, children A$10; by bus (return only), 80 cents; children, 20 cents.

SHOPPING. Brisbane has two main shopping areas, the city and Fortitude Valley. The major Australian department stores (David Jones, Myers, Waltons) are all there. There are duty free shops in the city (listed in the Yellow Pages of the telephone directory) and at the International Airport terminal. Several inner suburbs—including Chermside, Toombul, Indooroopilly, Brookside, Mt. Gravatt and Coorparoo—have drive-in shopping centres.

HOTELS AND MOTELS. Rates for a double room are categorized as follows: *Expensive:* A$70 and up; *Moderate:* A$50–69; *Inexpensive:* under A$50.

Lennons Plaza. *Expensive.* Queen St. City's premier hotel. 151 units and 19 suites with all modern conveniences, parking facilities, restaurants, bars. Modern with a traditional air.

Crest International. *Expensive.* Corner Ann and Roma Streets. 230 rooms, 13 suites. All modern conveniences, including pool and sauna.

Gateway Inn, 85–87 North Quay; **Parkroyal,** Corner Alice and Albert Streets; **The Ridge,** Corner Leichardt and Henry Streets; **Travelodge,** 355 Main Street; **Gazebo Terrace Hotel,** 345 Wickham Terrace (all five *Expensive); Metropolitan Motor Inn,* Corner Upper Edward and Leichardt Streets, and **Tower Mill Motor Inn,** Wickham Terrace (both *Moderate),* are all more or less equally good hotel/motels with shower and toilet in all units, plus restaurants, bars, baby sitting arrangements (for a fee).

Hotel Stradbroke. *Moderate.* Point Lookout, Stradbroke Island. Private facilities, TV, refrigerator; restaurant.

Tropic Isle Motel. *Inexpensive.* North Coast Road, Clontarf. Private facilities attached to all units; TV, refrigerator, swimming pool.

Waltzing Matilda Motel. *Inexpensive.* Margate Parade, Redcliffe. Private facilities, TV, kitchenette in some units; restaurant, refrigerator, telephone in rooms.

Koolamara Motel. *Inexpensive.* Woorim Beach, Bribie Island. Private facilities, TV, refrigerator; swimming pool; telephone in all bedrooms; restaurant.

DINING OUT. Brisbane has many restaurants specializing in ethnic food, Queensland's seafood, beef and tropical fruits and nuts. Excellent restaurants are located in the suburbs. Finer city restaurants include: *Top of the State.* 24th floor SGIO Building, corner Albert and Turbot Sts. The central floor revolves and presents a view of the entire city. *Cordon Bleu.* Cor. Leichhardt and Little Edward Sts. Long-established French restaurant. *Milano.* 78 Queen St. Dinner music and dance. *Gateway Inn.* 85 North Quay. Dinner music. *Raindrop Room.* Zebra Motel, 103 George St. *Room at the Top.* Top floor, Noah's Tower Mill Motor Inn, Wickham Terrace. *Heidelberg,* 46 Edward St. *Gambaro's,* 36 Caxton St., Petrie Terrace. One of Brisbane's busiest seafood restaurants using 1,200 mudcrabs a week.

Theatre restaurants: *Henry Africa's Theatre Restaurant,* Melbourne Hotel, 2 Browning St., West End. Nightly Tuesday to Saturday from 7 P.M. *Brentleigh Theatre Restaurant,* 497 Lutwyche Rd. Lutwyche, Wednesday to Saturday. *Dirty Dick's Elizabethan Rooms.* Corner Judge and Weetman Sts. *Petrie Terrace.* "Naughty" Elizabethan atmosphere. Dinner is served at long, wooden tables.

THE GOLD COAST

It takes only an hour's comfortable drive south from Brisbane to reach Australia's number one playground, the Gold Coast. This 42-kilometre. stretch of narrow land—in one part it is only half a kilometre wide—occupies 130 square kilometres, but almost all of it serves one purpose: to help the annual influx of 2,000,000 visitors relax and have fun. The Gold Coast is sometimes criticised as garish and flashy, a sort of upstart Miami. It is not a place for people who seek quiet and isolation to recover from the hectic tempo of modern life.

It is a place for people to enjoy their vacations *with* other people, not in solitude—at least not in that part of the Gold Coast where dozens of multi-storeyed luxury hotels and motels stand cheek by jowl with modest guest houses. Where caravan parks and supermarkets stand near expensive boutiques. Where self-service cafes stand next to elegant restaurants. Where one may dress formally, informally, or with casual abandon. For that part of the Gold Coast tries to provide for all tastes and all pockets. Well—nearly all of them.

But only a short distance from the beaches and the adjacent funlandia there is another Gold Coast along the man-made canals and the foothills of the mountains. This is the area where, in recent years, residential land developers have reaped huge profits. The Gold Coast region has the fastest growing population in the whole of Australia—13 percent a year. The permanent population of a few thousand a decade ago now exceeds 112,900.

Tourists are not alone in flocking there to enjoy an average of 287 sunny days a year and a mean temperature of 75°F (24° C). Thousands retire there; the number of these new settlers increases yearly. Besides climate and its many amenities, the Gold Coast has an added attraction for the not so young—Queensland has abolished death duties, an advantage which property salesmen are quick to point out. Prices of houses and home units (apartments) are not inexpensive; though real estate values have dropped somewhat recently, development of the region, which began in the 1950s, continues. Until about 30 years ago, the Gold Coast was mainly farm country with a few hotels, guest houses, and villas of well-to-do Brisbanites along the sea shore.

The main season is the winter months—June, July, and August—when people from the southern States as well as overseas flock to the Gold Coast. Nevertheless, the climate is quite pleasant throughout the year—December and January are especially popular—but February, March, and April may produce some spectacular downpours.

Where Fun Abounds

Southport, 80 kms. by road from Brisbane, marks the northern entry to the Gold Coast. The string of beaches along the Gold Coast include Surfers Paradise, Broadbeach, Mermaid Beach, Currumbin, Kirra and Coolangatta. The Gold Coast is, of course, well supplied with facilities for water sports as well as with bowling greens, tennis courts, and golf courses.

One of the region's least expected attractions is the mountainous hinterland—the MacPherson Range, with several national parks and wildlife sanctuaries. All are within easy driving distance of the coast and can be visited in a day. Most have well marked paths leading to lookouts over sweeping vistas, deep ravines, and waterfalls. Among those you might visit are:

Numinbah Valley National Park. Roads from Southport, Broadbeach or Burleigh lead through the charming hillside settlement of Nerang to the park 27 kms. away. The valley, situated between the steep face of the Springbook Plateau and the forests of Lamington National Park, is irrigated by the Nerang River which flows through it. The river forms natural swimming pools and there are many picnic areas on its banks.

Springbrook. About 40 kms. from the coast, this plateau contains two national parks. The best way to approach it is from Burleigh Heads through Mudgeeraba. Five kilometres beyond Mudgeeraba is the small Gold Coast Historical War Museum (with displays of tanks and other military equipment) and a boomerang factory where visitors over the age of seven can try their skill with this ancient Aboriginal weapon. Several attractions along this road serve meals.

Lamington National Park, 32 kms. from the coast, can be reached by two roads, one of which terminates at O'Reilly's "Green Mountain" guest house and the second at Binna Burra, where comfortable accommodations are available. Lamington is Queensland's best known national park and one of Australia's most beautiful reserves with some unique flora. The peaks of the mountains range up to 1,200 metres where the Antarctic beech—remarkable trees, some of them 3,000 years old—have survived the vicissitudes of time and climate. The region is the creation of violent volcanic actions in prehistoric times, and rain forests, flowering trees, and ferns thrive in the rich soil. Well graded paths lead to the interior of the park from O'Reilly's and Binna Burra where rather basic accommodation is also available.

Tamborine Mountain, 42 kms. from the coast, has 10 national parks with peaks of up to 650 metres. The parks preserve varieties of vegetation and have many picturesque waterfalls. Its most interesting plant, the macrozamia palm which grows on the western slopes, has retained its characteristics through millions of years. Some of the specimens on Tamborine mountain are more than 1,000 years old.

PRACTICAL INFORMATION FOR THE GOLD COAST

HOW TO GET THERE. *By air:* Regular air services from Brisbane, Sydney, Melbourne and Adelaide (with all-state connections) to Coolangatta Airport by Ansett, East West Airlines, and TAA. Connections from all other capital cities through Sydney and Brisbane.

By rail: Gold Coast Motor Rail Express from Sydney to Murwillumbah daily with connecting coach Murwillumbah to the Gold Coast. Carries passengers' motor cars which must be accompanied.

By road: Express coach services from Brisbane, Adelaide, Melbourne, and Sydney daily.

TOURIST INFORMATION SERVICES. Check with Queensland Government Tourist Bureau, 3177 Gold Coast Highway., Surfers Paradise 4217, Tel. 38-5988, and Coast House, Griffith Street, Coolangatta 4225.

PARKS. *Andalucia Park and Koala Village,* 2 kms. north of Surfers Paradise at Southport, features Spanish dancing horses, Australian birds and marsupials. Open daily 9.00 A.M. to 5.00 P.M. You can travel by car, bus or launch, which leaves from Cavill Avenue Jetty, Surfers Paradise, 2.00 P.M. daily except Saturday.

Currumbin Bird Sanctuary, 2 kms. south of Currumbin Creek, has thousands of brightly-hued lorikeets (small red and green parrots) which fly in from the bush twice daily to be fed plates of bread and honey held by visitors. Feedings during the daylight hours are mornings 8 to 10 A.M.; afternoons from 4.15 P.M. daily.

Sea World of Australia, the Spit, Southport, is 3 kms. north of Surfers Paradise. Daily events include shark and fish feeding 10.30 A.M. and 4.30 P.M.; Sea Arena dolphin show at noon and 3.00 P.M.; water-ski show at 11.00 A.M. and 4 P.M.; dolphin pantomime 2.00 and 4 P.M.; dolphin feeding at 12.30 and 3.30 P.M.

Fleay's Fauna Reserve, West Burleigh, is 3 kms. inland from Burleigh Heads. David Fleay, the noted Australian zoologist, displays Australian animals and birds. Open daily from 9 A.M. to 5 P.M. Koalas are fed at 2.30 P.M. and platypuses at 2.45 P.M.

Chairlift, Nobby's Beach (between Mermaid Beach and Miami), carries visitors to the Castle Lookout on top of North Nobby—330 metres—where one sees the Gold Coast and its hinterland. Open daily from 9 A.M. to 5 P.M.

TOURS. *Tropical Safari.* Passes through some of the finest scenery in the region including banana and pineapple plantations, pastoral farmland, and sub-tropical rain forests. Departure: Wednesday and Friday. Duration about 8 hours. Operator, Pacific tours, 40 Dalpurra St., Chevron Island, Surfers Paradise.

Lamington National Park. Travels through long stretches of tropical rain forests and visits O'Reilly's Guest House, Native Orchid Sanctuary, Mt. Tamborine, Binna Burra Lodge, and Talangi White Caves. Departs Sunday and Tuesday. Duration about eight hours. Operator, Holiday Services Pty, Ltd., Griffith St., Coolangatta.

Northern Rivers Tour. A tour to the northern rivers of New South Wales. Stops for morning tea at Murwillumbah; then travels to Uki, Nimbin, Lismore, and Byron Bay. Returns via Brunswick Heads, Kingscliff, and Chinderah. Departs Friday. About nine hours. Holiday Services Pty Ltd., Griffith St. Coolangatta.

Numinbah Valley Natural Arch. Travel via Natural Arch then to Murwillumbah Valley and return via the Tweed Valley. Departure: Thursday. Duration 8½ hours. Operator is Holiday Services Pty Ltd.

Daily Full-Day Launch Cruise to Stradbroke Islands. Tour includes launch cruise to Stradbroke Island and return. Barbecue lunch, fishing, swimming, included in fare. Operator Shangri-La Cruises, Cavill Ave., Surfers Paradise.

 SPORTS. Gold Coast *beaches* are regularly patrolled by surf life-savers. Fishermen (and women) can hire *motor boats* at Tweed Heads (just over the NSW border), Surfers Paradise, Tallebudgera Creek, and Southport.

There are *golf courses* at Southport, Surfers Paradise, Burleigh Heads, Tweed Heads, and Terranora Heights.

Bowls are available Musgrave Hill, Paradise Point, Southport, Surfers Paradise, Broadbeach, Moana Park, Mermaid Beach, Burleigh Heads, Palm Beach, Currumbin, Tugun, Coolangatta, Tweed Heads, also over the border.

Tennis courts are located all along the Gold Coast strip.

An international *motor racing* circuit operates at Surfers Paradise.

 NIGHT LIFE. Dining and floor shows at reasonable prices are provided at *Surfers Paradise, Tiki Village* (Cavill Ave.), *Roaring Twenties* (Gold Coast Highway), and *Ian Horton's Music Hall* (Cavill Ave.), as well as at the *Chevron Paradise.* At Broadbeach, there is usually a good floor show at the *Celebrity Room* of the *Broadbeach International Hotel.* Nightclubs at Surfers Paradise include the *Penthouse Club* and *Tuliana.*

Australian Accommodation and Tours (AAT) offers a tour of Gold Coast night clubs. Departure 7.30 P.M. Duration about four hours.

HOTELS AND MOTELS. Rates for double rooms throughout the rest of this chapter are: *Expensive:* A\$50 and up; *Moderate:* A\$30–49; *Inexpensive:* under A\$30.

Broadbeach

Broadbeach International. *Moderate.* About 3½ kms. from Surfers Paradise. Landscaped gardens, swimming pool. Special Spanish restaurant. Entertainment every night except Sunday. 100 rooms, a few family units which can accommodate 5 adults. 24-hour room service.

Hi-Ho Holiday Homestead. *Moderate.* One or two bedroom apartments with kitchen, bathroom, private balcony, refrigerator. Swimming pool, restaurant.

Burleigh Heads

Fifth Avenue Motel. *Moderate.* About 100 metres from the beach. Each room has shower and toilet, radio, TV, telephone, air conditioning.

Coolangatta

Beachcomber Motor Lodge. *Moderate.* Heated swimming pool; restaurant; each room has shower, toilet, colour TV, radio, telephone, refrigerator. Rooms can accommodate 3 persons.

Mermaid Beach

Camden Colonial. *Inexpensive.* Each room has private shower and toilet, TV, radio. Barbecue grill room; heated pool; baby sitters available.

Camelot Inn. *Inexpensive.* Each room can accommodate up to 3 adults; has private shower and toilet, TV, radio. Close to restaurants, golf, bowls, and tennis clubs.

Surfers Paradise

Some **70 hotels and motels,** most of them at least satisfactory quality. Recommended:

Chevron Paradise Hotel. *Expensive.* In the centre of the township, with all first-class hotel facilities. Two restaurants, 2 swimming pools, kiddies' pool with attendant, 7 bars, 24-hour room service, 166 rooms.

Iluka Quality Inn. *Expensive.* 17-storeyed; 112 one and two-bedroom motel units, each with private shower and toilet, colour TV, refrigerator, telephone, ceiling fans or air-conditioning. Heated pool, gardens, cocktail bar and grill room. Saunas and gymnasium.

Ambassadors Inn. *Moderate.* Near shopping centre and patrolled beach. Units accommodate 3 adults or 2 adults and 2 children. Each unit has private shower and toilet. Swimming pool.

Apollo Quality Inn. *Moderate.* 22 storeys, 120 suites (one and two rooms), swimming pool, kiddies' pool, cocktail bar and lounge, restaurant, 24-hour room service.

Chateau Quality Inn. *Moderate.* 18 storeyed; 144 one and two room suites. All facilities: coffee shop, cocktail bar and lounge, restaurant, games room, convention room, 24-hour room service, sauna.

 DINING OUT. The Gold Coast has a large choice of restaurants, from self-service cafes to all kinds of "national" eating places. French, Italian, Dutch, Viennese, Swedish, Chinese, Japanese, Bavarian, Lebanese, Belgian and Hungarian. The most reliable are the restaurants in the main hotels.

Toowoomba and Surroundings

Motorists who choose to travel from New South Wales to Queensland along the New England Highway (instead of the Pacific Highway) may do well to spend a day or two at Toowoomba, 186 kms. from the New South Wales border and 129 kms. from Brisbane. Situated on a brow of the Great Dividing Range at an altitude of 610 metres above sea level, Toowoomba is a pleasant town with tree-lined streets, a few good hotels and motels, and a friendly population of about 75,000. It is also an important industrial and commercial centre focusing mainly on agricultural products coming from the Darling Downs, the rich "Granary of Queensland," discovered in 1827 and first settled in 1840. Every September, Toowoomba holds a Carnival of Flowers when Queensland's "garden city" is a riot of flowers. The carnival, which draws large crowds and lots of visitors, is worth attending.

The Bunya Mountain National Park, 128 kms. from Toowoomba via Dalby, is the most beautiful nature reserve in this section of the Great Dividing Range. Its highest points are Mt. Kiangarow (1,129 m.) and Mt. Mowbullan (1,100 m.). The slopes are covered with bunya pines, tall, coniferous trees which produce large nuts. Aboriginals ate them roasted as delicacies. The mountains were once Aboriginal feasting grounds. When bunya nuts were harvested, members of different tribes gathered there and old grievances and enmities were forgotten and forgiven for the duration of the feasts. Other interesting flora includes tree ferns, coral trees, grass trees, wild orchids, staghorns, and elkhorns. Some 20 kms. of well graded paths lead to lookouts.

The small township of Dalby, which motorists cross en route to the Bunya National Park, played a part in the history of Australia's exploration. In 1848, the explorer Ludwig Leichhardt set out from nearby

Jimbour House to cross Australia from east to west—and never returned. Dalby is now developing itself as a tourist area.

The Warrego Highway from Toowoomba to Brisbane runs in the vicinity of Ipswich, 40 kms. west of Brisbane, a prosperous industrial and agricultural centre and the focal point of one of Queensland's most important coalfields. Originally a convict settlement founded in 1827, it is noted for its fine historic buildings. Ipswich is today a well laid out town of about 77,000 with many amenities including an Olympic swimming pool and a racecourse. Amberley, nearby, is the largest operational base of the Royal Australian Air Force (RAAF).

HOTELS AND MOTELS FOR TOOWOMBA

Telford's Toowoomba Hotel. *Moderate.* Licensed hotel at 554 Ruthven St. All rooms and suites provided with private bathrooms and toilets. Air conditioned. Reasonable restaurant. Baby sitting.

Coachman Motel. *Moderate.* Burmage St. All rooms with private conveniences. Swimming pool.

The Sunshine Coast and Hinterland

About 105 kms. north of Brisbane, there is another 60 kilometre stretch of beaches, inlets, lakes, and mountains which, a few years ago, acquired the name of Sunshine Coast. No one seems to know how it was named but the tag has stuck. For there is plenty of sunshine throughout the year.

The Sunshine Coast begins opposite Bribie Island in the south (see sections on Brisbane and Moreton Bay) and, in the north, it ends somewhere near Double Island Point. But its tourist and holiday sector is between Caloundra and Noosa. Scenically, this region is even more beautiful than the Gold Coast. And its hinterland—while it cannot match the grandeur of Lamington National Park—is also attractive in a more mellow way. Sunshine Coast resorts, however, are much quieter than those south of Brisbane. They are less commercialised and—if sophistication is measured by the number and quality of hotels, restaurants, and nightclubs—less sophisticated.

The Sunshine Coast is more for people who want to be physically active—yet relaxed during their vacation. Sports facilities (water and land) are as good north of Brisbane as they are south of the State capital. The costs of a holiday are about the same in both places. Hence, whether people choose one or the other is very much a question of personal taste.

The Bruce Highway is the main traffic artery which connects Brisbane with the Sunshine Coast. The highway itself runs inland but good bitumen roads branch off to the coast which is an average distance of 20 kilometres away. The turnoff from the Bruce Highway to the Bribie Island Bridge is 45 kms. north of Brisbane. It is near Caboolture, which is noted for a fine 18-hole golf course. Continuing along the highway, 24 kms. further north are the 10 steep trachyite cones of the Glasshouse Mountains, named in 1770 by Captain Cook who was reminded by the cones of the glass furnaces of his native Yorkshire. From Nambour (108 kms. from Brisbane) roads lead to the coast, to the mountains of the Blackall Range, and to the small, attractive Mapleton Falls and Kondalilla National Park. Gympie, another 72 kms. away, is the northern-most inland limit of the Sunshine Coast with good road connections to the chain of lakes north of Noosa where water skiing facilities and large flocks of water birds (including black swans, wild ducks, and cranes) may be found.

Sunshine Coast Resorts

There are a number of seaboard resorts along the Sunshine Coast going from south to north. Caloundra, at the meeting place of Pumic-stone Passage and the Pacific Ocean, has a series of excellent beaches extending over a dozen kilometres. Best for water skiing, swimming, and boating are Golden Beach and Bulcock Beach. For surfing, try Kings and Dickey which are regularly patrolled by surf lifesavers. Mooloolaba, at the mouth of the Mooloolah River, is one of the best fishing spots along the Sunshine Coast (the name means "the snapper's place"). It has facilities for all water sports and an excellent boat harbour. The resort is the finishing line of the Sydney/Brisbane Yacht Race and of the Single Handed Trans-Tasman Race. It is also the site of the annual Winter Series Off-Shore Races, and the base for a professional fishing and prawn-ing fleet.

Alexandra Headland has fine sand beaches. A road from there leads to the Bruce Highway and Buderim, a fast developing settlement which is now favoured as a permanent retirement place for well-to-do "south-erners." Buderim has a good golf course and Australia's only ginger factory. Adjacent to Alexandra Headland is Maroochydore, situated on the Maroochy River with first rate surfing beaches. At the estuary of the Maroochy River is a completely protected inlet which provides still-water swimming. A mass of cotton trees, decked in yellow blooms most of the year, borders the cove. For about 5 kms. between Cotton Tree and Bli Bli the tree lined road runs along the Maroochy River and provides spots for picnickers. There is good fishing in the river, especially in winter. Coolum beach lies at the foot of Mt. Coolum, where there are fine panoramic views of the coast and hinterland.

Noosa Heads has excellent surf because Laguna Bay faces north, rather than east. The still water of the estuary lagoon of the Noosa River offers pleasant swimming, good surf, estuary and rock fishing. Noosa-ville, on the Noosa River, is the gateway for tours to the famous multi-coloured sands in the 170 metre cliff face at Teewah. At Tewantin, on the Noosa River, a barge crosses the river and carries vehicles for trips to Teewah. Only four-wheel drive vehicles can make that journey.

Noosa National Park at Noosa offers a fine view from its crest, Tin-girina Lookout, and the picturesque spots along the park's oceanside walk, including Boiling Pot, Hell's Gates, Fairy Pool, Paradise Caves, Devil's Kitchen, and Alexandra Bay. North of Tewantin, a chain of lakes stretches for some 80 kilometres; the largest of them is Lake Cootharaba which is reached by a road running from Tewantin to Boreen Point. The lake is crossed by a launch (an 11 km. trip) and, from the other shore, a 2 km. walk leads to the sands. The lake itself offers swimming, fishing, and sailing.

There are two national parks worth seeing in the Blackall Range—a short distance from the seashore of the central Sunshine Coast; Nambour is a suitable starting point for visits to both. The Mapleton Falls National Park, about 10 kms. from Nambour, is a rain forest with fascinating birdlife and well marked tracks to splendid viewing areas. Kondatilla Park, about 22 kms. from Nambour (via Montville), is heavily timbered with all kinds of trees including bunya pines. The Kondalilla Falls cascades 75 metres into a rain forest valley. Easy walks lead to the head of the falls and to forest pools where the "living fossil," the Ceratodus (lung fish), may be found.

PRACTICAL INFORMATION FOR THE SUNSHINE COAST

 HOW TO GET THERE. *By air:* From Sydney daily by airlines of NSW and by East West to Maroochydore or by Ansett and TAA to Brisbane and connect with Unionair to Maroochydore. Henebery Aviation to Caloundra, or Noosa Air to Noosa.

By road: To all Sunshine seaside resorts there is a daily bus service by Skennars.

 TOURS. *River trips:* Cooloola Everglade Cruises, Noosaville, daily except Monday and Saturday. Maroochydore River Cruises, 269 Bradman Ave., Maroochydore, Monday, Wednesday, Friday and Saturday. Noosa Coloured Sands Tours, 182 Gympie Terrace, Noosaville, most days, morning and afternoon, depending on the tides. Teewah Coloured Sands Tours, 54 Gympie Terrace, Noosaville (daily, morning or afternoon).

Bus tours: Cotton Tree Tours, Maroochydore, daily except Sat. and Sun. Lookaburra Tours, Buderim, week days.

Scenic Air Flights: Air Maroochy, Maroochy Airport. Henebery Aviation Co., Caloundra Airport.

 SPORTS. *Bowls:* greens abound, visitors welcome.
Croquet: Buderim, Caloundra and Nambour.
Fishing: all kinds, boats for hire.
Golf: courses open to visitors at Beerwah, Bribie Island, Caloundra, Buderim (Headland Club), Maroochydore (Horton Park), Nambour, Cooroy, Tewantin.

Horse riding: Belli Park (via Eumundi), Caloundra, Cooroy, Mapleton, Marcoola, Northarm (via Yandina).

Sailing: Caloundra, Nambour, Maroochydore, Noosa.

Swimming: public swimming pools at Nambour, Marcoola, Peregian and Tewantin.

Water skiing: Caloundra, Currumundi Lake, Maroochy River, and at Tewantin.

HOTELS AND MOTELS

Alexandra Headland

Lauders by the Sea. *Moderate.* 120 Alexandra Pde. (Tel. 071-43-1939) 16 units, all with private bathrooms. Fans, TVs, radios, tea-making and cooking facilities. Laundry, pool.

Buderim

Mark Anthony. *Moderate.* 45 King St. (Tel. 45-1164). 26 air-conditioned units all with private facilities. Telephones, TV, radio, tea-making facilities—one unit has cooking facilities. Pool.

Maroochy Country Lodge Motel. *Moderate.* Situated just off a golf course and with three other golf courses within a 16 kilometre radius. The sea is only three kilometres away. Golf equipment for hire. All units are air conditioned and have private bath, toilet, refrigeration, TV. The restaurant is good.

Caloundra

The Dolphins Motel. *Moderate.* 6–8 Cooma Terrace. A comfortable, two storeyed motel; each unit has private shower and toilet, refrigerator, baby sitting.

Caloundra Safari. *Inexpensive.* Orsova Terrace and Minchinton St. Private bathrooms; room service; refrigerators, TVs.

Maroochydore

The Avenue Motel. *Moderate.* 106 Sixth Avenue. All units air conditioned and with private facilities. Service very good. Covered garage/carport for cars. Television in all units.

Mooloolaba

Twin Pines Motel. High standard motel. Private facilities attached to all units. Air conditioning in all bedrooms.

Noosa Heads

Noosa Parade Holiday Inn. *Moderate.* TV, radio, cooking facilities, pool.

Pine Trees. *Moderate.* A few yards from beach and river. Each unit is air conditioned and some have separate lounge room, full cooking and dining facilities, shower and toilet, telephone and radio. Heated swimming pool, restaurant, baby sitter. Hairdresser, clothing store, fishing gear store, boat hire.

Suncoast

Surfair Hotel. *Moderate.* One of the largest establishments of the Sunshine Coast; a 7-storey complex with 85 rooms. Facilities include seven bars, two restaurants, beauty salon, swimming pool, tennis court.

Highway of the Sun

Motorists who set out from semi-tropical Brisbane can drive almost 2,000 kms. to tropical Cairns along the Bruce Highway, nicknamed the "Highway of the Sun." This long route is studded with scenic stretches of sea and mountains, towns and villages of different sizes, and generally good accommodation. Several of the towns are also starting points for helicopter, plane and launch services to Great Barrier Reef islands and cruises and fishing excursions in the waters close by the Reef. Before setting out on a long trip, it would be advisable to obtain detailed information about the condition of secondary roads which the motorist might wish to take, and accommodation. The Queensland Government Tourist Bureau provides information of this kind free. Its head offices are at the corner of Adelaide and Edward Streets, Brisbane, and north of the capital at Alexandra Headland, 110 East St., Rockhampton; River St., Mackay; 320 Flinders St., Townsville; and 12 Shields St., Cairns.

The 172 kms. stretch of the Bruce Highway from Brisbane to Gympie is dealt with in the section on the Sunshine Coast. From Gympie, it takes about an hour to drive the 90 kms. to Maryborough—the next locality of importance.

Maryborough, a fast developing agricultural and industrial centre with some heavy industries, is situated on the Mary River. It is the gateway to holiday resorts in the *Hervey Bay* area and on *Fraser Island*. *Hervey Bay*, about 36 kms. from Maryborough, is called Australia's "Caravan Capital" because of the popularity of its resorts—Urangan, Torquay, Scarness, Pialba, Point Vernon, and Gataker's Bay—with people who prefer caravans to hotels and motels. Hervey Bay is one of the best fishing grounds on this part of the coast. Fraser Island is the largest (124 km. long) island off the east coast of Australia, and the largest sand island in the world with mountainous sandhills which rise to 290 metres. With some 40 freshwater lakes, the island is part Forestry Reserve, part National Park.

HOW TO GET THERE. *By air:* From Brisbane, the Sunshine Coast, Maryborough and Hervey Bay to Orchid Beach; to Happy Bay and Eurong from Maryborough and Hervey Bay. Barge services for 4-wheel-drive vehicles operate from Inskip Point (via Gympie) to the southern tip of Fraser Island; also from Urangan to Urang Creek on Fraser Island.

 ACCOMMODATIONS. Eurong: *Eurong.* Accommodation for 18 persons in nine twin units without private facilities. Also two self-contained flats, each for up to eight persons.

Orchid Beach: *Orchid Beach Island Village.* Overlooks Marloo Bay on the ocean side of Fraser Island. Double, twin, and three-bed units for a total of 79 guests. Family units with five beds, some accommodating up to six persons. Eurong, Happy Valley and Yidney Rocks offer spartan accommodations. Full board and holiday units are available at Happy Valley, Eurong, and Yidney Rocks.

Maryborough: *Arkana Inn.* A reliable motel in the Zebra group. Private shower and toilet in all units, air conditioning, TV. *Parkway.* Smaller than Arkana Inn but also good. Each unit has modern conveniences.

Bundaberg

A 52 km. detour off the Bruce Highway, 8 kms. north of the small locality of Childers, leads to the sugar centre of Bundaberg with its nearby seashore resorts. The combined output of the Bundaberg-Maryborough district makes up one-fifth of Australia's sugar harvest. Bundaberg Rum is a famous product of this city. The distillery can be inspected. Boyd's Antiquatorium has an interesting display of vintage cars and early model machinery.

Bundaberg has a number of fair motels. Most have at least some air conditioned rooms. Sun City, in Hinkler Avenue, has a pool and dog kennels. Evening meal by arrangement.

Gladstone

Another of Queensland's fast developing towns situated on a magnificent natural harbour, Gladstone is an export centre for beef, alumina, bauxite, fruit, tobacco, and peanuts and the location of the huge Queensland alumina plant. It is also the mainland port for Heron Island on the Great Barrier Reef.

Rockhampton

Situated on the Fitzroy River almost on the Tropic of Capricorn, Rockhampton is a "city of flowers." Its climate has been compared with that of Hawaii—pleasant in both winter and summer. The town was named after a barrier of rocks across the river which, in pioneer days in the 1850's, prevented navigation further upstream. The spot was first settled in 1855. Its Quay Street, between Fitzroy and Derby Streets, is one of the few surviving Australian townscapes of colonial times. Today the street is protected by the National Trust. Rockhampton's annual Capricana Springtime Festival is usually held in the second week of September. Rockhampton claims to be the biggest beef market place in Australia.

Motorists who don't mind roughing it may drive a roundabout route along the Capricorn, Gregory, and Flinders Highways 890 kms. to Townsville instead of continuing on the more civilised Bruce Highway. The roundabout will take the motorist across one of Australia's richest gemstone districts, open-mine coal fields, cattle stations, and the gold-rush town of Charters Towers. The going can be fairly rough along the 200 kms. of unsealed roads between Clermont and south of Charters Towers, and motorists are advised to take supplies of petrol and water.

Rockhampton has several very good hotels and motels:

Duthie's Leichhardt, Bolshover and Denham Sts. Fully air conditioned, good restaurant, TV, refrigerator, telephones. Excellent standard in Tower Wing.

Ambassador Motor Inn, Yaamba Road, North Rockhampton; **Central Park,** 224 Murray Street; and **Telford Fountain Motor Inn,** 161-165 George Street are three of the dozen motels to be recommended. All units have private showers and toilets and are air conditioned. Restaurants serve wholesome Australian meals.

Mackay

Although Mackay has become a sort of transit centre between the southern Australian capitals and the Great Barrier Reef region, it is a pleasant resort in its own right. The city, facing the Pacific Ocean and surrounded by lush green sugar cane fields, is situated on the banks of the Pioneer River. An excursion to the Eungella Range, 80 kms. west of Mackay, is well worth it even if it means spending a night in the town. Eungella National Park, 1,200 metres above sea level, is a tropical rain forest in cool mountain air. The name is Aboriginal and means "land of clouds"—which need not be taken literally. The park abounds in palms, elkhorns, staghorns, parasite figs, ferns, orchids, flowering vines, and shrubs. Accommodation of sorts is available at Eungella township on the crest of the range.

HOTELS AND MOTELS

Coral Sands Motel. *Moderate.* 40-42 Macalister Street. Two storeyed; 47 units air conditioned. All modern conveniences; restaurant.

Gorries. *Moderate.* 106 Nebo Road. Motel with 20 air conditioned units; private showers and toilets. Pool.

The Mackay Townhouse Motel. *Moderate.* 73 Victoria St. Air conditioned units with private shower (or bath) and toilet. Less expensive than Gorries. Restaurant.

QUEENSLAND

TOURS. There is a wide variety of flights and cruises to various Great Barrier Reef islands and to and over the Reef itself. The time of the flights is usually by arrangement. There is a regular launch cruise from Mackay to Brampton Island. It is advisable to contact the Queensland Government Tourist Bureau in River Street, Mackay, for arrangement of flights and confirmation of cruises. Both have very good safety records; the operators' guiding principle about weather conditions is, "if in doubt—don't fly or sail."

Proserpine

Proserpine, an attractive small town on the banks of a river of the same name, and Shute Harbour, 35 kms. east, are busy centres for transport to holiday islands of the Great Barrier Reef and the starting points of cruises. There is a daily helicopter service from Proserpine to islands of the Whitsunday group including Hayman where sightseers can spend a few hours at the island before returning to base. "Earlando," some 37 kms. northeast of Proserpine, is a seaside cattle station where paying guests can combine two kinds of holidays: surfing, fishing, sailing and horse riding in almost unspoiled bush. But they are for people experienced in the sports. The road to "Earlando" is officially termed "difficult to negotiate, particularly after rain." But the property can be approached by private plane or private launch. Proserpine has an Olympic swimming pool, golf course, squash courts, and bowling greens.

Bowen

This is a smallish agricultural centre with good surfing beaches and unpretentious accommodation. The Bruce Highway continues through Home Hill (101 kms.) and Ayr (12 kms.) to Townsville—Queensland's largest northern city.

Townsville

Despite its semi-tropical situation, Townsville (population 100,000) has a pleasant climate with an average maximum of 82°F (28° C) and an average minimum of 68°F (20° C) which partly explains how this city has fast grown from the site of a tallow plant in the 1860s into a pulsating centre of economic and academic activities. Its port is one of Australia's main export outlets of bulk sugar, beef, wool, and timber from the rich hinterland and of the products of Mount Isa Mines which exploit the world's largest copper-silver-lead-zinc deposits, 874 kms. west of Townsville.

The *James Cook University* in the city is Australia's only university in the tropics and it has become internationally recognised as one of the major research establishments in the veterinary and marine sciences connected with the tropical environment. The city has several well kept public gardens and also the Town Common, 4 kms. from the centre. Its flora and fauna, covering 3,240 hectares (8,006 acres), are especially worth seeing. National Parks with tropical forests are also close. They include *Mt. Elliot National Park* (22 kms. south), and *Mt. Spec National Park* (86 kms. northwest) with spectacular views. *Mt. Stuart Summit,* which presents a sweeping panorama of the city, the coast, and the islands, is well worth the 18 km. drive. *Castle Hill* remains Townsville's best vantage point. Townsville is the main approach to Magnetic, Orpheus, Hinchinbrook Island, Dunk and Bedarra Islands.

HOTELS AND MOTELS

Highway Motel Robert Towns. *Moderate.* 261-267 Stanley Street. All rooms air conditioned; private showers and toilets. Pool.

Lowths. *Moderate.* Corner Flinders and Stanley Streets. Licenced hotel in the centre of the city. 69 air conditioned rooms with all private conveniences. Also 6 suites (higher standard).

TraveLodge. *Moderate.* 75 The Strand. A very good motel with 180 air conditioned units with all private conveniences. Pool, baby sitting, restaurant.

If motorists find the 362 km. drive from Townsville to Cairns, where the Bruce Highway ends, too long, they can break their 352 kms. trip at several smaller towns en route: Ingham (112 kms.), Cardwell (170 kms.), Tully (209 kms.), Innisfail (263 kms.). From Innisfail, Cairns is only a hop of 90 kms. Recommended stops with suitable accommodation on the way, all with air conditioned rooms and private showers and toilets, are **Ingham,** *Herbert Valley Motel;* **Innisfail,** *The Roberts Johnstone* and *Moondarra* motels.

Cairns

The most northerly city in Queensland (population about 40,000) is a well laid out tropical resort with wide streets divided by flowerbeds and bushes. Cairns has smoothly working transport to other resorts and a big game fishing centre increasingly popular with the international set; but its existence is by no means based entirely on the tourist. Sugar and cattle country surround Cairns. During the sugar season, between June and December, the sweetish smell of burning cane stalks from the cane fields perfume the air; fires (lit to cleanse the stalks for the next day's harvest) circle the city with a fearsome but harmless blaze. Visitors who want to include as much sightseeing as possible would do well to choose Cairns as their base for trips to the outer Great Barrier Reef, the islands between the Reef and the mainland, and the scenically beautiful hinterland.

 HOW TO GET THERE. *By air:* There are daily services from Brisbane with connections to other capital cities.

By rail: "The Sunlander" from Brisbane runs from Monday to Saturday.

By coach: Daily services from Brisbane with interstate connections.

 TOURS. Palm Cove, 26 kms. north of Cairns, has one of Queensland's best quality guest houses—*The Reef House* for 22 guests. The large, attractively decorated bed-sitting rooms are air conditioned and have separate bathrooms. Guests eat the delicious meals together at lunch and dinner either in the air conditioned dining room or in the pool pavilion. Self-service bars are located in all suites, the community lounge, and the pool pavilion. Guests are picked up at Cairns Airport (free service for those staying 7 days or more. Others are charged the current taxi fare).

Kuranda. The 34 km. railway line between Cairns and Kuranda is the most spectacular in Australia. It was built between 1884 and 1888 through jungles and rocky mountains which had to be cut by 15 tunnels to lay the railway tracks. The steep, winding ascent is at the small township of Redlynch; from there, the motor train passes through jungles, over deep gorges and creeks. Views include mountain ranges, cane fields, and Great Barrier Reef islands. The trip is inexpensive and very worth while.

HOTELS AND MOTELS

Cairns has some two dozen hotels, many motels, and about 20 apartment houses at the visitor's disposal. Several are in the luxury class and, on the whole, accommodation and service are satisfactory even in the more modest ones.

Tuna Towers Motel. *Expensive.* 145 Esplanade. Licensed restaurant.

Adobe. *Moderate.* 191 Sheridan Street. A smallish establishment with air conditioned units, private showers and toilets, swimming pool, and well run grill room.

Bay Village. *Moderate.* 227-229 Lake Street. 33 air conditioned units, private shower and toilet; swimming pool.

Cairns Holiday Inn. *Moderate.* Cor. Sheridan and Thomas.

Atherton Tableland

Travellers wishing to embark on a road tour of the superbly beautiful Atherton Tableland may leave the rail motor at Kuranda for a connecting coach. Tickets should be reserved in advance. But the Tableland—a 600 to 900 meter high plateau of the Great Dividing Range southwest of Cairns—can also be reached by road directly from Cairns or from Innisfail. The name of the Tableland honours the memory of its first settler, John Atherton, who established a farm there in 1877. The climate is pleasantly mild during the day throughout the year, but evenings and nights can be cool so it is advisable to take warm clothing, especially in winter.

Dairy produce, maize, tobacco, peanuts, and timber including walnut, Queensland maple, kauri, and cedar are the main products. During World War II, the US Air Force had a Flying Fortress base on the plateau for operations against Japan in New Guinea and adjacent islands. Several scenic highways lead to the heart of the Tableland and detailed road maps (obtainable at most larger petrol stations) will be useful.

Mareeba

Driving from Kuranda towards Mareeba, at 23 kms. there is a branch road to Davies Creek Falls (6 kms.), an area of rain forest worth visiting. Mareeba itself (population over 5,000) is a prosperous, tobacco-growing area. The Mareeba Rodeo, held in July, is good fun; some of Australia's best rough riders participate.

Atherton

The commercial centre of the Tableland is Atherton with a population of about 3,000. Nearby (16 kms.) is the Tinaroo Dam which provides irrigation to the district from the captured waters of the Barron River. The dam is well stocked with fish and offers good opportunities for swimming and water skiing. There is a kiosk, which sells refreshment, and an attractive orchid garden.

Yungaburra

This small spot is well known both for its Curtain Fig Tree, an ancient and very large tree with curtain-like roots, and for two crater lakes nearby. A road through rain forest leads to Lake Eacham (6 kms.) at an altitude of 747 metres above sea level. It is 146 metres deep and provides pleasant swimming, water skiing, boating, and picnicking. Lake Barrine (8 kms.) is shallower (110 m.) but about twice as large as Lake Eacham and with the same facilities. The small locality of Malanda (14 kms. from Yungaburra) is known as the headquarters of the longest milk run in the world; it supplies areas hundreds of kilometres away, including Darwin, Mount Isa, and even New Guinea. From Yungaburra, a pleasant drive along the scenic Gillies Highway takes you to Gordonvale where the road joins the Bruce Highway for an easy run to Cairns.

There are a number of well maintained establishments in the area but none in the top hotel or motel class. Among them, the *Corn Cob,* at Tolga, has a fully licenced restaurant; *Lake Eacham,* at Yungaburra, with 32 units (all with private showers and toilets) and a restaurant has received favourable mention.

Cooktown

On the Endeavour River about 324 kms. north of Cairns, Cooktown stands on the spot where Captain James Cook repaired his ship "Endeavour," during his voyage of discovery in 1770. For a short while in the 1870s, it was the scene of a gold rush. Today, it is a sleepy tropical town with a certain charm. Air Queensland operates day tours from Cairns, including flights over the Great Barrier Reef.

The Queensland Outback

Where the Queensland "outback" begins is a question to which there are innumerable answers. For the average tourist, it may begin past Cairns on the seashore, somewhere beyond Toowoomba inland. Hence the Outback includes an enormous area, most of it untamed land, with rich and semi-arid pastures, artificial oases of pleasant mining towns, and deserts in between. It has its special fascination, especially for people who enjoy nature in the raw and don't mind occasional discomfort.

In the Outback, motorists may drive along thousands of kilometres of good bitumen roads but these may be broken by stretches that are "non-trafficable" after even light rain. A tour of the Outback is not a lightly taken drive but an expedition that needs careful preparation and execution. Such a tour does not present insurmountable difficulties, provided one has sufficient time, money and, above all, the necessary expertise. But, for the overwhelming majority of tourists, it will be simpler, more pleasant, and probably far cheaper to join one of the many tours organised by experts who know when, where, and how to undertake such a trip. Most of these safaris cross State borders and are planned to acquaint tourists with inland Australia and its people. For detailed information, see your travel agent or the Queensland Government Tourist Bureau.

THE GREAT BARRIER REEF

While there may be differing viewpoints about what to see in Australia, the Great Barrier Reef (more correctly "Reefs") must be high on any list. For the Reef—stretching for more than 1,200 kms. along the northern half of Australia's east coast from Gladstone to Cape York—is one of the world's most beautiful natural attractions.

There are more than 600 islands, ranging from tiny coral cays (low islets) to fair sized tops of submarine mountains in the Reef area of 207,200 square kilometres. The clear, warm, unspoiled waters which wash the Reef and the islands teem with all kind of fish—one of the many attractions for thousands of people who spend their holidays on the 18 reef islands developed as tourist resorts.

Visitors, fascinated by the Reef and its marine and bird life, will want to know a great deal about them; a fair amount of literature (for lay people) is available in most of the better mainland bookshops and in general stores at the resorts.

Here is a summary of some of the basic facts: The Barrier Reef has been built up through countless ages by tiny animals, the coral polyps. Their stomachs secrete lime from their food and this lime is deposited round the polyp forming a coral skeleton. A branch of dry coral appears as a delicate fabric of cells; a polyp occupied each cell with a thin membrane connecting the cells to each other so that the living coral consists of individual animals which form a sort of united body. Living corals have all kinds of pastel colours.

There are several hundred species of corals in the Great Barrier Reef, and nearly 900 species of fish, of which 250 are edible, in the Reef area. The nastier ones include sharks and rays; most of the sport fish belong to the swordfish and mackerel species.

Most of the islands are rich in bird life, including species which twice yearly cover the tremendous distances between the Queensland coast and Japan and Siberia, and others which are almost extinct on the mainland but thrive in the Great Barrier Reef havens. The 1,200 km. Great Barrier Reef is not an unbroken wall of coral; there are channels in between.

Whether the earliest European seamen sailing past Australia were aware of the existence of the Great Barrier Reef is not known. Therefore, it seems to have been discovered by Captain James Cook in 1770.

In mid-1985, rates for the resorts mentioned in this section ranged (per person, per week, for two adults sharing) from A$369 to A$1406, including full board.

Heron Island

One of the simpler spots (which does not mean less enjoyable), 72 kms. northeast of Gladstone, Heron Island is a true coral cay with several square kilometres of coral exposed at low tide. But an important warning: corals are razor sharp; never walk on them barefoot. Strong sandshoes are essential. The island is surrounded by sandy beaches where during nesting period—October to April—turtles can be seen at night when they crawl from the sea to lay their eggs. Trips in glass bottom boats and skin diving equipment are available as are snorkeling lessons. Underwater observation of the 1,100 species of fish is rewarding. There is a swimming pool and a tennis court equipped for playing at night. Heron Island Resort offers three kinds of accommodations: two classes of motel-type suites with private showers and toilets, and lodges with bunk beds for four and a nearby shower and toilet block.

Great Keppel Island

Just inside the Tropic of Capricorn, 48 kms. northeast of Rockhampton, Great Keppel is the largest of 27 islands which comprise the Keppel Group. Its 40 kms. of shoreline have several bays with gently sloping beaches, and the interior is wooded with several easy walks. The resort on Fisherman's Bay on the west side of the island has a swimming pool, shop, bar and tennis court. Dinghies for fishing or for trips to other beaches, glass-bottomed boats for observing marine life, and snorkel equipment are available for hire.

Brampton Island

A tropical paradise 32 kms. northeast of Mackay, Brampton offers all the water sports plus a tennis court, a practice golf course, and plenty of rain forest walks on gently graded hills. The resort accommodates 218 guests. All units have private bathrooms; executive suites have kitchenettes.

Lindeman Island

A highly recommended mountainous island in the Whitsunday archipelago, 67 kms. northeast of Mackay, Lindeman has good beaches, an interesting 6-hole golf course, a lovely wooded national park with charming lookouts, two yachts for cruising in and around the Reef, very good food, a pleasant staff, and efficient management.

Hamilton Island

One of the newest and best resorts in the Barrier Reef area, Hamilton Island has direct air connections with Australia's southern capitals (Sydney is 2 hours away, Brisbane 90 minutes). A wide range of accommodations—and prices—from the most luxurious to the more modest are offered. Visitors will find all water sports, plus tennis and squash.

Long Island (Happy and Palm Bays)

A scenically beautiful, mountainous island and one of the quieter places among the reef resorts, Long Island has accommodation for 71 guests in holiday cabins with private facilities. Happy Bay is a good centre for big game fishing, about 8 kms. from Shute Harbour. It has a tennis court and a 4-hole practice golf course. Visitors not looking for strenuous hiking will find the place enchanting.

South Molle Island

An "informal" resort, South Molle Island prides itself on providing accommodation for 243 guests "to suit most budgets," and there is an island bistro for casual meals. The island, 8 kms. from Shute Harbour, lies in the middle of the scenically beautiful Whitsunday Passage. It is hilly and has pockets of rain forests in between high grassland and native bush. There is a 25-metre swimming pool, a 6-hole golf course, and a tennis court. Visits are organised to coral gardens and to other islands. Speed boats are for hire.

Daydream Island

Five kms. off Shute Harbour is a scenically pleasant island in the Whitsunday Group. The general decor is Polynesian, with an 80 metre long salt water swimming pool (a tropical island bar in the middle) as the centre of social life for the 154 people that the hotel-motel establishment can accommodate. The vegetation is lushly tropical. Organised excursions in launches and glass-bottomed boats are frequently arranged. A very good place for snorkeling and skin diving.

Hayman Island

The most northerly resort in the Whitsunday group and the most sophisticated island in the Reef area. It is mainly for people who like round-the-clock action. Royal Hayman Hotel has accommodations for a total of 518 people in twin, double, and family lodges, all with private shower and toilet. Rates from A$43 includes all meals (accommodation for children under 1 year is free). The Island itself is hilly and tropical, and inhabited by some 80 species of birds. There are facilities for all water sports and coral reef viewing. Service is available to fill scuba tanks and there are dinghies for hire. Also tennis court, shops, banking facilities, nightclub. Rates are from A$68 per person.

Magnetic Island

Largest of the northern islands, 8 kms. from Townsville, is a national park with seven developed holiday resorts: Picnic Bay, Geoffrey Bay, Nellie Bay, Arcadia, Alma Bay, Radical Bay, and Horseshoe Bay. The best holiday accommodations, with all modern facilities, is at Hannaford's Mediterranean Village, inland from Nelly Bay. Hotels, guest houses, and self-contained flats can accommodate between 450 and 500 guests. There are about 24 kms. of sealed roads and the island has its own bus, taxi, and car rental service. It has complete facilities for water sport as well as dinghies and motor launches for hire. Visitors may take their own cars by ferry from Townsville. Other features include a 9-hole golf course, bowling green, tennis courts, shopping facilities, koala and animal sanctuaries, and marine gardens with outstanding displays of coral and reef fish.

Orpheus Island

A small, narrow island 80 kms. north of Townsville has accommodation for a maximum of 24 guests in bungalows and cabins, some with private shower and toilet. A quiet relaxing spot in the Hinchinbrook Channel, Orpheus Island has one of the loveliest landscapes of the Great Barrier Reef area. Facilities for fishing and other water sports are satisfactory. The resort has no liquor licence but the management will order liquor for guests. Rates are from A$120 (all inclusive) per person.

Hinchinbrook Island (Cape Richards)

Separated from the mainland by the narrow Hinchinbrook Channel, this mountainous island is the world's largest island National Park with mountain peaks, waterfalls, and forest areas. The resort at Cape Richards stands on the crest of a narrow peninsula and can accommodate about 60 people in 15 self-contained units. All units have a shower, toilet, full cooking facilities, refrigerator, linen, fans and fly screens. A shop stocks foodstuffs. Also available are the usual facilities for water sports and launch excursions on request.

Dunk Island

Described as "a beachcomber's dream," this tropical island off the coast of Tully in north Queensland was made famous by the distinguished Australian author E.J. (Ted) Banfield who lived there for 25 years before it became a resort. Now it can accommodate 200 guests in considerable comfort. All water sports are available as well as a 6 hole golf course, a tennis court, and facilities for horse riding, archery, and clay pigeon shooting. Cruises to other islands are provided. Rates A$92–120 per person.

Green Island

A true coral cay only 8 cm. above sea level and part of the Great Barrier Reef, Green Island is situated 27 kms. northeast of Cairns. A white sandy beach surrounds its small area which is covered with thick tropical vegetation. Up to 100 guests can be accommodated at the Coral Cay Hotel in single, twin, and family units for up to 5 persons. Some units have private shower and toilet; all are equipped with hot and cold water. Besides the usual water sports (snorkeling equipment is available for hire), the island's great attraction is the world famous underwater observatory where visitors can see marine life in its unrestricted and natural manifestations through 22 windows. (A similar observatory is further south on unsettled Hook Island which can be reached by launch.)

Lizard Island

A big game fisherman's paradise, this remote place 95 kms. northeast of Cooktown, accommodates 20 people. Lizard Island is only 16 kms. from the Great Barrier Reef and it was from here that Captain Cook discovered a passage through the maze of coral. The management provides a glass-bottomed boat and facilities for catamaran cruising and water skiing. Rates A$130–140 (full board) per person.

HOW TO GET THERE. By air: From Brisbane and other capital cities to Gladstone, Rockhampton, Mackay or Cairns on TAA or Ansett Airlines. Then to the individual islands by TAA, Air Queensland, Ansett, Lindeman Aerial Services, Helitrans Australia, Barrier Reef Airways and Safaris, and/or launch.

PRACTICAL INFORMATION FOR QUEENSLAND

HOW TO GET THERE. *By air:* There are direct International flights to Brisbane from the U.K., U.S.A., New Zealand, Singapore, Papua New Guinea, Solomon Islands, Hong Kong and Fiji with connections from Japan.

From Sydney and Melbourne, there are frequent daily flights by both Ansett Airlines of Australia and TAA to Brisbane.

By rail: Brisbane Limited Express from Sydney has connections from other capitals.

By road: From Sydney, express air conditioned coaches operated by Greyhound Express, and Ansett Pioneer provide daily service to Brisbane.

 WHEN TO GO. The best time to visit Brisbane, the Gold Coast, and the Sunshine Coast is between April and November; for the Great Barrier Reef, it is between April and October. However, there is plenty of sunshine all year round. The Gold Coast, for example, has an average of 290 sunny days a year. In January, February and March, Brisbane, Rockhampton, Cairns and the Gold Coast have a daily average of seven hours of sunshine; between April and July, Brisbane and Cairns average seven hours of sunshine each day, while Rockhampton and the Gold Coast average eight hours. From August to December, the daily average sunshine is eight hours for all four places.

 WHAT TO WEAR. Queenslanders like to dress casually. In summer, it is quite in order to wear lightweight suits, slacks and jackets, or tailored shorts and long socks even in the cities. However, some of the top hotels and restaurants insist that men wear a jacket and tie or scarf for the evening meal. Women should dress as they would in the warm months at home. In winter, slightly heavier clothing—what people would wear in the late spring or early autumn in North America or Western Europe—is advisable. Evenings may be rather cool even in summer, especially inland, and it would be wise to put a warm jumper or pullover into the suitcase at all times. Sandshoes are a must when walking on the reef.

 FESTIVALS. *February:* Food and Wine Festival, Surfers' Paradise.

April-May: Rock Swap Festival, Warwick; Vintage Wine Festival, Roma.

June: Pacific Festival, Townsville, and displays, mardi gras, street carnival.

July: Diver's Rally, Heron Island. Underwater sports, photography, scuba diving expeditions.

August: Royal National Show, Brisbane; Exhibition of the State's primary industry; rodeo events. Festival of Opals, Cunnamulla-Eulo. Displays of opals (popular with gem collectors).

September: Warana Spring Festival, Brisbane, the capital's own festival of sports, arts and cultural events. Capricana Springtime Festival, Rockhampton. Carnival, competitions, festival-princess election. Toowoomba, Carnival of Flowers. Dancing, floral displays, home garden exhibitions, floral floats, competition and parade. Caloundra Arts Festival. Exhibitions, awards for painting and craft items. World-famous Outback races, Birdsville.

October: Fishing Expo, Heron Island, Great Barrier Reef. Warwick Rodeo, the most important event of its kind in Australia.

November-December: Heron Island. One week's competitions, expeditions, photographic displays.

December: North Queensland Conservatorium of Music Festival, Innisfail. Arts and crafts exhibits, concerts, held over 3½ weeks. Special activities.

FARM HOLIDAYS. Queensland is a great State for holidays in rural areas. A number of farms and sheep and cattle stations accept paying guests. The Queensland Government Tourist Bureau (corner Adelaide and Edwards Streets, Brisbane 4000) provides an up-to-date list, and most travel agents will accept bookings. Typical examples of farm holiday homesteads include: *Rosevale,* via Charleville, a sheep and cattle station with colonial-styled homestead, swimming pool and tennis court. *Dalkeith,* 129 kms. west of Longreach, a huge sheep station where kangaroos and emus roam freely. The *9YE Holiday Ranch,* 160 kms. north of Brisbane and near the Sunshine Coast which offers horseback riding and instruction, excursions to nearby mountain gorges and streams, a rock pool, and transport to surf beaches. *Cherribah Mountain Resort* 28 kms. from Warwick or by air from Brisbane to the property airstrip. Air-conditioned accommodations, golf, horseback riding, sailing on lake.

 TRAILRIDING. There are many properties throughout Queensland which organise trail rides. In Brisbane, there are the High Chaperelle Riding Ranch, 245 Mt. Crosby Rd., Moggill, and Pineview Quarter Horse Stud, Bronson St. Aspley. Further out, the Reidvale Riding Ranch, Tallebudgera Dam Rd., Ingleside, and the Binna Burra Lodge in Lamington National Park, 90 kms. southwest of Brisbane are among the establishments which offer escorted trail rides. Belli Park via Eumundi also offers conducted trail rides.

 BUSHWALKING. There are magnificent bushwalks in Queensland, especially in the national parks. Those who want to camp there need a permit from the Department of Forestry, 41 George St. Brisbane. The Queensland Federation of Bushwalking, G.P.O. Box 1537, Brisbane or the Brisbane Bushwalking Club, G.P.O. Box 1949, provide information. Popular walking spots include: Fraser Island off Maryborough, a heavily timbered, large, sandy island with freshwater lakes; Lamington National Park, southwest of Brisbane, an easily accessible rain forest with waterfalls, birdlife, graded walking trails, and two lodges—O'Reilly's and Binna Burra; and Valley of Diamonds, a scenic gorge northwest of Toowoomba.

 CAMPING. The Queensland Government Tourist Bureau and the Royal Automobile Club of Queensland produce up-to-date caravan and camping guides. No tent camping is allowed in parks within a 25 km. radius of Brisbane; special permission to camp in national parks must be obtained from the Department of Forestry. Camping areas at the seaside include: Currumbin, Caloundra, Maroochydore on Sunshine Coast, Bowen, Townsville, Ingham, Mackay, Mission Beach, Hervey Bay, Shute Harbour and Cairns further north. At the lakes: Somerset Dam near Kilcoy, Lake Broadwater near Dalby, Moogerah Dam near Boonah, Tinaroo Dam, Lake Eacham and Lake Barrine, all near Atherton. In the country: Toowoomba and Roma on the Darling Downs, Palmerston National Park, Millstream Falls, Tully Falls on the Atherton Tableland, Lamington National Park, Cunningham's Gap National Park, and Springbrook National Park in the southeast.

 SPORTS. *Golf.* There are several public golf courses in Brisbane—including Victoria Park and Long Pocket—but they are heavily booked at holidays and weekends. Introduction from a golfer's home club will frequently (though not necessarily) result in an invitation for a game. For Brisbane clubs, consult the Yellow Pages of the Telephone Directory. For country courses, contact the

Queensland Golf Union, phone 221-5410. *Squash.* Centres are located in most major areas throughout the State. Most of them also rent shoes, rackets, and balls. In Brisbane, (and for advice about the country) contact the Squash Rackets Association, 492 Main St. Kangaroo Point. *Tennis.* Public courts are available for hire in Brisbane and in country areas. Contact the Queensland Lawn Tennis Association Hardcourt Centre, Sheard Park, Brisbane.

 WATER SPORTS. *Surfing.* There are dozens of popular surf beaches but the best are located south of Fraser Island where they are not sheltered by the Great Barrier Reef. Most surf beaches are patrolled by members of local surf life-saving clubs. Sea wasps are found only on far north Queensland beaches where there is no surf. For detailed information about surfing, contact the Surf Life-Saving Association, Surf House, PO Box 127, Brisbane South.

Canoeing. There are good flat water areas on the Brisbane River, and on the Mooloolah, Maroochydore and Noosa Rivers on the Sunshine Coast. The Townsville Canoe Club holds white water events on the Tully and other northern rivers, and races to various Great Barrier Reef islands. The club also organises full day, weekend, and extended trips open to visitors. *Sailing.* There are clubs in most larger coastal centres. Some provide reciprocal membership. An introduction will help to obtain an invitation to an outing, especially if the visitor comes from overseas. *Skin diving.* Excellent areas include Green and Heron Islands in the Great Barrier Reef, Moreton Bay, and beaches along the Sunshine, Capricorn, and Gold Coasts. The Bunker and Capricorn Island groups near Bundaberg are accessible for underwater photography and snorkeling. To rent equipment, divers must show evidence of qualifications. Seek help and advice from Underwater Adventurers' Club, Annie St., Kangaroo Pt., Brisbane; Underwater Skindivers and Fishermen's Association, 58 Maynard St., Bundaberg; and Underwater Research Group, PO Box 10, North Quay, Brisbane. Air filling stations are in Brisbane, the Gold Coast, Maryborough, Mackay, and Gladstone.

Fishing. The Queensland Government Tourist Bureau publishes a free pamphlet on fishing. The Wednesday edition of the Brisbane afternoon daily newspaper, *Telegraph,* lists fishing clubs which accept visitors. Game fishers are warned that most boats for hire are booked 12 months ahead. The main fishing season is between September and December but you can fish successfully anywhere between the Gold Coast and Cairns all year round. The waters abound in black marlin, barracuda, sail fish, wahoo, giant trevally, yellow fin tuna, Spanish mackerel, barramundi, and bonito. Inshore, the best fishing areas are Moreton Bay, North and South Stradbroke Island, Bribie Island, Nerang River, and off the coast within limits of the Great Barrier Reef. Summer catches include whiting, flathead, jewfish, dart; winter catches are tailer, bream, and whiting. Crabbing is also popular but watch out! Heavy penalties are imposed for taking female crabs. Popular freshwater fishing spots for barramundi, giant perch, and red bass include the estuaries of the following rivers: Dawson, Burnett, Boyne, Calliope, Fitzroy, Burdekin, Pioneer, Don, Barron, and North and South Johnstone.

CAR RENTAL. A large number of firms are in the business of renting cars, camping equipment, bicycles, boats, houseboats—even light aeroplanes, with or without pilot. Consult Yellow Pages of the Telephone Directory.

 TOURS. There is a large choice of organised group tours. In general, their reputation is good in this highly competitive market. As schedules, timetables, and prices change from time to time, it is advisable to check final arrangements with your tour operator a couple of days before departure. Accommodation along the main tourist routes is at least reasonable and occasionally quite good. But excursions to the outback—rewarding in other respects—may offer the traveller only the simple necessities of food and shelter. However, the travelling amenities—air conditioned coaches and expert driver-guides—are usually very pleasant and comfortable. Both of Australia's major internal airlines, Ansett and TAA, offer combined air-coach holidays which means that the customer is flown from any of a dozen or so places in Australia to the Queensland starting point of the coach tour and back again.

In recent years, "camping holidays"—in which participants spend the night either in parked caravans or in sleeping bags in tents—have become increasingly popular with coach-tour travellers. For example, a 14-day "camper" from Sydney to Cairns cost A\$886 in mid-1983.

Rail tours. The Daylight Rail Car Tour, Brisbane to Cairns (5 days) and vice versa, is a popular tour which operates between April and September. Price of A\$337 covers fare, meals, overnight accommodations and local sightseeing tours at various stopovers en route. Bookings for this tour and other railway information may be obtained from the Queensland Government Tourist Bureau or the Railway City Booking Office, Adelaide St., Brisbane.

Cruises. A number of operators conduct cruises in the Great Barrier Reef waters. They include McLeans Roylen Cruises (5 days) from Mackay on Mondays, from A\$466. The *Elizabeth E* also operates 4-day cruises from Mackay on Mondays, A\$445, over a similar route. From Shute Harbour and Airlie Beach a number of day, half-day and extended cruises operate along the beautiful Whitsunday Passage.

TASMANIA

An Island State

by
ANTHONY BERRY

Australians will tell you that Tasmania is just like England. English immigrants and visitors will dispute this.

The fact is, Tasmania is itself—an island state where the locals have a distinctive personality of their own; where officialdom has not taken over to such an extent as in the mainland; where the majority of people still know everyone in their home town, where they can get together for the common benefit.

In other words, in Tasmania, the native really is friendly. The getting together is shown particularly in the tourism industry, where Tasmania has shown the rest of Australia how government and private enterprise can act together to inspire everyone to welcome the visitor, to realise how important the visitor is to the economy.

Thus you will see in shops and restaurants and petrol stations (many of these spots themselves, members of the Tasmanian Tourist Council) the leaflets, *Let's Talk About . . . ,* which are available for visitors.

If one could sum up Tasmania in a few words, it would be like this: compact, ideal to explore by car or caravan (although twisting roads can be challenging), rural atmosphere and beauty combined with stark mining enterprises amid the wild grandeur of the western coast and ambitious hydroelectric projects in the high lakes and rivers of the inland mountains.

Tasmania records the history of Australia in the south, where Port Arthur has been partially restored to show what one of Australia's main convict settlements was like.

Being the southernmost state, Tasmania offers cooler weather in summer than many mainland states, but that's not to say it can't be hot. It isn't quite so cold in winter either, thanks to the influence of the sea all 'round.

Although mining is bringing money in, Tasmania expects tourism to be a great contribution to its economy, and craftsmen and artists are more and more flocking to Tasmania for its out-of-the-rat-race atmosphere and cheaper living.

The State has made sure of its natural heritage by devoting 2,125,000 acres (850,000 ha), more than any other State, to national parks.

Falling within the temperate zone, Tasmania has four distinct seasons as well as temperature variations between the milder coastal areas and the highlands.

Generally speaking, summer wear for beach or sightseeing should be light, with provision for something extra to put on in the cool of the evening. There is no winter freeze, although temperatures in both Launceston and Hobart can fall to freezing point overnight. Spring and fall can produce changeable conditions and hikers are warned that weather can be treacherous in highland areas.

Buildings and vehicles are normally heated. Heavy clothing is required only if you are spending time in the open—at race meetings or walking round Port Arthur. Office buildings, hotels, motels and bigger shops are air-conditioned for summer.

There is no wet season but a light raincoat or umbrella should be packed irrespective of time of year.

Night life clothing depends where you go but smart casual clothes will do for both sexes in most places. For men a jacket is necessary for evening admittance to the casinos and to some hotels.

Van Diemen's Land

Getting back to the beginnings, the real reason why Tasmania was settled was that the British didn't want the French to have it, even though it was discovered by a Dutchman.

Abel Tasman discovered the island in 1642 and named it Van Diemen's Land and that was that for 130 years. Between 1772 and 1803 when it was finally settled, no less than 10 exploring expeditions landed many Frenchmen, not to mention Captain James Cook, and George Bass who proved in 1798 that Tasmania was an island.

The last such explorer was Nicholas Baudin in 1802 who had previously enjoyed great hospitality from the British in Sydney. While extending this hospitality, the British governor in New South Wales wrote to the then Secretary of State for the Colonies, Lord Hobart, suggesting that a new colony should be formed down south.

Approval was given and Lieutenant Governor David Collins set out from the other side of the world. Before he could get there, however, the New South Wales Governor King, hearing rumours of French intentions to settle in southern Tasmania, decided to beat them to it and sent Lieutenant John Bowen who landed at Risdon, now a Hobart suburb, in 1803. Next year Collins arrived, landed in the same place, but decided on Sullivans Cove as the settlement headquarters, naming it Hobart Town. The British decided the settlement should also claim the northern half and this was subsequently done at Port Dalrymple. Thus, the island had two governors for a while. The island grew up in 1865 when responsible government was established and the name of the colony changed to Tasmania.

Historical associations still remain, however, for there is a distinct feeling among Tasmanians of belonging either to the south or the north, mostly because Hobart to the south and Launceston to the north have quite different characters and are the only two really well populated cities.

If you are travelling in Tasmania you will find the State divides itself up quite naturally into a variety of areas.

The best way to see Tasmania thoroughly without backtracking is to arrive at Launceston, travel right round the island seeing both east and west coasts, back to Launceston and then shoot down the midlands, diverting perhaps into the Cradle Mountain lakes area, and finish up with a few days in Hobart, flying back to the mainland from there.

A Cable-Stayed Truss Bridge

See the east coast first. This pretty, rolling, green area offers Tasmania's best beaches and good fishing.

Launceston was given its name by the founder Colonel Paterson, after the U.K. Cornish birthplace of the then Governor King. This city, second largest in Tasmania, is situated at the confluence of the South and North Esk rivers which here become the Tamar, also named after the river flowing by the English town. About 20 miles downstream, you might like to look at the Batman Bridge, one of the world's first cable-stayed truss bridges, which is dominated by the 330 ft high steel-frame tower.

In Launceston take a day out to the Cataract Gorge and ride the chairlift. The nearby Penny Royal Cornmill and the Gunpowder Mill offer a taste of colonial life with a little piratical high adventure thrown in. Both feature good accommodation and restaurants.

And at least have a drink in Australia's oldest licensed hotel, the Launceston, in operation since 1814, with many reminders in both print and artifacts tracing its past.

If shooting is your thing, properties near Launceston and Campbell Town offer hunters a chance at the elusive deer, in season, of course. To the northeast is Bridestowe lavender farm—best to see it in January for full colour effect. Travelers interested in historical connections should pause at Lilydale Falls Reserve en route to Bridestowe to see the two oak trees grown from acorns from the Great Park at Windsor (U.K.), planted on Coronation Day, May 12, 1937.

Going toward the east coast, the attraction is more natural than man-made—good fishing and attractive towns such as Scottsdale, where hopfields can be inspected nearby at Tonganah; there is also a museum and re-created tin-mining shanty town at Derby. Scamander is noted for its good fishing, both sea and river; St. Helens has shooting (ducks and wallaby) in season. While there see the museum, old mine workings, wildflowers, sea shells.

Farther along the coast, Swansea boasts the old Swan Inn, a delightful stop for the night or a meal. See there Morris' Store, the community centre, housing the only remaining full sized billiard table in Australia, and Australia's only restored bark mill.

Bicheno has gained a name for its crayfish and is one of Tasmania's most popular holiday resorts. First known as Waub's Boat Harbour, Bicheno was used as a shelter for whalers' boats and later settled as a coal mining port in 1854 with coal being pulled by horses along a half mile tramway from the mines. The remains of the convict-built bins can still be seen at the Gulch. See fairy penguins on Diamond Island (accessible only at low tide). Also visit the Sealife Centre and the East Coast Bird and Wildlife Park.

Granite Hills and Whaling Boats

Continuing on down the east coast, the scenery becomes more interesting. At Coles Bay there is some of the most spectacular coastal scenery in the State. Travelling on a road that was originally surveyed as a railway line, you come to the foot of the Hazards, hills of solid red granite from which the facings of several Hobart buildings have been quarried. It is a region of fine beaches, rocky cliffs and peaceful bush paths, a rewarding experience for a bushwalker.

Coles Bay is the starting point of Freycinet Peninsula National Park. Triabunna was a whaling station of some importance in the last century and a garrison town when Maria Island was a penal settlement. Now it is a base for many fishing boats which can also be used to visit the island.

On the way into Hobart, you'll see Buckland, whose most notable feature is the Church of St. John the Baptist, built in 1846. The beautiful east window is said to have been originally designed for Battle Abbey in England on the site of the Battle of Hastings. (The Abbey was badly damaged and never restored and the window was given to the first rector of Buckland.)

If you don't want to backtrack before you go into Hobart, take the Port Arthur Road crossing Eaglehawk Neck with its tesselated pavement and spuming blowhole. The Neck, a narrow strip of land joined to the Tasman Peninsula and containing the Port Arthur penal settlement, made escape for prisoners almost impossible. Guards with ferocious dogs would patrol the Neck. (One prisoner nearly made it by swimming the narrow stretch underwater. But it was his unlucky day. He swam against the tide; a hawk-eyed guard noticed ripples flowing against the stream and it was back to the prison again.)

Port Arthur is possibly the most interesting relic of Australia's days as a penal colony. It has a walkway through it as well as an audio visual performance and museum. The scenery around is quite beautiful. Guides explain that, contrary to what most people think, compared with the poor, free, working people in England of their time, the prisoners were well off. They had food and clothes and not too exhausting work, while their compatriots overseas would be starving, ill treated and overworked until they literally dropped.

Gateway to Antarctica

Hobart, Tasmania's capital city, is a town of history and scenery, and still has a small-town atmosphere. It is the starting point for Antarctic expeditions, the only Australian city with a school run by Quakers, the first city in Australia with a legal casino, and a good base for day trips to Bruny Island, Hastings Caves, Lake Pedder, Port Arthur and the Huon Channel district. Here you can swim in Hastings thermal pool and fossick (search for gemstones) in the Lune River with local collectors.

A drive up to the peak of Mt. Wellington, the backdrop of Hobart, is worthwhile in winter or summer (but beware of road conditions and don't go at night in winter) for a wonderful view.

While exploring this area the traveler will come across some weird names. The small township of Bagdad, 20 miles north of Hobart, for example, was named by early explorer Hugh Germain, who gave title to several villages from the two books he carried with him—the Bible and Arabian Nights. A small farming township on the main railway line 40 miles from Hobart, Colebrook, was originally named Jerusalem by Mr. Germain.

From Hobart, take the road to New Norfolk and Queenstown; the former is a pleasant little old town with the interesting Oast House to visit—see the modern art gallery, and buy hop pillows in season.

PRACTICAL INFORMATION FOR HOBART

 FACTS AND FIGURES. Hobart is Australia's second oldest capital city, founded 16 years after Sydney in 1804. Until 1881 its name remained Hobart Town and you can still see the ancient stone signs along the roadway marking the miles to Hobart Town. The first British settlement had been formed five months earlier at East Risdon upstream but was abandoned in favour of the place where Hobart now stands, with Risdon becoming, in time, a mere suburb.

Appropriately, Hobart's Town Hall in Macquarie Street now stands where the city was formally founded in February 1804 by Colonel David Collins. The name of Hobart was given to honour Lord Hobart, then Imperial Secretary of State for the Colonies. Population is now 170,000.

 HOW TO GET THERE. *By air:* Daily service by jet from Melbourne (the nearest interstate airport), one hour. Also direct flights from Sydney to Launceston and to Hobart, and from New Zealand to Hobart each Saturday.

By sea: Overnight cabin ferry three times a week (takes cars also), Melbourne to the northern port of Devonport.

By road: from Devonport as above, by bus daily. Journey takes minimum two/three hours by car, half a day by bus.

 HOW TO GET AROUND. Tasmanian Redline Coaches operates a service from the airport to the city, and two cab companies operate a "maxi-taxi"—a small bus—in addition to their regular cabs. Cab fare to the city will run around A$12.

TOURIST INFORMATION. Tasmanian Government Tourist Bureau at 80 Elizabeth St., Hobart, and the corner of St. John and Patrick Sts., Launceston, and in Devonport, Burnie, and Queenstown.

MUSEUMS AND ART GALLERIES. The State Library's *Allport Collection* houses what is probably Australia's finest collection of Tasmanian history, with notable household items. Closed weekends. Cnr. Murray/Bathurst Sts. *Tasmanian Museum and Art Gallery,* 5 Argyle St: Historical collection European/Australian glass, silver, china; emphasis on Tasmanian Aborigines and early colonial activities. Free. Closed Christmas Day, Good Friday, Anzac Day (April 25). *Van Diemen's Land Memorial Folk Museum,* Hampden Road, Battery Point, one of Hobart's earliest colonial homes housing Australia's first folk museum. Comprehensive collection features lives and times of pioneers. Open every day, limited holiday hours. *Post Office Museum,* 19 Castray Esplanade, sited in historic waterfront building, portraying history of development of post and telegraph services; also has fine philatelic collection. Free. Closed Sundays. *Maritime Museum* in historic "Secheron House" at Battery Point, by the harbour. The *Shot Tower,* Channel Highway, Taroona, 60 meters (200 feet) high. Museum, art gallery.

HISTORIC SITES. Hobart is the city to come to for historic sites. More than 90 buildings have National Trust classification, and of these 32 are in Macquarie Street, 31 in Davey Street. Only a few minutes from the city centre is *Salamanca Place,* with its terrace of restored warehouses dating back to the 1830s. Craft shops and restaurants now inhabit some of these old houses and on the wide street outside, open air stalls are set up on Saturday. Salamanca Place is part of the historic Battery Point waterfront area, which also includes *Arthur's Circus,* a backwater crescent of the tiniest cottages tucked behind Hobart's newer buildings. At Taroona, a suburb, is the Shot Tower, open 7 days a week. *Parliament House,* 1840, is one of the oldest buildings in Hobart. *Runnymede,* 61 Bay Rd., New Town, is a restored colonial home. Closed Mon/public holidays and during July.

TOURS. Walking tour of Battery Point, organised by National Trust, half-day; half-day coach or car tours to Mt. Wellington (magnificent views of Hobart and river); historic Shot Tower and Kingston, site of Australia's Antarctic research headquarters; Mt. Nelson signal station for views and city sights; historic town of Richmond; New Norfolk, hopgrowing centre and Oast House. Full day coach or car tours to historic penal settlement, Port Arthur, where a walker's tour includes audiovisual display; Hastings caves and thermal pool; for scenery, try the Russell Falls in Mt. Field National Park, or the grandeur of wild scenery and ancient outcrops of the tour to Lake Pedder.

Car tours are more expensive than those by bus, but all tours above, except walking tour, are organised by the Tasmanian Government Tourist Bureau (Tasbureau) at 80 Elizabeth Street. The historic towns of Richmond and Ross are easily reached by car.

GARDENS. *Botanical Gardens,* reached by bus from Liverpool St. in Hobart, dropping off at Tasman Highway and five minutes walk to main gates in Domain Road. Features conservatory, glasshouse, garden tea rooms.

MUSIC. The ABC (Australian Broadcasting Commission) features major orchestral concerts at the converted Odeon Cinema in Liverpool Street and also organises youth concerts at the same place. The ABC and the Conservatorium of Music run regular lunchtime concerts at the State Library Auditorium, Murray Street. "This Week in Tasmania," available at accommodation places, is a good guide to current performances and staging of rock, jazz and Musica Viva concerts. The Tasmanian University Musical Society also stages unusual concerts.

THEATRE. The Wrest Point Casino, four miles out of town at Sandy Bay, is the spot to go for cabaret shows, nightly performances of international stars, singers, comedy and revue specials. Cost can be as low as $15 for the show, depending on the guest performers, and dinner can be ordered à la carte. Regular performance at The Theatre Royal, 82 Campbell St., The Play House, Bathurst St.

CINEMA. Hobart boasts several modern cinema complexes, one drive-in, and the State Cinema on Elizabeth St., North Hobart, which often features reruns of classic movies or avant garde films.

BARS. Under Tasmania's licensing laws, generally considered to be the most liberal in Australia, owners of licensed hotels or restaurants may elect their own hours of trading, provided certain minimums are observed. As a result, trading hours vary enormously on all days except Sundays, when trading is restricted to between noon and 8 P.M.

CASINOS. Hobart boasts Australia's first legal casino at Wrest Point Hotel, open seven days a week from 1 P.M. until 3 A.M. where blackjack, French and American roulette, mini-baccarat, keno, mini dice and two-up are played to a maximum $500. A special suite operates on the lower ground floor for gamblers wishing to play for higher stakes. Launceston's new Federal Country Club Casino offers gamblers the same choice of games and true "country club" pursuits on its acres of grounds.

SPORTS. *Bowls* clubs at New Town, North Hobart, St. John's Park, Sandy Bay and Lindisfarne. *Fishing* can be arranged through the Tasbureau office, which can supply information for self-sail Cavalier 26 yachts. Charter tuna fishing boats operate Feb–June from Eaglehawk Neck. *Golf:* Tasmania has 60 courses with about 16 around the Hobart area. However, only Rosny Park, three miles from the centre of Hobart, is a public course. About half the courses insist the visitor must be a member of an affiliated golf club before playing. A few clubs, particularly in the Hobart metropolitan area, require a personal introduction by a member or production of a home course credential.

Horseriding is available at Gillingbrook, Acton, Sandville and Willunga Riding Schools. *Sailing* at Sandy Bay and Bellerive. *Swimming*—three Olympic-size pools at the Domain, Glenorchy and Clarence. *Squash* courts at Sandy Bay, New Town, Glenorchy, YMCA. *Tennis:* Domain Tennis Centre. *Ten pin bowling* at Moonah (24 lanes).

SPECTATOR SPORTS. Australian Rules football in winter, cricket in summer, and horse racing year-round. The sport that draws most spectators is the Sydney-Hobart Yacht Race, starting on Boxing Day in Sydney and ending around New Year's Eve before huge crowds in Hobart.

 SHOPPING. Shops in Hobart are open from 9 A.M. to 6 P.M. weekdays and from 9 A.M. to noon on Saturdays, when craft stalls also trade in Salamanca Place. Shopping is concentrated on and around the centre city block and many stores on the block have inter-connecting doors. Some lead out into Cat and Fiddle Square, a welcome oasis with its fountain and novelty clock. The City Council has completed a pedestrian mall by blocking off Elizabeth Street. In addition to established craft shops along Salamanca Place and the Saturday morning stalls, the city offers a variety of outlets for craft wares. *National Trust Gift Shop,* 25 Kirksway Place, has selected range of Tasmanian crafts, especially in rare Tasmanian woods, originally designed gift cards, diaries, cookbooks, notepaper. Galleries and gift stores specialising in Tasmanian crafts include *Handmark Gallery* on Hampden Road, Battery Point; *Fragments* on Elizabeth Street (notable brassware); and *Aspect Design,* Salamanca Place (closed Saturday afternoon and Sunday). Outlets for art work include *Salamanca Gallery* and *Coughton Gallery* on Macquarie Street (open daily). The *Country Women's Association* gift shop on Elizabeth Street has homemade goods for sale on weekdays. Suburban shopping centres such as *Sandy Bay* and *Eastlands* on the eastern shore have a full range of shops and, like city stores, are open Saturday morning.

 WHAT TO DO WITH THE CHILDREN. Those over 8 might like to see how chocolates are produced at *Cadbury's factory; harbour and river cruises* down the Derwent River; novelty clock at *Cat and Fiddle Arcade.* Visit the *Model Tudor Village,* 827 Sandy Bay Rd. Open 9 A.M. to 5 P.M. Take Taroona bus from Franklin Square to Stop No. 30.

HOTELS AND MOTELS Hobart has a good selection of hotels and motels, with price ranges for double rooms as follows: *Expensive:* A$50 and up; *Moderate:* A$35–49; *Inexpensive:* A$20–34.

Hobart and Environs

Four Seasons Downtowner. *Expensive.* Liquor room service. Licensed restaurant. 24 hr food service. City centre. Member Zebra chain.

Four Seasons Westside. *Expensive.* 156 Bathurst St. Liquor room service. 24 hr food service. Member Zebra chain.

Hatcher's Hobart Motor Inn. *Expensive.* Fountain Roundabout. Licensed restaurant. Central. Member Innkeepers chain.

Hobart Pacific Motor Inn. *Expensive.* Kirby Court, Knocklofty. Liquor room service. Licensed restaurant. Pool. Adjoins national park. Nr city centre, Mt. Wellington. Member MFA Homestead chain.

Lenna Motor Inn. *Expensive.* 20 Runnymede St. Liquor room service. Licensed restaurant. 24 hr food service. Overlooking harbour, at historic Battery Point. Member Flag chain.

Wrest Point Hotel-Casino. *Expensive/Deluxe.* 410 Sandy Bay Road, Sandy Bay. Depending on whether room in wing or in casino tower. Liquor room service. Licensed restaurant in revolving tower. 24 hr food service. Pool. Air conditioned. Nr beach, river, Mt. Wellington, golf course.

Argyle Motor Lodge. *Moderate.* Cnr. Lewis/Argyle Sts. Nr city and Oval.

Astor Private Hotel. *Moderate.* 157 Macquarie St. Pleasant, homey atmosphere. Central location, licensed restaurant.

Black Buffalo Hotel. *Moderate.* 14 Federal Street, North Hobart. Liquor room service. Licensed restaurant. 24 hr food service.

Blue Hills Motel. *Moderate.* 96a Sandy Bay Road.

Brisbane Hotel. *Moderate.* 3 Brisbane St. Rate includes hot breakfast. Licensed restaurant.

Four Seasons Motor Lodge. *Moderate.* 429 Sandy Bay Rd., Sandy Bay. Licensed restaurant.

Hadley's Hotel. *Moderate.* 34 Murray Street. Some cheaper rooms without private facilities. Liquor room service. Licensed restaurant. 24 hr food service.

Marquis of Hastings Hotel/Motel. *Moderate.* 209 Brisbane St. Licensed restaurant.

Motel Mayfair. *Moderate.* 17 Cavell Street. No restaurant. Nr city centre.

Prince of Wales Hotel. *Moderate.* 55 Hampden Road, Battery Point. Licensed restaurant. Set in historic area.

Southport Town House. *Moderate.* 167 Macquarie St. Liquor room service. 24 hr. food service. Central city.

Taroona Motor Hotel. *Moderate.* 178 Channel Highway. Liquor room service. Licensed restaurant. One minute from beach, five from casino.

Waratah Hotel. *Moderate.* 272 Murray St. Licensed restaurant. Central.

Black Prince Hotel. *Inexpensive.* 145 Elizabeth St. Liquor room service. Licensed restaurant. City centre.

Berriedale

Highway Village Motel. *Moderate.* 897 Brooker Highway. Liquor room service. Licensed restaurant. Own boat ramp and jetty. Member Flag chain.

Derwent Park

Hotel Carlyle. *Moderate.* 232 Main Road. Rate includes hot breakfast. Licensed restaurant.

Glenorchy

Balmoral Motor Inn. *Moderate.* 511 Brooker Highway. Off-season rates available. Liquor room service. Licensed restaurant. Nr racegrounds, trotting, showgrounds.

Howrah

Shoreline Motor Hotel. *Moderate.* Cnr Howrah/Rokeby Roads. Liquor room service. Licensed restaurant.

Montague Bay

Motel Panorama of Hobart. *Moderate.* Tasman Highway. No restaurant. Near golf course, swimming pool, beach.

Moonah

Lenton Lodge Motel. *Moderate.* 238 Main Road. No restaurant. Nr racecourses.

Mount Nelson

Mount Nelson Motor Inn. *Moderate.* 571 Mt. Nelson Road. Off-season rates available. Licensed restaurant. Overlooks city.

New Town

Hobart Tower Motel. *Moderate.* 300 Park Street. Off-season rates available. Near Hobart, Olympic pool.

Valley Lodge Motel. *Moderate.* 11 Augusta Road. Licensed restaurant. Pool.

Graham Court Holiday Apartments. *Inexpensive.* 15 Pirie Street. Kitchen facilities in rooms. No restaurant. Central.

DINING OUT. Hobart's restaurants are among the best in Australia. Prices for a 3-course meal, excluding wine, are as follows: *Expensive:* A$25 and up; *Moderate:* A$15–25. *Inexpensive* meals (less than A$15) can be had at many hotels serving counter lunches and teas.

Cock and Bull. *Expensive.* French cuisine, licensed, close to Wrest Pt. Hotel Casino.

Dirty Dick's Steak House. *Expensive.* Old world atmosphere. Steak size to suit appetite. Licensed.

Milan's. *Expensive.* Seafood and international cuisine in beachside mansion. Licensed.

Mondo Piccolo. *Expensive.* Italian dishes, veal a specialty. Licensed, lunch and dinner.

Mures Fish House. *Expensive.* Fresh seafood in intimate cottage. Licensed, reservations necessary.

Revolving Restaurant. *Expensive.* Wrest Pt. Hotel Casino. International cuisine, panoramic views, lunch and dinner.

Seafarers' Restaurant. *Expensive.* Seafood in appropriate "old salt" atmosphere. Licensed.

Stucki's. *Expensive.* Warm, rich decor. Fondues a specialty. Licensed.

Ball and Chain. *Moderate.* Colonial decor and service.

Chinese Lantern. *Moderate.* Special lunches and banquets. Licensed.

The Red Fox. *Moderate.* English meals in Tudor setting. Licensed, lunch and dinner.

A Lake That Drowned

If mountain scenery and man's use of natural power interest you, divert from New Norfolk into Maydena and travel the private road up through geologically ancient country to the hydroelectric scheme at Strathgordon and the drowned Lake Pedder whose end caused much controversy amongst conservationists a few years ago (1974). You can stay overnight at Strathgordon in the Lake Pedder Chalet (but book ahead), see the mighty dam and visit the underground Gordon power station.

Backtrack again through Bushy Park and continue on the mountainous twisting road through the Derwent River valley (sheer delight in colours in autumn) and into Queenstown. This mining town has been scoured out of the rocks and is not beautiful but to visit the mines and stand on top of the workings can be impressive. Beware of windy days, for the gales will suck the breath out of you if you stand on the rim of the open cut.

Strahan, 18 miles south, is now merely an echo of its glorious past during the copper boom. Even so, it is used today as the starting point for the breathtaking Gordon River trip by motor launch on which Tasmania's first penal prison, Settlement Island, can be seen.

Zeehan, on the way back to the north coast, and Burnie saw their greatest prosperity between 1903 and 1908 in the mining boom, a prosperity now being revived by the re-opening of the Renison Bell Tin Mine nearby. Many buildings of that era are now in use, including the once famous Grand Hotel (now apartments), Gaiety Theatre, Post Office, some banks and St. Luke's Church. The West Coast Pioneers' Memorial Museum houses one of the world's finest mineral collections.

Burnie, in the northwest, is an industrial town, but the surrounding "Cape Country" is full of green, rolling hills descending steeply to a wild and rocky coastline. The many small towns rely on the processing of farm products for their livelihood.

Burnie's pioneer museum is worth a visit and locomotive enthusiasts will enjoy a drink at the Loco Bar in the Burnie Town House Motor Hotel, where they'll be surrounded by photographs of early railwaymen and their steam engines.

In this area, too, visit cheesemakers, carpet factories and paper mills. At Devonport see the Tiagarra aboriginal project which traces the history of the extinct Tasmanian aboriginals and preserves some of their art, crafts and rock carvings.

The Devonport area is the centre of cave visits—Gunns Plains—but make sure they will be open; and Mole Creek, open daily and featuring glowworms. King Solomon caves are also open daily.

Temptation, Recreation, Salvation, Damnation

Once back in Launceston take the Midland Highway down the middle of the island—a road that calls through several worthwhile historic small towns. See Campbell Town and Ross—one of the State's finest and most attractive historic villages, whose dominant feature is the convict-built Ross Bridge. Stand in the centre of Ross and look at the four corners: Man O Ross Hotel—said to represent temptation; Town Hall—recreation; Church—salvation and the Gaol—damnation!

Travelling south to Oatlands, look for topiary (tree figures) lining both sides of the roads. Oatlands got its name because it reminded the early Governor Macquarie of his native Scotland and the grain which grew there, but as late as 1827 it was still only a site with a board bearing the name. Much of its development took place in the 1830s and it is said today that almost everyone in the town lives in an historic building.

Explorer Hugh Germain crops up again on the old road at Jericho. The settlement can be traced back to the 1820s when one early grant was given to William Pike, who arrived in 1823 and stayed to become the local catechist. Jericho even has "walls"—mud walls at the northern end of the town, which are the remains of the old probation station.

This, then, is the body of Tasmania. If you have extra time and money, try the outlying islands of King and Flinders in the north, reached by air services. These will be attractive, just for their peace and scenery.

PRACTICAL INFORMATION FOR TASMANIA

FACTS AND FIGURES. Named after its discoverer, Dutchman Abel Tasman, in 1642 but settled by the British in 1803, Tasmania is an island of 26,200 sq. m. The State capital is Hobart in the southeast; population is 170,000.

Set in the temperate zone, Tasmania has four seasons with temperature variations between the milder coastal area and the highlands. The eastern and southeastern half is rolling green hills, while the central and west and southwest is mountainous, wild and rugged.

Tasmania was nicknamed the Apple Isle for its profusion of apples, a main export until the west coast mines opened up areas of bush hitherto inaccessible to modern man. It has a network of fine standard roads, albeit narrow and turning, and is, because of its shape and island nature, the ideal place to explore by car.

HOW TO GET THERE. *By air:* Direct one hour flights from Melbourne into Launceston, Devonport and Wynyard on the north coast and to Hobart on the southeast with Ansett, T.A.A., or East-West Airlines. Direct flights from Sydney to Launceston and on to Hobart. Daily flights from Sydney to Hobart by East-West Airlines. Hobart has a new international airport for direct flights to and from New Zealand. Passport required.

By boat: from Melbourne only, where *The Abel Tasman,* a newcomer plies three times a week on a 15-hour overnight service to Devonport. All accomodations in cabins; cars are also carried. Advance booking necessary. Christmas holidays (Dec/Jan) booked about a year ahead.

HOW TO GET AROUND. Tasmanian Redline Coaches operates an airport bus service; taxis will complete the journey a little quicker, but at a price of A$12.

By air: Air Tasmania flies between Hobart, Queenstown Wynyard, Devonport and King Island.

By car: Tasmania's roads are generally 2-lane and in good condition, but allow extra time for journeys along the twisting coastal highways. Most car hire companies have unlimited mileage rates, including Budget, Avis, Autorent/Hertz, Costless, Curnow's, Thrifty, Concorde, Bewglass. Latter five are Tasmanian only, usually below national car rental rates. Campervans available from Tourmobile Rentals, Hobart; Tasmanian Mobile Motels, Launceston. Bewglass, Dolphin Enterprises, Motor Holidays, Tourmobile Rentals, Thrifty, Natcar, Van Winkle Campers. Tasmanian Mobile Campers are others. Speed limit in towns is 37 mph (60 km/h); outside 68 mph (110 km/h). Sounding of horn, except in emergency, forbidden in built-up areas. Use outside these areas when overtaking.

By bus: Circular Head Motor Services between Smithton, Wynyard and Burnie connect with Redline Coaches, continuing along the north coast to Launceston and southwards to Hobart. Daily.

TOURIST INFORMATION. More than any other State in Australia, Tasmania involves its inhabitants in the tourism industry on which it so heavily relies. Thus, the Tasmanian Visitors' Corporation, formed of government and private enterprise representatives has outlets for its informative booklets "Let's Talk About . . . " in cafes, historic homes, garages, shops of all kinds throughout the State. The Tasmanian Government Tourist Bureau has offices in all mainland state capitals and also in Hobart, 80 Elizabeth St; Launceston, cnr St. John and Paterson Sts; Burnie, 48 Cattley St; Devonport, 18 Rooke St; Queenstown, 39 Orr St. There is also a bimonthly *Travelways* newspaper crammed with detailed information available from the bureau or travel agents.

SHOPPING. Shops in most large towns and cities are open on Saturday mornings. There are many working galleries and craft centres open to visitors, where they can buy distinctly Tasmanian ware as gifts—copperware, pine wood carvings and utensils and hand made leather goods. And Salamanca Place in Hobart has open air stalls on Saturdays in summer.

Launceston has many boutiques and specialty shops in its arcades and in the Mall. *Emma's Arts,* 78 George St. sells Tasmanian made gifts; *I Spy,* 6 The Quadrant, has a great range of Tasmanian made souvenirs—17 different crafts. The *National Trust Old Umbrella Shop* and the *Tasmanian Design Centre* have unusual gifts; *Country Women's Association Gift Shop,* 129 St. John St; variety of arts and crafts made by members; *Hole-In-The-Wall,* 33 The Quadrant—locally made pottery toys and candles.

290

TASMANIA

St. Helens, *Bakers Oven Art and Craft;* all handcrafts including homespun and knitted garments; open Thursday/Fridays, more frequently in summer months; Deloraine, *Berry's Antiques*—antiques, paintings and craftwork; *Old Bowerbank Mill Gallery,* Bass Highway—weaving, knotting, furniture, pottery, paintings. Westbury, *Craft Corner,* Bass Highway; homespun wool garments, leatherwork, wood, copper and crocheting. Open Wed, Thur, Fri, Sun; *White House*—patchwork, needlework, bobbin lace, exhibition of old crafts. Carrick, *The Gallery,* Bass Highway once an inn, now art and craft gallery for 20 years. Displays of paintings, pottery, copper, leather, Tasmanian woods, minerals, cider, honey, lavender and embroidery. Open Tue-Sun, closed June. George Town, *The Grove,* 25 Cimitiere St—variety of local handcrafts. *Things,* 56 Main Road—antiques, jewellery, open weekends in summer.

Longford: *Kilgour Gallery,* 4 Archer St., paintings, pottery and sculpture.

Ross: *Ross Wool and Craft Centre,* Bridge St.—raw and spun wool, handspun and knitted garments, toys, glassware, copper, wood-work.

Evandale: *Colonial Art Gallery* has a representative collection of contemporary and historic art work, notably early Tasmanian paintings. *Evandale Antiques* also offers old treasures.

Lower Longley: *Mrs. Hops' Australiana Emporium.*

Scottsdale *Art and Craft Centre*—specialises in northeastern gemstones. Open Mon-Sat, varying times.

Pontville: *The Old Pontville Barracks*—crafts and Tasmanian work.

Port Arthur: *Maude Poynter Pottery*—watch potters at work daily. *Tasman Peninsula Craft Shop*—work of local people.

Richmond: *Saddlers Court Gallery*—original Tasmanian pottery, jewellery, woodturning, weaving, sculpture, paintings.

Burnie: *Art Gallery, Civic Centre*—permanent and specialist exhibitions, closed Mondays.

Devonport: *Impressions,* Best St.—selection of local arts and crafts, also exhibitions. Open 7 days a week 9 A.M.–5:30 P.M.

Marrawah: *Marrawah Gallery*—variety of crafts.

Smithton: *Art/Craft Centre*—many local crafts.

Ulverstone: *Weeda Copper Ware,* 39 Forth Rd—hand beaten copperware. *Crafts* 37, King Edward St—Tas. timber crafts, pottery, home-spun wool. *The Rock Shop,* Forth Rd—specialists in polished gemstones, both Tasmanian and others. *Westella Gallery and Teahouse,* Bass Hwy—fine range of arts of arts and crafts in National Trust home. Also serves Devonshire teas and light snacks.

 SEASONAL EVENTS. Regattas, golf and fishing tournaments are held year round all round Tasmania. Main events are: *January:Aquatic Carnival,* Stanley. *February: Royal Hobart Regatta Association Carnival* on the River Derwent. *October:* The *Launceston Agricultural Show,* about October 5, followed by *Royal Hobart Show,* about October 18–22. *November:* Woolnorth *Rodeo.* *December: Sydney to Hobart Yacht Race* starting from the New South Wales capital on Boxing Day and usually finishing three days later, in Hobart's fine old Constitution Dock. At about the same time the *Westcoaster,* Melbourne to Hobart yacht race, is run. Latrobe *Wheel Race*—one of biggest cycling carnivals in Australia. *Tasmanian Fiesta* in late December–early January features Hobart waterfront and sporting events.

 NATIONAL PARKS. Tasmania's Scenery Preservation Act in 1915, the oldest legislation of its kind in Australia, has resulted in the State having the highest percentage of any in Australia set aside as national parks, State reserves and conservation areas—a total of 6.1 per cent of the area of Tasmania.

Part of a geologically ancient country, Tasmania has, in one of its many national parks, a primitive wilderness area explored only by the hardy bushwalker. It is quite possible to walk where no other modern human has trod, even in these travel-conscious times. *South West National Park,* 1,105,000 acres (442,000 ha) is the largest in Tasmania. This park incorporated the flooded Lake Pedder, now a storage lake created by the hydroelectricity authority. Guided walks are conducted by private operators. It is wild rugged windy country. Don't venture in without a guide.

Cradle Mt.-Lake St. Clair National Park 330,000 acres (132,000 ha) is accessible by road at the southern end via Derwent Bridge. Superb lake and mountain scenery, with good fishing, forests of eucalypt and pine, extensive plains and mountains bedecked with summer alpine flowers are contained in the park. This park also has Tasmania's highest mountains. Furnished accommodation (no linen) cabins are available at *Lake St. Clair* at the southern end, although everything is supplied in chalets and cabins at *Cradle Mt.* at the northern end, where access is available by road. Prepare for bad weather. Blizzards can occur even in mid-summer. Discuss with ranger.

Mt. Field is 50 miles (82 km) from Hobart on a sealed road and has recreation and picnic area at entrance. Russell Falls are reached in 10 minutes walk; giant eucalypts border this track. By driving 16 miles into the park, visitors can get good skiing in winter at Lake Dobson. A ski tow is operated by Southern Tasmanian Ski Association. Four rustic cabins can be rented. *Ben Lomond National Park,* close (61 km) to Launceston, accessible by road, is developing as a ski resort by ski clubs and ski tows are in operation. *Mt. William National Park* covering 34,700 acres (13,800 ha), 15 km northeast of Gladstone, is the place to see the Forester kangaroo, but access is limited and there is no accommodation.

Located on the East Coast adjoining the town of Coles *Freycinet National Park,* 19,000 acres (7,541 hectares), provides a combination of a seaside resort, bushwalking and mountain climbing. Red granite outcrops and magnificent coastal scenery are features. Caravan and camping facilities are provided and a ranger is stationed here.

Franklin/Lower Gordon Wild Rivers National Park, subject of international attention since its listing as a world heritage area, features the untamed Franklin River and the enormous white quartz peak of Frenchman's Cap, southeast of Strahan. Experienced rafters can travel the Franklin during summer. Details from National Parks & Wildlife Service: 16 Magnet Court, Sandy Bay, Tasmania 7005. Ideal wilderness for bushwalkers entering from the Lyell Highway, but conditions change without warning. Huts at Lake Vera and Lake Tahune. *Hartz Mountains Park,* 21,000 acres (8,620 hectares), 80 km south west of Hobart via Huonville and Geeveston, is good for a one-day trip from the capital city. High moorland dotted with picturesque lakes and seasonal wildflowers attract visitors.

Rocky Cape is a small park of 7,500 acres (3,000 ha) on the northwest coast, accessible from the Bass Highway about 30 km west of Wynyard. Geology is the main interest of this park—many formations are more than 700 million years old. The park is also renowned for rare botanical specimens peculiar to the area and caves frequented by Aborigines about 9,000 years ago.

Tasmania has two island national parks: *Mt. Strzelecki* and *Maria.* The latter is off the east coast and was originally a penal settlement. The quaint little settlement of Darlington is in a good state of preservation and some dwellings are still occupied. Interesting marine fossils, splendid mountains and sheer cliffs on the coast are features. It is accessible by boat from Triabunna or by light aircraft from Hobart and Launceston. Mt. Strzelecki is the only national park on Flinders Island, with its entrance 15 km from Whitemark. A walking track leads to the 750 m peak.

CAMPING. Camping is not permitted in any roadside picnic areas or rest areas in Tasmania. Most campgrounds charge a fee. Tasmania can be cold and downright rainy and miserable in winter, so keep camping for summer and those golden autumn and tangy spring days only.

MUSEUMS AND ART GALLERIES. Apart from Hobart's museums (listed under the Hobart information), Tasmania has many small museums dotted round the island: at New Norfolk, the *Hop Museum;* an award-winning *Bark Mill Museum* at Swansea; *Piscatorial Museum* at Plenty; *Folk Museum* at Deloraine. Zeehan has a fine collection of minerals from all over the world. Burnie has its fine *Pioneer Museum;* East Devonport a *Maritime Museum,* Launceston a bigger museum showing early lifestyles and containing a Chinese joss house. All are related to the interests of each area. Launceston gallery, housed with the *Launceston Museum,* has a particularly exquisite collection of china and glass. Tasmanian and other Australian artists and craftsmen's work is displayed in many local galleries including *Saddlers Court* at Richmond, *Norfolk Galleries* in the Port Arthur area at Taranna and the *Bowerbank Mill Gallery* on the Bass Highway at Deloraine. *Coughton Galleries* in Hobart has regular exhibitions.

HISTORIC SITES. When Australians want to see history, they go to Tasmania. On your wander round Tasmania, make a point of looking in at Bothwell, Evandale, New Norfolk, Oatlands, Pontville, Ross and Stanley; Longford was recently classified.

Consistently Tasmania's number one historic attraction is Port Arthur, once the major penal settlement. The old asylum has been developed and has a visitor reception centre with audiovisual performance, scale model and small museum. *Isle of the Dead,* originally Opossum Island, became the burial ground for convicts and free people from Port Arthur. Boat trips across to the island from Port Arthur daily except July.

Bowen Park. Risdon Cove. A $1.2 million development honoring the founders of the first European settlement in Tasmania. Open daily. Films, displays and audio-visuals.

Evandale. Clarendon House, Nile, completed 1838, one of the great Georgian houses of Australia, designed in the grand manner and set in an extensive formal garden. Open daily except Christmas Day, Good Friday, and July.

Deloraine. Bowerbank Mill, Bass Highway. One of several flour mills, built 1853, whose production finally ceased in the 1930s. Now an art gallery exhibiting work by Tasmanian artists and craftsmen. Open Tues-Sun.

Hadspen. Military museum with vehicles, uniforms, photographs. Daily.

Richmond. A pleasant drive from Hobart through grazing country that once served as the state's "wheatbelt" brings the visitor to this historic township featuring Australia's oldest bridge, beautiful churches, galleries and tea shops.

George Town. The Grove, 25 Cimitiere St. Once the home of the port officer, the house has been lovingly restored and is open for inspection daily. Closed July. The owner and staff dress in period costume to guide, and supply refreshments.

Hadspen Village. Entally House, old home of great charm, furnished with prized antiques and set in delightful park. Collection of horse-drawn vehicles in out-buildings. Open daily except Christmas Day and Good Friday.

Bush Mill. Tasmania Peninsula. A replica of a 19th-century steam timber mill. Open daily. Audio-visuals and tea-rooms.

Hobart. Narryna (also known as Van Diemen's Land Memorial Folk Museum), built 1836, with many original features preserved. Open daily, closed for four weeks in winter. *Shot Tower, Taroona,* 11 km south of Hobart. Built to make shot for firearms. Interesting museum, locally made souvenirs. Panoramic views from top of tower.

Launceston. Franklin House, Franklin Village, Georgian house once a home and then a school. Open daily except Good Friday and Christmas Day. *Bonney's Inn* at Deloraine offers good food in a charming atmosphere, well-suited to the pace of life in this small rural town. *New Town. Runnymede,* 61 Bay Road. National Trust property, recreated home of 1860s. Open except Mondays, closed July. *New Norfolk. Old Colony Inn,* Montague St. One of Tasmania's most famous historic features, built 1835, but doubtful if it ever was actually used as a pub. Contains fine antiques and collection dating back to penal era. Huge walnut tree in the delightful grounds reputed to be 170 years old. Open daily. *Westbury. White House, Village Green.* Originally a store, now contains collection of 17th/18th century furniture. Garage houses early motor cars and horse-drawn vehicles. Display of miniature furniture, glass and china, model toys and playthings from 1850. Open daily except July–early August.

Gunpowder Mills, near Cataract Gorge, is simulation of 19th-century gunpowder mill with foundry, arsenal and ships of war. Open daily.

 TOURS. Tasmanian Government Tourist Bureau *(Tasbureau)* operates bus tours round the State, taking 7 to 15 days. These tours, together with those of mainland operators Australian Pacific, Trans Otway, AAT, Pioneer, and Centralian Staff, are packaged together with flights from Melbourne and the seagoing *Abel Tasman.* Similarly, there are self-drive packages offered by Tasbureau and the airlines Ansett, TAA, from Melbourne. Under-30s coach tours and camping tours are operated by Australian Pacific, and camping tours by Centralian Staff and AAT.

The *Arcadia II* travels the Pieman River to the Pieman Heads on the rugged west coast daily except Tuesday from Corinna. There's a two hour picnic stop at the Heads where the river meets the Indian Ocean. Other interesting river cruises operate out of Strahan up the Gordon River; magnificent river reflections and a visit to a 19th-century convict settlement are highlights.

Par Avion provides scenic flights over Cradle Mountain, northwest and west and southwest coasts and Bass Strait Islands.

Tasbureau can tell you about the seven-day, personally-escorted excursions through Cradle Mountain national park from Waldheim. These operate during summer months only. *Goondooloo* motor launch one hour cruises along the Tamar River operate daily from December to April. Paddlesteamer *Lady Stelfox* leaves regularly from Ritchie's Landing.

Tasmanian Chairlifts in Launceston run a chairlift ride of 500 yards along the beautiful Cataract Gorge, about a mile from the city centre. The central span of more than 300 yards is believed to be the greatest single span of any chairlift in the world. Impressive at any time, the gorge is best seen in spring for the colour of the flowers.

Each main centre in Tasmania has half and full-day tours to surrounding attractions. Devonport has car trips out to the hydroelectric scheme, to Gunns Plains Caves, Mole Creek Caves and scenic coastal tours.

From Burnie, all day tours by car run through magnificent mountain and forest scenery to Queenstown, to Savage River, where mines can be inspected (ladies wear slacks and low heeled shoes) and through rich farming communities to Launceston. Table Cape Boat Harbour tour gives an interesting run along the superb seascapes of Burnie's coast to the dramatic headland of The Nut and historic settlement of Stanley. The tour to Fern Glade goes through dense forest and is bordered by manferns and the Emu River.

From Launceston, half-day tours visit historic Entally House, and for mountain and coastal views to Mt. Barrow. City sights tour includes Cataract Gorge, National Trust House, Clarendon and a tour along the Tamar river with constant river and orchard views. Whole day trips from Launceston take in St. Helens on the east coast, visiting St. Columba Falls; the Great Lake 3,000 ft. above sea level and Poatina power station; the verdant farmland and rugged coastal scenery en route Table Cape.

Longer one-way tours last two or three days, finishing in Hobart. The shorter of these travels the gentler rolling farmland scenery of the east coast with its old villages. The three-day tour goes along the northwest coast and then south down the west coast to Queenstown. When available, a day-long cruise up the lovely Gordon River is included; at other times, more time is spent on the northwest coast.

For those who want to wander on their own, an "All Route" bus ticket can be bought as you board a bus; many bus routes go past or near visitors' attractions.

 INDUSTRIAL TOURS. More than any other Australian State, Tasmania encourages industries to participate in tourism. In the past few years visits to factories have risen high on the visitor attraction list of the state.

Going round the state in an anti-clockwise direction, here are the plants welcoming visitors (check times with the plant or Tasbureau first):

Bell Bay—*Comalco Aluminum.*

Launceston—*Waverley Woolen Mills,* conducted tours through a mill and salesroom, featuring quality woolen garments.

Devonport—*Edgell* processed vegetables; East Devonport—*Tascot Templeton,* carpets.

Russell Falls Trout Farm, 77 km from Hobart.

Mole Creek—*Tasman Golden Nectar Leatherwood Honey Factory.*

Port Latta—*Savage River Mines,* iron ore pelletising plant.

Burnie—*APPM,* paper and hardboards.

Wynyard—*United Milk Products; Table Cape* cheese factory.

Queenstown—The *Mount Lyell Mining and Railway Co.,* copper mining.

South Hobart—*Port Huon Fruit Juices,* cider.

Risdon—*Electrolytic Zinc Co.,* zinc plant.

Claremont—*Cadbury Schweppes Australia,* cocoa and chocolate.

Glenorchy—*Universal Textiles,* silk and textile printers.

Boyer—*Australian Newsprint Mills,* newsprint.

Scottsdale—*Kraft* food processing factory.

In the mountainous centre of Tasmania, the *Hydro-Electric Commission* provides viewing galleries for visitors at the following stations: Liapootah, Tarraleah, Tungatinah and Trevallyn. Guided tours are available at the Poatina underground power station in the north of the state and at Strathgordon.

 FAUNA PARKS. While Tasmania today has no major zoo, it has developed a series of small zoos, wildlife sanctuaries and deer parks to display both native and introduced fauna to its visitors and local public. The modern concept of presenting native and introduced fauna in a mostly open range situation, has proved to have great appeal.

At the deer parks, animals and birds go free in their native habitat, yet they are never too distant for the public to view or photograph. People can drive or walk through the parks to observe deer, kangaroo, wallaby, birds and fowl as they exist naturally.

Tasmanian Wildlife Park, 20 km from Deloraine, has animals roaming free plus a nocturnal house. Open daily. Features include a Koala Village.

Tasmanian Devil Park Tasman Peninsula, is the place to see this unique creature.

The *Longford Wildlife Park,* just out of Launceston in the North, features fallow deer and Tasmanian marsupials, including the giant Forester kangaroos, in their natural habitat. A road winds through the park and there are trails for bushwalking. Picnic, barbecue, and kiosk facilities are available. Closed Monday and Friday except during school holidays; open weekends only mid-June to the end of August.

Hadspen Park at Rhutherglen Holiday Village, west of Launceston on the Bass Highway, includes Tasmanian devils, wombats, and a large range of birds.

Bonorong Park at Brighton, just north of Hobart on the Midland Highway, has native Tasmanian animals, barbecue, and picnic areas.

East Coast Birdlife and Animal Park at Bicheno features pelicans, emus, rainbow lorikeets, and rare and territorial birds. Walk round the park or travel by mini train. Open daily.

Tasmanian Devil Park at Taranna near Port Arthur has native animals plus an old film of a Tasmanian tiger.

DRINKING LAWS. Under new laws, Tasmanian hotels can open for any part of a 24-hour period, but they must trade five days a week for at least eight hours on each of these days. And on Sundays many hotels are opening from noon to 8.00 P.M. Pubs near the waterfronts and in industrial suburbs open as early as 7.00 or 7.30 A.M. In the tourism mainstream they trade as late as 4.00 A.M.

SPORTS. Winter skiing, bushwalking, climbing, golf, yachting, pheasant shooting, but, above all, fishing are the sporting attractions Tasmania has to offer the visitor.

The Tasmanian snowfields have the advantage of being within about one hour's drive from the main cities so visitors can stay in town and be on the fields early next day.

Main *skiing* grounds are at Ben Lomond, 40 miles from Launceston, and Mount Field, 50 miles from Hobart. At the moment, no top class accommodation is available on the actual skifields but facilities are being developed by ski clubs and tows are in operation.

Contact the Tasbureau for information on conditions, accommodation and equipment hire. Or advance enquiries may be sent to Southern Tasmania Ski Association, GPO Box 702-G, Hobart or the Northern Tasmanian Alpine Club, P.O. Box 641, Launceston 7250.

For *golf,* Hobart's Rosny Park is the only public course offering prebooked starting times and equipment for hire. Tasmania has 60 courses, of which half require membership of an affiliated club; about 20 mostly in resorts and country clubs welcome visitors on payment of a green fee.

Fishing: Game fishing has three active clubs: Game Fishing Club of Northern Tasmania with headquarters in Launceston; The Tuna Club of Tasmania in Hobart; and the St. Helens Game Fishing Club.

The most common game fish is the southern bluefin tuna, caught off the east coast from St. Helens southwards, from late November to end of June. Other tuna common in these waters are striped tuna and the albacore.

The Yellowtail Kingfish is now being sought after; they are usually caught off the east coast but have been found around Cape Portland and the northeast coast. The Broadbill Swordfish has been sighted and Blue Pointer and one White Pointer sharks have been captured by game fishermen. Charter boats can be hired at St. Helens, Triabunna and Pirates Bay.

Saltwater fishing is available all round Tasmania. The main species caught are Australian salmon, trumpeter, perch, trevally, flounder, whiting, rock lobster, flathead, rock cod and black bream.

Along the northwest coast, *estuary fishing* is popular in the Duck, Inglis, Leven, Forth, Mersey and Rubicon Rivers; in the north east in the Mussel, Roe and Ansons Bay; at St. Helens, Scamander, the Douglas River, near Bicheno, Coles Bay, Swansea, Little Swanport and Prosser Bay on the east coast; in the Pittwater and Derwent River in the south; in the Huon River, at Dover and Southport in the Huon-Channel area; and in the Tamar River.

Surf fishing is found from the beaches of the north and east coast and on Flinders and Bruny Islands. The waters of the west coast are generally too rough.

Carp, trumpeter and members of the parrot fish family can be found by *skin diving* and *spear fishing* enthusiasts. Rock lobsters and abalone are the only salt-water fish on which there are restrictions on the number bagged. Also, licences are required for these.

Trout fishing: Tasmania's waters were stocked, first with browns, in 1864, and then with rainbows in 1896. There are about 2500 miles of streams and rivers within 40 miles of Launceston especially the Patrick River, the Macquarie River and Brumbys Weirs—which are renowned for dry fly fishing. In the Central Lakes, trolling and spinning are productive in lakes such as Sorell and Arthurs. The Lagoon of Islands has excellent rainbow. Catches of up to 10 kilos have been taken from Lake Pedder, now proving to be one of the State's best fishing areas.

Southwards, the Derwent system of impoundment gives good fishing, to *trolling and spinning.* Fly fishermen should try Bronte and Dee lagoons.

Bushwalking and climbing: Plenty of opportunities for both in the numerous national parks through Tasmania. Several local organisations welcome visitors and in some cases provide guide facilities. Contact Hobart Walking Club; Launceston Walking Club; North West Walking Club; Tasmanian Caverneering Club; Federation for Field Naturalists; Tasmanian Air Tours Association; or the nearest Tasbureau office.

Pheasant shooting is available only at a farm 45 miles out of Launceston.

 WHAT TO DO WITH THE CHILDREN. Take factory-minded youngsters on one of the factory visits listed under Industrial Tours, but note that children under 8 are not usually admitted. Watch craftsmen and artists at work at the *Maude Poynter Pottery* at Port Arthur. See copper beating at *Weeda's* in Ulverstone; join in youth activities during the *Salamanca Arts Festival* at Salamanca Place in late November. Take a ferry ride across the harbour in Hobart, or farther afield on organised cruises. Pick strawberries at *Hillwood Strawberry Farm;* visit Penny Royal World in Launceston to see a corn mill. Ride the chairlift in Launceston's *Cataract Gorge.* Inspect the *Lighthouse* at Low Head (check which days this is available). See fairy penguins at low tide on *Diamond Island* at Bicheno. See *sheep shearing* at Tullochgorum on the Esk Highway, late November. Look out for *tree figures* on the road from Oatlands northwards to Antill Ponds.

HOTELS AND MOTELS. Accommodation standards and prices in Tasmania vary from the basic (but clean), moderately priced, motel-style rooms to luxurious suites at the 2 casino-hotels. Price ranges: *Expensive:* A$50 and up; *Moderate:* A$35–50; *Inexpensive:* A$20–35.

Beauty Point

Astra Motel. *Inexpensive.* Golf courses, beach, fishing.

Beauty Point Motor Hotel. *Inexpensive.* Some cheaper rooms without private facilities. Liquor room service. Licensed restaurant. Adjacent beach, yacht club, fishing.

Bicheno

Homestead Holiday Estate. *Moderate.* Liquor room service. Licensed restaurant. Nr golf course, fishing, beach.

Silver Sands Hotel/Motel. *Moderate.* Liquor room service. Licensed restaurant. Pool. Overlooking beaches. Nr golf course. Member Flag chain.

Boat Harbour

Seaway Motel. *Moderate.* Off-season rates available. Licensed restaurant. Nr beach, national park, golf and bowling courses.

Burnie

Voyager Motor Inn. *Expensive.* Liquor room service. Licensed restaurant. Opposite beach. Nr golf, bowls, tennis. Member Flag chain.

Four Seasons Town House. *Moderate.* Liquor room service. Licensed restaurant. Member Zebra chain.

Motel Emu. *Moderate.* Pool.

Top of the Town Hotel/Motel. *Moderate.* Liquor room service. Licensed restaurant. Sauna. Nr beach, golf course.

Bayview Hotel. *Inexpensive.* Counter meals available. Cabaret Saturday night. Central, near beach.

Devonport

Gateway Motor Inn. *Expensive.* Liquor room service. Licensed restaurant. City centre. Nr beach.

Motel Argosy. *Moderate.* Liquor room service. Licensed restaurant. On main highway. Member MFA Homestead chain.

Shearwater Country Club Hotel/Motel. *Moderate.* Liquor room service. Licensed restaurant. Pool. Own golf course, tennis courts. Nr beach.

Sunrise Motel. *Moderate.* Near to the beach. A member MFA Homestead chain.

Hotel Formby. *Inexpensive.* Some cheaper rooms without facilities. Licensed restaurant. Nr beach, golf course.

Eaglehawk Neck

Penzance Motel. *Moderate.* Liquor room service. Licensed restaurant. 24 hr food service. Nr beach, two golf links, historic buildings.

Lufra Hotel Motel. *Inexpensive.* Licensed restaurant. Surf beach. Nr historic Port Arthur.

George Town

Mt. George Motor Hotel. *Moderate.* Includes hot breakfast. Licensed restaurant. Nr beach, golf course.

King Island

King Island Boomerang Motel. *Moderate.* Adjacent bowls, tennis courts.

Launceston

Launceston Federal Country Club Casino. *Deluxe/Expensive.* Casino, licensed restaurants, cabaret, pool, saunas, golf, tennis, squash.

Colonial Motor Inn. *Expensive.* Corner George/Elizabeth Streets. Licensed restaurant.

Four Seasons Great Northern Motor Inn. *Expensive.* Licensed restaurant features old tram.

Penny Royal Watermill. *Expensive.* 147 Paterson St. Atmospheric, restored and converted old watermill. Liquor room service. Licensed restaurant. Nr the Gorge. Has antique and gift shop and corn mill museum.

Abel Tasman Motor Inn. *Moderate.* 303 Hobart Road. Includes light breakfast. Nr golf course, airport.

Batman Fawkner Hotel. *Moderate.* 39 Cameron St. Liquor room service. 24 hr room service. No restaurant. Central.

Coach House Motel. *Moderate.* Kitchen facilities in rooms. Member Flag chain.

Commodore. *Moderate.* 13 Brisbane St. Liquor room service. Licensed restaurant. Opposite city park.

Hotel Tasmania. *Moderate.* 191 Charles St. Liquor room service. Licensed restaurant.

Launceston Hotel. *Moderate.* 107 Brisbane St. Liquor room service. Licensed restaurant. 24 hr room service.

Parklane Motel. *Moderate.* 9 Brisbane St. Kitchen facilities in room. Opposite parkland. Central. Member, Flag chain.

Riverside Motor Inn. *Moderate.* West Tamar Road. Includes light breakfast. Licensed restaurant. Nr golf, swimming pool, tennis courts.

St. James Hotel. *Moderate.* 122 York St. Licensed restaurant.

Village Motor Inn. *Moderate.* Westbury Road. Liquor room service. Licensed restaurant. Pool. Member Flag chain.

New Norfolk

Amaroo Motel. *Moderate.* Off-season rates available. Liquor room service. Licensed restaurant. 2 hr food service. Nr golf course.

Port Arthur

Four Seasons Motor Hotel. *Moderate.* Licensed restaurant. Member of Zebra chain.

Fox and Hound. *Moderate.* Licensed restaurant.

Queenstown

Four Seasons Silver Hills Motel. *Moderate.* Licensed restaurant.

Penny Royal Queenstown. *Moderate.* Motel or self-contained units.

Southport Motor Hotel. *Moderate.* Licensed restaurant. Central.

Southport Motor Lodge. *Moderate.* Licensed restaurant.

Westcoaster. *Moderate.* Licensed restaurant.

Savage River

Savage River Motor Inn. *Inexpensive.* Licensed restaurant. Nr Pieman River.

Scamander

Four Seasons Motor Hotel. *Moderate.* Licensed restaurant. Pool. Nr ocean beach.

Surfside Motel. *Moderate.* Licensed restaurant. Pool. Nr beach, golf course. Member MFA Homestead chain.

Smithton

Bridge Hotel-Motel. *Moderate.* Licensed.

St. Helens

Bayside Inn. *Moderate.* Coffee-makers, color TV, electric blankets, refrigerators. Licensed restaurant.

St. Helens Hotel/Motel. *Inexpensive.* Off-season rates available. Liquor room service. Licensed restaurant. Nr beaches, golf, bowls.

Swansea

Swan Motor Inn. *Expensive.* Liquor room service. Licensed restaurant. On beach. Nr golf, bowls.

Ulverstone

Beachway Motel. *Moderate.* Rate includes hot breakfast. Pool.

Stone's Hotel. *Inexpensive.* Rate includes hot breakfast. Liquor room service. Licensed restaurant.

Cradle Valley

Pencil Pine Lodge. *Moderate.* Hotel or cabin facilities. Licensed restaurant. On boundary Cradle Mountain national park.

Wynyard

Southport Motor Lodge. *Moderate.* Liquor room service. Licensed restaurant. Nr beach, golf.

Zeehan

Heemskirk Motor Hotel. *Moderate.* Licensed restaurant.

DINING OUT. Price ranges (3-course meal, excluding wine): *Expensive:* A$25 and up; *Moderate:* A$15–25; *Inexpensive:* A$6–15.

Burnie

Raindrop Room. *Expensive.* Extensive menu, children's servings available. Licensed. Serves breakfast, lunch and dinner.
Martini. *Moderate.* International cuisine, licensed; crayfish (lobster) mornay a specialty.

Campbell Town

Campbell Town Inn. Historic building. Lunches Mon-Fri.

Coles Bay

The Chateau. *Inexpensive.* Family place, fresh vegetables.

Devonport

Ruby's. *Expensive.* International cuisine, licensed, intimate cottage atmosphere.

George Town

The Grove. Historic building. Local dishes. Closed in evening.

Launceston

Aristocrat. Specialises in Greek dishes. BYO.
Matador. Spanish decor. Varied menu.
Penny Royal Watermill. Traditional English food in Owls Nest restaurant.
Shrimps. Licensed, seafood specialty.
Woofies. Macquarie House, Civic Square. A la carte, licensed.

Port Arthur

The Broad Arrow. Crayfish a specialty.

Port Sorell

Shearwater Country Club Hotel/Motel. Holiday club atmosphere, barbecues, smorgasbords round the pool. Dining and dancing at night.

Queenstown

Westcoaster Motor Inn. *Moderate.* Local fish and Tasmanian cheese.

Ross

Scotch Thistle Inn. Old world charm. Good food and wines.

Smithton

The Bridge Hotel. Choose your own steak.

Swansea

The Swan Hotel/Motel. Renowned for smorgasbord but book ahead.

NEW ZEALAND

NEW ZEALAND

Land of the Long White Cloud

by
JOHN P. CAMPBELL

A New Zealander, the author has traveled to every part of his country through his work with the New Zealand Tourist and Publicity Department. Currently focusing on travel writing, he contributes to a number of publications, including Travel Digest.

To think of the South Pacific is to conjure up visions of tropical isles, warm sandy beaches, waving palms, exotic forests, colorful Polynesians and lilting music. As a South Pacific country New Zealand has all these; yet it also contradicts the popular image. Its scenery rivals the best of other parts of the world, but it also has fine modern cities, and is a major exporter of food and manufactured products.

The atlas shows New Zealand as a slender, slanted outline close to the bottom of the world. Astride a line midway between the Equator and the South Pole, it appears small and isolated in the vast Pacific Ocean. In shape, it resembles California; in size it exceeds Britain and equals the area of Colorado. On the map, New Zealand seems to be dwarfed by the vast neighbouring continent of Australia; but Australia lies 1,200 miles to the west, and it is a source of pained but resigned irritation to New Zealanders that the two are often linked by the misleading term "Australasia". Naturally, there is some affinity between the two peoples, but

Australia and New Zealand are quite distinct, each having an individual character and landscape.

New Zealand comprises three main islands: the North Island (44,197 square miles); the South Island (58,170 square miles); and Stewart Island (676 square miles). From north to south the country is about 1,000 miles long, and no point is more than 70 miles from the sea. Two-thirds is mountainous; a region of swift-flowing rivers, deep alpine lakes and dense subtropical forest—known locally as "bush".

Lying almost half-way between the Equator and the South Pole, New Zealand has the best of both climatic worlds. The climate ranges from subtropical in the north to temperate in the south. There are no extremes of heat or cold, and snow is usually confined to the mountains and high country. Rainfall levels vary; but since rainy days are evenly distributed throughout the year, there is no unduly wet season to be avoided.

Topsy-Turvy Topography

To those living in the Northern Hemisphere New Zealand is an upside-down country. The north is warmer than the south and the seasons are reversed: summer is from December to March, fall from April to May, winter from June to August, and spring from September to November. Even the visitor's sense of time needs adjustment. New Zealand has a universal time zone, set 12 hours ahead of Greenwich Mean Time; which puts it ahead of most other places too: noon in New Zealand is 7 P.M. the previous day in New York, for instance. In the summer period, the difference is increased by one hour by New Zealand Daylight Saving Time, which extends from the last Sunday in October to the first Sunday in the following March.

New Zealanders like to think of their home as "God's own country." After creating the world, they say, He decided to make one ideal country for His own special enjoyment. And so He formed New Zealand, chiselled high mountains and sprinkled them with snow, gouged out deep fiords, filled the hollows with aquamarine lakes fed by fast-flowing clear rivers, clothed the slopes with thick verdant forest or lush grass, and plumbed beneath the earth's crust for geysers to serve as steam heating. He banished all deadly creatures—there are no snakes, poisonous insects, or dangerous wild animals, so even the thickest forest is entirely safe. For added security, He placed the country far from quarrelling nations.

For thousands of years, after its last land bridges sank beneath the Pacific, New Zealand remained isolated. Evolution went its curious way, undisturbed by man or beast except for sea-blown birds from other lands. Safe from predators, some birds became lazy and abandoned flight. Gradually their wings atrophied to small stumps and they walked the earth for their food. Best known is the kiwi (pronounced *kee-wee*, and named for its cry), which has become, although unofficially, New Zealand's national emblem. New Zealanders are sometimes referred to, and refer to themselves, as "Kiwis". About the size of a young turkey and rounded in shape, the Kiwi has strong legs and an unusually long bill with two nostrils close to the tip, which it pokes about in the undergrowth in search of grubs. Being nocturnal, it is seldom seen in the wild, but there are several places where it can be viewed in specially constructed houses.

An emu-like bird ten feet in height, the *moa,* once grazed in New Zealand. A main source of Maori food, and materials for clothing, it was hunted to extinction. The tuatara lizard, about 18 inches long and with a third vestigial eye, is a living fossil. It evolved before the giant dinosaurs roamed the earth, lives a hundred years or more, and still exists as a protected species on certain offshore islands.

Finding the Forgotten

Even today, because parts of the country are so heavily forested and difficult to explore, species which were believed to be extinct are occasionally discovered. In 1948 the *takahe,* a type of swamp bird, was rediscovered in the wild country of the southern fiords. Naturalists are now nurturing a small colony to save the species from final extinction. Today, about 75% of New Zealand's native flora is unique, and includes some of the world's oldest plant forms.

This was the virginal land first sighted by the adventurous Polynesian voyagers some 600 years ago. They called New Zealand by a more colorful name—*Aotearoa* ("Land of the Long White Cloud"). To them, near death from thirst and starvation in their sea-battered canoes on a migratory voyage across hundreds of miles of ocean, the land first appeared as a long, low white cloud on the horizon. To Abel Tasman, the first European to sight New Zealand, it appeared as "a great land uplifted high."

Both descriptions are apt. As you approach by air, New Zealand often does appear as a long low cloud joining the sky and the sea, especially when you are flying from Australia to Christchurch and the long line of the Southern Alps rises to meet you.

New Zealand was unknown to Europeans until 1642 when Abel Tasman, the Dutch navigator, sighted it when seeking a southern continent. He had trouble with the Maoris, however, and sailed away after drawing a wavy line as a crude chart. He gave the land the name of *Nieuw Zeeland.* No one was interested until 1769, when Captain Cook and a Frenchman, De Surville, rediscovered it almost simultaneously; though neither was aware of the other's presence on the opposite side of the islands. It was Cook who circumnavigated New Zealand and found that Tasman's wavy line was actually a group of islands. In general, his chart is amazingly accurate.

From 1790 onwards, adventurous Europeans arrived to take lumber, flax, whales and seals, and lonely settlements grew up in Northland and on the West Coast of the South Island. They were wild, lawless and isolated. The main European settlement and headquarters for the whaling fleets was Russell (then known as *Kororareka*) in the Bay of Islands. It became known as "the hell hole of the Pacific."

The newcomers traded muskets with the Maoris, and the traditional inter-tribal wars became blood-baths. But the newly-introduced European diseases took a heavier toll. Thousands of Maoris, having no immunity, died from epidemics of normally minor ailments, such as influenza and measles.

Arrival of "Law and Order"

Pressure was growing on Britain to make New Zealand a colony. The churches urged protection of the Maori people, and colonial reform organisations, which had bought land for settlements, wanted action. In addition, there was concern that the French, who had taken considerable interest in the country since De Surville's visit, might annex it.

Finally, the British Government acted by sending Captain William Hobson as Governor. On February 6, 1840, a week after his arrival, he officiated at the signing of the Treaty of Waitangi, by which the Maoris ceded sovereignty to the British Crown in return for the protection of law and order, and the rights of ownership of their traditional lands and fisheries for all time.

This event is regarded as the beginning of modern New Zealand history and the date is still observed as New Zealand's National Day. An impressive ceremony is held each year on this day at Waitangi in the shadow of the Treaty House, now an historic trust.

Britain's hand had also been forced by the New Zealand Company, formed in London to colonise the country with or without the consent of the Government. The first settlers arrived at Port Nicholson, now Wellington, on January 22, 1840. New Plymouth was founded in 1841, Nelson the following year, Dunedin by dissident Presbyterians in 1848, and Christchurch by the Church of England in 1850.

Then features of American history began to repeat themselves. Disputes over land developed between the settlers and the Maoris, culminating in the "Land Wars" of 1860. They flared up spasmodically for years, and the last sparks were not extinguished until 1872. There were many incidents of heroism and chivalry, as well as ruthlessness and cruelty, on both sides. The British Army Regulars never quite succeeded in subduing the Maoris. There was no final decisive battle. The conflict just gradually petered out. Technically, the settlers won, but the Maoris were never forced to a surrender as a beaten foe. Nor were they confined to nominated areas or reservations. Today the two peoples live as one.

The early settlers used English methods of arable farming, but the New Zealand countryside was not England. Except for Canterbury, the land was undulating or semi-mountainous, much of it thickly covered with native forest. Cultivation was formidable and backbreaking toil. When the land was eventually cleared they turned their efforts to sheep farming. Then gold was discovered in Otago in 1861, and on the West Coast of the South Island in 1865. Prospectors came in their thousands from Australia and North America. The gold-rush was short-lived, but it gave the South Island a lead in commercial and political development.

The Iceman Cometh

Then came an invention which was to ensure New Zealand's future prosperity—refrigeration. Now her farming could export not only wool, but also perishable items, such as meat, butter and cheese. The first shipment to Britain was made in 1882, and was a success. The cornerstone of New Zealand's economy was laid.

The heart of New Zealand's success in agriculture lies in its ability to grow superb grass and clovers, although the land as a whole is not rich in fertile soil. The large meat and milk-producing pastures are due to a climate which combines a remarkably even rainfall distribution with plentiful sunshine. Careful land management and regular applications of fertiliser from the air (known as topdressing) enhance these natural advantages.

The efficient New Zealand farmer applies modern business techniques and an impressive array of machinery. Electricity, which is available even in the remotest farming settlements, runs milking machines, shearing shed apparatus and irrigation machinery. New Zealand makes its own aircraft for aerial topdressing, as well as equipment for haymaking, ploughing, sowing and reaping. In addition, the farmer is backed by comprehensive Government advisory and research services.

Agricultural exports provide the major source of the country's income. It has become the biggest exporter of sheep meat and dairy products in the world, and the second largest exporter of wool. These three agricultural commodities account for 75% of the country's total exports, and a wide and expanding range of annual crops is also grown. More efficient use is now made of land. One-third of the total land mass is sown in grass, one-third can be described as marginal agricultural land (supporting grazing stock or planted in commercial forests), and the remainder is mountainous.

27% of the farms are smaller than 100 acres and include dairy and pig farms as well as vegetable producers. Farms of 5,000 acres or more make up 48 percent of utilised land. Many of these cover steep hill country that cannot be cultivated by machinery, but provide good grazing for sheep and cattle.

New Zealand is ideally suited to sheep farming. High-country farms concentrate on wool, while the more fertile lowlands (carrying up to 5 sheep per acre, and sometimes even more) raise lamb and mutton. With over 55 million sheep, it is not surprising that New Zealand is the third largest producer and second largest exporter of wool in the world. It is also the world's largest lamb and mutton exporter, contributing 65% of the market, and rears 6.5 million beef cattle.

Because of the equable climate, dairy stock do not have to be housed in winter, and grass grows the year round. There are some 2,080,000 cows in milk in New Zealand. Butter and cheese are the main dairy exports, followed by casein and skim milk powder.

Tamarillos, Feijoas and Passion Fruit

Most grain crops are grown for local consumption, but the large orchards in the sunny, dry and fertile areas of Hawke's Bay, Nelson and Central Otago, grow peaches, nectarines, plums, cherries and berry fruits for both local needs and export. Subtropical fruits (tamarillos, feijoas, Kiwi fruit and passion fruit) are grown in the north and air-freighted to overseas markets. Tobacco is grown in Nelson and blended with imported leaf to supply the local market.

Until World War II New Zealand was content to concentrate on agriculture and to import most of the manufactured goods it needed. Suddenly, sources of supply diminished or were cut off completely, and the manufacture of some essential goods began. This development continued after the war, and today New Zealand exports a wide range of manufactured articles to many parts of the world. About a quarter of the labor force is involved in manufacture, though most of the factories are small by overseas standards.

The biggest growths have been in light engineering, electronics, textile and leather goods, rubber goods, plastics, building materials, pottery and glassware, and furniture. One of the largest developments has been in carpets. High quality tufted and woven all-woollen carpets, made chiefly from the fleece of New Zealand crossbred sheep, have proved popular overseas.

Two recent major projects have been the establishment of a steel industry near Auckland to mine the extensive deposits of ironsand, and a large aluminum smelter in the lower part of the South Island. Another massive industry now exports pulp, newsprint, wood chips and lumber from the huge pine forests of the central North Island. Aided by a plentiful supply of labor during the depression in the 1930s, the New Zealand Forest Service (a Government Department) and private companies planted nearly 700,000 acres of *radiata* pine trees, which mature in New Zealand in about 25 years (much faster than in their native American habitat). The plantations include one of the world's largest man-made forests, the Kaingaroa Forest, which covers more than 364,000 acres. The harvesting, processing, and planting of these trees is now one of the country's major industries.

New Zealand takes pride in its harmonious race relations. There is no segregation or discrimination. The Race Relations Act of 1971 affirms and promotes racial equality, implementing the resolutions of International Convention on the elimination of all forms of racial discrimination. Discrimination on grounds of color, race, or national origins is unlawful, and it is an offence to incite racial conflict. A breach of any of the Act's provisions may be investigated by the Race Relations Conciliator, who is also empowered to intervene in racial misunderstandings.

Where Maori and English Mingle

While English is the universal language, the Maoris often use their own tongue in conversation or on special occasions. Interest in the language is reviving, and a number of educational institutions conduct courses in Maori, which are also attended by Europeans. Maori words are increasingly used in everyday conversation. "Pakeha", meaning "non-Maori", often applied to those of European origin, is perhaps the most common. A popular phrase is "kia ora" or "good luck".

A distinctive New Zealand accent and vocabulary have evolved. Perhaps the most familiar phrase is the all-purpose "fair go," which can be used, for instance, as an expression of surprise ("is that so?") or to mean a reasonable chance (as in, "give the man a fair go."). Another phrase frequently heard is, "She'll be right, mate", equivalent to "That's OK, buddy."

Although, like any other country, New Zealand is not free from crime, police do not carry guns on routine duty.

New Zealand is also fortunate in having almost entirely escaped the massive pollution problems which have beset heavily industrialised and densely populated countries, but is conscious that this good fortune must be backed by sound and imaginative environmental protection. To control growing pressures on natural resources the Government has strengthened anti-pollution measures. These include a Commission for the Environment, the appointment of non-governmental advisory bodies, and the requirement that major Government development plans be assessed for environmental impact, giving the public an opportunity to comment on proposals before decisions are taken. An increasing number of New Zealanders are working to ensure that their country avoids the errors that have been made elsewhere and safeguards its unique natural heritage.

From a population of only a little over three million, New Zealand has produced some internationally-known figures: Lord Rutherford, the first man to split the atom; Sir Edmund Hillary, conqueror of Mount Everest; Sir William Liley, who introduced the principle of early blood transfusions for Rh ("blue blood") babies; and in the field of sport John Walker, the first man to run a mile in less than 3 minutes 50 seconds.

Long Live the Queen

Although established as a British colony, New Zealand quickly achieved self-government and has long been a fully independent nation, and remains a member of the British Commonwealth by choice. The Head of State is Queen Elizabeth II, who is represented by a resident Governor General, appointed for a term of five years.

The New Zealand Parliament has a single chamber, the House of Representatives, comprising 92 members, amongst whom are four Maori members elected directly by Maori voters. The head of government is the Prime Minister, who is always the leader of the successful political party.

From the 1880s, New Zealand has often led the way in social welfare. It has even been described as "a welfare state which looks after its people from the cradle to the grave." This is neither Communism nor Socialism, but rather a sort of benign paternalism. Democracy and the capitalist system are alive and well in New Zealand.

New Zealand pioneered statutory provision for age benefits and has a system of benefits providing for general family welfare and all contingencies arising from sickness, accident, unemployment, death of a breadwinner and old age. The aim is to ensure that all citizens have a reasonable standard of living and that they are safeguarded against economic ills from which they may be unable to protect themselves.

The social security system includes a full range of health services. Public hospital treatment and maternity services are free, as is nearly all prescribed medicine. The State pays varying amounts towards the cost of medical attention, and contributes a portion of doctors' fees and private hospital expenses. School children receive free dental care from clinics.

Recent legislation provides compensation for accidents, and applies not only to New Zealanders but also to visitors from overseas. Upon arrival the visitor is covered, without charge, for personal injury by accident for 24 hours a day, even if the accident is his own fault, and wherever it occurs. Cover ceases when the visitor leaves the country.

If anyone suffers personal injury by accident, entitlement to compensation and rehabilitation (in New Zealand) is absolute, not determined by lengthy and costly litigation to determine fault or negligence. Consequently, an action for damages in respect of injury cannot be brought in any court in New Zealand. The right to bring such actions has been abolished.

Influence of the Military

Though far from Europe, New Zealand has not escaped its conflicts. In World War I New Zealand fought beside Britain, and more than 10 per cent of its 1,000,000 population of that time served overseas, 17,000 men being killed. World War II cost another heavy contribution in manpower and resources. In fact, the country mobilised a higher proportion of able-bodied men than any allied nation except Russia. Its land forces fought in Greece, Crete, North Africa, Italy and the Pacific, and more than 140,000 served overseas.

New Zealand became vulnerable as the Japanese began moving across the Pacific, but it did not recall its troops from the Middle East. Instead, it became a base for American forces. The Second Marine Division was based in Wellington, and it was from there that they embarked for what was to become the blood-bath of Guadalcanal. Many New Zealanders whose sons were fighting overseas took Americans into their homes and adopted them as their own, and when news of the grim casualties came back an air of grief enveloped the city. Many of the wounded returned to Wellington for recuperation, and some returned after the war, married New Zealand girls, and settled.

The years since 1945 have seen New Zealand's increasing involvement in international affairs, particularly through the United Nations, of which it is a founder member. New Zealand's horizons in diplomacy, defence co-operation and foreign aid to less-developed nations have been greatly extended. Inherited traditions of democracy and social concern have been moulded into a distinctive national character which, though introspective, in some respects, also welcomes contacts with the world beyond its shores.

In 1984, the New Zealand Labor Party came into power, pledging to make the nation a nuclear-free zone. This has led to a certain amount of tension between New Zealand and U.S. governments, since it could mean that American warships will be banned from New Zealand waters.

SEEING THE BEST OF NEW ZEALAND

It is easy to be misled by looking at New Zealand on an atlas. It appears smaller than it really is, especially when compared with its much larger neighbor Australia. But don't allow its size to persuade you that it can be seen in three or four days by taking excursions from the main cities. Its varied attractions are scattered throughout the thousand-mile length of the two islands, and are often remote from major cities.

New Zealand is roughly the same area as Colorado, and similar to California in shape. Visitors will miss a great deal if they do not allow enough time to see the best of both the North and South Islands. It is possible to glimpse some of the highlights in a week, but having invested in the cost of reaching New Zealand the wise traveler will allocate at least ten days or two weeks, or perhaps even longer.

Climatically and scenically, the islands are like two entirely different countries. Writing in the *National Geographic Magazine,* the well-known author Peter Benchley said New Zealand has "alps that rival Switzerland's, fiords reminiscent of Norway's, beaches as alluring as California's, plains more fruitful than England's, streams as laden with fish as Scotland's" and that it was "a pleasant, peaceful and robust bit of Europe in the South Pacific."

Because he was writing only about the South Island he did not catalog the unusual attractions of the North Island—the weird thermal geysers and mudpools, the mildly active volcanos, and the unique Glow-worm Grotto.

The only satisfactory way to enjoy these attractions is to travel progressively from place to place.

New Zealand's charms lie in the countryside, mountains and fiords rather than in the cities. In terms of European settlement, New Zealand is less than a century and a half old. So there are no ancient historic buildings, museums or art galleries; no quaint and colorful festivals based on historical events or native customs and religions.

Certainly, at least one day should be spent in the major cities, each of which has its own individuality and charm, but most of the time should be devoted to the scenic areas.

Driving for Fun

The main cities are linked by road, air and rail, but many of the most beautiful regions are in the mountain fastnesses and can be reached only by road or air. Because of the varied countryside, road travel is exciting. There are no long monotonous distances to be covered. Because of the hilly to mountainous terrain the roads weave through an ever-changing landscape, bordered by lush green pastures dotted with sheep and cattle, or clothed in native forest.

All the main roads and most of the secondary roads are sealed, well maintained and signposted, with route numbers. New Zealand has changed to the metric system, and all road signs are now in kilometers. To convert kilometers to miles, divide by 8 and multiply by 5; e.g., 80 kms. per hour (the legal speed limit) equals 50 mph.

Some of the road signs, which are peculiar to New Zealand, will cause amusement. For instance: "Dangerous Curves", "Soft Shoulders", "Beware of the Wind", and "Metal Road Ahead", (which means that the sealing ends for a stretch and is replaced by a gravel surface).

Road travel does, however, pose a problem to those with limited time. Although distances are not great, travelling times are longer than one might expect, as there are few long straight stretches and, in the interests of conserving fuel, all of which has to be imported, there is a speed restriction of 50mph on all roads. A combination of air and car travel is sometimes the best means, but there are also well-organised coach tours and scheduled road services, as well as courier-driver automobiles.

Every now and then you'll encounter flocks of sheep being driven to new pastures by a drover and a team of sheep dogs. The sheep outnumber New Zealanders by 80 to 1, so they have some right to the road! It is intriguing to see the dogs clear a way in obedience to the whistled, and sometimes forcefully vocal, commands of their owner. Or you may meet a herd of cows on their way to the afternoon milking.

If you are accustomed to the congested highways of America and Europe you'll be pleasantly surprised at the light traffic density. It is not due to the lack of automobiles—New Zealand is the third most highly motorised country in the world—but to the size of the population, which is small in relation to the size of the country.

Throughout New Zealand the air is clean and fresh, there are no extremes of heat and cold, and no health hazards. The water everywhere can safely be drunk from the tap, and there are no snakes, dangerous wild animals or poisonous insects.

To the English-speaking visitor language is no problem. English is the common language of all New Zealanders, Maoris included, although many still converse in their own tongue.

New Zealand has retained a large number of Maori place names. They appear formidable, but they are easily pronounced if they are broken into syllables, remembering to give each vowel its full value and that all words must end with a vowel. For instance, Lake Waikaremoana "(Sea of Rippling Waters") breaks down into: Wy–carry–mo–ana". The word Maori is pronounced "Mau-ree", with the accent on the first syllable, not "May-ori".

Getting Around Fairly Easy

New Zealand has an efficient network of air, road, rail and sea transport. The major domestic air carriers are the government-financed Air New Zealand, which uses Boeing 737 jets and F27 Fokker Friendship turbo-jet aircraft and services the main cities and provincial centers. Servicing the prime scenic resorts such as Rotorua, Mount Cook, and Queenstown are Mount Cook Airlines and Newmans Air. Mount Cook Airlines also continues to Te Anau in Fiordland. Modern motor coaches are used on coach tours and scheduled services, and the New Zealand Railways, Government owned, link the main and subsidiary centers. Group tours are operated by several companies. Rental cars are available at all the main centers, but the visitor should note that traffic travels on the left of the road. Motor caravans and campervans may be rented at the main centers.

THE NEW ZEALANDERS

From a Common Nationality

by
JOHN P. CAMPBELL

A survey of visitors' impressions carried out by the Pacific Area Travel Association showed that memories of "a warm, friendly people" did much to account for New Zealand's popularity with travellers in the South Pacific. Friendliness is undoubtedly one of its greatest charms. New Zealanders are fiercely proud of their country, and they enjoy sharing its delights with others. To them, a visitor is a guest—not just another tourist. The growth of tourism has not affected the New Zealander's spontaneous willingness to go out of his way to welcome and assist the visitor. His nature has enabled the people to become a distinctive, unique nation.

Like America, New Zealand accepted immigrants from European countries. Some established their own settlements: people from Norway farmed at Norsewood, Danes at Dannevirke, and Yugoslavs (then known as Dalmatians) formed communities north of Auckland to dig for the gum of the kauri tree, grow grapes, and make wine.

But, unlike American immigrants, such communities did not remain as individual and self-contained ethnic transplants. They became integrated. Though some communities retain traces of the origin of their early settlers (Scottish names are still common in Dunedin, for example), the modern generation is united by its pride in a common nationality.

Intermarriage between Maoris and Europeans is increasing. There are few full-blooded Maoris today, and most have adopted European names. Although there can be no "typical" New Zealander any more than there can be a "typical" American or German, certain characteristics have emerged as a result of the comparatively recent European settlement of the country, and its relative isolation from other lands.

The early settlers, and those who followed them, left Britain to escape from overcrowded slums, the limitations imposed by class barriers, and the lack of economic opportunity. These motives have formed the New Zealand character, and an egalitarian society. Few are very rich and none are really poor. There are no slums or tenements, and by overseas standards, unemployment is very low.

The Unimportance of Position

An egalitarian attitude is universal. New Zealanders do not take kindly to servility. The boss is never "Sir", but "Mr.", and is often known by his first name. Never call a waitress "Miss"—a polite "excuse me" will do the trick.

New Zealanders cannot abide being addressed by their surnames only; to them, this would imply inferiority. The title "Mr." is always used until first name terms are reached; which happens quickly, if not immediately. They value and respect people for themselves, not social status or wealth, which leave them unimpressed.

Most New Zealanders live well. Almost every family has television (color broadcasting began in 1974), and more than one radio. There is a telephone to every two people, and an automobile to every three. Most kitchens have electric or gas appliances, and most homes have washing machines.

Housing is generally of high quality, for New Zealanders spend much money and time on their homes. Seven out of ten are owner-occupied. The typical dwelling is a single-storey detached house, standing in its own garden of about one-eighth acre, although many town plots are smaller. It has a floor space of between 1,000 to 1,500 square feet; divided into three bedrooms, living room, dining room, kitchen, bathroom and laundry. Although multi-storeyed blocks are numerous, an apartment (usually called a "flat") is often part of a single-storey building.

Food is good and plentiful. The advanced agricultural economy and the temperate climate ensure a supply of meat and dairy products, and a great variety of fruit and vegetables is available throughout the year.

Rah Rah for Rugby

The New Zealander is an avid do-it-yourselfer and improviser—perhaps as an inheritance from pioneering days, when many articles were in short supply and most of the manufactured goods were imported, and therefore costly. He begrudges paying for his house to be painted or wallpapered, for concreting or carpentry, and minor repairs. He is an ingenious improviser if the proper materials are not to hand, or are, in his view, too expensive. Yet he is quick to accept innovations which will make life easier or more enjoyable. Making use of the fertile land and equable climate, he usually grows vegetables, and fills his home with blooms from the flower garden.

is leisure time. His
very Saturday and
Mondayised," mak-
outdoor man, he
ance of open space
ve. Popular sports
ound in the rivers
d mountains; and
ealanders sail: the
an-going yachts.
er cities contain
for no beach or

tball and horse
y overseas as a
who are named
y in school, and
ttended. As a
the ubiquitous
ew Zealander
alisator (pari-
many off-track

emands the
ucracy, but
y guards the
y not admit
ge fortune.
rather than
is pride of
er sophisti-
and is the

ne from.
y voyage
thought
ved that
theory
ositions

t long-
Maori

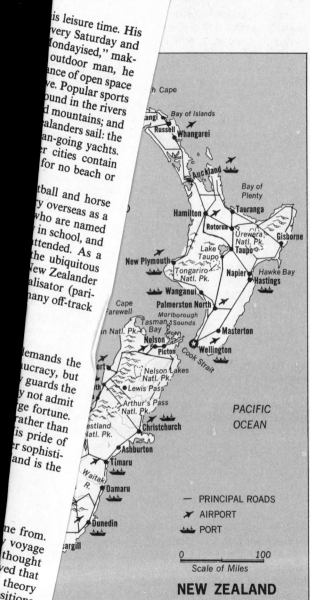

PRINCIPAL ROADS
AIRPORT
PORT

0   100
Scale of Miles

NEW ZEALAND

The New Zealander prizes and makes full use of h
jealously guarded five-day working week gives him e
Sunday free, and many public holidays have been "M
ing them long weekends. By nature essentially an
prefers participating in sports to watching. The abund
makes many kinds of recreation possible and inexpensi
include fishing for rainbow and brown trout, which ab
and lakes; hiking (known as "tramping") in the hills an
skiing. With the sea never far from home, many New Z
harbors and lakes are dotted with small boats and oce
Golf is also enormously popular, and even the larg
courses. Uncluttered beaches and picnic spots abound,
river may be privately owned.

But New Zealand's greatest passions are Rugby foo
racing. It is every boy's ambition to represent his counti
member of the "All Blacks", the national rugby team,
for their black jerseys. Young New Zealanders play rugby
many continue in later life. Matches are always well-a
spectator sport, horse racing takes pride of place, and
racecourses are crowded. Bookmaking is illegal, but the N
enjoys the thrill of testing his judgment against the tot
mutuel) at the courses, or placing his bets with one of the n
agencies in the cities and towns.

Rugged Country, Rugged Individualists

Above all, the New Zealander is an individualist. He
right to shape his own life as he wishes, and dislikes bure
believes it is inevitable and sometimes necessary. He jealousl
social and industrial benefits he has won; but, although he ma
it, he is more interested in enjoying life than amassing a la
Though at first he may appear a little reserved, he welcomes
resents strangers—just as long as they like New Zealand. H
country is deep, and though he may sometimes envy the great
cation of other nations, he steadfastly believes that New Zeal
best country in the world.

THE MAORI PEOPLE

No one really knows where the Maori people originally ca
Tradition has it that they sailed to New Zealand in a migrator
from a land they called Hawaiki, which was not Hawaii but is
to have been the Society Islands near Tahiti. It is generally belie
the islands of the Pacific were peopled from Asia, although on
is that the first settlers came from South America. All three prop
are matters of scholarly discussion and debate.

One thing is sure—the Polynesians were among the greates
distance sailors in the world. As Witi Ihimaera, a well-known
author, says in his book *Maori*:

"Long before Europeans ventured out of sight of land, thes
bold and restless ancestors of the Maori were making voyage
whether deliberate or accidental, of thousands of miles acros

the world's greatest ocean. Star-reading experts with remarkably efficient systems of navigation based on full knowledge of the trade winds and ocean currents, they gradually peopled a vast oceanic world."

If the traditional legend of migration is to be believed—and most New Zealanders, both Maori and *pakeha* (the Maori word for white man) would prefer to—it exemplifies the adventurous spirit, courage, stamina, and intelligence of the Maori.

Legend relates that the first Polynesian voyager to sight New Zealand was Kupe about 950 AD, who returned to Hawaiki and gave sailing instructions which were later followed by the migrating canoes. It is said that the next to come was Toi, in about 1150.

One of the reasons for our lack of positive knowledge is that the Maori had no written language. History was passed down by word of mouth, usually in the form of chants *(waiata)*. There was room, therefore, for imaginative embellishment.

Maori tradition has it that the great migration from eastern Polynesia took place about 1350 in seven canoes. They were named: *Tainui, Te Arawa, Aotea, Tokomaru, Takitimu, Mataatua,* and *Kurahaupo.* It is from these voyagers that most Maori claim their descent. About 40 tribes developed and were further divided into sub-tribes, and most Maori continue to express their identity in terms of their geographical and genealogical links.

No one knows why the migration took place, but it may well have been due to overpopulation and a shortage of food. If the great migration theory is believed, however, it is clear that the Maori knew of the existence of New Zealand and navigated to it in a voyage covering hundreds of miles—a remarkable achievement.

There is evidence that the immigrants found a race of Polynesians, the *Moriori,* living in New Zealand when they arrived. Where that race came from no one has the least idea, except that they were also Polynesians. Having an abundance of food from the *moa* (a huge, emu-like bird), other flightless birds, and fish from the sea, the Moriori lived peacefully. The more warlike Maori soon drove them farther and farther south until they eventually disappeared or were absorbed by intermarriage.

The Maori brought with him the *kumara,* a variety of sweet potato, the dog, and the rat. These were the first mammals to live in New Zealand. The Maori had an abundance of fish and birds, and established agriculture.

From these beginnings emerged a distinctive Maori culture and well-ordered tribal society, led by hereditary chiefs and a powerful priesthood.

The Maori lived in fortified villages *(pa),* usually built on a strategic land eminence which would give the occupants an advantage over attackers. Within palisades they built sleeping and eating houses and a main meeting house, all focused on a main courtyard, the *marae.* The *marae* was an important part of the village. It was here, in front of the meeting house *(whare runanga),* that matters of importance were debated and decided and that visitors were received.

Lore of the Tribes

The *marae* retains that importance and function today. Though they now live in European-style homes, any large settlement of Maoris will have a meeting house and a *marae* on which any important visitors will be received, and an ancient and impressive greeting ritual is still followed.

The visitors stand at the entrance to the *marae* as a warrior from the resident tribe advances, grimacing fearfully and brandishing a type of long club *(taiaha)*. He places a sprig of greenery at the strangers' feet and cautiously retires. If the visitors pick up the sprig they come in peace; if not, it is war. If the first, the visitors are greeted with a song of welcome. Even today the ceremony is treated with respect, and the audience is asked not to applaud when it is performed at Maori concerts.

Each tribe was headed by a chief, *ariki* or *rangitira,* whose prestige *(mana)* was believed to have been inherited from his predecessors. There was also a high priest, the *tohunga,* who was thought to be close to the gods and was credited with supernatural powers.

An important influence on Maori life was the concept of *tapu* (sacred). *Tapu* came from the gods, and was not to be taken lightly. A new meeting house was *tapu* until inaugurated by a *tohunga* in a special ceremony. All items under construction were *tapu,* as were burial grounds. A *tohunga* under *tapu* had to be fed by another with food skewered by a stick.

Intensely proud, the Maori also practised *mana* and *utu* (revenge). *Mana* was all-important and any insult or slight, however trivial, demanded retribution.

Intertribal warfare was frequent, either for *utu* or for more desirable land. The Maori revelled in fighting and excelled in hand-to-hand combat, for which he fashioned weapons. He did not use throwing spears. Instead, he used the *taiaha,* a sort of wooden broadsword about five feet long with a blade for cutting and a hilt sharpened for thrusting. The *taiaha* was wielded with two hands. For even closer combat the Maori warrior used a *patu* and a *mere,* clubs about the length of a man's forearm. They were made either of wood, whalebone, or the very hard greenstone.

Before engaging in battle warriors would perform a *haka.* While it has the appearance of a war dance, the *haka* was really a limbering-up exercise, much like a boxer uses to limber up before the start of a fight. A rhythmic stamping of feet is accompanied by chanting and vigorous hand and arm movements to a set pattern, which includes eye-rolling and protruding the tongue. Every part of the body is exercized. Today the *haka* is a popular item in Maori concerts and is often performed as a symbol of New Zealand by sports teams competing overseas.

The Felled Flagpole

Typical of the Maori's pride and courage is the incident of Hone Heke and the flagstaff, which took place at Russell in the mid 1840s. For years Hone Heke's tribe, the *Ngapuhi,* had prospered from trade with visiting ships and a harbor tax which they imposed. Then the Government introduced the first customs duties. Heke showed his resentment by cutting down the flagpole on Flagstaff Hill. A new pole was erected, only to be cut down again. A third pole was erected, a reward offered for Heke's capture, and "friendly" Maoris posted as a guard, but Heke marched straight through and felled the pole again. This time the governor sheathed the new pole with iron and surrounded it with troops. Undaunted, Heke enticed the troops away with a diversion and landed by night, and for the fourth time the flagstaff fell. He followed this by an attack on the town, leaving it in ruins. Heke was later defeated in a battle elsewhere and was pardoned. On his death he was given a Christian burial.

For clothing and baskets the Maori used the leaves of native flax. They were stripped and dried and woven into cloaks or rolled into long tubes to make skirts *(piupiu)*. The chiefs' cloaks were decorated with the feathers of birds.

The Maori developed a distinctive style of wood carving which he used lavishly. All Polynesians carved in wood but seldom reached the artistic standard of the Maori. Working with greenstone adzes and chisels, he carved great ancestor images as panels along the walls or as posts to hold up the ridge-poles inside meeting houses and at the entrances outside. He carved weapons, boxes, and ornaments, and painted the rafters red, black and white in symbolic designs. The design was not haphazardly chosen; each had a meaning and each carving told a story. The human figure was distorted and grotesque so as not to offend the gods by making a true image of a human being.

For a time it appeared that the carver's art would be lost, but some 20 years ago the Government established the Maori Arts and Crafts Institute at Rotorua, which has enabled exponents of carving to continue the tradition. Under a master carver young Maori from several tribes are instructed in the art and later return to their home regions to carve and to pass on the knowledge that they have gained. Girls are trained at the Institute in the art of weaving.

Tattooing was traditional to the early Maori. As a sign of status the warrior was heavily tattooed on cheeks, nose, and forehead in an intricate design of whorls. Women, too, were tattooed, but mainly on the chin *(moko)*. It was a painful process. The skin was cut, not pricked, with a chisel and coloring was rubbed into the wound. Tattooing has long died out, but the designs are now painted on to the face for performances at Maori concerts.

Pride, Dignity, Intelligence

The basis for the integration of the Maori into European society was laid when the Treaty of Waitangi was signed in the Bay of Islands on February 6, 1840. In full naval regalia, Captain William Hobson told 45 Maori chiefs what the treaty meant. In essence, it recognized that the chiefs' lands belonged to the Maori and guaranteed to them "full exclusive and undisturbed possession of their lands and estates, forests, fisheries and other properties which they may collectively or individually possess, so long as it is their wish and desire to retain the same in their possession." Any land they would be willing to sell would be sold only through the British Crown, which implied that the Crown was concerned with saving the Maoris from being cheated in private land deals.

The principles were laudable, but of course the treaty did not work. Representatives of the Crown wanted to buy the land for next to nothing; four years after the treaty was signed the Crown abandoned its right of pre-emption, and settlers were doing their own buying on their own terms.

The stage was set for what was to become a period of bitterness and strife. The wars over the sale and confiscation of land dragged on from 1860 to 1872. The conflict was a series of skirmishes rather than a national war over an unbroken period; it did not completely involve both races. Some Maori tribes were, in fact, friendly to the Government. Although land matters are still not fully resolved, land classified as Maori property totals about 4 million acres and is administered by Maori interests.

From those unhappy days the Maori increasingly moved into the pakeha world, but his innate pride, intelligence, and dignity helped him to preserve his racial identity.

Today he lives in full equality with other New Zealanders, and in the same type of home. He has taken much from the European culture and has given much in return.

Over the last two decades there has been an increasing emphasis on the expression of Maori identity and the Maori way of doing thing (*maoritanga*). Three basic concepts are fundamental to this movement: that Maori identity is important to the Maori people; that Maori culture is also a national heritage and therefore belongs to all New Zealanders; and that although New Zealand can be justly proud of its overall racial harmony, there are still some problems which require attention.

Some problems have arisen from the transitions associated with rapid urbanization. Solutions are often to be found only over the long term, but efforts are being made in many areas, including educational aid, legal assistance, trade-training programs, and provision of welfare services by governmental agencies, local authorities, and volunteer organizations. Other organizations, such as the New Zealand Maori Council, the Maori Women's Welfare League, and the Maori Education Foundation, all endeavour to promote *maoritanga* among their own people.

Songs, Dances, Oratory

At the personal level, cultural pride embraces preservation of ancestral land and traditional arts, including wood carving, weaving, and oratory. The Maori loved oratory almost as much as fighting, and to listen to a Maori elder speaking on a *marae* in Maori is to hear poetry, even if the words and meaning are not fully understood.

Songs, dances, and oratory are widely practiced in schools and clubs. A fairly recent development has been the instruction of *maoritanga* on urban *marae* or meeting places. This involves the teaching of such attitudes as obligation to the family, *aroha* (or love) for one another, hospitality, and the dignity of Maori etiquette.

The concept that Maori culture is a national heritage to be shared by all New Zealanders is widely accepted. In some areas it is well established—the use of Maori symbols and designs in art and architecture, for instance—but in others it has yet to make an impression. It is being assisted by the introduction a few years ago of Maori language and culture classes in schools, and many adult Europeans attend classes in Maori.

Since World War 2, in which Maori and *pakeha* served together, the Maori have inclined away from their traditionally rural life, learnt new skills, and become city-dwellers.

Once close to being a dying race, the Maori now total more than 227,000, or 9% of the New Zealand population. Most Maori continue to live in the North Island, and seven out of ten in the northern half.

Double Heritage of Culture

From the early days there was a good deal of intermarriage between Maori and pakeha, which has intensified over the last three decades. One result has been a greater drawing together of the two races in a desire to foster their bicultural heritage. As Witi Ihimaera says in his book:

"Today, one in every twelve persons in New Zealand is of half or more Maori origin. In addition, the non-Maori population includes another 50,000 people who are part but less than half Maori. On top of this, it can be safely estimated that most New Zealand families have relatives with Maori blood and more than cursory contact with Maori people.

"In effect, most New Zealanders now have a double heritage of culture. Rather than maintain the division between Maori and pakeha, many New Zealanders now seek a compromise world where Maori culture has an equal place with pakeha culture in New Zealand, where New Zealand is as bi-cultural as they are.

"There has been, therefore, a growing identification of many New Zealanders with Maori culture. This identification has tended to contest the question of what, in fact, constitutes a Maori. Intermarriage has meant that today there are few, if any, full-blooded Maori in New Zealand. For present census purposes he is one who states that he has half or more Maori blood. By the same token, none other than verbal evidence is required to substantiate a claim to being a Maori, which means that a Maori is a Maori if he says he is.

"The usual visual evidence of a brown skin is no longer the sole criterion, and some Maori today have such non-racial characteristics as green eyes and red hair. Such has been the success of integration."

As each Maori chief signed the Treaty of Waitangi Captain Hobson said, *"He iwi tahi tatau"* (we are one people). That ideal may not have been fully realized, but it is closer now than it has ever been before. Some problems still remain, but there is a great fund of goodwill between Maori and *pakeha,* which augurs well for a truly multicultural future.

Race relations may not be perfect in New Zealand, but they must be among the most harmonious in the world.

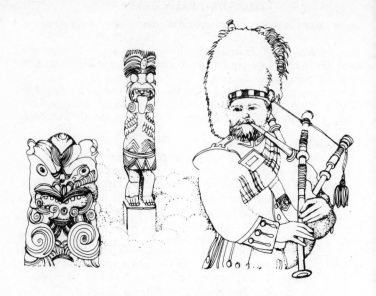

THE ARTS IN NEW ZEALAND

Singers and Woodcarvers

Art in New Zealand began with the Maori. All Polynesians carved, but the Maori brought a particularly high degree of skill and artistry to this form. He favored graceful, sweeping curves rather than angular shapes, and while many of the designs are grotesque in character they have a symmetry which is pleasing to the eye. Their carvers were men of rank and held in high regard. At the Maori Arts and Crafts Institute at Rotorua, visitors may see Maori carving being done by trainees under the guidance of master carvers.

Not only are the traditional arts being preserved, but the modern Maori also brings his distinctive ethnic background into all forms of art. The painters Selwyn Muru, Ralph Hotere, Cliff Whiting, Sandy Adsett and Arnold Wilson are outstanding, and have exhibited internationally; so also has Rangimarie Hetet, a traditional weaver.

Natural singers and musicians, the Maori have produced some first-rate operatic singers, the most notable being Kiri Te Kanawa, Michael Tairawhiti McGifford and the late Inia Te Wiata.

In the field of literature, Hone Tuwhare has become well established as a poet, and Witi Ihimaera has earned high respect as novelist and short story writer, and for his sensitive treatment of Maori-European relations in his recent book, *Maori.*

New Zealand's best known writers are undoubtedly Samuel Butler (1835-1902) and Katherine Mansfield (1888-1923). Butler was born in England, but emigrated to Canterbury in 1859, and became a successful sheepbreeder. *A First Year in Canterbury Settlement* is based on this experience, as is his great satirical novel *Erewhon,* in which a sheep-farmer stumbles upon an undiscovered country.

Katherine Mansfield, essayist and short-story writer, spent her childhood in Wellington and returned to New Zealand for two years as an adult. Her earlier stories contain memories of the society in which she grew up and portray the country as it was at the turn of the century.

Among contemporary writers, the late Dame Ngaio Marsh was one of the most celebrated authors of detective "thrillers." The first of her many books was published in 1933. Few New Zealand authors were internationally known until quite recently, but Janet Frame, Ian Cross, Sylvia Ashton Warner, Maurice Gee, and Maurice Shadbolt are now highly regarded overseas.

New Zealand Painting

New Zealand's beginnings in painting can be traced from the water colors and drawings made by European artists who accompanied the English and French navigators and naturalists during the 18th century. In the early 19th century three men, Richmond, Gully and Barraud, settled in New Zealand and are considered the first artists to devote themselves consistently to painting. They saw New Zealand through English eyes, but their works were the beginning of a New Zealand landscape tradition. An Austrian, Gottfried Lindauer, who came to New Zealand about 1873, has left a number of able and accurate portraits of the Maori people, as did Goldie.

Many artists today are inspired by the things they see about them, considers Stewart Maclennan, former director of the National Art Gallery, Wellington. They are, he says, interested in the natural beauties of the country, the mountains, the lakes, rivers and bush. In exhibitions there is evidence of the influence of overseas trends, but also an indication of a serious attempt to evolve a national art that represents a natural growth from the artists of last century. There are also many contemporary artists, such as Richard Killeen, Colin McCahon, Ralph Hoterer, Robert McLeod and Gretchen Albrecht who have adopted an international approach.

The last two decades have seen a remarkable growth in the professionalism at public art galleries and museums, with many provincial institutions housed in new and modernised buildings, such as in Nelson, New Plymouth, Palmerston North, Napier and Hamilton. The best endowed and largest of the metropolitan galleries is the Auckland City Art Gallery. Like the National Art Gallery in Wellington, it has a large collection of paintings, sculpture and works on paper, as well as photography, from New Zealand and overseas. The McDougall Art Gallery in Christchurch and the Dunedin Public Art Gallery also have significant collections and have active exhibition and educational programs. Important collections of early New Zealand paintings are held by the Alexander Turnbull Library in Wellington and the Hocken Library in Dunedin.

In concert with overseas trends, most of the larger cities have a substantial dealer-gallery network, which has grown significantly during the past 20 years. A flourishing group of print-makers, some using very advanced techniques, find a ready market for original prints.

324   **THE ARTS IN NEW ZEALAND**

The Other Arts

Pottery has developed rapidly and has become an important craft. New Zealand weavers make good use of a variety of native wools to produce garments, wall hangings and off-loom tapestries. Frequent craft exhibitions are held throughout the country, and works have toured overseas.

Performing arts groups flourish in many centers, and the main cities also have professional theater and dance. The Mercury Theater and Theater Corporate in Auckland, Centerpoint Theater in Palmerston North, Downstage and Circa theaters in Wellington, Court Theater in Christchurch and Fortune Theater in Dunedin offer main-bill productions throughout the year. Several of these theaters also have a second auditorium for experimental work.

Three dance companies regularly tour New Zealand. *Limbs* and *Impulse* are contemporary companies based in Auckland and Wellington, respectively, which perform exclusively indigenous repertoires. The New Zealand Ballet, also based in Wellington, performs a wide variety of works from the classics to works commissioned from New Zealand choreographers.

Concerts by the New Zealand Symphony Orchestra are always well attended, and in the four main centers semi-professional orchestras provide regional concerts and an accompaniment service. In 1978 professional opera activity was revived through the new National Opera of New Zealand.

Recent years have seen the development of film-making, and several productions have received acclaim and are being screened in theaters and on TV overseas.

Practical assistance in encouraging the arts is given by the Queen Elizabeth II Arts Council, an independent body that receives financial support from the Government. Advisory assistance and grants are given by the council in the fields of painting, print-making, sculpture, music, drama, dance, crafts, film and arts administration. Facilities are provided for training promising actors and dancers at the New Zealand Drama School and the National School of Ballet. Through the Regional Arts Councils, assistance is also made available to community groups to help promote participation in arts activities.

A council for Maori and South Pacific Arts was recently established within the Arts Council to foster and encourage the arts and crafts of the Maori and the South Pacific cultural traditions in New Zealand.

The Queen Elizabeth II Arts Council welcomes requests from visitors for information on events that may especially interest them. Contact: Kirk Motors Building, 110–116 Courtenay Place, Wellington; tel. 851–176.

NATIONAL PARKS

A Legacy of Grandeur

As early as the beginning of this century New Zealand began preserving some of its most outstanding natural assets. It now has ten National Parks, totalling over 5¼ million acres (one-thirteenth of the total land area) and encompassing forests and valleys, mountains and glaciers, inland lakes and coastal bays. Three are in the North Island and seven in the South Island.

Overall administration is carried out by the National Parks Authority, although each park has its own controlling board. The objective, set out in an Act of Parliament in 1952, is to preserve these areas in their natural state for the benefit and enjoyment of the public.

Inevitably, the tourist must visit or pass through some of these parks, as they contain many of New Zealand's most beautiful and unusual attractions.

Without exception, the parks suffer from the depredations of animals. There were no animals indigenous to New Zealand and, misguidedly, the early settlers introduced deer, opossum, stoat, and weasel; and, in the Mount Cook region, chamois and Himalayan thar. Having no natural enemies and finding the environment much to their liking, the immigrant species multiplied rapidly until they became menaces to the native vegetation and bird life. They still destroy the forest cover, resulting in erosion on steep slopes and flooding of rivers, while birds fall prey to stoats, weasels, and domestic cats that have run wild. Some of these have been declared noxious animals, but the nature of the terrain makes it almost impossible to implement an effective control program.

Tongariro National Park

The nucleus of Tongariro, New Zealand's first national park, was set aside in 1887 when a far-seeing Maori chief, Te Heuheu Tukino, gave the summits of three mountains to the Government to avoid inevitable sale to Europeans. "They shall be," he said, "a sacred place of the Crown and a gift for ever from me and my people."

Almost in the center of the North Island, the park has extremes of climate and terrain, ranging from forest to desert-like areas and geothermal activity. This central upland plateau has as its most prominent land forms three volcanic peaks rising almost in a straight line from north to south: Mt. Tongariro (6,345 ft.), a series of mildly active craters; symmetrical Mt. Ngauruhoe (7,515 ft.), the most active volcano; and Mt. Ruapehu (9,175 ft.), the highest mountain in the North Island, with an intermittently active crater from which radiate small glaciers. The park has an area of nearly 171,000 acres.

Tongariro National Park is the most accessible and easily seen of all the national parks. It straddles two main highways between Lake Taupo and Wellington on the east and Wanganui and New Plymouth on the west. It can, in fact, be circumnavigated by road with continuous views of the mountains.

Tongariro is also the most used of the national parks. Although only the upper part of Mt. Ruapehu is coated with snow in the summer and fall, the lower slopes are heavily covered in winter and form the North Island's most popular skiing resort. Skiers come from as far as Auckland and Wellington. About 40 mountain clubs have provided buildings in an alpine village from which a system of chair lifts, T-bars, and tows take skiers higher up the slopes.

The Tourist Hotel Corporation (THC) Chateau Tongariro is conveniently placed close to the main highway.

Egmont National Park

The second to be established, Egmont National Park of 82,836 acres surrounds the symmetrical cone of Mt. Egmont (8,260 ft.) and dominates the extensive and fertile farming country of Taranaki. It is easily reached by good roads from the main highways and is popular for skiing and climbing. Three roads run up into the park: from New Plymouth to the North Egmont Chalet; from Stratford to the Stratford Mountain House and plateau; and from Hawera to Dawson Falls and the Dawson Falls Tourist Lodge.

Geologists consider that Egmont may have been active about 220 years ago, but it is now dormant and its dense rain forest helps control the watersheds of 31 rivers that radiate from its slopes. The Maori hold the peak to be sacred. Skiers and mountaineers respect it as an excellent training ground.

Urewera National Park

By tradition the home of the Tuhoe tribe ("the children of the mist"), Urewera National Park lies in a remote region between Rotorua and Wairoa, on the east coast, and at 495,000 acres is the third largest of New Zealand's national parks and the largest in the North Island. A maze of confusing watersheds, it is noted for its Maori history, for the size of its area of virgin forest, and for its lake, Waikaremoana ("sea of rippling waters"), a vast, star-shaped lake of intense blue water and countless bays and coves some 2,000 feet above sea level.

The heavily wooded ranges include forest typical of the original vegetation. So vast and unbroken are the forests that the traveler does not have to go far from roads and tracks before he feels that no-one has been there before him.

Access to the park is by a highway linking Rotorua and Wairoa, but it is a slow, winding road which must be taken with care. There is no hotel, but there are camping facilities near the Wairoa end of the lake.

Mt. Cook National Park

The area of Mt. Cook National Park (172,739 acres) is not large by New Zealand standards, but its essence and quality are determined by the height and sheerness of the ranges and by the size and length of the glaciers, the great valleys they have gouged, and the rock debris they have spread. Waving tussocks, blue-green lakes fed by glacier water, tawny rocks and glistening snow add to the grace and breadth of the scene. The park is linked to Westland National Park by the ice-covered chain of the Main Divide of the Southern Alps.

The park is dominated by Mt. Cook, at 12,349 ft. New Zealand's highest mountain, and clustered around it are 17 peaks over 10,000 ft. The area has been a training ground for many mountaineers who have represented New Zealand in the Antarctic, the Andes, and the Himalayas.

The Alps were pushed up late in New Zealand's geological history, and have been sculpted into their present form by glaciers and streams. The degree of glaciation is outstandingly high. There are scores of glaciers within the park, but the most impressive are the Tasman (18 miles), the Murchison (11 miles), the Hooker (7 miles), and the Mueller (8 miles).

An exciting sightseeing event is a skiplane flight with a landing at about 7,500 feet on the vast snowfield at the head of one of the glaciers.

Accommodation is available at the THC Hermitage complex almost at the foot of Mt. Cook. Although the Hermitage and Glencoe Lodge are at 2,500 ft., snow does not cover the ground except occasionally in winter, and no special warm clothing is needed.

The Hermitage is roughly half-way between Christchurch and Queenstown, and is reached by road or the regular services of Mount Cook Airlines.

Mt. Aspiring National Park

South of Mt. Cook, Mt. Aspiring National Park is wild and rugged and visited mainly by enthusiastic hikers and hunters. The boundaries of its 680,000 acres extend along a 100-mile front, and its width is seldom more than 20 miles, but it effectively divides the eastern side of the South Island from the West Coast. The Haast Pass road to the West Coast traces the park's northern tip.

Like other South Island parks, Mt. Aspiring consists of glaciers and rocky mountains, thick bush, river flats and gorges, waterfalls and passes. It has some rivers so accessible that families may camp on the flats, and others so rough and inaccessible that only hardy hunters or hikers can reach them.

The park derives its name from its dominant feature, Mt. Aspiring, which rises to 9,931 ft. It is a distinctive peak, sheer and icy and rising to a needle point, not unlike Switzerland's Matterhorn.

The mountains may be comfortably seen across the lake from Wanaka, where the THC runs a well-appointed hotel. There are also motels.

Wanaka is reached by an alternative route from Mt. Cook to Queenstown, where the traveler turns off at a right angle at Tarras, reaching Queenstown through Wanaka and over the Crown Range. Wanaka is passed in the course of, or can be the starting point for, the journey through the Haast Pass to the West Coast.

Fiordland National Park

Fiordland National Park is the grandest and largest of all—over 3 million acres, virtually untouched and in some places unexplored. It is larger than the total area of the other nine parks and one of the largest in the world. Its western boundary is a shoreline indented by countless fiords and bays. So difficult of access is the land that it was here as recently as 1948 that a small colony of *Notornis (takahe* in Maori *)*, a swamp bird thought to be extinct, was rediscovered. It is also the only place in New Zealand where wapiti are established in the wild.

Fiordland has a wealth of history covering nearly two centuries and a great variety of people, from navigators, sealers, and whalers to explorers, surveyors, and miners. After rounding the southern point of the South Island on his first voyage, Captain Cook sailed *"Endeavour"* in March 1770 past the West Coast sounds but could not make harbor. At one place "dusk" intervened and at another the weather was "doubtful"; accordingly he named the sounds Dusky Sound and Doubtful Sound. On this voyage Cook left a few names on the map but never a footprint on the land.

The highlight of Fiordland is Milford Sound, a 10-mile long, narrow waterway biting into precipitous granite cliffs rising thousands of feet. Milford can be seen on a 1½-hour scenic flight from Queenstown or Te Anau or can be reached by road from Te Anau by a journey of 75-miles through exciting alpine scenery. The vastness of the sound is best appreciated from a launch cruise.

For those who enjoy hiking, the most rewarding way to explore Fiordland is on the three-day, 33-mile walk over Milford Track, with overnight stays at accommodation huts. The track passes the Sutherland Falls which, at 1,904 ft., are among the highest in the world.

The gateway to Fiordland, either by road or by the Milford Track, is Te Anau on the shores of the lake of that name.

The THC runs a comfortable hotel at the head of Milford Sound, and at Te Anau there is the THC Te Anau Hotel as well as several well-appointed motor hotels and motels.

Westland National Park

Westland National Park is dominated by the mountains and the sea. Its eastern boundary is the Main Divide of the Southern Alps, and from the sea on the west come rains that feed the forest and glaciers. The park's 219,000 acres are a mixture of high, snow-clad peaks, steep glaciers, lush rain forest, deep gorges, and cattle-farming country.

Westland's glories are the thick, verdant rain forests, attractive even in the rain, the backdrop offered by the long line of high, snow-covered peaks, and lovely, unexpected lakes.

The Franz Josef and Fox Glaciers, flowing from vast snow fields shadowed by peaks more than 9,000 ft. high, are among the largest glaciers in the temperate zone. They descend for seven and eight miles, respectively, past flanks of luxuriant bush to less than 1,000 feet above sea level and only ten miles from the sea.

By glacial standards the rate of flow is fast—1,000 feet an hour. The rate of flow varies according to the pressure of ice built up in the snow basins high in the mountains, but there is a time lag. The most recent advance and thickening of the two glaciers occurred in 1965, but thickening of the ice at the top of the icefall was noticed four years earlier. There has since been a recession of both glaciers. The specific rate of flow varies in different parts of the glacier, like the current of a river. The ice surges over itself, breaking and grinding and being forced up into pressure ridges by the movement of the flow.

The boundaries of the park are skirted by the traveler driving along the West Coast between the western portal of the Haast Pass and Hokitika.

There are hotels and motels at the Franz Josef and Fox Glaciers.

Arthur's Pass National Park

Arthur's Pass National Park comprises 243,000 acres and extends on both sides of the Main Divide of the Southern Alps between Canterbury and the West Coast. Its scenery, climate, vegetation, and development reflect its spread over contrasting areas.

Easily accessible, the park attracts people to its river flats, its forests, and, in winter, its snowy mountains. The main transalpine railroad, with its 5¼-mile Otira tunnel, and the main transalpine highway take a large number of people through the park.

Only 93 miles by road from Christchurch, Arthur's Pass is the shortest overland route to the West Coast and Hokitika, only 63 miles farther on. It is a popular skiing area in winter, and there are day excursions by road and rail from Christchurch.

The road over the pass can be closed by snowfall, floods, or landslides in winter, but it is open for most of the year. Farther north, the Lewis Pass has easier gradients and is less vulnerable to storms, but the scenery is less spectacular.

There is a small township, called Arthur's Pass, near the summit.

Nelson Lakes National Park

Nelson Lakes National Park is a very popular recreation area for New Zealanders. Nelson people used it as such long before it became a national park and a tradition of a holiday at Lake Rotoiti was well established. It is much used in this way today as there are excellent facilities for camping, boating, swimming, hiking, trout fishing, and hunting.

Comprising 141,127 acres, Nelson Lakes is predominantly a park of bush-clad mountains, quiet valleys, swift-flowing rivers and streams, the seven-mile long Lake Rotoroa, and five-mile long Lake Rotoiti. Forests here mark a stage in the transition of vegetation from the rain forests of the West Coast to the dry grasslands east of the Main Divide. The bush is principally beech forest.

Abel Tasman National Park

Just north of Nelson, Abel Tasman National Park, with only 47,373 acres, is the smallest of the parks. Much of it is coastline and outlying islands, and its unspoilt golden beaches make it popular with New Zealanders for camping holidays. Access is either by sea or by land, but there are no hotel or motel accommodations.

FISHING AND HUNTING

Trout, Marlin, Shark, Chamois and Thar

by
REX FORRESTER

New Zealand has long been renowned for its outstanding trout and big game fishing and for its hunting for deer, chamois, and thar. Even though the number of local anglers is increasing, the quality of trout fishing remains consistently high and big game fishing still yields some excellent fish. Hunting, however, is becoming more difficult because of measures to control herds and reduce damage to the natural forests, and as a result of the development of an overseas market for venison.

Fantastic Trout Fishing

By overseas standards New Zealand is underfished. Its innumerable fast-flowing rivers and streams of clear mountain water, and cold, clear lakes proved an ideal environment for the brown trout ova introduced and hatched in 1869 and the rainbow trout ova brought from Russian River, California, in 1877. Both species bred swiftly and were subsequently liberated throughout the country.

Fishery management by national and local wildlife authorities has maintained these qualities through sound conservation and hatching methods, and size and quality of trout are, in many cases, even improving.

So fast do trout grow in New Zealand that they rarely reach maturity until 14 inches long. In fact, all trout under this length must be returned to the water.

As an instance of this rapid growth, rainbow fingerlings weighing less than half an ounce each (forty to the pound) were liberated in 1971 in Lake Tarawera. When taken by anglers nine months later they weighed an average of 3½ to 4 pounds. Some grew 7 pounds in sixteen months. The wildlife authorities estimate that each year about 700 tons of trout are taken by anglers from Lake Taupo alone, the average weight being 4.4 pounds.

A check taken a year or two ago indicated that about 6,000 anglers visited New Zealand and caught about 14,000 trout, or better than two trout per angler—better still when it is realized that most fishermen returned unwanted trout to the water alive. These 14,000 trout at a conservative estimate weighed 14 tons, which proves that the claim "tons of trout" is no exaggeration.

For seven years Rotorua conducted a trout fishing competition for one week each year. Over the seven weeks, 5,018 trout were weighed and found to total 17,654 pounds—nearly 8 tons, or over a ton of trout each week. The fish averaged 3.52 pounds.

Lake Tarawera has a reputation for producing more 10-pound trout than any other lake in the world. The summer average, when the fish are feeding deep in this lake, is 5 pounds; but in May and June, when the trout come up from the deep and gather at the stream mouths to spawn, fly fishing comes into its own. In May and June of a recent year fish of 9 to 10 pounds were caught almost daily. The biggest was a female weighing 13.2 pounds.

The average brown trout passing through a fish trap on a Lake Taupo spawning stream weighs 6.71 pounds. In the South Island, browns average 2 to 3 pounds, although in such rivers as the Mataura, Clinton, and Hollyford, 5-pound fish are commonly caught.

The daily limit per angler differs slightly from one district to another, but is usually eight to ten trout a day, and trout under 14-inches long must be returned alive to the water. There is no limit on brown trout taken from Lakes Rotorua and Taupo. Rainbow trout taken in Lake Rotorua average from 2 to 4 pounds and in Lake Taupo from 3½ to 6 pounds. In Lake Tarawera the rainbow trout average 5 pounds, but weights of 8 to 10 pounds are not uncommon.

Whopper after Whopper

The main fishing areas of New Zealand are the lake systems of the North Island, including Lakes Rotorua and Taupo. Here the quarry is the rainbow and the usual method of fishing is with wet fly (streamer).

Most streams flowing into lakes are designated for fly fishing only, and sinking lines with lure-type flies are most favored. Trolling is popular and most productive, and during the summer floating lines are used for rising trout. Spinning is also popular.

In the South Island the brown trout is predominant and most plentiful in the southern lakes, rivers and streams of Southland. It is taken mainly by dry fly, or nymph. Rainbows and landlocked salmon as well as sea-run browns are also taken in the southern lakes. Here, spinning, trolling, and wet fly are used with success. Rainbows and browns average 2 to 2¼ pounds but run to 5 pounds in some areas. Rainbows of 10 pounds can be found and 11-pound browns are not unusual.

Although several areas, notably Lakes Taupo and Rotorua, are open all the year round, the main season is from October to the end of April (in some districts as late as the end of June).

Most serious anglers who try to avoid the January vacation period find that dry fly fishing is good in October, December, February, and March. Wet fly fishing in lakes, mainly at stream mouths, is good from October to December and in February-March and is excellent in rivers when trout start their spawning runs, from April through September. Trolling and spinning are both good from October through March.

Fishing licences are reasonably priced. In most areas day licences cost $3 and, for a week, average $10. A tourist licence is available to visiting anglers at a cost of $50. This allows the holder to fish anywhere in New Zealand for one month (with the exception of one Maori-owned lake where an additional day licence is needed).

Accommodations in the popular fishing areas are good, with many hotels and motels of high standard at Rotorua, Taupo, Turangi, Wanaka, Queenstown, Te Anau, Gore, and Invercargill. There are also fishing lodges at Lakes Okataina, Tarawera, Rotoroa, Makarora, and at Tokaa-nu. Camping and caravan sites are plentiful, and many small country hotels in fishing areas make the angler especially welcome. The roads to most fishing areas are good.

Scattered throughout the most popular areas are 60 or more professional guides. They provide all equipment needed, including first-class rods, lines, and reels. Many supply hipboots. Most have boats, from fiberglass 14-footers to 50-foot overnight launches, and many have passenger-licenced automobiles.

The average price of a top fly fishing guide supplying all equipment and vehicle to reach streams is $250 to $300 per day. Trolling guides operating 15-ft. boats with canopy and two motors run a daily average of $250 to $300. Fifty-ft. launches charter at $350 to $600 a day, or $36 to $60 an hour, plus $100 for overnight trips, plus meals, and can sleep up to six, who share that rate.

BIG Big Game Fishing

The coastal waters of New Zealand teem with fish of all descriptions. Those that can be regarded as big game are broadbill swordfish; blue, black, and striped marlin; mako, thresher, and hammerhead shark; yellowtail (or kingfish, as it is known locally); and tuna. Excellent light-tackle sport can be enjoyed with smaller varieties such as bonito, skipjack, and the famous *kahawai* (sea trout).

Big game fish are found mostly on the eastern coast of the North Island between North Cape and Cape Runaway in an area warmed by the Pacific tropical current. Here are found the big game fishing bases of Whangaroa, Bay of Islands, Tutukaka, Mercury Bay, Tauranga, Mayor Island, and Whakatane. All are less than 200 miles from Auckland and visitors with limited time can fly to them by amphibian aircraft.

New Zealand's big game fishing grounds are world famous for producing big fish; in fact, striped marlin, the most prolific of all marlin in these waters, average around 250 pounds. Black marlin average from 400 to 600 pounds: a 976-pound black marlin held the world record from 1926 to 1953. Pacific blue marlin range from 300 to 600 pounds.

New Zealand all-tackle records are: broadbill, 673 pounds; black marlin, 976 pounds; blue marlin, 1,017 pounds; striped marlin, 465 pounds; yellowtail, 111 pounds; thresher shark, 922 pounds; tiger shark, 947 pounds; hammerhead shark, 460 pounds; mako shark, 1,000 pounds; yellowfin tuna, 168 pounds; bluefin tuna, 519 pounds.

The trend in New Zealand fishing circles is to lighter tackle. For many years most charter boats used 130-pound (and heavier) line but most now carry 80-pound line, while enthusiastic sportsmen are taking records on lines of 50, 30, and even 20 pounds.

Top of the light-tackle fish are the yellowfin tuna, which run from 40 to 100 pounds. Second are the yellowtail closely followed by the skipjack, bonito, and *kahawai*. The *kahawai* is in fact eagerly sought by fishermen using fly rods and fly lure. Seasoned trout anglers say that *kahawai* fights better, pound for pound, than trout.

Kahawai is also the popular bait fish used by big game fishermen when trolling or drifting for marlin and shark. It is found in huge schools, often up to an acre in extent. At times, *kahawai* can be seen "boiling" on the surface at all points of the compass.

Charter boats are available at all the big game bases mentioned. Most are fitted with two chairs, outriggers, and ship-to-shore radio. Most boats are operated by owner-skippers who are fully conversant with the fishing and other conditions in their areas. Costs are around $450 a day.

Membership of any of the big game fishing clubs runs from $5 to $10 annually. It entitles one to use all facilities and to enjoy the general conviviality of such clubs everywhere. Visitors are made especially welcome. The season is from mid-January through April.

Hunting

Because of vastly reduced wild animal populations there are now few guides. The daily rate is $350, plus equipment and food, and an hourly rate of $600 for a helicopter (3 seats) to locate game and gain access. World-class trophy animals—chamois, thar, and deer (Red, Sika and Fallow)—can be hunted from lodges on game-management areas, where all hunting is controlled. Trophies of each species are guaranteed. The average price for each animal starts at $2,000 and increases on a point system, depending on the rating in the world record books.

Interested hunters can obtain lists of all guides from the Fishing and Hunting Officer, New Zealand Government Tourist Bureau, Private Bag, Rotorua.

FACTS AT YOUR FINGERTIPS FOR NEW ZEALAND

HOW TO GET THERE. The international airports at Auckland, Wellington and Christchurch have direct services to Australia, but most international flights arrive at Auckland. Air New Zealand, Pan Am, Continental Airlines, and UTA French Airlines have regular flights from North America (Air New Zealand and CP Air from Vancouver; at press time it looks as if United Airlines may take over Pan Am's Pacific runs); Qantas, flies from North America and Europe via Australia; Air New Zealand and Japan Airlines from Japan; Trans Australia Airlines from Hobart to Christchurch. Check with your travel agent.

CLIMATE. Subtropical in the North Island; temperate in the South Island. The north has no extremes of heat or cold, but winter can be somewhat cold in the south. The seasons are reversed: summer from December through February; fall from March through May; winter from June through August; spring from September through November.

Average Temperature (°Fahrenheit) and Humidity

Auckland	Jan	Feb	Mar	Apr	May	June	July	Aug	Sept	Oct	Nov	Dec
Average max. day temperature	74°	75°	73°	68°	63°	59°	58°	59°	62°	64°	68°	71°
Days of Rain	6	5	6	8	10	12	12	11	9	9	8	7
Humidity, Percent	64	65	65	65	70	71	69	69	66	65	64	66
Christchurch												
Average max. day temperature	71°	71°	67°	63°	57°	52°	51°	54°	59°	63°	67°	69°
Days of Rain	5	4	5	4	6	6	6	4	4	5	5	5
Humidity, Percent	57	59	63	65	71	70	70	63	61	56	55	58

TIME. New Zealand standard time is exactly 12 hours ahead of Greenwich Mean time, but from the last Saturday in October until the first Sunday in March the clock is put forward by one hour.

NATIONAL HOLIDAYS. New Year's Day (January 1), Waitangi Day (February 6), Good Friday, Easter Monday, Anzac Day (April 25), Queen's Birthday (first Monday in June), Labor Day (fourth Monday in October), Christmas Day and December 26. New Zealanders themselves vacation from mid-December through April, so its best to make all reservations in advance for this period.

CLOSING TIMES. Shops and banks are open five days a week and closed on Saturday and Sunday, but some shops are open on Saturday until noon. Shops are usually open from 9 A.M. to 5:30 P.M. and until 9 P.M. on Fridays.

MONEY. The monetary unit is the NZ$, approximately US$0.45 at the current rate of exchange.

TIPPING. Employed persons do not depend on tips for their income, but a small tip for personal services in a hotel or restaurant is appreciated. Taxi drivers do not expect tips. Neither service charges nor taxes are added to hotel or restaurant bills.

ELECTRICITY. 220-240 volts A.C., 50 cycles.

 FOOD AND DRINK. Food and water are clean and fresh everywhere. There are good local beers, and some fine local wines. All alcoholic beverages must be purchased from hotels or licensed stores, but hotel guests can obtain liquor at any time.

 MEDICAL FACILITIES. Public hospitals provide a very high standard of treatment. Hotels and motels usually have arrangements with doctors who will visit in the event of illness.

Visitors to New Zealand who suffer personal injury as the result of an accident are entitled to compensation, irrespective of fault. Benefits include reimbursement for expenses resulting directly from the accident, such as hospital charges.

 SHOPPING. The best buys for the visitor are greenstone jewelry, and sheepskin. Greenstone is a type of jade, deep or pale green in color. For centuries, the Maori made weapons and ornaments from it, and it is now used for attractive rings and brooches. Other, less expensive ornaments are fashioned from the irridescent blue-green shell of the *paua,* a large shellfish similar to the abalone.

Many imported products are sold duty-free to visitors throughout the country.

 PASSPORTS AND VISAS. All visitors, except Australian citizens, require passports, but visas are not necessary for Americans, Japanese, or residents of New Caledonia and Tahiti, provide they are bona fide tourists and do not intend to stay for more than 30 days. Some other countries are also exempt, and visitors should check with the New Zealand consul or British consulates in their own country.

All tourists are required to show that they have sufficient funds to maintain them during their stay without taking employment.

CUSTOMS. There is no restriction on the amount of foreign currency that may be brought into, or re-exported from New Zealand. No customs duty is payable on personal effects, or on a reasonable amount of photographic equipment. No duty on: 1 qt. of liquor; 1 qt. of wine; 200 cigarettes or 50 cigars.

TAXES. Apart from a NZ$2 departure tax on departing air passengers, the government imposes no direct charges on visitors, nor is tax added to hotel and restaurant bills.

 HOW TO GET ABOUT. *By air:* Air New Zealand has frequent services between the major centres. Scheduled flights to some of the outstanding scenic areas are run by Mount Cook Airlines and Newmans Air. New Zealand Railways Travelpass allows unlimited rail travel throughout both islands. At press time, cost is US$65 for 8 days (this pass and passes for high season, mid-Dec. –Jan. when costs are somewhat higher, must be purchased outside of New Zealand); US$85 for 15 days; US$114 for 22 days. Any of these can be extended up to 16 days for US$7 per day. You can buy more than one pass if you want to travel, stay somewhere for a time, then travel again. Contact New Zealand Tourist Offices.

By rail: The main towns and cities of both islands are connected by rail, and many of the routes are scenically attractive. Wellington and Auckland have commuter train services.

By bus: Scheduled coach service throughout the country. Rates run around NZ$12–17 for a half-day trip; NZ$18–40, for a full day, depending on length of journey. Reservations required.

By car: International Driving Licences are valid, and rental cars are available at reasonable rates in all the main centers. Remember to drive to the left. Roads to all the main centers and scenic areas are sealed and well maintained. Since the decimal system has been introduced to all measurements, gas is now sold in liters (1 U.S. gallon = 3¾ liters), and distances are now in kilometers (1 mile = 1.6 km). For information on roads, and motor vehicle insurance, and even accommodation reservations, contact Automobile Association at New Zealand (AA), 33 Wyndham St., or PO Box 5, Auckland 1.

By taxi: Cabs are available by phone or at particular stands. Rates average around 74¢/km.

By ferry: Ferries link North and South islands; travel is between Wellington and Picton and takes about 3½ hours.

USEFUL ADDRESSES. The New Zealand Tourist and Publicity Department has representatives in the following places: *North America:* Suite 970, Alcoa Building, One Maritime Plaza, San Francisco, California 94111; Suite 1530, Tishman Building, 10960 Wilshire Boulevard, Los Angeles, California 90024; Suite 530, 630 Fifth Avenue, New York, NY 10111.

Britain: New Zealand House, Haymarket, London, S.W. 1Y 4TQ.

Australia: United Dominion's House. 115 Pitt Street, Sydney NSW 2000; C.M.L. Building, 330 Collins Street, Melbourne, Victoria 3000; Watkins Place, 288 Edward Street, Brisbane, Queensland 4000; 16 St. George's Terrace, Perth, West Australia 6000.

Japan: Toho Twin Tower Building, 2F, 1-5-2 Yurakucho Chiyoda-ku, Tokyo 100.

Germany: New Zealand Government Tourist Office. 6000 Frankfurt A.M., Kaiserhofstrasse 7, Federal Republic of Germany.

Canada: New Zealand Consulate-General, 701 West Georgia St., IBM Tower, Vancouver, B.C. V7Y 1B6.

Singapore: 13 Nassim Rd., Singapore 1025.

FESTIVALS AND SPECIAL EVENTS. January— Auckland Cup Galloping race meeting; National Lawn Bowling Tournament (varies); N.Z. International Grand Prix, Auckland; Wellington Cup Galloping meeting; National Yearling Sales (bloodstock sale of about 450 selected yearlings, held concurrently with Wellington Race meeting); Anniversary Day Yachting Regatta (Auckland), reputed to be the largest one-day regatta in the world.

February—Auckland Cup Harness racing meeting; Festival of the Pines (New Plymouth), music, ballet and cultural arts in outdoor amphitheater; International Vintage Car Rally (varies).

March—Golden Shears Sheep Shearing Championships (Masterton), with leading shearers competing for the championship; Ngaruawahia Annual Regatta (Hamilton), the only Maori Canoe Regatta held; Wellington Galloping Race meeting.

March/April—Easter Show (Auckland).

April—Rugby football season opens; Highland Games (Hastings); Metropolitan Harness racing meeting (Christchurch).

May—Skiing season opens; World Ploughing Championships (Christchurch).

June—Great Northern Hurdles and Steeplechase meeting (Auckland); Agricultural Fieldays (Hamilton), displays of equipment.

July—Wellington Hurdles and Steeplechase meeting.

August—International Ski Championships (varies); Grand National Hurdles & Steeplechase meeting (Christchurch).

September—Cherry Blossom Festival (Hastings and Alexandra).

October—Hawke's Bay Agricultural Show (Hastings); Waikato A. and P. Show (Hamilton).

November—New Zealand Cup race meeting and Trotting Cup race meeting (Christchurch); Canterbury Agricultural and Pastoral Show (Christchurch).

 SIGHTSEEING. If you're interested in escorted tours, contact: *Royal Road Tours,* 2169-D Francisco Blvd., San Rafael, CA 94901; *Club Universe/Unitours,* 1671 Wilshire Blvd., Los Angeles, CA 90017; or *Maupintour,* 900 Maff St., Lawrence KS 66044; *Islands in the Sun/Guthreys,* 760 W. 16th St., Apt. L., Costa Mesa, CA 92627; *Tiki Tours,* Alcoa Bldg, Suite 970, 1 Maritime Plaza, San Francisco, CA 94111.

Because trips to the main cities alone will not do justice to the variety of attractions this country has to offer, listed here are some sample itineraries to help you get the most out of your trip. *North Island (4 days):* Day 1, Arrive Auckland; day 2, Auckland to Waitomo Caves to Rotorua; day 3, at Rotorua; day 4, Rotorua to Auckland. *South Island (5 days):* Day 1, arrive Christchurch; Day 2, Christchurch to Queenstown by air; day 3, at Queenstown; day 4, Queenstown to Mount Cook to Christchurch; day 5, depart Christchurch. *Both Islands (10 days):* Day 1: Arrive Christchurch; day 2, Christchurch to Lake Te Anau by air; day 3, day trip to Milford Sound by road; day 4, Lake Te Anau to Queenstown by air; day 6, at Queenstown; day 7, Queenstown to Mount Cook by air; day 7, Mount Cook to Rotorua by air; day 8, at Rotorua; day 9, Rotorua to Waitomo Caves to Auckland by road; day 10, depart Auckland. *Both Islands (17 days):* Day 1, arrive Auckland; day 2, at Auckland; day 3, Auckland to Paihia (Bay of Islands); day 4, at Paihia (catamaran or launch cruise or day trip to Cape Reinga); day 5, Paihia to Auckland; day 6, Auckland to Waitomo Caves to Rotorua; days 7 and 8, at Rotorua; day 9, Rotorua to Christchurch by air; day 10, Christchurch to Lake Te Anau by air; day 11, day trip to Milford Sound; day 12, Lake Te Anau to Queenstown; days 13 and 14, at Queenstown; day 15, Queenstown to Mount Cook by air; day 16, Mount Cook to Christchurch by air; day 17, depart Christchurch or fly to Auckland for departure.

Outdoor Action Holidays: *Golf:* Even small towns have golf courses, at which visitors are always welcome. Green fees range from about $5 to $10 per game. Golf is very popular and played year-round.

Skiing: New Zealand has fine ski fields, close to accommodations centers, and with the complete absence of tree hazards. The main season in the North Island is from about mid-July to the end of October and in the South Island from early July to the end of September. The main ski fields are at Mount Ruapehu in the North Island and at Coronet Peak, Queenstown, and Mount Hutt, near Christchurch.

Charter Yachts: Mainly in Auckland and the Bay of Islands, yachts may be chartered fully equipped with or without crews; only food and bedding are required.

Cruising: Fiordland Cruises Ltd., Manapouri, operate three-day cruises in Doubtful Sound in Fiordland. Charges include transport, accommodations and meals.

River Rafting: Heavy-duty inflatable rubber rafts similar to those used on the Colorado River are used for journeys down rivers and through countryside not normally seen. Trips vary from three hours to 12 days.

Jet Boats: Jet boat trips are operated on many rivers, ranging from one hour to a full day.

Snorkel and Scuba Diving: While good diving is available out of most cities and towns, the Poor Knights, off the coast of Tutukaka in Northland, offers the most spectacular diving.

Surfing: New Zealand's extremely long coastline offers surfers a wide variety of reef point, river bar and beach breaks. The best surfing is in Northland, the west coast of the North Island, Bay of Plenty, Gisborne, Wellington and the east coast of the South Island.

Mountaineering: Probably no country can offer such a wide scope and variety of mountaineering as the Southern Alps, where Sir Edmund Hillary, the first to climb Mount Everest, did much of his early training. Mount Cook and Westland, from the nature of their country, attract more overseas climbers than other places.

Backpacking: There are guided hiking trips in several parts of the country, but the most popular are the three- or four-day alpine "walks" over the Milford Track in Fiordland and through the Routeburn and Hollyford Valleys from Queenstown.

Alpine Guides (Mt. Cook) Ltd., Box 20, Mt. Cook, or New Zealand Government Tourist Bureau, Alcoa Bldg., Maritime Plaza, San Francisco, Ca. 94111, provide information on heliskiing, glacier skiing, Nordic skiing and Alpine ski-touring. Guided climbing, mountaineering courses and raft trips are available in summer.

Dane's Back Country Experiences, Ltd. P.O. Bx 230, Queenstown, NZ. Back-country specialists in whitewater rafting, hiking, fishing, airplane tours in the back country. Tours from three hours to five days. Sample rafting rates: NZ$145 2-day; NZ$318 4-day, including food and transportation.

Venturetreks Ltd., Box 3839, Auckland. Wanganui River Walk: A five-day guided walk/camping trip from Ohakune in the center of North Island. Costs include coach and jetboat transportation, tent accommodations, equipment, meals, guide fee. Adult NZ$240.

Special-Interest Tours: *New Zealand Farm Vacations,* P.O. Box 1436, Wellington; *Farmhouse and Countryhome Holidays,* P.O. Box 31250, Auckland. Accommodation in farm or ranch home, meals with the family. Three homecooked meals a day. Holidays in over 65 farm homesteads from 5–16 days; rates include transportation by rental car, sightseeing, day tours from farm. Write for details. Also contact *Farm Holidays Ltd.,* P.O. Box 1436, Wellington. Prices (for one person) around NZ$60–80 per day, with meals.

Milford Track: Tourist Hotel Corp. of New Zealand, P.O. Box 2840, Wellington. Departures from Te Anau on Mondays, Wednesdays, Fridays with extra parties scheduled as required. Trek is sold as a five day/four night package ending at Milford Sound. Prices: Adults NZ$450. Write: Southern Pacific Hotel Corporation, 1901 Avenue of the Stars, Suite 880, Los Angeles, Ca. 90067.

Kiwi Air Pass: Mount Cook Line, operators of New Zealand's airline flies to all the scenic resort areas in the country on scheduled Hawker Siddeley 748 jet prop planes. The Kiwi Air Pass, which must be purchased prior to arrival in New Zealand, allows 14 days of travel to: Bay of Islands, Auckland, Rotorua, Christchurch, Mt. Cook, Queenstown and the Southern Lakes. (Not valid for flight-seeing, ski-plane or charter operations.) Reservations are essential and must be made at the operator's offices in New Zealand. Tickets must be issued against the pass only by Mount Cook in New Zealand, and only for each separate stage of the itinerary. Rates are for air travel only, all other charges at passenger's expense.

Kiwi Coach Pass: Offers unlimited coach travel on a regular basis (no tours) from the following motorcoach companies: Mount Cook Line, NZ Railway Road Services, Hawkes Bay Motor Company, Newmans Coachlines, and Gibsons Motors. Pass must be purchased prior to arrival in New Zealand. Reservations for travel must be made through the local office of operator whose service is to be utilized. Tickets issued against pass by appropriate operator only in New Zealand and only for each separate stage of the itinerary. Maximum validity 28 days. Price is about US$90 for basic seven-day pass; extra days can be added for a minimal fee.

Mount Cook Line: Suite 1020 9841 Airport Blvd., Los Angeles, Ca. 90045. Operates catamaran cruises out of Auckland Harbour.

Mount Cook Northland: P.O. Box 40, Paihia, Bay of Islands. Operates cruises aboard catamaran *Tiger Lily II.*

Rotorua's Volcanic "Wunderflites," Box 118, Rotorua. Offers 30 min. flight of Rotorua area, lakes, craters and thermal phenomena. NZ$25/person. Also, City Tonic Flight, Taupo Great Lake, Nat'l Park and Active Volcano flights. Operates fleet of 4 Cessna 207's seating 6 and Cessna 172's seating 3. Additional flight landing on Mt. Tarawera, a dormant volcano, NZ$32.

FISHING AND HUNTING. Deep-sea fishing is one of New Zealand's most outstanding sports and fishing facilities are well developed. Boats, complete with all equipment, may be chartered at five major ports, all on North Island within 200 miles of Auckland. Main bases: Whangaroa Big Game Fishing Club keeps a masterbook of all bookings for the launches; for Russell and Otehei Bay, which are the Bay of Island bases, information is available from Secretary, Bay of Island Swordfish and Mako Shark Club, P.O. Box 55, Russell; Whangarei (contact Whangarei Deep Sea Angler's Club, Tutukaka, North Auckland) is a base 108 miles north of Auckland; the Mercury Bay Game Fishing Club, Whitianga, is based on the Coromandel Penisula, 100 miles southeast of Auckland; details available from the Secretary of the Club, P.O. Box 54, Whitianga; the Tauranga Big Game Fishing Club, Tauranga, is at the Bay of Plenty, 135 miles southeast of Auckland. The fishing base of the club is at Mayor Island, 20 miles off the coast. Inquiries: Secretary, Commercial Boat Owners Association, P.O. Box 333, Tauranga. Boat rates around NZ$450 per day. *Clubs:* Visiting fishermen are advised to join local deep-sea fishing clubs for the period of their visit. Local club members welcome the visiting angler; club membership averages NZ$4–8 for the season.

Trout Fishing is excellent in New Zealand's numerous rivers and lakes, which are abundant with rainbow and brown trout. Season varies somewhat in different areas, but all areas are open from Oct.–Apr., and Lakes Rotorua and Taupo have open season all year. Fishing license: NZ$7 for a week. Guides: NZ$18–24/hr.

Hunting. Experienced, registered guides providing all camping, hunting and transportation equipment can be obtained by writing to the Fishing and Hunting Officer, Tourist and Publicity Dept., Private Bag, Rotorua. Guides (costing around NZ$350 per day, plus food and equipment) will usually arrange for entry permits to National Parks or private land. Duck, Canadian geese, swan, pheasant and quail have a three-week to two-month season beginning the first Saturday in May.

THE NORTH ISLAND

"The Fish of Maui"

by
JOHN P. CAMPBELL

New Zealand is a land of startling scenic contrasts. The North Island has its weird geysers and bubbling mudpools, where underground steam sizzles through cracks in the ground as if from Nature's pressure cooker. Huge clouds of steam billow from the vast underground reservoir, which is now tapped to provide power for electricity.

The South Island has the dramatically impressive beauty of its alps and fiords, its forests and rivers, and its enchanting lakeland. But the North Island has its share of rolling pastureland and verdant forest-clad hills, so easy on the eye and restful to the senses.

In ancient Maori mythology the North Island is *Te Ika a Maui* ("the fish of Maui"). While fishing with his brothers, Maui, who was descended from the gods and had magical powers, fished the North Island from the sea. Disobeying his orders not to touch the fish, his brothers gnawed at it to assuage their hunger, causing the fish to writhe and thresh about and giving the island an undulating or mountainous landscape.

Auckland (pronounced "Orkland"), the arrival point for most visitors, divides the bulk of the island from the long peninsula of Northland. Being nearer to the equator than the remainder of New Zealand, Northland has a subtropical climate, with superlative seascapes and uncluttered beaches. It is a dairying region, with some sheep farms, but also has large citrus and tropical fruit orchards. It is the birthplace of New

Zealand as a nation, for it was here that the Maoris signed the Treaty of Waitangi, acknowledging British rule.

Most visitors travel south from Auckland through the center of the island to Rotorua to see the thermal activity, and to meet Maori people in one of their principal homes. A detour of some 46 miles is necessary to visit the Glow-worm Grotto of the Waitomo Caves (definitely not to be missed), but this is always included on organised tours, and is easy to visit either in a rented car, or by coach.

Wherever you travel in the North Island you'll pass through dairying and sheep raising country, and it begins soon after you leave Auckland. On the road you'll notice a number of large stainless steel tankers, some with trailers. They are not carrying gas or oil, but milk. These tankers collect milk from the farms every day and take it to factories which make butter, cheese, dried milk powder and other dairy products. One of the largest of these, a tall, gleaming modern building, is passed at Te Rapa just before reaching Hamilton, which stands on the banks of the Waikato River and is New Zealand's largest inland city.

To the left lies Tauranga, the Bay of Plenty and Poverty Bay on the east coast; to the right New Plymouth and Taranaki on the western bulge.

"An Endless Golf Course"

Beyond Hamilton you pass through some of the most fertile farming land in New Zealand. The rolling pastures and grass-covered hills are incredibly green, and dotted with fat, white woolly sheep—they appear like mushrooms in the distance—and sleek dairy cows. The countryside looks like an endless golf course, so immaculately kept are the pastures. They always draw comment, and coach drivers often joke that "as soon as they upgrade the local golf course they are going to turn it into a farm."

The lush fields result from scientific farming. High quality grasses and clovers are sown, but the soil still needs additional fertilizer. Superphosphate, occasionally mixed with other ingredients, is spread annually, and often twice a year. This once laborious task is now done from the air—"aerial topdressing" it is called. This has become a fine art. Aircraft can now land, load a ton of superphosphate, and be airborne again within one minute. Only by aerial topdressing can much of New Zealand's hill country be kept fertile. The chances are that you'll see aerial topdressing being done as you travel.

Abruptly leaving farmland behind, the road enters thick bush and climbs over the Mamaku Range. This magnificent stand of native forest remains just as it was hundreds of years ago. As you peer through the tangled undergrowth, and admire the graceful trees climbing from the deep valleys, you cannot help wondering how the Maoris first found their way through it. You'll also understand why people still get lost in it, and why animals introduced to New Zealand, such as deer, pigs and opossums, which have no natural predators, multiply so prolifically and have been declared noxious animals.

Rotorua is the center of a hot thermal belt which begins in the Bay of Plenty some 40 miles to the east and continues to Tongariro National

Park. Rotorua's thermal area, though vigorously active, is concentrated, and rather surprisingly, surrounded by rich green farms.

It was not always so. Until comparatively recent times the land, consisting to a large degree of volcanic ash and pumice, would grow little but scrub, but scientists discovered that the addition of small quantities of cobalt would make the soil productive. Topdressings of this and superphosphate have resulted in the development of highly intensive farming. The landscape has been transformed from a dull brown to a deep green.

World's Largest Man-Made Forest

It was also found that the pumice and volcanic soil supported pine trees, which mature here in 20 to 25 years, much faster than in other countries. The farming of these trees for lumber and pulp is now one of New Zealand's largest industries. Near Rotorua is the Kaingaroa Forest; 364,000 acres of pines, claimed to be the largest man-made forest in the world. There are other large forests at nearby Kinleith.

The trees are husbanded and harvested much like other crops. Replanting programs are followed, and the Government maintains a Forest Research Institute at Rotorua. All New Zealand newspapers, and many in Australia, are printed on newsprint made at a large plant at Kawerau, a few miles from Rotorua. Understandably, the plant makes use of natural underground steam for some of its power. You'll see the fringe of the forest as you drive from Rotorua to Wairakei and Taupo, and pass through towering avenues of pines.

Fire is a constant danger, and in the dry summer months fire-watchers are stationed in hilltop observation towers, and aerial inspections carried out. In the forests large roadside signs indicate the present degree of fire danger. Thoughtful people do not throw cigarette butts out of the automobile or coach windows. One cautionary sign says: "Chaperone your cigarette—don't let it go out alone."

If time presses, you can fly from Rotorua to Wellington or Christchurch, or even to Mount Cook and Queenstown, but the road journey south is full of interest.

Only 56 miles (90 km) from Rotorua is Taupo, on the northern shores of the lake of that name. Once little more than a sleepy village catering mainly for anglers (the lake is famous for the quantity and size of its trout) and summer holiday-makers, Taupo is today a thriving modern town. It owes its prosperity to the development of farming and the growth of forestry.

Entering the town you descend an incline and cross a narrow bridge over sluice gates. This is the beginning of the long Waikato River, which flows out of the lake. Here, unlike the muddy river seen on the journey from Auckland, the waters are crystal-clear with an icy blue-green tinge, for they flow from the vast snowfields and glaciers at the opposite end of the lake.

In spite of its commercial activity, Taupo is still a mecca for anglers. More than 700 tons of trout, mainly rainbow, are taken from the lake each year!

The road follows the eastern shores of the lake for 32 miles (45.5 km) to Turangi at the southern end. At Waitahanui, where a stream flows into the lake, you'll probably see a score or more anglers standing waist-high in the water, and almost shoulder to shoulder. At this particularly productive point, the congestion is known as "the picket fence".

The road then winds through a narrow gorge, thought to have been formed by an earthquake, and climbs to a plateau, at the end of which is an especially beautiful vista of the lake and the sacred island of Motutaiko, a Maori burial ground. On a fine day the lake is colored in pastel shades, as if a rainbow had been laid on the waters.

Like Taupo, Turangi was once a sleepy trout-fishing village, but it is now the center of a large hydro-electric development which is nearing completion.

Hard-to-pronounce Mountains

Within a few miles you enter the boundaries of the Tongariro National Park, with its three mountains—Ruapehu, Ngauruhoe and Tongariro. To the right, the road follows the western slopes to the Chateau, the North Island's most popular skiing resort, but the more direct route to Wellington is to the left. Some delightful forested valleys with tumbling mountain streams are passed before a long plateau is reached. This is known as the Desert Road, but it is nothing like a conventional desert. Overshadowed by three mountains and swept by winds, the area is arid and grows nothing but scruffy tussock in its pumice soil, although pine plantations are now being established. Anyone familiar with true desert would object to the description, but to New Zealanders, accustomed to grass-covered land, it is a barren wasteland. Near the center of the plateau the road is 3,600 ft above sea level, and is occasionally blocked by snow in winter. Waiouru, at the southern end, is the North Island's main military base.

Hill-Country Farming

Green pastures soon appear again, but the terrain is steep and rugged —a good example of what New Zealanders describe as "hill country farming." The hills were once covered with thick forest, which was burnt off and replaced with good grasses and clovers. Sheep clamber up the steep slopes like mountain goats.

Slowly, the hills give way to rolling pastures, and finally to an extensive plain which slopes from the mountain ranges to the sea. It is an area of concentrated sheep farming and dairying, and once again the large number of sheep in the fields demonstrates the fertility of the land.

Just past Waikanae, some 40 miles (64.4 km) from Wellington, there are fine views to the right of Kapiti Island off the coast. Once a stronghold of the infamous Maori chief Te Rauparaha, it is now a bird sanctuary. The land which appears, rising from the sea as you follow the coast to enter the suburbs of Wellington, is the northern tip of the South Island.

Most visitors tend to follow this central route and omit the delightful areas of the Bay of Plenty and Hawke's Bay on the eastern coast, and Taranaki on the west coast, because of the additional travelling time required. If time is not an important factor, it is a good plan to travel through the center of the island on the way south, and to return to Auckland from Wellington along the eastern or western coast.

In Hawke's Bay, Hastings and Napier are reached in one day by road or in 2 hours by air. The area is one of the largest vegetable and fruit producing regions in the country, and Napier is a delightful seaside city. From Napier one can travel through mountain passes to Taupo and Rotorua, or go up the east coast to Gisborne and through to Tauranga, in the Bay of Plenty, from which it is an easy drive to either Rotorua or Auckland.

The west coast route passes through the river city of Wanganui and on to New Plymouth, nestling beneath the slopes of Mount Egmont in Taranaki. The Glow-worm Grotto at Waitomo Caves lies close beside the main road to Auckland.

AUCKLAND

Rome was built on seven hills, Auckland on seven or more extinct volcanoes. Auckland is New Zealand's largest city, with a population of over 800,000. Situated on a narrow isthmus, it separates two seas, the Pacific Ocean and the Tasman Sea, and two harbors, the Waitemata and the Manukau.

Dominating the Waitemata Harbor *(Sea of Sparkling Waters)* is Rangitoto Island, a long, three-humped, former volcanic island, whose shape never changes from whatever angle it is viewed.

Like parts of the United States, Auckland was bought for a song. History records that 3,000 acres of land were purchased from the Maori for $110 in cash, 50 blankets, 20 pairs of trousers, 20 shirts, 100 yards of cloth, 10 waistcoats, 10 caps, 20 hatchets, a bag of sugar, a bag of flour, 10 iron pots, 4 casks of tobacco and a box of pipes.

A large population and an abundance of flat land gradually drew industry to Auckland, which is today New Zealand's largest industrial and commercial center. Thoughtful planning has, however, prevented most of the newer factories from becoming unsightly blotches, and the new homes from being too stereotyped.

The growth of industry called for more labor, and, seeking opportunities for employment and education, thousands of Pacific Islanders, who also hold New Zealand citizenship, have flocked to Auckland. From the Cook Islands, Tonga, Western Samoa, the Tokelau Islands and from Niue Island they came, to make Auckland the largest Polynesian city in the world.

Unlike the Europeans who settled earlier, the Polynesians have tended to retain their own culture and customs, and to live in their own communities. On Sundays especially you will see the women in long skirts and flowered straw hats, and the men in neat suits with white shirt and tie going to their own churches. Walk the length of Karangahape Road, to the north of the business center of the city, and you'll rub shoulders with as many Polynesians as Europeans.

They are mostly a happy, carefree people, but some have yet to adjust to the European way of life. They tend to congregate with their own compatriots, and some of the hotel bars have identified with them by painting their exteriors in the brilliant colors the Polynesians love, particularly reds and purples.

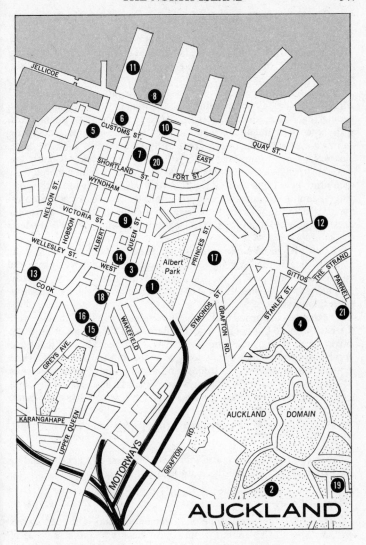

AUCKLAND

Points of Interest

1) Art Gallery
2) Botanical Gardens
3) "246" Shopping Center
4) Carlaw Park (Rugby League)
5) City Markets
6) Downtown Shopping Center
7) Duty-free Shops
8) Ferry Terminal
9) His Majesty's Theater
10) Post Office
11) Princes Wharf
12) Railroad Station
13) St. Matthews Church
14) Strand Arcade
15) Town Hall
16) Town Hall Theater
17) University
18) Visitors Bureau and Downtown Airlines Terminal and Shopping Center
19) War Memorial Museum
20) Queen's Arcade Shopping Center
21) Parnell Village Shopping Center

Queen Street: Narrow Valley Floor

Some New Zealanders consider that Auckland is humid in summer. There is some truth in this, but the humidity is nothing like as enervating as the humidity of New York, and there is usually the relief of a sea breeze.

Most of the principal hotels are close to Queen Street, the main street, which runs along a narrow valley floor, with side streets climbing off it like herring bones. Queen Street is a series of small shops, interspersed with larger department stores and some interesting arcades. One-storey and two-storey buildings are gradually giving way to modern office blocks. Of special interest is "246" (the street number). All floors are served by escalators, and each floor has varied shops which merge with each other on an open-plan style. It is well worth a visit for both shopping or simply strolling. Almost opposite is the Strand Arcade, a corridor of enticing shops rebuilt to resemble a colonial street of Victorian days. At the bottom of Queen Street is the downtown complex of modern shops.

Parnell Village, a couple of miles from the city, should not be missed. Here, an imaginative developer has transformed what was formerly a rather run-down part of Auckland into a delightful replica of early colonial days—not merely as a tourist attraction but as an attractive collection of shops.

Aucklanders are proud of their harbor bridge which links the city with the North Shore (a popular residential area and the main outlet to the north), even though they flippantly refer to it as "The Coathanger". Previously the only link was by ferry or a long journey by road. Opened in 1959, the bridge is 3,348 ft long, and its 800 ft navigation span rises 142 ft above the water. Within ten years the traffic flow had trebled, and extra lanes had to be added to each side to cope. It now has eight lanes.

EXPLORING AUCKLAND

Several half or full-day coach tours show the best of Auckland and its surroundings. All include the main features.

Mount Eden

The 643 ft symmetrical cone of an extinct volcano. The road spirals up the slopes to the summit, from which there is a complete circle of panoramic views of the city and outlying areas. From here one can look at two oceans with a turn of the head; on one side the Tasman Sea, on the other the Pacific Ocean. A table shows the direction and distances of the main cities of the world. Just below the lip is the deep red lava crater, fringed by grass, where sheep graze placidly.

One Tree Hill

This hill catches the eye from the city, with its single tree and a 70 ft obelisk honoring Sir John Logan Campbell, "the father of Auckland." On the crest of the hill is the Auckland Observatory. Like Mount Eden, it was formerly a Maori fortified village.

The Auckland Domain

Virtually in the city, this large expanse of parkland and sports fields contains the Winter Gardens and the Auckland Museum, which has a fine collection of Maori and South Pacific artifacts. There are authentic Maori houses, weapons, and an 82 ft war canoe.

Kelly Tarlton's Underwater World

Not to be missed is this attraction, which is far from a routine aquarium. The impression of actually being an underwater diver is strong as one takes the 8-minute trip on a conveyor through a 40-foot long tunnel lined with acrylic windows. Over 30 species of fish, including sharks and stingrays, swim beside and above you in a natural environment. There are also fish pools and a 12-minute audio-visual show. The complex is opposite Orakei Wharf, on a bus route, and close to the city.

Parnell Rose Garden

Famous for its rose gardens and profusion of blooms in season (November).

Zoological Gardens

By overseas standards the zoo is not outstanding, but New Zealand's unique bird, the kiwi, can be seen in a special nocturnal house. The kiwi forages for food only at night, and a special house has been built and lit to resemble its native habitat.

Museum of Transport and Technology

Don't let this forbidding title put you off. A fascinating collection of equipment and machines that have now largely disappeared, including a working tramway, a railway, vintage cars and carriages, and wartime guns and aircraft. It also contains the remains of what was probably the second aircraft to fly. A New Zealander, Robert Pearse, designed and built an aircraft which he twice flew in March 1903, just three months after the Wright brothers made the world's first powered flight. There is still argument whether Pearse did, in fact, fly first. Ancient vehicles have been painstakingly restored, and mounted on rails are old trolley cars and railroad locomotives. The camera and telephone exhibits are outstanding. If you grew up in the 1920s and 1930s you'll feel a pang of nostalgia to see the old type of gas pumps still bearing names like "Voco," and "Super Plume Ethyl" and even five-gallon cans labelled "Texaco" and "Shell." In another part of the museum about a mile away memories of World War II are revived by a Lancaster bomber, one of the type which carried out the daring raid on the Moehne, Eder and Sorpe dams in the Ruhr. Nearby are a Kittyhawk and a Vampire jet.

Vineyards

The Henderson area is renowned for its vineyards. They began in the 1890s when an immigrant from Lebanon, Assid Abraham Corban, brought with him a 300-year-old tradition in wine making and viticulture. Today, there are dozens of vineyards in a compact area, from large corporation enterprises to small individual holdings. A tour of some of the vineyards to taste the local product on the site is full of enjoyment.

Bus Tours and Harbor Cruises

Half- and full-day bus tours of Auckland and the surrounding area are run daily by Trans Tours-Grayline and Scenic Tours. There are harbor cruises by fast launches which leave regularly from the Ferry Building at the foot of Queen Street for parts of the Hauraki Gulf including Rangitoto and Waiheke Islands.

AUCKLAND HOTELS AND MOTELS

Airport Inn. Mangere (close to airport). 100 rooms, restaurant, bar, pool.

Airport Travelodge. 253 rooms, high quality. Restaurants, bars, parking, pool.

Barrycourt Motel. Parnell. 126 rooms. Restaurant, bar.

Hyatt Kingsgate. Prince Street and Waterloo Quadrant. 327 rooms, restaurants, bars, Jacuzzis, jogging track.

Mon Desir Hotel. 144 Hurstmere Road, Takapuna (on the North Shore). 37 rooms, restaurant, bar, pool, sauna.

Regent of Auckland. Albert Street. 332 rooms, restaurants, bars, parking, in this new, top-quality establishment.

Rose Park Motor Inn. 100 Gladstone Road, Parnell. 110 units. Restaurant, bar.

Royal International Hotel. Victoria Street West. 98 rooms, restaurant, bars, refrigerators in rooms.

Sheraton-Auckland Hotel. 85 Symonds Street. 410 rooms, 28 executive rooms. Top quality, central location, pool, bars, parking, sauna, spa, gym.

South Pacific Hotel. Customs Street. 184 rooms, restaurants, bars, refrigerators in rooms.

Takapuna Beach Motel. The Promenade, Takapuna. 28 units and studios with kitchens, bar; restaurant close by.

Townhouse Auckland. 150 Anzac Ave. 110 service units. Central location.

TraveLodge. 96 Quay Street. 198 rooms, restaurant, bars, parking.

Vacation Hotel. 187 Campbell Road. 222 rooms, restaurant, bar, parking, five miles from city.

White Heron Regency. 138 St. Stephen's Avenue. 75 rooms, restaurant, bar.

AUCKLAND RESTAURANTS

Antoine's. 333 Parnell Road. Traditional French colonial atmosphere, French cuisine.

Bonaparte Restaurant. Corner Victoria and High Street. Empire period decor, French cuisine and traditional New Zealand dishes.

Carthews. 151 Ponsonby Road, American cuisine, creole cooking.

Clichy Restaurant. 3 Britomart Place. French provincial atmosphere, all French cuisine.

Da Gino. 66–68 Pitt Street. Appropriate Italian décor and exclusively Italian food.

Deerstalker Inn. 153 Ponsonby Road. Hunting atmosphere, emphasis on good food, especially game and fish.

Fisherman's Wharf. Northcote. Harborside nautical atmosphere, predominantly seafood menu.

Gamekeeper's. 29 Ponsonby Road. Hunting lodge decor, game and local foods.

Le Gourmet. 1 Williamson Avenue, Ponsonby. Late-Victorian decor, limited specialized menu.

Harleys. 25 Anzav Avenue. New Zealand food, with embellishments.

Number Five. 5 City Road. Top quality, superlative French nouvelle cuisine.

Oblio's. 110 Ponsonby Road, Ponsonby. An "indoor garden" restaurant, tasteful décor and good food.

Oliver's. 18 Fort Street, Lavish ultra-modern decor, international cuisine.

Orient. Strand Arcade, Queen Street. Elegant Chinese decor with Chinese cuisine.

Orleans. 106 Symonds Street. French household cuisine; desserts a specialty.

Orsini's. 50 Ponsonby Road. Fine food in elegant surroundings.

Pelorus Jack. 27 Rutland St. Specializes in seafood.

Salters. 473 Khyber Pass Road, Newmarket. Attractive, restrained décor, good food.

Yamato. 183 Karangahape Road. Traditional Japanese food.

WELLINGTON

"Like San Francisco" say Californians when they survey the city from the surrounding hills. And it *is* rather like San Francisco. Its wide, circular harbor lies in a basin of steep hills, the shops and offices cluster near the waterfront, and it even has a cable car! As the lights glow at night it resembles Hong Kong.

Wellington stands at the south-west tip of the North Island, and only a 20 mile stretch of water, Cook Strait, separates it from the northern tip of the South Island. The gap is bridged by 4,000 ton passenger/vehicle ferries which cross the strait frequently every day.

It is known as "Windy Wellington". Cook Strait seems to funnel every breeze that blows and expand it into a wind. Most are gentle to moderate, but in the spring and fall they become strong. They are not unbearable, and at least they prevent air pollution. Other cities have a joke: "You can always identify a Wellingtonian because he grabs his hat when he rounds a corner".

Wellington is the capital city, and a large proportion of Wellingtonians work in Government departments, whose head offices are here—rather like Washington D.C. Many national business concerns also have their head offices in Wellington, though there is a gradual migration to Auckland, where the factories are tending to concentrate.

The combined urban areas have a population of about 354,000, making it the second largest city. The number in the city boundaries is, however, much less, as there are large residential and light industrial areas in the adjoining Hutt Valley and Porirua basin. Lower Hutt and Upper Hutt are cities in their own right.

Wellington is justly proud of its magnificent harbor, a huge circular basin reached through a channel from Cook Strait and hemmed by steep hills. As the settlement grew from its small beginnings problems arose. There just wasn't enough flat land. The extension of the business areas was achieved by reclaiming land from the harbor. One of the main streets, Lambton Quay, is no longer a waterfront and is now about a quarter of a mile from the docks. From the waterside the hills rise so steeply that in some of the modern buildings you can enter a shop or office block at street level, ascend in an elevator to the second or third floors and exit at a door, still at street level.

Finding sites for homes also posed problems, and many houses climb dizzily up the hills, clinging to apparently sheer slopes. Many are built on stilts, and some even have their own small private cable cars.

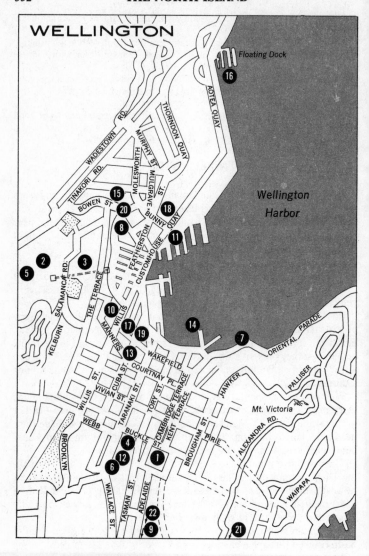

WELLINGTON

Floating Dock

Wellington Harbor

Mt. Victoria

Points of Interest

1) Basin Reserve (Cricket and
   Soccer)
2) Botanical Gardens
3) Cable Car
4) Carillon & Hall of Memories
5) Carter Observatory
6) Dominion Museum
7) Freyberg Pool
8) Government Buildings
9) Government House
10) Government Tourist Bureau
11) Main Docks

12) National Art Gallery
13) New Zealand Display Center
14) Overseas Shipping Terminal
15) Parliament House
16) Picton Ferry Terminal
17) Post Office
18) Railway Station
19) Town Hall
20) War Memorial
21) Wellington Airport
22) Zoo

There was only one way for the city to go—up. Wellington's two and three-storey office and shop buildings are giving way to small skyscrapers. The height of buildings was originally kept low, not because tall buildings were not originally needed, but as a precaution against possible earthquakes. Modern design and construction have, however, overcome the latter danger.

Named after the Duke of Wellington, who won the Battle of Waterloo between the British and the French, Wellington was settled by a company formed in England by Edward Gibbon Wakefield. The first ships arrived in 1840, and many of the streets are named after them or the British leaders of the day.

In 1865 Wellington became New Zealand's capital. It adopted as its motto *Suprema a Situ,* supreme by situation. In spite of Auckland's faster growth, it still holds proudly to that title. Certainly it is the geographical center of New Zealand.

Like Auckland, it has a population of Polynesians from the Pacific Islands, although in smaller numbers.

EXPLORING WELLINGTON

The best way to see Wellington is to take one of the half-day sightseeing coach tours run by Wellington Sightseeing Tours, or the Wellington City Transport Corporation. The former will call, by arrangement, at hotels and motels, and the latter leaves from Rotary Garden Court opposite the Town Hall. The main points of interest on these tours are:

Summit of Mount Victoria

Reached by a winding but well-made road through a residential area, the 558 ft. summit of Mount Victoria is the best known vantage point. From here the whole city and harbor seem to spread out like a gigantic relief map. To the west, the northern tip of the South Island can be seen on a clear day. In the roofed observation deck is a bronze bust of the Duke of Wellington staring austerely, not at the city named after him but, strangely enough, away from it. A short distance away is a stone cairn memorial to Rear Admiral Richard Byrd, an American explorer of the Antarctic who used New Zealand as a base for his expeditions. The stones embedded in the cement are from Antarctica.

Dominion Museum and Art Gallery

The Maori section contains many authentic carvings and artifacts, including a meeting house which is considered to be the finest surviving example of its kind. There are some relics of Captain Cook, including the original figurehead from his ship *Resolution,* which he used on his second and third voyages to New Zealand. The colonial section shows early European life in New Zealand and features an "Early Wellington House" complete with furnishings.

War Memorial Carillon Tower

Standing in front of the Dominion Museum, the carillon is the national war memorial and contains the Hall of Memories. A lamp at the top of the tower burns continuously. The carillon has 49 bells, and recitals are given periodically.

Lady Norwood Rose Garden

From summer through fall the Lady Norwood Rose Garden in the Botanical Gardens is a profusion of colorful blooms.

Kelburn Lookout

A ride on the cable car should not be missed for the magnificent views of the city and harbor from the 480-foot summit at Kelburn. The entrance to the city terminal is along a lane off Lambton Quay. Unlike the San Francisco cable cars, the car simply climbs a hill and then returns. It travels at a constant angle of about 15 degrees. Try to get seats on the left-hand side as the car ascends, and in the front for the best views as the car descends. The car passes through three short tunnels and makes three intermediate stops before reaching the summit. The cars run frequently, and the return trip can be made after you have enjoyed the view.

Parliament Buildings

Just above the Cenotaph, Wellington's war memorial, stand Parliament Buildings, the legislative center. The main marble buildings lack the towers which were originally intended but still present a solid dignity. At one end is a new circular building which looks remarkably like, and has therefore been christened, *The Beehive.* Inside, Government messengers will conduct you on a tour of the legislative offices.

Government Buildings

Below Parliament Buildings is one of the largest wooden buildings in the world. Of 100,300 square feet, the Government Buildings, which house several departments, are a source of pride to Wellingtonians.

Old St. Paul's Cathedral

This is one of the finest examples of a wooden church built in the early days by Church of England followers. Only a block away from the new modern cathedral, Old St. Paul's was so much a part of Wellington's history, and so beloved, that it is now preserved as a national shrine. The interior is exquisite.

Alexander Turnbull Library

This is almost as much a museum as a library in that it contains a priceless collection of historic documents and many rare first editions. Included in the displays are the original signed sheets of the Treaty of Waitangi.

Memorial Gates to the Second American Marine Division

As the Japanese began moving down the South Pacific, the Second American Marine Division made Wellington its headquarters. They were based at McKay's Crossing (a railroad crossing) near Paekakariki, some 30 miles north of Wellington on the main highway. From here they embarked for the blood-bath of Guadacanal. The Memorial Gates, recalling the 17 months spent there by the Division, stand at the entrance to the former camp.

Tramway Museum

Close by is a Tramway Museum, founded to preserve Wellington's trolley cars, now replaced by buses. The old trolley cars still run on a ¾ mile track in Queen Elizabeth Park.

WELLINGTON HOTELS AND MOTELS

Burma Motor Lodge. Burma Road, Johnsonville, 8 miles from city, 63 rooms, restaurant, bar, parking.

Forum Hotel. 110–116 Wakefield Street. 102 rooms, restaurant, bar, central.

Hotel St. George. Willis Street. 88 rooms, restaurant, bars, central.

Hotel Waterloo. Cr. Waterloo Quay & Bunny St. 85 rooms, restaurant, bar, opposite railroad station.

James Cook Hotel. The Terrace. 270 rooms, restaurant, bars, parking.

Melksham Towers. Cor. Brougham and Ellis Sts. Motel flats, 39 units. No liquor facilities or restaurant.

Sharella Motor Inn. 20 Glenmore Street. 66 rooms, restaurant, bar, parking, ½ mile from city.

Shaw Savill Lodge. Kemp Street, Kilbirnie. 122 rooms, restaurant, bar, parking, 4 miles from city, 1 mile from airport.

Terrace Regency. The Terrace. High quality, 122 rooms, suites, pool, bars, restaurant, parking.

Town House Motor Inn. 100 Oriental Parade. 122 rooms, restaurant, bar.

Parkroyal Hotel. Oriental Bay. 70 rooms, high quality, restaurants, bars.

Wellington Travelodge. 40 Oriental Parade. 78 rooms, restaurant, bar.

WELLINGTON RESTAURANTS

Acropolis. 37 Dixon St. Specializes in Greek food.

Amsterdam, 165 Riddiford St., Newtown. Early Colonial atmosphere. Good food, but a little off the beaten track.

Bacchus Restaurant. 8 Courtenay Place. Quiet, intimate, wide range of dishes.

Beefeater's Arms. 105 The Terrace. Tudor decor, popular for business lunches, specialty is rib of beef on the bone.

The Coachman. 46 Courtenay Place. Small and exclusive, concentrates on good food, quiet atmosphere, specialties are duckling, scallops, and crayfish.

Il Casino and Il Salone. 108 Tory Street. Good traditional Italian cuisine.

La Normandie. 116 Cuba Street. Elegant old-fashioned decor, New Zealand game a specialty.

Orsini's. 201 Cuba Street. Elegant, open fires in winter, quiet dining, seafood and steak.

Otto's Hafen Restaurant. Overseas Passenger Terminal. Harbor views, specialises in fresh seafood.

Pickwicks. Hannah Playhouse Bldg., Courtenay Pl. Simple but good.

Pierre's Restaurant. 342 Tinakori Road. Early settler decor, small, intimate, French cuisine, no liquor licence so bring your own wine.

The Packing Case. 191 Featherston St. Warehouse décor, with tables in packing case booths.

Plimmer House. 99 Boulcott Street. Gracious dining, Victorian decor, specialties are beef and seafood.

The Roxburgh. 18 Majorbanks St. Small, intimate, international fare, German emphasis; open fire in winter.

Shorebird. 301 Evans Bay Parade. Fresh fish caught from restaurant's own boat.

Skyline. At top of cable car. Good food with views of the city.

Windows on Wellington. Williams Parking Center, on 31st floor, Plimmers Lane. Ultra-modern, French and English cooking, seafood.

The Woolshed. Williams Parking Center, Plimmers Lane. Early provincial decor, replica of a woolshed, entertainment, quick service, steaks, lamb dishes.

NORTHLAND

"The winterless north" is how residents describe the long peninsula pointing north from Auckland. (Remember that seasons are reversed in the Southern Hemisphere). The claim is not strictly true, but the region is subtropical, and certainly warmer in winter than other parts of New Zealand. It is a productive dairying area and also contains New Zealand's only oil refinery, at Marsden Point.

Northland is often bypassed, as it is time-consuming to travel. Even though the route is circular, it takes six or seven days if sufficient time is allowed for sightseeing. Yet it repays a visit. Even just three days will allow a visit to the most interesting area, the Bay of Islands.

In pre-European times much of the land was covered with a unique tree, the kauri. Of huge size, it is branchless for much of its length, and was therefore especially favored by the early whalers for masts and spars. The Maoris made canoes more than 100 ft. long from it. And the Europeans plundered it—a tragedy, as it is a slow-growing tree and takes a thousand years to reach full maturity. Today, the remaining forests are rigidly protected. There are three stands where the kauri may be seen in all its magnificence—the Waipoua State Forest and Trounson Park on the western side, and Puketi State Forest, near Waitangi, in the east. Waipoua State Forest has the greatest kauri of all—Tane Mahuta (*God of the Forest*—167 ft. tall and 14 ft. thick, with the lowest branches 60 ft. from the ground, and an estimated age of 1,200 years.

Through splits in its bark the tree exudes a gum which runs down the trunk and into the ground. It hardens into solid lumps of amber-colored, clear resin, which is today used for carved ornaments. In the latter part of the last century, however, it was much used for making varnishes, and thousands of Yugoslavs came to New Zealand as gum diggers. They dug for the gum in the ground and scaled the straight trunks to extract it from the branch forks. Modern synthetics replaced the gum, and many of the Yugoslavs became absorbed into other occupations or became grape-growers and wine-makers, a calling they still follow.

A little more than half-way up the narrow peninsula on the east coast is the Bay of Islands—a large semicircular indentation serrated by many bays and beaches, as if some giant sea monster had bitten into the coast with a mouth of jagged teeth. Within the bay are some 150 islands—the exact number is a matter of dispute.

This is the birthplace of modern New Zealand history. It was here that the Treaty of Waitangi, establishing British rule, was signed on February 6, 1840. Waitangi Day is observed as New Zealand's National Day, and a colorful ceremony is always held on the sweeping lawn outside the Treaty House, now an historical reserve. It was here, too, that Christianity was first introduced to the Maori. On Christmas Day 1814 the Rev. Samuel Marsden conducted the first Christian service to be held in the country.

Further north on the west coast is the long stretch of Ninety Mile Beach (actually only 64 miles), and further up on the northernmost tip of New Zealand, Cape Reinga.

Between December and April marlin and shark appear off the eastern coast, and two points share popularity with other places further south for big game fishing.

Exploring Northland

Travelling up the east coast, your objective will probably be the Bay of Islands, but pause to try the thermal springs at Waiwera, which means "hot water," and see the busy city of Whangarei. Here the Clapham Clock Museum in Lower John Street is world-renowned for its collection of clocks, and should not be missed.

In the Bay of Islands, Paihia, close to the Treaty House, and Russell stand on opposite sides of the bay. There are regular launch services connecting them, but vehicles have to be punted across a stretch of water. Because of its wider range of accommodations Paihai has become the holiday center.

Russell, once known as Kororareka, is redolent with evidence of early history. It was once known as "the hell-hole of the Pacific," when in the early 1800s whaling ships began calling for provisions. They traded with the Maoris with muskets and liquor, and brawling was commonplace. Nevertheless, after the signing of the Treaty of Waitangi it became New Zealand's first capital and was renamed Russell, but in 1841 the seat of government was moved to Auckland.

Russell still maintains an old-world charm. Dominating the waterfront is what is known as Pompallier House, a graceful Colonial-style building which could almost have come from the deep South of the United States. It is commonly thought of as the home of Bishop Pompallier, a Frenchman and the first Roman Catholic bishop of the South-west Pacific, who arrived in 1838 to establish the first Roman Catholic mission. Actually, he never lived in it but in a building which has long disappeared. The present building bears no resemblance to the original two-storey structure made of rammed earth that was used to house the mission's printing presses. They produced several religious booklets printed in Maori. After the mission moved to Auckland it was used as a tannery for a time, but then sold to a local official, who transformed it into a fine residence. It was subsequently acquired by the Government, and the Historic Places Trust has turned it into a museum, which contains a number of interesting exhibits.

Outstanding sidetrips from Russell (or Paihia) are cruises to outlying islands by launch (formerly known as "Fullers Cream Trip") or by the motor-powered large *Tiger Lily* catamaran. The big thrill is a Piercy Island turnaround, with its famous "hole in the rock." Here the sea surges through a funnel-like hole about 30 feet long, 50 feet high, and 40 feet wide, and, with masterly maneuvering, the catamaran is edged slowly through the gap. Both the catamaran and the launch have comfortable cabins, hostess services, and bars. Take your lunch or order one when buying your ticket.

Across the bay is Waitangi, the birthplace of New Zealand history. On a grassy lawn sloping to the sea the Treaty of Waitangi was signed.

The Treaty House is fascinating. It was built as a home by the newly-appointed British Resident, James Busby, in 1833, and is typical of the type of home favored by the more prosperous of the early settlers. In addition to a collection of historic items, it contains the first piano brought to New Zealand. In front of the house a kauri flagstaff marks the place where the treaty was signed.

Of greater interest, however, is a Maori meeting house *(whare runanga)* which is unusual in that it contains carvings from many different tribes; a meeting house usually has only the carvings of its own tribe. Beside it is a 117 ft. war canoe built for the 1940 centennial celebrations. It is made in three jointed sections, cut from huge trees.

Relics from the Bottom

Two miles (3.2 km) beyond the Treaty House is Mount Bledisloe (376 ft) from which there are wide views of the Bay of Islands.

It is worth pausing near the Waitangi Bridge to see the Museum of Shipwrecks, housed in an old wooden ship sitting on the river bottom. Here a collection of what a diver, Kelly Tarlton, has brought up from the sea bed is exhibited.

Just a few miles away is the township of Kerikeri, one of the first mission stations. It is a prolific citrus-growing area, but a rich soil and kind climate also favor other subtropical fruits.

Almost on the river bank is the Mission House, the oldest building in New Zealand, which has been carefully restored, and the old Stone Store, still a store and in part a museum.

It's a full-day bus trip to New Zealand's northernmost tip, Cape Reinga. Part of the route is along the hard sand of Ninety Mile Beach and then up a shallow river bed. From the lighthouse at the cape you can watch the Pacific Ocean meet the Tasman Sea in a flurry of angry water. It was from here, the Maoris believed, that the spirits of the dead departed on their journey back to their Pacific homeland, Hawaiki.

Ninety Mile Beach is famous in New Zealand as a source of the toheroa, a type of clam which grows up to 6 inches long and from which is made a delicious green-colored soup. Unfortunately, this is hard to get, as restrictions have been imposed to conserve the toheroa beds, which were being depleted. More plentiful, however, is the tuatua, a similar but smaller type of clam, which is also mouth-watering.

The return to Auckland from the Bay of Islands is usually made down the west coast and through the Waipoua State Kauri Forest.

Waitomo Caves

Resist the temptation to say "when you've seen one cave you've seen them all." Certainly the Waitomo Caves have stalactites and stalagmites like so many others, but they also have a feature which is unique—the Glow-worm Grotto. Neither words nor pictures can capture the beauty and the atmosphere. A visit is a remarkable experience.

With a guide, you descend to a deep cavern through which flows a quiet, sluggish stream. You are warned to keep silent as the glow-worms extinguish their lights at noise. At a landing you take your place in a flat-bottomed boat, the electric light is extinguished, and the guide slowly pulls the boat by wires around a cornice and into a vaulted cavern festooned with thousands and thousands of pinpricks of light—tiny individually, but collectively strong enough for you to see your companions in the darkness. Except for the occasional sound of dripping water the silence is complete. Above and around you myriads of glow-worms shine their steady blue-green light, the dark, still waters glistening with their reflections like a star-studded carpet.

The Waitomo glow-worm is an unusual species, quite unlike the glow-worms and fireflies seen in other countries. While most other glow-worms shine their lights as a mating lure, the Waitomo glow-worm lights up to attract food. The hungrier it is, the stronger the light. Visitors are able to see the glow-worms at close hand in what is called the "demonstration chamber" close to the grotto.

The Waitomo Caves are 126 miles (203 km) from Auckland and 46 miles (74 km) off the main route to Rotorua. Such is their beauty that they are always included in an itinerary unless lack of time makes it impossible. It is possible to include the caves in a tour of other parts of the region, and they are also a convenient stopover point if one is driving from Auckland to New Plymouth or Rotorua.

ROTORUA

Rotorua is an area of contradictions. Gentle scenic beauty and violent thermal activity exist side by side. It has long been regarded as New Zealand's prime attraction, both for overseas visitors and New Zealanders themselves.

It has also remained one of the traditional homes of the Maori people, and it is the best place to meet them and to gain an insight into their philosophy and culture. But don't expect to see them living in native reservations or around the streets in their native costumes. They are completely integrated into modern society and live, dress and work the same way as Europeans. Far from there being any segregation, they mingle freely and on equal terms. But to entertain the visitor they don their traditional costumes to give Maori concerts at night. Few are fulltime entertainers; most of the men and women you see performing hold regular jobs as secretaries, shop assistants, radiographers, technicians or clerks. The girl you see performing intricate and graceful dance movements may serve you your breakfast in the morning.

(A reminder: Maori is pronounced "Mau-ree", not "May-ori". Not that offence is taken at a mispronounciation, but you might as well give a good impression by saying it right.)

Rotorua, 149 miles (239.8 km) south of Auckland, once relied on tourism, but forestry and farming are now major industries, and the city's population has grown to over 47,000. Don't be concerned at the smell as you approach. Because of the underground thermal activity there is frequently a pungent odor of hydrogen sulphide: the locals

Speak a foreign language in seconds.

Now an amazing space age device makes it possible to speak a foreign language *without* having to learn a foreign language.

Speak French, German, or Spanish.

With the incredible Translator 8000—world's first pocket-size electronic translation machines —you're never at a loss for words in France, Germany, or Spain.

8,000-word brain.

Just punch in the foreign word or phrase, and English appears on the LED display. Or punch in English, and read the foreign equivalent instantly.

Only 4¾" x 2¾", it possesses a fluent 8,000-word vocabulary (4,000 English, 4,000 foreign). A memory key stores up to 16 words; a practice key randomly calls up words for study, self-

testing, or game use. And it's also a full-function calculator.

150,000 sold in 18 months.

Manufactured for Langenscheidt by Sharp/Japan, the Translator 8000 comes with a 6-month warranty. It's a valuable aid for business and pleasure travelers, and students. It comes in a handsome leatherette case, and makes a super gift.

Order now with the information below.

To order, send $69.95 plus $3 p&h ($12 for overseas del.) for each unit. Indicate language choice: English/French, English/German, English/Spanish. N.Y. res. add sales tax. MasterCard, Visa, or American Express card users give brand, account number (all digits), expiration date, and signature. SEND TO: Fodor's, Dept. T-8000, 2 Park Ave., New York, NY 10016-5677, U.S.A.

sometimes jocularly refer to it as "Sulphur City". But the natural gas is harmless, and one quickly becomes accustomed to the smell.

For many years Rotorua was a popular spa resort, and many went there to bathe in the mineral waters. Modern medicine tends to discount the curative power of the waters, but it does not dispute their value in relieving minor aches and pains. There is nothing more relaxing than soaking in a hot thermal pool after a day's sightseeing. You'll sleep soundly. The Polynesian Pools near the center of the city have a variety of baths, and many hotels and motels have their own pools, as do some private homes.

Don't be alarmed by discolorations on the water taps and fittings. They are not dirty. Chemicals in the water tend to tarnish certain metals; in fact, you can often identify "Rotorua money" by the dullness of the silver coins.

The Hot-Water Belt

Rotorua sits on a huge bed of hot water and steam. You'll see it seeping from banks and culverts, from gutters beside the sidewalks, from clumps of bushes, and even from the middle of flower beds. It is not uncommon to see hot and cold pools side by side. In fact, hot earth is one of the natural hazards in the main golf course.

Residents of the "hot water belt" take full advantage of this by sinking a bore and harnessing the steam to heat their homes and pools, and even do some of their cooking. You'll often see thin pipes rising from gardens to let off surplus steam.

Rotorua is at the southern end of the 32 square mile lake of that name. Unfortunately, the name is not as evocative as it sounds. It simply means "second lake" *(roto* means lake and *rua* means second *)*. When the migrating Maori canoe *Arawa* landed on the east coast an exploring party moved inland. They found a large lake, Rotoiti ("first lake"), and then a larger lake, Rotorua.

The Arawa tribe settled in the Rotorua area, and it is still their homeland.

In the center of Lake Rotorua is Mokoia Island, the scene of the greatest of Maori legends, a love story that ended happily. Against the wishes of her parents, a Maori maid, Hinemoa, who lived on the shores of the lake, fell in love with a young chief, Tutanekai, who lived on the island. Her efforts to sail to her lover in a canoe were foiled, and night after night she listened to the sounds of Tutanekai playing his flute to guide her. Finally she could stand it no longer, and under the cover of darkness slipped into the water and swam the long mile to the island, guided by the sounds of the flute. Exhausted and cold, she dragged herself up the beach and sank into a natural thermal bath, which bears the name Hinemoa's Pool.

Tutanekai, who had retired for the night, was unable to sleep and sent a slave to a cold spring near the pool for a calabash of water. Disguising her voice, Hinemoa asked the slave for a drink of water. He passed the calabash, which she promptly smashed. He returned to Tutanekai and reported the insult, and Tutanekai seized his club and rushed to the pool to challenge the stranger, only to find his beloved. He placed his cloak around her and embraced her and led her to his hut, and they were married and lived happily ever after.

The love story is still related in song, and two streets in the city have been named after the lovers.

As Maori names are used so extensively in Rotorua, it is helpful to know how to cope with these seemingly tongue-twisting words. Break the words into syllables, give each vowel its full value, and remember that every word must end in a vowel and that "wh" sounds like an "f". For example, Whakarewarewa breaks down into *Whaka-rewa-rewa,* Tutane-kai into *Tu-tan-e-kai,* Hinemoa into *Hine-moa,* Whakaue into *Wha-cow-e,* Ohinemutu into *O-hine-mutu,* and Tamatekapua into *Tama-te-ka-pua.*

Apart from its thermal activity, Rotorua is also a popular area for trout fishing in the nearby lakes and streams.

Exploring Rotorua

No area in New Zealand has such a wide variety of sightseeing. Two or three days, or more if possible, should be spent here to enjoy all the area offers. Excursions are well organised and inexpensive.

Whakarewarewa

Commonly shortened to Whaka. It is essential that the tourist visit this weird thermal area, only a couple of miles from the city center. There are two entrances, but it is recommended that you enter through the replica of a fortified Maori village (a *pa*) beside the main highway. An ornately carved gateway straddles the thick palisades to the village. The two figures at the gateway depict the famous lovers, Hinemoa and Tutanekai.

From the entrance a well-kept path bordered by native shrubs twists its way through outcrops of steam and boiling mud and silica terraces. Tiny geysers hiss beside you, and spouts of boiling mud leap from the mud lakes like jumping frogs. In the center of the area is Pohutu Geyser, New Zealand's largest, which plays to about 100 ft, often for long periods. Its activity is heralded by the "Prince of Wales Feathers", three jets which play spasmodically to a height of 40 ft. Below all this feverish activity a small cold stream flows placidly along the floor of the valley. Just before you leave the thermal area you pass a number of Maori graves, concrete-encased above the ground because of the earth's heat, and reach a collection of hot pools in which the Maoris who live nearby still cook their food. Meat and vegetables are placed in a woven flax basket and immersed in the boiling water, or in a wooden or concrete box set into the earth to trap the steam; a sort of natural pressure cooker.

Maori Arts and Crafts Institute

This is situated beside the main entrance to the Whakarewarewa thermal area, and should not be missed. It is not a museum, but a living preservation of Maori art and culture. As the Maori acquired the European way of life there was a danger that the Maori arts would disappear; so, with Government assistance, the institute was formed some 20 years ago.

For a three-year course of training under a master carver, the school accepts four students of less than 18 years of age, chosen from four Maori tribes. They are paid the same wages as apprentice carpenters. Some of their smaller carvings can be purchased, but the larger pieces are destined to replace deteriorating carvings at meeting houses in various parts of the country.

Women are not permitted to carve by Maori ethics, but at the institute they demonstrate traditional Maori weaving with flax, the making of *piupiu* skirts (flax leaves rolled into tight tubes), and basket and mat making. Instructors now go all over New Zealand to teach. The institute is funded by the fees paid to enter Whakarewarewa. There is a kiwi house near the institute where live kiwis may be seen.

Government Gardens

It was left to the Government to beautify Rotorua in the early days (there were not enough local residents to meet the cost), which it did by forming what are still known as the Government Gardens, close to the center of the city. Rotorua was then much favored as a spa resort, and, in an effort to emulate the elegance of European resorts, a large and incongruous Elizabethan-style bath-house was built, and surrounded with lawns and flower gardens.

It is no longer used as such and contains an art gallery, museum, and restaurant. The formal flower gardens are delightful, and, surprisingly, steam often rises from stone cairns in the middle of them. There are also well-kept greens for playing lawn bowls and croquet in summer.

Ohinemutu Maori Village

Ohinemutu is truly a Maori village in that only Maoris live there. But do not expect to find native huts; they live in European-style houses. Nevertheless, it is one of the most fascinating places in Rotorua. Although it is on the edge of the cold waters of the lake, the land is pitted with harmless little geysers, and steam rises from crevices. In the courtyard stands a bust of Queen Victoria, surrounded by four decorated pillars and shielded by a canopy decorated with Maori designs and carving.

Two buildings are of special interest. Almost on the shore of the lake is St. Faith's Anglican Church, built in Tudor style in 1910. You cannot escape a feeling of reverence as you enter. The layout is traditional, but the decorations are distinctly Maori. Rich Maori carving is everywhere —on the pews, the pulpit and the altar. Hymn books are in Maori.

As you approach the sacristy move to the right and sit in the front pew. Before you is a large window fronting the lake. On it is etched the figure of Christ—a Maori Christ wearing a chief's robe—at such an angle that He seems to be walking on the waters. Near the entrance to the church hang several historic military flags.

If you can, attend a service. To listen to the liquid and sonorous Maori language and the harmonious singing is an emotional experience. It is also an opportunity to mingle with the Maori people in their own environment.

Opposite the church is the Tamatekapua meeting house, an ornately carved building containing some venerated work dating from about

1800. The house is named after the captain of the Arawa canoe, and the carved figures in the interior represent passengers in the canoe. The figure on the top of the center post is Ihenga, who claimed the hot lakes district for the Arawa people. Another figure represents Ngatoroirangi, the canoe's navigator and *tohunga* (priest).

Kuirau Domain

Just a short stroll from the city is Kuirau Domain, a pleasantly grassed area which has the inevitable boiling mud pools, steam vents and small geysers. More unusually, it has a shallow pool of thermal water which is used as a foot bath. It does indeed invigorate tired feet.

Polynesian Pools

Rotorua's natural thermal waters can be enjoyed at the Polynesian Pools in the Government Gardens. There are two public pools, one for adults and one for children, and 20 well-appointed private pools, all fed by the soft alkaline mineral waters of nearby Rachael Spring. There are also the Priest and Radium Springs, with their eight pools of different temperatures, bubbling out of the pumice. This spring water is acidic, and is well-known for relieving arthritis and similar ailments.

Maori Concerts

A Maori concert is an unforgettable experience. Their original chants *(waiata),* which usually describe the history and ancestry of the tribe, are monotonal, rather like a church litany, but they warmly embraced the European tone scale, giving to the melodies their own harmonic variations. Maori singing is truly sweet and rhythmic.

Maori concerts are given in full costume in most of the larger hotels, at the Maori Cultural Theater, the Tudor Towers in the Government Gardens and Ohinemutu. The THC Rotorua International Hotel adds spice by giving a Maori feast every Sunday evening, followed by a concert. For a reasonable charge non-guests can attend the meal and entertainment, but reservations are essential.

Pork, chicken, ham and vegetables are cooked in a *hangi* (oven) in the hotel grounds. A large hole is dug and partially filled with river stones which have been heated to a high temperature. Water is thrown on them to make steam, the food in flax baskets or other containers is placed on top, and covered with soil. That is the true Maori oven, but in Rotorua the natural superheated underground steam dispenses with the need for heating stones. The principle and effect are, however, the same. The food is taken into the concert area and eaten informally.

The concert always begins with the traditional Maori ceremony of welcome. Grimacing fearfully and brandishing a *taiaha* (a long club), a warrior from the host tribe advances to the visitors with a sprig of greenery. He places this at the feet of the leader of the visitors and cautiously retires. If the visiting leader picks up the greenery he comes in peace; if not, it is war. Needless to say, the sprig is always picked up at a concert. The host tribe then greets the visitors with a song of welcome—*Haere mai, Haere mai, Haere mai,* thrice welcome. The ceremony is held in respect, and guests are asked not to applaud.

So musical are the Maoris that they do nothing without singing. Lilting melodies accompany the graceful *poi* dances by the girls as they deftly twist and twirl balls of plaited flax.

It is impossible not to feel the blood stirred by the war dance *(haka)* performed by the men. The chant is in a simple rhythm and the tempo is kept by stamping feet—the Maori did not use drums. Every part of the body is brought into action in a set routine, even to protruding and wagging the tongue. The *haka* was intended to strike fear into the hearts of the enemy, but was also a "limbering up" exercise for hand-to-hand battle.

The concert always ends with the traditional Maori song of farewell, "Now is the hour" *(Po ata rau)*. It is not strictly a Maori melody, but Maori and *pakeha* alike have adopted it as a traditional New Zealand song. They sing it first in Maori and then in English, and as its plaintive notes die it is impossible to escape a feeling of sadness at parting.

Waimangu Round Trip

The Waimangu thermal valley gives a good idea of how the earth was formed. It contains both furious thermal activity and quiet bush with grass-covered slopes rising from placid pools. The main valley can be seen from a mini-coach on a half-day trip. An extension, which includes some walking, adds launch cruises on Lake Rotomahana, with its steaming cliffs, and Lake Tarawera, where you meet a bus for the return to Rotorua.

The Waimangu Valley was created by the violent eruption of Mount Tarawera in 1886. In the early hours of June 10 the northern peak blew up, splitting the range into a series of massive craters. The noise was heard hundreds of miles away. Ash and debris were strewn over 6,000 square miles, and the Maori villages of Te Wairoa, Te Ariki and Moura were destroyed. Maori legend tells that a phantom canoe was seen in Lake Tarawera just before the eruption.

Among other things, the eruption destroyed the famous Pink and White Terraces, glittering staircases of silica, and the Waimangu Geyser, once the world's largest, which played to a height of 1,600 ft.

But other remarkable sights remain or were created. The Waimangu Cauldron occupies a crater formed by a later and milder eruption and is a boiling lake of about 10 acres. The flow at the outlet is more than a thousand gallons a minute. Above the lake rise the jagged Cathedral Rocks, red-tinted and gently breathing steam. Ruaumoko's Throat (he was the god of the underworld) has an atmosphere of suppressed unearthly violence. Roughly circular, the crater is the bed of a pale blue steaming lake of unknown depth which overflows periodically at a rate varying from 200 to 3,000 gallons a minute. At times the water recedes 50 ft to uncover the beautiful white walls of the crater. Bird's Nest Terrace is aptly named, but has miniature geysers and a silica terrace formation. Surrounded by vegetation, the Warbrick Terraces are layers of orange, brown, black, white and green caused by algae and mineral deposits falling from the top platform.

Te Wairoa Buried Village

In contrast to geysers and hot mud pools, the Te Wairoa Buried Village is tranquil but interesting.

Once the starting point for the trip to the Pink and White Terraces, the village of Te Wairoa was buried under eight feet of ash in the eruption. It has now been partly excavated—a sort of miniature Pompeii. There are many interesting relics, but as one walks through the heavily grassed pastures fenced by tall poplar trees and English cherries it is hard to visualise the devastation which occurred.

Of special interest are the remains of a *tohunga's whare* (priest's house). The tohunga, who was reputed to be 110 years old, did not predict the coming disaster and was therefore blamed for it by the tribe, who refused to allow him to be rescued from his buried house. After four days they relented. Incredibly, he was still alive, but died a few days later. Relics of the eruption are still being excavated and are on display in a museum, which also includes displays of kauri gum and polished New Zealand rocks.

Tikitere

Appropriately named "Hell's Gate," Tikitere is an area of furiously bubbling pools and seething mud, including a mud waterfall. It is an eerie place, but intriguing.

Mount Tarawera Tours

When Mount Tarawera erupted it blew a 9¾-mile rift along almost its entire length, leaving a jagged chasm with walls up to 800 feet high. From the air, it is an awesome sight, and there are helicopter and fixed-wing aircraft tours that include a circuit of the mountain and a flight across the crater as part of a scenic tour, which takes in the surrounding native forests and lakes, the vast pine forests, the Blue and Green Lakes and aerial views of the city. Some aircraft land on a strip at the summit of the mountain. Another way of viewing the crater is by a four-wheel-drive cruiser that travels from Rotorua up the side of the mountain to the summit.

Lake Okataina

Lake Okataina, 19 miles from Rotorua, must be one of the loveliest lakes in New Zealand. Steep hills, thickly clad in subtropical forest, enclose the blue-to-turquoise waters and delightful sandy beaches. The place is alive with native birds, and deer roam the forest. Of human habitation there is only a tourist lodge, a launch and runabouts for enjoying a cruise and for fishing, for the lake is renowned for the abundance and size of its Rainbow trout.

The name means "place of laughing", but you are more likely to relax and absorb its serenity and beauty. The approach is impressively beautiful, through thick native forest and a tunnel of native fuschia, whose flowers form a red carpet on the roadway in the spring.

Trout Pools

Even if you don't catch trout you can see them at close quarters at Rainbow Springs and Paradise Valley Springs. Here they live a protected life in crystal-clear pools in native bush, gradually evolving from tiny fingerlings to 8 and 10 lb monsters. In some springs the path is below the pool, one side of which has a thick plate-glass window, through which you can see the fish cavorting beneath the water. It is enthralling to watch the trout, like performing dolphins, leaping from the water to seize small pellets of meat held above the pool on the end of a stick. Rainbow Springs also has a kiwi house where a live kiwi may be seen.

Taniwha Springs

Taniwha Springs, 7 miles from Rotorua, has dozens of busy waterfalls, gushing springs, glittering sandsprings, and several trout pools set in native bush. A short climb takes you to an old Maori fortified village site. It takes its name from a legendary water monster, the "taniwha."

Skyline Skyrides

An outstanding attraction is Skyline Skyrides, just a few miles from the city center. A 900-metre gondola lift, with a vertical rise of 200 metres, takes you up the slopes of Mt. Ngongotaha to a panoramic view and a restaurant and cafe. Descent can be by the gondola or a 1-km-long luge, or slide ride.

Agrodome

Even if you think you've seen enough sheep as you've traveled through New Zealand, a visit to the Agrodome, five miles from Rotorua, is well worthwhile. Here you can meet them at first-hand and watch performing sheep take the center stage and show off their rich fleeces. Top-class shearers describe the characteristics of 19 different breeds and demonstrate shearing techniques. But the sheep dogs steal the show as they muster sheep into a holding pen, often without a bark being heard.

Heli-Jet Tours

A Heli-Jet tour is an adventure, but safe. It is an unusual combination of helicopter sightseeing and a ride in a jet boat. A helicopter takes you to the unspoiled Lake Rotokawau, nestling amid towering native forest and tree ferns. You step from the helicopter into a waiting jet boat and then speed at up to 50 m.p.h. over the lake before returning to the airport by the helicopter. The tour takes about 1½ hours.

Waiotapu

While much of the thermal activity at Rotorua is vigorous, the phenomena at Waiotapu are quieter, but beautifully colored. The area is 19 miles from Rotorua and is conveniently visited when driving from Rotorua to Wairakei and Taupo.

Wairakei

There is no settlement of Wairakei—just a comfortable Tourist Hotel Corporation Hotel, a superb golf course, and a dramatic example of how man has harnessed Nature's vast underground heat for his own benefit. This is the site of the Wairakei Geothermal Steam Power Project, where scores of bores have been driven several thousand feet into the earth to tap huge underground reservoirs of super-heated steam, which is then piped to a powerhouse to make electricity. The steam drives turbines, which feed 192,600 kilowatts into the national supply.

You'll know when you approach Wairakei, 50 miles south of Rotorua. Huge clouds of steam billow above the trees from large concrete cylinders, silver-colored steam pipes arch over the road, and a sign warns of a visibility hazard from drifting steam.

The complex is unusual, to say the least of it, and its like can be seen in few parts of the world. A roadside information center graphically demonstrates the project, and an impressive view of the steam field can be obtained from the crest of a hill behind the area.

Lake Taupo

Six miles beyond Wairakei lie Taupo and the lake. On the way, a detour should be made to view Huka Falls on the Waikato River. The falls are not particularly high, but they are spectacular. Compressed into a narrow rock channel, the river boils and surges before it gushes over a 35 ft ledge into a maelstrom of white and green water.

Lake Taupo, New Zealand's largest lake, is 25 miles long and 17 miles wide and about 1,100 feet above sea level. It is almost the geographical center of the North Island. The Maoris called it *Taupo Moana* (the Sea of Taupo).

To anglers throughout the world the name Taupo is synonymous with trout, for it is famous for the abundance and excellence of its fishing both in the lake and in the numerous rivers and streams flowing into it. It is said that over 700 tons of trout are taken from the lake each year! The average weight is 4½ lb, and 7 lb and 8 lb fish are not uncommon. Charter boats are available for hire from the small natural harbor.

Until recent years the township of Taupo, at the northern end of the lake, was a sleepy village catering mainly for anglers and holiday-makers, but the development of farming and forestry have transformed it into a clean modern business town of some 13,000 people. It has also become a popular retirement place, with many fine homes.

From the lake's edge there are good views of the mountains in Tongariro National Park. Off the south-eastern shore of the lake is the island of Motutaiko, an ancient Maori burial place and therefore sacred.

Tongariro National Park

The most popular national park in the North Island, Tongariro National Park, some 60 miles south of Taupo, encloses 175,000 acres of brown tussock plains and native forest. Dominating the park are three mildly active volcanoes—Mount Ruapehu (9,175 ft); permanently snow-capped; Mount Ngauruhoe (7,515 ft); and Mount Tongariro (6,458 ft). Curiously, it is the lesser mountain which gives its name to the park. They huddle close together, as if for protection.

Ruapehu still has a steaming lake in its snow-fringed crater. Ngauruhoe, an almost perfect cone, still sends up occasional puffs of steam; and Tongariro, which "blew its top" countless years ago, still has warm slopes in places.

The park is a tribute to Maori generosity and wisdom. In 1886, to avoid other tribal claims and the inevitable sale of the land to Europeans,

Te Heuheu Tukino, hereditary chief of the Ngati Tuwharetoa tribe, gave the land to the Government ("It shall be a sacred place of the Crown and a gift for ever from me and my people"). There is a succinct tribal proverb: *Ko Tongariro te Maunga; ko Taupo te Moana; ko Te Heuheu te Tangata*"—"Tongariro is the mountain; Taupo is the sea; Te Heuheu is the man".

There are many Maori legends about the mountains, but the most popular is that there were once more of them in the park, and all were in love with the womanly Mount Pihanga, to the north. They fought, and the vanquished were banished, but they could move only during the hours of darkness, and now remain in parts of the North Island where daylight touched them. One, Mount Taranaki, hurried westward, scouring the course of the Wanganui River as he went, and by daylight reached the position by the sea where he still stands.

From late spring through fall the mountains are bare of snow except for the upper slopes of Ruapehu, but in winter all are deeply snow-covered. Ruapehu is the North Island's most popular ski resort and has chairlifts and ski tows to the upper ski fields. Many ski and mountain clubs have huts here.

There are pleasant walks through the native bush, and at the National Park Headquarters there is a fine exhibit of the park's geology, flora and fauna. There is also a good golf course, and tennis courts.

Tauranga

Finding the Maoris of the east coast of the North Island hospitable, Captain Cook named the area the Bay of Plenty. In the production of dairy products, meat and fruit, it is still a region of plenty. Its principal city and port is Tauranga, with a population of 48,000. Not far away is Maketu, the landing place of the *Arawa* canoe in the great migration from Hawaiki.

Tauranga's genial climate made it chiefly a retirement area, and centre for holidays and big game fishing. Now its character is changing, but it has lost nothing of its charm. It is now a modern, thriving city, supported by the export of lumber from the man-made pine forests near Rotorua, 55 miles away, and farming.

Two narrow entrances open to a sheltered harbor. The city is on the western side, and opposite, at the tip of a peninsula, is Mount Maunganui, standing like a sentinel at the entrance. Sweeping beaches and good swimming make this a popular holiday resort. Off the coast is Mayor Island, the main big game fishing center.

Tauranga was the site of the most chivalrous battle in the wars with the Maoris. In 1864, to prevent supplies and reinforcements reaching Maoris who were fighting inland, the Government sent troops to build two redoubts. Hearing this, the Ngaiterangi tribe hurried back and built a *pa* some miles inland. But no soldiers came. Mystified, the chief, Rawiri Puhirake, sent a letter to the commanding officer at Tauranga advising him of the presence of the *pa* and the fact that his followers had built 10 miles of road "so that the soldiers would not be too weary to fight." Still no soldiers came, so a second *pa* was built closer to Tauranga. It became known as Gate Pa as it stood near the entrance to the Christian mission.

The first two British assaults failed, and as night fell a remarkable incident of chivalry occurred. Hearing a wounded British officer begging for water as he lay near the outer ramparts of the *pa,* a Maori woman crept through the British lines with a rusty can, filled it at a small creek, and made the dangerous journey back to give it to the officer and four others. The British finally managed to storm the *pa,* but the Maoris had slipped quietly away to fight again elsewhere.

Tauranga Mission House

Better known as "The Elms," it was built between 1838 and 1847 by Archdeacon A.N. Brown, and contains the original furnishings.

Tauranga District Museum

A blacksmith's shop, a colonial section, and an exhibition depicting the development of Maori culture and the growth of Tauranga.

Gisborne

Because of its closeness to the International Date Line, Gisborne claims to be the most easterly city in the world, and the first on which the sun shines.

It was at Gisborne that Europeans first landed on New Zealand soil. Knowing that he must be near land, Captain Cook offered a gallon of rum to the first man to sight land, and promised that the part seen would be named after him. On October 7, 1769, Nicholas Young, a twelve-year-old cabin boy, sighted a headland, which was promptly named Young Nick's Head.

Two days later Cook led a party ashore at Kaiti Beach—the spot is marked with a memorial. A series of misunderstandings led to bloodshed, and Cook sailed away. He named the area Poverty Bay "because it afforded us no one thing we wanted."

Contrary to Cook's description, Poverty Bay is anything but poor, but a highly productive area for lambs, corn, vegetables, citrus fruit, grapes and wine.

Kaiti Hill Lookout

From the summit there are splendid views of the city and the long sweep of the bay, including Young Nick's Head. At the foot of the hill is one of the largest Maori Meeting houses in New Zealand.

"Star of Canada" House

The bridge of a 7,280 ton ship in a city street! In 1912 the "Star of Canada" was wrecked on Kaiti Beach. The superstructure was salvaged and reconstructed as a house, which is now used as a private residence.

Napier

Napier is a phoenix city, risen from the ashes. Without warning on February 3, 1931, a severe earthquake shook the province of Hawke's Bay, and was felt further afield. Much of the city and many houses in the suburbs were flattened and fire ravaged a good deal of what remained. Hills crumbled and crevices opened in the roads. The Ahuriri lagoon was raised and over 8,000 acres of new land arose from the sea bed. Today, factories and the airport are on this new land.

Out of the chaos order was restored in a surprisingly short time. Napier was rebuilt as a modern city, and now has a population of 50,000.

Standing at the center of the wide sweep of Hawke's Bay, Napier's pride is the Marine Parade fronting the city. Lined for two miles with graceful Norfolk pines, it has beautiful sunken gardens, a Dolphin pool, a concert auditorium, a roller skating rink and an aquarium.

On the parade stands the graceful bronze statue of Pania of the Reef. Maori legend has it that Pania, one of the Sea People, left them to live with her human lover, Karitoki. But she yielded to the constant calls of her people to return, and swam out to meet them. From the caverns of the sea they came to draw her down, keeping her forever from her lover. And so Pania sits, gazing forlornly out to sea.

Exploring Napier
Regular sightseeing tours are run by Cox World Travel, and also by taxi companies.

Bluff Hill and Lookout
From the Bluff Hill Lookout there are panoramic views of the bay, and on a lower ridge the City Lookout gives good views of the city.

Botanic Gardens
Formal gardens and a Kiwi house.

Cape Kidnappers Gannet Sanctuary
Cape Kidnappers, a cliff-faced promontory jutting into the sea at the southern end of Hawke's Bay, was named by Captain Cook as here the Maoris tried to kidnap his interpreter, a Tahitian boy.

Only recently has an overland route been opened to the gannet sanctuary. 22 miles (35.5 km) from Napier, it is the world's only mainland gannet colony. At the cape visitors can obtain excellent views of the gannets, and walk quite close to the nesting birds. There are between 12,000 and 13,000 birds at the sanctuary in the height of the season, which is between November and February.

A fully-grown gannet weighs about 5 lb. and has a wing span of 5 ft. Eggs are laid in October, and take about six weeks to hatch. The chicks are fully fledged at 12 and fly after 16 weeks. Migration of the chicks and dispersal of the adult birds occurs in February and March, and by April most birds have gone. Because of the rugged nature of the terrain, visits can be made only in special vehicles on tours run by Gannet Safaris.

Hastings
13 miles (21 km) south of Napier is Hastings, with a population of 51,000. There is friendly rivalry between the two cities; each has, for instance, its own daily newspaper.

It is a well-kept city, proud of its parks, gardens, and streets. Closer to the fertile sheep farming country of Hawke's Bay and to large vegetable and fruit farms, Hastings is more of a commercial center. There are a number of food processing plants, including Wattie's Canneries, which cans and quick-freezes huge quantities of vegetables and fruit. It is the largest and most complex plant of its kind in the Southern Hemisphere. Nearby meat packing plants process about three million head of sheep and cattle annually.

Although most New Zealand wine is produced in the Auckland area, there are large vineyards near Hastings and Napier. The larger wineries, which welcome visitors, include Greenmeadows, a Catholic mission which is possibly New Zealand's oldest vineyard. It produces a variety of excellent table wines. Vidals Wines were founded in 1902 in converted racing stables; their wines are now well known and also sold in Australia. At nearby Havelock North, T.M.V. Wines runs the oldest commercial vineyard in the country. North of Napier, Glenvale Wines are one of the largest producers.

Hastings is the host city for two popular annual events: the Cherry Blossom Festival in October, and the Highland Games at Easter, when the city resounds to the skirl of bagpipes and competitions are held in Highland dancing and sports.

New Plymouth

The perfect cone of Mount Egmont (8,260 ft.) dominates the province of Taranaki, which was also the Maori name for the mountain. It is a dormant, but not extinct, volcano. The ash from its ancient eruptions has made the land fertile, particularly for dairying, and Taranaki exports large quantities of cheese.

Below the north-eastern slope of the mountain is the city of New Plymouth (population 43,000). Though a commercial center, it is a well-planned and attractive city.

It is also New Zealand's main hope for new sources of energy. Oil was found in the suburb of Moturoa as early as 1856, only seven years after the first discoveries in the United States, but the yields were small. Drilling in what is known as the Maui field, some distance off the coast, is raising hopes of a more bountiful supply. In 1962 natural gas was discovered at Kapuni and is now piped to various points of the North Island and provides considerable quantities of oil condensate for shipment to the oil refinery at Whangarei, north of Auckland.

Pukekura Park

Once a wasteland, it was transformed by voluntary labor into a delightful park. One of the outstanding features is a small lake, surrounded by tree ferns, with the cone of Mount Egmont forming a perfect backdrop. At night an elaborate illuminated fountain plays in the lower of the park's two lakes and makes a colorful spectacle.

Adjoining Pukekura Park is Brooklands Park, where a natural amphitheater can seat over 16,000 people. A lake in front of the soundshell mirrors performances of drama, ballet, opera and music for the "Festival of the Pines" held in January and February.

Taranaki Museum

An excellent collection of early Maori sculpture and Maori carvings done with original stone tools may be seen in the museum, which also contains the stone anchor of the Tokomaru canoe, part of an early canoe fleet.

Pukeiti Rhododendron Trust

Any lover of flowers will be enthralled by this world-famous 900 acre park of rhododendrons and azaleas 18 miles (29 km) from New Plymouth. It is at its best between September and November. There are about 900 species, all of which grow better in this climate than in their native habitat. Japanese nurserymen have been sending seedlings to the extensive nursery of Duncan & Davies; from which, after two years, they are shipped back, having grown as much as they would in five years in Japan.

Wanganui

One of New Zealand's oldest cities, Wanganui (population 38,000), stands near the mouth of the Wanganui River, which rises in the Tongariro National Park in the center of the North Island. The river was used as a canoe highway by the Maoris, and until recent years was navigated for more than 100 miles by launch, but this mode of transport gradually declined as roads were built.

The real beauty of the river is a 20 mile section upstream from Pipiriki, 49 miles (79 km) from Wanganui, known as the "Drop Scene". Here the river is confined to narrow, fern-clad gorges, where small waterfalls cascade down through the bush, and the water is churned into foam by rapids. The full-day trip is now done by jet boats.

Durie Hill

Panoramic views of the city and surrounding countryside can be obtained from the tower on Durie Hill (300 ft). A road leads to the summit, which can also be reached by an elevator inside the hill.

Wanganui Museum

The Wanganui Museum has a good Maori collection, and New Zealand's first church organ, which has no keyboard and is operated like a pianola by a rotating cylinder.

Sarjeant Gallery

The Sarjeant Gallery displays a good selection of British and New Zealand painters of the nineteenth and twentieth centuries.

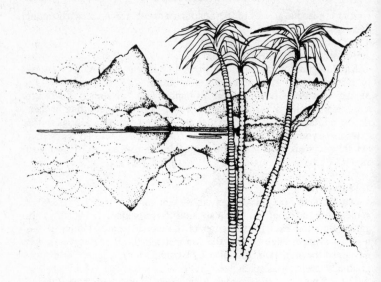

THE SOUTH ISLAND

"The Mainland"

The starting point of a journey through the extraordinary scenery of the South Island is usually Christchurch, which is reached by air from Rotorua, Wellington or Australia. It is a good point of arrival, as it typifies the different characteristics of the two islands. While Christchurch is a busy commercial city, it is more gracious than those in the North Island and the pace of life seems more relaxed. Its intense civic pride is exemplified by numerous city gardens and parks, and by the lovely gardens of private homes.

The South Island is larger in area than the North, and the South Island people like to refer to it as "The Mainland".

To the south, the main highlights are Mount Cook, Queenstown, Lake Te Anau, Lake Manapouri and Milford Sound. All can be reached by good roads, but almost a full day is required between each point, and most visitors use the regular services of Mount Cook Airlines, with its twin turbo-jet planes. The pilots add enjoyment by giving detailed commentaries as points of special interest are passed.

On a time-restricted itinerary it is possible to fly to Mount Cook, take a ski plane flight with a landing on the glacier, and be back in Christchurch that night, having included a glimpse of Queenstown. Changing planes at Queenstown one can even fly into Milford Sound. All, of course, depends on favourable weather, as this is alpine country, and weather can be changeable. But having come this far in the South Pacific, one should make the most of it and allow a week or more, to enjoy some outstanding scenic spectacles and sightseeing experiences.

As the plane leaves Christchurch the vast checkerboard of green and brown cultivated fields of the Canterbury Plains unfolds, and soon the plane is flying along the long chain of the permanently snow-clad summits of the Southern Alps. As far as the eye can see there is a jumbled mass of rugged peaks.

In a little over half an hour the plane crosses The Divide at about 7500 ft., and as it does so, the majesty of Mount Cook and the sister mountains clustering around her are suddenly revealed. Below is the 18-mile-long Tasman Glacier, down which the plane flies. Sheer icy cliffs rise beside and above you as the plane gradually loses height to land at the airport, whose altitude is 2500 ft. The clarity of the air makes the mountains seem almost at the wing tip; in fact they are a mile or more away.

From the Mount Cook airport the plane flies down the length of the Tasman River and over the green-blue glacial Lake Pukaki and swings to the right. On the left is the alpine plateau of the Mackenzie Country, named after a Scottish sheep-stealer who found a pass to it through the mountains; to the right is lovely Lake Ohau. Soon the blue waters of Lake Wakatipu and tree-studded Queenstown come into view, and the plane sweeps over the deep valleys, silver rivers and fertile farms to land.

From here, smaller planes fly the exciting scenic round-trip flight to Milford Sound, where one can stop overnight, and return next day by road. Alternatively, continue to Te Anau, and make that a base for a trip to the Sound by road.

That is the aerial tour for the visitor in a hurry, but he will miss some of New Zealand's most enchanting travel experiences. Mount Cook demands a day to absorb the grandeur of the surrounding mountains, and savour the ski-plane flight to the full. As one visitor put it, "Queenstown is good for the soul." An unhurried sampling of the wealth of beautiful and unusual sidetrips amply repays a visit of three days.

Milford Sound cannot be appreciated in all its majestic glory and grandeur on a flying visit, for unless a half-day is allowed for a launch cruise down the Sound a truly moving experience is missed.

Lakes Te Anau and Manapouri offer their own unique attractions. Each has its individual charm: Manapouri for its somber beauty and Te Anau for its glowworm cave. The road from Te Anau to Milford Sound must rank as one of the most spectacular scenic drives in New Zealand.

The Fertile Southland

Further to the south are Southland, so fertile that farmers can run up to eight sheep to the acre, and Invercargill, the southernmost city, famous for its succulent oysters. To the east is Dunedin, founded by the Scottish immigrants, and proud of its title of "the Edinburgh of the South."

If you look at a relief map of the South Island you will see quite clearly how the Southern Alps form a backbone for much of the length of the island. Only three passes give access to the West Coast. Consequently, this delightful region is too seldom visited, for it is a place of magnificent seascapes, tranquil alpine lakes, verdant subtropical forest, and the Franz Josef and Fox Glaciers.

From Christchurch the West Coast can be reached through the Lewis Pass and Arthur's Pass, both distinguished for natural beauty, and from

Queenstown through the Haast Pass, spectacular in an entirely different way. A popular route, especially for organised tours, is from Christchurch to the glaciers, through the Haast Pass to Lake Wanaka and Queenstown, Lake Te Anau and Milford Sound, back to Queenstown, and then on to Mount Cook and back to Christchurch.

The northern part of the South Island above Christchurch which is highly popular with New Zealanders, is often omitted by overseas visitors as it is apart from the main route. The Marlborough Sounds, a maze of sunken valleys, has hundreds of miles of inland waterways which afford excellent fishing. Nelson, a placid city, is the heart of a large fruit and tobacco growing area, with some of the most delightful beaches to be found anywhere and a climate that lures people into retirement there.

Although they have a common bond, the North and South Islands are entirely different. The South Island undoubtedly has the greater number of scenic attractions.

CHRISTCHURCH

"Gracious" is a fitting term for Christchurch, the South Island's largest city. With a population of over 300,000, it is the hub of the extensive Canterbury district, and the main point of arrival for travelers from the North Island and many from Australia.

Christchurch is often described as "the garden city of New Zealand," and richly deserves its title. Within its confines are about a thousand acres of parkland and gardens, and through the city itself meanders the small and restful Avon River, fringed with willows and bordered by sloping grassy banks. Householders take pride in their gardens, and competitions are held every year for the finest garden and best-kept street.

It has also been said of Christchurch that it is "more English than the English" and "the most English city outside England". Certainly many aspects of it and many of its buildings are reminiscent of England, for it was planned that way.

It was settled under the auspices of the Church of England and was planned for English people belonging to the Anglican Church. In 1850 the "First Four Ships" brought a group of English settlers to the port of Lyttelton, and the Canterbury pilgrims made their historic trek over the steep Port Hills to the fertile plains beyond. The older Canterbury families proudly trace their lineage to these ships, just as Americans are proud to claim that their forbears came over in the "Mayflower."

The settlers found their city already surveyed and laid out in broad regular streets, some named after Church of England bishoprics, such as Worcester, Hereford and Gloucester. Canterbury's planners saw the colony as part of England transplanted to New Zealand.

Colonisation went ahead rapidly. By 1865 all the available land on the Canterbury Plains had been cultivated and sheep farms carried more than a million sheep. In the 1880s the success of refrigerated shipping revolutionised farming in Canterbury. Small towns and villages, the centers of farming areas, grew up, an irrigation system solved the problem of watering stock, new areas were opened up by railroads, and the large holdings were divided to make land available for small farms.

Today, Canterbury is New Zealand's chief wheat-growing district, as well as the home of world-famed "Canterbury lamb."

Christchurch was planned and built around the beautiful Christchurch Cathedral. Like many of the city's early buildings, the cathedral is Gothic in design, and built of rough, grey local stone. The bells duplicate the upper ten of St. Paul's Cathedral, London. Gothic architecture, undergoing a revival when the first buildings of Christchurch were erected, was used for many of the early structures: schools, the museum, the old Provincial Council Chambers and Canterbury University College. There is a charm and stability about these early stone buildings, sheltered by English trees planted by the city's forefathers.

To the south of the city rise the Port Hills. From the 24 mile scenic Summit Road extending along their crests there are fine views of the Canterbury Plains and the Southern Alps and, to the east, the peaceful bays of Lyttelton Harbor and the hills of Banks Peninsula. The French established a colony on the peninsula in 1840, and had they done so a little earlier they could well have claimed New Zealand for France before the Treaty of Waitangi was signed, establishing British sovereignty over all New Zealand. The French attempt was abandoned nine years later.

Christchurch has long been a New Zealand base for exploration of the Antarctic. The British explorer, Robert Falcon Scott, whose party of five reached the South Pole in 1912, left from here (his statue stands by the Avon River), and it is now the headquarters of "Operation Deep Freeze". From the international airport non-stop 2,200 mile flights are made in summer to McMurdo, the main United States base in Antarctica. New Zealand itself exercises control over the Ross Dependency and maintains Scott Base, near McMurdo.

EXPLORING CHRISTCHURCH

Scenic Tours

Afternoon bus tours are run by the Christchurch Transport Board. Easy two-hour morning and afternoon escorted walking tours of the city's main attractions or escorted tours in your own vehicle are available from Personal Guiding Services at US$10.50 for a half day. Contact the Government Tourist Bureau or Canterbury Information Center.

Cathedral Square

Cathedral Square stands at the very heart of the city, and all the main streets radiate from it. Once a busy bus terminal, it has now been cleared of traffic and made into a delightfully decorated pedestrian area. A "speaker's corner" where those who have a cause to advocate can give their message is popular at lunchtime.

Christchurch Town Hall

This is less an administrative building than a cultural complex containing a concert auditorium, a theater, a banquet room and a restaurant. It was opened in 1972, and is one of the finest in the Southern Hemisphere. It incorporates the latest in theater and auditorium design, and its pleasing exterior is well set off by a small lake and fountain.

Canterbury Museum

An entire Christchurch street after the style of the 1850s can be explored. Shop windows display their goods, cottages are fully furnished, and there is even an old fashioned horse cab. The ornithological section is particularly well designed, with birds displayed in realistic dioramas.

The Hall of Antarctic Discovery contains a well-displayed history of Antarctic exploration and a superb collection of equipment used by successive parties which have visited Antarctica. A graphic idea of the scientific knowledge that has resulted can be gained from static and moving diagrams, dioramas of penguins, seals and whales and sound recordings of them.

Botanical Gardens

In keeping with the "garden city" reputation, the Botanical Gardens are a delight. A section is devoted entirely to New Zealand plants, and the rose, water, azalea and rock gardens are outstanding. Tropical plants may be seen in the Begonia House, and there is a splendid display of cacti in the Succulent House.

McDougall Art Gallery

Just behind the museum is the McDougall Art Gallery, which contains classic paintings of the Maori by the noted artists Lindauer and Goldie.

Sign of the Takahe

Henry George Ell, who died in 1934, was a visionary. He planned a series of rest houses along the Summit Road of the Port Hills and began three. Only one, the Sign of the Takahe (a New Zealand bird) was completed. It takes the shape of an English baronial hall of the Tudor period. Made of stone quarried from the Port Hills and from native timbers, the building was fashioned by hand. Its fine carvings, coats of arms, heraldic shields and stained glass windows bring a touch of old-time England to these southern hills.

Ferrymead Historic Park & Transport Museum

Still in the process of development, this technological museum is a journey into the past. There are displays of old trolley cars and railroad locos and horse-drawn vehicles. The "Hall of Wheels" houses vintage autos and machinery and early century appliances.

Orana Wildlife Park

Animals from various parts of the world have been assembled in this 10-acre drive-thru wildlife park, not far from the center of the city. Lions, tigers, camels and others roam freely in a natural environment.

Willowbank Wildlife Reserve

Contains probably the largest collection of birds and animals in the South Island, and includes mountain lions, camels, donkeys and deer. A farmyard section has Scottish highland cattle, primitive sheep and other ancient livestock breeds, as well as old farm implements and vehicles.

CHRISTCHURCH HOTELS AND MOTELS

Admiral Lodge Motor Hotel. Pages Road. 20 rooms, motel flats, restaurant, bar, parking.

Australasia Motor Inn. 252 Barbados Street. 30 rooms, restaurant, bars.

Avon Motor Lodge. 356 Oxford Street. 86 rooms, restaurant, bars, parking.

Blenheim Road Motor Inn. 280 Blenheim Road. 20 rooms, motel units, stoves and refrigerators, parking. Licensed restaurant, bar; pool.

Canterbury Inn. Mandeville Street. 45 rooms, restaurant, bars, parking.

Chateau Regency. 187 Deans Ave. 98 rooms, rest., bars, suites, parking.

Christchurch TraveLodge. Memorial Ave., 110 rooms, restaurants, bar, parking, pool.

Clarendon Hotel. 78 Worcester Street. 76 rooms, restaurant, bars.

Coker's Hotel. 52 Manchester St, 37 rooms, restaurant, bars.

Commodore Motor Inn. 447 Memorial Avenue. 66 rooms, restaurant, bars, close to airport and putting green.

DB Redwood Court Hotel. 340 Main North Road. 22 rooms, restaurant, bars, parking.

Gainsborough Motor Lodge. 263 Bealey Ave, 52 rooms, restaurant, bar, parking.

Hotel Russley. Roydvale Avenue. 69 rooms, restaurant, bar, pool, adjacent golf course.

Kingsgate Vacation. Colombo St. 90 rooms, restaurants, bars.

Latimer Motor Lodge. 195 Worcester Street. 29 rooms, restaurant, bars, parking.

Noah's Hotel. Cr. Worcester St. & Oxford Terrace. 214 rooms, restaurants, bars, suites.

Park Hotel. 50 Park Terrace, 60 rooms, restaurant, bar, parking.

Shirley Lodge Motor Hotel. 112 Marshlands Road, 63 rooms, bar, restaurant, parking.

White Heron TraveLodge. Memorial Ave. 114 rooms, bar, restaurant, parking.

CHRISTCHURCH RESTAURANTS

Allegro. 108 Hereford Street. Elegant decor, Italian food.

Cascade Restaurant. Main foyer of Town Hall. Modern atmosphere, Chateaubriand a specialty, smorgasbord.

The Civic Regency. 198 Manchester Street. Elegant, refurbished civic chambers specialising in Continental and Chinese cuisine.

Dux-de-Lux. Corner Montreal and Hereford Sts. Vegetarian.

Guardsman Restaurant. 103 Armagh Street. Contemporary dining, barbecued lamb cutlets a specialty.

Kurasaki. Colombo St. Japanese food and atmosphere.

Leinster. 158 Leinster Rd. Game food, varied.

Michaels. 178 High St. French Mediterranean food.

Paul Revere's. 813 Armagh St. Traditional cooking.

Samuels. 115 Armagh Street. Quiet, romantic atmosphere, spaghetti dishes a specialty.

Sign of the Takahe. Dyers Pass Rd., Cashmere Hills. Elegant atmosphere and European cuisine. A taxi ride from town.

Mount Cook

This towering pinnacle of 12,349 ft, is New Zealand's highest mountain. The Maoris called it *Aorangi* (the Cloud Piercer). But it is now, of course, named after Captain Cook, who never actually saw it.

Mount Cook is in the very heart of New Zealand's most spectacular mountain region, almost in the center of the long chain of permanently snow-capped Southern Alps stretching down much of the South Island. Yet it does not stand alone—surrounding it are 17 peaks, all exceeding 10,000 ft.—and Mount Sefton, Mount Tasman and Mount La Perouse are only a little lower.

Rising to what appears to be a sharp point (though there are three peaks on the summit ridge), Mount Cook is indeed a monarch among mountains, its steep slopes glistening with ice and snow. Those who first saw it thought that it would never be climbed. It was—but not until Christmas Day 1894. It has since been climbed many times, and by the first woman, Freda du Faur, in 1913. It was here that Sir Edmund Hillary, the first to conquer Mount Everest, did much of his early mountaineering.

Glaciers abound on the mountain slopes, including the 18-mile Tasman Glacier, longest in the Southern Hemisphere. From the hotel, 2,500 ft. above sea level and well below the snow line, it is not uncommon to hear the dull roar of an avalanche high in the mountains, particularly on Mount Sefton, but by then it is usually too late to locate the source and see the falling snow and ice.

Two natural inhabitants are of interest. The area is one of the homes of the kea, a New Zealand bird rather like a large parrot with deep green plumage and a vivid crimson breast. They are amusing birds, inquisitive and fearless, but beware of leaving anything bright or shiny about; it will quickly disappear or be pecked to pieces by their strong beaks. The name comes from the sound of their cry. Although they are not large, they have the reputation of being sheep-killers. It is said that a flock will chase a sheep until it is exhausted and then alight on its back and dig with their cruel beaks for the kidneys.

Seldom seen except by hunters, thar and chamois also inhabit the mountains. Liberated in 1904, they found the environment similar to their native Himalayas, and thrived to such an extent that they have been declared noxious animals because of the damage they do to vegetation.

Growing profusely on the alpine slopes are the delicate white flowers of what are known as "Mount Cook Lilies". This is not, however, a true lily but a variety of *ranunculus lyallii.* It is used as the insignia of Mount Cook Airlines.

Arriving by road (or flying from Mount Cook to Queenstown) you pass through or over a large plateau of brown tussock and grass bounded by long ranges of hills. This is the Mackenzie Country, named after a Scottish sheep stealer. Mackenzie, who spoke only Gaelic, found a pass through the mountain barrier in the mid 1800s and would sneak with his dog down to farms in the lower levels, round up sheep, and drive them back to the plateau. Caught eventually, he was given a five year jail sentence. He begged to be allowed to take his dog with him to prison but was refused. The dog was taken south and her offspring were eagerly sought by shepherds. Mackenzie escaped three times in the first year, and was finally released on condition that he left the country and never returned.

Good sheep dogs were indispensable to the early settlers in this remote and spartan area. At Lake Tekapo, at the edge of the Mackenzie Country and just off the main road from Christchurch on the way to Mount Cook, stands a bronze statue of a sheep dog, erected as a tribute.

Here too is the charming rural church of the Good Shepherd, built of stone as a memorial to the pioneer sheep farmers of the region. The backdrop to the altar is a large window, filled with a magnificent panorama of the blue-green waters of the glacial lake and the mountains behind.

Ski Plane Flights

A wonderful way to see the New Zealand scenery. Where else in the world can you take off at 2,500 ft. and within 20 minutes land at about 7,000 ft. on the vast snowfields at the head of a glacier? Many tourists go to Mount Cook as much for this flight as to see the mountain.

The aircraft has wheels for use at the Mount Cook airport, but it is also fitted with retractable skis. You take off from the airfield in front of the hotel, and within minutes you are flying amid peaks sheathed in perpetual ice, over snow valleys, and beside glittering icefalls. The slopes seem close enough to touch, but distances are deceptive in the clear mountain air, and they are actually at least a quarter of a mile away. Below you the rock-strewn surface of the Tasman Glacier gives way to pure ice, hundreds of feet deep, and then you are above the huge snowfields at the head of the glacier.

The skis are lowered, and the plane glides on to the snow and hisses to a stop. You get out into the soft snow—and find yourself in complete silence, in a place that once only mountaineers could reach. Armchair mountaineering if you like, or, as one visitor put it, "Instant Hillary". Only the most insensitive could fail to be emotionally stirred.

After a time to take photographs the plane takes off again and you fly around Mount Cook, with a view of the two glaciers flowing down the opposite side into native forest and the Tasman Sea. Then down the Meuller Glacier and back to the airport. Known as "The Grand Circle", the flight takes an hour, and no special clothing is needed.

The ingenuity of a New Zealander made this flight possible. The late Harry Wigley (later Sir Henry), head of Mount Cook Airlines and its coach-touring company, had flown light planes in this region before and after the war, during which he was a well-known pilot. He designed his retractable skis, had his company workshops make a prototype, and on September 22, 1955, Wigley and one of his men made the first ski plane landing. As he writes in his book "Ski Plane Adventure":

"For several seconds not a word was said. We just sat and looked at each other. Then we slowly opened the doors and stepped out into the deep, soft, powder snow almost up to our knees. We felt like two blowflies sitting on the South Pole."

Now, landing on the glacier is commonplace.

Skiing and Mountain Climbing

Skiing and mountain climbing in the area are superb. Alpine Guides, at Mt. Cook Village, offer heli-skiing, glacier skiing, ski touring, cross-country skiing, and a school of mountaineering.

National Park Headquarters

Here you can see collections of mountaineering equipment and exhibits of local flora and fauna and specimen rocks peculiar to the region.

Christchurch to Mount Cook by Road

Mount Cook is 211 miles (339.5 km) from Christchurch by road—a good day's drive. For about 60 miles (96.5 km) the road heads straight through the rich Canterbury Plains, which were formed by the wearing down of the high country by snow or glacier-fed rivers rising in the Southern Alps. Some of these are quite large, and all are swift-flowing and change their courses continuously—hindering the efforts of soil conservation authorities who have tried to confine the waters to regular channels with protection works of willow and embankments, but a delight to anglers, as the rivers are the haunt of brown trout and quinnat salmon. The Selwyn River is unusual in that it flows underground for much of the year.

The road then swings inland into the rolling lamb country of Canterbury and Fairlie, nearly a thousand feet above sea level, and in coaching days a staging place on the journey to Mount Cook. It then follows the pleasant Opihi Valley and climbs through Burke's Pass to 2,000 ft. The long chain of the Southern Alps is now clearly in view.

A gentle downhill grade brings you to Lake Tekapo, 15 miles long and 620 ft. deep, the site of a glacier that flowed in prehistoric times. 30 miles (42 km) on is Lake Pukaki, 1,588 ft. above sea level. Both Lake Tekapo and Lake Pukaki are sites of extensive hydro-electric developments.

On the 36-mile (52 km) run to Mount Cook the road follows the shore of Lake Pukaki for 15 miles and then heads up the mountain-flanked Tasman Valley to the Hermitage complex. In clear weather the views of the high alps are breathtakingly beautiful.

Mount Cook to Queenstown by Road

After following the Tasman River for 36 miles (52 km) to Lake Pukaki, turn right and head south. For 26 miles the road crosses comparatively flat country, through which the Ohau River flows. The river drains Lake Ohau, another glacial lake and also a source of the Waitaki River.

After leaving the township of Omarama there is a fairly steep ascent to the 3,300 ft. summit of the Lindis Pass through hills covered with brown tussock and grass, then a descent through the Lindis Gorge. From ancient times a well-worn track used by the Maoris ran from Wanaka over the Lindis Pass and down the banks of the Waitaki River to the coast.

From the township of Tarras, after 112 miles (180 km), there are two routes to Queenstown. To the right the road leads to Lake Wanaka and then climbs over the 3,676 ft. Crown Range, dropping down to Arrowtown and continuing to Queenstown. The more popular route, however, is straight on to Cromwell at the junction of the Clutha and Kawarau Rivers. This was the scene of intense gold mining activities in the 1860s, and dredging is still carried on in the Clutha River.

The next 22 miles is through the winding Kawarau Gorge, with its many relics of the gold mining days. Of special interest are the Roaring Meg Stream, which operates a tiny powerhouse, and, about a mile further on, a natural bridge across the river, used for years by the Maoris. The remainder of the journey is through pleasant farm country. At the crest of a hill, pause to admire tree-ringed Lake Hayes, famed for its lovely reflections.

As the route is sparsely populated, it is a good plan to have the hotel give you a box lunch, as there are many lovely picnic spots.

Queenstown

"Picturesque" is a word too frequently used in tourist brochures, yet it is difficult to find a more appropriate adjective for Queenstown. It is a small, well-kept township of 3,000 permanent residents, but thronged with visitors throughout the year. Most leave with regret that they have not allowed enough time to enjoy it more. Though reliant on tourism for its prosperity, it has avoided gross commercialism. The outstanding quality of the scenery and the variety of sightseeing make exploitation unnecessary.

Queenstown delights the mind as well as the eye. It stands on the middle shores of Lake Wakatipu, facing two imposing peaks and flanked by the saw-toothed 7,500 ft. range of The Remarkables. It is often difficult to believe one is not at an alpine lake in Switzerland.

Queenstown can be enjoyed in all four seasons. In winter it resounds to the laughter of young skiers, in spring the trees begin to show their greenery, in summer it is a place for swimming, sunbathing and boating, and in the fall it is a blaze of color. The early settlers planted deciduous trees in this originally treeless area, and as fall arrives the willows and poplars, elms and larches, sycamores and maples splash the brown landscape with a riot of color.

Lake Wakatipu, shaped like a giant letter S, is 52 miles long and varies from one to three miles in width. It is 1,016 ft. above sea level, and its greatest depth is 1,310 ft., which means that its floor is 294 ft. below sea level. It has been called "The Lake that Breathes", as its waters rise and fall 3 inches every 15 minutes. The Maoris noticed this and created a legend. In revenge for carrying off his bride-to-be an angered lover set fire to a giant as he lay sleeping in the fern. The pain of the fire caused the giant to draw up his knees, and so intense was the heat that he sank deep into the earth and burned until nothing remained but his ashes and his heart, which kept beating. The rains and rivers filled the chasm, but the outline of the lake retained his figure. The waters of the lake, says the legend, still pulsate to the beating of the giant's heart.

Hard-headed scientists, however, give a more prosaic explanation. The pulsations, they say, are caused by wind or variations in atmospheric pressure. A pity. The Maori legend is more colorful.

High in the affection of Queenstown residents and much admired by visitors is the T.S.S. "Earnslaw", a steamer built in 1912 and still in service. Her gleaming white hull and red funnel capped with a black band blend harmoniously with the mountain and lake backdrops. "The Lady of the Lake" they call her. Of 335 tons, she was prefabricated in Dunedin in 1912 and assembled at Kingston, at the southern end of the lake. Until a road was cut around the lake comparatively recently, she was the only means of servicing the lakeside farms, and she worked hard transporting not only stores but also sheep and cattle. If you have time, don't miss a half-day or full-day cruise up the lake. If you're mechanically minded, you'll enjoy peering down at the engine room, with its gleaming, lovingly maintained machinery, watching the boilers being stoked with coal to drive the twin screws and smelling the pungent clean smell of hot oil.

In spite of the then difficult access the first settlers established sheep farms, but in 1862 an event occurred which changed the history of the area. Gold, in plentiful supply, was found, and New Zealand's biggest gold rush began. The Shotover River was termed "the richest river in the world." Thousands of miners converged from many parts of the world.

Gradually, the bounteous supplies dwindled, and the miners either settled or left. A little gold is still found, but the finest gold in Queenstown today is the burnished leaves on the trees in fall. Everywhere, however, are interesting relics of those days of gold fever—abandoned workings, crude stone cottages, culverts to carry water for washings, and the huge mounds of stone "tailings" from the dredges.

Exploring Queenstown

Queenstown has such a wide range of beautiful and unusual sidetrips that a week could be spent doing something new every day.

Queenstown Domain

Sometimes called the Government Gardens (they were developed by the Government), the Queenstown Domain extends along a peninsula occupying one side of the bay and presents a colorful display of bright flower beds, lily ponds, exotic shrubs and trees, and a sports area. Near the tip is a large glacial boulder commemorating Captain Robert Falcon Scott, the Antarctic explorer. On it are inscribed his last words as he deliberately walked from the tent to his death to try to save his companions.

Skyline Chalet

From almost anywhere around Queenstown you'll see a chalet perched on Bob's Peak 1,530 feet above the town. It is reached by an aerial cableway with small gondolas, and from the restaurant at the top there are spectacular panoramic views.

Queenstown Motor Museum

Close to the base terminal of the cableway, this museum displays a very good collection of vintage cars—a 1903 De Dion, a 1909 Renault and a 1922 Rolls Royce Silver Ghost, to name a few.

Feeding the Trout

Pause where the jetty juts from the land at the foot of the pedestrian mall, and below in the clear water you'll see monster trout lazily cruising and waiting for food thrown by visitors. They seem to know it is a prohibited fishing area.

Lake Cruises

Launches, jet boats and a hydrofoil run short cruises on the lake from the jetty.

Farm Visits

Dominating the opposite side of the lake are two lofty peaks—Walter Peak (5,936 ft.) to the right and Cecil Peak (6,477 ft.) to the left. Both are sheep and cattle ranches of over 50,000 acres. A half-day trip to Walter Peak Station by launch, the only means of access, is well worth while. Hosts explain how the steep hills are farmed and how trained sheep dogs are able to muster the animals from "the tops." Sheep dog demonstrations are given. Launches leave from the jetties.

Shotover River Jet Boat

For an unusual and thrilling experience a half-hour jet boat ride on the upper reaches of the Shotover River is hard to beat. Invented by a New Zealander, the boat has no propeller but is driven by a concentrated jet of water under high pressure, rather like a jet aircraft. They can travel in only 4 inches of water, and maneuvre quickly and easily through shallows and rapids, even turning in their own length.

Carrying up to nine passengers, the boat speeds through a narrow gorge, dodging boulders, over rapids and along shallow stretches only 1 foot in depth. Passengers wear life jackets, but this is purely a precautionary measure and there is no real danger. If the boat did happen to strike a boulder it would dent but not puncture. The trip starts below the Edith Cavell Bridge at Arthur's Point, about three miles from Queenstown, to which transport is provided at the Mount Cook Tourist Offices.

Coronet Peak

One of New Zealand's most popular ski fields, Coronet Peak, is 11 miles from Queenstown. Coaches leave the Mount Cook Tourist Offices at 9 A.M. and 2 P.M., or you can drive in your own automobile. From the road terminus at 3,800 ft. a chairlift rises 1,600 ft. to the summit, from which there are spectacular views. Coronet Peak is snow-covered only from June through September, and summer visits are worthwhile. The Coronet Cresta Run is a thrilling toboggan ride on brake-controlled sleighs down 1,800 feet of a stainless steel track.

Cattledrome

Just past the Edith Cavell Bridge is the Cattledrome, where cattle have been trained to walk into the large exhibition hall and mount steps to their allotted pens. Seven breeds of beef cattle and three cows of leading dairy breeds are displayed. A focal point is the milking of the cows by machine at eye level. The show includes a film, "The Grass Growers", showing how New Zealand has led the world in developing pastures. Shows are held at 9.30 A.M. and 4.15 P.M.

Skippers Canyon

While highly interesting, this trip should be taken only by those with strong nerves. A warning road sign "Extreme Care Necessary" does not exaggerate. But if you go by one of the regular tour coaches it is safe, though scary. The narrow road twists around a steep gorge past abandoned gold prospecting sites and relics to a turning point. It was from this part of the Shotover River that a great amount of gold was taken.

Arrowtown

Just 12 miles from Queenstown, Arrowtown, now little more than a village, was once a booming gold rush town. Its main street is lined with sycamores, which lay a golden carpet of leaves in the fall. Many of the old stone cottages and wooden buildings have been preserved and are still lived in, giving this sleepy village an air of realism while it still retains its history.

Deer Park Heights

Deer, chamois, thar, wapiti and mountain goats may be seen close at hand in a natural setting about 10 miles from Queenstown. In the April mating season you can hear the stags roaring their challenge to each other.

Raft Trips

There are two types. One is a gentle floating cruise on the placid portion of the Kawarau River, and the other is for the adventurous and physically fit who don't mind getting wet as the raft leaps through wild rapids.

Milford Sound Scenic Flight

This is unquestionably one of the highlights. It is a 1½ hour return flight, with 20 minutes on the ground at Milford Sound, flying over and through some of the most spectacular alpine scenery imaginable. The plane flies to the head of the lake and then enters the rugged terrain of Fiordland. You pass the Sutherland Falls, at 1,904 ft. one of the highest in the world, descending in three great leaps, and make a brief landing at Milford Sound.

The return flight takes you up the sound, past Mitre Peak and the Stirling Falls, through the entrance and a little out to sea and then, in a circular sweep, over Coronet Peak and back to Queenstown.

It is also possible to fly into Milford Sound and return by road in a day excursion coach. Like the ski planes at Mount Cook, the flights are operated by Mount Cook Airlines.

Golden Terrace Mining Town

About a mile from Queenstown, this reproduction of an old mining town displays, under cover, a general store, bank, livery stables, blacksmith and farrier's shop, old Colonial cottage, school, carpentry shop and lumber yard, hotel, newspaper office and beauty parlor. Outside is a gold mine, with traction engine and hydraulic sluicing equipment, and wagons.

Queenstown Sound and Light Museum

An audio-visual lasting about 20 minutes in three rooms, each presenting a different aspect of early immigration and early Colonial life in

Queenstown during the gold-rush days. Room 1 is in a ship's cabin, Room 2 in a gold mine, and Room 3 in a canvas hotel with a display wall incorporating silent movies, slides and artifacts.

Guided Hiking

Two outstanding guided scenic hikes (known here as "walks") operate from Queenstown. The Routeburn Walk covers 25 miles of track or trail over four days through Fiordland and Mount Aspiring National Parks, with accommodations and meals provided in mountain lodges. The four-day Hollyford Valley Walk is also through alpine scenery, although in a different direction. The walks are from November through April.

Full-day Milford Sound Trip

New Zealand Railways Road services run a daily return trip to Milford Sound by road. It's a long day, as the coach leaves Queenstown at 7:30 A.M. and returns at 9 P.M., but the spectacular scenery makes it well worthwhile. There's time for a launch cruise down Milford Sound.

Heli-Jet Trips

Combine two modern means of transportation by taking a helicopter flight to a waiting jet boat for a fast ride on the Kawarau River.

Lake Cruises

In addition to the "Earnslaw" cruises, there are pleasant lake cruises by a hydrofoil and 2½-hour cruises by a fast launch to the head of the lake and two large, lakeside ranches.

Trail Rides

For those who like horseback riding, the half-day trail rides operated by Moonlight Stables from Arthurs Point into the old gold mining district of Moonlight are something unusual. Transport is by courtesy coach to and from the stables.

Trout Fishing Safaris

The lakes and rivers around Queenstown abound in Rainbow and brown trout and quinnat salmon. If you're an expert you can arrange to be taken on a guided fly fishing tour, and if you're just an amateur but would like to try your luck you can go trolling or spinning from a jet boat. Fishing gear is supplied on all charters.

Queenstown to Te Anau By Road

The road follows the Frankton Arm of Lake Wakatipu to the airport and then drops gently down to the Kawarau Dam Bridge over the outlet of the lake. The dam was constructed in 1926 to lower the waters of the Kawarau River so that the alluvial gold-bearing deposits could be worked. The scheme was not successful and has long been abandoned.

For a time you follow the flanks of The Remarkables and the eastern shore of the lake before arriving at Kingston, about 30 miles from Queenstown at the southern tip of the lake.

The way then lies through the barley-growing and seed-producing region of Garston, and after passing several little settlements descends to Five Rivers, which is little more than a gas station. Watch for the signposted right-hand turnoff to Te Anau, as the main highway continues to Lumsden and further south, and if you are not alert you could fly past it and add miles to your journey by having to turn inland at Lumsden. If you set your speedometer at zero at Queenstown it should be reading about 97 kilometres at Five Rivers.

The main road from Lumsden is joined at Mossburn, 20 miles on, and a right-hand turn is made for Te Anau. Much of the journey is through rolling farm country and some tussock. On the left are the Takitimu Ranges, said in Maori legend to be the petrified hull of the canoe "Takitimu."

Te Anau is 118 miles (190 km) from Queenstown, and it is a pleasant 2½–3 hour drive.

Fiordland

Some of New Zealand's most spectacular mountain and lake scenery is found in Fiordland National Park on the south-west corner of the South Island. Over three million acres in area, it is one of the largest national parks in the world, and the terrain is so precipitous and heavily forested that parts have never been explored. The land still holds secrets. In 1948 a bird long believed to be extinct, the Takahe (*notornis*), was discovered in a remote valley. It is now being nurtured to preserve the species. In 1947 a glowworm cave was discovered.

A flight over Fiordland will show why much of it is virginal. Towering peaks and sheer rock walls are jumbled together as if to keep man at bay. The steep rock walls slide into narrow valleys, and the luxuriant rain forest is almost impenetrable.

In Dusky Sound Captain Cook rested his crew after a two-month voyage, made tea from the manuka shrub, brewed a sort of beer, and boiled a native celery plant as antidotes to scurvy. It was here, too, that the first house was built by a European, bagpipes were first played (by one of the sailors), and where the first musket was fired by a Maori.

Queenstown, and Te Anau, are the starting points for a journey into Fiordland. The highlight is Milford Sound, which can be seen in a 1½ hour scenic flight, but to really appreciate the dramatic and outstanding scenery you should travel by road down the eastern shore of Lake Wakatipu to Lake Te Anau and thence through the mountains to the sound.

From October through April there are full-day return trips by coach, although a one or two-day stopover at Te Anau is well worth while. Alternatively, you can travel by road to Milford Sound, stay overnight, and return to Queenstown by air.

The road journey to Milford Sound is more exciting than the return, as the scenery opens before you more impressively. A two or three-hour launch cruise down the sound should certainly be undertaken.

Milford Sound

Milford is magnificent. There is no other way of describing the primeval grandeur of this region sculptured by Nature. The majesty of the scenery makes the visitor feel very insignificant.

Thousands of years ago great glaciers gouged out the land from granite rock, forming a deep basin. As the glaciers receded, the sea flowed in, filling a great depression. From the water's edge almost vertical cliffs rise several thousands of feet. They are mostly bare rock, yet here and there vegetation clings somehow to the sheer slopes. In many places valleys high above the sound end abruptly in a U-shape. These are known as "hanging valleys", and were formed when the glaciers feeding the main glacier receded and disappeared.

Milford Sound is 10 miles long and about 1½ miles wide at its broadest point. At its deepest the floor is 1,280 ft. below sea level. So deep are the waters that the largest cruise ships can enter the sound, but there is only one place, Harrison Cove, where they can anchor.

Like a forbidding guardian, Mitre Peak rises 5,560 ft. to dominate the sound. Opposite, the Bowen Falls explodes in a great spout of water which soars high into the air before tumbling 520 feet into the sound in a flurry of spray. Further down are the Stirling Falls (480 ft.) which flow from hanging valleys in a series of leaps before they too plunge into the sea.

To appreciate the beauty of Milford Sound to the full a regular launch cruise should be taken. Only in this way can a sense of the vastness of the encircling cliff faces and the towering heights of the mountains be gained.

Milford Sound has one irritating defect—it is heavily populated with voracious sandflies, so go armed with insect repellent.

The Road To Milford Sound

The road to Milford Sound from Te Anau is probably the most scenically exciting in New Zealand, and should be travelled if possible. The distance is only 75 miles, but it will take you three hours or so—not that the road is difficult or dangerous, but there are many points where you will want to stop to admire the view or take photographs.

Shortly after leaving Te Anau, the road crosses the Upukerora River, a noted trout stream, and for the 17 miles to the Te Anau Downs sheep ranch there are views of the South Fiord, Center Island and the Middle Fiord. The road then enters the Eglinton Valley and follows the Eglinton River for some miles. A magnificent forest of beech trees, some from 70 to 90 ft. high, flanks the road between the serrated peaks of the Earl Range on the left and the Livingstone Range on the right.

Suddenly, you enter the Avenue of the Disappearing Mountain. At the end of a long avenue of beech trees a mountain slowly disappears from view instead of growing larger as one would expect. This effect is caused by an almost imperceptible rise in the road, and is startling to say the least.

From Cascade Creek Camp, 47 miles (69.5 km) from Te Anau, the outstanding beauty of Fiordland begins. Two small forest-ringed lakes, Gunn and Fergus, are passed, and then the Divide is reached. As you round a big bend the Crosscut Range comes into view and a little further on Mt. Christina, over 7,000 ft., suddenly appears, its sparkling peak rising above the skyline framed by forest.

High, stark granite cliffs, snow-capped and laced with waterfalls, close in as the road follows the floor of the Hollyford Valley and gradually climbs to a large basin of stark granite cliffs.

Like a pinpoint in the massive barrier, the portal of the Homer Tunnel appears. The construction of the tunnel was a daunting undertaking. In winter the area is subject to mountain avalanches, and twisted hunks of reinforced concrete testify to their destructive force where a protective canopy was caught in an avalanche and crumpled out of recognition. There is, however, no danger, as the road is closed when there is a danger of avalanches.

Although it is perfectly safe, the tunnel appears a little fearsome at first sight. There is no graceful facade—it is simply a hole in the rock. Its walls are of rough-hewn rock and there is no lighting. Headlights have to be used, and the traffic is one-way for 25 minutes of each hour. When almost at the center you can hear the roar of a hidden waterfall.

The Homer Tunnel is 3,000 ft. above sea level at its eastern portal and descends for three-quarters of a mile at a grade of 1 in 10. It is only 12 ft. high and 22 ft. wide. As you emerge from the tunnel it is as if the backdrop of a stage were being raised to reveal the beautiful Cleddau Valley.

The road snakes down the moraine in a series of zig-zags and, still dropping, follows the floor of the valley, flanked by lovely forest and occasional waterfalls. The towering mountains of the Sheerdown Range, Mt. Underwood, the Barrier Range and Barren Peak almost enclose the valley. From Tutoko Bridge there are fine views of Mt. Tutoko (9,042 ft.). Then, as you round a corner, Milford Sound springs suddenly into view, like a slide being thrown on to a screen.

The Milford Track

"The finest walk in the world" is the description often given to this three-day, 33-mile hike from Te Anau to Milford Sound. It was not until 1888 that a Scottish immigrant, Quintin Mackinnon, discovered a mountain pass that made land access possible to Milford Sound. This route is now one of the most popular hikes in New Zealand, if only because of the spectacular scenery through which it passes.

The walk is made in three stages, with comfortable overnight accommodation in well-equipped huts. With a guide, it is taken in easy stages and is within the capabilities of anyone who is reasonably fit and used to walking. The season is from mid-December through March. As parties are restricted to 40 persons, reservations are necessary.

The lake steamer leaves Te Anau in the early afternoon and takes you to the head of the lake, from which a half-mile bush track leads to Glade House, where the first night is spent.

The first section of the Milford Track has been likened to a Sunday afternoon stroll, for the path is broad and rises only 500 ft. in 10 miles. After crossing the swing-bridge over the Clinton River you follow the river through the Clinton Canyon. On the left are the Pariroa Heights, which reach 5,000 ft. For the last mile of the journey the saddle of the Mackinnon Pass can be seen framed in the converging walls of the canyon ahead. The night is spent at Pompolona Huts.

The track becomes steeper after leaving Pompolona and the beech forests give way to ribbonwood. The bushline is left behind as you approach Mackinnon Pass, and at 3,400 ft., the saddle, the highest point in the journey is reached.

The view from the Mackinnon Pass is ample reward for the climb. Three thousand feet down on one side is the bush-clad canyon of the Arthur River, and on the other, just as sheer, is the great cleft of the Clinton Canyon, the bed of an ancient glacier, pointing the way back to Lake Te Anau. Lake Mintaro glitters far below, and the Clinton River threads its way along the valley floor, with the rock walls of the canyon towering thousands of feet on either side. More intimate beauty is provided by the sub-alpine flowers which grow in the pass—mountain lily and daisy and the thin wiry snowgrass make a wonderful show among the rugged hills. Descending from the pass, the track leads under several mountains and ends at Quintin Huts, where the night is spent after the 9¼ mile hike.

A sidetrip to the Sutherland Falls is normally included. The track enters the bush from beside the huts and rises gradually through beautiful ferns and beech trees. The roar of the falls steadily increases, and after a walk of a little over a mile they come into view.

The third day consists of an 11 mile walk and a launch journey of two miles to the jetty in Milford Sound.

Most hikers travel back to Te Anau by motor coach.

Lake Te Anau

Built on the edge of the lake, the township of Te Anau is the land gateway to Fiordland and Milford Sound. At the foot of high, rugged, forest-clad mountains, the lake has three long narrow arms. It is the South Island's largest lake, being 33 miles long and six miles wide at the widest point. Its greatest depth is 906 ft., making the floor 212 ft. below sea level.

Lake Te Anau shares with Waitomo the distinction of having a glow-worm cave, but the two differ in many respects. While the Waitomo glow-worms extinguish their lights when disturbed by noise, the Te Anau glow-worms continue shining above a noisy torrent of water.

Te Anau is a contraction of the Maori name *Te Ana-au,* which means "cave of swirling water." No one knew of this cave until in 1947 a curious resident, Lawson Burrows, went exploring and entered a cavity where water was flowing out of a hill.

A visit to the cave is now an essential part of Te Anau stopovers. The trip takes about 2½ hours and can be undertaken after dinner.

The caves are reached after a half-hour launch cruise. The entrance is low, and one has to crouch for about 20 yards to reach a higher chamber where the river plunges over a man-made dam, necessary to float a steel punt. A series of concrete ramps are climbed and a second boat boarded to enter the glowworm grotto itself. As at Waitomo, the ceiling and walls are covered with thousands and thousands of brightly shining glowworms.

Lake Te Anau is a popular weekend resort for residents of the city of Invercargill, about 100 miles away, many of whom have cottages on the lake shores and boats on the waters. It is popular, too, with anglers, as its waters are full of rainbow and brown trout and Atlantic salmon.

From Te Anau, day trips can be taken by coach or hired automobile to Milford Sound, and scenic flights are also operated.

Te Anau is not far away from New Zealand's "Kentucky country", the Hokonui Hills. There were no feuds, but illicit whisky was distilled there some years ago. Objecting to paying tax on liquor, a Scottish family decided to make their own. The terrain of the hills is such that a successful surprise raid was difficult, but occasionally the "revenooers" paid a visit. They sometimes found the still, but seldom the distillers, who had quietly melted away. The story is told that on several occasions the stills were dismantled and sold to recover costs. And who bought them? The distillers, of course, who took the parts back to the hills for reassembly and went happily back to distilling. Older residents still talk about the potent "Hokonui whisky".

The crude but distinctive label featured a skull and crossbones with the words:

Ergo Bibamus
Free from all Poisons
OLD HOKONUI
Passed All Tests except the Police
Bottled by ME for YOU
Produce of SOUTHLAND
Supplied to all Snake Charmers

You might be able to pick up a label—but not the whisky.

Lake Manapouri

"The lake of the sorrowing heart" is the meaning of the Maori name. The legend tells of two sisters who, near death in the high forests, held each other and wept. Their tears divided the hills and formed the lake.

Flanked by the Cathedral Mountains, it is studded with small islands clad in native bush. It has many moods. On a clear morning or in the late afternoon it can be peaceful and serene, with the tranquil beauty of its surroundings mirrored in the waters and the stillness broken only by the call of the tui or bellbird. Or it can have an air of mystery when lying beneath a curtain of mist.

Lake Manapouri is long and narrow. With a coastline of over 100 miles, it is 20 miles long and six miles wide at its widest point, and the deepest part is 872 ft. below sea level. Rainbow and brown trout and Atlantic salmon are plentiful in the lake.

Lake Manapouri became the focal point in one of New Zealand's most heated controversies over the environment. Some 10 years ago the Government decided to divert some of the lake waters to a power house, mainly to produce the large amount of electricity required by a new aluminum smelter 100 miles away. This meant raising the level of the lake by several feet to provide water storage, thus burying vegetation at the water's edge and submerging some of the small beaches. A vociferous and effective body, "The Guardians of the Lake", was formed, and a petition with some 265,000 signatures was presented to Parliament. The battle was not completely won, but significant modifications were made to the plan.

The hydro-electric plant is unusual in that the powerhouse is 700 ft. underground. The lake waters are channelled down into the powerhouse and discharged into Doubtful Sound on the west coast of the island. Fiordland Travel Ltd. runs a four-hour trip which is full of beauty and interest. Leaving the natural boat anchorage at Pearl Harbor, near the Manapouri township, the launch "Fiordlander" threads its way through the islands to West Arm. From here passengers are taken by coach down a 1¼ mile road, which spirals down to the powerhouse 700 ft. below. The powerhouse is a cavern hewn out of solid rock, 364 ft. long by 59 ft. wide. The water drawn from the lake falls nearly 600 ft. to turn the turbines and then passes through a 6¼ mile tailrace to discharge in Deep Cove in Doubtful Sound.

An extension of this trip goes by coach over the 2,200 ft. Wilmot Pass and down into Deep Cove.

Invercargill

Invercargill (population 50,000) is New Zealand's southernmost city. The Maoris called it Murihiku ("the end of the tail"). The name is formed from the combination of "Inver", from the Gaelic "mouth of the river", and "Cargill," after Captain William Cargill, the first superintendent of the province of Otago. Most of the settlers were of Scottish descent and have left their mark on those streets named after Scottish rivers or places.

For 30 years Invercargill was a "dry" area, a prohibition city where no liquor could be sold, but some 25 years ago it went "wet" in an experiment that has now been followed in several parts of New Zealand. Instead of allowing private enterprise to establish liquor stores, a Licensing Trust was formed, and all profits are devoted to improving the city's amenities.

For many years the Southland area was the largest oat-producing region in New Zealand, but now that the horse has been replaced by machinery it concentrates on sheep-raising and dairying. Four large meat-packing plants process nearly six million lambs annually, most of which are exported from the port of Bluff, 17 miles to the south, where an 84 acre island was built in the harbor to provide docks and loading facilities. Across the harbor a large smelter produces 110,000 tons of aluminum annually, powered by electricity from Lake Manapouri.

Fifteen miles across the restless waters of Foveaux Strait lies Stewart Island, New Zealand's third and most southerly island. Stewart Island is so small and sparsely populated that even New Zealanders are inclined to overlook it and forget that New Zealand comprises three and not two islands. It has a population of less than 400 concentrated in one area, and only about 16 miles of road. Rugged and heavily forested, it is indented with many lovely bays and beaches and is a bird sanctuary. The Maoris called the island *Rakiura* ("sky glow") from the superb sunsets for which it is famed.

Off the coast, mutton birds (Sooty Shearwaters) are harvested in April and May. The birds are very fatty and have a very strong fishy taste.

Not so, however, the large, plump Stewart Island oysters dredged from the waters of Foveaux Strait. They are much larger than rock oysters and perhaps not as sweet, but if oysters are your dish you'll find a dozen almost a full meal. They are marketed throughout New Zealand, but there is a special gastronomical joy in eating oysters freshly dredged from the Strait.

DUNEDIN

Dunedin shows a Scottish influence. The original plan of the new Edinburgh to be founded in Otago was made by the Lay Association of the Free Church of Scotland. It was to be a truly Scots settlement where the Kirk would be the basis of community life.

Like Christchurch, the city was surveyed and laid out before the colonists arrived. The surveyor was instructed to reproduce features of the Scottish capital, and Dunedin has as many associations for the Scots as Christchurch has for the Englishman. Many of the streets bear familiar names—Princes Street, George, King, Hanover, Frederick, Castle and Queen Streets—and the little boulder-strewn stream flowing through the north-east corner of the city is called the Water of Leith.

In the early 1880s gold was discovered in the province. Thousands of prospectors poured in from all over New Zealand and from Britain, Australia and even California. Dunedin's population jumped from 2,000 to 5,000 and the population of the Otago Province from 12,000 to 75,000.

Dunedin was the center where prospectors met and prepared to leave for the goldfields. The township became blocked with shanties and tents packed on to all vacant sections. Miners swarmed down every track leading to the goldfields, travelling by bullock wagon, on horseback, and on foot. As much as $200 a week (a substantial sum in those days) could be made, and in the first four wild years Otago exported $14,000,000 worth of gold.

Dunedin boomed. But even in the middle of this dizzy prosperity the canny Scots citizens gave thought to the future, and when inevitably the boom ended the settlement had something permanent to show for the years of precarious good fortune.

The citizens needed all their determination and resourcefulness in the years that followed, for they had to find new and more permanent means of making their living. They established flourishing industries and developed fruit growing and farming in the province. New prosperity was found after the first shipment of frozen meat left Port Chalmers in 1882.

Today Dunedin has a population of about 120,000, and is New Zealand's fifth largest city. Its progress has been steady, if less spectacular, over the last three-quarters of a century. Stone buildings replaced the wooden shanties of gold-boom times, and Dunedin's beautiful churches and schools are among the finest in the country.

First Church, Gothic in design, stands in Moray Place right in the center of the city, and when the spire is floodlit the building is an impressive sight. St. Paul's Cathedral dominates the Octagon. The main block of the Otago University, the oldest university in New Zealand, is also Gothic; a stately grey stone building with a tall clock tower.

Railroad Station

Railroad enthusiasts will find the railroad station fun ("railway" is the New Zealand term). Its architect was dubbed "Gingerbread George," and the station is a fitting monument to him. He seems to have wanted to leave nothing undecorated. Heraldic lions corner the massive copper-capped tower, the NZR (New Zealand Railways) cypher is engraved on window panes everywhere, ornate scrolls surround the ticket office windows, and stained-glass windows depict locomotives approaching at full steam.

Lanarch Castle

Built in 1871 and copied from an old Scottish castle, Lanarch Castle is a living memento of the Victorian way of life. William Lanarch had married the daughter of a French duke, and, being wealthy, he set out to provide her with the sort of lavish home he thought she should have. It is said to have cost about $300,000, which was a very considerable sum in those days. The interior is a mass of ornate carving and mosaics, elaborately decorated ceilings, and marble fireplaces. The most notable feature is a Georgian hanging staircase. There is even a dungeon, where Lanarch is said to have locked up poachers caught on the property. It is situated on the Otago Peninsula nine miles from the city and is included in sightseeing tours, or can be visited by taxi or private automobile.

Olveston

This stately mansion, built between 1904 and 1906, stands in a beautiful setting of trees and formal gardens. In the Dutch influenced Jacobean style, Olveston has some 35 rooms, and contains an unusual collection of domestic art: paintings, ceramics, ivory, bronze, silverware and furniture. It is only one mile from the city.

Royal Albatross Colony

Taiaroa Head, at the tip of the Otago Peninsula about an hour's journey from the city, is the only place in the world where this magnificent bird breeds close to human habitation and can be seen at close quarters. One of the largest of birds, it has a wing span of about 11 ft., weighs up to 15 pounds, stands about 30 inches high, has a bill about 7 inches long, and may live 70 years. It does not breed until it is about seven years old, and then only on alternate years.

The birds arrive from their migration in September and settle down to lay a single egg, which is white, about 5 inches long and weighs about a pound. The parents share sitting duty for about 11 weeks, and the chick may take three days to struggle free from the shell. It is not fully fledged for about a year, when it flies as far as Tahiti in search of squid. Eight years pass before it returns to start a new breeding cycle.

The colony is rigidly protected, and bookings must be made in advance through the Government Tourist Bureau, 131 Princes Street; parties are restricted to 10 persons. The season is usually late November through mid-March, but may be cancelled without notice to protect the birds.

There is no public transport, so you may need a taxi or rental car. From January, when the chicks have hatched, there is an afternoon coach tour, usually on Mondays, Wednesdays, and Saturdays only.

Weather conditions at the colony are often boisterous, and 40 to 50 knot winds are not unusual. Warm clothing and walking shoes are recommended, and binoculars are available for observing the birds.

DUNEDIN HOTELS AND MOTELS

Abbey Lodge Motor Inn and Motels. 680 Castle St. 38 rooms, 12 motel apartments. Restaurant, bar, parking.

Adrian Motel. 101 Queens Dr., St. Kilda (close to beach). 10 units, swimming pool, spa.

Alcala Motel. Corner George and St. David Sts. 21 motel flats, parking.

Commodore Hotel. 932 Cumberland St. 12 motel units, attractive decor, parking, close to restaurants.

Leisure Lodge Motor Inn. Corner Great King and Duke Sts. 50 rooms, restaurant, bar.

Pacific Park Motor Inn. 23 Wallace Street. 60 rooms, restaurant, bar.

Regal Court. 755 George St. Eleven motel flats in different ethnic styles, parking.

Southern Cross Hotel. Princes Street. 94 rooms, restaurant, bars.

Townhouse Motor Inn. Upper Moray Place, 55 rooms, restaurant, bar.

DUNEDIN RESTAURANTS

Blades. 450 George St. Simple, intimate; excellent French food.

Carnarvon Station. Prince of Wales Hotel, 474 Princes St. Impressive, authentic railroad setting.

The Huntsman. 309 George Street. Old English setting, booth seating, specializes in steaks.

Rogano. 388 Princes St. Specialises in seafood.

La Scala. Alton Avenue, Musselburgh. Attractively furnished, specializes in Italian food.

Savoy. Corner of Princes Street and Moray Place. Victorian-style furnishings, specializes in New Zealand foods.

Terrace Cafe. 118 Moray Pl. Small and quaint; specialises in vegetarian dishes.

The Roads to the West Coast

Like a long spine, the Southern Alps divide the west from the east coast. There are only three ways across them—the Lewis Pass and Arthur's Pass from Christchurch and the Haast Pass from Queenstown and Wanaka.

By the Lewis Pass, the northern route, it is 208 miles (335 km) to Greymouth. The ascent to and descent from the 2,840 ft. summit lie through glorious beech forests.

By Arthur's Pass it is 159 miles (258 km) to Greymouth. The first pass to be negotiated is Porter's Pass which, at 3,102 ft., is 77 ft. higher than Arthur's Pass on the Main Divide. It is the boundary between Canterbury and Westland and the center of Arthur's Pass National Park. The mountains are pierced by a 5¼ mile railroad tunnel, an outstanding engineering feat. One portal appears at Otira as you leave the pass.

Neither pass poses difficulties to the driver, although the descent from the summit of Arthur's Pass to the west coast is winding and steep.

The Haast Pass, at 1,849 ft., is the lowest of the alpine passes and many find it more restful to the eye. The road passes through beautiful forest and mountain scenery, with good views of Mount Brewster (8,264 ft.) and the Brewster Glacier. As there is no settlement of any size between Wanaka and the Fox Glacier 180 miles away, take a picnic lunch.

The opening of the Haast Pass road in 1965 has opened a circular route from Christchurch through to the West Coast, to the glaciers and through the Haast Pass to Queenstown. Before then it was necessary to return from the glaciers to Greymouth in order to reach Queenstown.

Franz Josef and Fox Glaciers

The main attractions of the West Coast are the Franz Josef Glacier and the Fox Glacier, which flow down from the Southern Alps. Only 24 miles apart, they are the lowest in the Southern Hemisphere, and are unusual in that they descend to the edge of native forest. Both have receded in recent years, but the recession does not make them less beautiful. Scenic roads lead almost to the terminal faces, from which you can take a guided walk on the ice if conditions are suitable. Boots are provided by the hotel. The walk at the Franz Josef is now quite a rugged one.

The Franz Josef Glacier was named after the Emperor Franz Josef of Austria by the geologist, Sir Julius von Haast, in 1862.

The glacier's broken surface ends abruptly in a terminal ridge. Here the ice beneath the covering shingle is grey, but only a short distance above it is clear white. From an ice cave at the foot of the glacier the turbulent Waiho River ("smoky water") gushes out and flows for 12 miles to the coast. The water appears milky from the particles of rock ground to dust by the glacier, and a layer of mist sits above the surface, formed by the sudden chilling of the warm air as it meets the ice-cold river. A short distance from the source of the river is a small hot mineral spring, which emerges beside cold water.

The glaciers start at the crests of the Southern Alps and are fed by heavy snowfalls brought by westerly winds. The steep mountain slopes account for the glacier's precipitous fall—about 1,000 ft. a mile.

Unlike other New Zealand glaciers, the Franz Josef's surface is almost clear of debris. The surface is marked by deep crevasses and jagged pinnacles, due to tension caused by the more rapid motion of the middle of the glacier, or by its movement over steep slopes in the rock floor of the valley. The crevasses are usually confined to the upper layers of the ice where the pressure is not great enough to force the ice to flow.

Ice is solid, but the movement of a glacier resembles that of a viscous fluid. The movement of the Franz Josef Glacier varies from 1½ to 15 ft. a day.

Be sure to visit the small church in the bush, St. James Chapel. A large window behind the altar gives a magnificent view of the bush and mountains.

Aerial sightseeing trips are run from the air strip, and ski planes are used for landings on the glacier snowfields.

The Fox Glacier was named as a compliment to Sir William Fox, who visited it during his term as Premier of the colony. The Fox River emerges from the terminal face and flows westward to join the Cook River on its journey to the sea. The Cook River Flat is good sheep and cattle country.

Nearby Lake Matheson is famous for its reflections of Mt. Cook and Mt. Tasman. The best time to see these is in the early morning. The return walk through the native bush surrounding the lake takes about 40 minutes.

Hokitika

Hokitika now has a population of only a little more than 3,000, but in 1864 and 1865 it was a booming gold rush town of thousands. In those years over 1.3 million ounces of gold were exported. But the rush declined as quickly as it began when rich deposits were exhausted. Although small quantities of gold may still be found, Hokitika now mainly relies on farming and lumber.

But it was left with one natural asset—greenstone, a type of jade. New Zealand Greenstone, as it is called, is found in rivers near Hokitika, and helicopters are used to bring out boulders from inaccessible sites in the mountains. A 12 ton boulder was recently dragged from the sea.

Greenstone is extremely hard and can be cut only by diamond saws. The Maoris called it *pounamu* and used to raid the area to obtain it for their war clubs and ornaments. A visit to the Westland Greenstone Factory to watch the stone being cut, fashioned and polished, is well worth while. Greenstone jewelry and ornaments may be purchased at the factory (as in most souvenir shops throughout New Zealand), but, like other kinds of jade, it is not inexpensive.

Hokitika is also a prime source for a popular New Zealand delicacy—whitebait. A type of smelt, it is netted in spring at the mouths of and on the banks of rivers as it swims upstream. The fish is usually cooked in batter as fritters or patties.

Greymouth

Greymouth, with a population of just under 8,000, is primarily a coal mining town and the main business center of the West Coast. Seven miles south is "Shantytown", a convincing replica of a goldfield town at the height of the boom. Authenticity has been observed as far as possible, both in the buildings and the replicas on display. Some of the buildings were restored from those actually used, and there is an 1897 locomotive which hauls a couple of passenger cars a short distance through the bush.

Traces of gold are still found in the area, and you can try your luck in panning for gold at "Shantytown." Even if you don't find a nugget, which occasionally happens, you can be reasonably sure of leaving with a few glittering specks in a tiny phial of water. Transport can be arranged through the West Coast Public Relations Office, Mawhera Quay.

Marlborough Sounds

North of Christchurch and at the northern tip of the South Island are the Marlborough Sounds, an enormous jigsaw puzzle of sunken valleys forming over 600 miles of waterways. Three of the largest are Queen Charlotte, Pelorus and Kenepuru Sounds, Pelorus being the most extensive (34 miles long). The hills, headlands and peninsulas rising from the sheltered waters are in many cases densely wooded, and everywhere there are secluded bays and beaches. Some of the hills have been turned into sheep farms which can only be reached by water.

Understandably, the Sounds are a popular holiday center for both Wellington and Christchurch residents, for although they are 217 miles (339.5 km) by road from Christchurch they are only 52 miles from Wellington by sea. The opportunities for swimming, sailing, boating and exciting sea fishing are limitless. Those who like the amenities of a township will base themselves at Picton (population normally about 3,000, but rising to 10,000 at the height of the holiday season between Christmas and the end of January); those who prefer relaxing in quiet scenic beauty by the sea "away from it all" or enjoy boat fishing or surf-casting will choose a place like The Portage in Kenepuru Sound.

The ubiquitous Captain Cook entered Queen Charlotte Sound in 1770 and anchored his ship "Endeavour" near the northern entrance in "a very safe and convenient cove" (Ship Cove). On an island he hoisted the flag and announced he was taking possession of New Zealand in the name of King George III, after whose Queen the Sound is named. Cook returned to the Sound four times.

Passenger-vehicle steamers of over 4,000 tons sail regularly each day from Wellington to Picton. The voyage takes 3½ hours, but only two hours are spent in Cook Strait itself. The last hour is entrancing, after the steamer has swung through a narrow entrance and cruises down the narrow Sound, whose banks are dotted with sheep farms.

From Picton there are launch cruises to various parts of the Sound and organised fishing trips.

Nelson

Only 40 minutes by air from Wellington and 73 miles by road from Picton, Nelson is one of the sunniest places in New Zealand, with 2,407 sunshine hours a year. Its climate and lovely beaches make it highly popular for holidays and retirement.

In 1858, although it had a population of less than 3,000, Nelson was declared a city by Queen Victoria when she ordained that it should be a Bishop's See. A cathedral was duly built. Today Nelson has a population of over 42,000.

Nelson is the hub of one of New Zealand's largest fruit growing areas. Orchards are to be seen everywhere, and it exports over a million cases of apples each year, mainly to Britain. It is here, too, that New Zealand's tobacco is grown, as well as hops for brewing.

Nelson is proud of being the birthplace of Lord Rutherford, the first man to split the atom. He received his early education at Nelson College and went on to do research into radioactivity at McGill University, Montreal, and later at Cambridge University, England. He was born at

Brightwater, 12 miles south of Nelson.

Near outlying Takaka is one of the largest fresh water springs in the world, Pupu Springs. Water bubbles out of the sand at a reputed 200 million gallons a day and a constant temperature of 52°F.

PRACTICAL INFORMATION FOR NEW ZEALAND

 HOTELS AND MOTELS. New Zealand does not have "super luxury" hotels, but the better hotels are somewhat similar to the Hilton type, although styles vary. The average room rate ranges from NZ$85 to $145, and motels from NZ$45 to $60. The cities and scenic resorts are well served with good quality hotels and motels, but advance reservations, especially from Christmas through February, are advisable.

Many motels have fully-equipped kitchens where you can cook your own meals; others have only tea and coffee-making facilities; some serve breakfast.

Some remote scenic areas are served by Tourist Hotel Corporation hotels (prefixed by the letters THC), which have high-quality accommodations, in the middle of mountains, lakes or fiords.

NORTH ISLAND

Gisborne

DB Gisborne Hotel. Huxley and Tyndall roads; P.O. Box 113. 26 rooms, restaurant, bars.

Sandown Park Motor Hotel. Childers Road. 35 rooms, restaurant, bars.

Hamilton

DB Glenview. Ohaupo Road. 18 rooms, all facilities, restaurant, cocktail bar.

DB Riverina Hotel. Grey Street. across the river, 12 doubles, 31 singles, restaurant, cocktail bar.

Waikato Motor Hotel. Main highway at Te Rapa. 18 rooms, all facilities, restaurant, cocktail bar.

Hastings

Angus Inn Motor Hotel. Railway Road. 58 rooms, restaurant, bar, parking, 5 minutes' walk to the city's center, adjacent to the racecourse.

Fantasyland Motels. Sylvan Road. 19 rooms, private facilities but no restaurant or bars.

Napier

Masonic Hotel. Marine Parade. 18 rooms with facilities, 49 without, restaurant, bars.

Tennyson Motor Inn. Emerson Street. 42 rooms, restaurant, bars, parking.

TraveLodge. Marine Parade. 60 rooms, restaurant, bars, parking.

New Plymouth

Devon Motor Lodge. 382 Devon Street. 135 rooms, cabaret, pool, sauna, gym.

DB Bell Block Hotel. 15 Bell Block. Restaurant, bars, pool.

The Plymouth. Leach, Hobson, and Courtenay streets. 75 rooms, suites. Restaurants, bars, parking.

Westown Motor Hotel. Maratau Street. Restaurant, bars, pool.

Bay of Islands (Paihia)

Autolodge. Marsden Rd. 50 rooms, restaurant, bar, parking.

Bushby Manor Motor Inn. Marsden Rd. 17 suites, nearby restaurant, pool, parking.

Casa Bella Motel. McMurray Rd. 16 units, parking.

Paihia Sands Motor Lodge. Marsden Rd. 8 units, restaurant, parking.

THC Waitangi. 111 rooms, restaurants, bar, parking.

Rotorua

DB Rotorua Hotel. Fenton Park. 74 rooms, restaurant, bars, heated pool.

Geyserland Motor Hotel. Fenton Street. 76 rooms, restaurant, bars, thermal pool, massage facilities golf course, pool.

Kingsgate. Eruera St. Deluxe resort in beautiful lake setting with 233 rooms, Health center, some Jacuzzis, restaurants, bars, parking.

Sheraton-Rotorua Hotel. Fenton St. 144 rooms, restaurants, bars, roof-top pool, entertainment, spa, parking; top quality.

THC Rotorua Hotel. Froude St.. 150 units, restaurant, bars, refrigerators in rooms, thermal baths and pool.

TraveLodge Motor Inn. Eruera Street. 210 rooms, restaurant, bar, thermal pool.

Voyager Resort, Ranolf St. 42 hotel rooms, 44 motel rooms. Restaurant, bar, parking.

There are also a large number of good quality motels, all rooms with private bath and toilet, some with thermal pools.

Taupo

Berkenhoff Tourist Hotel. Corner Duncan and Scannell Sts. 1½ miles from town, restaurant, bar, parking.

De Brett Thermal Hotel/Motel. Napier Highway. 2 miles from town, restaurant, bar, parking.

Huka Lodge. 2 miles from town on banks of Waikato River. Mainly for anglers, restaurant, bar, parking.

Manuels Motor Inn. Lake Terrace. Restaurant, bar, parking, pool, fishing, sauna.

Suncourt Motor Hotel. Northcroft St. 52 units, restaurant, bar, parking.

Tauranga

18th Avenue Motels. 50 18th Avenue. 21 rooms, no bars or restaurant, but breakfast available.

Willow Park Motor Hotel. Willow Street. 44 rooms, restaurant, bar, parking.

Tongariro National Park

THC Chateau Tongariro. A Tourist Hotel Corporation hotel on the slopes of Mount Ruapehu, 84 rooms, all facilities, heated, restaurant, bars.

Wairakei

THC Wairakei Hotel. 75 rooms, restaurant, bar, thermal swimming pool, golf.

Waitomo Caves

Waitomo Country Lodge. 17 rooms, restaurant, cocktail bar.

Waitomo Hotel. Run by the Tourist Hotel Corporation, an oldish but redecorated hotel featuring solid comfort and good meals, 26 rooms with facilities, 17 without, restaurant, cocktail bar.

Wanganui

Bryvern Motor Inn. 321 Victoria Avenue. Restaurant, bars, parking.

Hurley's Grand International Hotel. 99 Guyton Street. Restaurant, bars.

Wangunui Motel. 14 Alma Rd. Restaurant, bar, pool.

SOUTH ISLAND

Franz Josef Glacier
THC Franz Josef Hotel. 45 rooms, restaurant, bars, parking.
Westland Motor Inn. 47 rooms, restaurant, bar, parking.

Fox Glacier
Fox Glacier Hotel. 53 rooms, restaurant, bars, parking.
Kingsgate Hotel. 55 rooms, restaurant, bar, game room, shop.

Greymouth
Ashley Motel & Motor Inn. 70-74 Paroa Rd. 54 serviced units, restaurant, bar, parking.
DB Greymouth Hotel. 68 High Street. 26 rooms, restaurant, bar, disco.
King's Motor Hotel. 88 Mawhera Quay. 177 rooms, restaurant, bar, pool, parking.
Revington's Hotel. Tainui Street. 25 rooms, restaurant, bar.

Hokitika
DB Westland Hotel. 2 Weld St. 28 rooms, restaurant, bar, parking, close to railway terminal.
Hokitika Hotel. 22 Fitzherbert St. 3 rooms, 13 units with kitchens, breakfast available.

Invercargill
Ascot Park Hotel/Motel. Corner Tay St. and Racecourse Road. 77 rooms, 23 motel units, spa, heated indoor pool, restaurant, bar, parking.
Don Lodge Motor Hotel. 77 Don Street. 24 rooms, restaurant, bar, parking.
Grand Hotel. 76 Dee Street. 62 rooms, restaurant, bar.
Kelvin Hotel. 16 Kelvin Street. 82 rooms, restaurant, bars.
Swan Lake Motor Inn. 217 North Road. 15 motel-type rooms, restaurant.

Marlborough Sounds
DB Terminus Hotel. High Street, Picton. 20 rooms, restaurant, bar, parking.
The New Portage Hotel. Kenepuru Sound. 11 rooms with facilities, 22 rooms share bath, restaurant, bar, parking, informal atmosphere.
Picton Motor Inn. Waikawa Road, Picton. 70 units, boating available, pool, restaurant, bar, parking.

Milford Sound
The Tourist Hotel Corporation has a well-appointed and comfortable hotel (the THC Milford) with restaurant and bar at the head of the sound, but as that is the only accommodation available, advance reservations are essential.

Mount Cook
As Mount Cook is within a national park, only the Tourist Hotel Corporation is permitted to operate hotels. The Hermitage, regarded as the best resort hotel in New Zealand, is so built that each room has excellent views of Mount Cook and other mountains and is furnished to a very high standard. It has restaurants, bars and parking.

Nearby Glencoe Lodge, Mount Cook Motels and Mount Cook Chalets are less luxurious, with lower rates. The popularity of the area, and its remoteness from a town of any size, makes it essential to reserve accommodations in advance.

Nelson

DB Nelson Hotel. 270 Trafalgar Square. 38 rooms, restaurant, bar, parking.
DB Rutherford Hotel. Trafalgar Square. 95 rooms, restaurant, bar, pool, parking.

Queenstown

A-Line Motor Inn. 27 Stanley Street. 56 rooms, restaurant, bar, lake view.
Hotel Esplanade. 32 Peninsula Street. 21 rooms, restaurant, bar, on lake shore.
Kingsgate. Frankton Road. 83 rooms, top quality.
Lakeland Regency. Lake Esplanade. 116 rooms. Restaurant, bar.
Mountain View Lodge Motel. Frankton Road. 1 mile from town, 32 motel apartments, restaurant, bar, parking.
Country Lodge. Fernhill Rd, ½ mile from town. 25 rooms; restaurant, bar, parking.
Resort Hotel. Lake Esplanade. 117 rooms, restaurant, bars, parking.
TraveLodge. Beach Street. 140 rooms, restaurant, bars, parking, sauna, on lake shore.
Vacation Hotel (Frankton). Vewlett Crescent. 87 rooms, restaurant, bars, 5 miles from Queenstown, adjacent to airport.
Vacation Hotel (O'Connell's). Beach St. 65 rooms. Restaurant, bar.

Te Anau and Manapouri

Campbell Autolodge. 42 Te Anau Terrace. 23 rooms, motel flats, restaurant, parking.
Fiordland Motor Lodge. Highway 94. 106 rooms, motel flats, restaurant, bar, parking.
Grand View Hotel. Manapouri. 15 rooms, restaurant, parking.
Luxmore Lodge. Milford Road, 69 rooms, restaurant, bar, parking.
DB Manapouri Motor Inn. 56 rooms, restaurant, bar, parking, lake swimming.
Vacation Safari Lodge. Mokonui Street. 44 units, restaurant, bar.
THC Te Anau Hotel. Lakefront. 102 rooms, restaurant, bars, parking.
Trans Hotel. Milford Road. 63 rooms, restaurant, bar, parking.
Vacation Hotel Te Anau. Te Anau Terrace. Box 133. 96 rooms, restaurant, bar, parking, jacuzzi. Summer resort.

 RESTAURANTS. New Zealand has few first-class restaurants of the quality one would expect to find in the larger cities of Europe and America. Although sophisticated cuisine is hard to find, good food is not, for New Zealand has an abundance of excellent and relatively inexpensive raw materials. Plainly cooked steak, lamb and seafood are the basis of most local menus. New Zealand wine, like American, is variable in quality, but some reds and a great many white wines are well worth trying.

All the major hotels contain restaurants, and the larger cities, especially Auckland and Wellington, contain smaller establishments that serve attractive meals. You may pay anything from NZ$15 to 30 per person for a three course meal, but the cost is usually determined by the quality of the food rather than the reputation of the chef, or current fashion in dining.

By New Zealand law, restaurant staff are paid a living wage, and do not depend upon tips for their livelihood. It is not necessary, then, to leave a tip, but your kindness will be appreciated if you do.

There are a number of smaller restaurants of the "diner" variety where a meal of steak and French fries can be had for as little as NZ$5. In these, however, you cannot obtain alcoholic beverages. Many more expensive restaurants also lack a liquor licence, but some will allow you to bring in your own wine.

NORTH ISLAND

Rotorua

All the larger hotels have good quality restaurants, and there are some interesting restaurants in the city.

Aorangi Peak. 7 miles from city, half-way up Mount Ngongotaha, magnificent views, good food.

Bushman's Hut. 167 Tutanekai St., decorated as such, seafood and wild game.

Caesar's. Arawa St. Excellent food; bring your own wine.

Friar Tuck. Corner Arawa and Tutanekai Sts., quiet atmosphere, good steaks.

Landmark. 1 Meade St. Early colonial decor, elegant, top New Zealand food.

Lewishams. 115 Tutanekai St., tastefully quiet, personalized service, good food.

Ruedi's. 41 Arawa St., French decor and cuisine.

Tudor Towers. Government Gardens, Polynesian feast, concert.

Tauranga

DB Mount Maunganui. Girven Road. New Zealand dishes.

Sierra Bianca. Marine Parade, Mount Maunganui. Continental dishes, steaks, lobster.

The Stable. Cameron Road. Steaks and seafood.

Top Hat International Restaurant. Main Road, Mount Maunganui. Steak and seafood.

Willow Park Motor Hotel. Brown Street. Steaks and seafood.

SOUTH ISLAND

Invercargill

Bogart's. 5 Dee St. French cuisine.

The Fodder House. 38 Dee St. Steaks and local seafood.

Queenstown

Country Lodge. Fernhill, 3 miles from township. Views down south arm of the lake, whitebait a specialty.

La Rochelle. Beach St. French cuisine.

Packers Arms. About 4 miles out of Queenstown. Genuine old stone cottage tastefully decorated, venison ragout a specialty.

Roaring Meg's Restaurant. Shotover St. Informal atmosphere; specialises in scallops, salmon, whitebait, venison, and lamb.

Sablis Restaurant. Beach St. French cuisine.

Skyline Restaurant. Top of cableway. Panoramic views and good cuisine, specialty is crayfish mornay.

Upstairs/Downstairs. Arcade in center of town. Modern restaurant with semi-Victorian decor, specialty is fillet steak with tomato, cheese, and onion.

Westy's. Center of town. Gourmet food, yet casual atmosphere.

 FARM HOLIDAYS. If your taste lies toward breaking away from the main tourist areas for a while and living with New Zealanders, you'll enjoy a farm holiday. About 300 farmers offer accommodations to visitors for overnight or longer stopovers on normal working farms, not "dude ranches." If you stay for a while you'll become part of the family and join in social activities.

While many farms have "cottages," where the visitor has to provide his own food and linen, probably the most suitable is the "live-in" arrangement where the visitor stays with the farmer and his family in their own home, takes meals with them, and possibly joins in with farming activities. The visitor has his own bedroom, many with private facilities, and takes nothing but personal belongings.

Bookings can be heavy during the main school holidays from mid-December to the end of January, and it is wise to reserve in advance. Reservations may be made through travel agents or through

Farm Holidays, Ltd., Box 11–137, Wellington;
Home Holidays, Box 31–250, Auckland;
Homestay Ltd., Box 630, Rotorua; New Zealand Home
Hospitality, Box 309, Nelson.

THE SOUTH PACIFIC

FRENCH POLYNESIA

The Bustling Paradise

by
JAN PRINCE

A resident of Tahiti since 1971, Jan Prince works as a free-lance journalist and tour guide. Her voyages to the remote islands of French Polynesia provide first-hand information for her articles.

Flowers! The heady, sweet scent of tropical blossoms permeates the air you breathe as you enter Tahiti. Whether you come by airplane or ship, you are greeted by leis of Tiare Tahiti gardenias or the fragrant frangi pani. Smiling Tahitian beauties welcome you to their island in their high musical voices as they place the flowers around your neck and you are happy to have arrived in Paradise. After clearing immigration and customs and learning that there is "No Tipping!" in Tahiti, you cheerfully proceed to your hotel by taxi or escorted tour bus. If it should be in the daylight hours when you arrive, you will be sitting back in the car when you suddenly become aware of something—what is that noise?

Welcome to modern day Tahiti! That's just what it is—noise. Hundreds of motorcycles, motorbikes, Vespas, trail bikes, automobiles and trucks all zoom along, zigzagging in and out of the traffic, trying to get there first. There is even a small section of freeway cut through the mountains now, giving two lanes that are usually made into five lanes by the speed happy motorists.

Look out into the lagoon and there is more noise. Even the traditional outrigger canoes have engines on them, as well as the power boats and, the most annoying of all, the racing boats that whine round and round the once calm (oh, how long ago!) lagoon.

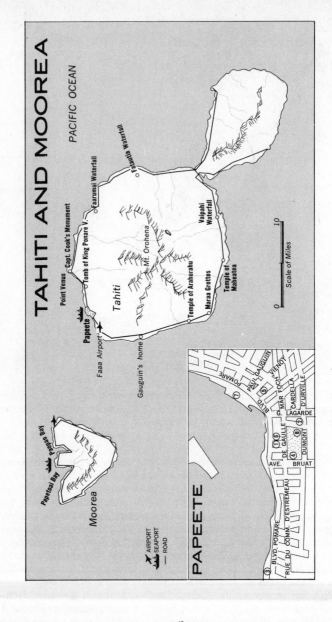

TAHITI AND MOOREA

PACIFIC OCEAN

Moorea

Papetoai Bay · Paopao Bay

✈ AIRPORT
⚓ SEAPORT
— ROAD

Faarumai Waterfall
Fatautia Waterfall
Point Venus
Capt. Cook's Monument
Tomb of King Ponare V.
Papeete
Faaa Airport
Gauguin's home

Tahiti

Mt. Orohena
Vaipahi Waterfall
Temple of Arahurahu
Marea Grottos
Temple of Maheatea

Scale of Miles
0 _____ 10

PAPEETE

BLVD. POMARE
RUE DU COMM. D'ESTREMEAU
AVE. BRUAT
DE GAULLE
DUMONT
LAGARDE
CARDELLA
MAR LOCH VENOT
PAUL GAUGUIN
POMARE
G. D'URVILLE

Points of Interest

1) Bougainville Park
2) Cathedral
3) Cultural Center and
   Auditorium
4) High Commissioner's
   Residence
5) Market
6) Post Office
7) Sea Passenger
   Terminal
8) Territorial Assembly
   and Convention
   Auditorium

The other noise that tourists once complained about is still here also—
that of the roosters crowing at all hours of the night and the mynah birds
fussing outside the hotel windows in the early morning hours. Compared
to the machines, though, these natural noises are like music to the ears.

Take a stroll downtown. What has happened to dear old "Papeete
town"? It has almost vanished forever. Gone are the old landmarks,
many of the centuries old trees, and whole blocks of once familiar
Chinese stores, replaced by modern shopping centers or buildings under
construction.

When the most famous bar in the South Pacific, Quinn's, was torn
down in 1973, "Papeete town," as it was known to hundreds of seamen,
voyagers, adventurers and South Seas characters, ceased to exist. The
urge to build shopping centers and apartment buildings seemed to affect
everyone with money to invest, and a rash of fires on the waterfront
speeded up the process of changing the face of Papeete. And that's what
it is now; Papeete, a true city, bustling and noisily busy. The town that
was once the land of "aita pea pea" (Who cares?) and "haere maru"
(Take it easy) has become the city of "dépêchez-vous" and "ha'a viti viti"
(Hurry up).

Paradise Found

But don't despair. Take heart, for the good old days do still exist and
can easily be found outside of Papeete. There are some 130 islands in the
vast area known as French Polynesia. To some people all this is collectively known as Tahiti, meaning more a state of mind than any geographic location. However, it is not necessary to leave the island of Tahiti to
seek your ideal of a tropical setting. Just get away from the downtown
area, take a tour around the island and you will find all the beauty,
tranquillity and color you could wish for.

Go to Point Venus and see where the first known Europeans set foot
on the island that later came to be known to the world as "paradise."
Today it is a big park with monuments, a museum and a lighthouse,
surrounded by the lagoon and a large black sand beach. It was here, on
June 23, 1767, that Captain Samuel Wallis of the British Royal Navy,
and his crew of 150 men aboard H.M.S. "Dolphin," anchored in Matavai
Bay, five days after first sighting the tall mountains of Tahiti and following the coastline to seek a safe anchorage. The exhausted and scurvy-
ridden men aboard the 32-gun frigate had left England eight months
before in search of Terra Australis Incognita, the great land mass that
King George III and his geographers were convinced lay somewhere
between Cape Horn and New Zealand, in balance with the northern
hemisphere. Imagine their surprise and joy the following morning when
they found their ship surrounded by "upwards of five hundred canoes"
containing four thousand athletic paddlers and loaded with fruit, coconuts, fowl and young pigs. But the most astonishing sight to their sea-
weary eyes was that of the fair young girls, standing in the middle of each
canoe, nude to the waist, "who played a great many droll, wanton
tricks." While the hungry sailors were enjoying the free strip-tease, the
Tahitians began to hurl fist-sized stones at the men on board the "Dolphin." The sailors retaliated by firing the ship's cannons at the canoes,
killing forty or fifty of the Tahitians and sinking a great number of the

canoes. After a second attack that the men of the ship easily won, the Tahitians decided to be friendly and peaceful.

As Wallis was too weak from scurvy to claim the new land in the name of the King, the second lieutenant, Tobias Furneaux, hoisted a pennant on a long pole and took possession of the island, calling it "King George's Island." The remainder of the five-week visit was spent trading earrings, nails and beads for foodstuffs. However, the men of the "Dolphin" began to wholeheartedly engage in "a new sort of trade . . . it might properly be called the old trade," according to George Robertson, master, whose journal is the best account given. When the men had emptied their sea chests to exchange their possessions for the ladies, they began to pull out the iron nails and cleats from the ship. The initial cost of such carnal exchange was a 20 or 30 penny nail. This rose to a 40 penny as demand outgrew the supply, and some women demanded as much as a seven- or nine-inch spike. Very soon two-thirds of the men had no nails to hang their hammocks on. The "Dolphin" sailed back to England soon afterward, without looking further for the southern continent.

Here at Point Venus is a marker for Captain Wallis and another one for the French explorer Louis Antoine de Bougainville, who was the second visitor from Europe to claim Tahiti for his country. Bougainville, captain of the French ships "Boudeuse" and the "Etoile," had been searching also for the mythical Terra Australis Incognita and sought refuge on the windward side of the island off the district called Hitiaa, arriving nine months after Wallis' departure. His short visit, lasting only from April 6–14, 1768, was very much a repetition of the reception Wallis had received. One unusual incident marked this landing, when the Tahitians spotted among the 314 officers and men of the two ships a woman who had made the voyage disguised as a man. When one big Tahitian man grabbed her up to run off to the hills, her secret became known. Her name was Jeanne Baret and she had sailed as the personal valet of Bougainville's botanist, amongst all those French sailors, without any of them knowing there was a woman on board. She became the first white woman to visit Tahiti and to circumnavigate the world.

Bougainville, not knowing that his new island had already been "discovered" by Wallis and claimed for England, proclaimed French sovereignty over the island he called New Cythere or the New Island of Love. He found many similarities between the ancient worship of Aphrodite-Venus, whose birthplace was the Greek island of Cythere, and the Tahitian love rites.

Before Bougainville sailed away, his botanist named the scarlet and violet paper-like flowers they saw growing in such profusion Bougainvillea, after his captain. And when the "Bodeuse" left, there was a young Tahitian man from Hitiaa named Ahutoru, who sailed with her. He became the first Tahitian to discover Europe.

The following year Tahiti had her third visitor. Lieutenant James Cook, who later came to be known as England's most famous explorer, anchored in Matavai Bay in H.M.S. "Endeavour" on April 13, 1769. After 25 years at sea, half in the merchant marine, Cook had so impressed his superiors in the Royal Navy (he is credited with originating the art of making charts) that they took the almost unprecedented step of transferring him to the command of a very important mission, promoting him from the ranks to lieutenant.

This expedition assigned to Cook was to take an astronomer either to the Marquesas Islands or to New Zealand for the purpose of observing the transit of the planet Venus across the disc of the sun. This event was to take place on June 3, 1769, and there would be no further opportunity to witness such a phenomenon again until 1874. Astonomers were anxious to take advantage of this rare occurrence as it would enable them to ascertain the distance of the earth from the sun, the fundamental base line in all astronomical measurements, and which was imperfectly known. Expeditions organized by the Royal Society had been sent to various parts of the world, but Cook's was the only one to the southern hemisphere and was therefore of special importance.

Two months before Cook left for the South Seas, Wallis returned to England with the disappointing news that he had not found the great southern continent. When he learned of the imminent voyage Cook was to command, Wallis suggested King George III's Island as the ideal spot to establish an observatory. There Cook and his men would find hospitable natives and an abundance of food and water.

Cook's expedition consisted of eighty-four officers and seamen and eight civilians. The civilians included Joseph Banks, a young botanist who later became president of the Royal Society; Dr. Daniel Solander, an eminent Swedish botanist and zoologist who had studied with the great Linnaeus; and astronomer Charles Green, who, in addition to supervising the observation of Venus, provided Cook with precise estimates of longitude, indispensable on such a discovery voyage.

When Cook and his noteworthy assistants anchored in Matavai Bay, seven weeks before the transit of Venus was expected, the "Endeavour" was given an enthusiastic welcome by the Tahitians. Crowds of natives greeted the ship with the now customary friendliness and immediately recognized four of the officers who had visited the island with Wallis.

The first thing Cook did upon arrival in what was then known to the English as King George III's Island was to erect a fort to protect the astronomer and his instruments. He chose the same site that Wallis had selected, the strip of land between the beach and the river. In less than three weeks' time the 150 foot long and 80 foot wide fort was finished, complete with five foot high walls and two four-pounder cannons.

These precautions proved superfluous, however, for the Tahitians, especially the women, were so friendly and hospitable that the British sailors forgot their duties. Cook had posted regulations concerning trade with the natives to prevent a repetition of Wallis's nail-removing fiasco. It was ordered that no iron be exchanged except for provisions. He also asked his men to treat the natives with "all imaginable humanity" and to use every fair means of cultivating their friendship. The natives appreciated this treatment and came to know the Englishmen affectionately by their "Tahitianized" surnames—Tute (Cook), Opane (Banks), Tolano (Solander), and so forth.

The major problem Cook encountered was constant pilfering. From time to time he was obliged to take one or more of the chiefs hostage against the return of pilfered objects. The most important item taken was the quadrant, an essential instrument for astronomical observation. Although the instrument was eventually returned, the culprit had removed it from its box and taken it apart to see what made it tick and it proved of no use in the operation.

On the day of the observation, there was not a cloud in the sky and the scientists were able to witness every phase of the transit from the fort at the place named Point Venus in honor of the occasion. However, it was subsequently found that the readings taken in Tahiti and other places were of little value because of unforeseen optical distortion caused by the irradiation of the sun.

Cook's expedition stayed in Tahiti for three months, during which time he learned much about the Tahitian way of life. He made precise observations of native customs, manners, religion and law. He described the people's appearance (explaining their tattoos), cooking methods, foodstuffs and apparent social and political order. He also made a trip around the island and drew a complete and accurate map of the whole coastal region of Tahiti.

By this time Cook had learned what the natives called their island and began using the name he understood it to be—Otaheite. When he asked them the name, they replied, "This is Tahiti," and in their language it sounded like Otaheite. Actually, the full name is *Tahiti-nui-i-te-vai-uri-rau*, "Great Tahiti of the many-colored waters."

Several of the things Cook learned about the Tahitian way of life shocked the 41-year old seaman. "It is this," he said in his Journal, "that more than half of the better sort . . . have enter'd into a resolution of injoying free liberty in Love, without being Troubled . . . by its consequences. These mix and Cohabit together with the utmost freedom, and the Chilldren who are so unfortunate as to be thus begot are smothered at the Moment of their Birth." He noted that couples lived together for years, destroying all children. His reference was to the Areoi Society that was in existence at that time, and their meetings during which "the Women in dancing . . . give full Liberty to their desires." He was also aghast that "both sexes express the most indecent ideas in conversation without the least emotion" and that "chastity . . . is but little valued. The Men will very readily offer the Young Women to Strangers, even their own daughters, and think it very strange if you refuse them; but this is merely done for the sake of gain."

However, the Tahitian people were suffering consequences of having enjoyed free liberty in love. Cook found, to his distress, that many of them, as well as his own men, were suffering from venereal disease. How they had caught it is a toss-up between the men on Cook's ships or the former discoverers. The English blame the French and vice-versa.

In years to come, the ravages of venereal disease, as well as other illnesses the Europeans introduced to the islands such as tuberculosis, small pox, measles and alcoholism, as well as the guns they brought to the natives, helped to reduce the population at an alarming rate. Cook gave the estimate of the population at over 200,000. Just 36 years later it was determined to be 8,000.

Cook and his men sailed away from Tahiti on July 13, 1769. Heading westward, he discovered the islands of Huahine, Raiatea, Tahaa and Bora Bora. He named them the Society Islands "because they lay contiguous to one another." He then sailed on to New Zealand and Australia, discovering many islands in the process. He was to return to Matavai Bay again, as Captain Cook, on three separate occasions in 1773, 1774 and 1777, during his second and third voyages of exploration. Today there is a monument to this great discoverer at Point Venus.

"Breadfruit Bligh" and the Bounty

In the following years many ships called at Tahiti, some anchoring in Matavai Bay and others stopping at Tahiti-iti, the peninsula which means "little Tahiti." One of the most famous ever to drop anchor in these waters was the H.M.S. "Bounty," commanded by Lieutenant William Bligh. The *Mutiny on the Bounty* saga is well known as it was imaginatively told by co-authors James Norman Hall and Charles Nordhoff, two Americans who moved to Tahiti after fighting in World War I. The "Bounty" story, starring Marlon Brando, Trevor Howard, and the Tahitian beauty, Tarita, was filmed at Point Venus in 1961, and a 1980's version, with English and Australian actors, was filmed on Moorea.

Bligh, who had been to Tahiti previously with Cook on his third voyage, aboard the "Resolution," was married to a lady whose uncle had a number of large plantations in Jamaica, was well connected in government circles and was the owner of several ships. A petition was made to King George III by English merchants in the West Indies, asking that the breadfruit tree be transplanted from Tahiti to their islands. Cook and others had spoken highly of the breadfruit as a substitute for bread and had told of how healthy and strong the Tahitians were, who ate it as their staple diet. The merchants believed it would be a cheap and nourishing means of feeding their slaves. The petition was approved and Bligh was appointed to command the voyage. There was no problem in signing on a crew as the reputation of the friendly and voluptuous Tahitian ladies was well known in Europe by that time.

By the time the "Bounty" arrived in Matavai Bay, October 26, 1788, there had already been problems aboard between captain and crew. For five months they stayed in Tahiti, waiting for the breadfruit to reach the right stage for transplanting. During this lengthy stay the discipline slackened while the sailors lived among the happy Tahitians, who were not accustomed to let work interfere seriously with their many pleasures and amusements.

As the time drew nearer for their departure, Bligh became excessively severe with his men. And on April 4, 1789, when the "Bounty" weighed anchor and steered towards the leeward islands of the Society group, he carried a reluctant crew.

The magic of Tahiti proved too strong a magnet and Bligh's insults to his officers, especially to acting Lieutenant Fletcher Christian, too harsh to endure. Thus, on the early morning of April 28, Bligh was awakened by four of his men, hauled out of bed, tied up and dragged on deck. There he learned that a mutiny was being staged, under the leadership of Christian, and he was put into a launch, along with eighteen of his officers and men, a 28-gallon cask of water, 150 pounds of bread, some wine and rum, a compass, a quadrant, some canvas, lines and sails. Then the mutineers cast the boat adrift in the open ocean, a few miles from Tofua in the Tongan Islands. Bligh made one of the most notable open boat voyages in history, sailing 3,600 miles to Timor and Batavia in the Dutch Indies, losing only one man during this grueling voyage. Six others died after reaching safety.

The mutineers first tried to settle at Tubuai, in the Austral Islands, but the natives were so hostile that the "Bounty" turned back to Tahiti three days later to resupply and reconsider what to do next. The twenty-five men who remained in the "Bounty" consisted of two parties: those who had taken an active part in the mutiny and those who had not. On June 6 the ship once again anchored in Matavai Bay, where she remained for ten days, loading pigs, goats, a cow and a bull, dogs, cats and fowl. When she sailed for Tubuai again, the mutineers were accompanied by nine Tahitian men, eight women and nine children, many of whom were stowaways.

Life with the aggressive Tubuaians proved impossible (about 100 natives were killed in skirmishes), so the mutineers finally decided to retreat to Tahiti. Some of the men remained there and Fletcher Christian led eight of his fellow mutineers, with six Tahitian men, one little girl and twelve Tahitian women, aboard the "Bounty" and they sailed away to eventually settle on the uninhabited island of Pitcairn. There they burned the ship and were not heard of again for 18 years.

Meantime 16 of the original "Bounty" crew lived in Tahiti, some taking wives and having families. Here they were discovered in March, 1791, when H.M.S. "Pandora" sailed into Matavai Bay, in search of the mutineers. Two of the "Bounty" men had died by the time the "Pandora" reached Tahiti, but Captain Edward Edwards arrested the remaining 14. On their way to England for their trial, the "Pandora" was shipwrecked and four were drowned. A court martial inquiry was held in England and three men were condemned to death and hanged, while the remaining seven were allowed to live as free men. During his confinement, one of the men, Peter Heywood, wrote the first Tahitian dictionary while awaiting trial.

Even after all the troubles he had been through on the "Bounty," old "Breadfruit" Bligh didn't give up on his mission. He appeared again in Matavai Bay on April 10, 1792, as Captain Bligh and commander of H.M.S. "Providence" and her armed tender, the "Assistance."

When he arrived there was a native war going on and he was afraid it would make it hard for him to collect the breadfruit. Finally he went ashore to supervise the building of storage sheds for his plants.

During the three months he was in Tahiti on this visit, Bligh had ample time to note the changes that had occurred. He was disappointed to learn that "little of the ancient customs of the Otaheitans remains ... It is difficult to get them to speak their own language without mixing a jargon of English with it, and they are so altered that I believe in future no Europeans will ever know what their ancient customs of receiving strangers were." He also felt that their method of dress had degenerated and they were "no longer clean Otaheitans, but in appearance a set of ragamuffins with whom it is necessary to observe great caution."

By July 18, Bligh had collected 2,126 breadfruit plants and about 500 others and set sail for the West Indies with no major problems. There, in St. Vincent and in Port Royal, Jamaica, the breadfruit seedlings were planted. But when the trees grew and bore fruit, the Negro slaves, for whom the breadfruit was intended, disliked the taste and refused to eat it.

Heathen and Missionary

Thirty years after Captain Wallis discovered Tahiti, a shipload of an entirely different type of conquerors arrived in Matavai Bay. These were the missionaries. Composed of Presbyterians, Methodists, Episcopalians and Independents, the newly formed London Missionary Society left England in 1797, bound for Tahiti. This island was chosen as their first foreign country because they felt the society should begin its work in some place where "the difficulties were least."

By the time their ship, the "Duff," anchored in Matavai Bay, on March 5, 1797, a Sunday morning, more than a hundred natives were dancing and capering on the decks, crying "tayo, tayo" (friend). Even though they were unarmed, the captain ordered the ship's guns to be hoisted. The Tahitians cheerfully assisted in placing them in their carriages.

As the 18 missionaries settled into their new quarters on Point Venus, formerly the house of Lieutenant Bligh, they began to realize the immensity of their task in imposing bleak, puritanical ideas on the uninhibited, idolatrous islanders. They soon became aware that there was "more to apprehend from being caressed and exalted, than from being insulted and oppressed."

There were only four ordained ministers in the group, while the rest were carpenters, weavers, tailors, shoemakers, bricklayers and a harness maker. Most of them were in their early twenties and only five of them were married and had their families with them. Therefore, it is not surprising that the first problem to face the new settlers was how to deal with the beautiful and alluring Tahitian women. Even though they agreed that it would be sinful to marry a heathen woman, some of the men succumbed to the weakness of the flesh and committed the unforgivable sin of fornication.

The missionaries' life was not an easy one, in that they never learned the Tahitian language well enough to preach the gospel in an intelligible manner. The natives would scoff and ridicule them and laugh when they tried to convince the Tahitians that Jehovah was the only true God and their pagan rites and human sacrifices should be abolished. It took the missionaries more than 15 years to make their first convert, even though they had some 2,300 natives attending their meetings and instructions. Some of the Tahitians felt that the missionaries should pay them to attend the mission schools. The missionaries also quarreled among themselves and many of their number left for other islands or back to England. They made the mistake of taking sides in the local power struggles and usually supported the wrong chief for the wrong reasons.

After baptizing the powerful chief, Pomare II, whom the missionaries thought of as king of Tahiti, the other people followed suit and their idols and temples were destroyed in favor of the Christian religion.

For almost forty years the Protestant missionaries enjoyed tremendous success in Tahiti before any competition arrived. They had gained strong political control and some had lined their pockets well.

Therefore, when a small band of Catholic missionaries arrived in Tahiti with the intent of opening a new mission, the Protestants used all their influence to prevent this from happening. The first Catholic group landed on the island of Mangareva, 900 miles away, in 1835. One of them was sent to Tahiti disguised as a carpenter. The Protestants protested when they learned his true mission and they were even more incensed when two French Catholic priests arrived on the scene the following year.

The priests were asked to leave the island but refused. Queen Pomare IV, the illegitimate daughter of Tahiti's first Christian convert, who was now in power, wrote a letter to the French priests, ordering them to leave on a ship that was in port. When they again refused, the two men were forcibly removed from the island and placed aboard the ship.

The Brink of War

This action began a series of events that almost brought England and France to the brink of war. When the French government learned of this affair, it was decided that the "scandalous treatment" of the two priests could not go unpunished. Thus the frigate "Venus," under the command of Captain Abel Du Petit-Thouars, was ordered to proceed to Tahiti to demand "a full reparation" from the Queen for "the insult done to France in the person of our compatriots." The punishment called for the Queen to write a letter to the King of France, apologizing; an indemnity of 2,000 Spanish dollars was to be paid for losses suffered by the two priests and the French flag was to be hoisted and saluted with twenty-one guns. The Queen wrote the letter but had neither the money nor the flag nor the powder. Du Petit-Thouars provided the flag and the gunpowder for the salute and George Pritchard, the most prominent missionary, and two other English residents gave the money.

The French Commander also proposed that a treaty of perpetual peace be drawn up between Tahiti and France and that Frenchmen of every profession would be allowed the right to come and go and to trade in all the islands composing the government of Tahiti. He also proposed that Frenchmen should be "received and protected as the most favoured foreigners."

As soon as the Venus had sailed, Queen Pomare and four of her principal chiefs wrote to Queen Victoria asking for British protection. This was not the first time the Queen of Tahiti, persuaded by George Pritchard, had asked the Queen of England to make Tahiti a British protectorate. But England was having her own troubles with France and Queen Victoria "expressed deep concern at the difficulties under which Queen Pomare appeared to labour," but decided it would be impossible for her to "fulfill, with proper punctuality, any defensive obligations towards the government and inhabitants of Tahiti." For that reason, she was unable to make Tahiti a protectorate of Great Britain, but she would always be glad to "give the protection of her good offices to Queen Pomare in any differences which might arise" with any foreign power.

Queen Pomare began having serious problems with a foreign power very soon after this letter was received from the Queen of England. A Frenchman who was also a Catholic, M. Moerenhout, had been appointed as the French Consul. While the queen was visiting in Raiatea and while the former missionary, George Pritchard—who was now the British Consul—was away in England, Moerenhout took advantage of the opportunity to trick four of the chiefs into signing a document he had composed, asking that Tahiti be made a French protectorate.

When the French government received this request, they found it suited their needs at the time, since they were looking for a base in the Pacific for the warships, whalers and merchant vessels sent out from France. They had already decided to take possession of the Marquesas Islands. So Rear Admiral Du Petit-Thouars, aboard the flagship "La Reine Blanche," was chosen to establish the French protectorate in Tahiti as well.

Despite the protests of Queen Pomare and her chiefs, who admitted they didn't understand what the document was about that they had signed, the French began to install themselves very firmly on the island. With threats and troops, Du Petit-Thouars obtained the signature of the Queen on a letter accepting "the proposal to place the government of Queen Pomare under the protection of His Majesty Louis Philippe, King of the French." He then set up a provisional government of three—the Commissioner Royal, a military governor and a captain of the port of Papeete.

When news of the French protectorate reached England six months later, the matter was brought up in Parliament, and the decision was made to accept the French protectorate as long as the Protestant missionaries would be allowed to carry on with their work.

However, when it was learned in England and in France that Du Petit-Thouars had not merely established a protectorate in Tahiti but had actually taken full possession in the name of the French king, this far-away island became the main topic of conversation on both sides of the Channel. The issue was debated even more heatedly when it was learned that the Tahitian flag had been replaced by the French flag after 500 French troops surrounded the palace, and Queen Pomare had been dispossessed and forced to flee to the safety of an English ship in the Papeete harbor. But all of England was outraged when Pritchard arrived on July 26, 1844, in H.M.S. "Vindictive" with the news that he had been arrested and deported.

The matter was heatedly discussed in all circles and given much publicity in the newspapers of both countries. Both the French and English governments found it difficult to avoid war as both sides felt they had been humiliated. Finally King Louis Philippe offered to pay Pritchard 25,000 francs out of his own pocket, hoping that he could maintain the "entente cordiale" with Great Britain. This offer was rejected and accord was maintained between the two governments when France apologized to England for the treatment given Pritchard and an "equitable indemnity" was paid for his loss and sufferings.

This affair was kept alive in the French parliament for three more years and contributed to the eventual overthrow of the government and monarchy in the famous revolution of February 24, 1848.

While England and France were carefully avoiding war back in Europe, the Tahitians were staging a lot of skirmishes with the French troops in Tahiti, and sometimes getting the upper hand. Their queen sought refuge in Raiatea, where she wrote to Queen Victoria, pleading for help in regaining her sovereignty. The letters were never answered and she realized that she would have to fight alone. The natives, however, never gave up hope that Britain would come to their aid. They could not believe that England had deserted them and they refused to submit to the French protectorate.

The protectorate had been re-established and the Queen's sovereignty restored in early 1845, after France and England had come to terms over the George Pritchard affair. But Queen Pomare refused to return to Tahiti under French rule. Finally, in February, 1847, she gave up the useless struggle when she heeded the advice of a Tahitian chieftainess and agreed to accept the French protectorate. Thus she was brought back to Tahiti, where she was little more than a figurehead until her death on September 17, 1877.

King Pomare V, the last of the dynasty to carry this title, was totally unfit for even the most nominal duties of kingship. He preferred drinking and gambling and had none of his mother's pride in the Tahitian heritage. Therefore, it was easy to get him to abdicate, with the promise of an annual pension for himself, his wife and two brothers.

The century-old rule of the Pomares formally came to an end on December 30, 1880, and Tahiti became a full-fledged French colony, when the French government accepted Tahiti and her dependencies as forming one and the same country with France.

In 1903 the whole of the French establishment in the Eastern Pacific was declared one colony and was called French Oceania. In 1957 the status was changed from a colony to a Territory and the name was changed to the present, French Polynesia.

Modern Polynesia

Before you leave Point Venus and the site where white man first stepped ashore to change the lives of these 'noble savages,' take a moment to look up at the green peaks of Mt. Orohena, Tahiti's tallest mountain of 7,353 feet. Follow the line of the mountains around to where the hotel Tahara'a is situated on top of the famous "One Tree Hill," so named by Captain Cook. Here you have the continuity of the magic of Tahiti, bridging the unknown past with the uncertainty of the future. Eight million years have passed since these mountains first rose from the blue waters. Radio-carbon dates indicate that human history began in what we now know as the Society Islands around A.D. 850. As there was no written language until the missionaries devised an alphabet for the natives, very little is known about their origins. Scientists have learned some interesting things about their ancient culture by studying their language and by excavations that have revealed their temples, called "maraes," and their stone adze heads, fishhooks and artifacts.

In modern times, after more than 200 years of white man's influence, the Tahitian and Polynesian culture is very much alive. A leisurely drive around the island of Tahiti reveals many of the same attractions that brought romanticists to these shores—writers and artists such as Robert Louis Stevenson, Jack London, Somerset Maugham, Rupert Brooke, Paul Gauguin, Henry Adams—who were, each in his own way, trying to capture the "same charm of light and air." There are the several rivers and waterfalls; the fern covered mountains; coconut plantations and taro fields; the simple Tahitian "fares" built of bamboo and pandanus roofs; the soft featured and golden skinned women, clad in their bright "pareos" and with flowers behind their ears, washing clothes in a stream or holding a baby on their hips and gossiping alongside the road; and there are the friendly and athletic men who still fish on the reefs at night and play their guitars and drums. The "tamure" and other traditional dances are still performed with skill and enthusiasm even though the modern French Polynesian eagerly adopts the latest dances from Europe or America and performs them with vigor and an abandon seen nowhere else.

It is true that the faces of Tahiti have changed from the days when Wallis and de Bougainville and Cook first came ashore. With the arrival of the Europeans in 1767 and the Chinese—who were first introduced to these islands during the American Civil War to work in the cotton plantation where the golf course is today—there has been more racial intermingling than in any other part of the Pacific except Hawaii. With the exception of the Chinese community, who are the merchants of these islands and who still try to maintain their tradition of marrying within their own race (although it is increasingly difficult to control), there are no financial, racial or social barriers.

Even though many of the couples who live together are not legally married, the population continues to grow, so that more than half the population of 167,000 in French Polynesia is under the age of 20. There is no stigma for an unmarried girl to have a baby and there are few unwanted babies. Tahitians love any tiny infant, cat, or dog, as long as they are very young. Life is not so easy for the growing youngster or animal, however, in many cases.

As you end your tour of Tahiti you find that you have stepped back into modern day Papeete, just in time for the evening rush hour to begin as the workers go home from their offices. The euphoria that surrounded you around the island as you walked through the botanical gardens, picked a flower, watched the surf breaking on the reef, listened to the wind whistling through the casuarina trees at the edge of a black sand beach, drank the cool liquid of a coconut, or viewed the mountains of Tahiti from the plateau at Taravao on the isthmus, begins to dissipate as you enter the downtown area with its high rise shopping centers and parking meters.

But if you can keep that magic around you and get to the waterfront area undisturbed by the noise, then you will be amply rewarded as the sun begins to set behind the peaks and spires of Moorea, that land of "Bali H'ai," just 12 miles across the bay. As you sip a tall cool one at one of the sidewalk cafés and watch the sky turn all shades of red, pink and orange, the last of the traffic disappears and you can see the outrigger canoes in the harbor, where their vigorous paddlers are practicing for their next race. When you finish your drink and before you return to your air conditioned hotel room, walk down the waterfront to the corner across the street from the Tahiti Tourist Board. Here, in a thatched-roof "fare," you will find a tradition that has existed ever since there have been Tahitians. The old women are sitting on the floor, making crowns of flowers for the merrymakers to wear when they go out that evening, dining and dancing. This scene is one of the last remnants of "Papeete town."

For the curious traveler who doesn't adhere to the belief that "if you've seen one island, you've seen them all," French Polynesia is a veritable treasurehouse. Because it covers such a large area of the eastern Pacific and the five archipelagoes are at different latitudes, choices can be made from the high volcanic islands of the Society group, the low coral atolls of the Tuamotus, the remote and mysterious islands of the Marquesas, or the temperate climate of the distant Australs.

Many a visitor has made the mistake of allowing too little time for visiting the outer islands of French Polynesia and quite often the complaint is heard, "Oh, how I wish I had come here first."

At the Tahiti-Faaa airport in Tahiti there are lockers where it is possible to store luggage while visits are made to the other islands. Also the hotels are very good about keeping your bags while you are away from Tahiti.

The islands most frequently visited are those with first class hotels. They are: *Tahiti, Moorea, Bora Bora, Huahine* and *Raiatea* in the Society Islands; and *Rangiroa* and *Manihi* in the Tuamotus. The following information will enable you to determine which ones suit your desires most, and includes some of the lesser known islands.

Moorea

This sister island just 12 miles from Tahiti is the most frequently visited one after Tahiti. There are several launches that leave daily from the Papeete harbor for the 45-minute crossing, returning to Tahiti in the afternoon. Also there is an air taxi service that will land you on Moorea in just seven minutes flying time. Once there, you can choose from several hotels, most of which are located on white sand beaches.

In Moorea, as on the other islands, most of the activities are centered around the clear waters of the lagoon. A coral reef several yards offshore protects the lagoons from the pounding surf and, as a result, the lagoons are usually as calm as a giant swimming pool.

If you're not a swimmer, snorkeler or diver, then you can ride a bike around the island or take a tour arranged by the hotels. It is also well worth the money to rent a car and drive the 37 miles around the island and up into the valley of Opunohu, passing coffee plantations and pineapple fields. Be sure to drive up to "Le Belvedere," a lookout spot where you will be well rewarded with a magnificent view of Moorea's jagged mountains and Cook's bay, also called PaoPao and of Opunohu Bay, also known as Papetoai Bay. On all the tours the mountain called "Bali H'ai" by the tourists will be pointed out. This is a needle shaped mountain named Mou'aroa that appeared in the movie "South Pacific" as the mythical Bali H'ai.

Most of the nighttime activities take place in the hotels, where there are regular Tahitian feasts, called "tamaaraas," dance shows or singing to the accompaniment of guitars and ukuleles. There is discotheque dancing aboard a refurbished old schooner anchored at the Hotel Kia Ora, and Pimm's Disco is located on the other side of the island, across from Hotel Moorea Village. The once-popular "One Chicken Inn," where one could dance Tahitian-style, has now closed.

Bora Bora

More "purple prose" has been written about this little island than any other in the South Pacific and justly so. Situated 143 miles northwest of Tahiti, it can be reached in 55 minutes by Air Polynesie, plus another 45 minutes by launch from the airport to the main village of Vaitape. Or you can go by an air-conditioned ferry that leaves Tahiti twice weekly, stopping at Huahine, Raiatea, and Tahaa enroute, and arriving in Bora Bora the following day.

The island is fringed by small islets, called "motus," and boasts one of the clearest and most colorful lagoons anywhere, with a variety of coral gardens that can be viewed through glass bottom boats or while snorkeling and diving. The two highest mountains, Mt. Otemanu at 2,379 feet and Mt. Pahia at 2,165 feet, can be seen from many vantage points as one travels the 17 miles around the island on a partially paved road.

There are two rental car locations that have bicycles and motorbikes, as well as jeeps and cars. Bicycles are a popular method of transportation in Bora Bora and can facilitate the many stops you will need to make to visit the villages, the old barracks and seaplane base built by the Seabees, the ancient temples, called "maraes," or to inspect the curios at the many souvenir stands around the island. You will want to stop for a drink at the Bloody Mary Restaurant and make reservations to return for a seafood dinner, cooked and served in a setting right out of a South Seas movie.

The largest hotel, the Hotel Bora Bora, offers all types of water sports, and frequent Tahitian dance shows or slide shows. The Club Mediterranée, with over-water bungalows, also has a full range of activities, including picnics and swimming on a nearby "motu." The Hotel Marara was built to house a movie crew while filming a Dino DiLaurentiis movie, *The Hurricane*. Upon completion of the film the Marara (Tahitian for flying fish) was opened to the public. It faces toward Tahaa and Raiatea. Next door is a new Climat de France Hotel. The Hotel Oa Oa has eight bungalows near the principal village and the Bora Bora Marina Hotel is located on Motu Mute, the islet where the airport is built. The Hotel Matira has housekeeping bungalows, complete with individual outrigger canoes, built beside the island's prettiest beach.

If you just want to lie back and take life easy, this island is an ideal place to do just that. There is no hustle and bustle unless you want to create it yourself. Serenity is the password on Bora Bora, which means "firstborn-of-silent-paddle."

Huahine

Promising to become French Polynesia's most popular island in the not too distant future, Huahine is only 40 minutes by air from Tahiti, or just an overnight trip by inter-island schooner.

This quiet and peaceful island, which is actually two islands, called Huahine-Nui (big Huahine) and Huahine-Iti (little Huahine) is only 20 miles in circumference. There are mountains over 2,000 feet high and two lakes, where it is easy to dig for clams and crabs. Most of the island's population of 3,900 fish and farm for a living and produce watermelons and cantaloupes for the market in Tahiti.

The principal village, called Fare, is reminiscent of an old western town from some cowboy country. There are a handful of Chinese stores lining the tree-shaded waterfront, plus a cinema that shows Kung Fu movies once a week. Snacks or full meals can be purchased from the "roulottes," or lunch wagons, in the village or a good hamburger can be had at the snack stand built by the beach. The Hotel Huahine overlooks the impressive turquoise harbor and Chez Lovina, next to the Bank of Tahiti, offers clean rooms at affordable prices.

When the copra boats arrive four days a week, there is much excitement in the village, with truckloads of Tahitians coming to town for market day. The rest of the week the village takes on a somnolent air with only a few people strolling under the big almond trees.

The first class Hotel Bali H'ai Huahine can be reached in just five minutes from the village by walking on a path alongside the strip of white sand beach that stretches from the village past the hotel.

Rental cars or mopeds can be ordered at the Hotel Bali H'ai, Hotel Huahine, or with Lovina. Also there are guided tours from each place around the island, or visits to the village of Maeva, an old Polynesian village built over the water on stilts. Many interesting Tahitian temples or "maraes" are located in or near this village.

Five miles from Fare is the Hotel BelleVue, with 15 colonial-style bungalows and eight double rooms, a swimming pool, and a restaurant that features locally caught seafood prepared Chinese-Tahitian style.

At the south end of Huahine-Iti two hotels were opened in mid-1985 near the pretty village of Parea. The Huahine Beach Hotel and the Relais Mahana are built beside long white sand beaches and offer 12 bungalows each, plus restaurant, boutique, all water sports, and other activities. Parea has a few "pensions" where guests share the Polynesian lifestyle, including children and dogs.

Raiatea

This second largest island in the Society group is only a 45 minute flight from Tahiti or an overnight passage aboard the "Raromatai Ferry," an air-conditioned passenger and car ferryboat that departs Tahiti twice weekly. The inter-island schooners *Temehani II* and *Taporo IV* also service the Leeward Society Islands, with a true Polynesian atmosphere.

Although there are not many white sand beaches to be found on this island, many visitors favor Raiatea because of the friendly people and the historic landmarks. It was from the river called "Faaroa" located here that the original Maoris set off for New Zealand. This was also the former educational and religious center for the ancient Tahitians, and the most famous temple or "marae" called "Taputapuatea," is located on the southeast point of the island.

The Hotel Bali H'ai chain offers first class accommodations with many over-water bungalows, all water sports, bicycles, a swimming pool and games area, as well as being the center for the nightly social events and dancing.

The Raiatea Village, with 12 bungalows complete with kitchenettes, opened in late 1983 by the Faaroa River. A restaurant is planned and by the end of 1985 there will be 32 rooms. Although this small hotel is not close to the village it does offer a peaceful beauty.

There are various tours available at both hotels, including speedboat trips to the nearby island of Tahaa, where time seems to have stopped a hundred years ago.

A lot of fun can be had just by walking or biking into the principal town of Uturoa. There are Chinese shops to explore and the public market, in the center of town, is interesting to visit during the early morning hours of market days. Even though Raiatea has a population of 7,400 and Uturoa is the second-largest town in French Polynesia, there is little nighttime activity except on weekends, when the young Raiateans head for the disco or local nightclub to dance the night away.

Another kind of dancing is performed on special occasions at the Hotel Bali H'ai, when the firewalking ceremonies recreate the ancient rites of walking barefoot across white-hot stones.

Tahaa

Tahaa is the sister island of Raiatea, sharing the same lagoon. It is nearly circular in shape and is only 15 miles in circumference, half the size of the main island of Raiatea. From Tahaa you can easily see Huahine, Raiatea and Bora Bora. It is necessary to go to Raiatea first if flying and take the Rainui Ferry, with daily service, for the short trip to this still-unspoiled island.

Most tourists visit Tahaa for the day only as there is no longer any hotel on the island. A few rooms are available with local families. Speed canoe excursions, fishing, and sailing trips can be arranged at hotels in Raiatea. The *Raromatai Ferry* and the copra ships *Temehani II* and *Taporo IV* call at Tahaa.

Tetiaroa

Tetiaroa is the atoll that belongs to Marlon Brando, just a 20-minute flight from Tahiti. Due to extensive damage during several hurricanes in 1983, the hotel was closed and is presently open for day tours and one-night weekend stays only. Accommodations include 11 bungalows and 5 A-frame rooms built of coconut trees. Meals are served picnic style since the restaurant has not been rebuilt. Beautiful beaches and an interior lagoon are the natural attractions here.

Tuamotus

The Tuamotu archipelago, also called the Low or Dangerous archipelago and comprising 78 low islands called coral atolls, is scattered over several hundreds of miles of the eastern Pacific that is part of French Polynesia.

Thirty of these atolls are uninhabited, while the rest are very sparsely populated. The islands rise only some six to twenty feet above the water and are surrounded by coral reefs with rarely a pass or break in the reef; when there is a pass it is usually navigable only at certain tide levels. The reefs are graveyards for the many boats that didn't make it through the passes. Life on these remote atolls is simple and often lonely, because of the lack of people or visiting boats. The diet of the people consists mostly of fish, coconuts and canned food.

There is airplane service to several of the atolls—Rangiroa, Manihi, Arutua, Hao, Tatakoto, Pukarua, Reao, Nukutavake, Fangatau, Puka Puka, Kaukura, Mataiva, Apataki, Napuka, Fakarava, Takapoto, Anaa, Makemo and Tikehau—but there are no first class hotels on any except at Rangiroa and Manihi. There are facilities available with Tahitian families on the other atolls, for those travelers who don't require too many comforts and services.

Rangiroa is a perfect example of a coral atoll. The reef encloses a lagoon 42 miles long and 14 miles wide at its extreme width. Air Polynesie has flights six days a week from Tahiti to Rangiroa and in only one hour you are there, in a completely different world, surrounded by blindingly white sand beaches, with the multi-colored lagoon on one side and the pounding surf of the Pacific on the other side of this narrow strip of land.

The atoll life can be observed in the villages of Tiputa and Avatoru on Rangiroa, where there are the churches, schools, the usual Chinese stores and ancient bakery still producing long loaves of French bread daily. Tiputa can be reached by speedboat from the Kia Ora Hotel in a few minutes. Avatoru is located on the same atoll as the airport and the hotel can be reached by car. There is a pass into the lagoon at both Avatoru and Tiputa. Many visitors and locals enjoy swimming through the passes as the extremely powerful tide rushes through. You can see hundreds of tropical fishes, as well as sharks, who are swept along with the current.

The hotels Kia Ora Village, Rangiroa Village, and La Bouteille a la Mer are located on the main atoll, and the small hotel Sans Souci is across the lagoon on a private islet.

These atolls of the Tuamotus are often ravaged by hurricanes or cyclones. Their limpid lagoons have been found to be the perfect place to farm the famous South Seas black pearl, which is sold in Tahiti.

For the diver, a trip to these waters is a dream come true, for it offers some of the finest diving in the world.

Marquesas

The twelve islands that comprise *Les Îles Marquises* are little known to the world and are considered to be strange and mysterious by the outsider. The first white man to discover any of these high volcanic islands was Alvaro Mendana de Neira of Spain, who arrived in 1595 and discovered four of the southernmost islands. He named the group in honor of the Viceroy of Peru's wife, the Marquesa de Mendoza.

Before the missionaries converted the people to Christianity, the Marquesans fought many wars among themselves and were noted cannibals, but the diseases and vices introduced by white man had a more devastating effect on the population than earlier practices had. The population was once more than 100,000 but numbers 6,500 today.

For 40 years prior to the French government taking over, the Marquesas group was ravaged by whalers, traders, blackbirders (slave traders) and others. Finally the Marquesan chiefs asked France to help, and a treaty was signed between the chiefs and Admiral du Petit-Thouars in May 1842.

Today, the Marquesans are noted for their native handicrafts, especially for their wood carvings. They also earn money from copra and the sale of shells.

The island of Nuku Hiva can be reached by airplane from Tahiti. This 5-hour flight normally runs each Friday with a stopover in Rangiroa. There are additional flights often added during high season, operating on Thursdays. It is advisable to make reservations well in advance. There are internal flights within the Marquesas islands, connecting Nuku Hiva with the islands of Hiva Oa, Ua Pou and Ua Huka. The Aranui, a 264-foot long cargo/copra/passenger ship departs Tahiti each month for 16-day round trips to the Marquesas, with two brief stops in the Tuamotus enroute. This is the best way to visit the Marquesas; the ship is comfortable, clean, and air-conditioned, with a French chef, and the Aranui calls at each principal Marquesan island and at isolated valleys.

There are a few small hotels on some of the islands, as well as a room or two in village homes. For those adventurous enough to visit these still-peaceful islands where wild horses, cattle, goats, sheep, and pigs roam through the mountains, the trip will be an experience.

Australs

For those who want to see French Polynesia but prefer their climate a bit cooler than is usually found in the Society Islands, then perhaps the Austral group will be just what you're seeking.

The five inhabited and two uninhabited islands form a chain that extends from the southwest to northwest over a distance of about 800 miles. The nearest island to Tahiti is Rurutu, which is 300 miles south, placing it in a temperate zone where potatoes and strawberries grow instead of mangoes and papayas.

Rurutu, as well as Tubuai, can be reached by plane from Tahiti in less than 2 hours. The flights leave on Mondays and Thursdays, returning the same day. A passenger-cargo schooner, the *Tuhaa Pae II*, makes regular trips between Tahiti, Rurutu, Tubuai, Raivavae and Rimatara. The round trip takes 10-12 days. A 15-17 day round trip is made between Tahiti, the above islands and Rapa every three months.

On the island of Tubuai there are numerous accommodations in Tahitian style bungalows close to the beach. There are bicycles, horses and outrigger canoes to rent for exploring this oval shaped small island that is only six miles long by three miles wide. This is the island where the "Bounty" mutineers attempted to make a settlement but were forced to leave when the natives became violent. Today, the people of the Australs are very friendly and love to include the visitor in their daily events.

On Rurutu there is a hotel that opened in February, 1982. Each of the 16 bungalows includes a sunken bathtub, lush carpets, bedding and towels. A fresh water swimming pool and excellent food are part of the hotel's offerings for the visitor who wishes to explore Rurutu in comfort and style. There are also lodgings available with the local people in the three villages of Moerai, Avera and Hauti. Here the islanders build their own schooners and carry their produce of taro, arrowroot, copra and vanilla to the other islands to sell. The woven hats from Rurutu are very well made and bring a high price in the stores of Papeete.

Anyone planning to visit these islands of the Austral group that Captain Cook discovered should bring a heavy cardigan and warm clothes, especially during the months of May through October.

PRACTICAL INFORMATION FOR FRENCH POLYNESIA

FACTS AND FIGURES. French Polynesia covers an area as big as Europe without Russia (1,545,000 sq. miles) and consists of some 130 islands with a land area of only 1,544 sq. miles. These islands, many of which are uninhabited, are divided into five archipelagoes: the Society Islands (Windward and Leeward Islands), the Austral Islands, the Tuamotu-Gambier Islands and the Marquesas Islands. Total population is 167,000.

Tahiti, the largest island, is the seat of government and the capital, with Papeete (pronounced Pah-pay-ay-tay, meaning 'water (from a) basket') the major city and harbor. Population for Tahiti is 116,000, consisting of Polynesians of Maori origin representing 69%, Polynesians mixed 14%, Asians 4% and Europeans (including Americans) 13%.

French Polynesia is administered as an overseas Territory of the French Republic. The High Commissioner is appointed by France to serve for three years. A 1984 revision to the constitution allows more internal autonomy, with a local president and council of 10 ministers elected by the 30 Territorial Assembly members for 5 years. The Territory is represented in France by a senator and two deputies to the National Assembly.

WHEN TO COME. There are only two real seasons in French Polynesia—the warm and rainy season from November to April and the cooler and drier season from May through October. The daytime temperature in the hotter time of the year averages 82°F. and during the cooler months the average is 76°F. The flowers and fruits are at their best during the warmer months but the tropical winds are usually blowing during the months of April through August.

Average Temperature (°Fahrenheit) and Humidity

TAHITI Papeete	Jan	Feb	Mar	Apr	May	June	July	Aug	Sept	Oct	Nov	Dec
Average max. day temperature	86°	86°	86°	85°	83°	82°	82°	82°	82°	83°	84°	85°
Days of Rain	14	11	9	8	7	7	6	5	6	8	9	13
Humidity, Percent	79	79	79	79	80	79	78	76	77	77	79	79

WHAT WILL IT COST? Due to the strength of the U.S dollar at time of publication (168 French Pacific francs to US $1) the cost of visiting Tahiti and her Islands is now lower than it has been for several years.

LANGUAGE. The official language is French, although Tahitian is usually spoken by the Polynesian population, especially away from Papeete. English is spoken in many of the shops and in all the hotels.

 TIPPING. Signs are posted at the airport in Tahiti in three languages, "No Tipping." In other places, such as hotels and travel brochures, you will read that tipping is contrary to Tahitian hospitality. This is true and it is not the custom to tip; however, the employees of the larger hotels in Tahiti, as well as tour escorts and drivers, do graciously accept occasional tips.

 WHAT TO TAKE. Lightweight summer clothes are used all year round as it is normally warm to hot. A light sweater or jacket feels good in the evenings during the cooler months of May through October. Rarely is a man seen wearing a jacket and tie in Tahiti. The standard attire for men even at dinner parties is simply slacks and shirt. The women usually wear pretty long dresses in the evenings and normal resort wear around the hotels. "Pareos" (brightly colored and versatile) are worn in most of the outer islands around the hotels, but Tahiti is a bit dressier. Tennis shoes or plastic beach sandals for walking on the coral reefs and in the lagoons. If you're going to some of the remoter islands, take your own supply of tobacco and cigarettes. Suntan lotion, dark glasses and mosquito repellant come in handy. Bring lots of money because this place is trés cher!

 ELECTRICITY. Most of the hotels use 220 volts, 50 cycle, with 110 volt outlets for razors only. Some of the older hotels still use 110 volts. Converters can sometimes be borrowed from reception desks in the hotels.

 HOW TO GET THERE. *By air:* The airport at Tahiti-Faaa is served by six international airlines. UTA leaves Los Angeles four times weekly direct to Tahiti, and also has service from Sydney, Noumea and Auckland, plus a weekly Honolulu–Tahiti–Honolulu flight. Air New Zealand flies from Los Angeles to Tahiti twice a week and has three flights weekly from Auckland, one of which stops in Fiji and the Cook Islands. Qantas flies 747s from Los Angeles to Tahiti three times weekly and three weekly flights arrive from Melbourne and Sydney, Australia. Lan Chile arrives on Wednesdays from Santiago, Chile and Easter Island. South Pacific Island Airways flies from Honolulu to Tahiti each Friday and returns early Saturday mornings. Polynesian Airlines connects Tahiti with the Cook Islands, American and Western Samoa with weekly flights that arrive in Tahiti on Thursdays and depart on Fridays.

By sea: Several international ships call at Tahiti but on an infrequent basis, offering connections from Europe, South Africa, Panama or Australia. These ships are from the lines of Sitmar, Cunard, Holland America, Norwegian America and Bank Line. A few cruise ships leave from San Francisco or other California ports, as well as New York and Florida, and stop in Tahiti. Royal Viking Lines, the *Pacific Princess, Queen Elizabeth II,* and *Sagafjord,* among other passenger ships, cruise to Tahiti and beyond. A few Windjammer Barefoot Cruise boats, such as *Yankee Trader,* pass through infrequently.

430   **FRENCH POLYNESIA**

 TOURIST INFORMATION SERVICES. There are some fifteen travel agencies in Tahiti that can provide information and assistance for anyone wishing more specific information on French Polynesia. Some of the larger ones are: Tahiti Nui Travel, B.P. 718, Papeete; Tahiti Tours (the American Express Agency), B.P. 627, Papeete; and Tahiti Voyages, B.P. 485, Papeete. The best source for information and brochures would be the Tahiti Tourist Development Board, B.P. 65, Papeete, Tahiti, or one of its branches throughout Europe, Japan, New Zealand, Australia and the United States.

 HOW TO GET AROUND. *By air:* Air Polynesie, the domestic airline, connects Tahiti with neighboring islands (Moorea, Huahine, Raiatea, Bora Bora, Maupiti), distant islands of the Gambiers, and remote archipelagoes (Tuamotu atolls of Rangiroa, Manihi, Takapoto, Anaa, Makemo, Tikehau, Hao, Kaukura, Apataki, Mataiva, Fakarava, Tatakoto, Pukarua, Reao, Nukutavake, Fangatau, Napuka, Arutua, and Pukapuka; Austral Islands of Rurutu and Tubuai; and the Marquesas Islands of Nuku Hiva, with connections to Ua Pou, Ua Huka and Hiva Oa), using F-27 turbo-prop and Twin Otter planes. There is also an air taxi service between Tahiti and Moorea, operated by Air Tahiti, with planes leaving frequently throughout the daylight hours.

By sea: Inter-island connections can be made within French Polynesia on the many copra boats and schooners that make regular trips throughout many of the islands. Between Papeete and Moorea there are daily connections and between Papeete, Huahine, Raiatea and Bora Bora there are a car ferry and two cargo ships that take passengers on a twice-weekly basis. The *Tuhaa Pae II* cargo ship takes passengers to the Austral Islands, and the air-conditioned, 17-cabin ship *Aranui* offers 16-day round trip cruises to the Marquesas Islands.

By car: On the islands of Tahiti, Moorea and Bora Bora, it is relatively easy to rent cars, except on busy weekends or holidays. In Huahine and Raiatea one may find a rental car, but the chances are lessened because of the small number available. In Papeete, Avis, Budget and Hertz have agencies, as well as the local agencies of Robert Rent-a-Car, Andre and Pacificar. There is taxi service available in Tahiti, Moorea, Huahine, Raiatea and Bora Bora, the most visited islands. The fares in Tahiti are high and the prices double between the hours of 11:00 P.M. and 5:00 A.M. except for runs between the airport and the hotels. Le "TRUCK": Local buses, called "trucks," offer an inexpensive and often entertaining way to get around Papeete. They leave from the central market downtown and go in all directions, making stops all along the way, up back roads and alleys, taking people home. They operate on no schedule at all. There is service available to and from all hotels by this means between 6:00 A.M. and 6:00 P.M. Often you will find some trucks on the streets even much later at night.

 TOURS. *Air Polynesie,* Box 314, Boulevard Pomare, Papeete. Operates Fokker F-27s, Britten-Norman Islanders, and De Havilland Twin Otters. Rates one-way from Papeete to: Bora Bora Fr9.490; Maupiti Fr10.665; Hauhine Fr6.950; Moorea Fr2.100; Raiatea Fr7.995; Rangiroa Fr11.460; Manihi Fr15.850; Anaa Fr13.190; Takapoto Fr17.590; Tikehau Fr10.810; Apataki Fr13.395; Makemo Fr18.590; Hao Fr25.540; Gambiers Fr44.000; Tubuai Fr18.965; Rurutu Fr16.975; Marquesas Fr39.000.

American–Hawaii Cruises, 550 Kearny St., San Francisco, CA 94108. The 715-passenger ship *Liberté* is scheduled to begin year-round 7-day cruises in November, 1985, between Tahiti and Rangiroa, Hauhine, Raiatea, Tahaa, Bora Bora, and Moorea. Ship includes casino, pool, nightclub, conference center and TV sets, plus round trip airfare program of $299 from Los Angeles to Tahiti.

Exploration Cruise Lines, 1500 Metropolitan Park Bldg., Olive Way at Boren Ave., Seattle, Wa. 98101, offers island hopping aboard the *Majestic Tahiti Explorer.* First-class 4-, and 5- and 7-day cruises from Tahiti to Moorea, Huahine, Bora Bora, Tahaa and Raiatea, aboard 152-foot, 44-stateroom, 4-deck ship. Fly and cruise programs available in cooperation with UTA from Los Angeles.

Islands in the Sun (Ted Cook Tours Inc.), 2814 Lafayette, Newport Beach, Ca. 92663. Offers cruise aboard 65-foot cruiser *Danae III* for 14 days in French Polynesia. This plan includes all meals during the 6-day sailing portion of the itinerary; low-season rates are also offered between Los Angeles and Tahiti. Departures guaranteed with no minimum number of passengers required.

Moana Adventure Tours, Nunue, Bora Bora. Glass-bottom boat trips, water skiing, speedboat rides, visits to coral reef, fishing, scuba diving inside lagoon and outside reef.

Sea and Leisure, P.O. Box 65, Papeete. Operated as a branch of the Tahiti Tourist Development Board, this floating office along the Papeete waterfront has information on every aspect of water sports in Tahiti and her Islands. Boats, fully equipped for deep-sea fishing for marlin, sailfish, tuna, and other game fish can be chartered here. Sailboats, Hobie Cats, surfboards, and windsurfing equipment, glass-bottom boats, waterskiing and diving expeditions can all be arranged.

South Pacific Yacht Charters, Inc., PO. Box 6, Smithfield, Utah 84335. A bareboat sailing fleet of Peterson CSY 44-ft. yachts, Nautical 39-ft. boats, and Endeavor 37-ft. boats can be chartered out of Raiatea for sailing to Leeward Islands of Society group. Provisions, captain, cook, and crew available if desired.

Tahiti Aquatique, BP6008, Faaa, Tahiti. Double Polynesian canoe used as glass-bottom boat for lagoon cruises, snorkeling, sunset of "funset booze cruise," dinner cruises. Complete line of nautical sports including scuba diving and underwater photography lessons. Located at Maeva Beach Hotel.

Tahiti Yachting, Arue Nautical Center, P.O. Box 363, Papeete. Offers 28- to 37-foot sailboats for rental on daily or weekly basis.

Voile Charters, Tepua, P.O. Box 110, Uturoa, Raiatea. Sailing charters aboard 56-ft. Columbia ketch *Aita Peapea* for 10-day cruises through the Leeward Islands of the Society group. Captain, crew and all meals included. Shorter or longer itineraries available, as well as smaller yachts with or without crew.

Circle Island Tour: Full-day tour includes stops at One Tree Hill, Point Venus, Museum of Discovery, Monument of the Missionaries, Blowhole of Arahoho, waterfalls of Faarumai. After lunch (not included in price of tour) visit to botanical gardens of Papeari, Gauguin Museum, Atimaono Golf Course, Maraa fern grotto, and old Polynesian sacrificial temple.

Moorea by boat: The new *Keke III,* a 100-foot air-conditioned launch, travels daily between Tahiti and Moorea, bringing the visitor to Cook's Bay. The *Keke III* also makes more direct connections between the two islands on twice-daily round trips, along with the *Tamarii Moorea II* and *Moorea Ferry,* two large ferry boats.

 SEASONAL EVENTS. The inhabitants of French Polynesia delight in any opportunity to go "ue ue" (pronounced as way-way); that is to have a good time, dancing and singing. Contests are also very popular, especially those to elect a "Miss" from the local beauties. Here is a sampling of the activities.

February: Chinese New Year Carnival, celebrated by the Chinese community, featuring legendary dances and fireworks.

April: Local handicraft contest; *Miss Bora Bora Contest* held on her island. Election of *Mr. Tahiti* and *Mr. Muscles.*

May: Annual day of the "Maire," a Tahitian fern found in the valleys, with a ball following the exhibits.

June: Election of Miss Moorea on her island, with an all-night big ball.

Early July: Election of Miss Tahiti and Miss Tiurai (Miss July), the coronation of Tahiti's prettiest girl of the year, who will represent French Polynesia in international beauty contests, and her local representative, who reigns over the July festivities.

July 14: Bastille Day celebrations throughout all French Polynesia, with the festivities lasting two weeks on the islands of Tahiti, Moorea, Bora Bora, Raiatea, Tahaa and Huahine. There are parades, games, contests, dances and singing competitions. In Tahiti it's an all-stops-out affair, with gambling and dancing all night. The offices, banks and shops are closed for July 14, but the hotels, restaurants and airlines still operate.

August: Mini-"Tiurai" at Hotel Tahiti Beachcomber, featuring winners of singing and dancing competitions during Bastille Fête competitions over 3- or 4-night period of feasts and entertainment.

September: Night of the Woman and the Flower, when Tahitian lovelies attend a ball dressed in a floral mode.

October: Ball featuring costumes from Tahiti of Old Times.

November: Harrison Smith Flower Show, with exhibitions of the many flowers of Tahiti; a different theme each year, such as orchids, flowers of the banana family, or anthuriums. Biggest flower show of the year.

December: Tiare Tahiti Day. Tahiti's national flower, the white gardenia, is featured, with a gardenia being presented to everyone on the streets of Papeete, in the hotels and at the airport, culminating in an all-night ball with Tiare Tahiti flowers decorating the ballroom, the tables and even the performers.

December 31: New Year's Eve is celebrated in Tahiti with the illumination of the Papeete waterfront, running competitions in the streets of downtown and all night dancing in all the hotels and nightclubs.

CAMPING. There are two sites for camping on Tahiti where tents can be pitched and one site on Moorea and Huahine. If you wish to camp outside an organized area, seek permission from the owner of the property before setting up your tent.

SPORTS. The climate is very favorable all year for outdoor sports, and the lagoons are the centers of sporting activities. In Tahiti there are sailboats for rent by the hour, day or week at Tahiti Yachting and Sea and Leisure's floating office on the waterfront. There are water sports facilities located at the Tahiti Beachcomber and Tahiti Aquatique, at the Hotel Maeva Beach. Both locations have small *sailboats, water-skiing, sightseeing lagoon tours, glass bottom boat rides, line fishing* in the pass or on the coral reef and *deep sea fishing* available. Tahiti's official organization for fishermen, called the "Haura Club," is associated with the International Game Fish Association.

On the waterfront in downtown Papeete there are numerous deep-sea fishing boats for hire. For scuba divers, complete diving equipment can be rented at Tahiti Aquatique, from Moana Adventure Tours in Bora Bora, The Kaveka Village Club in Moorea, and from the Hotel Kia Ora Village on the Tuamotu atoll of Rangiroa, where guests enjoy diving in the passes along with hundreds of sharks.

A bowling alley is located between Papeete and the Tahara'a Hotel.

For the *golf* enthusiast, the course at Atimaono, 45 minutes by car from the center of Papeete, is open year round and is located between the lagoon and the mountains in a very colorful setting. There are 18 holes (6,950 yards) and par is 72 for men and 73 for women. A club house with bar and snack bar, pro-shop, lockers, driving range, clubs, hand cart rentals and lessons are all provided.

Tennis courts are available in Tahiti, Moorea, Raiatea, Huahine, and Bora Bora, and *riding* is available in Tahiti, Huahine and Moorea. There is a *mountai-*

neering club in Tahiti, and an *aero club,* where licensed pilots can make arrangements to fly the club's planes.

SPECTATOR SPORTS. *Soccer,* the favorite sport of Tahitians, can be seen on almost all the islands. In Tahiti, enthusiastic crowds gather at the Fautaua Stadium near Papeete on week nights and during weekends to cheer their team to victory. *Horseracing.* Tahitian style horseracing is held on special occasions at the Pirae Hippodrome, where jockeys sometimes ride bareback, wearing only a brightly colored "Pareo" and a crown of flowers. Parimutuel betting exists, but the payoffs are very small. *Cockfighting* is another Sunday afternoon event. Although officially illegal, the fighting rings are out in the open and all the hotels can help you to find out where the action is taking place. Recent spectator sport to thrill the trail bike enthusiasts is the opening of an international motorcross course at Taravao. Other regularly scheduled spectator sports include *archery, bicycling, boxing, outrigger canoe racing, volleyball, sailboat racing* and *track* events.

HOLIDAYS. All government offices, banks, and most private offices are closed —sometimes on the day before and after, too. January 1—New Year's Day. March 5—Anniversary of arrival of the missionaries. Easter holidays. May 1— Labor Day. Ascension Day, Whit Sunday and Monday.

July 14—Bastille Day/National Day: Games, contests, dances and carnivals at the fairgrounds. Celebrations also held on Raiatea, Tahaa, Huahine, Bora Bora, and Moorea. November 1—All Saints Day. November 11—Armistice Day. December 25—Christmas Day.

MUSEUMS AND GALLERIES. *Musée de Tahiti et Des Îles* at Pointe des Pêcheurs in Punaruu, about 10 miles from town, is located on the site of a former "marae" and has displays of the ocean floor and the Polynesian islands. The bountiful nature that exists in these islands is featured—life on the coral reefs and in the lagoons, in the highlands and on the atolls, as well as the flowers and trees. The history of Polynesia after the arrival of the Europeans is also a main theme here. The *Museum of the Discovery* is located at Point Venus, 8 miles northeast of Papeete. This exhibit shows wax figures of Wallis, de Bougainville and Cook, and figures of the Tahitian chief and dancers at the time of the white man's first arrival in Tahiti. There are also several artifacts and engravings. The *Paul Gauguin Museum* is located 30 miles southeast of Papeete in the district of Papeari. This is Tahiti's most famous museum. The story of this famous artist's life and artistic activities is told with the help of photographs, reproductions of his most famous works, documents and furniture. *Tahiti Perle Center,* on Blvd. Pomare, is a jewelry store and a new museum for the black pearl.

Art Galleries in Tahiti are *Galerie Winkler* on Rue Jeanne D'Arc, *Galerie Vaimantic* in the Vaima Centre, *Galerie des Artistes* above Bata Shoe Store, and *Galerie Noa Noa* on Boulevard Pomare. In Moorea the *Galerie* of artist Aad Van der Heyde is definitely worth a visit. The *Galerie Api* combines paintings with jewelry and handpainted clothes. On Bora Bora, Rosine Temauri's *Galerie d'Art* at Matira Point is very interesting.

GARDENS. The Harrison W. Smith *Botanical Gardens* are located adjacent to the Gauguin Museum in Papeari, 30 miles from Papeete. In these 340 acres you will find hundreds of varieties of trees, shrubs, plants and flowers from tropical regions throughout the world.

SHOPPING. With the introduction of shopping centers in Papeete, the merchandise displayed in the stores is very much what you find in Parisian boutiques, including the price tag. There are no real bargains to be found here. French perfumes are less expensive than in the United States. There are some local products such as the exquisite Marquesan wood carvings, the dancing costumes, shell jewelry and Tahitian perfumes that will make nice gifts or souvenirs of your visit to Polynesia. An especially nice inexpensive purchase is the Monoi Tiare Tahiti, which is the coconut oil scented with Tahiti's national flower. This can be used as a moisturizing lotion, a perfume, suntan lotion, mosquito repellant, hair dressing, massage lotion—some people have even considered drinking it! The brightly patterned "pareu" fabrics that make the traditional Tahitian "pareo" are available in dozens of shops.

The largest shopping center is the Vaima center, where you will find *Polynesian Curios* for local wood carvings and mother-of-pearl jewelry; *Islands Treasures* for authentic Polynesian artifacts and dance costumes; *Polynesia Perles* for the South Sea black pearls; *Pareu Shop* for beach wear; *Librairie Hachette* bookstore; *Choisir* for crystal, china, gifts; *Anita* for Italian shoes and deluxe ladies clothes; *Vaima Shirts;* and photo shops. *Aline's,* Tahiti's only department store, has a shopping mall. It is located on the waterfront. *Tahiti Art* and the *Bikini Shop* have new shops in this mall. Shopping around the public market in downtown can turn up some unexpected finds in the many Chinese stores, as well as presenting the possibility of paying a little less. For the hand painted fabrics and dresses that are so popular in Tahiti, try *Aloha, Hawaii, Marie Ah You* and *Augustine.* The boutiques in Moorea carry a better selection of this type dress, however, as most of the designers live on Moorea. For beautiful Tahitian fabrics, try *Tapa.*

 NIGHT LIFE. Papeete is a swinging town after dark and the crowds in the restaurants and nightclubs seem to really enjoy themselves. Most of the hotels feature Tahitian dance shows several times a week and a band that plays dance music nightly. For discotheque dancing, go to the Club 106 above the Moani Iti Restaurant on the waterfront downtown, the Rolls Club in the Vaima Centre, the young "jet-set" Mayana Club in the Centre Bruat, the Piano Bar and the Bounty Club on Rue des Ecoles, ½ block from the waterfront, or to the Zizou Bar downtown. For more of the local ambiance try La Cave at the Hotel Royal Papeete, the Pitate Bar, or Le Pub on Avenue Bruat; or go to the Matavai nightclub on weekends. The Hotel Tahiti also has dances on Saturday nights, lasting all night.

 HOTELS. Accommodations in French Polynesia range from the air conditioned, carpeted deluxe rooms with telephones and room service, similar to what you can find throughout most of the world, down through your thatched roofed bungalow "fares" and your Tahitian pensions, where you share a room and the bathroom may be outdoors with cold water showers or a barrel of water that you splash on with half a coconut shell. The Hotel Sofitel Maeva Beach and Climat de France in Tahiti have television sets in the rooms, as well as in-house video programs. Some of the hotels in Tahiti and the outer islands now have a big-screen video for evenings and rainy-day entertainment.

In Tahiti, most of the hotel rooms are conventional in that they are in buildings easily identified as hotels. In the outer islands, the resort hotels normally have individual gardens and overwater bungalows and rooms, many of which are built of bamboo with pandanus roofs and a porch or veranda. These all have large bathrooms with showers. Bathtubs are found only in the deluxe hotels in Papeete and one or two others of the expensive category. Swimming pools are becoming more popular, even in some of the outer islands, although they are still not standard amenities. However, there is usually a lagoon nearby where one can swim in clear water.

The listings below are ranged according to price categories. The rates for the island of Tahiti are based on double occupancy, without meals and the ranges are *Deluxe,* $90 and up; *Expensive,* $77–86; *Moderate,* $35–64; *Inexpensive,* $18–35. The rates for all accommodations in the outer islands vary widely and are often more expensive than deluxe-rated hotels in Tahiti. The classification given is based on double occupancy, without meals, although in some remote islands meals are included. *Expensive,* $65 and up; *Moderate,$46–64; Inexpensive,* $20–36. Hotel Tax is 4%.

Tahiti

Maeva Beach Hotel. *Deluxe.* P.O. Box 6008. On the west coast of Tahiti, on a man-made white sand beach, 4.5 miles from Papeete. One 7-storied building, totally air conditioned with elevators, 2 restaurants, 2 bars, meeting rooms, beauty parlor, boutiques, 5 acres of gardens, swimming pool, tennis, all water sports. TV sets in all rooms with in-house video and new direct distance dialing telephone system. Suites available. Tahitian dance shows several times weekly.

Tahara'a. *Deluxe.* P.O. Box 1015. Five miles northeast of Papeete, 8 miles from airport, this hotel is built on the famous "One Tree Hill," commanding one of the finest views in Tahiti. All rooms have terraces that overlook Matavai Bay and the island of Moorea. Air conditioned, elevators, restaurant, bar, banquet-and-bar facility, meeting room, beauty parlor, boutiques, 10 acres of gardens, pool, tennis, skeet shooting, jogging trail, beach club and black sand beach at bottom of cliff reached by stairs built in the cliff or by beach buggy from hotel entrance. Tahitian dance shows nightly.

Tahiti Beachcomber (Formerly *TraveLodge*). *Deluxe.* On the west coast of Tahiti, 4.3 miles from Papeete with good view of Moorea. Air conditioned, overwater bungalows and suites available, pool, tennis, 9-hole golf course, all water sports, conference room, boutique, beauty parlor, 2 bars, restaurant-coffee shop, free slide shows, Tahitian dance shows, refrigerators and coffee maker in rooms. Small white sand beach. Very pretty location.

Royal Tahitien. *Expensive.* 2.5 miles east of Papeete on very long black sand beach located in large tropical garden, air-conditioned, beach restaurant and bar.

Climat de France. *Moderate.* Opened Dec. 1983 on hill across from Maeva Beach, overlooking lagoon and Moorea. 40 rooms with TV and video, swimming pool, two tennis courts, restaurant and bar.

Matavai. *Moderate.* 1.2 miles from center of Papeete at Tipaerui. Formerly Holiday Inn. Air conditioning, elevators, pool, squash, restaurants, bars, night clubs, meeting room, game room, boutique.

Princesse Heiata. *Moderate.* On east coast of Tahiti, 2.5 miles from Papeete, five-minute walk from large black sand beach, pool, restaurant, bar, dancing on weekends until 4:30 A.M.

Puunui. *Moderate.* Operated by Hotel Best Western Tahiti, it opened in 1985. Situated in the mountains of Tahiti-iti, under varying stages of completion are 84 rooms, some with kitchenettes, restaurant, bar, boutique, pool, and tennis. A water sports marina and restaurant are built at sea level.

Royal Papeete. *Moderate.* In center of Papeete, air conditioned, pool, restaurant, bar, boutique, night club. The nightclub, "La Cave," is one of the most popular places for dancing until the wee hours. But the hotel walls are thick as it was formerly a warehouse. Across street from Moorea boats.

Te Puna Bel Air. *Moderate.* On west coast of Tahiti, between Tahiti-Beachcomber and Maeva Beach Hotel, sharing same white sand beach. Rooms are in buildings and in Tahitian style bungalows, many air conditioned. Natural spring-fed swimming pool, restaurant, bar, boutique, Tahitian dance shows on Friday nights and public dancing Tahitian style each Sunday afternoon.

Tahiti. *Moderate.* On the lagoonside, at Auae, 1.2 miles from Papeete. This was once the most popular hotel in Tahiti, before the three deluxe hotels were built. Still has a lot of appeal with the lacy woodwork, huge thatched roofed bar and restaurant where the locals come to dance on weekends. Air conditioned rooms, refrigerators, pool, gardens, swimming dock, boutique.

Kon Tiki. *Inexpensive.* Highrise across street from Moorea boats. 45 air-conditioned rooms with private balconies facing harbor or mountains.

Mahina Tea. *Inexpensive.* Near the center of Papeete, behind Gendarmerie. Private baths. Restaurants and shopping nearby.

Moorea

Bali Hai Moorea. *Expensive.* At entrance of Cook's Bay on very small white sand beach, 6 miles from Moorea's airport, Tahitian style bungalows in 4 acres of gardens, busy and popular bar, restaurant, boutique, outrigger canoes, bicycles, volley ball, tennis, diving, excursions on raft "Liki Tiki," frequent picnics, friendly management and personnel, Sunday noon Tahitian feast with Tahitian dances. New addition is a swimming pool and bar with stools in the pool. Tahitian music nightly.

Kia Ora Moorea. *Expensive.* Located on white sand beach facing Tahiti. 5 minutes from airport in Moorea. Suites, 2 restaurants, 3 bars, boutique, all water sports, glass bottom boat, outrigger canoes, picnics, tennis, frequent Tahitian shows. An unusual attraction is the discotheque, aboard a famous old sailing schooner called the "Vaitere." Lots of fun.

Captain Cook Hotel (formerly Maui Beach). *Moderate.* 18 miles from Moorea airport on very large white sand beach near Club Mediterranée. Tahitian style bungalows, gardens, restaurant, bar, disco, nearby tennis courts, all water sports.

Climat de France. *Moderate.* Next door to Hotel Residence Tipaniers, along white sand beach. 40 rooms in two motel-style buildings, with air conditioning or fans, plus 33 bungalows with kitchenettes. Rooms are homey and cheerful, with fridges and some bathtubs. Restaurant, bar, swimming pool, tennis, water-skiing, windsurfing and all other water sports. Nightly movies on large video screen, often in French.

Club Bali Hai. *Moderate.* Located on a small white sand beach, this hotel is on the famous Cook's Bay, and was formerly known as the Aimeo Hotel. It is now managed by the Bali Hai group as a time-sharing condominium. The most centrally located hotel in Moorea, close to the village of Pao Pao, with a new swimming pool and tennis court. Restaurant, two bars, boutique, outrigger canoes and a young atmosphere.

Moorea Lagoon. *Moderate.* On a very long white sand beach between Cook's Bay and Opunohu Bay, 2.5 miles from village of Pao Pao, 9.5 miles from Moorea airport. Tahitian style bungalows in 12 acres of garden, pool, restaurant, bar, boutique, bicycles, outrigger canoes, friendly staff, Tahitian music nightly.

Club Mediterranée. *Moderate.* 45 mins. by bus from Moorea airport on large white sand beach at Haapiti. The completely rebuilt village opened in March 1985 with 700 beds, a huge restaurant, bars, boutique, disco, theatre, and sports complex.

Hotel Ibis-Kaveka Village Club. *Moderate.* Part of the French hotel chain ACCOR, this combination of two hotels offers 100 rooms in Cook's Bay near *Keke III* pier. Built in a Polynesian and "neo-colonial" style with two restaurants, two bars, swimming pool, and all water sports.

Moorea Village. *Moderate.* 19 miles from Moorea airport on large white sand beach at Haapiti. This hotel is the farthest away from the airport. Tahitian style bungalows, pool, tennis, restaurant, bar, boutique, frequent Tahitian shows, all water sports. Ideal for families as many bungalows have complete kitchen facilities.

Hotel Residence Tiahura. *Moderate.* Located 300 meters before Club Med across street from beach. Unscreened Polynesian-style bungalows with kitchenettes and fridges. Small swimming pool, tea shop and pancake bar, bar, boutique.

Hotel Residence Tipaniers. *Moderate.* In district of Haapiti close to Club Mediterranée on white sand beach. Nine of the 17 bungalows are complete with kitchens. Waterskiing center located here.

Chez Albert. *Inexpensive.* In village of Pao Pao, facing Cook's Bay and with a lovely view of the mountains. 8 houses furnished with kitchenettes, stores and restaurants nearby.

Bora Bora

Bora Bora. *Expensive.* 4.4 miles from village of Vaitape, 45 minutes by boat from airport. Situated in 15 acres of gardens, the Tahitian style bungalows are adjacent to a very long and very white sand beach. Over-water bungalows and suites available with refrigerators. 2 bars, restaurant, beach restaurant, boutique, conference and lounge room, many complimentary activities such as bicycles, outrigger canoes, snorkel equipment, games, tennis, basketball, volleyball; ride on outrigger sailing canoe. Music nightly, frequent slide shows or films. Full choice of water activities available, including trips to uninhabited islets for picnics. Demonstrations of Tahitian arts and crafts and garden tours given free. One of the prettiest sites to be found anywhere.

Hotel Marara. *Expensive.* P.O. Box 6. Part of Sofitel chain—the food and atmosphere are very European. Bungalows are in gardens, along white sand beach and over water near village of Anau. Tennis courts and nightly shows. Emphasis is on water activities—there's a special speedboat excursion around island, with visits to reef and very popular shark-feeding show, where you can actually go into water with sharks.

Bora Bora Marina. *Moderate.* The first "motu" hotel in Bora Bora, opened in May 1980. Located two minutes from the airstrip on Motu Mute. Cottages are duplexes and have an Oriental flair. Both beach and garden accommodations available. Entertainment brought over from island of Bora Bora for Saturday night show under the stars. All the normal water sports are available.

Climat de France. *Moderate.* 36 rooms with restaurant, bar and boutique. Nine blocks of 4 rooms each in gardens and on beach next to Hotel Marara. The rooms and grounds are attractive, but noises can be heard from room to room as walls are not completely closed at ceiling. Many water activities plus nightly video shown on big screen.

Club Mediterranée. *Moderate.* On lagoon near village of Vaitape, 45 minutes by boat from Bora Bora airport. Over-water bungalows, large restaurant, bar, nightclub and boutique. Dancing daily, sailing, picnics, glass-bottom boat, excursions on lagoons and to mountains, private swimming dock. No beach, but there are several trips made daily to a nearby islet where there is a nice white sand beach.

OA OA. *Moderate.* 5 minutes from village of Vaitape, 45 minutes by boat from Bora Bora airport. Eight bungalows situated on lagoon with restaurant, bar, meeting room. Glass-bottom boat, windsurfing, and all other water sports.

Chez Aimé Mare. *Inexpensive.* In village of Vaitape. House with rooms and beds, kitchen facilities or you can eat with Tahitian family. Join owner's activities in fishing, expeditions into valley, shelling, etc.

Chez Fredo Doom. *Inexpensive.* In village of Vaitape, 3 housekeeping bungalows on lagoon, also house where you can rent a bed with kitchen privileges. Low rate for bed and breakfast. Popular with French military.

Hotel Matira. *Inexpensive.* On most popular white sand beach in Bora Bora, "Matira Plage," 5 miles from village of Vaitape, 45 minutes by boat from airport. Housekeeping bungalows with outrigger canoes available. Restaurant close.

Huahine

Bali Hai Huahine. *Expensive.* Near village of Fare (0.6) mile on large white sand beach and adjacent lagoon. 1.8 miles from airport. Tahitian style bungalows, very nicely constructed with indoor gardens in all bathrooms, in 2.5 acres of gardens and lakes, crisscrossed with bridges. The total impression is one of enchantment. Restaurant, boutique, bar, Tahitian music nightly. Excellent swimming in turquoise lagoon. Large swimming pool with a thatched-roof bar.

Huahine Beach Hotel. *Expensive.* New 12-bungalow American owned hotel on 8 acres of tropical gardens and white sand beach next to Parea Village on Huahine-iti. First class accommodations include restaurant and bar with big screen video, boutique, drink-stocked fridges in rooms, piped-in stereo system, waterskiing, windsurfing, picnics to "motu," deep sea fishing, and free transfers between hotel and airport.

Hotel Bellevue. *Moderate.* In district of Maroe, 8 km. from airport of Fare. One story building with 8 rooms. Each has balcony, bathroom and electricity. Also several new individual bungalows around a swimming pool, overlooking Maroe Bay and surrounding hills.

Hotel Huahine. *Moderate.* 2 story building near beach in the village of Fare. Private baths. Restaurant and bar. Overlooks the lagoon and harbor. Frequent Saturday night dancing with locals and yachting crowd attending.

Relais Mahana. *Moderate.* 12 individual bungalows on long, white sand beach at lovely Avea Bay on Huahine-iti near Parea village. Restaurant, bar, tennis, windsurfing, pedalboats, and Hobie Cats. Hotel scheduled to open May 1985.

Chez Albert Temeharo. *Inexpensive.* In village of Parea, one hour from airport and Fare. 7 rooms in clean building, family-style dining, shower and toilets in common. Long white sand beach nearby, shelling. English spoken.

Chez Lovina. *Inexpensive.* In the middle of "downtown" Fare, next to the Bank of Tahiti, this 7-room accommodation is clean and convenient to the true local life of Huahine. Lovina speaks good English and serves meals.

Chez Urua Viri (Pension Mémé). *Inexpensive.* In village of Parea, one hour from airport and Fare. Accommodations for 10 to 15 persons, shower and toilet in common. Local chief of village. Family style cooking and dining in European and Tahitian cuisine. Trips to islet for snorkeling and shelling. Long white sand beach close by. Don't stay here if you do not like children because there are many grandchildren of all ages around all the time. And Tahitian children adopt strangers very easily, and have a habit of following them about and gazing through the windows into the guest rooms.

Raiatea

Bali Ha'i Raiatea. *Expensive.* On the lagoon 0.6 miles from village of Uturoa, 1.9 miles from airport. One-storied buildings and Tahitian style bungalows, many over-water. A sitting pool, bar, restaurant, boutique, bicycles, tennis, volley-ball, badminton, table tennis, all water sports, Tahitian music nightly. No beach at hotel, but trips to nearby "motu" offer white sand, shelling, and good swimming.

Raiatea Village. *Moderate.* 12 bungalows with kitchenettes located at Faaroa River in district of Avera, 11 km. from Uturoa. Additional bungalows and restaurant/bar planned for near future, but meals are presently served from owner's house across street. Far from village but a quiet and pretty locations.

Tetiaroa

Tetiaroa Village. *Moderate.* Open for day tours and one-night weekend stays only, while hotel is being rebuilt following 1983 hurricane damage.

Rangiroa

Kia Ora Village. *Moderate.* 15 minutes by boat from village of Tiputa. 15 minutes by bus from Avatoru, 10 minutes by bus from airport, on long white sand beach, 30 beach bungalows in Tahitian style, restaurant, bar, barbeque, boutique, all water activities, including complete diving facilities, glass-bottom boat, Tahitian music 3 times a week. Specialty is fish from the abundant and clear waters of the huge lagoon. Good service and friendly management who take special care to see that their guests enjoy their visits to the utmost. Excellent French chef. Delicious meals.

La Bouteille a La Mer. *Moderate.* 11 beach bungalows in typical thatch-roof and bamboo-wall design, near airport on lagoon side. Family-style meals. French atmosphere, with emphasis on do-it-yourself entertainment, with water sports the main theme.

Hotel Rangiroa Village. *Moderate.* 9 traditional bungalows on white sand beach 0.5 mile from Avatoru village. Restaurant, bar, water sports, and lagoon excursions.

Manihi

Kaina Village. *Moderate.* Tahitian-style bungalows over water. Very friendly island. Restaurant, bar, snorkeling in the pass and lagoon. Excellent food. Trips to nearby pearl farm. Line fishing available in lagoon.

Marquesas

Hiva Oa (Bungalows Guy Rauzy). *Moderate.* 3 bungalows in center of village of Atuona, bedroom, veranda, shower and toilet, paraffin lamps, riding, boat excursions.

Nuku Hiva (Keikahanui Inn). *Moderate.* Within easy walking distance of Taiohae Village, rooms, house, and 3 bungalows for rent. Meals served in restaurant/bar or cook yourself. Owners are American yachtsmen.

Ua Huka (Chez Vii Fournier). *Inexpensive.* Located in village of Hane. Kitchen, refrigerator, toilet, comfortable beds. Bring mosquito repellant.

Rurutu (Austral Islands)

Rurutu Village. *Moderate.* 16 bungalows with all the amenities. Carpets, luxurious bedding, draperies, sunken bathtubs, freshwater swimming pool, excellent cuisine, tours by horseback, jeep or hiking. Opened in 1982, all fresh foods and juices from the island.

Tubuai (Austral Islands)

Ermitage Sainte-Helene. *Inexpensive.* Close to main village of Mataura, housekeeping bungalows, refrigerator, hot water, electricity, horses, boats, bicycles, picnics available.

Bungalows Caroline. *Inexpensive.* Located in main village of Mataura, 6 bungalows in Tahitian style, electricity, warm showers, bicycles, boat excursions.

 RESTAURANTS. Dining out in Tahiti is one of the most popular pastimes for visitors and residents alike. Since there are so many cultures, it naturally follows that the choices of foods available are varied and interesting ones. The most popular restaurants for visitors are usually those serving French food—Papeete is noted for its French restaurants. Chinese food is a favorite anywhere and Tahiti is no exception, as shown by the many Chinese restaurants scattered over town. Tahitian food is a little harder to find, because it is usually prepared at home by the families. Many of the hotels do feature Tahitian feasts or "tamaaraas" frequently to give the visitor a taste of smoked breadfruit, taro, "fei" or mountain bananas, "fafa," their version of spinach which is very good when cooked with chicken and served with their young suckling pig, and "poisson cru," or marinated fish served with coconut milk, or "poe," a starchy pudding made of papaya, mango or banana.

Good old fashioned steak and French fries can be purchased almost anywhere that serves food and the quick-service hamburger shops have discovered Tahiti, with the opening of Big Burger and several stand-up sidewalk shops. A very popular place to eat, especially at night with the locals, yachties or those on low budgets, is on the "trucks" called "Les Roulottes." These are lunch wagons that are parked on the waterfront where the boats load for Moorea. Some have stools and they all serve basically the same foods—steak and fries, chicken and "poisson cru," brochettes or shish-kabobs, which are heart of veal barbequed on the spot. For breakfast or a snack, try the French pastries found in the "salons de thé."

Price categories are as follows: *Deluxe,* over $20. *Expensive,* $14–20. *Moderate,* $6–$14. *Inexpensive,* $4–$6.

EDITOR'S CHOICES

Rating restaurants is, at best, a subjective business, and obviously a matter of personal taste. It is, therefore, difficult to call a restaurant "the best" and hope to get unanimous agreement. The restaurants listed below are our choices of the best eating places in Tahiti, and the places we would choose if we were visiting.

ACAJOU   *Continental*

On the waterfront downtown, this indoor/outdoor restaurant is usually filled with a lively group of American tourists or residents. Owner-chef Acajou, formerly with Pitate, is famous for his French onion soup, seafood cassoulet, steak roquefort, shrimp in champagne sauce and delicious pepper steaks. Very friendly personnel who speak English. *Expensive.*

LA PETITE AUBERGE   *French Cuisine*

A small, intimate place with very special service not usually found in Tahiti. Foods and wines from Normandy and Brittany are featured. Red and white checked linens and curtains, plus a fireplace, lend a cozy atmosphere to this air conditioned restaurant. On corner of Rue General de Gaulle and Rue des Remparts. *Expensive.*

JADE PALACE   *Chinese Cuisine*

Conveniently located in the Vaima Centre in downtown Papeete, this small but elegant restaurant serves the most delicious Chinese dishes in town. It has become very popular with tourists and local diners, so reservations are required. *Expensive.*

L'AUBERGE LANDAISE   *French Cuisine*

A small elegant restaurant on the waterfront just west of downtown Papeete that advertises the "best French food in town." Owner Philippe Gion is always on duty to insure that his food and service live up to the reputation of the restaurant. He speaks good English and has special menus for tourists, which include a welcome cocktail, a choice of homemade fish soup or salad, prime sirloin steak with pepper sauce or fresh seafood of the day, accompanied by rice or potatoes and followed by apple-pie or ice cream. His French menu is extensive and exquisitely prepared. *Expensive.*

LE BELVEDERE   *Continental Cuisine*

Located 1800 feet high in the mountains, this restaurant offers the best bargain for tourists as the price includes transportation to and from hotels, a delicious meal with wine, coffee and dessert, a swimming pool and happy atmosphere. The beef fondue is a specialty. Second and third helpings of beef, French fries, salad and wine are cheerfully brought on request. Other selections include French onion soup, mahi mahi, "cous-cous" and pepper steak. The ride up the mountain is an unforgettable experience as the bright yellow "Le Truck" winds around the numerous curves, overlooking all of Papeete and the harbor. *Moderate.*

GAUGUIN RESTAURANT   *Continental and Polynesian*
A favorite luncheon stop for people touring island, this beautifully located restaurant in Papeari is close to the Paul Gauguin Museum. Roger and Juliette Gowan serve fresh and deliciously prepared hot and cold dishes, varied buffets, plus fruits and homemade pies. Most tourist groups eat here. *Moderate.*

Other recommended restaurants:

Lagoonarium. *Expensive.* Seafood specialties served in spacious setting over water, accompanied by frequent dance shows. Visit to underwater observatory included. Located in Punaauia five minutes from Hotels Beachcomber and Maeva Beach.

Moana Iti. *Expensive.* Blvd. Pomare on waterfront. French cooking, with servings of rabbit in white wine sauce, roast lamb, seafoods and pepper steak.

Dragon d'Or. *Moderate.* Very popular Chinese restaurant on Rue Colette in Papeete. Specialty is Ta Pen Lou, or Chinese fondue.

Le Gallieni. *Moderate.* Located in the Hotel Royal Papeete on Blvd. Pomare in Papeete. Noted for excellent breakfasts. California prime rib featured for lunch or dinner three days a week. Other specialties include "cous-cous," pineapple duck, and hot apple pie.

Le Gauguin. *Expensive.* Located in the Hotel Maeva Beach, the elegant atmosphere, good service and equally good food make this one of Tahiti's nicest places to dine.

Lou Pescadou. *Moderate.* Noisy and lively Italian pizzeria that also features specialties from south of France. Very popular with young international set. Located on Rue Anne Marie Javouhey, three blocks back of Papeete waterfront.

Mandarin. *Moderate.* Rue Fres-de-Ploërmel. A nicely decorated air conditioned restaurant serving excellent Mandarin style food. Ask to be seated in the dining room upstairs, which is even more elegant and offers excellent service.

THE SAMOAS

Under Two Flags

by
ROBERT GILMORE

Robert Gilmore, Auckland Star *columnist, has been traveling the South Pacific for 30 years. He first visited the Samoas by flying-boat (on the pioneer Air New Zealand "Coral Route," from Fiji to Tahiti) when Western Samoa was a New Zealand colony.*

Among nations, the Samoas are as fortunate as San Francisco is among cities. In the past century, few of consequence have written anything but warm words of the people and the landscape. Credible witnesses write with rancour of Rome, with contempt of Tahiti ("Tobacco Road beneath palm trees"). But not of the Samoas or Samoans.

Samoas—plural? One cohesive Polynesian race under two flags: American Samoa (administered by the U.S. Department of Interior) and independent Western Samoa, formerly New Zealand Samoa and, before that, German Samoa. The division occurred at the end of the last century. Families extend over the oceanic dividing-line and links are intimate and easy, despite a growing gap between life-styles. American Samoans, by the way, are U.S. *nationals,* not *citizens.*

Robert Louis Stevenson's Haven

The Samoans' first major booster in modern times was Scottish author and poet Robert Louis Stevenson. He spent the last four years of his life at Vailima, a property 600 ft. above the Western Samoa capital of Apia. Vailima is now the official home of the head of state. From the lawn one can see Stevenson's tomb atop Mount Vaea. Engraved on the tomb is his requiem: "Under the wide and starry sky/Dig the grave and let me lie

... Home is the sailor, home from sea/And the hunter home from the hill."

In 1888, after fruitless attempts to conquer tuberculosis by living in Switzerland, Stevenson, his wife (an Indianapolis divorcee, 11 years his senior), his mother-in-law, and stepson chartered a yacht in San Francisco to seek a home and workplace in the Pacific. Thirteen years earlier he had been advised, in England, and had noted the advice in a diary, that he should quit Europe for the Samoan islands, "beautiful places, green forever ... perfect shapes of men and women, with red flowers in their hair; nothing to do but study oratory and etiquette, sit in the sun and pick up the fruits as they fall ... absolute balm for the weary." From San Francisco the Stevensons sailed to Apia—and stayed.

They poured Stevenson's copious earnings into "my beautiful shining windy house." They imported fine furniture from Scotland and wines from France. They dined by candlelight and, on formal occasions, dressed their table servants in lavalavas (wraparound Samoan single-piece garments) of Royal Stuart tartan, which Stevenson thought blended best with Polynesian skin. Two hours before the family rose, the author was at work every morning, writing. In four years of failing health, he wrote and published 700,000 words, among them the texts of "Catriona" and "The Wrecker." He died preparing mayonnaise for dinner.

Samoans called him "Tusitala," teller of tales. So close was his association with Honolulu that a street off Kaiulani Avenue is named Tusitala for him.

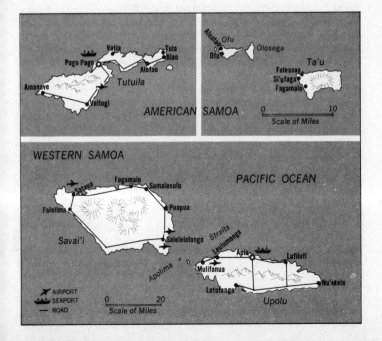

Stevenson, his mother-in-law, his wife, his stepson, his stepdaughter and at least one employee wrote books on Samoa. But the most illuminating was produced by his wife, Fanny, and not discovered until 1952 when the American scholar Charles Neider found the manuscript in a museum at Monterey, California, and realised it had never been published. He used infra-red photography to reveal censored words—mostly allusions to minor and wholly normal domestic spats. The work was published in 1956. Fanny died in California in 1914—20 years after her husband, and willed that her ashes go to Mount Vaea, where they rest beneath her husband's words about her: "Teacher, tender comrade, wife/ A fellow-farer true through life/ Heart-whole and soul-free/ The august Father gave to me."

Stevenson's head is on a 1939 sevenpenny and on a more recent 12 sene stamp. His tomb and Vailima have been depicted on various stamps.

In 1978, Samoa's ruling chiefs declared 900 acres, embracing Vailima and Mount Vaea the nation's first national park, to be known as Tusitala Nature and Historic Reserve.

Of the Samoans, whom he knew intimately, he wrote: "They are easy, merry and pleasure-loving; the gayest, though far from the most capable or the most beautiful of Polynesians . . . Song is almost ceaseless."

"Rain"—Still a Best-Seller

American Samoa became known to fiction readers when British author W. Somerset Maugham (1874-1965) published in 1921 a volume of short stories, "The Trembling of a Leaf." Of these, the most famed is "Rain," since dramatised and filmed as "Sadie Thompson." Sadie was a prostitute in Pago Pago (pronounced Pango Pango), capital of American Samoa, where she seduces a missionary marooned in the same boarding-house. Through its title and its tropical atmosphere ("It did not pour, it flowed"), "Rain" made much of the world aware of Pago Pago.

In the lower Fagatogo (pronounced Fahngatongo) area of Pago Pago is Valupac Foods. In 1916 there were rooms to let upstairs and it is almost certain that Maugham and his male lover-secretary, American Gerald Haxton, stayed there on their way from Hawaii to Tahiti to research the Gauguin story for the novel "The Moon and Sixpence."

Before his death, Maugham told American biographer Wilmon Menard that he and Haxton travelled to Pago Pago on the American liner *Sonoma*. A fellow passenger was an American prostitute, a refugee from a police clean-up of Iwilei, Honolulu's red-light district at the time. "She was tall, bosomy, over-painted . . . . She drove the other passengers to distraction with her portable gramophone, drinking and carousings with the crew. . . .

"There were two missionary couples aboard the *Sonoma* and one of them fascinated me; he looked like an embalmer of cadavers. The more I watched the blond trollop and this Holy Henry the more I became intrigued with the circumstances of their coming into emotional conflict. . . .

"In Pago Pago, then run by the United States Navy, an embargo on travel, because of a measles epidemic, tossed us all together in a mouldy hotel on the outskirts of the steamy port . . .

"The royalties on my 'Miss Thompson,' as a play and a film, amounted to more than a million dollars."

In both Samoas, Maugham found the real-life characters for three other classic short stories, "The Pool," "Red," and "Mackintosh."

"Coming of Age in Samoa"

A third major creator of Samoa-awareness in the world was American anthropologist Margaret Mead (1901–78). Her *Coming of Age in Samoa,* published in 1928, depicts a society of virile, highly intelligent people following a 1,000-year-old life-style. Mead's Samoans are casual, tension free, peaceable, and guilt free in adolescence. In 1983, a world expert on Samoa, New Zealand anthropologist Professor Derek Freeman, published *Margaret Mead and Samoa: The Making and Unmaking of an Anthropological Myth.* Freeman argues Mead is wrong. Freeman's Samoans are prickly, violent, jealous, and prone to rape, violent assault, homicide, and suicide.

But expert witnesses, though perhaps starry-eyed, generally write warmly of the people. New Zealand-born anthropologist Felix M. Keesing wrote four decades ago: "Samoan life has a repose . . . that seems a wise human adjustment to tropical conditions."

More recently, New Zealand educator George Irwin wrote: "In their incorrigible optimism, their fierce pride and above all in the poetry of their animal spirits . . . they resemble Homer's dark-eyed Greeks. And perhaps it is because they are so like the ancient Greeks that Samoa is the heartland of the Polynesian Pacific as Greece was of the Mediterranean."

Another New Zealander, former Chief Judge C. C. Marsack, while writing with warmth, identifies a Samoan trait which irks tourists: "The Samoan is a totally unpredictable character. Not for nothing is his country called the Ireland of the Pacific . . . . The Samoan shows two notable characteristics which set him apart from men of other races: his dignity and his response to discipline. It is hard to reconcile the Samoan's open-handed generosity with his inordinate propensity for thieving. Very possibly the root cause is that the doctrine of individual ownership of property is a new one to the Samoans."

"Facts and Figures on American Samoa," published by the Government of American Samoa, alludes directly to this practice and in so doing alludes indirectly to the only other Samoan practice of which strangers disapprove—accurate and deadly stone-throwing. "Don't leave any valuables unattended while swimming. There are good people and bad in every territory. If they should come for you, raise your arm and pretend you are going to throw a stone at them. The very motion will probably prove discouraging. If you're with a Samoan, he'll be able to handle the situation very nicely. Our aim is exceptionally good."

The Heartland of Polynesia

Both geographically and emotionally, the Samoas are the heartland of Polynesia. Draw a line from Polynesian Hawaii to Polynesian New Zealand and the Samoas are two-thirds of the way down. Nine main islands spread east and west over 290 miles (464 kms.). Western Samoa is the bigger of the two Samoas, with a land area of 1,090 square miles (2,831 sq. kms.). American Samoa's land area is 76 square miles (197 sq. kms.). Savaii, biggest island in Western Samoa, is one of Polynesia's largest islands outside Hawaii—703 square miles (1,821 sq. kms.). Its highest peak, Mount Silisili, is 6,095 ft. Upolu is second in size in Western Samoa. Remaining land area mainly comprises the smaller islands of Manono and Apolima.

American Samoa's largest island, Tutuila, is 54 square miles (140 sq. kms.) with its highest peak, 2,142 ft. Mount Matafao, rising above Pago Pago bay. American Samoa's remaining 22 square miles (57 sq. kms.) include the three islands of the Manua Group. Margaret Mead's Tau is a short air journey from Pago.

A Western Samoan government handout reads: "The Samoan is the purest surviving Polynesian type. He is conservative and unspoilt. In character, the Samoan has a reputation of being upright and dignified, is friendly to visitors but expects his customs to be respected. The majority of Samoans can be seen living their lives in traditional native fashion, almost entirely unaffected by contact with another civilisation, enjoying the food which they themselves can produce and coveting little else.

"Samoan life has been traditionally leisurely and the Samoan is prone to be content with his few possessions. The point has been made that if a Samoan has healthy children, a neat and comely wife, a house of his own, a canoe, a coconut tree, banana trees and a few pigs, he has intelligence enough to know he is well off."

The equivalent document from the Government of American Samoa, discussing the "fa'a Samoa"—the Samoan Way, states: "As a result of increased travel and education, Samoa's new generation is acquiring a desire to enjoy the American standard of living, which cannot be fulfilled under the old subsistence way of life."

As the same language is used in both Samoas, the same customs survive, and many families overlap from one Samoa to the other. There are many basic similarities. But differences proliferate.

First-time visitors normally are astonished at their exposure to Samoan domesticity on the ride from Faleolo airport to Apia. From bus or taxi you see, along the route and close to it, in addition to 72 churches, hundreds of Samoan fales (pronounced far-lay), oval private homes comprising a platform sheltered from sun and rain by a thick thatched roof. The walls, or substitutes for walls, are blinds of woven leaf that in daytime seem to be lowered only to exclude driving rain. This is ancient Samoa, despite the successive German and New Zealand presences, with their Caucasian emphasis on privacy.

Along comparable routes on the main island of American Samoa, the fale is made from concrete blocks, has a roof of corrugated sheet-steel and, instead of leaf-blinds, has jalousies.

Western Samoa is poor and has high unemployment. American Samoa is rich (by South Pacific standards) and has full employment.

As former "subjects" of New Zealand, Western Samoans have only limited immigration rights in New Zealand. But American Samoans enjoy the enormous advantage of free entry to the United States.

The "Matai" System

As might be predicted, young people in American Samoa are more restive than those in Western Samoa—impatient with the values that have bound Samoan society firmly and amiably for at least 1,000 years. They appear to resent the "matai"—a pyramidal structure of social organization that depends on the "chief" as the administrator of village affairs. It is actually a system of extended family. The unit of Samoan life is the aiga (pronounced *eye-ing-a*), an extended family that may encompass several thousand kinsmen and in-laws. Social security within the aiga is total. Nobody has needs. The family selects, or endorses, a matai (chief). By behaviour and performance, he is required to bring honor to the aiga. He even decides (and his decision normally is unquestioned) who will provide the pigs for a family wedding, the entertainment, the dress, and the presents.

The matai system extends upwards. Above the extended family chief are high chiefs, high talking chiefs, and paramount chiefs. Among the combined population of the Samoas—188,000, chiefs number in excess of 8,000. Scoffers from western democracies should remember that the system works and has worked for many centuries for a virile, rugged, and bloody-minded race.

Along with the ancient matai system in Samoan life, goes the contemporary white man's religion. Like Fijians and Tongans, Samoans embraced missionaries' primitive Christianity with joy. The Samoas have more church buildings per capita than anywhere else in the world, more even than in Catholic Italy. Most Samoans are active members of a church, attending services twice on Sunday and choir practice once a week. Most Samoans know the Bible as western man knew it two or three generations ago.

The most chauvinistic of Samoans will agree that the alien import, Christianity, is as firm a binder of traditional Samoan society as anything from the Polynesian past. In what American news magazines label the post-Christian society, the visitor from the United States, enquiring into the finances of church building and church funding in Samoa, is liable to regard the old established missions as exploiters. But at least one modern mission, American in origin, gives incomparably more than it receives, tithe-based though it is. That is the Mormon mission.

A Mormon Outpost

Polynesia is a main area of Mormon endeavor. Twenty years after the foundation of Mormonism in the United States in 1830, Mormon missionaries landed in Hawaii. Now, an official Mormon publication writes of the "Mormon Axis of the Pacific" and describes the proliferating Mormon establishments in Polynesia and the fringes of Polynesia as "Mormonia." Recent erection at Apia of a Mormon temple established the Samoas as the center of "Mormonia."

Why do the Mormons, who until 1978 denied Blacks entry into their priesthood, solicit the Polynesian? By "continuing revelation," a pillar of Mormon belief, the Mormons became "aware" that the Polynesians are of the Children of Lehi, and hence among the Chosen People.

Why does this unorthodox creed with its demand for self-denial and self-discipline appeal to happy-go-lucky young Polynesians and, in particular, Samoans? Obvious answers include the Mormons' genuine respect for and encouragement of Polynesian culture, defiled by most missions in the past; their ardent interest in genealogy (for the purpose of "vicarious baptism of the dead") which aligns itself with Polynesians' obsessive interest in family trees; Mormon encouragement of dancing (damned by many missions in the past) and sport; and, the Mormons' policy of offering village children in the South Pacific the opportunity of education—from primary school to university in Hawaii and Utah.

An excitingly beautiful new religious structure on a hillside nine km south of Apia is the nine-sided Baha'i House of Worship, one of six in the world. It is by Iranian architect Husayn Amanat, whose work includes the Iranian embassy in Beijing. By day, the dome, of crystalline coral limestone from Niue island, captures the glow of the sun; worshippers looking upward see blue sky. By night it is softly iridescent from internal lighting; reflections of interior light on glass and interplay of shadows create a mosaic of light on the bush-hammered, textured white concrete interior, which is accented in the local timber ifilele. In the manner of a Samoan fale, the dome sits on nine pairs of buttresses clad in soft red granite. Ribs are of mirrorglass.

A Western Samoan Government publication says: "Churches are the centre of the way of life in these islands. Fusion of religious principles and traditional values makes the Samoan the proud possessor of a culture where the old people are respected, the young are looked after, and each member knows his place in the community."

"Aitu"

Samoans' ready embracing of many brands of Christianity has not demonstrably affected their belief in witches—"aitu" in their own tongue. Medical records of big Samoan expatriate communities in California, Hawaii, and New Zealand show that the Samoan immigrant in industrial societies is highly liable to be aitu-bedevilled. Aitu can be the spirits of dead relatives or they can be national identities. One such is Telesa, a beautiful young witch with long brown hair. Telesa is unusual, although not unique, in that she must be dealt with through a medium. The name Telesa is well-known in psychiatric clinics in all overseas cities with Samoan populations.

Code for Tourists

Samoa, both Samoas, are still so attached to tradition that both Governments issue the travel trade a behavior code for tourists. Here is an amalgam of the slightly different Apia and Pago Pago official codes:

1) Don't wear shorts or other revealing garb except when swimming or climbing coconut palms (in fact, disapproval of shorts, if they are not too short, is waning).

2) When in a Samoan home, don't speak to Samoans while standing. Also, don't eat while standing or walking.

3) While sitting, Samoan fashion, on a woven mat on the ground, don't stretch your legs straight out in front of you. If you can't tuck your legs beneath you, Samoa fashion, lay a mat over them before stretching them out.

4) If you pass an open *fale* in which a group of middle-aged or elderly men obviously are holding a meeting, you should assume they are chiefs in conference. If you are carrying an umbrella, or a load on your shoulders, lower the load to hip level and fold the umbrella (even if there is a downpour) while walking past the house. If you are in a car, get out and walk.

5) Don't enter a *fale* while an *aiga* (extended family) is at prayer. Wait outside.

6) During the early evening hours, even if swimming offshore, avoid noise that could interrupt Samoans' prayer period.

7) When you stay in a Samoan home (liable to occur if you evince genuine interest in Samoan life) remember that grace is said before every meal and that most families devote at least 10 minutes in the evening to prayers and a hymn.

A Government of American Samoa publication adds: "In some villages *sa* time is enforced. It is a prayer time usually lasting 10 to 15 minutes in the early evening. People are expected to go into their homes; vehicles must stop. Usually three gongs are sounded. The first is the signal to return to the house, the second is for prayer, and the third sounds the all-clear. In some villages, swimming and fishing are forbidden on Sunday." [To cope with growing juvenile delinquency, attributed usually to unemployment, the Western Samoan Government, with Matai approval, seeks to enforce for all Samoans a 10:30 P.M. to dawn curfew. Village elders enforce the curfew. The curfew signal can be a blast on a conch shell or the striking of a free-suspended oxy-acetylene cylinder.]

8) If you have the good fortune to be invited to stay in a Samoan household, remember the rigid rules. On leaving you make a gift, a *mea alofa,* literally a thing of love. The American Samoan Government suggests $5–8 dollars a day per person but stresses that this should not be regarded as payment for hospitality and that, when offering the money, this should be made clear. For part of the *mea alofa,* you might like to substitute shirts, belts, or a dress-length fabric. As Samoans are most hospitable, the neighbors probably will invite you to stay with them. Don't accept, as your abandoning the *fale* of your primary hosts can bring shame to them. Make known from the first day your intended day of departure and hence preclude risk of offence.

9) Remember the immortal injunction in a Pan Am global guide book for American travelling salesmen of nearly 20 years ago: "Be humble— even if it kills you."

If you attain anything akin to intimacy with Samoans, you may be invited to a *kava* ceremony—a genuine one, as distinct from those laid on for tourists.

Kava is a water emulsion of piper methysticum extract. Containing the lactone marindinine, it can induce a state of apathy. It is the traditional tipple of most of Polynesia and much of Melanesia. Its taste has been described variously as weak milk flavored with cloves and pepper, magnesia with a dash of pepper, rhubarb and magnesia laced with sal volatile, and weak, soapy water with a dash of carbolic. It is made from the pulped roots of the pepper-like piper methysticum, dissolved in cold water.

Within living memory, kava was pulped by having young virgins with sound teeth and free of colds masticate the fresh root and spit it into the kava bowl, after which the chewed pulp was strained through a fibrous mesh of hibiscus. This charming custom has passed into history, as have village virgins, to judge from the high rate of ex-nuptial births.

If you attend a genuine kava ceremony, don't sip until you tip a little kava from its coconut shell cup onto the ground immediately in front of you, while saying "manuia" *(mah-noo-ee-ah),* meaning good luck. Don't drain your cup. Leave a little and tip it out before handing the cup back to the server. Remember that to the Samoan, kava-drinking is a solemn, even sacred, ceremony in Western society. You might not relish the taste, but it will do you no harm. Westerners living in Polynesia often enjoy it and many swear by it as a rapid hangover cure.

If you become involved in Samoan life, you had better learn the word "musu," and become aware of its meaning rather than question it (its direct equivalent in Tahiti is "fiu"). Musu is a male state of mind for which the only term in the Queen's English is bloody-mindedness (in American English, "moody"). But in Anglo-Saxon communities, once bloody-minded, always bloody-minded. In Samoa and Tahiti, "musu" and "fiu" seem to be biochemically triggered. Your pleasant, friendly guide or host can become, within seconds, sulky, silent, intractable. Do nothing, say nothing. He will snap out of it as inexplicably and suddenly as he snaps into it.

Something else common to Samoa and Tahiti is the transvestite. In Tahiti (or rather in French Polynesia's Isles Below the Wind, as they are rare in Tahiti itself), they are known as "mahu." In Samoa, the word is "fa'afafine," meaning boy-girls. They often are reared as girls from birth by families wishing to balance the male-female ratio. From age 3 or 4, they dress as girls. They become dressmakers, laundresses, baby-sitters and house servants. To meet the modern entertainment tastes of the western world, they form entertainment troupes (the most notable in the Samoas is the Matautu troupe in Apia). Samoans tend to regard them tolerantly. Many fa'afafine ardently seek the company of male western tourists.

PRACTICAL INFORMATION FOR THE SAMOAS

FACTS AND FIGURES. The rocks married the earth and the earth became pregnant. Salevao, god of rocks, observed motion in the *moa,* or centre, of the earth. A child was born and named Moa, from the place where it was seen moving. Salevao provided water for washing the child and made it *sa,* or sacred, to *moa* hence "Samoa." In another legend, the land was flooded by the sea and everything died but the *moa,* the chickens. A daughter of a senior god declared them reserve chickens, *sa moa*—and so on.

The state motto of **Western Samoa** is "fa'avae i le atua Samoa," meaning "Samoa is founded on God," and that of American Samoa is "Samoa, Muamua Le Atua," meaning "Samoa, let God be first."

American Samoa's territorial plant is the *kava* (Piper Methysticum), known as *'ava* in Samoa, and the territorial tree is the *lau fala* (pandanus).

Apia is Western Samoa's capital. The state population is 155,000. Pago Pago (pronounced Pango Pango) is American Samoa's capital.

Average Temperature (°Fahrenheit) and Humidity

AMERICAN SAMOA

Pago Pago	Jan	Feb	Mar	Apr	May	June	July	Aug	Sept	Oct	Nov	Dec
Average max. day temperature	87°	86°	86°	87°	85°	84°	83°	83°	84°	85°	86°	86°
Days of Rain	25	22	22	24	20	18	19	18	18	22	21	23
Humidity, Percent	76	76	76	76	76	77	75	74	73	76	76	75

General hints: The tourist season starts April/May; June to October are considered the most pleasant. Remember, Samoa is close to the equator and the weather is tropical, warm and humid. It rains most of the year but the bursts last only an hour or so.

WESTERN SAMOA

Apia	Jan	Feb	Mar	Apr	May	June	July	Aug	Sept	Oct	Nov	Dec
Average max. day temperature	86°	86°	86°	86°	86°	85°	84°	84°	85°	85°	86°	86°
Days of Rain	24	24	19	24	13	13	11	11	21	18	15	22
Humidity, Percent	84	85	84	84	83	82	80	80	80	82	83	84

General hints: There is little climate variation between the two Samoas, although American Samoa has a heavier rainfall. Best time for visit in Western Samoa is June through November.

HOW TO GET THERE. To reach **American Samoa** (where Pago Pago's Tafuna field is the only international airport in the Samoas) travel by air or inter-island ferry. *By air:* From Honolulu, South Pacific Island Airways; Hawaiian Air and Samoa Inc; from Western Samoa, Polynesian Airlines and South Pacific Island Airways; from Suva, Air Pacific; from Rarotonga, Air Nauru; from Tahiti, Polynesian Airlines and South Pacific Island Airways; from Tonga, South Pacific Island Airways and Hawaiian Airlines. *By sea:* Thrice weekly ferry from Apia.

To **Western Samoa.** *By air:* From Melbourne, Qantas via Nadi; from Sydney, Air Vanuatu via Port Vila; from Fiji, Air Pacific and Polynesian Airlines. From American Samoa, Polynesian Airlines and South Pacific Island Airlines. From Tonga, Polynesian Airlines; from New Zealand, Air New Zealand and Polynesian Airlines; from Nauru, Air Nauru. From Honolulu via American Samoa, SPIA. *By sea:* Thrice weekly ferry from Pago.

HOW TO GET AROUND. *By air:* In Western Samoa, local flights are provided by Polynesian Airlines Ltd. In American Samoa, by South Pacific Island Airways.

Car rentals: In Western Samoa, Gold Star, Retzlaff. Pavitt's U-Drive, Apia Rentals Ltd., Lobers Transport Ltd., Vatco Ltd., and Avis. Motorcycles may be rented from Gold Star. In American Samoa, Holiday Rental Car, Royal Samoan, Budget, Avis, and Scanlan's Rent-a-Car.

By bus: In both Western Samoa and American Samoa, use simple commuter buses for fun, to know the Samoans, and to enjoy a travel bargain.

In Apia, timetables exist but it is best to ask the traffic police at the old market bus stand in the middle of town for advice about a bus to the village or the route of your choice. Start in the early morning to give yourself time to reach your destination, spend a few hours exploring (take a picnic lunch from the hotel), and to get a bus back in mid-afternoon.

The same is true for Pago Pago, even to catching the bus at the market place in downtown Fagatogo (pronounced fahngatongo). In American Samoa, bus services cease after about 4.30 P.M. If you are stranded, hail a cab by telephone. In every village you are certain to find a phone at the home of the Pulenuu, who is government agent and mayor as well as a chief.

In both Apia and Pago Pago a wide choice of bus tours is available.

TOURIST INFORMATION. In **Western Samoa:** the Western Samoa Visitors Bureau, Box 862, Apia. In **American Samoa:** Office of Tourism, Government of American Samoa, P.O. Box 1147, Pago Pago, American Samoa 96799.

 MONEY. In **Western Samoa,** the WS $1 (called the tala and equal to 100 sene) = US $0.60 at time of writing. Tala denominations: 1, 2, 10. Sene denominations: 1, 2, 5, 10, 20, 50. But American paper currency is freely negotiable and readily acceptable. Carry plenty, especially at the weekend. The currency of **American Samoa** is that of the United States.

The Bank of Western Samoa and the Pacific Commercial Bank are open daily, except Saturday and Sunday, from 9.30 A.M. to 3 P.M. In American Samoa, the Amerika Samoa Bank and the Bank of Hawaii are open from 9 A.M. to 4 P.M., Monday through Friday, with the Bank of Hawaii having a special service counter open to 4:30 P.M. Friday.

SHOPPING HOURS. In Apia, 8 A.M. to noon and 1.30 to 4.30 P.M., Monday through Friday, and 8 A.M. to 12.30 P.M., Saturday. Pago Pago shopping hours are 8:30 A.M. to 5 P.M., weekdays, and 8:30 A.M. to noon, Saturdays.

SEASONAL EVENTS. January through March: Cricket Season; unorthodox version of the English game played by some 50 to 100 barefoot participants. The game is accompanied by songs and dances to the rhythm of kerosene tin drums. **Mid-April:** In **American Samoa,** *Flag Day,* April 17, is American Samoa's July 4—its commemoration of April 17, 1900, when the Stars and Stripes was raised for the first time in what was then called Eastern Samoa. Since then, April 17 has been a state fair beneath the coconut palms with Samoan singing, dancing, fautasi (long boat) racing, and fun. If you're not there for Flag Day, make a point of visiting a school within walking distance of your hotel for flag-raising any weekday morning (you'll be welcome) to hear the singing of "The Star-Spangled Banner" in rich-vowelled English, and the local anthem "Amerika Samoa" in Samoan. Take a tape-recorder. If you don't own one, buy one (American Samoa is duty free), and familiarise yourself with its operation before going to school. There is no better way to launch yourself on the rewarding pastime of recording the rich sounds of travel.

January (entire month): In **Western Samoa:**—Cricket Games: Men and women's competitions each Saturday in Apia.

March–July—Rugby Season: Regular games played each Saturday in Apia and outside villages. Inter-school rugby games played each Wednesday afternoon.

June: The nation celebrates the first three days in June with great gusto as *Independence Days* (independence from New Zealand). Singing, dancing, rugby football (inherited from New Zealand and played with great skill), horse racing and fautasi (longboat racing). A good time to visit. Book well in advance.

July (entire month)—Inter-Secondary Schools Athletic Competition.

August (First or second week)—Samoa International Golf Tournament: (Fagalii) held at the Royal Samoa Country Club.

October: *White Sunday,* common to Western and American Samoa, is the second Sunday in October. For Samoan children, it is a sort of second or preliminary Christmas. Brought to the Samoas by the London Missionary Society, it is now observed by most Protestant denominations. White Sunday is literally Children's Day. In the two Samoas, there are slight differences but, in the main, children lead morning church services and, in afternoon services, children read the lessons, deliver sermons, and act in religious plays. The children are dressed in immaculate white. They march, singing, to church where they occupy seats of honour.

Seek advice from the offices of tourism as to where you may share in these beautiful observances. This is another Samoan event worth recording with a good tape recorder.

Rising of the palolo—two days in late October to early November every year. Palolo is the coral worm, the caviar of the South Pacific. When moon and tide are just right, the worms emerge from the reef very late at night in an annual bid to propagate the species. With gas lanterns, nets, and cheese cloth, Samoans venture forth—strangers are welcome—in reef waters to gather an annual gourmet feast. Arrange with your hotel desk to be invited. A few old Samoans forecast with uncanny and consistent accuracy the rising of the palolo.

December: In Western rather than American Samoa, *Christmas-New Year* is a week of good fun, uniquely Samoan. Song and dance troupes go from village to village. The "social clubs" which are a pleasant feature of Samoan life hold end-of-year dances. Strangers are genuinely welcome but especially so if they dance well, are informal, and appear respectful of Samoan traditions and standards. Strangers are liable to be wide-eyed at the strongly religious, rather than commercial flavor of Christmas.

HOLIDAYS. All government offices, banks, and most private offices are closed —sometimes on the day before and after, too.

American Samoa. January 1; February—(3rd Monday: Washington's Birthday); Good Friday; Easter.

April 17—(Flag Day: the biggest holiday in American Samoa); May—last Monday (Memorial Day); July 4; September—(1st Monday: Labor Day).

October—2nd Sunday (White Sunday: Dressed in white, children attend church services and later in day hold seats of honor at family feasts); October— (2nd Monday—Columbus Day); October—(4th Monday—Veterans' Day); November—(4th Thursday—Thanksgiving Day); December 25.

Western Samoa. January 1-2—New Year Holidays. Easter Holidays. April 25—ANZAC Day: Observed in commemoration of those killed in World Wars I and II.

June 1-3—Independence Anniversary Celebration: (Apia) Activities include long-boat races, singing, dancing and marching competitions. Also horse races.

December 25—Christmas Day. December 26—Boxing Day: Friends visit, picnic and celebrate end of Christmas holidays.

 SPECTATOR SPORTS. Whatever the dynamic Samoan has taken from the white man he has adapted to his needs and his culture. He has quietly added Samoan witchcraft to many Christian faiths. And he has wrought remarkable change to the ancient English game of *cricket,* even switching its name to *kirikiti.* Instead of a quiet and stylish game for 22 immaculately clad men, it is a community game for young and old, male and female. Since the American presence in Eastern Samoa, the game has become a combination of English cricket and American baseball—an exciting, if sometimes puzzling spectator sport. More than half a century ago, Robert Louis Stevenson wrote: "Cricket matches where 100 played upon a side endured at times for weeks and ate up the country like the presence of an army." More than 60 years later, a New Zealand educator assigned to Western Samoa, wrote that the three-sided bat keeps players and spectators "in a state of suspense," that wickets "look like peasticks" and that the balls normally are made from strips of raw rubber bled from local trees. The educator added: "A defeated team can buy itself back into the competition with another entrance fee. The host village may collect $2,000 in fees but be eaten out of food." Samoans take their cricket seriously. During one inter-village match, a visiting batsman was given 'out' when he was caught by a young spectator. Singing and dancing (the usual accompaniment to a match) stopped while the indignant batsman protested. But the umpire, proud, as it happened, of his young brother (the spectator in question), stuck to his decision. He is probably the only umpire in the history of cricket to lose his life for doing so. He was fatally felled on the spot with one swipe of the bat.

Longboat races in American Samoa on Flag Day and Western Samoa on Independence Day are exciting. The 50-oarsmen craft are 100 feet long, start five miles out to sea and enter the home stretches through foaming gaps in reefs.

 SPORTS. *Fishing* is primary. There is some difference in emphasis between Western and American Samoa—because of the different economies. In each Samoa, but particularly American Samoa, the stranger has ready access to close-at-hand exciting fishing for marlin, tuna, wahoo, skipjack, sailfish, and mahimahi (called dolphin in American Samoa as in Hawaii but, in fact, the dorado). In Western Samoa, fishing is a way of life rather than a sport. People catch fish to sell or to eat.

For *bowling, golf* and *tennis,* enquire at your hotel.

Watch Western Samoan high school *rugby football.* And watch American Samoan high school American *football* and *basketball.* In American Samoa, you could find yourself alongside college and professional scouts from the United States mainland. Under the headline SHAKE 'EM OUT OF THE COCONUT TREES, normally unexcitable *Sports Illustrated* magazine some years ago posed the possibility that "Samoans are about to do for US football what oil did for Oklahoma." *Sports Illustrated* also thought a Samoan incursion into mainland basketball could be in the offing. The magazine identified a "swarm of Polynesian warriors—not your run-of-the-reef gin mill flamethrowers, but strong fierce men, six to seven feet tall, who seem to have stepped into the 20th century from some secret museum of oceanic antiquities. As in fact they have . . . the only island group where the Polynesian race has survived virtually intact." A forerunner of the "swarm" of the late seventies was Al Taa who, under the name of Al Harrington, made a name for himself at football at Stanford in the late fifties. Al, who majored in history while playing football at Stanford (and since then has exploited his physique by playing Ben Kokua in "Hawaii Five-O") is quoted as attributing American Samoan youths' new stardom in football to racial pride—standard-bearers for fa'a Samoa, the Samoan way of life. In legend, the Polynesian seeks an easy life. That may go for the Tahitian and the Maori, but not for the Samoan. He is a competitor—in everything. He hates to lose. "In consequence," says *Sports Illustrated,* "U.S. football looks like the rainbow's end for many Samoan teen-agers."

Swimming and *skin diving* are available almost wherever you go in the Samoas. But remember—lower middle class English and Australian missionary standards of modesty of a century ago obtain. Also, as a general rule, don't swim where Samoans don't swim. Rarely do they swim beyond the reef and they are highly respectful of known undertows.

In Apia, within easy bus or taxi ride of the main hotels, you may have memorable year-round swimming in the sea, in lakes, in waterfalls in mountain streams. Palolo Deep, a short distance from Aggie's Hotel, is in the lagoon on the eastern front of Pilot Point. It is perfect for swimming (remember to take water goggles for the coral formations and the tropical fish) and for under water photography.

Vaiala beach is a mile (1½ kms.) fom Aggie's and Mulinuu beach is a mile (1½ kms.) from Hotel Tusitala.

Fatumea pool is at Piula Methodist Theological College, on the east coast, half an hour's drive from Apia. It is an oval natural pool, with fresh, cool, clear water flowing from a cave at the foot of a cliff below a church. The fresh water meets warm sea water. A pool for connoisseurs. The college makes a small charge.

Laulii and Solosolo black sand beaches, 5 miles (8 kms.) from Apia are for *experienced* surfers. In heavy surf, the undertow is frightening!

Papaseea sliding rocks, 6 miles (10 kms.) from Apia in a rushing mountain stream are, in effect, a natural slippery slide, water-lubricated, into a cool pool. Generous nature has provided separate chutes for men, women, and children.

Ever fancied swimming in a goldfish pond? You can do it, hygienically, in Lake Lanotoo, a crater lake teeming with gold fish, 12 miles (19 kms.) from Apia.

TOURS. Western Samoa. *By air:* Destinations on the Samoan Archipelago's "Big Island" of Savaii are variously 7 minutes and 35 minutes by scheduled air service from the airport of Apia, and 90 minutes by Government car ferry (on which you may take your rental car). The Western Samoan Government Department of Economic Development "advice for visitors" bulletin says: "Savaii is for the hardy. But you will always remember your adventure. Allow yourself a leisurely two-day visit and observe Polynesia at its truest." Contact Polynesian Airlines, Ltd., P.O. Box 599, Apia.

Bus and car tours on Upolu officially recommended by the West Samoan Government are operated by Retzlaff's Tours, Samoa Scenic Tours, Janes Tours, Gold Star Travel, and Tours and Union Travel. Check in Apia to see who is using air-conditioned vehicles. On most tours it is necessary to order a package lunch and something to drink from your hotel or guest-house the night before departure.

By road: Vailima, just out of Apia, one may see the home built by author Robert Louis Stevenson. Modified many times since, it is now the official home of Western Samoa's Heads of State. The grounds may be visited with official permission. But the path to the graves of Stevenson and his American wife above Vailima, a strenuous climb, is always open. Vailima is without architectural merit. But the site is enviable. And the author's fans still abound.

A standard tour from Apia is to Falefa Falls, Mafa Pass, Fuipisia Falls and the Aleipata district, a 40 mile (64 km.) east coast drive. This is instant Samoa, complete with 180 ft. waterfall, white sand beaches, an old village, and four offshore islets.

Lefaga Village, on the southwest coast of Upolu island is the comely oceanside village where, in 1952, the Gary Cooper film "Return to Paradise," based on the James Michener book, was filmed. Access is by a cross-island road.

By sea: Passenger and vehicle ferries ply between Apia and Pago Pago and between Apia and Savaii. This is an excellent way to see islands and people. But definitely not for the comfort seeker. You'll be traveling with locals carrying chickens, vegetables, other items that take space on the deck. Only suggested for the adventurous.

Royal Viking Line, One Embarcadero Center, San Francisco, CA 94111. (800) 422-8000 nationwide. Offers 4, 14-day cruises between Sydney and Auckland. The South Pacific itineraries vary east and west bound so that you could combine 2 14-day cruises to make a 28-day cruise without repeating ports. Ports of call include, Wellington N.Z., Christchurch, N.Z.; Hobart, Tasmania; Adelaide, Australia; Melbourne, Victoria; Nou'mea, New Caledonia; Vila, Vanuatu; Suva, Fiji; Nuku'Alofa, Tonga; Parhia, N.Z.

Royal Viking Line also offers a "Pacific Plus" package that allows you to connect with segments of the cruises. Write for details concerning their free round-trip air fare and complimentary pre- or post-cruise land packages. Write Royal Viking Line.

P & O Princess Cruises, 2029 Century Park E., Los Angeles, Ca. 90067. Offers cruises to the South Pacific. Ports of call include Honolulu; Bora Bora; Papeete; Moorea; Niuao'ou; Apia; Pago Pago, Auckland, New Zealand; and Sydney, Australia. Contact your travel agent.

Dateline Tours, Inc., P.O. Box 1755, Newport Beach, Ca. 92663, offers tours to Samoa in connection with tours to New Zealand and Australia. Contact your local travel agent.

Samoa Tours & Travel Agency, Inc., P.O. Box 727, Pago Pago, American Samoa. Offices in Rainmaker Hotel lobby. Two- to three-day tours of Samoan way of life; overnights in High Chief Guest House in village. Includes meals and bedding with share facilities. Deep-sea fishing and cable-car rides to Mt. Alava arranged. Also special tour to Manu'a Island, the King Tauimanu'a Faasamoa Tour (1–2 days).

Samoan Holiday & Travel Center, P.O. Box 968, Lumanai Bldg., Pago Pago, American Samoa 96799. Sightseeing by air to Manua Islands $50 round trip, with overnight in Manua $80. Harbor sailing $25/person, including lunch, other sports available. Tours with emphasis on native handcraft-manufacture include: Tula Tour, which passes through market place, handicraft center, and coastline tour— 2½ hours $33.20/car or $11/person. All-day tour to villages to see native life and coastal areas. $13.10/person with evening *fia fia* (feast and entertainment) $25/person. Other specialized tours to hospitals, canneries, etc. available.

By car: From Solo Hill, on minute's taxi ride (a very warm walk in Pago's humidity) from the Rainmaker Hotel, there is a 12-passenger aerial tramway that climbs to the 1,609 ft. summit of Mt. Alava, the other side of Pago Pago Bay. This skyride is not for the fainthearted. It is claimed to be the world's longest single-span aerial cab ride. Originally built to take construction crews to the television transmitter atop Mt. Alava, it affords long-distance viewing every day of the week, 8 A.M. to 4 P.M., except Sunday, or when winds exceed 45 knots. At starting and closing times, it is often possible to see Western Samoa clearly and also the Manua Islands of American Samoa. Fainthearts may use a new smooth road to the summit.

Solo Hill itself, starting point of the cable cab ride, is an ideal picnic ground from which to relish the beauty of Pago Pago Bay. Picnic tables are behind the tramway house.

From Mount Alava, where the cable cab ride ends, those in good physical condition, with stout non-skid footwear, may hike down a mountain trail to Vatia village at sea level, 1,600 ft. below. The trail is muddy, stony, and impeded with tree roots and descent can take from 2 to 3 hours. You can either climb back to the summit, an extremely arduous ascent, or await one of the 2 small boats a day which go from Vatia to Pago Pago. Or, you may spend the night with a village family. But this should be organised properly and with appropriate respect. The Office of Tourism in Pago Pago will arrange for a guide for about US$10 a day. Make sure that you understand from him the obligations of a guest in a highly formal—although very warm—traditional society.

For scenery fans, there is a rewarding drive by good road from Pago Pago Bay to the remote north side of Tutuila through the snake-like *Fagasa Pass.*

On foot: Just across the road from the Rainmaker Hotel is the heart of American Samoa's world-famed instructional television system (guided tours Monday to Friday, 2–5 P.M.). In an experiment unique in the world, American Samoa teaches school by TV and uses the same plant at night both to entertain and educate adults. There are three color channels, which cover both Samoas. One-week-old videotaped American programs are screened.

NIGHTCLUBS AND RESTAURANTS. Samoans' love of music and dancing, aligning with the presence of a mainly young transient expatriate population, has generated proliferation of nightspots. In a South Pacific manner they come and go and hence total accuracy is impossible. In alphabetical order, Apia's serious eating places are Amigo's, Apian Way, Aggie Grey's Hotel, Leung Wai, Jade Garden, Pizza Palace, Hotel Tusitala, and Wei's Chinese restaurant. Cabaret-bars are Hotel Tusitala, Jerome's Cove, Tanoa, Otto's Reef, Emilio's Go Go and, out of town, Mount Vaea. Fiafia (Samoan dancing) night at Aggie's and Tusitala on Fridays is usually memorably cheerful. In American Samoa, Pago Pago places include the Bamboo Room (matey little bar liked by locals), Seaside Garden Club (despite bourgeois label, island proletarian in a nice way and right on the edge of the ocean), Pago Bar (inclined to be rowdy), Tunna Palace and Teputas (good bands playing the latest from the States with supersteam) and the 11th Frame (on the first floor of the Pago bowling alley). Soli's & Mark's American and Chinese Restaurant and Disco (open to 1:30 A.M.) offers stunning views through jungle-covered green slopes that dive sharply to the sea; it serves octopus cooked in coconut milk. Good Chinese cuisine is available at the downtown Golden Dragon. Polynesian dancing is a feature of the Pago nightclubs Tepatasi Club, Purple Onion Club, Leilani Club, and Tiki Club.

 DRINKING LAWS. In **Western Samoa**, sale of liquor on Sundays is permitted only to hotel guests and their guests. So if you are organising a picnic, do your shopping on Saturday—and be discreet with any Sabbath drinking in public, remembering Samoan respect for the Sabbath. **American Samoa** is more flexible.

 SHOPPING. Easiest shopping for quality artifacts is done in **Western Samoa** at the Government-sponsored Handicrafts Corporation in downtown Apia (it provides income and employment in the villages) from family stalls in the "J New Market" and from small stores in Beach Rd. In **American Samoa,** visit the beautiful complex of fales at the southern end of Pago Pago park called the *Elderly Center.* This is a government-sponsored enterprise in which the elderly of American Samoa keep alive the artifacts of the country. They work on-site and sell their work there. But the discriminating shopper with time will roam the villages. In largely duty-free American Samoa Japanese audio and optics are available at more-or-less Singapore and Hong Kong prices.

Samoa's best buys, and they are best in Western Samoa, are "fine mats" from pandanus fibre, which is scarcely wider than a linen thread and woven without loom. Within Samoa, these mats have great ceremonial importance as gifts between families or clans. Each mat is a woman's spare-time work for months or even years. The highest quality article, normally available to non-Samoans when it is given as a gift to foreign dignitaries, rarely appears on the market. But "never ask, never get."

More readily for sale are the woven and plaited ware and tapa cloth of great variety and consistently high quality as well as hand-painted fabrics in tapa designs, tortoise-shell products, shell necklaces and—a good buy if you are flying in an airline that does not watch the baggage scales-tanoa (or kanoa) kava drinking bowls, that can be used as big salad servers. They are made of very hard, close-grained hardwood, polished with cowrie shells to a high gloss. They stand on short legs.

CUSTOMS REGULATIONS. American Samoa. Free import, 200 cigarettes; 50 cigars or one pound tobacco; one U.S. gallon of five bottles of liquor or wine; reasonable amount of perfume. **Western Samoa.** Free import. For persons 16 years and older, 200 cigarettes or 50 cigars up to 1–½ pound tobacco; for tourists only: one bottle of 26 fl. oz. spirits.

 HOTELS AND MOTELS. In the Samoas, accommodations range from the Rainmaker in Pago Pago, owned by the Government of American Samoa, managed by Inter-Continental, then Americana and now independent, to Tusitala and Aggie Grey's in Apia, to a small galaxy of little-grass-shack establishments, some of them admirable.

Rates, based on double occupancy, are below US$35. Devaluation of the West Samoan dollar brings it to about US 60¢ (mid-1985) and hence all accommodations are inexpensive.

WESTERN SAMOA

Apia

Aggie Grey's. *Inexpensive.* 110 air-conditioned rooms, but still old South Seas atmosphere. On seafront. Pool. Golf close. Within walking distance of downtown Apia.

Tusitala. *Inexpensive.* Modern and Western. Striking architecture in Samoan style, with 96 air-conditioned rooms. Within walking distance of shops and business centre. Seafront. Pool.

Tiafau Hotel. *Inexpensive.* Small but modern, 5 minutes by cab from downtown.

Apian Way. *Inexpensive.* Bed and breakfast. Small and modest.

Samoan Hideaway Beach Resort. *Inexpensive.* P.O. Box 1191. Samoa's only beach resort. 18 double rooms. Restaurant, bar, pool, Samoan feasts. About 45 minutes from Apia by cab. Diving is organised, excellent, and cheap.

Savaii Island

Safua Hotel. *Inexpensive.* At Lalomalava. 11 fales with banana-leaf folding "walls" which do not always exclude dogs and chickens. A "culture immersion experience" where guests dine —well— at one long table with owner Moelagi Jackson, staff, and fellow guests from many lands. The holder of two chiefly titles, Moelagi can organise whatever you seek, from tapa-making to a walk along a blowhole coast.

Salafai Inn. *Inexpensive.* Near Saleloga ferry jetty. Dormitory and seven western-style rooms.

AMERICAN SAMOA

Pago Pago

Pago Pago Rainmaker. *Moderate.* On shore of Pago Pago harbor, superbly sited, facing Rainmaker mountain. Duty free shopping within hotel.

Herb and Sia's Motel. *Inexpensive.* In the heart of town. Nightclub with Polynesian entertainment, Wednesday and Friday.

THE COOK ISLANDS

Instant Paradise?

Sudden aggressive publicizing in late 1977 of the Cook Islands, next-door neighbor of Tahiti, as a new away-from-it-all, English-speaking, hygienic, friendly, politically stable, ultra-beautiful tropical resort, makes one wonder why the islands have never aroused tourist interest in the past. The simple answer is accessibility and beds. Only in 1973 did New Zealand create a jet airport in its former colony (now liberated) and only in the second half of 1977 was a resort hotel conforming to international standards established here on New Zealand's initiative, to provide revenue for the insolvent ex-colony and to generate traffic for New Zealand's international airline.

The Cooks and Tahiti have the same attractions—human and topographical. Why, then, did New Zealand—which owned the Cooks from 1901 to 1965—refrain from creating its own Tahiti? The reason is that New Zealand had no relish for imperialism. At the turn of the century, a chauvinistic, British-born Prime Minister of New Zealand talked his motherland into quitting the profitless and remote Cook Islands and giving them to New Zealand. Until some gentle political agitation of the 1950's, most New Zealanders were as unaware of their neglected colony as most Americans are unaware today of their not neglected colony of American Samoa.

The Cook Islands government does not pretend to welcome tourism. A former government tourist authority spokesman said: "We're too small to open our doors and be flooded. Agriculture must remain our number one activity." But this attitude is eroding.

Tourism Is a Necessity

The Cook Islands are belatedly in the tourism business as a consequence of the independence for which they clamoured. The mini-nation is broke. Today, more than half the people born in the Cook Islands are in New Zealand—seeking a better life and more open space. As New Zealand grants unrestricted access, the Cook Islands' population steadily falls and, with it, the rate of agricultural production. Of the 18,500 people still living in the Cooks, 10,000 live on Rarotonga.

New Zealand contributes NZ$ 10 million a year in direct financial aid, plus at least as much again in budgetary aid. Shipping and air-freight subsidies are also provided. One consequence is surprisingly comprehensive medical service for a population so small and dispersed. The doctor population ratio is 1:1000.

Pros and Cons for Tourists

Whether tourism will "flood" the increasingly deserted Cook Islands is doubtful. For the tourist, pluses are the rugged oceanic beauty comparable to that of nearby Tahiti and Moorea; a lively Polynesian population closely akin to the Tahitians; easy jet access from Los Angeles, Honolulu, Papeete, Pago Pago, Apia, Nandi and Auckland; low costs by South Pacific standards; and a tranquil, unhurried atmosphere. Minuses are that only 5 of the 15 Cook Islands—Rarotonga, Aitutaki, Atiu, and Mauke—offer tourist accommodations; an indication of tourist interest, however, could change that situation. Another minus is the absence of a Cook Islands' tradition of fine cuisine as there is in French Polynesia. Too often, tourists assume, as they feast in Tahiti, that the French taught the Tahitian how to cook. But, as Herman Melville recorded a century and a half ago, Tahitian cuisine was both rich and delicate and its presentation elegant and gracious long before the French arrived. The good news is that the international hotel in Rarotonga and the two operations on the island of Aitutaki serve fine food.

The Cooks, half way between Hawaii and New Zealand and half way between Fiji and Tahiti, occupy 93 square miles (241 sq. kms.) of land but are widely scattered through 751,000 square miles (1,945,090 sq. kms.) of the Pacific Ocean. Islands of the southern group, including the main island of Rarotonga (main town, Avarua) are volcanic extrusions, towering folds of basalt squeezed from the seabed. The northern group, except Aitutaki, are true coral atolls.

A Hermit . . .

One of the atolls, remote Suwarrow (given a Russian name in 1814 by far-from-home Mikhail Lazarev), had, until his death in 1977, only one inhabitant, New Zealand-born self-proclaimed hermit Tom Neale. He has written a book which reports persuasively the happiness of the hermit in a paradisical environment.

. . . or a Father Figure

One island, Palmerston, discovered and named by Capt. James Cook in 1774, is the homeland of an English-Polynesian tribe, the Marsters. Of its 87 inhabitants, 62 are Marsters. William Marsters, farm boy from Gloucestershire, England, settled there in 1862 with a Cook Island wife and her sister. When the sister-in-law complained of loneliness, Marsters proclaimed himself a minister of the Episcopalian church (Church of

England in the British Empire) and, with his wife's ready consent, took his sister-in-law as his number two wife. When wife number one became pregnant, a sister from a distant island, versed in midwifery, came to attend her. With the consent of wives one and two, Marsters extended his matey little commonwealth by taking her as wife three.

Within 18 years, Marsters had 60 children, all of fine physique, copper-skinned, with Anglo-Saxon features, and all speaking perfect English in the mellow manner of Gloucestershire, softened even further by the full Italianate vowels of Polynesia. In 1946, the New Zealand Government estimated that Marsters' children and grandchildren numbered 2,508, plus roughly 3,000 great-grandchildren. As a result, the transient is unlikely to spend a day in the Cook Islands without meeting a Marsters. And the name (far from common in England) recurs in New Zealand telephone books.

Mangaia, southernmost of the Cooks, used to be noted for the sexuality of its people. American anthropologist Donald S. Marshall has written in *Psychology Today* magazine: "Sex—sex for pleasure and sex for procreation—is a principal concern of the Polynesian people on tiny Mangaia. . . . There is great directness about sex, but the approach to sex is correspondingly indirect. Among the young there is no dating, no tentative necking in the American sense. A flick of the eye, a raised eyebrow in a crowd, can lead to copulation, without a word . . . Sexual intimacy precedes personal affection."

Sex vs. Evangelism

Female sexuality in the Cook Islands enraged Protestant missionaries 130 years ago. London Missionary Society archives, recording forcible head-shaving of adulteresses by missionaries, noted: "The moment the fine flowing locks were cut off, the head would be immediately adorned with a wreath of flowers in many colours, which seemed to embolden the erring creatures."

The missionaries welcomed epidemics and earthquakes as warnings against fleshly pleasures. A dysentery epidemic that killed children by the hundreds was accepted as a divine scourge and an aid to conversion —anything that scared the "natives" was turned to advantage. Another epidemic was hailed as a "solemn dispensation." A destructive hurricane was "a merciful chastisement of the people."

The late Professor Ernest Beaglehole, New Zealand historian, calls the authors of these sick sentiments "lower middle class evangelical English puritans" who sought to create in the Cooks "a replica or a mirror of lower middle class England."

As Polynesians, Cook Islanders are akin to Hawaiians, Tongans, Samoans, New Zealand's Maori, and Chile's Easter Islanders. In physical appearance, culture, language, and character Cook Islanders are close to both Tahitians and Maoris. Their national legends mesh most closely with those of the Maori. According to legend, Cook Islanders, setting out from Rarotonga to the uninhabited New Zealand in a small fleet of canoes about 1350 A.D. became the forerunners of the New Zealand Maori race. The migration, complete with women and children, was induced by population pressures, food shortages, and inter-tribal warfare.

The Cuisine

To the detriment of cuisine in the Cook Islands, there are almost no Asians in the community. This situation derives largely from the prejudice of former New Zealand Prime Minister Richard Seddon, who contrived the switch in ownership of the Cooks from Britain to New Zealand. His anti-Asian xenophobia was undisguised. A New Zealand Government hardback publication of 1900, reporting on a visit by Seddon to the Cooks, Tonga and Fiji, cites, without attribution but with obvious approbation, the story of a Chinese in Rarotonga who contracted leprosy. This was an embarrassment to a sprinkling of Chinese residents, tolerated at that time by the British administration. The Chinese filled two Cook Islanders with gin, told them the Chinese cure for leprosy was to bury the sufferer alive, and promised them more gin if they bundled the sufferer into a cornsack and buried him. This the Cook Islanders did. A subsequent legal process, according to this official New Zealand Government document of the year 1900, returned a verdict of "justifiable homicide" on the grounds that the spread of leprosy was stemmed. The New Zealand Government document concludes: "This episode had one effect, namely that Chinese are not numerous in the Cook Group." The same document quotes Seddon as saying at the time to Queen Makea and a group of high chiefs of the Cook Islands: "I wish to bring under your notice restriction of Chinese. If Asiatics come here in large numbers it means deterioration of your race. They bring evils among you worse than bubonic plague. It may be strong language to use, but I would rather see a case of plague here than see one hundred Chinamen land. They bring leprosy with them, gambling, immorality and opium-smoking. They get hold of young people and teach them these bad habits. The result is that the whole of the race will be degenerated. . . . In their quarters you see filth. In their habits they are dirty."

The only relevance of this account to the traveller in the Cooks is that in the absence of Chinese or other Asians, the Chinese cuisine of Papeete and the Chinese and Vietnamese cuisines of Noumea, Port Vila and Santo do not exist to do justice to the fruit, seafoods, and vegetables of the islands.

PRACTICAL INFORMATION FOR THE COOK ISLANDS

WHEN TO GO, WHAT TO TAKE. Highest temperatures at Rarotonga average 84°F in January and February but, throughout the year, the southeast trade winds keep the weather from being uncomfortably hot. December through March is known as the "hurricane season," but world weather changes seem to make the term meaningless. Heaviest bookings are June through September, when Australians and New Zealanders escape their winter in neighboring tropics. Take easy-care cotton clothing, medication, and any unusual photographic equipment. Both black-and-white and color processing are sent to New Zealand. Take sturdy old tennis shoes for reef exploration, which is a favorite tourist occupation, and to protect feet against slow-to-heal coral cuts. There are several duty-free shops in Rarotonga.

Average Temperature (°Fahrenheit) and Humidity

Rarotonga	Jan	Feb	Mar	Apr	May	June	July	Aug	Sept	Oct	Nov	Dec
Average max. day temperature	84°	84°	83°	81°	79°	77°	77°	77°	77°	79°	80°	82
Days of Rain	15	15	16	14	13	11	10	11	11	12	13	14
Humidity, Percent	79	81	80	79	77	77	75	74	73	74	75	76

General hints: The best tourist season is May through October. Temperature is warm and humid, tempered by trade winds.

WHAT WILL IT COST? The New Zealand dollar is used in the Cook Islands, with an exchange rate at press time of NZ$1-US$0.45. At Rarotonga's top hotel, the *Rarotongan,* first class ceiling fan rooms with bath start at twin NZ$56 a day. Motels, New Zealand style (meaning very completely equipped by international standards), with electric range and refrigerator, some with air-conditioning, start at NZ$20 a day but NZ$30 is more usual. Some rent or lend outrigger canoes. Small Japanese and British rental cars cost NZ$40 a day. Drive on the left, as in British countries, and give way to pedestrians. Japanese 90 cc motorcycles rent at NZ$45 a week, with no mileage charge. Pedal cycles are NZ$4 a day. Green fees at nine-hole golf courses at Rarotonga and Aitutaki are $2 a round. Clubs can be rented. Movie admission is less than NZ$1. The state monopoly betting shop will take 25¢ bets on horse races in New Zealand, win, place and doubles (instant results by short-wave radio).

POST AND TELEGRAPH. Mailing, cabling, and telephoning are done most conveniently through hotels.

TIPPING. None. No one wins gratitude by trying to force tips on those who have served them.

WHAT TO SEE. There's much to observe: on Rarotonga, the daily life of a small Pacific town; the Cook Islands capital, Avarua; the ever-lively waterfront with its emotional farewells as small craft leave for the outer islands; life in small villages in the valleys (readily accessible in cheap taxi, bus, rental car or on rental motorcycle). On Sunday, visit any church to share in or just sense the fervour of the old-time religion and the joyful hymn-singing. Note, when touring Rarotonga, the custom of putting a metal roof over a front-garden grave and the lanterns, water jugs and blankets on the graves. At Arai-te-tonga marae (meeting area), just outside Avarua, ask to see the ceremonial stone where prisoners' brains used to be bashed out. Go to the spirited island dance displays at the Tamure Resort and Rarotongan hotels. Bare-back horse racing on Muri beach on New Year's Day, Easter Monday and at random dates during the year is memorable fun. Much lower key, but also delightful is a song-and-dance contest, held mainly inthe evenings, during Constitution Week, which celebrates independence from New Zealand. There are tableaus depicting island legend. Dance troupes come from outlying islands for occasions that almost match Tahiti's Bastille Day celebrations. If you like Polynesian dancing, this or the dance-festival week in the second week of April could be the best times to visit. On Aitutaki, enjoy the lagoon cruises (snorkel gear is available from the hotel but remember to bring those old tennis shoes from home). Cook Islandair and Air Rarotonga provide scheduled and charter flights to the outer islands. Reputable tour operators are in business.

FESTIVALS AND SPECIAL EVENTS. New Year's Eve—open-air dancing; New Year's Day, bareback horse races on Muri beach.

Third week in **February**—Cultural Festival Week.

Second week in **April**—Island Dance Festival Week.

Easter Monday—races again at Muri beach.

Friday before **August** 4 and then for 10 days—Constitution Celebrations, which are mainly festivals and sporting activities to mark self-government and independence from New Zealand.

October 26. Gospel Day, commemorating missionaries' arrival in 1823. Open-air religious plays ("nuku").

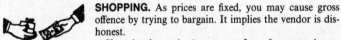

SHOPPING. As prices are fixed, you may cause gross offence by trying to bargain. It implies the vendor is dishonest.

Shopping hours in Avarua are from 8 A.M. to 4 P.M., Mondays through Friday, 8 A.M. to 11:30 A.M., Saturday. Village stores often are open at night.

Curio stores offer carvings in wood and pearl shell and delicate weaving in pandanus fibre.

The Women's Craft Center sells what is made only in the Cook Islands and in French Polynesia—bedspreads known as tivaevae (in French Polynesia tifaifai), made with a unique combination of Polynesian and European skills. In the manner of an intricate mosiac, a wide range of fabrics is cut into matching shapes and sewn together in what is usually a harmonious and attractive pattern. Another procedure is to draw on a piece of plain cotton fabric flower designs with accompanying foliage, or sometimes a purely abstract design. The designs are cut from different materials of contrasting colours and appliquéd onto the master print. Often a team of women will work on a tivaevae as, in other days, they would have made tapa by team effort. Normal size is 8 feet square.

Another good buy is the high-crown woven coconut fibre hat, worn in the islands by both men and women, often with a band of small shells, threaded with exquisite skill. For free, at South Seas Distillery testing room near the post office, try Ara, a potent and potable distillate from pineapple. Lace it with coke.

At Avarua's six-days-a-week market the display of oranges, papaya, bananas and coconuts is superb.

BEACHES. The best beaches for swimming are Muri lagoon and Titikaveka. Some are for viewing only. Get local advice on coral heads. Beside being an effective safeguard against coral cuts, old tennis shoes will protect you against the thorny stone fish and the crown of thorns star-fish, which are seen rarely.

TOURS. *Exham Tours.* Rarotonga. A must tour for anyone traveling to the Cooks. Exham Wichman, owner, takes you on a lifestyle tour through Arorangi Village and plantations. Exham's way of presenting how people live in the villages and his own personality make for an outstanding adventure. Tour ends at Wichman's home, where his wife serves afternoon tea. Great opportunity to actually feel life as it exists in the Cooks.

Union-Citco Travel Ltd., P.O. Box 54, Rarotonga, Cook Islands. Arrangements for small groups or individuals. Transfers, sightseeing, barbecues and guided walking tours. Visits to other islands. Booking agent for major air, sea and land services, "Island-style Meet-the-People Evenings," day tour to Aitutaki by air, across-island walks, reef walks, line fishing, scuba diving, and guided snorkelling. Unspoilt Aitutaki island, 60 miles north of Rarotonga, is a must—be it for a week or a day.

Air Rarotonga, P.O. Box 79, and *Cook Islandair,* P.O. Box 65, operate scheduled and charter services throughout the Cooks.

South Seas Travel, P.O. Box 49 offers round-the-island motorized buggy tours, diving and game-fishing tours. Bicycles and motorcycles for hire. *Tipani Tours,* P.O. Box 4. Big-game fishing, round-the-island coach and car tours. reef walks.

Nature Expeditions International, P.O. Box 11496, Eugene, OR 97440. Offers outstanding naturalist and cultural trips to the Cook Islands and Fiji. Stay in homes in traditional villages and resort hotels. Tourists participate in daily life of typical Polynesian family. Tours led by prominent anthropologists and naturalists and geared for both first timers and experienced travellers.

Ocean Voyages, Inc., 1709 Bridgeway, Sausalito, Ca. 94965, offers a variety of cruises through the Cooks. They offer cruises small boats, which carry only 4 to 8 passengers.

Dive Rarotonga, Box 38. Daily dive trips. Hire and sale of equipment.

Game fishing is offered by *Aquaholics IV, Daniel Webb, Seafari Charters, Blue Water Adventures, Don Beer,* and *Pacific Marine Charters.* At Aitutaki, it is offered by *Capt. Kavana* and *Aitutaki Scuba.*

 HOTELS AND MOTELS. Double occupancy rates are classified as follows: *Expensive,* NZ$70 and up; *Moderate,* NZ$40–69; *Inexpensive,* below NZ$40. In package deals effective rates can be much lower. And there are high and low season rates. Ask a travel agent for the very detailed *Explorair* catalogue.

Rarotongan. *Moderate.* 150 rooms with ceiling fans. Restaurant, bar and disco. Swimming pool. On a fine beach 6½ miles from town. Offers "Club Rarotonga," a meals-inclusive, multi-activity program inspired by Club Med.

Aitutaki Resort Hotel. *Moderate.* On an island linked by causeway, provides the pleasant hilly banana-producing northerly island of Aitutaki with its first international-quality accommodation.

Rapae Cottage Hotel. *Inexpensive.* On a beach at Aitutaki. Government-owned and operated and very popular. Big dance floor by open-sided restaurant. Many rate this one of the best meet-the-people opportunities in the region.

Little Polynesian Motel. *Inexpensive.* At Titikaveka village, 8 miles from Avarua, offers superb swimming in a turquoise lagoon.

Tamure Resort (formerly Trailways/Reef). *Inexpensive.* 35 rooms, none air conditioned but all with fans. Restaurant and bar. Swimming pool. On shore-front 1½ miles from town but no beach. Friendly and informal. Offers "Club Pacific" multi-activity program.

Excellent New Zealand-style motels proliferate. They include Puaikua Reef Lodges, Edgewater Motel, Moana Beach Lodges, Beach Motel, Palm Grove Lodges, Orange Grove Lodges Arorangi Lodge, Muri Beachcomber, Little Polynesia, Lagoon Lodges, and Kii Kii. Aitutaki motels are Torino Villa and Aitutaki Guest House. And there are new motels on the islands of Atiu and Mauke. Write Cook Islands Tourist Authority, Box 14, Otera, Rarotonga, Cook Islands, for list of hotels and rates.

WHERE TO EAT. After a slow start in the 70s, eating houses proliferated. There are combinations of lounge, bar, dance floor, and even mini-golf (Tere's 18 holes). The Rarotongan Hotel has the most formidable menu and wine list. Banana Court is the number-one night spot and in daytime you may drink there while betting on New Zealand races in the next-door legal betting shop. Big band music every night but Sunday, Monday, and Tuesday.

NUMISMATISTS. The minting of coins has created a great deal of special interest. Their coins are collectors' items throughout the world.

PHILATELISTS. Stamp sets, which are produced by the Philatelic Bureau in Avarua, are a major source of revenue.

SPORTS. Fishing, golf, horseracing, horseback riding, lawn bowls, sailing and skin diving,

The Cook Islands Sports Association, Box 440, Rarotonga, welcomes all sportsmen who may wish to participate in activities. They can make arrangements for teams who would like to visit.

The Deep Sea Fishing Club welcomes visitors and offers advice and facilities to them. Visitors who want to see the capture of flying fish (maroro) can see them being netted at night in outrigger canoes equipped with bright lights. Arrangements are made through local tour agencies. (During certain phases of the moon only.)

Rarotonga Sailing Club at Muri Beach is open to tourists from noon to 6 P.M. daily, except Sunday, for snacks and cold beer. Anything that floats is for hire.

Rarotonga Marine Zoo amenities range from an "oceanarium" to lagoon scuba diving lessons for beginners, from the famed Piri Puruto running up coconut palms to barbecues and cold beer.

HOLIDAYS. All government offices, banks, and most private offices are closed —sometimes on the day before and after, too.

Cook Islands. January 1—New Year's Day: Horse races at Muri Beach. Evening dances and floor shows.

Good Friday: Special church services throughout the islands.

Easter Monday: Horse racing at Muri Beach as well as various sporting activities, evening dances and floor shows.

August 4—Constitution Day: Commences with formal ceremony and parade of uniformed organizations. Day ends with formal State Ball.

October 26—Gospel Day: Commemorates arrival of first missionaries. Features all day open-air religious plays.

December 25—Christmas Day: Special church services. Main shops closed but village stores open. December 26—Boxing Day: Horse races at Muri Beach. Dancing and entertainment at night. Main stores closed but village shops open.

TONGA & NIUE

A Taste of Simple South Seas Life

When you land at Tonga's single strip international airfield on a rainy day, you wonder why you came. Puddles and slush. Your camera case, baggage, and shoes grow green mould in the customs queue. Battered and rusty old cars. Hard-up but cheerful and handsome people.

But disembark from a cruise liner on a sunny day on a common in front of the royal palace and you wonder why you didn't come years before to be among a happy, never-colonised Polynesian people who probably resemble the Hawaiians before the Americans came, the Tahitians before the French came, the Samoans before the Germans came, and the Maori before the British came.

The Only Island Monarchy

Proud poor Tonga is a political freak, the last of the Polynesian kingdoms. Two centuries ago, the crowned heads of Europe recognised as fellow monarchs the kings or queens of Hawaii, Tahiti, Samoa, the Cook Islands, Tonga and, on the fringes of Polynesia, Fiji. Now, the only remnant of the island monarchies is the royal family of Tonga. It has been ruling for 1,000 years.

Tonga is the only Polynesian or Melanesian territory that has never been colonised. This is partly good luck. It lacked riches comparable to the nickel of New Caledonia and the pastures of New Zealand. It had no "coaling station" comparable to Pago Pago.

Now, in the 1980's, this means that Tonga is not on the conscience of any imperialist power, past or present. But aid, especially in creating an international airport, is promised from sources as diverse as Japan, the USSR, Libya, Taiwan and the EEC.

Tonga is poor because the world market for her main crops, coconuts and bananas, is erratic and because her population increases at a rate of

3.6 percent a year—more than twice the world average. There are few jobs for the young when they leave school and only a trickle of Tongans are permitted entry by New Zealand.

Tahitians and New Caledonians may migrate anywhere within the still vast French Community. American Samoans may come and go within the United States. Western Samoans, as former New Zealand subjects, have limited access to New Zealand. Cook Islanders have unrestricted access to New Zealand. Tongans are cooped up at home. The fact is profoundly demoralising to an energetic people who find diminishing outlet at home for their energies.

Tonga—On the Map at Last

The western world suddenly became Tonga-conscious in 1953 while watching the televised coronation of Queen Elizabeth II of Great Britain. Following the British Queen, the star of the outdoor procession was the portly, smiling Queen Salote of Tonga (now deceased). She rode in an open carriage through drenching rain, graciously acknowledging Londoners' cheers on all sides.

Subsequently, through two decades of student and social unrest in the west, it was fashionable to depict Queen Salote's kingdom as an enviable repository of traditional values, a happy and stable society which painlessly had grafted Christianity onto a sort of primitive feudalism-beneath-the-coconuts.

An Economic Bind

That was a pretty picture which the world seemed to need. It was substantiated in a way by a century-old constitution which guaranteed to every Tongan male reaching 16 a lifetime title to eight and a quarter acres of farmland and a fifth of an acre within village or town for a home. When this advanced scheme was introduced a century ago, Tonga's population was 25,000. Now, thanks to modern medicine and freedom from war, it is more than 98,000. So Tonga has run out of land. That would not matter so much if its people could emigrate.

Also, the "cosy kingdom" image was dispelled between the end of Queen Salote's long reign and the introduction of air transport which made it possible for large numbers of young Tongans to meet nearby New Zealand's need for a short-term brown proletariat at that time. The transient Tongans benefitted both themselves and the Tongan economy by sending home part of their high earnings from menial jobs. But they returned home—sometimes literally bundled to the airport by police— aware of the sharp disparity between the high living standards generated by a leisurely existence in New Zealand and the enduring poverty that resulted from a life of drudgery in Tonga.

In the newer democracies of Polynesian or Melanesian societies, an aggrieved community could attain political remedy or action. But Tonga is feudal. Tonga has 33 "nobles" (English translation) who elect 7 of their parliament's 14 members. The remaining 7 are elected by the 90,000 commoners, which means that each "noble" has more than 2,000 times the political clout of a commoner. The King may also add any number of ministers he chooses to the cabinet. In addition, the establishment of trade unions is illegal. The result? The young men of Tonga are restless.

Tonga's present King, Taufa Ahau Tupou IV, son of Queen Salote, holds a law degree from Sydney University. Despite his 308 pounds (he normally books two adjacent seats in a commercial aircraft), he is hyperactive, both mentally and physically, and attempts ceaselessly to promote the economy of Tonga abroad. The obstacles, however, are formidable.

The Sabbath Is Sacred

A key clause in the Tongan Constitution of 1875 reads: "The Sabbath Day shall be sacred in Tonga forever and it shall not be lawful to work, artifice, or play games, or trade on the Sabbath." Tonga's Order in Public Places Act reads, in part: "Whoever shall do any work on the Sabbath day, such as engaging in any trade or the purchase or trade of any goods or chattels, house-building, boat-building, gardening, fishing, or conveying anything by boat or wagon, except in cases of emergency, and whoever shall discharge a firearm in the town or country or engage in game such as cricket, football, lawn tennis, golf, bowls, or similar games and dancing, lakalakas, and such pastimes shall be liable to fine not exceeding ten dollars or be imprisoned with hard labor for not more than three months in default of payment."

Avoid Tonga on Sunday might seem to be one valid piece of advice. But many tourists in Tonga have found themselves agreeably reminded of the quiet Sabbath of their youth in the small towns of America. Those who have taken the advice of hotel staff and gone to church—Wesleyan, Catholic, Episcopalian, Adventist, Mormon—for the beauty of the singing, the spiritual experience, or whatever they might seek, are liable to be invited home to lunch by a Tongan family. This will be a beautiful meal, gracefully served by people who are by western standards poor but who enjoy and offer bounties of the spirit.

The Tongan "Loop"

A curious by-product of the Tongan passion for observance of the Sabbath is the dilemma of the Seventh Day Adventist Church there, publicized in the late 1970's. The church says it is troubled and puzzled by a loop around Tonga that puts Tonga west of the international date line, despite the fact that Tonga lies east of the 180th meridian and is almost due south of Samoa. Yet it is a day ahead of Samoa. Thus, the SDA's, as they are known respectfully in the South Pacific, assert that Sunday in Tonga is really Saturday, that they are pained to attend church on what is really Sunday, and that they cannot find in international law any validity for the Tongan loop.

Irksome enforcement of the Sabbath law affecting tourists can range from being ordered out of the sea when swimming to being refused permission to remove one's own baggage from an inter-island government passenger ship. There is no public transport into, out of, or within Tonga on Sunday. You might want to visit a friend in hospital, only to learn that it is illegal to hire a taxi on the Sabbath. Yet the roads are busy with the private cars of the Tongan "nobles." However, this happens only one day a week.

It can be said that, while Tonga escaped colonisation, it was victimised by Wesleyan missionaries who are a lasting embarrassment to modern adherents of that now liberal faith. In 1831, Tonga's top chief, Tupou, and his wife were baptized by Wesleyans from Sydney under the names of George and Salote (Polynesian rendering of Charlotte, consort of the then reigning British King George III). As King George I of Tonga, Tupou created the "modern" Christian state with the Cross dominating its flag, and with the rigorous constitutional clause regulating observation of the Sabbath. Late in life, this same King George I of Tonga permitted himself to be dominated by a so-called missionary, the Rev. Shirley Waldemar Baker. Baker came from Sydney in 1860. By the time Britain (which enjoyed an inert "protectorate") engineered his deportation to New Zealand in 1890, he had been Premier, Foreign Affairs Minister, President of the Court of Appeal, Auditor-General, Minister of Lands, Minister of Education, and Medical Adviser to His Majesty. After a 10 year exile, during which a British Colonial Office troubleshooter patched up Tonga's ravaged finances, Baker returned as a lay reader licenced by the Anglican Bishop of Auckland. After he died in 1903 his children raised a statue in his memory that remains the largest monument in Tonga.

Niue, Newest Hideaway

Niue (pronounced new-ay, rhyming with day) is a 100-square-mile cliff-ringed coral island in the southwest Pacific, 300 miles east of Tonga, 350 miles south of the Samoas and 580 miles west of the Cook Islands. Its people are friendly English-speaking Polynesians, akin to Hawaiians, Tahitians, Samoans, Tongans and Maoris. Until recently it was a colony of New Zealand and is still closely linked to and dependent on New Zealand.

Niue is one of the diminishing number of safe, friendly and readily accessible islands that offer the traveler a taste of the simple South Seas' life of other days.

It is reached by scheduled air services from Western Samoa by the Western Samoan flag-carrier, Polynesian Airlines.

Niue has one hotel, the 20-room Niue, which costs only US$17 double but has swimming pool, nine-hole golf course, grass tennis courts, big game fishing (tuna, swordfish, Spanish mackerel), skin-diving off coral reefs and swimming in deep reef pools, and a twice-weekly cabaret-bar. The new Hinemata motel costs only US$7.50 double.

Local delicacies include ugu (coconut crab) and all tropical fruits. Specialties at Bob Rex's Crab Inn restaurant include island fish cooked with taro, breadfruit, and yam in an earth-oven. Owned by the Premier's son. And visitors are welcome at the well-appointed golf club's weekly bash.

PRACTICAL INFORMATION FOR TONGA

FACTS AND FIGURES. Tonga's total land area is 269 square miles (697 sq. kms.), covering a total sea area of 100,000 square miles (259,000 sq. kms.). Population is estimated at 98,000. The name of the capital, Nukualofa, meaning Land of Love, was chosen by King George Tupou I and is assumed to have its origin in Capt. James Cook's designation of the Tongan islands as the *Friendly Islands.*

HOW TO GET AROUND. *By air:* Local flights are provided by South Pacific Island Airways and Tonga Air.
Car rentals: Gateway Rental, Mr. Paul Fukukofuka, P.O. Box 596, Nukualofa, Tonga.

Inter-island ferries: They are small but you need have no qualms. For centuries, Tongans have been superb sailors.

TOURIST INFORMATION SERVICES. Tongan Visitors' Bureau, Box 37, Nuku'alofa, Tonga. It is worth writing for a copy of their free leaflet *Tonga Handicrafts.*

CURRENCY. Tonga's currency unit is the pa'anga, equivalent at press time to US$0.67. Credit cards not accepted except for American Express at the Dateline.

HOLIDAYS. All government offices, banks, and most private offices are closed —sometimes on the day before and after, too.

January 1—New Year's Day.

Easter—Magnificent choral singing.

April 25—Anzac Day: Military parade.

May 4—Birthday of Crown Prince Tupouto'a: Military parade, at which the Crown Prince is the reviewing officer. This ceremony is held at Mala'e Pangai. Mid-May–Red Cross Week and Grand Ball.

June 4—Emancipation Day: Honors Tonga's unity under one King. Also commemorates Tonga joining the Commonwealth in 1970. July 4—Birthday and Coronation Day of His Majesty King Taufa'ahau Tupou IV: A military parade is held at the mala'e pangai, at which His Majesty is the reviewing officer.

Late August—Royal Agricultural Shows, tropical county fairs, on all main islands; attended by the King.

November 4—Constitution Day: In 1875 King George Tupou first established the Tongan constitution, modeled on the British constitution.

December 4—King Tupou I's Birthday: Tongans celebrate birthday of country's first king.

December 25—Christmas Day: Tongans, ardently Christian, celebrate this season like no other, and it is a time for visiting relations and friends.

TOURS. Mostly by car and boat. On outer islands, tourists are still expected to use horses, "unschooled" and without saddles. Obviously not for beginners.

Goodtravel Tours, 5332 College Avenue, Oakland, California 94618. Specializes in tours that focus on music, dance and traditional culture. Write direct for itineraries and costs.

Shipping Corp of Polynesia, Warner Pacific Lines, and private ferries provide regular interisland service between Nuku'alofa and several Tongan islands.

Mamafa'o Enterprises, P.O. Box 229, Nukualofa, Tonga. Can arrange all types of tours: visits to plantations, villages, small islands for day picnics and swimming, Tongan feasts with entertainment, handicraft center. Individual or group tours. Accommodations also arranged.

South Pacific Island Airways, offers regular flights four times weekly between Pago Pago, Vava'u, Ha'apai, 'Eua and Nuku'alofa-Vava'u and Nuku'alofa-Ha'apai. Planes are also available for charter and air sightseeing trips.

South Seas Travel, P.O. Box 581, Nuku'alofa, offers wide variety of local tours.

Tonga Air. Scheduled and charter services to the islands of 'Eua, Ha'apai and Vava'u.

South Pacific Yacht Charter, at Neiafu, Vava'u, has a 44-ft. yacht, fully-equipped, sleeping 6 adults, ideal for visiting small islands. It can be skippered by charterer if certified, or skipper provided. Day charter (for up to six), US$300.

WHAT TO SEE. *Royal palace and chapel.* The residence of the King of Tonga, His Majesty King Taufa'ahau Tupou IV. The timber palace was built in 1867 and enlarged slightly in 1882 when the royal chapel was added. The coronations of the last three monarchs took place in the chapel.

Royal tombs. Near the middle of town, where Tongan royalty has been buried since 1893. By modern standards, the statuary is impressive.

Flying foxes. In a grove at Kolovai village, 11 miles (18 kms.) from the capital, thousands of flying foxes hang head downwards all day like fruit from trees.

Blow holes. Nine miles (14 kms.) from the capital, along a wildly rocky terraced coast, ocean rollers send water spouting 60 ft. high through narrow apertures. The stretch of coast is called the chiefs' whistle. Go at high tide.

Ha'amonga Trilithon. Tonga's 'Stonehenge'. Erected about 1200 A.D., it comprises two upright coral slabs 16 ft. high topped by a horizontal connecting slab 19 ft. long, each stone weighing 40 tons. Tonga's King, a scholarly man, believes he has found their purpose—a seasonal calendar. Notches carved on the lintel point directly to the rising sun on the longest and shortest days of the year.

Haleluliku caves. Underground caves of stalactites and stalagmites through which a deep river flows. Near the village of Haleluliku, 13 miles (21 kms.) from Nukualofa.

Oholei Beach. White sand at the foot of sheer limestone cliffs. Good swimming. Showers and toilets. Ask at the Dateline Hotel for traditional night feasting and entertainment in a great natural amphitheatre formed from an old blowhole. This is on Wednesday and Friday nights and is conceivably the best beach barbecue offered to tourists anywhere. It is simple; suckling pig is the main offering. The band plays from a torch-lit platform up an ancient tree. The dance-and-song show is in the cave, which has remarkable acoustics.

Nuku Island, 75 minutes by boat from Nuku'alofa. A major new resort is being created here by a New Zealand developer.

CLIMATE. Marginally cooler than most tropical areas. Temperatures range from 60–70°F (16–21°C) in June–July to 80°F (27°C) in December–January, with mean humidity 77 percent. Mean rainfall is 70 inches.

Average Temperature (°Fahrenheit) and Humidity

Nuku'alofa	Jan	Feb	Mar	Apr	May	June	July	Aug	Sept	Oct	Nov Dec
Average max. day temperature	83°	84°	83°	82°	79°	78°	76°	76°	76°	78	80°	82°
Days of Rain	17	17	20	15	14	12	12	12	12	12	12	14
Humidity, Percent	76	78	79	77	74	74	72	72	71	70	71	73

General hints: Best tourist months are May through November. Heavy rains begin in December and last through March; humidity is high in this period. It's a good idea to have a sweater along for the cool July and August evenings.

SHOPPING. The most convenient and duty free shopping is at the International Dateline Hotel, at the airport and at A3Z radio shop at Nukualofa. But the fine artifacts of Tonga may be bought freely all over the kingdom, often from those who have made them. Tongan tapa cloth, mats, and basketware, woven from pandanus and coconut fibres, are distinctive and of consistently high craftsmanship. Tongan tapa is firm and flexible, and durable as wall, table, or even bed covering. But to collectors, the tapa's chief attraction is its warm tones. There are two main decorative styles. In one, the design is painted in bold freehand on the off-white raw tapa cloth. In the other, it is "printed" on the tapa by either preparing a large "block," 5 ft. by 4 ft., in wood, with a formal design boldly incised on it, or the design can be formed by sewing together dried pandanus leaves and then sewing coconut leaf midribs over them to form a somewhat fragile block. Tapa cloth is spread over the wooden or leaf block and its surface is gently rubbed with coconut-husk fibres, lightly impregnated with natural vegetable dyes to produce the imprint of the design in much the manner of ancient tombstone "rubbings" in England. The tapa decorator then goes over the whole piece again, brushing in by hand more definitely those parts of the design which are to be accentuated, using a darker, more glossy pigment in dark brown or even black.

Pay particular attention in Tonga to the fine woven floor coverings.

Ask also to see the snowwhite bleached pandanus To'a vala pandanus mat with fringed pandanus edge, with no design, intended as a girdle for ceremonial occasions.

Other Tongan artifacts, all fine, include table mats, linen baskets, Ali Baba laundry baskets (Air Pacific advertises that it takes particular care of Ali Babas in its freight compartments), woven sandwich and bread trays, goblets and ashtrays from polished coconut shell, and model outrigger canoes.

Women interested in the making of Tongan artifacts should, in the first hours of their stay, ask at the hotel to be put in touch with the Langa Fonua, a women's organisation under royal patronage which keeps alive the ancient crafts and has its own retailing centers.

The seas around Tonga are virtually forested with black coral, increasingly rare in the rest of the Pacific. Coral Head Diving can take divers to the seabed. In Nukualofa visit the workshop of Imua Pacifica, where a small pendant costs the price of a bottle of beer.

 HOTELS AND MOTELS. Rates for double rooms can be classified as follows: *Expensive,* T$40 and up; *Moderate,* T$30–39; *Inexpensive,* below T$30.

Nuku Island Resort. *Expensive.* 1¼ hours from Nuku'alofa.

International Dateline Hotel. *Moderate.* 76 air-conditioned rooms. Nightly entertainment. Swimming pool, duty-free shop, P.O. Box 39, Nuku'alofa.

Paradise International Hotel. *Moderate.* On the island of Vava'u, an international hotel and beach resort. All 38 units are Tongan fales. Air-conditioned, dining room, cocktail lounge, boutique, Tongan entertainment. Fishing boats, excursion boats, bicycles, horses, skin diving. Club Med-like package of accommodations plus sailboats, windsurfers, scuba and mopeds. P.O. Box 11, Neiafu, Vavau.

Pangaimotu Island, *Moderate.* 2 kms from the captial and 15 minutes by boat, offers 32 acres of escape territory. Good swimming and snorkeling. All meals included.

Ramanlal Hotel. *Moderate.* Downtown. Efficiency units. Disco. P.O. Box 74, Nuku'alofa.

Captain Cook's Vacation Apartments. *Inexpensive.* On Nuku'alofa waterfront, six fully self-contained two-bedroom apartments. Canteen, postal services, laundry. P.O. Box 838, Nuku'alofa.

Fafa. *Inexpensive.* An excellent new resort, 35 minutes from Nuku'alofa by daily ferry. Sailing, windsurfing, swimming and diving. Remarkable (for the South Pacific) cellar of international wines. Outstanding German and Polynesian cuisine (try cold avocado-and-onion soup). International dialing telephone in the bar.

Friendly Islander Motel. *Inexpensive.* Immaculate. 3 kms from downtown. 12 modern suites with bath, kitchen, private balcony, small swimming pool, radio and telephone. Lounge room by pool. Tonga's only squash court. Weekly and monthly rates. P.O. Box 142, Nuku'alofa, Tonga.

Nukuma'Anu Motel. *Inexpensive.* 2 kms from downtown along the waterfront. Individual fales (cottages) containing one, two or three bedrooms. Kitchen. Monthly rates on request. P.O. Box 290, Nuku'alofa.

Stowaway Village *Inexpensive.* On Vava'u island, 12 rooms in four Tongan-style houses, each house with bath. Boats and bikes to rent. P.O. Box 5, Neiafu, Vava'u.

Accommodations are proliferating fast on Tongatapu and the smaller islands. Contact the Tonga Visitors' Bureau, P.O. Box 37, Nuku'alofa, Tonga.

Boardinghouses are popular among tourists, both for great economy and for the opportunity to live comfortably and simply. Typical is **Sela's Guest House,** 20 minutes' walk from Nuku'alofa center. Five double rooms and 7 single. Charming 40-ish Sela is the wife of Tonga Development Bank accountant Atolo Tu'inu-kuafe, who helps run the small shiplike operation. A typical meal includes fonu (grilled turtle), feke (grilled octopus or squid) in coconut sauce, devilled clams, 'ota (raw fish marinated in lemon juice), lobster, avocado salad and tropical fruit. The price, including all meals is T$20 per person, per day.

 NIGHTCLUBS AND DINING OUT. Tonga being a puritan society, the night scene has been sedate. Tonga's Beautiful People dance in the pleasant nightclub of the International Dateline. But the jumping place is the disco at the new Indian Ramanlal Hotel. Establishment of diplomatic relations with Taiwan has led to sudden appearance of two serious Chinese restaurants, the Tonga Hua and the Hua-Hua. Potato pancakes are an unexpected special at the German-managed restaurant on top of Joe's Tropicana Hotel. Sea View Restaurant, in an old sea-front bungalow near the Royal Palace, specialises in seafood. Twenty miles out of town, Good Samaritan Inn, run by two Frenchmen, offers Tahiti-quality meals and superb swimming. Farther along the same road is Australian-run Ha'atafu Beach Motel, whose good restaurant overlooks a Tongan rarity—a good surfing beach.

Precaution: Appearing shirtless in public is an offense against the law.

HOW TO GET THERE. *By air:* South Pacific Island Airways from Honolulu via Pago Pago; Air New Zealand, Polynesian Airlines, and Air Pacific from Auckland; Air Pacific from Suva; Air New Zealand and Polynesian Airlines from Apia.

By sea: Royal Viking Lines and P & O Cruises have ports of call at Nuku'alofa. See also "Planning Your Trip."

FIJI ISLANDS

Crossroads of the South Pacific

by
JAMES TULLY

James Tully is Pacific Affairs correspondent of the Auckland Star, New Zealand. *He has travelled widely in the South Pacific, and visited Fiji several times. He studied the region in depth when obtaining his postgraduate degree in history at Auckland University.*

A cluster of tropical islands straddling the 180° meridian, 1100 miles south of the equator, Fiji is usually portrayed as a Pacific paradise—an ideal destination for the traveler seeking an escape from urban civilization.

Fiji, the tourist cliché continues, is a sun-drenched land of unpolluted, uncrowded islands with friendly people and the bonus of duty-free shopping.

Seasoned travelers usually dismiss the rhapsodic descriptions of travel agents, but the proof of the publicity is in the visiting.

With Fiji the cliché is remarkably accurate. But of course, there is far more to this fast-developing mini-state at the crossroads of the South Pacific.

Fiji is an archipelago of more than 300 islands, ranging from tiny coral atolls and rugged limestone islets, to the two islands of Viti Levu and Vanua Levu which together comprise 6/7 of the group's total area of 7022 sq miles. About 105 islands are inhabited.

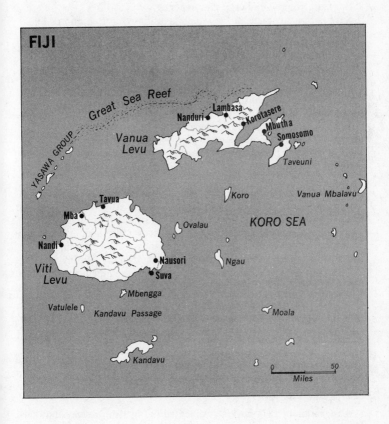

The group lies on the main North American air route to Australia and New Zealand, 3,183 miles from Honolulu and 5,611 from San Francisco. Suva, the capital, is 1,960 miles by air from Sydney to the southwest and 1,317 miles from Auckland to the south.

Most of Fiji's 700,000 (approximate) live on the coasts, especially in and around the capital Suva, and the other sugar-producing towns. Sugar is the main commercial crop and export.

Suva is the only place in Fiji which gives the visitor an impression of urban bustle, with its busy docks, light industrial zone and thriving shopping centre. With a population of about 175,000 the Suva-Nausori urban area is home to just over one-fifth of the total population.

It is mainly in the towns that the visitor can see the ethnic variety of Fiji society. There are powerfully built Fijians dressed in wrap-around sulus, numerous Indians, men in Western clothes, women in colourful saris, and a scattering of Europeans, Chinese and other Pacific Islanders.

Fijian legend tells of the great chief Lutunasobasoba leading his people across the seas to the new land of Fiji. Most authorities agree that this handsome race of Melanesians came into the Pacific from South-East Asia via the Indonesian islands. Pre-colonial contact with neighbouring Tonga resulted in an admixture of Polynesian blood and attitudes.

The islands were discovered gradually by European seafarers over a period of about 300 years. The Dutch explorer Abel Tasman sighted islands and reefs in the Fiji group in 1643, and English navigators, including Captain James Cook in 1774, discovered others. Most of the credit for the European discovery of the islands goes to Captain William Bligh, who sailed through the group after the Bounty Mutiny in 1789.

European contact increased steadily through the nineteenth century: traders in search of sandalwood, settlers in search of land, missionaries in search of souls. The rapid conversion of the Cannibal Isles to a gentle and generous Christianity was a miracle of missionary endeavour.

Because of the unstable conditions of life, a British consul was appointed in 1857 to aid the traders and missionaries in Fiji. Seventeen years later the islands were voluntarily ceded to Great Britain, which continued to administer them until independence in October 1970.

The Alien Majority

Annexation in 1874 not only cemented the British presence, but heralded an era of migration that was to change the nature of Fiji society profoundly.

When the first Australian and British planters sought labour for their cotton and sugar plantations they found that Fijians had no wish for money and no relish for labour other than tribal enterprises.

By the 1860s the growth of the plantation economy had created a demand for man-power that outstripped supply. The solution was to import labour; mainly from the New Hebrides and the Gilbert Islands, until the British Government forcibly disapproved of "blackbirding". Fiji's first governor, Sir Arthur Gordon, took the initiative after 1874 by introducing contracted labour from India.

Under contract, Indians were imported to Fiji as "coolies", with a right to repatriation to India. Only a third of the 62,837 Indians imported between 1879 and 1916 elected to return home.

In 1923 there were only 39,000 Indians in Fiji, but with free migration until the 1930s, and a high birth rate, they outnumbered Fijians by 1946. Today they make up just over half the population.

Indians form the majority in the towns and dominate commercial and professional life. The nation's shopkeepers, taxi-drivers, importers, lawyers and doctors are mostly of Indian descent. In the country they produce most of the sugar cane and rice, on land leased from Fijians. Indians own only about 2% of the freehold land available in Fiji.

Though some of the age-old customs remain, particularly in rural areas—marriages may still be arranged by the parents—the migration to Fiji brought changes in the Indian community. The Hindu caste system was shed, and women were freed from many restrictions hallowed by custom and religion.

To speak of Indian culture in Fiji implies the existence of a subcontinent of India. All the provinces are represented. Ten Indian dialects are still recognised. There are Hindus, Muslims, Sikhs and Christians.

There is little inter-marriage between Fijians and Indians and, generally speaking the two races do not mix socially, yet race relations have been harmonious since independence.

Fire-walking: A Double Act

It is an odd coincidence that two races—one indigenous, the other "imported"—should both practise the rare rite of fire-walking.

Fijian fire-walking arises from a belief in a legendary spirit god who passed on the gift of resisting heat to the Sawau tribesmen, who live in four villages on the southern side of Beqa Island, just off the main island of Viti Levu. It is said that only the Sawau people can walk on the white hot stones with impunity—but the tribe has been known to adopt outsiders who have been able to perform the ceremony successfully.

Visitors can see the men of Sawau walk bare-footed over stones heated by an enormous log fire at special occasions on Beqa Island, or at several hotels on the Coral Coast.

The Fijian fire-walking has its origin in legend, but Indian fire-walking is done for religious reasons. Trial by fire is regarded as a cleansing of the spirit, and the ceremony is the climax of a 10-day ritual practised by the Madrasis sect of the Hindu religion.

During the ceremonies held by the followers of *Maha Devi* (the Divine Mother) all are clad in yellow. Devotees selected to walk on the hot coals daub their faces with vermilion dye and yellow turmeric powder which they consider a symbol of prosperity and power to destroy disease. Their bodies are pierced with needles and skewers. The fire-walking is preceded by 10 days abstinence.

Young children are sometimes carried through the fire in the arms of devotees to satisfy vows taken by their parents when the children fall seriously ill.

It is only fairly recently that tourists have been invited to attend the ceremonies, usually held in August. Although admission charges are made "in keeping with the spirit of the times" the ritual remains, for the devotees of Maha Devi, a religious penance and not merely a tourist attraction.

Kava Drinking

Throughout Fiji—and also in most parts of Polynesia—the drinking of *Yaqona* (pronounced Yanggona), or Kava is a common ceremonial and social custom.

Yaqona is made from the root of the pepper plant. In the past the drink was prepared by the young maidens of a village, who chewed the pieces of root into a soft pulpy mass before water was added. Today the root is pounded in a pestle and mortar, or ground to powder by a machine. After the addition of the water, the gritty pieces of root are strained by passing the liquid through a bundle of vegetable fibre.

The Yaqona ceremony is still important in the Fijian way of life but has also become a social drink. *Yaqona* drinking is very common in Fijian villages, and it is usual for the men to gather round the kava bowl *(tanoa)* and swap yarns as the astringent liquid is passed around in the *bilo,* a half coconut shell.

In old Fiji, birth, marriage and death all called for correct ceremonies; as did installation of chiefs, welcoming important visitors, and launching of canoes.

The ceremony is performed by the hosts, and the *yaqona* mixed in the presence of the guest of honour is presented in a complicated ritual. This ceremony is not performed indiscriminately by Fijians and cannot be regarded as a spectacle. Not all visitors to Fiji are fortunate enough to see it. However, social drinking of *Yaqona* is very informal.

The Road Ahead

Fiji is the most populous and economically advanced of the South Pacific Island groups, and the most important communication centre.

Though a new figure on the world stage, Fiji has participated enthusiastically in the various international organizations to which it belongs—the Commonwealth, the United Nations, the South Pacific Forum, the South Pacific Conference, and the Lome Convention, which links it with the European Economic Community (Common Market). For six years a battalion from the Royal Fiji Military Forces served in Lebanon as part of the United Nations peace-keeping force.

Fiji is a parliamentary democracy with an elected House of Representatives (Lower House) and an appointed Senate (Upper House). The Senate's general purpose is to review legislation from the Lower House, and it has one particularly important power as far as the Fijian people are concerned—to adjudicate matters involving their land.

The complicated electoral system is designed to ensure a racial balance and guarantee the status of Fijians as the original inhabitants of a country where they are outnumbered.

Fiji's first and only Prime Minister is Ratu Sir Kamisese Mara, a hereditary chief, educated at Oxford University in England. A Catholic of 65 yrs. with six children, he is a scholarly statesman of world stature who has personally guided Fiji into nation-hood.

Ratu Mara's Alliance Government was actually defeated in the April 1977 elections. But the Governor-General re-appointed him Prime Minister because he felt Ratu Mara was the man best able to command a majority in the House after an election which saw the mainly Indian National Federation Party win 26 seats to the Alliance's 24. At a new election in September 1977 the Alliance swept back to power with 36 seats. They were reelected in July 1982.

Fiji's economic growth has centred on agriculture, chiefly sugar, and tourism. More than 400,000 tons of sugar are harvested each year. The government-owned Fiji Sugar Company crushes the cane and partly refines it for export. Tourism is the other principal earner of overseas funds-F$161 million in 1984. In 1985 a record 250,000 visitors were expected.

Coconuts, grown for their oil and copra content, are the next most important crop, followed by cocoa and ginger.

Timber will be increasingly important to the Fijian economy. A scheme to plant more than 180,000 acres with pine is under way, and the production of wood chips, pulp and timber is expected to become the third major export earner.

Fiji has for many years been a small producer of gold at the Emperor Mine at Vatakoula on the north coast of Viti Levu.

Fiji's development plans have put great emphasis on rural development in an attempt to reduce the drift to the towns where there is insufficient work for the unskilled. The Government hopes that better health and educational facilities and electrification will encourage people to stay on the land. The new five-year plan is also directed at rural development and includes measures to open up large areas of land which are still inaccessible and largely unused.

A hydro-electric power project in the highlands of Viti Levu is greatly reducing Fiji's reliance on imported fuel.

Exploring Fiji

Nadi International Airport on the west coast of Viti Levu is the gateway to Fiji. This is an area of dry hills, sweeping plateaus and mountains. The feeling of being in the tropics is strongest on the shoreline where palm trees sway. The rainfall on this the "dry" side of the island is about 60 inches annually, half that of the eastern side.

Not far from the airport are a dozen or so first-class hotels. Duty-free shops lining Nadi's main street are the only real attraction for the tourist. But Lautoka, 20 miles to the north, is of more interest. Fiji's second largest city and port is the setting-off point for several small island resorts, and cruises to the almost untouched Yasawa Group.

Life is casual on the island resorts off Nadi and Lautoka. Visitors stay in Fijian-style thatched or tile-roofed *bures*. There are white sand beaches for sunning and swimming. The calm waters behind the coral reefs offshore are safe for diving and snorkeling.

Beachcomber Island, just five sandy acres, is the most informal of the resorts and is popular with the younger set. Other resorts include Plantation Island, Treasure Island, Castaway Island, Club Naitasi, Mana Island, and Musket Cove.

Viti Levu is circled by a 317-mile road. The part running westwards from Suva to Lautoka is called Queen's Road, and the other section King's Road.

Heading from Nadi to Suva 132 miles away, you will immediately notice that you are in the sugar belt. The tall green cane stretches for miles. Narrow railway lines take trucks laden with cut cane to the huge sugar mill at Lautoka.

A little way out of Nadi there is a rough winding road that climbs into the Nausori Highlands from which there are arresting views of the south-west coast of Viti Levu.

Forty miles from Nadi is Sigatoka, market centre for the fertile Sigatoka Valley. A 33 mile gravel road follows the meandering river upstream past scallop-shaped river flats chequered with crops. There are large terrace forts on the valley sides.

Beyond Sigatoka the road hugs the so-called "Coral Coast". This 60-mile stretch of white sand beaches has been developed into a major resort area, with almost a third of Fiji's hotel beds.

Of special interest is the Pacific Harbour Development, a "leisure-oriented satellite town" 30 miles from Suva. In this Mediterranean-type resort, the first of its kind in the South Pacific, you may own or rent a villa. There is an 18-hole, par-72 championship golf course, the only one in the South Pacific to be fully irrigated and offer electric golf carts.

Nearby is Navua, a sleepy riverside town from which you can cruise upriver, through rapids, to a Fijian village.

By now you are in the wet belt around Suva and the open grasslands have become thick forest and evergreen grass. Heavy black rain-bellied clouds seem always to be overhead.

A mixture of old colonial and brash eighties, Suva sits on a point jutting into Laucala Bay: a busy port, thriving commercial centre, and focus of government.

The downtown shopping area has dozens of duty-free shops with electrical gear, cameras, hi-fi sets, perfumes, jewelry, sports equipment.

For a more peaceful atmosphere there are the museum and botanic gardens in the domain next to Government House, home of the Governor-General. The museum has an excellent collection of Fijian artifacts including pottery fragments from sand dunes at the mouth of the Sigatoka River dated as being about 2000 years old.

The University of the South Pacific, sited on what was once an air force base at Laucala Bay, is a regional educational centre for the South Pacific. Students from many island groups study there.

Five miles from Suva is Orchid Island; an island in a river with extensive collections of tropical plants as well as plots of coffee, tea and vanilla. Fauna includes mongoose, rare iguanas, monkeys and local snakes.

Seven miles from Suva is Colo-I-Suva forest park with its nature walks, picnic areas and swimming holes in Waisila Creek.

A short hop by air takes you from Suva to Ovalau Island, where you can visit the historic town of Levuka—the original capital of Fiji.

The King's Road passes through Nausori—site of Suva's airport—and heads north-east up the coast to Korovou, where the road branches through Lodoni to Natovi, where a ferry service to Ovalau operates. Or you can cut inland from Korovou to Vunidawa on the Rewa River.

King's Road continues around the island to Rakiraki, Tavua and Ba before joining Queen's Road at Lautoka. Two roads branch off at Tavua Bay—one to the timber-milling highlands of Nadarivatu, the other to the gold-mining town of Vatakoula.

Vanua Levu and Taveuni

The great appeal of the accessible outer islands, Vanua Levu and Taveuni, is their peace and beautiful scenery.

The main villages on Vanua Levu are Savusau, in the south, and Labasa, in the north. In between are coconut plantations, tropical vegetation and a mountain tableland.

Labasa (population 5,200) is the busier of the two, with its market and sugar mill. Vanua Levu's major road goes south from Labasa to Nabouwala at the island's southernmost point.

Savusavu is a sleepy little town of 1,800 people and a handful of shops. A good road called the "Hibiscus Highway" travels east to Karoko via Buca Bay, where there is swimming and snorkeling.

Fiji's third largest island, Taveuni, is not on the main tourist trail. Visitors stay at the only hotel at Waiyevo. The 35-mile road that connects copra plantations takes the visitor through rural villages that have changed little in the last 100 years. Behind Waiyevo is a mountain with a small crater lake. The unique Tagimaucia flower is found only on the shores of this lake. Fuchsialike, the plant has bunches of red flowers with a white centre.

On the north end of Taveuni there are mysterious earth works of a large scale. The island is one of several areas in Fiji where there are rock carvings.

PRACTICAL INFORMATION FOR FIJI

FACTS AND FIGURES. Fiji is an independent sovereign state with a population of around 700,000 living on 105 of its 320 or more islands. More than 60% of its population is under 25 years of age. The capital is Suva.

Average Temperature (°Fahrenheit) and Humidity

Nadi	Jan	Feb	Mar	Apr	May	June	July	Aug	Sept	Oct	Nov	Dec
Average max. day temperature	88°	88°	87°	87°	85°	84°	83°	83°	84°	85°	86°	88°
Days of Rain	21	19	24	20	17	14	10	12	14	14	16	17
Humidity, Percent	75	78	80	80	77	79	76	71	69	66	67	69

Laucala Bay (Suva)	Jan	Feb	Mar	Apr	May	June	July	Aug	Sept	Oct	Nov	Dec
Average max. day temperature	86°	86°	86°	84°	82°	81°	79°	80°	80°	81°	83°	85°
Days of Rain	12	13	15	14	9	7	6	5	8	8	10	10
Humidity, Percent	81	81	83	82	80	81	79	78	79	78	78	79

General hints: Usually comfortable all year round. April through October are best tourist months. January through March is hot, humid and rainy with a chance of hail or hurricanes.

 HOW TO GET AROUND. *By air:* Air Pacific maintains a 30-minute shuttle service between Nadi and Suva's airport at Nausori. Typical fare with 20kgs of luggage is F$34.

Regular inter-island services are available with Air Pacific and Fiji Air. Fiji has more than 15 airports. In addition, Turtle Airways offers seaplane sightseeing and flights to island resorts. Tours by helicopter are operated by Pacific Crown Aviation. Sunflower Airlines services several centres from Nadi.

By road: Buses operate right round Viti Levu and on the other main islands, as well as town and suburban routes. Bus between Nadi and Suva is F$15 one way. Taxis and rental cars are readily available. Taxis are metered in towns and are required to carry a fare table for long distances. Visitors with a current domestic licence are eligible to drive in Fiji. Rental car agencies require a minimum deposit of the estimated rental charge. Petrol is extra. Rates vary from about F$15 to F$40 a day.

Fiji has about 1950 miles of roads, about 700 of them are all-weather.

By boat: Government and local shipping companies operate freight and passenger services linking the outer islands. Cruises to off-shore islands leave Nadi/Lautoka and Suva. Yachts and cabin cruisers are available for charter. Intending passengers on inter-island vessels should not expect luxury.

TOURIST INFORMATION. The Fiji Visitors Bureau head office is on Thompson St., Suva. Complete information about Fiji's activities, accommodation and travel services are available. Telephone Suva 22–867 or write P.O. Box 92 Suva. There is a visitors information booth at Nadi Airport.

Other Bureau offices are in Auckland, Box 1179; Sydney, 38–40 Martin Place (telephone 231–4251). North America: Fiji Consulate General Office, 3701 Wilshire Blvd., Los Angeles, CA 90010. Great Britain: Marketing Services (Travel and Tourism) Ltd., Suite 433, High Holborn House, 52–54 High Holborn, London WC1V 6RL (telephone 242 3131).

The Fiji Visitors Bureau produces brochures with reliable information to help you plan your holiday. A useful brochure is *Fiji Calls.*

Inquiries regarding hotel accommodation should be addressed to the Secretary, Fiji Hotel Association, P.O. Box 2001, Government Buildings, Suva.

CURRENCY. Fiji's unit of currency is the Fiji dollar. In June 1985, US$1 = F$1.18.

HOLIDAYS. All government offices, banks and most private offices are closed —sometimes on the day before and after, too. In 1984, the following were public holidays:

January 1—New Year's Day.

April 5–8—Easter Holidays.

June 17—Queen Elizabeth's Birthday, August 5–Bank Holiday; October 7—Fiji Day: Celebrations throughout the country; November 11—Prince Charles' Birthday; November 12—Diwali Festival.

November 25—Prophet Mohammad's Birthday: special day of prayer for all Muslims (usually in January).

December 25—Christmas Day: Feasts and special church services. Christmas carol programs. December 26—Boxing Day.

SEASONAL EVENTS. January-April—Cricket Season: Matches can be arranged for overseas touring teams.

March to **October**—Sports season: rugby, soccer, hockey, basketball. In **June/ July/August** there is fire-walking by Hindu followers of Maha Devi.

July—Bula Festival (Nadi).

August—First week Hibiscus Festival (Suva). A week of festivals with Fijians, Chinese, Indians and Polynesians presenting traditional entertainment. Sports events, youth rallies, fashion show, baby show, bands, marching girls and a procession of floats. Week ends with Hibiscus Ball and crowning of Miss Hibiscus.

First week Fiji Open Air New Zealand Golf Tournament over 72 holes.

September: Suva Orchard. Flower shows.

October—Trooping the Color by the 2nd Battalion Fiji Infantry Regiment: regiment troops its Queen's color before His Excellency the Governor General of Fiji. A very colorful ceremony staged in Albert Park: led by the Royal Fiji Military Forces Band, the troops march through the city of Suva. Monthly (first week)—Government House Guard Change Ceremony: The Royal Fiji Military Forces Band leads the new Guard in a march through the city of Suva terminating at Government House gates where the Changing of the Guard ceremony takes place.

October to November—Diwali Festival. "The Hindu Festival of the Lights" is preceded by an annual spring cleaning of houses by Hindus. Then oil lamps and coloured lights decorate the houses. Hindus celebrate the holy festival with devotion. Fasting is observed and prayers and offerings of sweets and fruits are given to Lakshmi the Goddess of Wealth.

TOURS. *Fiji: Islands in the Sun Fiji,* c/o John Holmes, P.O. Box 126, Ross, Ca. or P.O. Box 364, Lautoka, Fiji. Offers a variety of ways to discover the islands in the South Pacific. You can cruise from Lautoka to Treasure or Beachcomber Islands and stay in bure (island style) accommodations. Rates include all meals.

You can also explore the islands of Fiji on cruises. *Islands in the Sun Fiji* offers a three day/three-night cruise through the Mamanutha and Yasawa Island groups off Nadi Bay. Sails from Lautoka Saturdays and Wednesdays and costs from about F$275/person, including meals. The M. V. *Matthew Flinders* picks up passengers from Beachcomber and Treasure so visitors to Fiji can combine an island stay with a cruise. The three-day cruise is a relaxed, informal affair with opportunities to stop off at islands along the cruise route to swim, snorkel, explore caves or just plain relax on the deserted beaches.

A seven-day cruise by the recently launched, 54-metre, 66-passenger *Yasawa Princess* covers more ground and lingers longer in this island paradise.

Diver Service of Fiji Ltd., P.O. Box 502, Lautoka. Offers dive or snorkeling trips daily. Dive-gear hire and water-taxi service provided.

Oolooloo Cruises Ltd., P.O. Box 2034, Suva. The 3½-hour tour leaves from Suva daily at 9:30 A.M. Includes coral viewing, live coral and fish display, complimentary morning tea, stop at Tradewinds Hotel and Nukumarau Island. Time for swimming and basket weaving demonstration. Cost: F$13. Twilight cruise departs at 5:45 P.M., returns 9:15 P.M.; includes licensed bar, barbecue dinner entertainment. Cost: F$22.

Orchid Island-Fijian Cultural Centre, Dominion Development Corp., Ltd., P.O. Box 1018, Suva. Offers half-day tour by coach to Orchid Island. Opportunity to see Fijian history, culture and enjoy the Yaqona (kava drinking) ceremony.

Blue Lagoon Cruise: P.O. Box 54, Lautoka, offer four- and seven-day cruises to the Yasawa Islands and Vanua Levu departing daily from Lautoka. Three-day cruise from F$275 plus tax per person for twin berth; seven-day, F$575 plus tax.

Tropic Cruises (FIJI) Ltd., P.O. Box 852, Suva. Operates glass-bottom cruises aboard the *Tropic See* or *Coral See II.* Departs 9 A.M. from Tradewinds Hotel. Buffet luncheon included. Ships stop in reef lagoon for coral viewing, swimming, beachcombing, snorkeling. Cost F$22 full-day, F$13 half-day (no lunch).

Rainbow Tours (phone 314634). Offers half-day tours of Rewa delta including Nasilai village with Fijian pottery demonstration.

Scuba Hire Ltd., G.P.O. Box 777, Suva. Offers resort course and certification course instruction as well as night diving. Can arrange special interest in underwater photography, shell-collecting, shark hunting, etc. Owns compressors, full medical air decanting facilities, hire gear for up to 30 persons. Daily trips around Suva reef. Hand-feeding of tame tropical reef fish is featured.

Wilderness Adventures (Fiji) Ltd., Box 1389, Suva. A day's rafting down the Ba River in rubber rafts. Cost F$55 including lunch.

Deep Sea Fishing Ltd., P.O. Box 44, Korolevu. The *MV Commander One* twin diesel 44-ft. luxury gamefishing vessel is available for charter at around F$180 a half-day or about F$350 a full day.

Coral Coach Express (Fiji) Ltd., P.O. Box 9172, Nadi Airport. Offers full range of sightseeing tours in air-conditioned cars and coaches. Scheduled service between major hotels in Nadi and Suva daily. Offers scheduled daily express service between Suva/Pacific Harbor/Hyatt Regency/Korolevu/Reef Hotel/The Fijian/Nadi Airport and vice versa. Departs Suva and Nadi Airport 9 A.M. Arrives Nadi Airport and Suva 2:30 P.M. Rate: Nadi Airport/Suva F$15 one way.

Emperor Gold Mining Company Ltd., Vatukoula, Fiji. Guided tours Monday, Tuesday, Thursday and Friday. The gold mine is situated on Viti Levu Island, 58 miles from the Nadi Airport.

South Sea Island Cruises Ltd., P.O. Box 718, Nadi. Cruises to Mana, Plantation and Castaway Islands; gamefishing; a half-day jungle cruise (F$11 per person); scuba diving and snorkeling.

Nature Expeditions International, Dept. JKB, 599 College Ave., Palo Alto, Ca. 94306. Offers 23-day expeditions to study the people, folk art and history of Fiji and the Cook Islands. Accommodations include both home stays in traditional villages and resort hotels. Provides unique cultural experiences and participation in daily lives of the Pacific islanders.

Veiseisei Village. Afternoon tour departs from The Regent for village founded by the first Fijian settlers. Sights include native house, church and chief's home. Visit Fijian handicraft center en route.

Around Suva. The Fiji Museum. Located in the Botanical Gardens at the east end of town, the small museum has exhibits on the history, customs and handicrafts of the Fijians and other Pacific Islanders. Handicrafts and recordings of Fijian band music are sold in the gift shop. Open daily. Small admission fee.

NIGHT LIFE. There are numerous places in Suva for wining and dining apart from the hotels. These include *The Lifeboat,* which specialises in seafood, and *Scotts,* with its silver service. For Chinese cuisine try *Lantern Palace,* the *Peking, Wan-Q,* and the *Bamboo Terrace.* Suva nightspots include *Lucky Eddies,* which appeals to the younger set, and the more sophisticated *Rockefellers.* Generally, entertainment centres out of the hotels.

SPORTS. With a tropical climate and endless shorelines there are limitless opportunities for fishing, boating, water-skiing, and other water sports. Charter boats for big game fishing operate from Coral Coast resorts and from Taveuni, at cheaper rates.

Diving: Scuba and snorkeling gear is available for hire at several resorts.

Horseback riding: Available at several resorts.

Golf: There are golf courses in Suva, Nadi, Lautoka and several other towns and resort hotels. Visitors usually need only pay green fees. The Fijian Resort Hotel has a nine-hole course with clubs for hire. The par-72 course at Pacific Harbour is up to championship standard.

Spectator Sports: From May to October Rugby football, soccer, hockey and netball are the main sports. After October the focus is on cricket and tennis. Fiji Day (October 10) is a good opportunity to see Fijian sportsmen in action.

SHOPPING. Duty-free shopping is a tourist occupation in Suva, Nadi and Lautoka. The duty-free shops pay 10% fiscal tax on all imported goods. Fiji's national association of duty-free dealers advises tourists to shop around on their own initiative and not be guided by touts, guides, taxi-drivers or tour operators. It is also wise to procure cash sale dockets to assist you in obtaining a warranty service back home as well as going through customs procedures. The Suva Duty Free Merchants' Association has introduced a certificate of membership to be displayed in members' shops. Members promise to protect and safeguard the interests of duty free customers.

Fijian handicrafts are attractive, relatively cheap, and popular with tourists. Mats, baskets and fans are woven from pandanus leaves. The boldly decorated tapa cloth is made by beating the inner bark of the paper-mulberry tree until it is of tissue-paper thinness and then joining together several layers of these fine sheets by further beating. Indian artisans produce shell jewelry and ornaments.

There are two types of artifacts made from carved wood. One is carved from hard wood by village craftsmen mostly on outlying islands-*yaqona* (kava) bowls, clubs and other traditional weapons. The other has developed recently and has attracted overseas interest. Carvers use the rain-tree (known in America as the monkey-pod tree), a wood with an attractive grain and silken texture to produce figures, heads and various inlaid objects.

RECOMMENDED READING. *Indians in Fiji,* by Adrian C. Mayer; *Fijian Way of Life,* by G.K. Roth; *The New South Pacific,* by R.G. Crocombe.

HOTELS AND MOTELS. There are many small, inexpensively priced hotels throughout the islands: Increasing numbers are offering dormitory accommodations at cheap rates—F$4–F$10. Some will allow up to two children free if they occupy the parents' room with no extra bed. So, for the traveler who does not want a resort, there are plenty of other choices. Fiji Visitors Bureaus have a list of accommodations in the inexpensive through moderate range.

Based on April 1985 prices for double accommodation, hotels are graded: *Expensive,* F$50–120, *Moderate,* F$25–49; *Inexpensive,* up to F$25.

OVALAU ISLAND

Levuka

Mavida House. *Inexpensive.* Friendly atmosphere. Communal bath and toilet, dining room.

Old Capital Inn. *Inexpensive.* Bed and breakfast.

Ovalau Guest House. *Inexpensive.* Bed and breakfast. Children under 12 half rate. Other meals—dinner $2 and lunch $1.

Rukuruku

Rukuruku Holiday Resort. *Moderate.* P.O. Box 112, Levuka. Cottages on beach F$10 includes meal. Licensed dining room and bar. Incorporates a holiday camp.

TAVEUNI ISLAND

Castaway Taveuni, *Expensive.* P.O. Box 9246, Nadi Airport. Restaurant, bar, nightly entertainment and dancing, swimming pool. At Waiyevo on Taveuni's west coast.

Qamea Beach Club. *Expensive.* Eight rooms in an idyllic setting.
Kaba's Guest House. *Inexpensive.* Cooking facilities.

VANUA LEVU ISLAND

Labasa

Grand Eastern. *Moderate.* Bar, restaurant, swimming pool. Recently upgraded and 24 rooms added.
Takia. *Moderate.* Restaurant, bar, swimming pool. 36 self-contained rooms.

Savusavu

Namale Plantation. *Moderate.* 120-acre beach resort. Working coconut plantation that can be rented entirely by one group of up to 16 people. Bar, dining room, swimming pool, tennis court.
Kon Tiki Lodge. *Inexpensive.* Amid 150-acre copra plantation. Self-contained cabins for self-catering. No restaurant or bar.

VITI LEVU ISLAND

Ba

New Ba Hotel. *Moderate.* Bar, dining room, swimming pool.

Coral Coast

The Crow's Nest. *Expensive.* Luxury villas overlooking beach. Fully licensed dining room. Swimming pool. Villas that sleep 4 have kitchens. Toll-free (800) 272-3282.
The Fijian. *Expensive.* Resort hotel on 100-acre island 35 miles from Nadi. Dining rooms, bars, swimming pools, tennis courts, 9-hole golf course, sailboats, water skiing, dancing nightly, shops. Has undergone a million-dollar face-lift and is now the most deluxe resort in Fiji, with all amenities of an international resort. A one-stop holiday spa. Outstanding hotel staff. Good food.
Hyatt Regency. *Expensive.* A 240-room luxury hotel on beach with man-made off-shore island. Opened 1980. Airfield nearby. Full facilities; game-fish excursions.
Naviti Beach Resort. *Expensive.* Vaviti Bay. Coral Coast. On beach 18 miles from Sigatoka. Restaurant, bars, swimming pool, stables, 9-hole golf course, five all-weather tennis courts, shops. Deep sea fishing boats by arrangement, bicycles.
Hide-A-Way Resort. *Moderate.* P.O. Box 233, Sigatoka. Informality stressed. Restaurant, bars, swimming pool, shops. Dormitory accommodation F$8. Mini-golf, swimming pool.
Reef Hotel Resort. *Moderate.* Restaurant, bar, dance band every night, stables, swimming pool, coral viewing.
Korolevu Beach. *Moderate.* On shoreline 19 miles from Sigatoka. Rooms and *bures,* swimming pool, 9-hole golf course, nightclub, dining room, firewalking every Friday, deep sea fishing.
Sandy Point Beach Cottages. *Inexpensive.* Cottages and pool on beach. Caters to longer staying visitors at budget rates.
Sigatoka. *Inexpensive.* Most rooms share facilities. Dining room.

Deuba

Beachcomber Hotel. *Expensive.* Set in 11 acres tropical gardens overlooking Beqa Island. Restaurant, bar, swimming pool.

Beachside Apartments. *Expensive.* Adjacent to Beachcomber Hotel where all facilities are available. Self-contained units, swimming pool.

Fiji Palm Beach Resort. *Expensive.* Two-bedroom self-contained apartments. Swimming pool. Access to Pacific Harbour activities. Time-share available.

Coral Coast Christian Camps. *Inexpensive.* Self-contained units 100 yards from beach. No alcohol permitted. Dormitory accommodation.

Lautoka

Anchorage Beach Resort. *Moderate.* Also has dormitory accommodations at F$12 plus cooking facilities. Swimming pool.

Cathay. *Moderate.* Dining room, cocktail lounge, swimming pool. Babysitting service.

Lautoka. *Moderate.* Dining room, cocktail lounge.

Sawene Beach Hotel. *Moderate.* Self-contained units on beach 12 minutes from Nadi. Dormitory accommodation $6. Dining room, bar, private and share facilities.

Lautoka-Offshore

Beachcomber Island Resort. *Expensive.* 11 miles off-shore. *Bures,* communal lodge and dormitory. Meals included in rates. Dining room, bar, water sports.

Mana Island Resort. *Expensive.* 22 miles off-shore. Dining room, bars, water sports, nightclub, *bure* accommodation.

Treasure Island Resort. *Expensive. Bure* units and bungalows. Dining room. Dancing nightly, swimming pool, water sports.

Castaway Island. *Expensive.* 15 miles off-shore. *Bures,* dining room, cocktail lounge, water sports, sailing, boat excursions, deep sea fishing.

Plantation Village. *Expensive.* 20 miles off-shore. *Bures,* dining room, bar, water sports, tennis, horseback riding.

Club Naitasi. *Expensive.* New resort at Malolo Island with bures and luxury villas. Restaurant, bar and sports facilities.

Musket Cove. *Moderate.* Only off-shore island facility with kitchens. Each cottage has bath, main bedroom, living room. Grocery store on premises. Restaurant, pool.

Nadi (also spelled Nandi)

The Regent of Fiji. *Expensive.* Luxury beach resort. Restaurant, bars, steak house, shops, swimming pool, water sports, deep sea fishing, sailing, firewalking.

Tanoa. *Expensive.* P.O. Box 9211, Nadi Airport. Dining Room, bar, swimming pool.

Nadi Airport TraveLodge. *Expensive.* Dining room, bar, swimming pool, tennis.

Dominion International. *Moderate.* Restaurant, bar, swimming pools, pitch and putt golf course.

Castaway Gateway. *Expensive.* Recently renovated. Ideal transit hotel close to airport.

Fiji Mocambo. *Moderate/Expensive.* Dining room, bars, swimming pool.

Seashell Cove. *Moderate.* 17 kms from Nadi on white sand beach. Swimming pool, tennis courts. Campers welcome. Dormitory F$6.

Westgate. *Moderate.* Transit hotel. Dining room and swimming pool.

Sandalwood Inn. *Inexpensive.* Downtown Nadi. Some rooms share facilities. Restaurant.

Fong Hing Private Hotel. *Inexpensive.* Restaurant with Chinese and European food.

The Melanesian. *Inexpensive.* Dining room. Bar, swimming pool, excursion boats. Dormitory accommodation $5.

Nadi Youth Hotel. *Inexpensive.* Member International YHA.

Rakiraki

Nawawa Bay Bungalows. *Moderate.* Self-contained cottages Nananu-i-ra Is.

Rakiraki Hotel. *Moderate.* Dining room. Swimming pool.

Betham's Beach Cottages. *Inexpensive.* Self-contained cottages on Nananu-i-ra Island.

Macdonalds Beach Cottages. *Inexpensive.* Self-contained cottages on Nananu-i-ra Island.

Suva

Suva Courtesy Inn. *Expensive.* Downtown. Dining room, cocktail lounge, swimming pool.

Suva TraveLodge. *Expensive.* Superior rooms. Dining room, snack bar, cocktail lounge, swimming pool. On water's edge near town center.

Grand Pacific. *Moderate* but with expensive suites. Somerset Maugham atmosphere. Restaurant, cocktail lounge, swimming pool.

President Hotel. *Moderate.* On hillside overlooking bay, dining room, bars, Fijian entertainment nightly. Swimming pool.

Southern Cross. *Moderate.* Licensed dining room, swimming pool.

Townhouse Apartment Hotel. *Moderate.* Self-contained apartments. Also restaurant and bar.

Tradewinds Hotel. *Moderate.* Ocean front. Dining room. Bars, swimming pool, water sports, excursion boats.

Fiji Youth Hostel. *Inexpensive.* Dormitory accommodation, communal facilities.

Miller's Private Hotel. *Inexpensive.* Fijian atmosphere. American Plan.

Sunset Apartment Hotel. *Inexpensive.* Rooms with kitchen. Bar and restaurant.

Other Areas

Naigani Island. *Islanders Village. Expensive.* Luxury villas. An hour by air from Suva. Excursions to Ovalau Island.

Toberua Island: *Toberua Resort. Expensive.* Dining room specialising in local seafood and native foods, bar, swimming pool. Fishing and excursion boats, coral viewing.

Yasawas. *Turtle Island Lodge. Expensive.* Set in the beautiful Yasawa group 60 kms north of Viti Levu, the main island. Rates include meals.

Kadavu Island: *Reece's Place. Inexpensive.* On Galoa Island 20 minutes from Kadavu. No electricity.

Tailevu: *Tailevu Hotel. Inexpensive.* 32 miles from Suva. Dining room, bars, outdoor bowls.

Tavua: *Tavua Hotel. Inexpensive.* Dining room, bars, swimming pool.

Waya Island. *Last Resort. Inexpensive.* In Yasawa Group 50 miles north-east of Viti Levu. Minimum stay of one week. Guests bring own food. Gas lighting and cooking.

CAMPING. Those with a taste for the outdoors and tropical nights under canvas can stay at licensed campsites. The main ones are at Rukuruku, the Colo-i-Sava recreational area near Suva, Nukulau Island, just off Suva Point, and at Seashell Cove resort between Nadi and Sigatoka.

Special permission is required to stay at Colo-i-Savu (Forestry Dept., tel. 22777) and Nukulau Island (Ministry of Lands, tel. 25081). At Rukuruku, tents are for hire. Campers provided with bedding, gas stove, and utensils.

KIRIBATI & TUVALU

Recently Independent Nations

by
ROBERT GILMORE

Until 1976, the Gilbert and Ellice Islands were a British colony and transportation companies treated them as one territory. But they are now independent and separate. They have new names. The Gilberts are Kiribati (pronounced "kiribas") and the Ellice Islands are Tuvalu. Most Kiribati people call their republic Tungaru.

Strung across the equator, none of the mini-atolls or islands of the group, except for Ocean Island, which seeks to secede from the Gilberts, rises more than 15 feet above sea level. All are, in the geographer's term, coral atoll-lagoons, arcs of coral sand, devoid of hills or streams. Were it not for masses of towering coconut palms, they would appear as little more than sandbanks.

Devotees of organic gardening observe with admiration how, in the inorganic coral sand, the islanders have, over generations, built up humus in deep pits by mulching. Here they grow taro and bananas. But they live mainly on uncultivated coconut, breadfruit, and seafood. Shortages of rain have created dependence on concrete tanks and brackish wells. Two year droughts have made survival difficult.

Although the present inhabitants of the islands are peaceable and pleasant, violent combat dominated their history until the coming of American missionaries in 1856. Even today, an occasional rough practice survives. You may read in the law reports of a husband being charged with biting off the nose of a straying wife—a traditional punishment.

Also within living memory, male adulterers have been punished by being put in a canoe without food, water, or paddle in a strong offshore wind—normally a sentence of slow and painful death.

The 56,000 Kiribati who occupy 28 inhabited islands and own 20 uninhabited islands with total land area of 252 square miles (720 square km) are Micronesians. The 8,000 Tuvaluans who occupy nine islands, with a land area of 10 square miles (26 square km), are Polynesians.

Because of World War II, the G&EIC, as they were known in the South Pacific, are more familiar to Americans than to the British who owned them, for the reason that roughly two years after the Japanese armed forces landed on Tarawa (now the capital of Kiribati) in 1941, the Americans set up an advanced base on Funafuti (now the capital of Tuvalu) and, on November 21, 1943, in Operation Galvanic, launched their first penetration of Japan's ring of island defences. At dawn, the United States Second Marine Division landed on the Tarawa islet of Betio.

After four days of fighting, as severe as any in the Pacific war, the marines overwhelmed a strongly entrenched Japanese garrison. The Japanese lost 5,000 men killed in action or dead by suicide and the Americans suffered 990 fatalities and 2,296 wounded. Once again, the Americans dispelled the Japanese legend that Americans were afraid to die.

Weapons and Artifacts

Among tools of war, the Kiribati shark-tooth sword is claimed to be unique in concept and craftsmanship. The swords, in great demand by collectors of both artifacts and militaria, are of polished coconut wood, with drilled shark teeth, filed to razor sharpness, lashed to the two edges. The hilt and sometimes the entire length of the sword is covered with finely woven dye-patterned pandanus into which, for good luck, a plaited strand of a girl's hair is sometimes woven. Length varies from 12 to 36 inches.

Another collectors' item is the shark-tooth glove, a mailed-fist with teeth imbedded in it. Only reproductions are now made. Genuine Gilbertese weapons are more likely to be found in the old mercantile households of Fiji and Samoa, even of Australia, than in islands that were occupied by the Japanese and became World War II battlefields.

A prized Tuvalu artifact is the carved wooden *tuluma,* also spelled *Turama,* an oval miniature sea-chest, 18 to 24 inches in diameter, with hermetically fitting lid, in which treasured possessions were carried on transoceanic canoe journeys. Miniature models, of 4 to 10 inches in diameter have, for decades, been used in the South Pacific as humidors and, in recent times, as containers for cameras. A comparable sea-chest in the Gilberts is named *bookai.*

American veterans wishing to view World War II battlefields in which American and Japanese hardware is still conspicuous, may take boat trips from Tarawa and Funafuti at modest cost. Hardware abounds at Nukufetau, Nanumea, Abemama, Tarawa, and Butaritari (which the American military labelled Makin). But a concentration of war relics may be found in Betio, at Tarawa, a cheerful islet on which 6,000 people occupy one square mile. You can circumnavigate Betio on foot along its beaches in about an hour (remember to wear sunglasses). If you seek portable war memorabilia, seek it at low tide and wear old tennis shoes to minimise the risk of gashing your feet on anything from shards of barnacle-encrusted coke bottles of the mid-1940's to torn metal.

The folk dancing at village meeting houses in Tarawa is wildly beautiful—completely unmodified for any foreign presence. And a wonderful voyage from Tarawa to a distant island can be undertaken in a *baurua* —a large, twin-sailed, ocean-going outrigger canoe, centuries old in design.

As of mid-1984 most of the area in these 2 mini-nations is best toured by backpackers and the hardy, or ardent, seeking "unspoilt" South Seas. Of more general appeal is Kiribati's Christmas Island, reached through the Marshall Islands by Kiribati's Air Tungaru service. Outstanding fishing (wading for bonefish; surf-casting for trevally, grouper, shark, snapper; off-shore angling for tuna, wahoo, sailfish), seabird watching, and accommodations are here.

An Unexpected Cuisine

As in much of Polynesia, Micronesia and Melanesia, there is a dismaying tendency to regard imported uncooked canned corned beef as a luxury. Diplomatically make known you're allergic to it. Memorable local delicacies you might hope for in the southern islands of Kiribati include the boiled fruit of pandanus (screwpine), sliced thin and spread with fermented coconut cream. Some find it tastes like dates. In Tuvalu, hope for palu sami, supreme delicacy of Polynesia. It is coconut cream with sliced onion and a dash of curry powder, wrapped in taro leaves from which spines and ribs have been removed, pressure-cooked in an earth-oven stashed with seaweed. It can be a vegetarian dish by itself or served with roast pork or chicken.

PRACTICAL INFORMATION FOR KIRIBATI AND TUVALU.

WHEN TO COME. Central Kiribati has a maritime equatorial climate. Islands to the north and south are tropical. Mean annual temperature is 80°F (26.7°C) and both annual and daily ranges are small. March–October is the season of north-east trade winds, with the lowest humidity and greatest comfort. December–March is a wet season, mainly in the north. In Tuvalu, north-easterly trades bring dry cool air from March through October. Westerly gales bring rain and sticky discomfort from November through February.

PASSPORTS AND VISAS. Passports required for everyone. Visa required but is available upon arrival enabling you to stay for a maximum of four months. You must have onward tickets and sufficient funds for maintenance. Kiribati has no airport tax; Tuvalu A$2.50.

HOW TO GET AROUND. Buses or taxes are available from hotel to the airport at $1.50 upward depending upon distance. Air Tungaru operates a special service for arriving and departing passengers to and from airport from all points from Bairiki eastwards. Fare is $2.50.

Taxis are available only in urban Tarawa. Hire cars available only in urban Tarawa and Christmas Island. The gregarious visitor will have no difficulty in making inexpensive transport deals on land and sea.

DRINKING WATER AND ELECTRICITY. Drink only boiled or bottled water or the palatable and wholly sterile water from a newly opened coconut. Electricity is geared for Australian and British-type outlets on Tarawa. American appliances may be used at the Captain Cook Hotel on Christmas Island.

WHAT TO WEAR. Lightweight casual clothing, preferably cotton. Bikinis are not recommended except for swimming. Women's shorts are seldom seen. Men usually wear walking shorts and cotton open-necked shirts; long trousers are worn only in the evening and for formal occasions.

 HOLIDAYS. January 1—New Year's Day; Good Friday; Easter Holidays include Saturday, Sunday and Monday; June 9—Queen's Birthday; August 4—Youth Day; December 25 Christmas; December 26 Boxing Day.
In Kiribati: July 12, Independence Day; and in August, Britain's floating bank holiday.
In Tuvalu: second Monday in March, Commonwealth Day; October 1 and 2, Tuvalu Days; November floating date, Prince of Wales' birthday.

MEDICAL FACILITIES. Tungaru Central Hospital on Tarawa caters for all islands on major health problems. Dispensaries exist on all islands for treatment of minor ailments. All facilities are run by the government; there are no private doctors.

CURRENCY. At present the Australian dollar is used. A$1 = US$0.68, mid-1985.

LANGUAGES. Local tongues and English. Because a local courtesy is not to speak English in the company of anybody who does not speak it, the traveler should be prepared for one-to-one conversations.

RELIGION. The population is almost equally divided between Catholics, predominant in the Northern Islands, and Protestants, predominant in the Southern Islands. There are also Mormons, Adventists, Bahais, and the Church of God.

 ACCOMMODATIONS. The *Otintai Hotel* on Tarawa has 20 air-conditioned rooms. If aircraft arrive simultaneously from Honolulu and Nauru, which sometimes happens, single-room guests must be prepared to live 3 to a room—most do so cheerfully. A$40 for a single. Hotel on coral atoll facing lagoon. A new Tarawa hotel is the *Kiribati,* at Betio, well spoken-of, but prices not available at press time. The *Captain Cook Hotel* on Christmas Island has 24 air-conditioned rooms. Rates are A$40 single, A$48 double. Outstanding evening entertainment by island song-and-dance troupe. The *Robert Louis Stevenson Hotel* at Abemama is A$46 a day for a double, including meals. The hotel consists of simple thatched cottages on a lagoon. (For all reservations and tours write Kiribati Visitors' Bureau, TX KI 039 a/b Resources, P.O. Box 64, Bairiki, Tarawa, Republic of Kiribati, Central Pacific.) Tuvalu's only hotel is the *Vaiaku Langi* near the airstrip at Funafuti, with 7 rooms. Singles from A$25, A$5 extra for air-conditioning. New hotel is scheduled for 1986.

ENTERTAINMENT. Film shows, island nights with dancing, feasts in Maneabas (local meeting house).

TIPPING. Not encouraged.

SHOPPING. Handicrafts of all sorts, baskets in all sizes, table mats, fans, cups, etc. are made from pandanus leaves, coconut leaves, coconut shells, turtle shells and seashells. Seashell necklaces are common on the islands. Business hours are Monday-Friday 8 A.M. to 12 noon and 1 P.M. to 5 P.M. Saturday hours are 7 A.M. to 12 noon.

COMMUNICATIONS. Post Office hours are Monday to Friday 8:30 A.M. to 12 noon and 1:30 P.M. to 4 P.M. Cables service in Betio is from 8 A.M. to 7 P.M. Government service to outer islands is Monday to Friday 8 A.M. to 4 P.M.

TOURS. *Ministry of Natural Resource Development,* P.O. Box 64, Bairiki, Tarawa. Offers organized 7-day wildlife tours. Chartered boats leave from the London Wharf for visits to bird colonies of Cook Island and Matu Tabu. Also excursions by road to wildlife reserves. Captain Cook 30-ft. launch and other boats for hire with skipper. Approximately A$15 per hour. Wildlife conservation unit guide every tour. 7-day fishing holidays also organized. 20-ft. Fiberglass fishing boat with twin 70 hp engines for hire. One night lobster fishing included. Pickup trucks and cars for hire, are available.

Air Tungaru, 3049 Valena St., Suite 910, Honolulu, HI 96819. Operates regular tours to Kiribati. Tel. (415) 332-7850.

Valor Tours, Lt., Schoonmaker Bldg. Sausalito, Ca. 94965.

Until recent suspension of Air Tungaru one-hour service from Honolulu to Tarawa, *Fish and Game Frontiers Inc.,* P. O. Box 161, Wexford, PA 15090, were offering 12-day/11-night and 5-day/4-night packages to Christmas Island. Watch for resumption of service.

How To Get There. By Air Tungaru from Majuro, Marshall Islands, and Tuvalu to Tarawa; and by Air Nauru from Nauru to Tarawa. Be sure to double-check air schedules before travelling, as in mid-1985 Air Nauru routes and flights were being slashed.

SOLOMON ISLANDS

Battlefields in the South Pacific

by
DON HOOK

The Solomons were first visited by Europeans in 1568 but it took a bloody battle almost 400 years later to introduce the islands to the Western world.

Alvaro de Mendana, on a voyage from Peru, gave the islands their name, hoping to stimulate interest in his discovery by inferring that the legendary King Solomon had gained his wealth in these faraway outposts. Mendana returned in 1595—27 years later—to find a settlement at Graciosa Bay in the Santa Cruz Islands. The village, however, beleaguered by internal strife, was soon abandoned following a fever epidemic. Mendana, himself, was a victim.

Other Europeans, including Abel Tasman, visited the Solomons but it was not until the end of the 19th century that traders and missionaries began to arrive. At the same time, large numbers of the islanders were recruited to work on sugar plantations in Fiji and Australia. Here they were treated like slaves and appalling stories of cruelty drifted back to the Solomon Islands. In retaliation, many Europeans were murdered.

To stop the bloodshed, the British Government established a protectorate in 1893 embracing the islands of Guadalcanal, Savo, Malaita, San Cristobal (or Makira), and New Georgia. The islands of the Santa Cruz group were added later while the Shortland Group, Santa Isabel (or Ysabel), Choiseul, and Ontong Java were transferred by treaty from Germany to Britain in the early 1900's.

The first British resident commissioner, appointed in 1896, set up office on the island of Tulagi, north of Guadalcanal. The headquarters of the British Solomon Islands Protectorate (BSIP) remained at Tulagi until World War Two when, like many other settlements in the Pacific, it was blasted off the face of the earth by American and Japanese shelling.

World War II

The Japanese advance across the Pacific reached the far western islands of the Solomons in early April, 1942. For the first time, places like Guadalcanal, Henderson Field, "Bloody Ridge," and the Coral Sea became household words around the world.

The Japanese began building an airstrip on Guadalcanal in July, 1942. In August, 1942, American marines landed on Red Beach, took the airstrip within 24 hours and, within a fortnight, the strip was operational. It was named after Major Lofton Henderson, an American hero of the Battle of Midway.

Late in August, the Japanese counterattack led to the famous battle of Edson's Ridge (or "Bloody Ridge" as it was known to the troops). The war on Guadalcanal ended early in February, 1943 when the Japanese evacuated the island and gradually, were forced out of the Solomons island by island. Thereafter, Guadalcanal became a huge American supply base and training centre for the remainder of hostilities. Stark reminders of the war are still to be seen—ships, tanks, vehicles, guns, and aeroplanes—rusting away on the beaches and in the jungle. Iron Bottom Sound, between Guadalcanal, Savo and Florida islands, is probably the world's largest graveyard of men, ships, and planes. Memorials have been built at various battle sites and American and Japanese war veterans often return to the Solomons to pay homage to their fallen comrades.

The war brought great change to Solomon Islands. Honiara (on Guadalcanal) replaced Tulagi as the capital; new roads, bridges, and airstrips were built; the land was opened up to tourists and other visitors; and the beginnings of a national unity began to be felt.

People of the Solomons

The country's population is 220,000. About 200,000 are Melanesian. There are also Polynesians, Gilbertese, Europeans and Chinese. Most Melanesians live on the main islands with the Polynesians living in the outlying islands to the south and east.

Although there have been many developments and incursions in the past 100 years, most Solomon Islanders still live in a traditional way, with each family growing its fruits and vegetables, catching its own fish, and building its own house. Some, however, have adopted the urban life of Honiara, attracted by job opportunities and the "bright lights." In addition, many Solomon Islanders are playing an increasingly active role in the development of their country. The Solomon Islands became independent July 7, 1978. The first Prime Minister was New Zealand-educated Peter Kenilorea. The present Prime Minister is Solomon Mamaloni.

PRACTICAL INFORMATION FOR SOLOMON ISLANDS

WHEN TO GO. The tropical climate of Solomon Islands is made more moderate by the expanse of ocean around them. Southeast trade winds blow from April to November. During the rest of the year, the winds are from the northwest and occasionally develop into cyclones. On Guadalcanal and the larger islands, the cool night breeze sometimes lowers the temperature to 66°F (19°C). Day temperatures are usually in the 80's, sometimes as high as 88°F (31°C). Rainfall in Honiara averages 85 inches a year with the heaviest rain between January–March. Some of the other islands average up to 140 inches a year.

Average Temperature (°Fahrenheit) and Humidity

Honiara	Jan	Feb	Mar	Apr	May	June	July	Aug	Sept	Oct	Nov	Dec
Averge max. day temperature	87°	86°	86°	87°	87°	86°	86°	86°	87°	87°	87°	86°
Days of Rain	N/A	N/A	N/A	N/A	N/A	N/A	N/A	N/A	N/A	N/A	N/A	N/A
Humidity, Percent	73	73	80	N/A	N/A	N/A	73	73	73	73	73	73

WHERE TO GO. Honiara, the capital of Guadalcanal offers most: museum, botanical gardens, and Chinatown. There are World War II relics in and around the town and noticeboards indicate major battles and incidents that took place during the battle for Guadalcanal. Villages and scenic drives are within easy reach. Three travel agencies are available to take visitors around Guadalcanal and other islands. Popular tours are available to the battlefields and the Betikama carving centre, Chapuru and Tambea villages (all Guadalcanal), and to Laulasi and Alite village (on Malaita). There are no regular tours to other islands but visitors may easily organise their own excursions.

HOW TO GET AROUND. A rented car from *Avis* is SBD20 per day plus km. Airport transfer by bus is about SBD1. Taxis are available for SBD30 per mile or SBD5/ hour, but be sure to negotiate beforehand. *Solomon Islands Airways Ltd.* has scheduled and charter service throughout the Solomon Islands and five-times-weekly flights to Kieta, Bougainville. Offers service between Honiara and Espiritu Santo.

HOW TO REACH HONIARA. Most tourists enter Solomon Islands by plane to Honiara. From Brisbane, Solomon Island Airways; Espiritu Santo (Vanuatu), Solomon Island Airways; Kieta (Papua New Guinea), Solomon Island Airways; Nadi/Suva, Air Pacific; Nauru, Air Nauru; Port Moresby (Papua New Guinea), Air Niugini; Port Vila, Air Pacific, Solomon Island Airways. Airport tax is SBD5 per person.

ACCOMMODATION. Accommodation is generally easy to obtain in Honiara, where there are three hotels—the *Mendana* (first class; on the beach and with a swimming pool), the *Honiara* and the *Hibiscus*. 28-miles west of Honiara by road is *Tambea Village Resort.* Still on Guadalcanal, is the *Tavanipupu Island Resort*, in the Marau Sound, which is accessible by air and sea. There is accommodation available in the Reef Islands (*Ngarando Rest House),* Western Solomons (*Kasolo Hotel* in Gizo and *Munda Rest House* in Munda), and Malaita (*Auki Lodge,* Auki), and at the *Anuha Island Resort,* a 15-minute flight from Honiara. A full list detailing facilities and tariffs is available from the Solomon Islands Tourist authority, P.O. Box 321, Honiara.

HONIARA NIGHT LIFE. Honiara is a comparatively quiet town—a feature which suits many visitors who go there with the idea of getting away from it all. The residents tend to entertain at home or spend the evenings in the town's three clubs. Thus, there is not a great deal going for the visitors who want a "night on the town". However, Honiara does have a number of restaurants which offer good European and Asian dishes. The clubs offer temporary membership to visitors at a very low fee. The clubs run dances and film nights and have a number of sporting facilities ie. snooker, darts, tennis and swimming. Liquor licensing hours are liberal. A number of restaurants also offer good European and Asian dishes.

CULTURE. Most Solomon Island dances and songs depict the early traditions and customs, or are based on history and mythology. For example, there are Melanesian dances about head-hunting raids and sharks. On some islands, the people once worshipped sharks. Bonito fishing in the Eastern Solomons is linked with the traditional rituals of the people, as are the dolphin drives off Malaita. Many Solomon Islanders are skilled woodcarvers.

CUSTOMS. Permitted are usual personal effects plus 200 cigarettes or ½ lb. tobacco, and three bottles of wines/spirits with a limit of two bottles of spirits.
Tipping is neither customary nor encouraged.

DUTY-FREE SHOPPING. A number of stores offer a limited selection of duty-free goods; The Trading Company and Quan Hong are the largest. Alcohol and electrical appliances are good buys.

TOURS. *Guadalcanal Travel Service,* P.O. Box 114, Mendana Avenue, Honiara, Guadalcanal, Solomon Islands. Can arrange for groups and individuals. Accommodations, diving tours and snorkeling tours and all other sightseeing arranged. Make reservations well in advance. Booking agent for all international airlines and shipping lines operating in the Solomons.

Hunts of the Pacific (S) *Ltd.,* P.O. Box 104, Honiara, Solomon Islands. Visit the battle grounds of WWII, and many primitive islands. Special bird watching, photographic, or skin diving tours arranged for groups. Most all other travel services also available.

Solomon Islands Airways Ltd. P.O. Box 23. Honiara, Solomon Islands. Will arrange for scheduled and charter service throughout the Solomons. Agents for services are Air Nauru and Air Nuigini, Air Pacific.

Melan-Chine Shipping Co. Ltd., P.O. Box 71, Honiara, Solomons. Operates freighter/passenger services throughout the Solomons. Room for 40 passengers but cabin facilities for only four; others have deck space. Not recommended for the comfort seeking. There are ships on the line that carry up to 70 passengers with different facilities and schedules.

Valor Tours, Schooner Point Bldg., 2nd floor, Spring St., Sausalito, Ca. 94965. World War II battle zone specialists with organized programs for units that served in both the Pacific and European Theaters. With the help and cooperation of national and civic leaders of the host countries, plans are underway for a series of reunions for a number of units who served in the Pacific. Visits: Australia, New Zealand, Papua New Guinea, Solomon Islands, Marianas (Saipan), Micronesia (Truk), New Caledonia, Vanuatu, Japan, Korea, Hong Kong, Singapore and Malaysia. Valor Tours will also arrange any individual tour—just tell them where you want to go, for how long, the approximate number of persons travelling

SOLOMON ISLANDS

together and when you would like to travel. They will plan your itinerary and provide a cost estimate.

Shipping – Local companies operate scheduled services to a number of islands and several other companies provide non-scheduled services. The Government Marine Department runs scheduled and non-scheduled services and like the commercial operators mentioned can carry a limited number of passengers. The most regular services run from Honiara to the Western Solomons and Malaita. (Refer to Inter-Island Ships in *Planning Your Trip* section.)

The following are tours most popular with visitors to the Solomons and most can be arranged after arrival; however, it is usually wise to make reservations well in advance if possible. Prices below are approximate.

Town Tour: (1½ hours) Visit Honiara Market, Chinatown, Vavaya Ridge, Botanical Gardens and Kakabona Village. Approx. US$12. *Honiara and Environs:* (4 hours) Visit Solomon Islands National Museum, Botanical Gardens, Point Cruz, Holy Cross Cathedral, Skyline Ridge. Approx. US$30. *Tambea Village Resort:* (Full Day) Coastal drive along the West Guadalcanal shore, through villages and coconut plantations, visiting Vilu Village enroute. Bungalow facilities available at Cape Esperance. Swimming, shell-collecting, and lunch. Approx. US$35. *Battlefields of WWII and Betikama Carving Centre:* (4 hours) Visit underground hospital, Bloody Ridge, Red Beach, battlefields and Swiss Memorial. Lunch included. Approx. US$35. *East Guadalcanal:* (6 hours) Tours of oil palm, rice and cattle projects, Henderson Field, Bloody Ridge, Red Beach and Henderson Field. Approx. US$35. *West Guadalcanal:* (6 hours) Tour west coastline and plantations, Vilu Cultural Village to view traditional buildings, tropical gardens, WWII relics. Picnic lunch included. Approx. US$35. *Alite Village, Manmade Island, Langalanga Lagoon, Malaita:* (Full day) *Solair* flight over Iron Bottom Sound, Indispensible Strait, old capital Tulagi, Taiyo factory, transfer by war canoe, stone age factory, Malaita shell money. Approx. US$100. *Laulasi Adventure Tour:* (Full day) 30-minute flight to Auki on Malaita Island, transfer to motorized war canoe for 40-minute cruise through Langalanga Lagoon. At Laulasi, reconstructions of traditional tribal tabu houses. Native-style feast. Approx. US$80. *Western Solomons:* (3 days) Departs Honiara Sunday for Gizo, calling at 10 intermediate ports en route. Twin berth-cabin, passengers provide own meals. Arrive Gizo at 6 P.M. Monday; overnight in a/c Kasolo Hotel. Return flight Tuesday.

CLOTHING. Light summer clothes are worn all year round. For women, long dresses, and for men, slacks and short-sleeved shirts are the regular attire for evening functions. Visitors are discouraged from wearing bikinis, swimming trunks, brief tops and shorts and similar attire around towns and villages as residents may be offended.

SPORT. Golf, tennis, bowls, skin diving, sailing, and fishing.

SWIMMING. The sea around Honiara is not recommended. A number of swimming pools are available. There are also some good river and beach spots 10 to 20 miles (16-32 kms.) west of town.

WATER. Safe to drink throughout Solomon Islands.

LANGUAGE. The official language is English, taught in schools throughout the country. There are about 40 different languages spoken by the inhabitants of the various islands but Pidgin is the medium most frequently used by the people from different language areas to communicate with each other.

WILDLIFE. Solomon Islands are rich in bird life—parrots, sun birds, kingfishers—in all about 140 species. The most common animals are wild pigs, opossums, and bush rats. Crocodiles and lizards also abound in the coastal areas. Snakes are mainly small and the majority are not venomous. Sharks are fairly common around the islands and, for this reason, bathing in the open sea is not advised.

NUMISMATISTS & PHILATELISTS. With the Solomons issuing their own currency, the fresh, newly minted money will probably become collectors' items. Most likely there will be an increased interest to collectors in the already attractive stamps.

HOLIDAYS. There are no national scheduled events. However, July 7, 1978 became independence day and celebrations are held to mark national day.

CURRENCY. Solomon Islands currency is the dollar, expressed in writing as SBD, e.g., $10 is written as SBD10. US$1 equals approx SBD1.30.

WALLIS & FUTUNA

Outposts of France

by
ROBERT GILMORE

Wallis and Futuna, an "overseas territory" of France, are two small groups of islands of volcanic origin between Fiji and Samoa. Their total land area is 107 square miles (171 sq. kms.)—Wallis has 6,000 inhabitants, Futuna 3,000. Wallisians' speak a modified Tongan, pointing to their long ago migration from Tonga. The people of Futuna, who speak a modified Samoan, are believed to have come from Samoa in the distant past.

Creation of a weekly air service from Nouméa, via Nadi, has opened Wallis—modestly—to tourism. Within a decade it could be a high-grade mini-resort for those seeking a peaceful Pacific backwater, plus pleasant people, French cooking, and a skin-diving paradise.

Envision a small verdant island within a coral lagoon. On the water's edge the French tricolor flying limply above the modest administrative center of Hahake. Above the palm-shaded hamlet lie three dormant volcanoes, their craters now clear jungle lakes. The scents of copra and wine.

To enter New Caledonia for up to 31 days, travelers with a valid passport from the U.S. or Canada and most western nations require only a return air ticket with return booking confirmed. But at outward passport control in Nouméa and Port Vila, the French normally want to know the business of a non-French national with a ticket to Wallis. Resolute tourists should, therefore, secure in advance written entry permission from the Chief Administrator for Overseas Administration of the French Republic in the Pacific, Nouméa, New Caledonia. Or, if they prefer to go to the top, the address is Commissariat à la Promotion des Departements et Territoires d'Outre-Mer, 83 Boulevard du Montparnasse, 75006, Paris.

More About Wallis

Wallis's volcanic origin is disguised by such erosion of its contours that the highest point of the main island, Uvea, is only 420 feet. Five miles wide by 10 miles long (8 by 16 kms.) it is surrounded by a coral reef which protects the coastline from the deep Pacific swell. Wallis has no rivers; for water, its people depend on rain and the springs along the beaches. The climate is hot and damp, with its average temperature dropping from 88°F to 83°F (31°C to 28°C) between July and September, the southern hemisphere winter.

Wallisian men are tall and strong, gold-complexioned, with slightly wavy hair and bold profiles. Women are smaller and less handsome, although invariably amiable. They often wear their hair long and elaborately plaited.

Wallisians lead a simple life, raising subsistence crops and fishing. But migrant Wallisians' exposure to the relative urbanity and prosperity of nearby nickel-rich New Caledonia (at time of writing in recession) has induced change—and discontent.

The Wallisian King lives in Mata-Utu in a modest, two-story stone house. A substantial stone cathedral proclaims the undisputed and unshared spiritual dominance of the Marists, a French Roman Catholic religious society.

Soon after Pearl Harbor, the United States installed a naval air station on Wallis. From 1942 to 1946, an average of 5,000 American servicemen were deployed to that area and life has never been the same since. Hihifo, the Wallis airfield, was built by the Americans.

Rugged and verdant Futuna is different. Mountain chains and rounded peaks enclose deep valleys and streams. Even smaller than Wallis, Futuna is settled mainly in villages strung along a narrow coastal plain. Alofi, the other island in the Futuna group, 3 miles (5 kms.) away, normally is uninhabited because of lack of water. Like the Wallisians, Futunans have worked in New Caledonia and Vanuatu (formerly New Hebrides) since the establishment of the air link.

The white sand beaches of Wallis and Futuna are ideal for water sports and skin diving. Inland, crater lakes are an attraction for climbers. But almost the only people who enjoy these pleasures are ocean yachtsmen because of the lack of amenities throughout the islands.

An event in 1977, however, might change the character of both island groups during the next decade.

The occasion was the air freighting, by Vatican decision, of the bones of Saint Peter Chanel, the first Pacific saint, from the Marist Fathers' Motherhouse at Lyons, France, to the little presbytery and convent at the village of Poi, on Futuna, decreed by the Vatican to be Chanel's final resting place. A national shrine will be established there.

Chanel, a Marist priest from Cras, France, was chopped to death at Poi on April 28, 1841, after five years of arduous missionary work, while preparing medicaments for villagers. Members of Futuna's ruling family, fearing that the missionary's moral authority was undermining their temporal powers, dispatched a murder squad to his mission hut.

As the Chanel remains travelled to Futuna through Australia, New Zealand, and Fiji, there were great displays of veneration, suggesting that the demand for pilgrimages to the Chanel shrine at Poi will be extensive. For this reason, either the church or the French administration will be obliged to provide accommodations and scheduled air transport on a continuing basis.

In the French-style garden of the small presbytery and convent at Poi, there is a grapevine from France, believed to have been imported and planted by Chanel. Application of its leaves, as they grow or as a moist mash, is said to bring remission of symptoms for a wide range of ailments.

Enquiries about facilities for future pilgrimages could be addressed to the Apostolic Vicar of Wallis and Futuna Islands, Lano Seminary, Wallis Island, via Nouméa, New Caledonia.

Nobody on Futuna other than "religious" speaks English.

HOW TO GET THERE. One flight a week from Nouméa via Nadi by Nouméa-based Air Caledonie International.

The Compagnie Wallisienne de Navigation's 15-passenger freighter *Moana* makes a monthly voyage: Noumea–Futuna–Wallis–Futuna. Sometimes the order of calls is shuffled and sometimes there are calls at Suva and Port Vila. Arrive by ship and you are liable to have to seek far for the gendarme who stamps passports—if you want yours stamped.

HOW TO GET ABOUT. Irregular "native" bus or rental car at about US$33 a day, gasoline negotiable.

HOTELS AND RESTAURANTS. The little hotel-restaurant **Lomipeau,** has 15 air-conditioned rooms with bath or shower, US$35 double. The hotel can arrange Wallisian dances, scuba, windsurfing—and a visit to the king. The **Moana Hou Hotel,** has 4 rooms, US$25 double; fans and communal toilet. Closer to the beach, is the **Hotel Tanoa** (seven rooms), owned and run by Jean-Pierre and Josette Defer. Rates are roughly US$25 single and US$35 double, but, like rates all over the Pacific, they are liable to increase with the cost of oil-generated electricity.

Food is outstanding and prepared in the French colonial style at the Lomipeau. A specialty is baby scallops, cooked in coconut oil with garlic and parsley. There is also a new Vietnamese restaurant.

At Futuna the church accommodates pilgrims simply but hospitably.

CURRENCY. The unit of currency used in Wallis and Futuna is the French Pacific Franc (C.F.P). 100 C.F.P. = US$.62.

NEW CALEDONIA

The Island of Light

by
KATHLEEN HANCOCK

New Zealander Kathleen Hancock is a free-lance journalist and photographer, covering travel, trade and current affairs in the island territories of the South Pacific.

Note: On the eve of enlarged Melanesian participation in government, there have been confrontations between French settlers and Melanesian tribes over land disputes and the extent of the franchise in the proposed referendum on independence. Disturbances have been largely limited to the upcountry districts and the Loyalty Islands. Tourists have never been involved. Neither Noumea, nearby offshore and country resorts, nor the Isle of Pines were affected at the time of writing. Consult your travel agent on the current state of affairs.

When Captain James Cook discovered New Caledonia in the course of his second voyage to the Pacific in 1774, he found a stone age Melanesian culture. The population of this 250 mile long, cigar-shaped island was estimated to be about 50,000 and consisted of a number of warring tribes speaking more than twenty mutually unintelligible dialects. Papuan/Australoid in racial type, the New Caledonian was a rugged warrior, and in times of war a headhunter and a cannibal.

However, the tribe that met Cook when he landed at Balade on the east coast were unarmed and shy.

D'Entrecasteaux followed in Cook's wake some years later. He heard the night cries of seabirds on reefs north of the Loyalty Group off the big island's east coast, and hastily made off in the other direction to anchor at Balade in 1793. However, unlike Cook, he found the people surly, dishonest and warlike and could hardly believe Cook's report of them. But it seems that this extraordinary alteration in the tribes of Balade was caused not by any basic change in the nature of the New Caledonians, but by the famine, drought and inter-tribal wars that had intervened.

No one worried much about New Caledonia for the next 50 years. Then French Catholic missionaries established themselves at Balade in 1843, but they and the traders that followed them met with a warm reception. Pillage, arson and murder were the order of the day and cannibalism was commonplace. Many a sandalwooder was killed, baked and eaten with a side dish of yams. However, a little research into early accounts of the goings on of sandalwood crews and traders reveals that their behaviour wasn't calculated to create a friendly climate in these islands, and it was generally their own fault that they ended up in the earth oven.

Hot on the heels of the missionaries, John Paddon, English ex-seaman, set up as a trader in New Caledonia and in 1845 he bought Ile Nou and established his trading station there. Dealing in sandalwood, whale oil and tortoiseshell, he brought groups of settlers from Australia to the as yet unclaimed island in his own ships. It looked as though the scene was set for a new British colony.

But the British delayed; neither the Colonial Office nor Queen Victoria were interested in acquisition. And the French had their own ideas about this remote island. The massacre of 17 naval personnel in the northwest in 1850 had enraged public opinion in France. Further, the establishment of a naval base in the southwest Pacific seemed a good thing. Finally, most pressing of all, the setting up of a prison colony with a climate less hostile than the pestilential vapors of infamous Guiana was felt in Paris to be an urgent matter.

So in 1853 the tricolore was raised at Balade by Admiral Febvrier Despointes. Ten years later the first shipload of convicts were building their own prison on Ile Nou, sold by Paddon to the French for a tidy sum. About this time the French realised that three British missionaries were firmly established in the Loyalty Islands only 50 miles off the New Caledonian mainland. A small "force de frappe" set off for Lifou, where they were confronted by 500 islanders led by the Rev. Macfarlane, a fiery Scots parson. After a bit of skirmishing, the better armed French subdued the islanders and their leader, declaring the group French territory.

Until penal transportation was abolished in 1898 there were, in any year, between seven and ten thousand able bodied criminals in the colony, engaged for the most part in mining the nickel that had been discovered by Jules Garnier in 1865. They were also employed on public works— many of New Caledonia's older public buildings date back to this time.

The deportees' lot was regarded in those days as not too uncomfortable. It wasn't unusual to see 50 prisoners controlled only by a man in uniform carrying a white umbrella. And 20 years later, George Griffiths, an English traveller, found Nouméa's nonchalant acceptance of the concerts provided by the prison band in the Place des Cocotiers "quite bizarre". He remarked that the "chef d'orchestre" had cut the heart out of a man he considered his rival in his wife's affections, got her to cook it, and dined off it with her before revealing its origin.

Legend has it that a Comte des Baue, at Les Beaux, in Provence established this gastronomic precedent . . . , serving the head of his wife's lover to his adulterous spouse.

But not all the deportees were common criminals. The Communards, who were sent out in their thousands after the collapse of the Paris Commune, were birds of a very different feather, honest workers and intellectuals for the most part. The Arabs who were exiled after the Kabyle revolt in Algeria were also political prisoners. But few of these were imprisoned at Ile Nou. Some were confined on the Ducos peninsula, but most finished up on the Isle of Pines where they enjoyed comparative freedom on one of the loveliest and healthiest islands in the Pacific. The great majority of Communards were pardoned and returned to France after the amnesty of 1879.

For a good while after annexation, the Melanesians resisted the French, but there was only one uprising of any importance—the great "canaque revolt" of 1878, which cost the French 200 lives during a guerilla campaign lasting more than a year. There is no record of Melanesian losses, but many villages were burned and crops destroyed during a long drawn out campaign which finally drew to a close when the Canala chiefs threw in their lot with the French.

From this time on the great mineral wealth of New Caledonia was developed in earnest. To fill the gap in the labour pool Indonesian, Japanese and Indo-Chinese indentured labourers were brought into the country on contract. Many of the Japanese remained, when their time was up, inter-marrying with European and Asian women. Most of the Vietnamese however, chose to return after the end of World War II, when the French held a referendum enabling them to make a choice between returning to South East Asia or remaining in the Pacific.

The Modern Scene

The outbreak of war in the Pacific led to great changes in this French colony. The island was stunned by the fall of France and shocked by the presence of the Vichy government in Nouméa. Feeling ran high, and finally Henri Sautot, French Resident Commissioner in the nearby New Hebrides, now Vanuatu, took steps. Supported by most of the populace of Nouméa and a great force of "broussards" or bush farmers, from the interior, he deposed the pro-Vichy regime and firmly placed New Caledonia on the side of Free France. In March 1942 he cordially received General Patch who arrived in the sleepy harbour with 40,000 men in 15 large battleships, 10 cruisers and several escort vessels.

Nouméa became an important American base, rated second for tonnage in the Pacific after San Francisco. Admiral Nimitz called the country the bastion from which the American offensives in the Solomons and the Philippines were launched. In New Caledonia they described it differently. "You couldn't pee behind a tree without peeing on an American," they complained. And no wonder, with something upward of 250,000 American troops in and around Nouméa at one time. But let it be said that there is still a great reservoir of good feeling and gratitude towards the thousands of Americans and New Zealanders who passed through New Caledonia during the war years.

As in all French territories, there's much excited political talk in Nouméa. At the time of writing France is offering the territory self-government, with a referendum in 1989 to choose between autonomy and complete independence.

Education is free and compulsory for all up to the age of 16 years. The little blue mini-buses that scurry round Nouméa day and night are used by citizens of every color and income level. Round the tables at the city's restaurants and nightclubs you'll see blue-black Somalis and pale Europeans; sloe-eyed Vietnamese and sturdy Melanesians; dusky Martiniquai and Chinese-Tahitians. It's an atmosphere you can breathe in.

The Economy

Upcountry New Caledonia is pretty well a solid lump of minerals for the whole of its 200 mile length. It's a case of scratch a mountain and you find a mine in this big cigar-shaped island. Nickel, iron, cobalt, chrome, coal, manganese, antimony, copper, lead and gold. You name it, they have it. Heading the list however, in vast quantity, is nickel, closely followed by chrome. The drop in world demand for chrome in the sixties caused the bottom to fall out of chrome mining, in spite of large deposits which are 50% pure ore. Today nickel has hit another low, and tourism is playing the major part in the country's economy. However, the big chrome mine at Tiébaghi has now reopened, mainly supplying the Chinese market.

Following their occupation of New Caledonia in 1853, the French wasted little time in investigating the mineral resources of the island. Jules Garnier, a government mining engineer, was sent out in 1863 and covered on foot and on horseback practically the whole of the wild and mountainous terrain of the new colony. He reported huge deposits of iron ore, copper and chrome, but he is famous principally for his discovery of the nickel ore which now bears his name—Garnierite. His report on his findings, published in 1867, is an historical document, and he also developed methods of smelting nickel ore which were used by the first smelters built near Nouméa.

Garnier's discoveries were followed by the establishment of the Société le Nickel by John Higginson, an Irish-born entrepreneur who later became a French citizen. "Le Nickel" was well established by the late 1870s and until a few years ago the company enjoyed a virtual monopoly in New Caledonia. There are a good many independent mine operators, known locally as "petit mineurs", in spite of fortunes running into millions. The "petit mineurs" sell a lower grade ore direct to Japan where it is processed in Japanese smelters, but this market is threatened today by recent nickel finds in the Philippines and Malaysia that are worked by cheap labour.

Most of the big mines are located on the island's east coast, where the nature of the terrain makes the delivery of ore to ship a comparatively simple matter. Mining is open cast, usually high in the mountains or on plateaux well above the narrow shoreline. The ore is recovered by excavators, bulldozers and power shovels and carried by immense 45 ton trucks to conveyors which send it directly down to the nickel ships on the coast. This economical and efficient method of working the rich deposits was born of necessity. New Caledonia could not produce a labour force large enough to cope with the demand, and almost total mechanisation was the only answer.

The "Société le Nickel" draws on many countries for the raw materials required to operate this huge concern. Tankers bring fuel from the Persian Gulf; coal for the coking plant comes from Australia; gypsum is bought from Mexico; New Zealand provides timber for the company's housing schemes.

New Caledonia can view with satisfaction her reserves of ore which have been estimated to be the world's greatest. And "le Nickel" proposes to reopen one of the shut-down furnaces shortly. This promise, together with the reopening of the chrome mine at Tiébaghi, has given New Caledonia's faltering economy a welcome boost.

There are said to be many millionaires among Noumea's 60,000 citizens. But in spite of all the money lying around, most New Caledonian housewives do their own work. They have to, because the labour shortage that has existed here for nearly a century, together with the highest wage scale of any other Pacific island territory, combine to reduce the domestic labour pool to less than a puddle.

Basic foods are pegged against inflation and of course, in this French community, wine heads the list of basics. Bread is about the same price as in the U.S. The big difference here is that it comes warm, crusty, and fresh from the ovens twice daily, including Christmas Day, saints days (of which there seem to be one a week) and all other holidays.

Compared to their Australian and New Zealand neighbours, New Caledonians pay a modest income tax. There's a solid payroll tax for all employers, worked out at from 25% to 30% of the pay-packet. This tax, from which all wage earners are exempt except for a 5.5% contribution towards old age pensions, covers the child benefit, pensions, maternity allowances, a workers' housing scheme and sundry other social security measures. If you're self employed—a doctor or lawyer for instance, you don't incur this tax, but you don't benefit from social security either.

Two notable developments in New Caledonia have been the increase in the population, which rose from 87,000 in 1963 to around 140,000 in 1979; and the development of tourism during the last ten years. The Melanesian population has risen during this period from about 41,000 to around 60,500, while an influx of immigrants, mostly from France, and also from former North African colonies, has boosted the European sector from 33,000 to around 50,000. Today Polynesians from Wallis and Tahiti number 17,000, while Vietnamese, Indonesians, ni-Vanuatu and others amount to nearly 12,000.

In the last 15 years or so tourism has seen its position in this territory change from that of a Cinderella neglected in favour of its rich ugly sister, mining, to a position where it's regarded as a welcome partner in the economy. Nearby Australia and New Zealand provide most of the holiday visitors to New Caledonia, but the slightly scruffy charm of the city of Nouméa combined with the beauty of the beaches, the reef and the outer islands, are rapidly making this a destination for travelers from further afield, mainly Japan. Considering the world economic scene, the cost of a holiday in these parts hasn't escalated nearly as much as might have been expected.

It does seem that things are pretty good for most people in this mineral rich island. As far as tourists are concerned, exchange rates are extremely favorable at the time of writing for visitors from Australia and the U.S., owing to the fall of the French franc.

Government

Today New Caledonia is a French Overseas Territory and an integral part of France. This status was gained in 1958 following the crisis in French politics which brought General de Gaulle to power. In response to de Gaulle's call for a Yes/No vote, 96% of the registered voters turned out and 74% of these opted for the new status.

All New Caledonian citizens of whatever race have French nationality, electing a President of France and sending to Paris two deputies, a senator, and a representative to the Economic and Social Council. The Mitterand government has made a start in buying back large tracts of land to hand over to the Melanesian people, the cost being shared by the territory and metropolitan France. Participation in government has also been increased for New Caledonians.

South Pacific Commission

Nouméa is also headquarters of the South Pacific Commission, housed in the old U.S. Army buildings at Anse Vata Beach. The Commission is a kind of small United Nations of the South Pacific and it is a heartening example of cooperation between the nations who administer territories in the South Pacific, the island territories themselves, and the increasing number of independent Pacific nations. Its staff of experts advise and assist the territories in their area with problems of health, social and economic development. It is a non-political body and gives its services only on demand. A visit to its operational headquarters at Anse Vata is well worth while for those interested.

Food and Drink

Eating is a passion in New Caledonia and you'll probably be given plenty of advice on where to find the best *crabe farcie,* the best *quenelles,* the best *couscous.* But since there are around 126 bistros, restaurants and shrines to "haute cuisine" on the island, there's not the slightest possibility of your being able to sample the lot. Moreover the scene changes frequently—they do say in these parts that a new restaurant opens every week and an old one closes. Space forbids a full catalogue of eating in Nouméa in our *Practical Information* section, later. But one thing's for sure—you'll eat well. Costs can vary from moderate to as high as you care to go, but whichever way you play it, you'll revel in the cuisine. And when your liver or your wallet protests, Nouméa's excellent delicatessens and groceries will provide you with a delicious picnic lunch for a very small outlay. With a *baguette* of crunchy bread, a *tranche* of Valmeuse, and a bottle of *vin ordinaire,* it's no hardship to economise at lunchtime.

See the *Dining Out* section for editor's choice. Check closing days—they differ.

Exploring New Caledonia

There are lots of good reasons for a holiday in New Caledonia. Obviously ones like sun and sea and fishing, gourmet cooking, the beat of the *tamoure* in dark Tahitian night clubs, the scruffy charm of the city of Nouméa, all these spring instantly to mind. But what you don't expect to find is courtesy, kindness and that easy going amiability that's a peculiarly Pacific thing. In this intriguing French Pacific territory, believe it or not, even the taxi drivers are polite!

Early explorers had a name for this island that lies above the Tropic of Capricorn on the fringe of the Coral Sea. They called it the Island of Light. And whether you fly in from Australia, New Zealand or Fiji, your first sight of land is breathtaking. The strange colors of mineral deposits streak fairytale peaks. A hundred promontories serpentine their way out to sea. Ten miles offshore the second biggest reef in the world glows jade and turquoise in the translucent ocean. As the aircraft loses height, you glimpse occasional sugar-white beaches between the green belt of coconut palms and the aquamarine waters of the great lagoon.

You're in a different world the moment you step out of the plane at Tontouta. Gendarmes in képis and very short shorts give the place a foreign legion air. But there's nothing military about their duties here—they simply hurry you through entry formalities.

Even at the airport you get a taste of the fascinating complex of peoples that makes up the population of this Pacific outpost. Chic Frenchwomen mingle with brown Melanesians. There's a sprinkling of Indonesian sarongs and a few tiny women wear the floppy black pants and white jacket of Tonkin. A group of Tahitians straight out of Gauguin stand next to a blue-black Somali off to Paris in a neat business suit.

A new shorter road to Nouméa cuts through rolling country covered with niaouli, cousin of the Australian eucalyptus. In the gullies blue smoke curls from the native houses roofed with the blotting paper bark of this tree. Breadfruit and banana grow by the wayside, and the gardens round the long, low settlers' bungalows vibrate with op-art colors—hot-pink hibiscus, magenta bougainvillea, scarlet poinsettia and citron yellow allamanda riot everywhere.

Nouméa

For most tourists their first sight of Nouméa is a big surprise. You expect to find a drowsy, humid, tropical town meandering round the shores of the harbour. But the reality is quite startling. Nouméa is a busy little city where the thermometer hovers pleasantly in the mid-seventies. The town clusters round a central square shaded by flame trees. A few tall palms give the "Place des Cocotiers" (Coconut Square) its name. Colonial buildings of faded pink stone nudge sparkling new structures of glass and concrete. There are chic boutiques with readymades from the great fashion houses of France. Dark little Indonesian or Tahitian shops are hung with shell necklaces, pandanus hats, and batik or pareu cloth. Chinese stores sell everything from incense burners to men's socks. In the back streets bougainvillea and Burmese honeysuckle spill over garden walls. Here and there among the shuttered houses you catch a glimpse of a cool courtyard.

The citizens of this tropical island are a multi-racial mixture—French, Melanesian, Indonesian, Tahitian, Arab, Martiniquais, Somali. In this atmosphere integration is no problem. The population is divided up almost half and half European and Melanesian; with a sizeable section of Polynesians from Tahiti and the Wallis Group. Vietnamese, Indonesians and "others" make up the rest of the total.

One of the foremost attractions of Nouméa is the transport system. From the bus depot on the Baie de la Moselle little blue mini-buses scuttle round town and out to the beaches and suburbs. There is no timetable—the bus leaves when it's full and the standard fare will take you anywhere in town or the suburbs. The drivers—Martiniquais, Somali, French, Melanesian or Indonesian—are an obliging lot, and a round trip on a bus is an entertainment in itself.

Within the precincts of the town you realise that there's nothing sleepy about this little "Paris of the Pacific". It moves! At 6 A.M. all Nouméa starts thinking of work, for shops and offices open at 7:30 A.M. and for a good half hour before that cars, scooters, and mopeds whizz along the narrow streets in a continuous stream. Most of the population seems to be on wheels, but the standard of living is high in these parts and no-one rides the lowly bicycle. At this hour of the morning the balmy air is filled with a truly Gallic blaring of horns and screeching of brakes.

Mind you, all this bustle is largely on the surface—indulged in, one suspects, because of the lovely noise it makes. There's always plenty of time in this part of the Pacific, and the Caledonians have their own ideas about the important things in life—there'd be a riot if those long loaves of bread didn't issue from the bakers' ovens all day long.

The hubbub comes to an abrupt end at 11 A.M. Nouméa goes home, with a loaf of the mid-day baking under-arm, and settles down for a lengthy French lunch and siesta. This is where the visitor has to look sharp. Eleven-thirty is the hour for lunch—and alas for the hapless tourist who wanders into a restaurant around 1:30 P.M. hoping to be fed!

New Caledonians live on and in the water. The yacht harbour is a forest of masts. Swimming in the limpid waters that surround this big island, skin diving off the reef, toasting on the white beaches—this is the New Caledonian way of life.

From the bays just out of town you can board a cruiser or catamaran for a day trip to Amedée atoll—a good way of enjoying all the charms of this informal sport-loving island. This isn't a trip for worshippers of muscular activity, it's for lotus eaters—though you can swim round the tiny atoll if you feel inclined. No, it's a place to lie on the sugar-white sand under a hau tree, dunking yourself in the translucent sea at intervals. Either the *Samara* or *Mary D* makes a good trip. *Samara* captained by Jack Owen, provides the best lunch, cooked by his delightful Tahitian-Chinese wife, Christine, and accompanied by songs from the Tahitian crew. A new addition to Nouméa's nautical scene is the ingenious Aquascope. Crouched off the Club Med jetty like a huge aluminum seabird, this unique machine has a windowed underwater viewing area in its belly—it will take you into the lagoon to get a real close-up of the fishy and coralline inhabitants.

Patrick and Minerva Helmy can organise a luxury cruise aboard their *Motor Ship California* which boasts a French chef and provides all types of water sports. Or, more down-to-earth, there's atoll living for naturists on M'Ba Island not far offshore in the great lagoon, offering swimming, snorkelling, volley ball, and other games (through Hoki Mai Cruises). You can eat superbly in Nouméa and dance on any night of the week. You'll try Tahitian fish, Indonesian curries, Italian pasta, Spanish paella, and Chinese specialties. You can sample every style of French cooking. The traditional French preoccupation with food and wine leads, of course, to the traditional French malaise—"le foie". To hear one of the locals bemoaning the state of his liver while consuming an epicurean meal washed down by copious draughts of good red wine—this is an experience. "Too much exercise", mutters the sufferer, spearing another delectable morsel.

Between Anse Vata beach and the Baie des Citrons Dr. Catala's world famous aquarium attracts scientists from all over. A new wing dramatically displays the vivid colors of the unique collection of living deep-sea corals, creating the effect of being actually submerged on the night-dark floor of the ocean home of these extraordinary creatures. You will probably have to be dragged away from the fishy and coralline wonders that are displayed here with such taste.

On weekends sturdy Melanesian women provide a free show with their cricket matches at the square near the gendarmerie. French citizens of every race and colour play *Pétanque,* a kind of bowls, under the spreading palms in the Place des Cocotiers. Eating can be expensive at night, but a picnic lunch will more than even things up. And you can dance all night in the city's *boîtes* for the price of a drink or two. Tipping is absolutely forbidden in this civilised island.

Down at the docks you can still find the traditional bead-curtained bistros, where a beer or an apertif can lead to an amiable encounter with the locals. And there's entertainment at the wharves where inter-island ferrys are crowded with outer islanders in a dazzle of gay *muumuus.*

Outside Nouméa

But however intriguing Nouméa may be, it's not the whole story. If you're one for open spaces, Melanesian villages, trade stores, deserted beaches fringed with rustling palms—in fact all the atmosphere beloved of old Pacific hands, then you've got to make another choice. You can fly to Poindimié on the East Coast with Air Calédonie and potter up north, either by country bus, if you're rugged, or private car.

Up country, inns are small and informal; the plumbing works, in spite of a tendency for the towel rail to fall to the floor. The food is generally first rate, with the accent on local fish, crab and oysters. It will be good French bourgeois cooking and what more could you want? In these parts you come across old churches that look like illustrations to a book of fairytales, and the Melanesian villages have a picture book quality too.

Finally a geological surprise awaits the visitor to Hienghène, further up the coast. The road winds through light forest hung with exotic parasites, along shores bordered with casuarina and coconut palms. Bronze hedges of "beefsteak" plant mark the sites of villages gay with hibiscus, cassia, poinsetta and tiare. Blue bignonia and magenta bougainvillea clamber over the tiny huts roofed with layers of white bark.

Suddenly Hienghène's stark seascape explodes in the lagoon. Oddly unrelated to the mainland, sheer black rocks rise abruptly from the sea to a height of more than 400 feet. From one side you can see them as the towers of Notre Dame. From another you get a picture of a gigantic sitting hen.

A new road has recently been built from Hienghène to loop around the top of the island, connecting up with the west coast road at Koumac. The northern scenery above Poum is spectacular—white beaches, offshore atolls, a denser rain forest—the road up the west coast is sealed as far as Koumac and work is proceeding on the mountain pass between Bourail and Poindimié. Unsealed roads are reasonable, and the surface is good.

Tribal life in upcountry New Caledonia goes on much as it always has—gardens are tended, a new house built from time to time. Coffee plantations shelter under the bigger trees of the forest all the way up the island, and at the right time of the year, villagers busy themselves drying the beans for market. In the valleys and on the east coast the old life of "the bush" still survives—it's a warm and friendly place. A fisherman on the reef may offer you part of his catch without the least thought of reward. In the small inns tucked away among the palm trees you can really relax over a meal of fresh caught fish and a bottle of vin d'Alsace.

The east coast is a favourite area for campers, especially for French families from Nouméa. Apart from mosquitos, there are no stinging or biting things in this favoured island and beaches and river banks are often bright with gay blues, yellow and multi-coloured stripes of smart French tents.

From Hienghène you can fly straight back to Nouméa if you wish, over the great mountain chain that marches down the centre of the island's two hundred and forty odd miles. Huge deposits of the island's great mineral wealth lie just beneath the surface of the gaunt mountain tops. From the small Air Calédonie plane you can see the winding russet trails traced by prospecting bulldozers. At Thio the towers and turrets of the immense opencast nickel mine look from the air like the red ruins of some ancient city, but as you fly southeast you soon see the familiar ribbon of white coral sand edging the blue-green bays and inlets.

Beyond Nouméa

You can't really leave this area without staying a night or two at an outer island. Ilot Maître, 30 minutes from Nouméa, within the great lagoon, is easiest to get to. White-roofed bungalows are dotted among the light bush of this little atoll, whose waters are a marine reserve. On the lee side a sandy beach, on the windward side rock pools for fossicking. The cuisine is first rate, served in a beamed, high-ceilinged restaurant overlooking the lagoon. Birds are returning to this island—it's a charming place to unwind.

Isle of Pines

The day trip to this beautiful island with Air Calédonie shows you some of the loveliest beaches in the Pacific. Its sugar white sand skirts blue-green lagoons and its beauty is world famous. Lunch is included on this excursion and divers will also find plenty of scope at the Nauticlub, where Swiss-born Albert Thomas and Hilary Root from New Zealand offer picnics (local fish barbecue, diving, swimming and shelling, on off-shore islets). Diving tuition is available and the rustic ambiance is warm and friendly.

Since the closure of the *Relais de Kanumera,* a number of "gîtes", or rural lodgings, have been built on this lovely island. They are small complexes of 3 to 5 bungalows, which are well constructed by members of the local tribes. Meals can be provided—by arrangement—or you can do for yourself. At the Bay of Ouameo, M. Lepers, a former plumber from Paris, dispenses simple but hearty hospitality at the Gite de Kodjeue—sturdy bungalows, excellent meals at a long table under a thatched shelter, a safe beach, plus fishing, pirogues. M. Lepers has extended his domain to a charming rustic restaurant just a step from the fabulous white beaches of Kuto and Kanumera. He will drive guests over for the day—great food and a changing room for swimmers. Also available are trips to Grottoes (Captain Cook's vessel is said to have been spied at sea by islanders peeping through a gap in the wall of one of these caverns) or a visit to the century-old mission at Vao. Nataiwatch is in a leafy grove a few yards from a white beach, and each bungalow is allotted its own private shower and toilet in a nearby block.

No visitor to the Isle of Pines should leave without exploring the prison ruins, cemeteries, water works, and other relics of the "deportation". Most of the ruins are to be found in the light bush near the isthmus of Kuto.

PRACTICAL INFORMATION FOR NEW CALEDONIA

WHAT WILL IT COST? Room costs in this territory are moderate in Nouméa and reasonable in the outer islands and upcountry. Food can be an expensive item, according to your tastes, but in most restaurants in the cheaper price range, the set menu is pretty reasonable at about 750–1250 C.F.P. The top class gourmet places will charge you about what you'd pay in similar restaurants at home for three courses and coffee. A bottle of Beaujolais or Riesling will cost around 1600 C.F.P. a bottle. You will eat fine food and the wine list will be extensive.

Drinks aren't cheap either, but it's necessary to remember that by most standards they are doubles—then the price doesn't seem too high. Soft drinks and beer are comparatively expensive and cost nearly as much as a carafe of wine. The remedy is obvious. If you're looking for your money's worth alcoholically speaking, a liqueur is the best buy. They are more like triples and you won't forget in a hurry your first sight of a New Caledonia-size cognac or Benedictine. Night-club drinks are expensive, as everywhere, but there is no cover charge as a rule and you can sit or dance over a drink or two all night without being hassled to buy more.

Local transport is fairly reasonable. The bus ride from Tontouta airport to your city hotel costs 1,500 C.F.P. The remarkable bus service charges a flat rate of 80

C.F.P. from town to Anse Vata beach and runs from 5:30 A.M. to 7:30 P.M. Taxis charge 420 C.F.P. daytime, after 6 P.M. 450 C.F.P. for the 2-mile trip from Anse Vata to the city. Air Calédonie's rates are reasonable. Rental cars are a bit more expensive than Fiji, but cheaper than Tahiti.

Sightseeing tours will cost around 4,600 C.F.P., including lunch and wine, for the all day Amedée lighthouse trip. A three hour fishing tour will run to 3,000 C.F.P., while a whole day's scuba diving will set you back about 9,900 C.F.P. It costs 300 C.F.P. to enter the aquarium and the same for entry to the big Olympic swimming pool. At the time of writing, US$1.00 = 169 C.F.P.

 WHEN TO GO. New Caledonian weather is pleasant all year round. December to March are the warmest months, fairly humid but only moderately rainy. Temperatures around 28°C. April to November is generally drier, with an average temperature of 22°C. June, July, August can be quite cool at times and you may need to pack a sweater or a wrap of some kind for going out at night. Visitors swim all year round. The locals prefer the summer months of November to March.

TOURIST INFORMATION BUREAU. Office du Tourisme, 25 Avenue du Maréchal Foch. Phone 27.26.32. Telex: N.C. Turism 063 N M. Tourist information and literature: Syndicat d'Initiative, Place des Cocotiers, Phone 27.27.03. Also: PO Box 688, Nouméa.

LANGUAGE. French is the official language but English is widely understood.

WATER. Modern pipeline supply. Safe in all areas.

HOLIDAYS. Legal holidays in New Caledonia are on January 1st, Easter Monday, 1st May, Ascension Day, Whit Monday, 14th July, 15th August, 24th September, 1st November, 11th November, 25th December. Watch out for saints days—they crop up often.

CLOSING TIMES. 7.30 to 11.00 A.M. and 2.00 to 6.00 P.M. Every shop and office closes at lunch time. Milkbars and restaurants stay open. Lunch 11.00 A.M. to 1.00 P.M. Banking hours 7.20 A.M. to 3.45 P.M. Closed Saturdays.

LAUNDRY & DRY CLEANING. A 48-hour service is available in most hotels throughout New Caledonia. Some hotels provide same-day service.

SERVICE NUMBERS. Police: 17. Radio Taxis: 28.35.12 and 28.53.70. Surcharge 50 CFP for telephone taxi.

CONSULATES. Australian Consulate, 19–21, Avenue du Maréchal Foch; New Zealand Consulate, 4 BD. Vauban.

RELIGIOUS SERVICES. Catholic services at: Cathedral St. Joseph 6, 8, 9 A.M., and 6 P.M. Church of the Vow, 7, 9 A.M., and 6.30 P.M. Protestant: at 9 A.M.

TIPPING. No tipping, please.

MUSÉE DE NOUMÉA. Well worth a visit—well displayed collection of Melanesian artifacts.

PASSPORTS AND CUSTOMS. Valid passport required. Visa not required for stay of up to 30 days provided visitor has return or onward ticket. Visa may be obtained for stay of up to three months, good for multiple entries and extendable upon arrival. Visas can be obtained from French consulate or embassy. Two photos needed. 200 cigarettes, 50 cigars or 250 grams of tobacco, 1 bottle of alcoholic beverages may be imported duty-free.

LOST PROPERTY. Contact Nouméa Police Station, rue de Sebastopol. Phone 27.22.53.

POST OFFICE. For letters, stamps, parcels, cables and telephone: Baie de la Moselle.

ELECTRICITY. A.C. 220 v. 50 cycles (2 prongs).

HEALTH: Smallpox vaccination required only if arriving within 14 days from infected area. Nouméa has 1 public hospital, 3 private clinics and 17 chemists. Contact your hotel for English-speaking doctor or dentist.

ART GALLERIES. Galerie Galleria Cr. Rues Gallieni and Republique L'Encardrerie, 2 bis Rue de Verdun, La Traboule, Le Village, Ave. Foch, Galerie Arenco, 21 Avenue Foch. L'Atelier, 51 Rue Jean Jaurès.

FESTIVALS AND SPECIAL EVENTS. *January 1*—New Year's Day is a public holiday and celebrated throughout the country. *Easter* usually starts the sport season with events throughout the New Caledonian "winter" season. *May 1*—Labor Day public holiday. *May 20*—Ascension Day Public Holiday. *July 14*—Bastille Day, celebrated throughout the country. Military parade and public ball. *August 28–30,* Agricultural Fair at Bourail. *September 24*—New Caledonia Day. Sports events. *November 1*—All Saints Day. Families place flowers at grave sites. Public holiday. *November 11,* Armistice Day. *Mid-November*—Round New Caledonia Auto Safari. Teams from Australia, New Zealand and Japan compete in this highly contested car rally. *December 25*—Father Christmas parades through Nouméa streets in the evening.

SPORT. Access to the Tennis Club du Mont. Coffyn, the Cercle Nautique and the Cercle d'Etrier (riding) must be provided by a member. The new Squash Club at the Baie des Pécheurs welcomes visitors—bring your own whites—all other gear is available on the premises. The Olympic pool behind the Chateau Royal is open daily. The Spear Fishing Club has information on outings to the Barrier Reef. Water-skiing and wind-surfing can be arranged from your hotel. Noumea Yacht Charters provide bareboat and skippered charters, day sail picnics and diving expeditions in superb Beneteau First 30 and First 38 yachts. Provisioning optional, but reasonable. An enchanting sailing area. Box 848 Noumea, telex 055 NM.

AQUARIUM. Unique in the world for its magnificent fluorescent corals, colorful fishes and tropical fauna from the nearby lagoon (Anse Vata), from 1.30 P.M. to 4.30 P.M. Adults 300 C.F.P., students 150 C.F.P., children 50 C.F.P.

WHAT TO WEAR. Light, informal clothes—women will find sophisticated dressing along these lines in the better restaurants. Long trousers for men at night in restaurants and clubs. Only the Casino requires jacket and tie.

CLIMATE: Dry season from April to December. Rainy season early February to late March.

AVERAGE TEMPERATURE:

	Jan	Feb	Mar	Apr	May	Jun	Jul	Aug	Sep	Oct	Nov	Dec
°F	83.5	84.2	82.9	79.7	77.0	74.5	72.3	72.9	74.1	77.9	80.6	82.6
°C	28.6	29.0	28.3	26.5	25.0	23.6	22.4	22.7	23.6	25.4	27.0	28.1

AVERAGE RAINFALL: (inches)
4¾   4   4¾   5   4¼   3¾   3¼   3   2   1½   1½   2¾

HOW TO GET THERE. *Flights from:* Paris (via Singapore), *U.T.A.* two times weekly; *U.T.A.* flies two times weekly and *Qantas* once weekly from Sydney; *U.T.A.* has one flight weekly from Auckland (New Zealand) and two flights weekly from Los Angeles via Papeete. *Air N.Z.* has one flight weekly from Auckland. *Air Calédonie International*, once weekly from Melbourne and Brisbane, twice weekly from Nadi, five flights weekly from Vanuatu. It is best to check with your air carrier as to which of the smaller lines can meet your needs.

HOW TO GET AROUND. *By air: Air Calédonie* maintains regular service from Noumea to various points on New Caledonia and the surrounding small islands. Points served: Isle of Pines; Mare Lifou, Ouvea and Tiga in the Loyalty Group, the East and West Coasts. Rates from C.F.P. 6,000–11,000.

By sea: Mary D, 60 passenger tourist boat operated all day; scheduled lighthouse cruises every Sunday or on request; also lagoon cruises, diving and fishing trips. 35-passenger boat *Samara* for charter, with Jack and Christine Owen, 33 Rue de Paris, Val Plaisance. Day trip on well run boat, with great food.

Bus system: From the bus depot buses leave every five minutes for the following destinations: Baie des Citrons, Anse Vata, Port Despointes. Trianon, Motor Pool, Magenta Airport. Fare: 75 C.F.P. for any distance, any direction. Pay the driver on leaving the bus. There is a handy bus stop on the square outside new Town Hall.

Car rental: Avis, Europcar, Mencar, Hertz, and *Vata Location* offer reasonable self-drive rates throughout the island. Enquire at your hotel. A current valid driver's license is required. Drive on the right.

Radio-taxis: Phone 28.35.12 and 28.53.70. Fare Anse Vata to town around 420 C.F.P., 450 C.F.P. after 6 P.M. Drive on the right, give way to the right.

TOUR OPERATORS: *Center Voyage,* 27 Avenue du Marechal Foch, tel. 28.40.40; *Tour Royale,* Route de la Baie des Citrons, near Nouméa Beach Hotel, tel. 28.29.71 and 28.28.42; *Amac Tours,* 2 Rue d'Alma, tel. 27.41.53 and 28.65.10.

DUTY FREE SHOPPING. At Tontouta International Airport and in Nouméa at the licensed duty free shops which are listed on a brochure published by the New Caledonia Tourist Office and also identified by window stickers.

SHOPPING. Shopping in Nouméa is fun, and for women, at any rate, first thoughts in this French territory are of clothes. And clothes, whether dresses or tops or skirts or underwear are an eyepopping temptation as you explore town. On this sport-loving island the emphasis is on casual gear—cotton knits, slacks, swimwear.

Look for the sign "Soldes"—a sale. In Nouméa a sale is a sale. You may pick up a $120 dress for $60 at one of the boutiques displaying the sign.

Océanie, the big supermarket, is fun to rummage in for everything from Dijon mustard to Italian cotton knits. *Barrau* and *Ballande,* one time trade stores, are now transformed into department stores—the former is now Prisunic-Barrau. *Ballande's* kitchenware department will probably fill some gaps in your "batterie de cuisine."

Perfume is sold almost everywhere in town, but *Rozanne* in the Rue Georges Clemenceau just off the square has a tremendous range and is duty free as well. Delightful accessories here too. *Marlene* in the Rue d'Alma and *Bricoles* at the top end of the square are both well-established duty free shops, and this is one area of shopping where a 30% discount really matters.

There are plenty of elegant specialty shops for the well-heeled locals where you can pay the earth—the jewelery at *Veyret* on the Rue d'Alma will make your mouth water. But further up the street *Cendrillon* is a treasure house filled with all kinds of precious trinkets within the reach of most travelers. Opposite, *Anémone* displays a most intriguing selection of costume and semi-precious jewelry. *Hippocampe* in Ave. Maréchal Foch for unusual bibelots modestly priced.

French and Italian leather handbags are a great buy in Nouméa and many of the duty free shops carry them. Real leather is the rule not the exception and *Le Bagage Calédonien* has a large range at good prices. Ballande's duty-free shop has a wide range of bags, clothing, perfume, cosmetics, and even shoes.

French children's clothes from birth to adolescence are just as enticing. From doll size dresses for doll size French babies to chic toddlers clothing and fashionable gear for teenagers, French designers have something the others haven't got. But watch out for differences in sizing by years. Multiply by two if you're buying for hefty Anglo-Saxon children. Then shoes! Perhaps, with perfume and handbags, these are the best buy in Nouméa. They run from amusing casual footwear to silver and gold slippers that would grace *Maxim's*. You can buy most of the top French shoe designers—Pierre Cardin, J.B. Martin and Jourdan—starting at US$60. The *Boty* shops and the Bettina Arcade have the biggest range. On the Rue d'Alma, *First* for Italian and French shoes, and *Les Champs Elysées* for ready-mades and sportswear from the Paris couturiéres.

In this town the male shopper isn't catered for as extensively as the female, but casual gear is a good buy, if a trifle expensive. St. Trop in the Rue Vauban isn't cheap, but quality menswear here is good value.

The duty free shopping is geared to make the traveler's life easier. There is an excellent duty free store at the airport, but you can also obtain a 20% to 30% discount in a number of licensed shops in Nouméa on purchases totalling 2000 C.F.P. or over. The Duty Free Shopping Guide, published by the Tourist Office, supplies a list of these shops, a map of Nouméa with them clearly marked, and a set of rules applying to the purchase of duty free goods before departure. The range includes jewelery, perfume, clothing, handbags, shoes, cosmetics, cameras and electronic gear. Tourists must not forget to hand in their duty-free receipts to Customs at Toutouta on departure.

TOURS. Tours of Nouméa can be booked by telephone from local agents. Most Nouméa companies have their own cars for touring; some operate buses. The most popular tours are listed here. Tours around the city and environs range from around $ US17 to $ US30 or so, the latter price including lunch. The *Isle of Pines* day trip, including air fare, will be around $US90. Two- to four-day trips up-country from $ US135 to $ US240.

City-Day Tours of Nouméa and environs: The following tours are available by car limousine from local agents. *Nouméa city tour with Aquarium:* (3 hours) Includes drive through downtown shopping area and suburbs; the world famous saltwater Aquarium de Nouméa, with tanks duplicating biological conditions of the reef; St. Joseph's Cathedral, built by convict labor; Place des Concotiers, the central square with its flaming poinciana trees; first settlement of Vallée des Colons; Magenta Bay; Mt. Coffyn Heights for spectacular city-harbor view. Daily. *Mt. Koghi Tour:* (4 hours) Travel through tropical jungle to Mt. Koghi for view of Nouméa peninsula, lagoon and barrier reef. Short jungle walk through rain forest to area waterfalls. Refreshments at mountain inn included. Daily 11 A.M. *Mt. Dore Tour:* (3 hours) Travel through country, viewing coastal scenery around the Mountain of Gold. Stops at Mission of St. Louis with its native village of thatch-roofed bungalows and dairy farm and La Conception, the oldest church in Nouméa. Daily. *Mt. Dore Bougna Feast:* (5 hours) Same as Mt. Dore Tour above, with lunch feast provided at a private residence. Bougna feast includes chicken, banana, pawpaw, taro and other vegetables cooked under preheated stones and served with a rum punch and French wine. Wednesday at 11 A.M. *East Coast Tour* (Full day). Visits cattle-raising area on the west coast, turning at Boulouparis, crossing high central mountain chain to the east, with a stop at a nickel-producing area. (*Note:* New Caledonia is the third largest nickel-producing country, after Canada and Russia.) Visit old mission villages and ghost towns. Lunch at restaurant along the way, then on to coffee and fruit growing country. Daily, on request. *Alize-Raid* is a new enterprise run by an experienced pair of operators who organize overland trips of one to four days, taking their passengers into the real back country. Meals, tents and all sporting equipment are provided. 13 Rue Tabou. tel. 26.26.41. From $ US50 to $ US260 (approx.) all inclusive. *Three-Day East Coast-Hienghene: 1st day* —Transfer from Nouméa hotel to airport for flight to Hienghene. Stay at Relais de Koulnoue; *2nd day* —Excursion to native village, grottos and lookouts; *3rd day* —At leisure until return afternoon flight to Nouméa. Monday, Wednesday and Friday. *Lighthouse Excursion* (out of Nouméa): Full-day tour. Travel by launch to Amedee Lighthouse, built during reign of Napoleon and shipped in pieces to New Caledonia. View coral formations and fluorescent fish. Tour lighthouse before lunch is served under banyan trees. Time for swim, snorkeling, siesta. Daily at 7:45 A.M., approx. $ US33 with lunch. Enjoy water sports on the luxury *Motor Ship California* or, more simply, with M. Plancade and Hoki Mai Cruises.

Air Calédonie, Magenta Airport, Nouméa, B.P. 212, New Caledonia. Offers regular service to various points within the country: Isle of Pines, Mare, Lifou and Ouvea in the Loyalty Group, the East and West Coasts. The Isle of Pines daytrip is well worth while.

For general help and information, the Syndicat d'Initiative is now located in the old "Mairie," or Town Hall, Rue Jean Jaurés, on the Place des Cocotiers.

 HOTELS. Most are smallish and intimate, with tariffs ranging from moderate to very reasonable. The newer hotels at Anse Vata and the Baie des Citrons are right up-to-date, and so are a few of the newer bungalow hotels upcountry and in the outer islands. Outside Nouméa at certain times of the year it's wise to carry your own mosquito repellent and a packet of mosquito coils, though the management can usually supply the latter. Hotel categories: *First Class,* US$40–50; *Moderate,* US$30–39; *Inexpensive,* under US$30.

NOUMÉA

Escapade. *First class.* Atoll resort within the lagoon, 25 mins. from town by launch. 44 bungalows, swimming, snorkeling, windsurfing, hobie cats, pool, floor shows twice weekly. Excellent restaurant.

Isle de France-TraveLodge, Anse Vata. *First Class.* 63 rooms, airconditioned, refrigerator, coffee making facilities. Bath as well as shower. 7 suites with kitchenette. Restaurant, bar, pool with snack service. Conference facilities. Down a quiet cul-de-sac, 3 minutes from Anse Vata beach.

Noumea Beach, Baie des Citrons. *First Class.* Charming hotel, excellent restaurant and snack bar, sidewalk café overlooking sheltered beach. Also Japanese restaurant. Rates include American breakfast, water sports, cycles.

Le Surf. Anse Vata Beach. *First Class.* Rocher a la Voile. Delightful ambiance, coffee shop, restaurants. Pool, casino.

Lantana Beach. *Moderate.* The old Lantana completely rebuilt with two more floors, color T.V., video, bar. No restaurant but many nearby. On Anse Vata Beach.

Nouvata, Anse Vata Beach. *Moderate.* Recently modernised beachfront hotel, 85 rooms, airconditioned, refrigerators. 2 restaurants, one French, one Chinese. Pool, with snack service. Pleasant garden setting. Charlie's American Bar a popular rendezvous.

Mocambo, Baie des Citrons. *Moderate.* Your host will be M. Lombard of "La Rotonde" restaurant. Completely refurbished. Air conditioning, color TV, tea and coffee-making facilities. Free transfer to "La Rotonde", one of Nouméa's top restaurants. Telex. Conference rooms.

Noumea Village Hotel. *Moderate.* Apartments, parking, restaurant, right in town. Daily poolside buffet lunch good value, free bus to Kuendu Beach.

Le Lagon, Route de l'Anse Vata. *Moderate.* Air conditioning. Private facilities. Attractive roof-top restaurant with terrace overlooking Anse Vata beach. Tea and coffee-making facilities. Telex, convention facilities for 150. Recently refurbished.

Paradise Park Motel. *Moderate.* A charming complex in the Valée des Colons; set in 3 acres of garden. Big pool, bar, restaurant, coffee shop. Air-conditioning, kitchenette. Shuttle bus to town and beaches 4 times a day.

Le Paris, Rue Sebastopol in town. *Moderate.* Convenient hotel, a few deluxe rooms, desk, telex, etc. Caters to business clientele, but families welcome, two nightclubs in complex, restaurant, hairdresser.

Hotel La Pérouse, in town near top of Place des Cocotiers. *Inexpensive.* Small, basic, 30 rooms, 18 with shower, air-conditioning extra. Snack restaurant and bar.

Motel Anse Vata, Val Plaisance. *Inexpensive.* 19 Rue le Laroque. 22 fully equipped one room motel flats with bath and kitchen. Airconditioning, balcony. Residential area, few minutes walk from Anse Vata Beach. Good food shops and restaurants adjacent.

Club Mediterrannée, Anse Vata Beach. 550 beds, 3 miles from town. The Club Med. recipe as before, great for investigating Club Med. but investigation of Nouméa and the hinterland frowned on. Plenty of well-organized spontaneity, lots of yé yé, as the French have it, good food at set hours. A bargain package.

YOUTH HOSTEL. Situated on a hill behind the city. 60 bunk beds in dormitories. Communal facilities. Lounge, dining room and recreational centre. Around 600 C.F.P. per night. Non-Y.H.A. members also accommodated.

WEST COAST COUNTRY HOTELS

Evasion 130, Sarramea. *Moderate.* About 80 miles from Nouméa, in the hills behind La Foa. 8 small bungalows, private facilities. A la carte restaurant, superb food, bar, pool. Walks, climbing, villages nearby. Not far from La Foa, where seafood is a specialty at l'Hotel Banu and Le Relais Melanésien.

Koniambo Hotel, Koné. Near the airfield; Nouméa gourmets fly up for Sunday lunch. Bar, pool, riding, if the quality of the mounts doesn't matter; rodeo 2 or 3 times yearly, cowboy country.

Madona Hotel, Koumac. A charming little inn tucked away in this cattle town. A good base for visits to northern beaches.

Les Paillottes de Ouenghi. *Moderate.* Quiet country retreat on Ouenghi River. 15 bungalows; pool, tennis, riding, canoeing, good food. Only 60 kms. from Bourail—a fascinating area for students of history and World War II.

Tontoutel. Airport motel. Modern, pool, good food.

EAST COAST COUNTRY HOTELS

Hotel de la Plage, Poindimié. *Inexpensive.* 15 rooms with private facilities. Off the main road. River nearby. Walks to tribal villages. Vieux Touho and Poyes 20 miles north are worth a visit.

Relais d'Amoa, Poindimié. *Inexpensive.* On the beachfront, 5 bungalows and 5 rooms in annex, all with private facilities. Bar, restaurant. Manager keen fisherman. Cuisine features local seafood. Hotel completely equipped with diving gear. Delightful setting, pool and good beach.

Relais de Koulnoué, Hienghène. *Inexpensive.* On beachfront, 10 bungalows, 25 rooms, all facilities, in beautiful gardens. Restaurant, bar, pool, tennis. Excellent cuisine. M. Fairbank is an amusing host, welcomes tennis partners. Picnics to nearby atolls.

Note: In most up-country hotels, double and single rooms cost the same.

 DINING OUT. Limitations of space prevent a comprehensive listing. So we will therefore present our own choices ranged in rough order of price—which leads to another problem.

It's not easy to categorise New Caledonian restaurants in terms of cost. First class and even the second rank of eating houses are not cheap, for the raw material of any meal you eat will cost your host a pretty penny. Most meat and vegetables are imported by air from nearby New Zealand and Australia and sometimes even from the west coast of the U.S.

The "elegant décor" required for de luxe rating will often be lacking. But instead, your surroundings will be individual and attractive, and the cooking itself in the better restaurants rates a "super de luxe" listing. Fine food is a passion in this country and even the humblest shack on a dusty country road may conceal a "cordon bleu" cook.

We have therefore not attempted to rate restaurants according to the décor but according to food and service—though in this offbeat French territory you will find that service will mostly be slow. Haste is a bad word here, as it is in most Pacific islands. But one thing is certain—you'll be able to indulge in an orgy of gourmet eating and sample Italian, French, Spanish, Indonesian, African, Chinese cooking. And when your liver or your wallet protests, the excellent delicatessens and groceries in town and at Anse Vata beach will provide you with mouthwatering goodies for a picnic lunch for very little cost.

Price categories: Expensive: US$18.00 and up; *Moderate:* US$12.00 to US$16.00; *Inexpensive:* US$8.00 to US$10.00.

(Check closing days—they differ.)

Expensive

Le Berthelot. In charming house in the Vallee des Colons. Fine cooking, interesting menu.

Centre Club. Another shrine for gourmets—cordon blue cuisine in town.

Dodin Bouffant. Named for the Paris restaurant of gourmet fame. Popular with lovers of fine food.

L'Eau Vive. Something different—an unpretentious restaurant run by a missionary order of nuns. Superb food. Moderate prices on the ground floor, fairly expensive upstairs. The sisters import their own wine. Faubourg Blanchot.

Le Petit Train. Baie des Citrons-gourmet cooking, superb outlook.

La Truffière. First class cuisine, specialising in the dishes of Périgord. Rue Gabriel Laroque, Val Plaisance, near Anse Vata Beach.

El Cordobes. Spanish dishes a specialty. Try their fish clothed in flaky pastry.

Moderate

Aux Trois Bonheurs. First class Chinese cuisine.

Brasserie St. Hubert, Toulouse Lautrec setting for this bar-restaurant in an old colonial building at the top of the Square. A reasonable set menu. Place des Cocotiers.

Mayflowers, Nouvata Hotel. High-quality Chinese food, friendly. Anse Vata Beach.

Nouvata Hotel Restaurant. Popular with tourists and locals too. Lively bar, the Monins great hosts.

Esquinade. This fish restaurant is a favourite eating place for old Nouméa hands. Attractive décor, good cooking. Rue de Sebastopol, Baie de l'Orphelinat.

Isle de France Restaurant. In the hotel of the same name. Small, attractive, popular bar.

La Grande Muraille. Good Chinese food in small colorful restaurant.

Les Helices, Magenta. Specializes in seafood, popular with locals.

Le Lagon Hotel Restaurant. In the hotel of the same name. The proprietor and his Vietnamese wife were in the hotel business in Vietnam for many years.

Ocean Palace. Excellent Chinese food, Szechuan style.

Santa Monica. Abuts the nightclub of the same name. Set menu the best value in Nouméa, as is the carafe wine.

Maeva Beach. Excellent cooking and a reasonable set menu. Overlooks the Baie des Citrons.

La Vacherie. Magenta. Phone 277044 and they'll send a free car or deduct taxi fare from your bill. Excellent cooking in a rustic ambiance.

La Voile Snack. Coffee shop at Le Surf; open 6:30 A.M. to 10:30 P.M.

EATING OUT OF TOWN. Almost every wayside café in New Caledonia can offer an attractive meal, but there are a few outstanding restaurants you may like to investigate if you drive to the east coast or even just out of town for the day.

Vallon d'Or. A traditional meeting place for Nouméa's teenagers, chaperoned by watchful parents. Excellent lunches and dinners, and the Sunday tea dance is lots of fun. Madame Rosa, late of the Poindimié Hotel is in charge. 14 miles from Nouméa on the Mont Dore road.

Inexpensive Snacks

Béarno. In town, quick service, reasonable. You can get the usual minute steak, but also such dishes as sausages and lentils. Rue d'Alma.

Biarritz. Right on the beach, especially good for a quick lunch after swimming.

Jamico. Unassuming little snack bar, friendly service, superb omelettes, as well as hamburgers, steak Tartare, etc. Super Vata Shopping Complex.

La Pergola, Rue du Général Mangin. Just off the square, attractive decor, steaks, omelettes, nems and so on. Reasonable prices, cheerful service.

Anse Vata Beach has blossomed lately with snack bars, pizzerias, boutiques and a couple of excellent cafés. The problem of a light lunch no longer exists in this area.

NIGHT LIFE. *Commodore Star Truck.* This disco is popular with the young. Tea dancing Sundays 3 P.M. to 7 P.M. Entry week nights about $US2.50, Friday and Saturday $US 3, which includes your first drink. Promenade Anse Vata.

Casino Royal. The only casino in the South Seas. Everything from poker machines to blackjack or roulette. Tie and jacket required for the gaming room. In Le Surf Hotel grounds, Anse Vata Beach.

Etoile. In Le Paris building right in town, drinks cheaper here than in the Papa Club, favored by tourists looking for chacha, tango, and so on. Ask at your hotel for a card to enter these clubs.

Le Black Jack. Private club in the Commodore complex. (But your hotel can get you a card to most of the private clubs in Nouméa, if you can afford the prices.) Popular with Nouméa's gilded youth. Promenade Anse Vata.

Le Métro Club. Attractive decor, really swings from about 11 P.M. Handy to all beach hotels. Drinks around $US 5.

Papa Club. In the Hotel Le Paris Building. All black glass and subdued glitter. Drinks around $US 5. Offbeat shows Thurs., Fri., Sat. around 10 P.M., dancing after 10:30.

Santa Monica. An institution in Nouméa and with visitors too. A really Tahitian atmosphere, small, dark, fabulous music from a group, most of whom sit in each night. No entry charge, drinks around $3.50 or so. Pay when you get your drink—there is sometimes confusion if you leave it till later.

Le Soleil. Perhaps the most sophisticated discotheque in Nouméa; worth a visit. Drinks around $US5.

Le Joker. Swinging disco, popular with young Nouméa. Le Surcouf building off Rue Sebastopol.

Night life in Nouméa is fun and everyone on this island loves to dance. The standard of the bands is high and in the discotheques the records are French and fascinating. You can dance for an hour or two over a couple of drinks and no one will breathe down your neck or hassle you to order more. As with restaurants, closing days vary, so check with your hotel.

WE WANT
AND APPRECIATE
YOUR COMMENTS

Errors are bound to creep into any guidebook. Hotels and restaurants can suffer instant or gradual decline in the quality of their service, acts of governments or God can change the travel picture, and in many ways, items that we presented as gospel will now appear to be untrue.

For these reasons we greatly appreciate letters from you, the reader, telling us of your travel experiences, chastising us, if you will, for our errors, or advising us of our oversights. We want to know! (We also appreciate words of praise, and we receive a lot of those too.) Your letters help us improve our coverage, but they also give us that essential "consumer's eye view," which is so helpful. We want to produce the best-possible travel guide series—and you can help us do it.

Please send your comments to
>> Research Director
>> Fodor's Travel Guides
>> 2 Park Avenue
>> New York, N.Y. 10016

VANUATU
(NEW HEBRIDES)

by
KATHLEEN HANCOCK

In 1606 Pedro Fernandez de Quiros, best navigator of his time, came upon Espiritu Santo, northernmost island of the New Hebrides group, thinking he had discovered the great southern continent hinted at by Ptolemy and Marco Polo, outlined on ancient maps as stretching right across the South Pacific. The Portuguese Quiros was looking for land and gold for his sponsor, King Philip III of Spain, and souls for the Church of Rome.

Not a man to be intimidated by immensities of ocean, he had christened the Pacific the "Gulf of Our Lady of Loreto" on leaving the coast of Peru. And four months later he made landfall in the northern New Hebrides at Gaua in the Banks Group. Gifts were exchanged with the friendly local people, but in the Spanish manner Quiros took hostages against the chance of sudden attack, putting them in the stocks for the night and, worst indignity of all for a Melanesian, shaving their heads and beards.

Sailing south, Quiros found more land and a great bay with a good port. The terrain was mountainous and he was sure this was the continent he sought. He named it Terra Australis del Espiritu Santo. A great gathering of Melanesians lined the beach to see the strange creatures in their huge ships of 150 tons! The local people refused to let the Spaniards approach them on the beach, but laid down their bows and arrows, and indicated that the visitors could get water, giving them presents of fruit and vegetables.

But soon there was trouble. Muskets were fired in the air to frighten the increasing numbers of excited people who gathered in the surrounding bush. A Spaniard fired too low and killed a Melanesian. There was some parleying. A line was drawn in the sand, and a chief indicated that his people would lay down their arms if the Spaniards would do the same. But Quiros' admiral, one Torres, mishandled the situation, arquebuses were fired and a chief dropped dead. He was hung from a tree "that he might be seen by all".

From this point there was never a chance of reconciliation between Quiros' men and the people he called "courageous and sociable". He broke the most sacred tabus of the people, beginning with the shaving of heads on Gaua. At Espiritu Santo his men stole carefully husbanded supplies of food from hill villages where they might have bartered for them successfully. Small boys were kidnapped to take home to Spain. And "he even broke the rules of war so far as to kill a chief". (Tom Harrisson:"Savage Civilisation").

Quiros took possession of the "continent", named the great anchorage the Bay of St. Philip and St. James, set up an altar and christened the city-to-be Nuova Jerusalema. But there were more killings, kidnappings and ambushes. Local resistance persisted. Many of Quiros' men fell ill with fish poisoning. Discontent, unrest and nostalgia for home unsettled the crews. Fifty days after their arrival in Espiritu Santo the Almiranta sailed out of what is now called Big Bay, bound for South America and ultimately Madrid. After seven years spent petitioning the King of Spain for recognition of his great discovery and compensation for its cost, Quiros died penniless and without honour.

For some reason Quiros' findings were suppressed and it was 162 years before these islands were visited again by European explorers. Bougainville sighted Maewo, Pentecost, Espiritu Santo and Malekula in 1768, and established clearly that this was no continent. Four years later Captain James Cook discovered the southern islands of the group and charted the whole archipelago, giving the islands their inappropriately dour Scottish name.

A mixed bag of missionaries, whalers and sandalwooders followed Cook, then the "blackbirders" moved in with their ugly trade. By 1885 missionaries and planters, mostly British and French were settling in increasing numbers on most islands in the group and problems arose over their personal safety. Murders were commonplace, with missionaries and traders the usual victims.

In 1877 John Higginson, an Irish-born trader, but a naturalised French citizen, was urging the French Government in New Caledonia to take over the New Hebrides, but this idea met with cries of outrage from the well established British missions and especially from neighbouring Australia. Finally the British and French governments got together in 1888 and set up a joint naval commission to keep law and order in the group. Then German interests appeared on the scene with a vigourous campaign to extend their influence in this part of the Pacific. To counter this threat the French and British governments set up the Franco-British Condominium in 1906.

Joint "Pandemonium"

This jointly controlled administration known in the Pacific as the "Pandemonium" with its two sets of laws, two education systems, two official languages and pidgin as well, was clumsy, expensive to run and functioned at a pace that any self respecting snail could have bettered. But it did keep the peace and introduce limited education and a system of hospitals and clinics to a wild and remote part of the Pacific.

News of World War I took three months to reach the remote New Hebrides and had little effect on these islands. But the outbreak of World War II was a different matter. The French administration of the New Hebrides was among the first of France's overseas territories to rally to de Gaulle. And when Japan entered the war in 1941, these islands became a forward base for U.S. troops, with attention concentrated on Espiritu Santo.

The Segond Channel, a strait between Espiritu Santo and Aore, was found capable of harbouring hundreds of ships. Roads, airfields and docks were built. Workshops, floating cranes, hospitals and sawmills were set up. The rain forest was cleared to establish hundreds of acres of market gardens to feed the troops in the New Hebrides and the Solomons. On Espiritu Santo the village of Luganville (or Santo, as it's commonly known) was the staging point for U.S. Army, Navy and Marine forces advancing on the Solomons. In 1943 there were around 40,000 U.S. troops in Santo, later joined by about 1400 New Zealanders, mostly airmen. Men, ships and supplies poured into the once sleepy backwater. French planters sent their nubile daughters to a safer island.

Independence was granted by Britain and France to the duly elected government of the New Hebrides on July 30, 1980, and the new state was christened Vanuatu, meaning "our land." In the first flush of independence there was some political unrest on Espiritu Santo and Tanna, but both are now back to normal. Efate was never affected.

The ni-Vanuatu (the new name for the Melanesian inhabitants) are now emerging from a confused and confusing period of sporadic contact with a motley array of European explorers, traders, sandalwooders, missionaries, colonists, civil servants, soldiers, sailors and airmen. Within the passing of less than a century they have left the stone age behind to confront European living, languages and legal systems. Whatever the rate of emergence into the hard light of social, economic and political reality, one thing is for sure. The great Melanesian gifts of common sense, goodwill, honesty and humour will prevail.

These are a sturdy, proud and independent people, with a strongly developed sense of fair play. Even a fleeting encounter with them is a rewarding experience for the traveller looking for a different scene. In these islands it's worth considering the answer given to an early missionary by a man of Tanna. "Why do you put that paint on your faces?" asked the missionary. "Why do you put those clothes on?" asked the Tannese. "This is our way of clothing, that is yours."

The Economy

Vanuatu is a potentially rich area. These islands are incredibly fertile, and the climate, though tropical, is a pleasant one with a predictable rainfall. Copra heads the list of exports, with fish not far behind, and cocoa coming on strong. A good way behind come beef and coffee, but production here is increasing and capable of much greater development. The recent growth of tourism has brought another source of income to the group, and the popularity of the area as a tax haven has also had a considerable effect on the economy.

Most of the meat eaten in Vanuatu is produced locally and there are great strides being made to improve local herds. Cattle were first introduced as a cheap form of weed control in the coconut plantations, but both European planters and Melanesian villagers have discovered that a little care in sowing good grasses, and the purchase of good quality breeding stock makes for an extra source of income at not much additional expense. With the introduction of pedigree Charolais and Hereford bulls, as well as Brahmin cross bred cattle, herds have improved greatly.

Plantation labor is pretty scarce in these islands. It's one of the few Pacific territories that is underpopulated and to aggravate this, local workers have long been accustomed to spending fairly long periods in New Caledonia where nickel is king.

Life in Vanuatu and especially in remote Espiritu Santo still ambles on in the same lazy way that it has for nearly a century. In Vila you can buy luscious brandied cherries at the trade stores and ivory and jade and gold jewelery at the Chinese shops. But in the bush villages elsewhere in the group, pigs are both capital and power. While a jazz combo belts out its rhythms on a hotel dance floor, not far away in the hill villages the thump of a hundred feet shakes the ground in a "custom dance".

Exploring Vanuatu (formerly the New Hebrides)

Captain Cook was never much of an original thinker when it came to christening all those islands he discovered in the Pacific 200 years ago. But he seems to have struck rock bottom when he gave such an unimaginative name to the 80 islands of that enchanting archipelago known as the New Hebrides. Now, of course, his error has been corrected by the new independent government.

This offbeat, slightly raffish, totally fascinating collection of islands lies east of the Coral Sea, scattered north to south in the Southwest Pacific like confetti. This is a territory where tourists are not yet processed, where you can still wander along a white beach on the edge of an impossibly blue lagoon with only the lap of the tide to break the silence. The two resort hotels in Vila modestly face the lagoon; a little investigation will disclose a few gourmet restaurants and the ambiance is as near to the traditional picture of a South Pacific island as you're likely to find.

On the short flight to Vanuatu from Australia, New Caledonia, Fiji, or New Zealand, it's hard to imagine that in about two or three hours you will be descending over Efate Island's endless acres of coconut palms. Your first hint of the important part these islands played in the Pacific war comes as you disembark at Bauer Field, named in honour of a gallant American airman. Melanesian officials, brown and sturdy, in their new green uniform, whisk you through the few formalities with a minimum of fuss.

Old Vila hands stay at *Le Lagon,* that lovely cluster of thatched roofs on Erakor Lagoon. This is a notable hotel in anyone's language. At the height of the winter season, or ticking over quietly between times, *Le Lagon* never gives any sign of hustle or crowding. You can hobnob with your fellows around the pool, or splash together in that translucent lagoon, meet in the bar or on the golf course. But for lovers of peace and solitude, the rooms and bungalows dotted among huge trees and slender palms provide a blissful escape from the worries of day to day life.

The *Intercontinental Island Inn* at Tassiriki is set at the far end of the lagoon. The need for more rooms for visitors to Vila has been obvious for some time, since the word about the fascinations of Vanuatu began to filter through the Pacific, and this new hostelry will certainly help to meet the growing demand. There is an excellent hairdresser here and a lively disco operates nightly in the Ravenga Room. Visiting businessmen tend to stay in town at *Rossi's* on the waterfront. A snack menu is available on the terrace. Another modestly charming hostelry near Vila township is *Solaise*—also a favourite gathering place for locals. If economy is uppermost in your mind, one of the small rooms in this single story complex set around a shady swimming pool could well suit you. Or the *Kaiviti Hotel* a short walk from town might be the answer. Overlooking beautiful Vila harbor, this complex includes family units with cooking facilities at a moderate tariff. The *Vate Marina,* a few minutes from the post office, is a good place for budget-conscious travellers. And the old *Vate Hotel* (renamed *The Olympic*) right in town has been almost gutted and totally refurbished with excellent cooking facilities. Yves Rossi of the well-known hotel family has taken over the restaurant here, providing first class cuisine.

If you want a change from your hotel, take off aboard trimaran or ketch for a three day cruise around Efate and the small offshore islands, visiting tribes, buying mats, diving, fishing, and picnicking. Ask at your hotel's tour desk about this. If one day on the ocean is enough, try a relaxing sail on a cruiser with a picnic lunch and all the sun you can soak up to loosen those knots you came here with.

Excursions by road outside Vila are not as smooth as excursions by sea. But if you are looking for a day out, drive around the island either by rental car or with one of the many tours, stopping at Eton Beach for a swim and lunch.

Closer to Vila, Susan Barnes' *Whitesands Country Club* at Rentabao offers riding through the rain forest, swimming 200 yds from the Clubhouse. Succulent lunches are available on order. An idyllic scene, the mounts are first rate, both experts and beginners are welcome. Or you can eat at *Nagar Hall* right on the beach at Paunagisu, where fresh seafoods, grills, and chicken feature on a moderately priced menu.

Among resorts near Vila is *Hideaway,* a minuscule island retreat on a five-acre atoll about half an hour by water taxi from the township, or less if you drive the 15 minutes by road to the jetty that looks over toward the island. But don't settle for a day trip—stay a few nights. Lush vegetation and your own private piece of lagoon make this an informal resort to dream about. Snorkel, go coral-viewing on Mele Bay. The surrounding waters are densely populated with marine life. Diving is becoming a feature of this small resort island. The emphasis is on local foods, admirably cooked.

Erakor Island, set on an atoll opposite "Le Lagon," is a delightful little bungalow resort run by Australian Val Ireland in conjunction with Erakor village. Great food, comfortable accommodations and an extra bonus in the form of a ruined chapel and missionary graves.

Manuro Paradise is different—30 miles from Vila, with the most unusual beach scene in the area. The Pacific has carved a rectangular lagoon through the coral rock, sloping up to a sugar white beach. Bungalows dot the grassy sward, and the food is great.

Back at Vila, shopping in the little township is an adventure. Travelers browse in the Chinese and Vietnamese shops, dark aromatic treasure houses. Serious collectors of artifacts and shells investigate Island Crafts and Handikraf Blong Vanuatu. A colorful market opposite the Government Building sells shells, artifacts, clothing and produce on Wednesday, Friday and Saturday. The Cultural Center has an interesting display of artifacts and shells.

French influence ensures you'll eat well in this far flung series of dots on the wide Pacific. There's a handful of excellent restaurants in Vila. Good French cooking is the norm, varied by Italian, Vietnamese and European. You can also buy delicious cheeses and fresh bread in town or collect takeaways at the *Solaise Motel.*

It's a relaxed scene in Port Vila. The atmosphere is informal, there's no tipping, and tariffs are very moderate by today's standards. This is a duty-free area too, and bargains abound.

Leave yourself plenty of time in these islands. This is a destination where things tend to crop up, adventures materialize, opportunities arise. You'll meet a new kind of people—warm-hearted, eccentric, generous and hospitable. It's Jack London country, large as life and twice as crazy.

The Outer Islands—Tanna

The next stop on your exploration programme could be Tanna, where Captain James Cook saw the glow from the sacred volcano Yasur miles out to sea. The copper-skinned Tannese call their lush island "the navel of the world". You can fly down to Tanna from Vila with Air Melanésie in about an hour, with a possible way stop at Erromanga, "the martyr isle", dubiously distinguished for wholesale murders of missionaries last century.

The plane approaches Tanna over a coastline jumble of red and black boulders washed by the aqua and emerald colours of the reef. You skim over the treetops of the rain forest. From the air the grassy airstrip looks like a cricket pitch, but it's twice the size of the one I landed on the first time I visited Tanna a few years ago.

At the reed and thatch bungalows at Epul Bay, *Tanna Beach Resort* offers good accommodations, a Vila-class restaurant, and cold beer from the bar. It's a lovely spot—rustic, but civilised. The bungalows are scattered among the coconut palms on grassy slopes rolling to a spectacular black sand beach.

At Whitegrass, Chief Tom Numake's bungalows overlook a rocky cove. A small restaurant serves wine and food, and your host will arrange excursions.

In the hill villages behind Epul Bay a cautious approach will pay dividends. These are proud and dignified people, not to be intruded upon with impunity. But as everywhere, good manners are a key to friendly acceptance. A pocketful of candy helps, too.

Villages are the ultimate in primitive living. Bamboo and nipa huts stand a mere 5 feet at the ridgepole. A rough barrier of logs keeps the pig population out of the dark and smoky interiors. Once Tannese reserve is breached you may be given oranges, and you can occasionally buy a mat or a Tannese grass skirt. If your village neighbours approve of you, there's a chance you might be invited to a "custom" dance—a nightlong feast of primeval music, colour and excitement.

The island is incredibly fertile. Tanna's ten foot topsoil grows yams six feet long. In the rain forest the margin of a deep pool makes a perfect picnic spot. The indigo ocean crashes in white foam on glistening beaches, black and white. Herds of magnificent wild horses roam at "White Grass" and the mighty stallions snort defiance at you, as you are driven by the tourist bus over the high plateau.

There's even a pocket volcano thrown in, with performance almost to order. The area around the volcano is also the headquarters of the "Jon Frum" movement, a cargo cult that originated on Tanna during the war. A belief arose that "Jon Frum" would ultimately appear, probably by plane, in the form of refrigerators, trucks, canned food, cigarettes and all the enormous variety of material goods that had suddenly begun to pour into these islands as part of the American war effort. "Jon Frum" symbols, which include crosses painted red, may be photographed but should not be touched. Permission to climb the volcano must be obtained from the neighboring village. Tour Vanuatu and Air Tropicana run day tour.

The Outer Islands—Ambrym

Ambrym has always been a mysterious island with its two live volcanoes, black soil, stone carvings, and monumental slitgongs. Ritual and custom are alive here, and for the first time travellers can find, not only accommodation, but an exciting experience. Superb food, guided trips to bush villages, splendid mounts for riding, hikes up the lava river bed to the base of the volcano (only the intrepid make the final climb), bathing in nearly hot springs—it's a scenario second to none in the South Pacific. Air Melanesie offers a weekend package.

The Outer Islands—Espiritu Santo

You can find a lot of adventure in a couple of weeks in Vanuatu; Espiritu Santo, largest island in the group, presents a picture totally different from either Efate or Tanna.

You fly into Santo from Vila with Air Melanésie or from Honiara with Solair, over a canopy of rain forest, interrupted here and there along the coast by the orderly ranks of coconut plantations. Relics of the Pacific war are everywhere on this island. The remains of fighter planes rust in the dense bush. And the jungle has overtaken the miles of market gardens that once supplied New Zealand and U.S. troops. However, the dogs of war are silent now in the Coral Sea, and today Santo sleeps in the sun.

Bokissa Island is a real hideaway, separated from the Santo mainland by the big island of Aore. Fifteen minutes by runabout and you find a Crusoe situation, but with all the amenities. Great swimming and diving, easy walks, a pool, and excursions. Good cooking, a varied library, and all the board games you've ever heard of.

The Hotal Santo will be your base on the mainland. It's small, modern, but full of atmosphere. The locals gather at the bar before lunch and dinner. You'll hear tall tales of the Pacific from Scottish supercargoes, Fijian first mates, Melanesian administration officers, Chinese storekeepers. Look around at the paintings, the "montages", the ancient artifacts on the walls. Decoration is by Marcel Moutouh, who completed his paintings for the 22 bedrooms in an incredible two month burst of effort.

Your choice of restaurants in this little township is limited, but the food is as intriguing as Santo itself. Down at the end of the main street, is "Pinocchio", a typical French bistro. "Little Saigon" is new, too, with a Vietnamese menu. The formidable Mme. Harbulot dispenses fresh local food in the French manner at a new venue at "Chez Lulu."

This island is a storehouse of local custom and wartime history. It's for travelers who like to find their own adventure. Shorter trips include Fanafo village, and the heavily forested South Santo coast where you may still see a "man bush" in traditional dress walking along the coral road. Santo isn't the thriving copra and cattle center it was before independence—only 200 Europeans remain there now—but for the adventurous traveller it still offers much of interest.

Divers will find plenty to do in Santo. There are myriads of fishy wonders, an infinite variety of shells to be gathered, and also the immense wreck of the 32,000 ton troopship "President Coolidge" to be explored. She lies on her side in the Segond Canal, the bow in 80 ft., the stern in about 240 ft. of water. This area is an underwater paradise for both reef and wreck divers. Their contact will be Allan Power, who can be reached at the hotel. Resident in Santo ten years now, and keeper of the local underwater monuments. Power is a world-famous diver who knows the wrecks and the fish who inhabit them. His underwater photography has been featured in *International Photography*.

In Santo there's lots of lovely gossip, as in all Pacific outposts. The coconut wireless may give a garbled version of the truth, but what it lacks in accuracy, it makes up for in colour. Given access to local rumour, you'll never need to open those paperbacks you brought with you. Regional half-truths are much stranger than fiction.

PRACTICAL INFORMATION FOR VANUATU

CLIMATE. Semi tropical with average of 70 May-October, 80 November-May. Humid and often rainy January-February.

Average Temperature (°Fahrenheit) and Humidity

Vila	Jan	Feb	Mar	Apr	May	June	July	Aug	Sept	Oct	Nov	Dec
Average max. day temperature	85°	87°	85°	83°	81°	80°	78°	79°	79°	82°	83°	85°
Days of Rain	22	20	23	20	19	18	17	14	16	15	17	19
Humidity, Percent	75	76	78	76	74	73	72	70	70	68	69	69

General hints: Note that the seasons are reversed from the Northern Hemisphere. May to October are good months for tourists. Humidity is high year-round.

CLOTHING. Informal the year round. Daytime, cotton dresses or slacks for women, slacks or shorts for men. No ties. Evening, light long or short dresses for women; for men, slacks.

HEALTH. Medical services available in most areas likely to be visited. It is advisable to take anti-malarial tablets once weekly, starting one week before arrival and continuing for four weeks after leaving the area. As in all tropical regions, it is advisable to equip yourself with remedies against upset stomachs. There are no dangerous animals or insects in Vanuatu.

TIPPING. Not in Vanuatu, please. It is contrary to Melanesian customs.

LANGUAGES. English and French are spoken. Pidgin English and many other dialects are also used in Vanuatu.

CURRENCY. Monetary unit the vatu; current rate: 110 vatu=US$1.00.

EVENTS AND CELEBRATIONS

14th February. John Frum, Tanna Island. John Frum Cargo cult rituals on Tanna Island, mainly at Sulphur village, include dances, parades, feast for the expected return of John Frum.

May (generally). Land-Divers of Pentecost Island, several times yearly. Diving from 70 ft. tower built around a tree. Vines are attached to ankles to break the fall. Usually performed by the pagan village of BUNLAP (South Pentecost). Arranged by Tour Vanuatu, Vila, at a high cost.

30th July. Independence Day, Military parade, speeches, ball at night.

End of August. Toka Dance, Tanna Island. Impressive native feast according to custom. Includes dances, killing of pigs by clubs, etc. Circumcision ceremonies are usually held during this period at Tanna.

September. Tanna Agricultural Show.

October. Vila Agricultural Show.

23–25 December. Christmas Festivities. Arrival of Père Noel at Vila. Church services, choir singing and ball in main centres.

HOLIDAYS. All government offices, banks, and most private offices are closed —sometimes on the day before and after, too.

January 1—New Year's Day. Easter; May 4th—Ascension Day. July 30th—Independence Day. 23rd–25th December—Christmas holidays.

DANCING. *Le Privé,* Erakor Road; *Le Lagon* (Saturday night disco and dancing in the Pilioko Piano Bar nightly); *Intercontinental* (disco nightly in the Ravenga Room); *La Cascade,* informal entertainment and occasional dancing at the piano bar; *Sol Wata Klab,* Vila Bay, popular with younger ni-Vanuatu.

SPORTS. *Vila Tennis Club; Le Lagon Golf Club* (free to guests); *Port Vila Golf Club,* Mele Beach (green fees 500 vatu); *Squash Courts* (BESA Club); Horse riding, 2nd Lagoon and Whitesands Country Club; skin-diving (*Dive Action, Nautilus*); sailing (*Yachting World*); game Fishing (see *Hotel Rossi*); cruising and big-game fishing on Charlie Laub's *Rendezvous II* or Gordon Neal's *Pacific Dream.*

POLICE. Central Police Station. Tel. 2222.

HOSPITALS. *Central Hospital.* Tel. 2100. Outpatients in town tel: 2512/2514.

HOW TO GET THERE. Flights from: New Caledonia—Air Caledonie International 4 times weekly; New Zealand—U.T.A./Air Caledonie; Sydney—Air

Vanuatu 4 times weekly; Honiara—Solair twice weekly; Brisbane—Air Pacific twice weekly; Nadi—Air Pacific twice weekly; Apia—Polynesian Airlines; Melbourne—Air Vanuatu once weekly.

HOW TO GET ABOUT. *By air:* Air Melanésie flies regular schedules to many parts of the group; charter services available. Air Tropicana also covers groups on regular basis or charter. *By car:* Taxis, depot in town, available from all hotels. Rental - Avis, tel. 2533; Hertz, tel. 2244, Box 128. National Car Rental at Socametra, tel. 2977; Budget Rent-a-Car, Mini Mokes, tel. 3170.

In Santo, *by bus and car: Buses:* regular service from wharf to town on cruise-ship days and mini-buses operated by hotels, transfers to Pekoa airstrip. *Taxis:* large number of taxis fitted with meters, reasonable charges. Check fare for longer trips before hire. Melanesia Rent-a-Car—contact Mary Miu, tel. 325.

 TOURS. *Vanuatu Visitors Bureau,* P.O. Box 209, Port Vila, Vanuatu. Contact your travel agent or the above bureau for advice concerning the two tours listed below.

Pentecost Land Divers: This event, usually held in May, can be scheduled for special occasions at different times of the year. A trip worthwhile to see these fabulous Pentecost divers. Men dive from 70-foot tower (head first) with vines attached to their ankles to break the fall.

Vila Township: (1½ hours) Drive covers downtown Vila, residential area, courthouse, college, police barracks and a native village. Before returning to hotel, tour continues to top of Klems Hill for a harbor view of Vila with a short stop at another small village. *Mele Village:* (Full day) Travel to Mele Village. Meet local people. Trip also includes ride on outrigger canoe. Time for swim, shelling, snorkeling or loafing. Picnic lunch (included in price) before returning to Vila. *Efate Safari:* (Full day) Travel 76-mile route through some of the most rugged terrain of Vanuatu. Tour east coast past beaches to Forari for a view of the islands of Mao, Pele and Kukula. Visit Church of all Denominations, drive through several villages and plantations. Picnic lunch before returning to Vila. *Volcano Skyrama:* (2½ hours) An extensive view of Vanuatu's volcanoes. *Air Melanesia* aircraft leaves at 5:30 A.M. and flying between the peaks of Mataso Island, heads toward the island of Tongoa to view underwater volcano. Tour continues toward Lopevi, one of the most active volcanoes in the islands, to see red hot lava flowing down sides into steaming sea. View the island of Ambrym to see smoking volcano Benboy and other nearby volcanoes, back to Vila, passing coast of Malekula, home of primitive Big Nambas tribe. *Glass-bottom Boats:* (2 hours) Tour sea world of Erakor Lagoon aboard *Coral Sea* glass-bottom boat. Underwater life specialist describes tropical coral and sea life. *Primitive Tanna Island:* (Full day) Fly *Air Melanesia* or *Air Tropicana* to Tanna Island. Transfer to four-wheel Land Rover for plantation tour, then continue through dense jungle bush through the mountains to Kings Cross (the island center). Cross the ash plain of Siwi Lake to Yasur volcano. Drive almost to crater edge for view of lava. Also visit subterranean volcanic tubes, until recently considered tabu. *Hideaway Island Cruise:* (Full day) Cruise aboard 41-foot catamaran to Mele Bay to Hideaway Island. Snorkel, swim before lunch at resort before return to Vila harbor via Pango Coast and Fila Island. Departs Sunday, Tuesday, Thursday. *South Pacific Cruises:* 3-day cruise round Efate, outlying islands; or 6–12 days to Ambrym, Pentecost, Santo in sailing ship *Coongoola. Vaterama:* (45 min.) *Air Melanesia* flight with panoramic views of Efate, the capital island of Vanuatu. Follow coast road by air with views of the outlying islands of Mele, Nguna, Mataso, Moso, and Hat Island. Also views of wartime airstrip of Coin Hill and Havannah, with pass over the international hotel "Le Lagon." *Air Tropicana* for variety of Air Adventure Tours—Tanna, Santo, Ambrym and local sightseeing round Efate.

Valor Tours, Schooner Point Bldg., 2nd floor, Spring St., Sausalito, Ca. 94965. Specializes in veterans tours with organized programs throughout the South

Pacific (and the world). Plans for 1985 include sending a number of units who served in the Pacific Theater to that area. They work with national and civic leaders of the host country. Write for complete details on individual or group tours to World War II sites.

Other tour operators include *Tour Vanuatu,* tel. 2745; *Frank King Tours,* tel. 2808; *Pan Tours,* tel. 3160.

TOURS AROUND VILA. Reef, fishing and sailing expeditions. Try the sailing canoe trip to Emae or Pele Island. *Frank King:* glass-bottom boat, sunset cruise, wine and cheese, coral viewing by underwater floodlight. *"Escapade":* a 43 ft. game fishing cabin-cruiser, twin Diesel fitted for diving, top class fishing equipment, day-trips and charter. *Teouma Village Tour:* Raft down Teouma River, snorkel at river mouth, tea and cakes at Teouma Village. *Nautilus Dive Shop,* N.Z. U.A. instructors, scuba diving, snorkelling for both experts and beginners. Tel. 2398. Other tours: *Vila Roundabout Bus Tour; Nature Walk; Visitors Club,* free services and restrooms for tourists; located opposite the market.

SHOPPING. Vila may be small, but the real traveler with an enquiring mind, a degree of patience, and a nose for a bargain can have loads of fun in the shops, boutiques and trade stores in between swimming in that fabulous lagoon and indulging the flesh in the town's restaurants and night clubs. Vila is a tax-free area for most luxuries. When budgeting be prepared for local 10% tax on tourist services and a 1000 vatu (approx. $US10) departure tax.

If artifacts are your thing, and you yearn for a puppet from Malekula, an ancestor figure from Ambrym, or an intricately carved comb from Tongoa, then your first stop in Vila town will be at *Island Carvings,* Judith Wood's crowded shop, now located in former U.T.A. premises on the Olympic Hotel Corner. You know you'll get the real thing here—this lively Australian does her own buying on trips that range from Tonga to the Trobriands, with emphasis, of course, on local Melanesian crafts. Prices are realistic and a chat with Judith Wood is an added bonus—she is one of the most knowledgeable dealers in the Pacific.

A mile or so from Le Lagon Hotel along the road skirting the lagoon lies a trap for art lovers. The thatched "atelier—musée" of Nicolai Michoutouchkine sits among a collection of immense slit-gongs in the midst of a tangle of tropical trees and herbiage. French born, of Russian parentage, Michoutchkine is a painter of originality and power. You can almost feel the miasmic vapours of the rain forest in his wildly colourful oils. His companion, Pilioko, comes from the island of Wallis, and was once the painter's protegé. These days this muralist, weaver of tapestries, designer of fabrics, stands on his own feet. In their shop in the Pilioko Building you can buy shirts, dresses, and pareos designed by Eliza Keil and Hand printed by Vanuatu's most famous couple.

There are dozens of Chinese merchants and up the narrow nameless streets of Vila. Jade, gold, ivory, transistors, tape recorders, portable hair dryers, cameras—all at duty free prices. At the two big trade stores, British and French, look at kitchen gear, fabrics and perfume; buy French cheese and patés to eat for lunch with a loaf of French bread; investigate the range of French and Spanish wines and bottles of tiny mandarines or plums in cognac. For stereo and electronic gear, *Sound Centre* is helpful.

In the Pilioko building *Sun Fashions* sell informal wear for women. *Rococco* across the main street is good for all kinds of trendy gear. All these are small establishments, the range won't be wide and you'll probably have to hunt for your size. Big news on the fashion scene is Australian Trudy Pohl for top-class leisure and swim wear from Europe and Israel.

Prouds, duty free shop on the main street, sells jewelery, silver and trinkets of every kind.

Natalie has a selection of attractive dresses, swimsuits, accessories, while Aquaverde at Palm Court has an intriguing selection of chic clothing from the U.S. and France. Handbags from Italy can be found at *Leather Showcase.*

Rossi's is for jewellery, crystal, les "must" de Cartier; *French's,* past the Fung Kwei building, for chic leisure clothes.

Here in this casual ambience you can drift in and out of the stores. Vila is heaven for shoppers.

HOTELS AND MOTELS. By world tourism standards, no Vila hotel comes within the "expensive" category, and as the highest price (for a lagoon-side bungalow) is US$58 single, US$77 double, we omit the "expensive" category from this report; prices from U.S.$58 single to US$40 single are considered *Moderate;* those below US$40 are considered *Inexpensive.*

Vila

Intercontinental Island Inn, Erakor Lagoon. *Moderate.* 166 rooms, airconditioning, all facilities, room service, 2 restaurants, 2 bars, pool. Shops, hairdresser, tour desk. Golf (9 holes) tennis. Conference facilities. Bank, boutique, disco.

Le Lagon. Erakor Lagoon. *Moderate.* 115 rooms, 25 bungalows on Erakor Lagoon. Airconditioning, all facilities, refrigerator. Some suites, to accommodate 5. The Michoutouchkine restaurant for fine cuisine and a verandah cafe. 2 bars, pool. All water sports, golf course (9 holes), cruises, films, dancing daily in the Pilioko piano bar. Conference facilities. Shops, tour desk. Both restaurants offer excellent cuisine.

Marina Motel. *Inexpensive.* In town on Erakor Road. 12 airconditioned apartments, pool, harbour view.

Olympic Hotel, *Moderate.* Right in town, popular with business people. Well-equipped apartments overlooking town and harbor. Secretarial services, telex.

Rossi's, Rue Higginson. *Inexpensive.* Oldest established hotel in Vanuatu. 32 rooms, airconditioning, and all facilities. Restaurant, bar. Undergoing extensive modernization.

Solaise, Rue Picardie. *Inexpensive.* 16 units 5 mins. from town, each with shower-room, refrigerator. Light breakfast included. Fans. Restaurant, bar, pool, garden. Weekly rates after two weeks. Varied menu, excellent cooking.

Coral Apartments. *Inexpensive.* Self-contained studio apartments; 5 mins. town.

Erakor Island, P.O. Box 24. In the lagoon of the same name. *Moderate.* Simple bungalows, great food. 24 hr. boat service to mainland.

Out of Town

Hideaway, Mele Island. *Moderate.* 6 miles from Vila, 3 minutes ferry service to island. 10 bungalows, restaurants, bar, tariff all-in. Swimming, snorkeling, diving, good food.

Manuro Paradise. *Moderate.* Sturdy bungalows and longhouse accommodations, great beach, swimming, excellent cuisine.

Teouma Village Holiday Resort. *Moderate.* Charming garden complex of 2 bedroom apartments on Erakor Lagoon. Safe swimming, babysitters.

Vila Chaumieres. *Moderate.* Bungalows, good facilities, popular bar.

Santo

Hotel Santo, Luganville, Santo. *Moderate.* Ten minutes from airport. 22 rooms. French restaurant, bar, swimming pool, curio shop, game room. Airconditioned. Tours arranged.

Tanna

Tanna. *Economical.* 11 bungalows at Epul Bay. New management. Licensed bar and restaurant, fresh local food,—lobster, fish, steak. Volcano excursions, wild horses.

Chief Tom Numake's Bungalows. Small restaurant and bar. Tours to volcano, wild horses; Tom's a good host.

Ambrym

Relais d' Ambrym. Six rustic bungalows, basic plumbing, restaurant bar. French host Jean-Pierre Fischer offers horseback trips to volcano. An unspoilt and interesting island, home of carvers in wood and stone.

DINING OUT. Vila. Even though Vila is a small town of around 15,000 inhabitants, these include about 10,000 Melanesians, 2,000 Europeans, and a smattering of Vietnamese, Chinese, Gilbertese, Fijians, Tahitians and Tongans, and eating out is therefore an adventure. It must be stressed that in these remote islands changes are frequent. But you are pretty certain to find good and often superb cuisine in the unpretentious eating houses of your choice. Service will not be swift in this languorous ambiance, but it will be pleasant, and after all this is not a place to come if you must rush madly around. We note the best of a surprisingly wide choice of restaurants and snack bars. Price categories for dinner (wine not included): *Expensive,* US$18–22; *Moderate,* US$14–18; *Inexpensive,* US$6–14.

Expensive

L'Houstalet. French cuisine. Erakor Road.

Michoutouchkine, Le Lagon Hotel. Extensive menu, wonderful outlook over Erakor Lagoon.

Pandanus. Beautiful setting at the head of the lagoon.

Tassiriki Room, Intercontinental Hotel. Charming "restaurant intime." You need to book.

Café de Paris. Small French restaurant right in town. Lots of atmosphere, good food, lively bar.

La Cascade. Restaurant/piano bar. Good cooking, lively impromptu entertainment for after dinner guests.

Le Rendezvous. Ground floor Olympic Hotel. Delightful décor, first class cuisine, a notable cellar.

Kwang Tung. Good Chinese cooking. Rue Carnot (Chinese Alley).

Pisces. Opposite Kai Viti Hotel. Excellent cooking, fish a specialty, exceptional service, plus a great view.

Moderate

La Hotte. Lots of atmosphere. Excellent and imaginative food. This well-established restaurant has kept up its standards without too much escalation in costs. Airport road.

Ma Barkers. Familiar menu, excellent fish and grills, well presented. Reasonable.

Rossi's. Blackboard menu at reasonable prices. On The Terrace overlooking Vila harbour.

La Cabane. Rustic restaurant on Erakor Road, good food, Tahitian ambiance, a warm welcome from Felix Tehei. Spontaneous music after dinner most nights.

Waterfront Restaurant. A roundhouse set on the shore of Vila Harbour, a step from town centre. Select your own steak, fish, or chicken to be barbecued; big salad bar.

Inexpensive

Binh Dan. Vietnamese specialties; new and popular.

Bloody Mary's. At the market. Excellent quick food, reasonable.

Cafe Vila. Open 7:30 A.M. to 8 P.M. Snacks, light meals.

Chalet. Excellent snacks, also main dishes like goulash and wiener schnitzel cooked under the eye of M. Brenner, late of Czechoslovakia via Papua-New Guinea.

Ichise. Delicious traditional Japanese food and service.

Solaise. A blackboard menu in a relaxed ambiance, a short walk from the centre of town. Pizza, crêpes, fresh caught fish. Also takeaways. Rue Picardie.

La Tentation. Salon du The in Raffea Building. Sinfully delicious patisseries.

La Terrasse. Rue Higginson. Snacks, French-café ambiance, excellent menu, reasonable.

Why Not. In new arcade past Fung Kwei's building. Interesting French food at reasonable prices. Outdoor terrace overlooking harbour.

SANTO

In a township that is little more than a hamlet—you can still eat well. Check for new restaurants when you arrive—like Vila, but on a much smaller scale, the eating out situation in Santo changes frequently. If the cook hasn't just left, the food will be excellent, and prices will be moderate.

Chez Lulu. Mme. Harbulot's famed cuisine features local foods. Access by boat. Tel. 4215 Santo. Good eating here.

Little Saigon. A shoebox of a restaurant serving tasty Vietnamese food.

Hotel Santo Restaurant. Not the gourmet restaurant it once was, but reasonably good plain food.

Pinocchio. A new addition to the Santo scene. Small French café-bar-restaurant, attractive menu changes daily. Seafood is a specialty.

Oceania. Good Chinese food, next to Hotel Santo.

PAPUA NEW GUINEA

A Prodigality of Pleasures

by
DON HOOK

Travelers who think they have "seen everything" will think again on visiting Papua New Guinea. As some slight hint of its variety, here are a few of this vast island nation's features:

Languages—There are more than 700 distinct languages, yet English, together with its cousin, Pidgin (pronounced "pisin") is widespread. For a few cents, you can buy a Pidgin phrasebook and you're on your way. Place names vary from the exotic to the plain: Popondetta and Port Moresby; Bulolo and New Britain.

Landscape—There is no end to the variety of topographical features. Not far inland from some dazzling beach, you can stand in a tropical rain forest and look up at snowcapped peaks. Volcanoes, both dormant and extinct, are numerous: Simpson Harbour at Rabaul is itself the crater of an extinct volcano. There are islands one can walk across and a river that is navigable for 700 miles.

Flora and Fauna—There are 2,000 varieties of orchid and more than 200 species of rhododendron, on view in their natural settings or in a number of botanical gardens in the cities. Cassowaries and birds of paradise are only two of the exotic birds to be seen, and every kind of tropical wildlife, including "shy" crocodiles, is to be found somewhere in Papua New Guinea.

Cultures—An anthropologist's dream, Papua New Guinea's civilization encompasses areas that were classified as Stone Age in their way of life a mere few decades ago. Yet at Lae there is a University of Technology. There are many stages of social evolution in between, with arts and crafts of high quality and unique design. There is of course a liberal infusion of European and North American artists, entrepreneurs, and professionals.

An Island Embrace

True, in sharing its main island with the Indonesian province of Irian Jaya, Papua New Guinea bears some resemblance to Haiti or the Dominican Republic, which divide Caribbean Hispaniola. But Papua New Guinea is much larger than all of Hispaniola and is also embraced by a great semicircle of islands, from Manus to the north to Bougainville (now the North Solomons) to the east. Between them and completing the vast crescent lie the large islands of New Britain and New Ireland. With all its striking features and its warm generous people, Papua New Guinea indeed offers the visitor a prodigality of pleasures.

Wantok Bilong Mi ("My Friend")

It has been said of the people of Papua New Guinea that "The English words 'my friend' hardly begin to describe the power of the wantok principle. It means someone united to you by an unbreakable bond—a debt of honour, a kinship, a blood brotherhood. . . . " Thousands of visitors have testified that the friendliness of the people is perhaps the highest of all the pleasures to be experienced in Papua New Guinea.

So—armed with your phrasebook, a ready smile and a friendly gesture or two—enjoy this finest aspect of life in Papua New Guinea today.

A Capsule History

The island of New Guinea was first sighted by Spanish and Portuguese fishermen, venturing out from the Moluccas or Spice Islands, in the early sixteenth century. Meneses, a Portuguese governor of the Moluccas, was the first to land on the shores of West New Guinea (now Irian Jaya) and he referred to the place as "Ilhas dos Papuas" meaning "Island of the fuzzy haired men", and it was thus that the people of this country came to be known as Papuans. In 1545, the Spaniard, de Retes, named the island "Nueva Guinea" or New Guinea. It was not until much later that Europeans began to explore and settle on the island.

The Dutch annexed the western half of New Guinea in 1828, but other than formal annexation changed little until the 1890's.

In 1871, the first Christian missionaries arrived and settled in the Loyalty Islands in the Torres Strait. In 1873, Port Moresby and Fairfax Harbour were discovered by Captain John Moresby.

The eastern half of New Guinea continued to be virtually ignored—except by the Australian colonies, which did not want a hostile foreign power only 100 miles from their northern shores across the Torres Strait. Continual pressure was placed on England by Australia and in 1884 the British annexed the southeastern coast, which became known first as British New Guinea. A few days later, the Germans annexed the north coast and the large northern islands which became known as German New Guinea. In 1901, British New Guinea was transferred to Australia and renamed Papua.

During the First World War, Australian forces occupied German New Guinea and in 1920 Australia was granted a mandate by the League of Nations to administer New Guinea.

Between 1920 and 1942 Papua and New Guinea were administered by Australia as separate entities. During World War Two, New Guinea was occupied by Japanese forces, but they were repulsed by American and Australian forces from occupying Papua. War relics can still be seen strewn on beaches and in forests along the New Guinea coast.

After the surrender of the Japanese, civil administration was re-established as a unified administration and in 1949 the country became known as the Territory of Papua and New Guinea. In 1973, Australia granted the territory self-government and on September 16, 1975 Papua New Guinea became an independent nation.

EXPLORING PAPUA NEW GUINEA

With its dazzling variety of beautiful and interesting places, Papua New Guinea beckons the visitor from all directions. As with many other fascinating lands, it's best to start from the hub of cultural, economic and political activity:

Port Moresby, the capital of Papua New Guinea, houses the National Parliament and is the point of arrival for most visitors.It is situated on magnificent Fairfax Harbour and only forty kilometres by road from the cool Sogeri plateau in the Owen Stanley Ranges.

Port Moresby is not connected by road to any other major centre of Papua New Guinea, but Air Niugini provides daily flights to most of the larger towns.

The city has a population of 122,000, 15,000 of whom are Europeans. As the administrative centre of the nation and the largest urban area Port Moresby is not truly representative of the nation's lifestyle. But, nearby along the coast are a number of interesting Papuan villages—many built on stilts over the water.

Swimming, skindiving and sailing are popular pastimes and the city also has two golf courses, bowling greens and several tennis courts.

Sightseeing is both easy and uncommonly rewarding in Port Moresby and the Central Province. Among the highlights:

National Museum—Opened in 1977 and a gift from the Australian government on Independence, the museum is an interesting example of modern architecture. It is situated at Waigani close to the government office complex. Although it will be a few years at least before all the exhibits are completed, the already established exhibits of pottery from all provinces and birds of paradise make it well worth a visit.

National Parliament—The new Parliament House at Waigani was opened in August 1984 by Prince Charles, heir to the British throne, before a gathering of Commonwealth leaders. Apart from a break in 1980–82, the country has been led since independence in 1975 by Michael Somare, a former schoolteacher and journalist. Somare is leader of the Pangu Party. There are more than 100 members in the National Parliament and proceedings are conducted in three languages, English, Pidgin and Motu. If Parliament is in session, a visit to the public gallery is recommended.

Botanical Gardens and University Campus—The modern University of Papua New Guinea is situated at Waigani and its grounds include the Botanical Gardens where a display of Papua New Guinea's world famous orchids and other tropical flora can be seen. Open 8 A.M. to 4 P.M. except Saturdays.

Catholic Cathedral—Built in Sepik haus tambaran style.

Koki Market and Village—A wander through Koki Market, only three miles from the town centre on the coast, entrances most visitors. Vegetables, fish, crayfish and wallabies are on sale, and the market has become a social gathering place for many Port Moresby residents.

Hanuabada Village—On the coast close to the town centre, Hanuabada was once the largest village in the Motu area. Most of the houses are built on stilts over the sea.

Bomana War Cemetery—Nine miles from town on the Sogeri road, the cemetery is situated in beautifully kept gardens.

The Kokoda Trail and Sogeri—The Kokoda Trail, where Australian troops fought the Japanese during World War Two, is a forty kilometre drive from Port Moresby. The Sogeri road has many magnificent views including that over the Rouna Falls, and winds through rubber plantations. Many visitors make it a day outing with lunch at the Kokoda Trail Motel where the most popular dish is barbequed crocodile meat.

Wairiata National Park—Also on the Sogeri road, the park has many bush walks and panoramic views of the Port Moresby area.

Moitaka Crocodile Farm—Situated only a few miles from town, behind Jackson's Airport, the crocodile farm is open to visitors on Friday afternoon to watch feeding time.

Village Arts—A government owned artifacts retailer, Village Arts, boasts a stock of over 20,000 items and the best artifact collection in the country. It is situated at Six Mile, close to the airport.

Loloata Island—Near Port Moresby. Swimming, diving, boating.

Sea Park Oceanarium—Dolphin and sea lion training sessions daily at 11 A.M. and 3 P.M. except Thursdays.

Side Trips from Port Moresby

Tapini—A short plane trip from Moresby, Tapini is tucked high in the Owen Stanley Ranges. There are several walking tracks to tempt bush walkers. And it's accessible to 4-wheel-drive vehicles. A small resort hotel and a group of holiday cabins provide accommodation.

Yule Island—About 80 miles by road from Port Moresby, the route follows the coast through picturesque coconut plantations. Yule Island was one of the earlier mission stations, settled in 1885.

Rigo—The road to Rigo follows the coast east from Port Moresby through several Papuan villages.

Lae and the Morobe Province

An hour's flying time from Port Moresby and situated on the north coast is Lae, Papua New Guinea's second city and an important commercial centre and seaport. Lae is the terminal for two major road systems—the Highlands Highway to the west which passes through the Markham Valley and the Kassam Pass to the valleys and plateaus of the highlands, and the Wau-Bulolo road south through timberlands to the site of goldfields at Bulolo and Wau.

Things to See at Lae

The *Botanical Gardens* established in 1949 occupy 130 acres of parkland within walking distance of the town centre. Adjacent to the gardens is the *War Memorial* and cemetery marking the resting place for some 3,000 Allied soldiers.

Markets—There are two markets at Lae: the *Main* market, south of the airstrip is where Morobe and Highlands people sell their produce and handicrafts. The *Butibum* market, located on Butibum Road, is decorated with traditional murals.

Lo'Wamung, or first hill, is a lookout for views of the Huon Gulf and Lae city. It was the hill used by early German settlers and named Fortress or Burgberg Hill. The Japanese army used the hill for the same purpose constructing a number of subterranean tunnels.

Wagan or *Malhang Beach*—This is five miles from town, near the Ampo Mission on Busu Road. The black sand beaches were used as an entry point for the 51st Japanese division in 1943. The remains of the landing barge, the "Myoko Maru' are still visible. Permission to enter the beach should be obtained from the Wagan villagers.

Ampo Lutheran Mission—This was the site of the Japanese camp during the war. It is located two miles north of the town on the Busu Road. Japanese shrines have been erected near the mission by returning servicemen.

Outside Lae

Wau—Situated in a pine ringed valley, Wau was formerly a heavily populated gold mining centre. Gold is still being sought, on a smaller scale, in Edie Creek and gold panners can be seen at work along the roads. Well worth a visit is the Wau Ecology Institute, on Edie Creek Road a few miles from the town centre, where there is a large collection of butterflies, insects and local flora. Other things to see include McAdam National Park and Mt Kaindi.

Bulolo—Now a small company town, Bulolo is the site of the nation's forestry college, a plywood mill and the remains of massive gold dredges.

Finschhafen—An unusually pretty coastal town, Finschhafen was originally settled by German missionaries and several buildings from that era remain. Unfortunately very limited accommodation is available for tourists. The Tami Islands, whose people are renowned for their carvings, is easily accessible from Finschhafen. The islanders have built a guest house-shelter on the beach of one of their islands and accommodation can be arranged through the Welfare Office at Lae.

Sialum—This is situated on a particularly attractive area of coastline known for its coral terraces. A new resort, Paradise Springs Holiday Inn, now caters for tourists with comfortable units and lounges and dining area of native materials. Sialum can be reached by plane from Lae through Tolair.

The Highlands

A journey into the highlands is a fascinating step back into history. The majority of the country's population live in the highlands, yet this was the last area contacted by European colonisers. The people of the highlands saw their first white man, their first steel implement and first wheel in 1937. It is a civilization that has just left the stone age.

The five highlands provinces offer a diversity of scenery and population. Mt. Wilhelm, the country's highest mountain, is often powdered with snow, yet is less than 700 kilometres south of the equator; the rich soils enable the people, who are still mainly subsistence gardeners to grow their sweet potatoes, taro and bananas in a mass of tiny neat fields fenced with sharp stakes; pigs, being a traditional wealth item, snout their way down roads and through fields and villages; people still wear only brief aprons to their knees and a bunch of leaves behind ("arse grass" in Pidgin) and carry bows and arrows for hunting; and tiny villages of low round thatched houses are scattered through valleys and breast hilltops.

The Highlands Highway runs from Lae and provides access to most highlands areas. The highway links the major towns of Kainantu, Goroka, Kundiawa and Mount Hagen, while there are a variety of feeder roads leading to the smaller towns and then into the more remote areas. A trip along this highway by bus or a tour with one of the operators (see Practical Information section) is a pleasant and interesting journey.

Leaving Lae on the coast and travelling through the Markham Valley and the Kassam Pass you first enter the Eastern Highlands, which provide the commercial and agricultural nucleus of the upland plateau with extensive coffee plantations and processing factories. Travelling through the town of Kainantu, past coffee plantations and innumerable villages, Goroka, the provincial capital of the Eastern Highlands is reached after some five hours. Accommodation of internationally accepted standards is available at Goroka and a few days could be well spent there taking day trips out from the town. The highlands weavers can be visited where one can watch being made and purchase woven mats and clothing. The *J. K. McCarthy Museum* features highlands masks, weapons and instruments and the Goroka Technical College can be visited to see students at work, particularly in the art and crafts field.

The *Market* in Goroka provides a wide variety of agricultural foodstuffs, live pigs, and clothing. A tour can also be arranged through tour operators in Goroka to visit the famous Mud Men at Asaro and watch them perform traditional dances. Every other year Goroka hosts the *Highlands Singsing*. This alternates between Mt Hagen and Goroka and is held in July or August of each year.

Leaving Goroka and the Eastern Highlands province the highway passes through the Simbu province, where in November of each year the *Pig Kill Festival* is held with a series of singsings in several villages. Simbu is characterised by rolling hills covered with multi-coloured wildflowers. More than 2,000 acres have been set aside as national parkland surrounding Mt. Wilhelm. Walking tracks through the parkland and rest houses along the footpath provide facilities for bushwalkers. At Chuave, about two hours drive off the highway from Kundiawa at the foot of Mt. Elimbari, are limestone cliffs, burial grounds and caves.

From Simbu, the highway enters the Western Highlands province. Provincial capital is Mt. Hagen where good accommodation is available. Mt. Hagen is settled in the Wahgi Valley amid coffee and tea plantations. The people of the valley are relatively less westernised than those of

Goroka and the *Town Market* is a fascinating spectacle with people in traditional dress selling their pigs and vegetables. The *Nondugl Bird of Paradise Sanctuary* at Banz (about one hour's drive from Mt. Hagen) and the *Baiyer River Bird of Paradise and Wildlife Sanctuary,* also within easy reach of the town, are interesting day trips from Hagen.

The Enga province includes the rugged area around Wabag and Wapenamanda. These can be reached via the Highlands Highway from Mt. Hagen. The scenery in this province is some of the most exciting in the country and a good hotel is located at Wabag.

The road trip from Mt. Hagen to Mendi, in the Southern Highlands province, is also impressive. It includes views of Mt. Ialabu, Mt. Giluwe and interesting villages, waterfalls and rivers. Cultural attractions include a Muruk farm (cassowary reserve), traditional villages, singsings and pig kills.

If time does not permit road travel, each of the major centres along the highway can be reached by plane. Regular daily flights leave Port Moresby and Lae for Goroka and Mt. Hagen.

The Islands Region

New Britain, New Ireland, Bougainville and Manus Islands lie to the east and north of mainland PNG. All the islands are lush, volcanic in origin, mountainous and rich in timber, copra, cocoa and palm oil.

New Britain is the largest island of the group. Rabaul is its major town and was once the capital of German New Guinea. The town still bears witness to the early orderly layout with carefully planted gardens, neat rows of frangipani trees, and wide avenues. The harbour at Rabaul, formed when a huge volcano exploded centuries ago, is one of the finest and most beautiful harbours in the Pacific.

Rabaul is surrounded by volcanoes—the *Mother, the North and South Daughters* and *Rabalankaia.* Serious eruptions occurred in 1878 and 1937 causing severe damage and loss of life. The town was hardly restored after the 1937 eruption when the Japanese invaded in 1942 and made Rabaul their headquarters in the South Pacific area. Rabaul still bears many traces of the *Japanese Occupation* and subsequent recapture by the allies. Many war relics can be visited in the town centre, including the Japanese naval command and bunker which today is a war museum, and out of town crashed zero fighter planes and the skeletons of barges nestled into artificial tunnels.

Rabaul Market should be on everyone's itinerary. The vegetable products are displayed in great quantity and at low prices. Avocados sell at about 40 U.S. cents each and pawpaws at about 50 cents. Rabaul is also a major game fishing centre with a number of record catches.

Accommodation is excellent on New Britain and the road system is probably the best in the country.

New Ireland, just off the northern tip of New Britain, is a tuna fishing, copra, cocoa, rubber and timber producing island. Kavieng, the capital, has a good airport and is a typically pretty South Seas town.

Bougainville (now known as the North Solomons Province) lies to the east of New Britain. It is famous for its enormous *open-cut copper mine* at Panguna. The island is rich not only in copper but also in cocoa and copra and due to its heavy rainfall an all year lush greenness. Fishing is good and accommodation of internationally acceptable standards is available at Kieta and Arawa.

Buka, on the northwestern end of the island, used to be well known for its artistic basketware. Today, such basketware is keenly sought by tourists. Accommodation is available at Buka in a modest guest house.

Manus Island lies to the north of the mainland and although one of the most beautiful places in Papua New Guinea, it unfortunately offers limited accommodation.

There are regular flights from Port Moresby and Lae to all of the islands.

Madang

Madang province is situated on the north coast of mainland Papua New Guinea. The town of Madang is built on a coral promontory which shelters a fine deep water harbour. The volcanic islands of Manam, Karkar and Long Island are scattered along the coast.

Madang, like Rabaul, is the site of an early German settlement and subsequent Japanese invasion. Many traces of both German colonisation and Japanese occupation remain. The Germans left great shady trees which lend an aura of seclusion to Madang town, whilst many rusting war relics have been left by the Japanese.

Madang offers a fine golf course and many squash and tennis courts. Scuba diving around the coral reefs is also popular as are sailing and water skiing. Game fishing is excellent.

Local sightseeing is highly rewarding:

Madang Market—Produce and handicrafts are sold and the market is a social gathering place, especially on Saturdays. Across from the market is the old cemetery of the first settlers who were felled by disease and hardship. Many of the tombs bear bullet scars from World War Two.

The Elizabeth Sourbly Memorial —contains beautiful orchid gardens and is located in town adjacent to the Madang Hotel.

Tusbab High School—has a small but fascinating museum with a fine collection of local and Sepik artifacts. The students have a singsing dance group which frequently performs for visitors.

Outside Town

Yabab Village—Accessible from Modilon Road, the village is well known for its terracotta pottery.

Siar Village—This is located on the north coast road past the airport. The village sits in a lagoon on the fringe of a coconut plantation. Singsings are frequently held for visitors and a small artifact shop is always open to guests.

The Sepik

For adventurous tourists, and connoisseurs of primitive art, the Sepik probably has more to offer than any other part of Papua New Guinea. Some of the finest and most vigorous woodcarvings and pottery come from the Sepik region and the towering *Haus Tambarans,* or spirit houses, with their decorated gables and richly carved pillars have pride of place in villages presenting fine examples of the people's artistic abilities. The great Sepik River, a mile wide at its mouth and navigable for nearly all its 700 mile (1,100 kilometres) length, is a reservoir of animal, reptile, insect and bird life. A trip down the Sepik in motorised canoe (for the hardy tourist) or luxurious houseboat is a memorable experience.

The centre of the East Sepik region is Wewak, set on white sandy beaches and connected by road to Maprik and Pagwi, on the Sepik River.

The West Sepik region bordering on Irian Jaya, is relatively undeveloped and largely inaccessible to tourists. The provincial capital Vanimo is within reach of Aitape, known for an abundance of war relics and its fine beaches. Also accessible from Vanimo is Telefomin, an inland patrol post and about as remote as one can get in Papua New Guinea.

Fanning Out from Wewak

A short distance from the Wewak town centre is Cape Wom Memorial Park marking the spot where Japanese Lieutenant-General Hatazo Adochi signed a document of unconditional surrender on September 13, 1945 in the presence of 3,000 Australian troops.

From Wewak one can travel by road to Pagwi where a houseboat or canoe can be arranged for the journey down the Sepik River. En route to Pagwi is Maprik, known as Haus Tambaran area. A cultural centre and museum is in the process of construction at Maprik.

The road following the coast from Wewak and terminating at Dagua, a Catholic mission station, is particularly scenic passing villages set on beaches and plantations.

Outside Wewak is Karawari Lodge set on the Karawari River, a tributary of the Sepik. Accommodation is in bush material units fitted with all modern conveniences. Side trips can be made to the Chambri, Yimas and Muruk Lakes, and villages known for their pottery and carvings in the area.

Angoram is located on the Sepik River and in the past has been a highlight of tours to the East Sepik. There is a hotel at Angoram and a trading centre for crocodile hunters and artifact buyers.

Milne Bay Province (Trobriand Islands)

The Milne Bay province includes 650 islands and atolls and extends well into the Solomons Sea. The most accessible to the tourist is the Trobriand Group and in particular the largest island of Kiriwina. The Trobriands are best known for the *Kula Ring*—a ceremonial traditional trade system operating throughout the islands which exchange white armshells, shell necklaces, pottery and yams. The Kula ritual embodies magic, mythology and tradition.

There is a comprehensive road system on Kiriwina and a small guest house caters for tourists. The Trobriand people are also well known for their art style: *Massim Art*. It is highly decorative employing intricate designs in carvings on ebony and other local timbers, and paintings contained within gables or yam houses and on war shields. Canoes are also ornamented with carvings and cowrie shells.

Elsewhere in the Milne Bay Province tourist facilities are available at the provincial capital of Alotau and the island port of Samarai, just off the tip of the mainland.

Northern Province

A short flight from Port Moresby is Popondetta, the provincial capital of the Northern Province and the starting point for the keen hikers who tackle the wartime Kokoda Trail. A word of warning—the Kokoda Trail, beginning at Kokoda, a short distance from Popondetta and finishing at Sogeri, forty kilometres north of Moresby, is not a casual stroll but a tough five-day hike. Fitness and preparedness are of vital importance.

Elsewhere in the Northern Province is Mount Lamington, active volcano visible from Popondetta, which erupted in 1951 causing widespread damage to property and claiming 4,000 lives.

Coastal scenery in the Northern Province is spectacular with deep fjord type inlets. Catering for tourists is a delightful village guest house at Tufi, built from local materials and reached from the airport by canoe. There are white-sand beaches in the area and the people of the Yariyari clan, who run the guest house, will take visitors fishing and sightseeing on their outrigger canoes.

At Wanigela on Collingwood Bay, there is a plantation resort with a guest house catering for tourists.

Fine quality tapa cloth, which compares favourably with that from anywhere in the Pacific, is hand-made in the Northern Province. It makes an easy souvenir to pack and carry.

Gulf and Western Provinces

These two large provinces cover the whole of the western part of what was formerly Papua, right up to the Irian Jaya border. Largely inaccessible and with a small population, they yet have a potential major role to play in the nation's economic development. Projects include drilling for oil and gas in the Gulf of Papua, feasibility studies for a major copper and gold mine at Ok Tedi in the Star Mountains, and for a major hydro-electric project at Wabo to harness the power of the Purari River.

The Western Province includes the great Fly River which flows south from the centre of New Guinea for 650 miles through the whole of the Western District. The river is fifty miles wide when it reaches the sea.

The principal visitor attraction in the area is the Bensbach Wildlife Lodge, near Weam, and close to the Irian Jaya border. The Bensbach River offers rich fishing including barramundi, black bass, saratoga— and numerous crocodiles. The plains have herds of Rusa deer and dozens of varieties of birdlife including Birds of Paradise, the Bensbach Rifle Bird and cassowaries. The lodge may be reached only by air from Port Moresby or Mount Hagen.

PRACTICAL INFORMATION FOR PAPUA NEW GUINEA

FACTS AND FIGURES. Papua New Guinea's population is approximately 3 million and is increasing at a rate of 2.7 percent a year. More than 90 percent of the people live in rural areas, in clan or village communities. It has been estimated that as many as 700 different languages are spoken. Population densities vary considerably from 0.6 persons per square kilometre in the Western Province to more than 38 per square kilometre on the Gazelle Peninsula of East New Britain.

The mainland and islands of Papua New Guinea lie entirely within the tropics, with a total land and sea area of more than 2.2 million square kilometres (850,000 sq. miles). Rich in natural resources, the country derives much of its revenue from copper, timber, copra, coffee, cocoa and tea. Secondary industry is being developed and there is a growing interest in tourism.

 HOW TO GET AROUND. Papua New Guinea's rugged terrain has prevented the establishment of a cross-country road network, but all main centres are connected by frequent air services. In addition, the Highlands Highway connects Lae with the major highlands centres of Goroka, Kundiawa, Mt. Hagen and Mendi. There is also a seasonal road between Lae and Madang.

By Air: Service from Honolulu by *SPIA, Qantas. Air Niugini* has services to all major centres and this is supplemented by services offered by third-level airlines *Talair, Panga Airways* and *Douglas Airways.* The addresses of the airlines' head offices are:

Air Niugini, P.O. Box 7186, Boroko, Png Tel. 259000.
In the United States write to: 5000 Birch St., Suite 3000 West Tower, Newport Beach, California 92660. Tel (714)-752-5440.
Talair, PO Box 5350, Port Moresby Tel 255799
Douglas Airways, PO Box 1179, Boroko Tel 253499

It is wise to book ahead in the November–February period.

Internal air travel is quite expensive although fares and airport tax have dropped in recent years. Main domestic route fares are:

Port Moresby–Lae US$70
Port Moresby–Rabaul US$144
Port Moresby–Kieta US$174
Port Moresby–Goroka US$88
Port Moresby–Madang US$99
Port Moresby–Wewak US$138.

The airport charge at Papua New Guinea, for international travel is K10, or approx US$10.

There are no railways.

By Car: Renting is not a problem in major centres. Avis-Nationwide, Hertz and Budget Hire Car are represented in Port Moresby, Lae, Rabaul, Mt. Hagen, Madang, Wewak and Kieta.

By Bus: Bus services operate in major towns and Highlands Buslines provides a bus service along the Highlands Highway from Lae to Mt. Hagen.

By Sea: For Inter-island ship information, see *"Planning Your Trip."*

TOURS. Major tour operators provide all-inclusive package tours throughout the country or day tours in individual centres. Bookings can generally be made through your travel agent or at hotel receptions.

Air Niugini, 5000 Birch St., Suite 3000, West Tower, Newport Beach, CA 92660, (714) 752–5440, can assist you with details on individual tours in cooperation with major ground operators. Papua New Guinea is one destination where it is wise to purchase the all-inclusive package whether planning a tour throughout the country or making a day tour to individual centers. Pre-planning is important. The following operators and tours are available in conjunction with Air Niugini. Contact Air Niugini above, or write to the tour operator directly.

The most popular local tours within various regions include the following.

PORT MORESBY TOURS. *Port Moresby & Environs:* (Half day) City sights include National Parliament and Museum, with opportunity to see parliament in session. Musuem includes one of the largest collections of Melansian art in the world. Continue past the Sir Hubert Murray Sports Stadium and the Cultural Center to the campus of the University of Papua, New Guinea, with visit to Orchid Gardens. See Central Government complex at Waigani, Koki Market and

Girl Guides artifacts store. K9. *Halifax Harbour & Surroundings:* (Full day) Transfer from hotel to harbor, cruise past Koki village (built on pylons over sea), glass-bottom boat viewings of the coral reef at Manubada Island. Lunch at "Loloata" with time to swim and snorkel. Return via Lion's Head Island and Bootless Bay. K16.50. *Kokoda Trail & Owen Stanley Range:* (Full day) Follow Sir Hubert Murray Highway past Jackson Airport to Bomana War Cemetery, then continue alongside the Laloki River, Rouna Falls hydroelectric power station; on to Varirata National Park to see some of the traditional-style houses, including a tree house of the Koiaris clan. Lunch at Kokoda Trail Restaurant before inspecting the end of the Kokoda trail, rubber plantation and lookout point of coastline. K20.

LAE—MOROBE PROVINCE. *Lae and Botanical Gardens:* (3 hours) Visits Lae War Memorial Cemetery, then proceeds to Lae Botanical Gardens, native markets, then up to Mt. Nuaman for sweeping view of Huon Gulf and Markham Valley. Also visits Japanese War Memorial Cemetery, beached cargo ship and relics of WWII. K10.50. *Bulolo-Wau-Bulolo:* (Full Day) Commences through tree-lined drive, past golf course and cocoa plantations set in surroundings of tropical jungle scenery. After leaving Highlands Highway, proceed across Markham River and climb 1000 meters through mountainous country. Stops at Mumeng for visit to Lutheran Mission then Bulolo in time for lunch at Pine Lodge. After lunch, visit Plywood Mill and gold dredges. Lunch included in cost. K45. *Lae-Boroka:* (Full day) Leave Lae by regular coach bus between Lae/Goroka/Mt. Hagen. Follow Highlands Highway through Markham Valley, up Kassam Pass into Eastern Highlands Province, past Kainantu, arriving in Goroka in late afternoon. Picnic lunch provided. Coach is not air-conditioned. Departs 8 A.M. K26.

GOROKA—EASTERN HIGHLANDS PROVINCE. *Mud Men and Asaro Valley:* (Half day) Tour leaves Goroka along Highlands Highway, past Kabiufa, the SDA Mission Station to Asaro. Inspect Makenhuku Village, meet people and see Mud Men perform their ritual, as legend is told by guide. Great opportunity for photographers. See fire-lighting demonstration plus bow and arrow shooting before returning to Goroka. Departs Tuesday and Thursday 2 P.M. K17. *Goroka & Environs:* (3 hours) Visit Goroka Technical College to inspect art class where students are being trained in the traditional arts, then on to J. K. McCarthy Museum where an excellent collection of carvings, traditional dress and ancient stone implements are displayed. Visit coffee plantation and processing factory, then a Highland village and locally owned handicraft shop. On Saturday and Wednesday also visit Goroka Council markets. Departs 9 A.M. K10. *Goroka-Mt. Hagen:* (Full day) Leave Goroka by Highland Bus Lines for drive through Asaro Valley over Daulo Pass, past villages of Watabung, Chuave, Sina Sina to Kundiawa, headquarters of the Chimbu province. In late afternoon, bus continues through fertile Wahgi valley to Mt. Hagen. Picnic lunch provided. Departs Sunday, Tuesday, Friday 8 A.M. K40.

MT. HAGEN—WESTERN HIGHLAND PROVINCE. *Mt. Hagen & Environs:* (3 hours) Visit township, which was previously an airstrip, then follow old highway past villages to Ogelbeng, rejoining the new Highlands highway and returning to Mt. Hagen past Kagamuga. Visit a Mission station, coffee plantation and people of Western Highlands. On Wednesdays and Saturdays, the tour includes tour of the markets. K10. *Baiyer River Wildlife Sanctuary:* (Full day) Drive through township past Ogelbeng, past Highland villages, then descend through Baiyer Gorge to thick rain forests where the sanctuary is located. See famous "Birds of Paradise" and animals indigenous to country. Lunch and admission costs included. K28. *Mt. Hagen-Goroka:* (Full day) Take Highlands bus through Wahgi Valley, past Kundiawa, headquarters of Chimbu province. Continue past villages of Sina Sina, Chuava and Watabung, over Daulo Pass and through Asaro Valley to Goroka. Picnic lunch provided. K40. *Mt. Hagen-Kundiawa:* (Full day) Scenic drive through tea and coffee plantations. Picnic lunch beside the Joronegal River and visits to Burial Caves and Pari Village. K26 with lunch.

MADANG PROVINCE. *Madang & Village Tour:* (Half day) Follow Coronation Drive bordering Bismarck Sea to Coastwatchers' Memorial lighthouse, then through pleasant, shady avenue of Madang township, past lagoons, market area and old German Cemetery and Chinatown. Leave Madang on Gogol Road and stop at Totary Lookout for view of Astrolobe Bay and Rai Coast. Pass Japanese Memorial and Overseas Telecommunication stations. See traditional pottery being made at BilBil Village, then travel North Coast road past copra and cocoa plantations onwards to Sia village. Visit Tusbab High School where students maintain aviary of indigenous birds. *Harbor Cruise/Reef Viewing:* (3 hours) Transfer to wharf to board pontoon cruise. During morning visit some of the harbor islands, view underwater life through glass-bottom panels and see many relics from WWII. Swim at Siar Island. K20 includes lunch.

WEWAK & SEPIK PROVINCE. *Wewak & Environs* (3 hours) Visit Cape Wom, local Sepik villages, Cultural Center, Catholic Mission and coast viewpoint. K8. *Maprik:* (Full day) Travel by coach over Sepik plains to Maprik in the East Sepik province. Visit Haus Tambarans (Spirit Houses), richly carved and painted. K25.50. Optional lunch extra.

From Angoram (Wewak and Sepik Province)—*Kambaramba Village:* (4 hours) Travel by rivercraft upstream past Migendi village to village of Kambaramba, situated on backwaters of Sepik. Village has been built entirely on stilts, and gardens are grown in canoes. Children learn to swim before they walk. K16. *Murik Lakes:* (Full day) Rivercraft travels downstream, past Catholic Mission at Marienberg, out along a baret to Murik Lakes, situated along the coast just north of the Sepik River. Meet people of area and see their daily routines. K45. *Angoram-Amboin:* (Full day) Leave Angoram by rivercraft, follow Sepik upstream past the villages of Migendi, Moin, Tambanum, Mindibit, then up the Karawari River to Amboin. Picnic lunch provided. K45–50.

From Amboin (Wewak and Sepik Province)— *Yimas Lakes:* (3 hours) Visit beautiful Yimas Lakes situated on upper reaches of Arafundi River, home of the magnificent Sepik blue orchids. See prolific bird life and visit villages of Yimas and Kundiman. K16. *Amboin-Pagwi:* (3 hours) Leave Amboin by rivercraft, rejoin Sepik River at Mindibit, then continue upstream past Chambri Lakes, Kanganaman, Yenthcen, Korogo, Japanau. Arrive at Pagwi in late afternoon to make road connection to Maprik and Wewak. Picnic lunch provided. K45–50.

From Ambunti (Wewak and Sepik Province)—*Upper Sepik:* (Full day) Opportunity to visit the interesting villages in the Washkuk area. K45–50.

Trans Niugini Tours, P. O. Box 371, Mt. Hagen, Papua New Guinea. In the United States: Trans Niugini Tours, c/o Greg Stathakis, 408 East Islay, Santa Barbara, CA 90131. Offers tours throughout the country. Special *Southern Highlands Extension* by 4-wheel-drive into remote areas. Also excursions to *Baiyer River Bird of Paradise Wildlife Sanctuary* and village cultural tours. Write or telephone *Australia Travel Service/Tour Pacific:* in California, (800) 232–2121; US (800) 423–2880; Los Angeles or Canada, call collect (805) 569–2448.

The following firms offer special-interest tours:

Culture: National Cultural Council, P.O. Box 7144, Boroka. *Bird-watching:* The Secretary, Papua New Guinea Bird Society, P.O. Box 1598, Boroko. *Butterflies:* Insect Farming & Trading Agency, Div. of Wildlife, Dept. of Lands & Environment, P.O. Box 129, Bulolo. *Orchids:* Mrs. A. Millar, Nat'l Capital Botanic Gardens, P.O. Box 4677, University of Papua New Guinea, Waigani. *Shells:* Brian Parkinson, Shell Project Officer, P.O. Box 385, Rabaul ENB. *Pearls:* Mr. Dennis George, c/o Post Office, Alotau, Milne Bay Province. *Diving:* Bob and Dinah Halstead, Tropical Diving Adventures Pty Ltd., P.O. Box 1644, Papua New Guinea. *Bush-walking:* Sobek Expeditions Inc., P.O. Box 761, Angels Camp, Calif. 95222. (Also *River Running.*) *Gold Mining:* Dept. of Minerals & Energy, Geological Survey Div., P.O. Box 778, Port Moresby. *War Relics:*

Aviation Maritime & War Branch, National Museum & Art Gallery, P.O. Box 635, Port Moresby. *Volcanoes:* Rabaul Volcanological Observatory, P.O. Box 386, Rabaul. *Fishing:* Moresby Game Fishing Club, P.O. Box 5028, Boroko. Marketing Services (Travel & Tourism) Ltd., Suite 433, High Holborn House, 52-54 High Holborn, London WC1V 6RB England, offers a free brochure describing most of the activities already mentioned.

Valor Tours, Ltd., Schoonmaker Point Bldg., Foot of Spring St., Sausalito, Calif. 94965. Specialists in veterans tours with organized programs throughout the South Pacific (and the world). Special return-of-the-veteran tours to Papua New Guinea/Solomons. Write for itineraries and rates.

Also offers *Coastwatcher Cruises* for 6 days, 5 nights from Rabaul, New Britain, to Guadalcanal, or the reverse. Includes Florida Islands, Munda, Leva, Lavella, and islands in the "slot." This WWII special interest tour includes accommodations, meals, transfers.

Cruise price includes accommodation on a share basis in twin-bunk cabin, with adjoining bathroom; all meals while aboard the MV *Coastwatcher Cruiser;* lectures; films shown on video; excursions on shore and aboard the ship's tenders.

The *MV Melanesian Explorer* accommodates 36 passengers in AC twin-bunk cabins with adjoining bathroom. All cabins have their own wash basins with hot and cold water. There is a comfortable AC lounge and separate dining room equipped with a video cinema. A large covered carpeted upper deck provides additional space and deck-chairs. Meals include fresh lobster, reef fish, choice of meat. Each cruise includes a traditional mumu (feast) cooked in a village.

Some cruises are designed in combination—additional cruises can be taken following a set cruise. A 5% discount to prices combining more than one cruise.

South Seas Travel, Inc., 62 West 56th St., New York, N.Y. 10019. Offers special 14-day "Discover Papua New Guinea" tours. Journey is through Upper Sepik region from Ambunti, the last "civilized" outpost. You will visit secluded tribes, villages, and participate in a sing-sing celebration and feast. This is safe, rugged bush country. Accommodations and conditions will be very basic. Best time is June through October. Tour includes Port Moresby, Goroka (mudmen), Mando Village (snakemen), Chimbu (Chimbu players), Mendi Village (Southern Highlands), Mt. Hagen, Karawari Lodge, Sepik River, Black Water Lakes, Chambri Lakes, Angoram, Wewak, Madang. Write for details and price.

Bougair Air Services Pty. Ltd., P.O. Box 986, Arawa, Kieta, Bougainville. Flights to government and mission stations throughout Bougainville. Scenic flights of the copper mine at Panguna and Mt. Bagana on request. Scheduled service between: Kieta-Buin; Kieta-Torokina-Kieta with Tonu-Boku-Wakunai as options; Kieta to Torokina. Scheduled flights to Buka via Wakunai, Unus and Sabah. Write direct for rates.

Talair Tourist Airlines of Niugini, P.O. Box 108, Goroka. Operates 60 aircraft serving major centers and outstations with scheduled service to all provinces.

Douglas Airways, P.O. Box 1179, Boroko, Port Moresby. Operates 19 aircraft in Gulf, Central, Western and Sepik Provinces. Aerial safaris are offered K220–500 hour depending on size of aircraft.

 SEASONAL EVENTS. Papua New Guinea's annual singsings held in the Highlands towns of Mt. Hagen and Goroka have become world famous. But if a visit cannot be timed to coincide with these you may able to attend some of the singsings and other cultural activities which mark national and local holidays throughout the country. The following is a guide to scheduled events throughout the country—dates may undergo year to year changes.

Chinese New Year: Chinese community in major centers stages festivities such as fireworks and traditional dragon dances.

April through June: Yam Festival, Kiriwina sub-province Papua. This annual event of the Trobriand Islands is to celebrate the harvest of yams (sweet potatoes) which are a staple crop of the area. Singsings and ceremonial gift exchanges are held.

May: Frangipani Festival, Rabaul. Three days of celebration including a parade, mardi gras, Frangipani Ball and beauty contest.

June: Queen's Birthday weekend. Port Moresby: *National Capital Show,* cultural, agricultural and industrial displays. Madang: *Maborasa Festival,* weekend of cultural events, including music festival, dance and drama performances and art show.

September 16–18: National Day celebrated throughout the country, marked by yacht races, singsings, cultural performances, art and craft displays. *Hiri Moale* (Port Moresby): Festival to mark the early voyages of the Motu people who travelled along the Papuan coast. Weekend event has canoe races, beauty contest and singsings; *Papua New Guinea Festival* (Port Moresby): Month long event with guest performers from other Third-World countries participating in traditional and contemporary arts program.

September–October: Tolai Warwagira Kavieng. Malagan Festival. Traditional performances for two weeks. Exciting festival held at East New Britain Province's major center. Weekend fireworks displays, singsings, fire-dancers, string band competition and performances by choral groups; *Morobe Show* (Lae): Weekend of cultural and agricultural displays. Major singsing is staged on the Sunday of the weekend. Many highland groups travel great distances to participate in the event.

November: Pig Kill Season. From the beginning of November until Christmas the Simbu people, near Kundiawa, stage traditional feasts within their village communities. Hundreds of pigs may be slaughtered for one such event. A moveable feast marked by singsings moving from village to village. *Pearl Festival* (Samarai-Milne Bay Province): Weekend long festival celebrated by beauty contests, art and craft displays, canoe races and junior sports events.

December: Tolai Warwagira, Rabaul, East New Britain. An annual festival including string band competitions, yacht races, and performances by drama and choir groups. A major singsing is held during which a duk-duk dance is performed to represent all Tubuan (secret) Societies near Rabaul.

\$P£   **CURRENCY.** The Papua New Guinea currency is the *kina* (about A\$1.45 and US\$0.80 in summer 1985) and *toea.* Pronunciation is 'keener' and 'toya.' The currency circulates in the form of K20, K10, K5 and K2 notes and the K1 with the hole in the centre. The *kina* is divided into 100 *toea* with coins of 1t, 2t, 5t, 10t, and 20t.

Banks represented in PNG include: *ANZ, WESTPAC, Bank of South Pacific, Papua New Guinea Banking Corporation,* and *Hong Kong Shanghai.* Banking hours are Monday-Thursday 9 A.M. to 2 P.M. Friday 9 A.M. to 5 P.M. No Saturday banking. Airport currency exchange service every day.

Travellers cheques are accepted by most shops, hotels, etc. Credit cards (American Express, Diners Club) are useful, but inquire in advance whether your particular hotel accepts them.

CUSTOMS REGULATIONS. Free import, one litre alcoholic beverage (persons 18 or older); 200 cigarettes or 250 g. cigars or tobacco; reasonable quantity of perfume.

   HOW TO DRESS. Dress in Papua New Guinea, as in most tropical areas, is informal. During the day open-neck short sleeve shirt and shorts or slacks, are the most common attire for men, while for ladies sleeveless dresses of cotton or cotton/synthetic materials are found to be the most comfortable. In the evenings some hotels expect men to wear long trousers, but ties are rarely seen. For ladies, long gowns appear on more formal occasions.

THE CLIMATE. On the coast the temperature rarely rises above 30°C (86°F) by day or falls below 23°C (73°F) at night. The sun is strong between 9 A.M. and 4 P.M. and a barrier lotion is recommended if you are prone to sunburn. A wide brimmed hat will protect your face from the vertical sun around noon. Coastal rainfall varies widely, with the "wet" in most districts occurring between November and March (but from April to October in Lae and Wewak). In the Highlands areas, the days are warm but nights can be cool—25°C (77°F) falling to 14°C (57°F). Light woollen slacks and sweaters may be necessary. Due to the higher altitude, ultra-violet rays of the tropical sun are accentuated and fair skins should be protected.

Average Temperature (°Fahrenheit) and Humidity

Port Moresby	Jan	Feb	Mar	Apr	May	June	July	Aug	Sept	Oct	Nov	Dec
Average max. day temperature	97°	97°	95°	93°	92°	93°	92°	92°	94°	95°	97°	97°
Days of Rain	16	18	18	15	8	7	6	7	7	7	8	14
Humidity, Percent	77	81	80	82	79	78	77	74	73	69	68	73

TIPPING is not customary and is not encouraged

SPORTS. *Golf, tennis, skin diving, sailing* and *fishing* are readily available.

SHOPPING. Papua New Guinea offers a wide range of craftwork made by its people in wood, copper, pottery, shell and basketwork. Artifact shops can be found in every centre. In the country they can be bought through missions or direct from village craftsmen. An artifact centre not to be missed is the government owned *Village Arts* in Port Moresby—it boasts a range of over 20,000 items, most of them purchased directly from villagers throughout the country. Village Arts is located at Six Mile, near Jacksons Airport. There is stringent control on the export of artifacts of national historical or cultural significance, so care should be taken when purchasing articles directly from villagers. A visit to the town market in each centre is an experience which should not be overlooked. A wide variety of local fruits and vegetables can be purchased for only a few toea.

Main centres also offer a wide range of shops and supermarkets, and there are many Chinese trade stores throughout the country offering cane and camphor-wood gifts as well as furniture and oriental fabrics. The introduction of duty-free shopping is presently under consideration.

MAIL AND TELEPHONE SERVICES. There is no home mail delivery service in Papua New Guinea—individuals and businesses rent post office boxes and collect their mail daily. As a visitor, you can have your mail forwarded care of your hotel or nearest post office. Telegrams are normally phoned through to the recipient and then left for collection at the post office. Telephone trunk dialling facilities link most parts of the country, and through international trunk dialling you can talk to Australia. Overseas mail charges are extremely reasonable.

CHURCHES. Papua New Guinea is a Christian nation and most Christian denominations are represented with regular church services in all main centres.

LANGUAGE. There are three national languages: English, Pidgin (pronounced *pisin*) and Motu. English is spoken in all shops, hotels and restaurants. A Pidgin phrase book is handy in the highlands and New Guinea coastal areas.

GENERAL HINTS. Do not expect everything to happen on time—the pace of tropical life is leisurely.

Do not be afraid to bargain, especially when purchasing artifacts in villages. Do not wander alone at night.

Drive carefully, especially in the country. If you are involved in an accident and someone is hurt, do not stay at the scene but drive to the nearest police station.

HOLIDAYS. All government offices, banks and most private offices are closed —sometimes on the day before and after, too. January 1—New Year's Day. Good Friday and Easter: Day of prayer and feasting among families and small communities throughout the country.

Mid-June—National Capital Show (Port Moresby): Annual event held on capital's new showgrounds (9 miles from city center). Events include singsings with village groups, equestrian events, cultural and agricultural displays. Celebration coincides with Queen's Birthday. Mid-June—H.M. Queen Elizabeth's Birthday.

August 15—Constitution Day, national holiday.

September 16—Independence Day: Celebrations actually take place all week in all 19 provinces. December 25—Christmas Day. December 26—Boxing Day.

HOTELS AND MOTELS. Adequate and comfortable accommodation is available throughout Papua New Guinea, and hotels of internationally accepted standards are in most major centres. But accommodation is relatively more expensive than in most Asian centres and Australia. As a guide: *Expensive,* K50 and up; *Moderate,* K25–49; *Inexpensive,* K25 and below.

Alotau (Milne Bay Province)

Masurina Lodge. *Moderate.* Located close to beach, unlicensed restaurant.

Amboin (East Sepik Province)

Karawari Lodge. *Expensive.* Accommodation is bush material huts fitted with all modern conveniences. Located on Karawari River, a tributary of the Sepik River. Licensed restaurant. Outstanding facility. Worth staying a week here. Rates include river-boat excursions, sing sing dances, meals, laundry. Swimming pool. Artifacts shop. Not really expensive if you consider it covers everything.

Angoram (East Sepik Province)

Angoram Hotel. *Expensive.* Air conditioned, licensed restaurant.
Kaminibit Lodge. *Expensive.* On middle of Sepik River near Chambri Lake.

Banz (Western Highlands Province)

Banz Hotel/Motel. *Inexpensive.*

Buka (North Solomons Province)

Buka Luman Solto Guest House. *Inexpensive.* Close to beach, guest house reached by ferry from Buka Island. Unlicensed restaurant.

Bulolo (Morobe Province)

Pine Lodge Hotel. *Moderate.* Air conditioned, pool, licensed restaurant.

Daru (Western Province)
Wyben Hotel. *Moderate.*
Daru Guest House. *Inexpensive.*

Goroka (Eastern Highlands Province)
Bird of Paradise Hotel. *Moderate.* Located in town centre. Licensed restaurant, lounge. Main hotel. Popular with businessmen.
Country Womens Association Cottage. *Inexpensive.* No restaurant, but kitchen facilities available.
Lantern Lodge. *Moderate.* Restaurant, lounge.
Minogere Hostel. *Inexpensive.* Restaurant, lounge, pool. Pleasant bushland setting, restful atmosphere.

Hoskins (West New Britain Province)
Hoskins Hotel. *Moderate.* Fairly new. Tours arranged of oil-palm industry and nearby hot springs.

Kainantu (Eastern Highlands Province)
Salvation Army Flats. *Inexpensive.* Cooking facilities.
Kainantu Lodge. *Inexpensive.*

Kairuku (Yule Island Central Province)
Yule Island Guest House. *Inexpensive.*

Kavieng (New Ireland Province)
Kavieng Hotel. *Moderate.* Airconditioned. Restaurant.

Kieta (North Solomons Province)
Arovo Island Hotel. *Expensive.* Air conditioned, with private suites.
Davara Motel. *Expensive.* Air conditioned. Pool, licensed restaurant, lounge.
Hotel Kieta. *Inexpensive.* Handy to Kieta Town.

Kimbe (West New Britain Province)
Palm Lodge Motel. *Moderate.* Pool, licensed restaurant, lounge.

Kundiawa (Chimbu Province)
Chimbu Lodge. *Moderate.* Licensed restaurant, lounge. Very central.
Kundiawa Hotel. *Inexpensive.* Restaurant, lounge,

Lae (Morobe Province)
Huon Gulf Motel. *Moderate.* Airconditioned, pool, lounge, licensed restaurant.
Melanesian Hotel. *Moderate.* Airconditioned, pool, lounge, licensed restaurant.
Buablung Haus. *Inexpensive.*
Hotel Cecil. *Inexpensive.* P.O. Box 12. Licensed restaurant.
Klinkii Lodge. *Inexpensive.* Unlicensed restaurant.
Lae Lodge. *Expensive.* Pool, tennis, lounge, licensed restaurant.

Lorengau (Manus Province)
Lorengau Hotel. *Moderate.* Restaurant.

Losuia (Trobriand Islands, Milne Bay Province)
Kiriwina Lodge. *Inexpensive.*

Madang (Madang Province)
Madang Resort. *Expensive.*

Smugglers Inn Motel. *Moderate.* Located on beautiful sea frontage. Airconditioned, pool, licensed restaurant lounge.

Coastwatchers Motel. *Moderate.* Airconditioned, licensed restaurant, lounge.

Hotel Madang. *Moderate,* Airconditioned, pool, lounge, licensed restaurant.

Country Womens Association Cottage. *Inexpensive.* Kitchen facilities.

Maprik (East Sepik Province)

Maprik Waken Motel. *Inexpensive.* Unlicensed restaurant.

Mendi (Southern Highlands Province)

Hotel Mendi. *Expensive.*

Minj (Western Highlands Province)

Tribal Tops Inn. *Moderate.* Restaurant, golf, swimming. Own collection art and handicrafts; lush gardens.

Mount Hagen (Western Highlands Province)

Hagen Park Motel. *Moderate.* Licensed restaurant, lounge.

Highlander Hotel. *Expensive.* Licensed restaurant, lounge. Largest hotel in town. Good location. Village Wing recommended.

Airport Hotel. *Moderate.* Licensed restaurant, lounge.

Kimininga Hostel. *Inexpensive.* Unlicensed restaurant. Ideal for children.

Namatanai (New Ireland Province)

Hotel Namatanai. *Moderate.*

Popondetta (Northern Province)

Lamington Hotel. *Expensive.* Airconditioned rooms available, licensed restaurant, lounge.

Port Moresby (Capital of Papua New Guinea—National Capital Province)

Davara Motel. *Expensive.* Airconditioned, pool, opposite beach. Licensed restaurant, lounge.

Gateway Hotel. *Expensive.* Opposite airport. Licensed restaurant, lounge.

Islander Hotel. *Expensive.* Airconditioned, pool, licensed restaurant, lounge. Close to government buildings, 6 miles from town centre.

TraveLodge Motel. *Expensive.* Restaurants, swimming pool, panoramic views.

Boroko Hotel. *Moderate.* Airconditioned, licensed restaurant, lounge.

Loloata Island Resort. *Moderate.* 14 miles from Port Moresby. All meals included. "Escapist" resort. Swimming, snorkelling, scuba diving, fishing.

Papua Hotel. *Moderate.* Very central, excellent dining room, music, dancing.

Civic Guest House. *Inexpensive.* Meals included.

Country Womens Association. *Inexpensive.* Cooking facilities available.

Devon Lodge Apartments. *Inexpensive.* Opposite beach, cooking facilities.

Konedobu Hotel. *Inexpensive.*

Mapang Guesthouse. *Inexpensive.* Meals included.

Salvation Army Hostel. *Inexpensive.* Kitchen facilities available.

YWCA Hostel. *Inexpensive.* Unlicensed restaurant.

Rabaul (East New Britain Province)

Motel Kaivuna. *Moderate.* Airconditioned, pool, licensed restaurant.

TraveLodge Motel. *Moderate.* Airconditioned, pool, licensed restaurant, lounge. First-class hotel.

Hotel Ascot. *Moderate.* Airconditioned, licensed restaurant, lounge.

Hamamas. *Moderate.*

Kulau Lodge. *Moderate.* Located 10 kilometres from Rabaul. Licensed restaurant, lounge.

New Britain Lodge. *Inexpensive.* Unlicensed restaurant.

Orims Camp. *Inexpensive.*

Rabaul Community Hostel. *Inexpensive.* Unlicensed restaurant.

Rouna

Rouna Hotel. *Inexpensive.* Twenty-two miles from Port Moresby.

Sialum (Morobe Province)

Paradise Springs Holiday Inn. *Moderate.* Licensed restaurant, close to beach. Seaside resort, individual units of high standard.

Samarai (Milne Bay Province)

Pacific View Guest House. *Moderate.* Meals included. Close to beach. Licensed restaurant.

Sogeri (Central Province)

Kokoda Trail Motel. *Moderate.* Pool, licensed restaurant. Crocodile steaks!

Sogeri Salvation Army Cottage. *Inexpensive.* Cooking facilities available.

Tufi (Northern Province)

Kofure Village Guest House. *Inexpensive.* Recommended. From airstrip to guest house by outrigger canoe. Fishing traditional style with spears and nets. Excellent skindiving.

Mirigina Guest House. *Inexpensive.* Pool, unlicensed restaurant.

Vanimo (West Sepik Province)

Narimo Hotel. *Moderate.* Airconditioned, licensed restaurant, lounge.

Wau (Morobe Province)

Wau Lodge Hotel. *Moderate.* Recently redecorated, licensed restaurant. Cool mountain air. Only game safari lodge in Papu New Guinea.

Wau Ecology Institute. *Inexpensive.* Cooking facilities available. Natural setting at the ecology institute overlooking the gold mining town of Wau.

Wau Hotel. *Inexpensive.* Licensed restaurant, lounge, built in 1930's.

Wabag (Enga Province)

Kaia Orchid Lodge. *Expensive.* Ten miles from Wabag. Includes all meals. Great views.

Wabag Lodge. *Moderate.* Licensed restaurant, lounge.

Malya Hostel. *Inexpensive.* Confortable accommodation in pleasant surroundings.

Wanigela (Northern Province)

Waijuga Park. *Moderate.* Unlicensed restaurant. Located in four acres of gardens with view of Owen Stanley Range. Canoe trips up Murin River, glass bottom boat tours to view the coral reefs and marine life.

Weam (Western Province)

Bensbach Wildlife Lodge. *Expensive.* Unique fishing and hunting lodge in one of the most remote areas of PNG. Fishing rods, guns, boats, and guides available for hire.

Wewak (East Sepik Province)

Sepik Motel. *Moderate.* Airconditioned, lounge, licensed restaurant. Refrigerator in each room.

Wewak Hotel. *Moderate.* Airconditioned, licensed restaurant.

Windjammer Motel. *Moderate.* Airconditioned, licensed restaurant, lounge located on white sand beach.

Woitape (Central Province)

Ororo Guest House. *Inexpensive.* 30 minute flight from Port Moresby—well known to orchid collectors.

 DINING OUT. Traditional cuisine of Papua New Guinea is confined to root crops such as taro, kaukau and yams; sago; pig (cooked in the earth on traditional feasts), and is generally uninteresting. There are no restaurants which specialise in Papua New Guinean food. However, most hotels have good dining facilities and the larger towns include Asian restaurants.

Port Moresby's Ela Beach ex-servicemen's club and the Royal Papua Yacht Club also cater to visitors in their dining rooms and bars.

The seas around Papua New Guinea swarm with fish, and particularly good are barramundi, crayfish, prawns and crabs. Local fruit should also be tried—pineapples, pawpaws, mangoes, passionfruit and bananas.

Port Moresby

Papua Hotel. *Deluxe.* Douglas Street. American international, dancing.

Moonlight Restaurant. *Moderate.* Open-air poolside, fully licensed, features Chinese cuisine.

Korobosea

Shanghai Gardens. *Deluxe.* Gavamani Mall. Cantonese cuisine, with dancing.

Akbar. *Inexpensive.* Indonesian cuisine.

Konedobu

Galley II Restaurant. *Moderate.* Aviat Club. American international cuisine.

East Boroko

Kwangtung Village. *Moderate.* Exclusive Chinese cuisine. Fully licensed.

INDEX

(The letter H indicates hotels and motels. The letter R indicates restaurants.)